Maged S.A. Mikhail is Associate Professor of History at the California State University, Fullerton. His research focuses on Late Antiquity, the Early Islamic period, communal interactions under Islamic rule, and Coptic Christianity.

FROM BYZANTINE TO ISLAMIC EGYPT

Religion, Identity and Politics after the Arab Conquest

MAGED S.A. MIKHAIL

I.B. TAURIS
LONDON · NEW YORK

Published in 2014 by I.B.Tauris & Co Ltd
6 Salem Road, London W2 4BU
175 Fifth Avenue, New York NY 10010
www.ibtauris.com

Distributed in the United States and Canada
Exclusively by Palgrave Macmillan
175 Fifth Avenue, New York NY 10010

Library of Middle East History 45

ISBN: 978 1 78453 481 3

A full CIP record for this book is available from the British Library
A full CIP record is available from the Library of Congress

Library of Congress Catalog Card Number: available

Typeset in Garamond Three by OKS Prepress Services, Chennai, India

For Reagan Renee

CONTENTS

Acknowledgements viii
Abbreviations x
Nomenclature and Conventions xii

1. Charting the Course 1
2. The Conquest: Event, Text, and Memory 16
3. Christian Elites: The Dialectic of Duty and Faith 37
4. Religious Conversion and Social Cohesion 51
5. Language, Identity, and Assimilation 79
6. The Long Eighth Century: A Cultural Bridge 106
7. Muslim Elites, Urban Administration, and Rural Justice 136
8. Metamorphosis of the Muslim Community 160
9. Ideologies and Jurisdictions 177
10. A Church and Community in Transition 204
11. Polemics and the Construction of Communal Identities 232
12. Webs of Significance 255

Notes 272
Select Bibliography 383
Papyrological Index 406
Index 409

ACKNOWLEDGEMENTS

This study began some years ago as my dissertation at the University of California, Los Angeles. Since then it has grown and evolved on nearly every front. Throughout this process, I have enjoyed the generous encouragement and feedback of Michael G. Morony, whose guidance and example have been invaluable. Claudia Rapp's direction and continuing support over the years have also been deeply appreciated. For several years, I enjoyed reading Coptic with Antonio Loprieno and the intellectual rigor of James Gelvin's approach to the study of history.

A special thanks is due to Tim Vivian, who was kind enough to read through an earlier version of this monograph. Over the course of my research, I have also benefited from the suggestions and observations of colleagues and friends who have read sections of this study or have discussed a host of issues in person, over email, or at professional conferences. I am especially thankful to Febe Armanios, Phil Booth, Fred Donner, Gawdat Gabra, Edward and Fadia Hanna, Marek Jankowiak, Fr. Tadros Y. Malaty, Mark Moussa, Chase Robinson, Lennart Sundelin, Mark Swanson, and Ramses Wassif. Likewise, I am grateful to the anonymous reviewers of this monograph for their generous feedback. Tomasz Hoskins, my editor at I.B.Tauris, has been a paragon of patience and professionalism. Over the years, I have also enjoyed the encouragement of His Grace Bishop Serapion, Coptic Orthodox Bishop of Southern California and

Hawaii. Habitually, I have drawn upon the resources at the library of the Saint Shenouda the Archimandrite Coptic Society (Los Angeles), which awarded me several stipends during my graduate studies. I am extremely grateful for the resources the Society and its president, Mr. Hany Takla, have placed at my disposal, though certainly the analysis and conclusions forwarded here are my own and in no way reflect the views of that organization.

Words fail to describe my gratitude to my parents, Samir and Juliette, whose decision to immigrate to the United States has been a labor of love; they labored and sowed, my brother Sameh and I reaped. My wife Reagan has been generous and patient in her editorial assistance and in providing me with time to work on this study. That was no easy task given the rambunctiousness of our boys, Lucas and James. It is to her that this book is dedicated.

Maged S.A. Mikhail,
16 July, 2013

ABBREVIATIONS

BSAC	*Bulletin de la Société d'archéologie copte*
BSOAS	*Bulletin of the School of Oriental and African Studies*
CMR	*History of Christian-Muslim Relations*, ed. D. Thomas, *et al.*
CoptEncyc	*Coptic Encyclopedia*, ed. A.S. Atiya
CPR	*Corpus Papyrorum Raineri*
CSCO	Corpus Scriptorum Christianorum Orientalium
DOP	*Dumbarton Oaks Papers*
EI^2	*Encyclopedia of Islam*, 2nd edition
GCAL	*Geschichte der christlichen arabischen Literatur*, ed. G. Graf
HCME	*History of the Churches and Monasteries of Egypt/ Tārīkh al-kanā'is wa al-adyurah*
HP	*History of the Patriarchs* I.1–4 = *History of the Patriarchs of the Coptic Church of Alexandria*, ed./trans. B. Evetts. PO 1.2, 1.4, 5.1, 10.5 II.1–3 = *History of the Patriarchs of the Egyptian Church*, ed./trans. O.H.E. KHS-Burmester and Yassā 'Abd al-Masīḥ. III.1–3 = *History of the Patriarchs of the Egyptian Church*, ed./trans. O.H.E. KHS-Burmester and Antoine Khater.

	IV.1–2 = *History of the Patriarchs of the Egyptian Church*, ed./trans. O.H.E. KHS-Burmester and Antoine Khater. Cited according to continuous pagination
HP (Primitive)	*Severus ibn al-Muqaffaʿ*, ed. C.F. Seybold. Hamburg, 1912.
IJMES	*International Journal of Middle East Studies*
JAOS	*Journal of the American Oriental Society*
JESHO	*Journal of the Economic and Social History of the Orient*
JJP	*Journal of Juristic Papyrology*
JNES	*Journal of Near Eastern Studies*
JSAI	*Jerusalem Studies in Arabic and Islam*
OCP	*Orientalia Christiana Periodica*
PO	Patrologia Orientalis
ROC	*Revue de l'Orient Chrétien*
SC	Sources Chrétiennes
SLAEI	Studies in Late Antiquity and Early Islam
ZDMG	*Zeitschrift der Deutschen Morgenländischen Gesellschaft*
ZPE	*Zeitschrift für Papyrologie und Epigraphik*

NOMENCLATURE AND CONVENTIONS

There is no shortage of labels to describe any constituency in Egypt during the centuries surveyed here. For example, those who refused to accept the decrees of the Council of Chalcedon have been labeled "Theodosians," "Eutychians," "Severians," "Jacobites," "non-Chalcedonians," "anti-Chalcedonians," and "Copts," not to mention the more inflammatory designations of "Theopaschites," "Monophysites," and "heretics". The designations employed throughout this study are as follows: "Arab(s)" identifies the Arab conquerors of Egypt, all of whom are believed to have been Arabic-speaking and overwhelmingly Muslim;[1] "Muslim(s)" designates adherents of the Islamic faith regardless of "ethnic" identity or origins; "Copt(s)," "anti-Chalcedonian(s)," and "Miaphysite(s)" are used interchangeably to refer to the Christians of Egypt who rejected the formulations of the Council of Chalcedon and adhered to the Alexandrian hierarchy that recognized patriarchs Dioskoros I and Theodosios I as orthodox.[2] "Melkite(s)," "pro-Chalcedonian(s)," and "Greek Orthodox" designate Christians (of various backgrounds) who accepted the Council of Chalcedon as binding. On occasion, scholars have criticized "Copt" and "Melkite" as polemical labels; however, even a cursory reading of the *History of the Patriarchs* or the *Naẓm al-jawhar* (*Annals*) of Saʿīd ibn Baṭrīq (Eutychios) demonstrates each community's acceptance and endorsement of the traditional nomenclature without reservation.

Purposely abandoned here are the terms "monophysite" and "dyophysite," which have been historically employed as polemical epithets by each confession to disparage the other.

Orthography of Greek names conforms to that found in the *Oxford Dictionary of Byzantium*, while Arabic names and terms adhere to the standards of the *International Journal of Middle Eastern Studies*. For Coptic, the standard transliteration of the Greek alphabet has been supplemented with ϩ/h, ϣ/sh, ϭ/ch, ϧ/kh, ϫ/j, and ϯ/ti. That said, strict transliteration has proven impossible, particularly for individuals who are attested in Greek, Coptic, and Arabic sources, or for names whose orthography or vocalization changed over time (cf. Khaīl which has variants of Khaël, Khayl, Kha'īl, Mikha'īl, and Michaēl). In such instances, or where the Latinized version has proven too ingrained, consistency rather than absolute accuracy became the goal. In regard to chronology, unless otherwise noted, dates are routinely cited in accordance to Hijra/Common Era (CE) or in Common Era only.

A problematic issue, circumvented here wherever possible, is the enumeration of patriarchs. In early Greek and Coptic texts, apostles, who comprised a unique fraternity whose authority and jurisdiction superseded that of bishops, were not enumerated among the lists of archbishops and patriarchs. At some point, however, possibly in the tenth century, both the Copts and the Melkites began to enumerate Saint Mark as their first patriarch. This led to two problems. The first pertains to the enumeration of patriarchs in general: whereas Eusebios identifies Demetrios as the eleventh Bishop of Alexandria, the *History of the Patriarchs* designates him as the twelfth. The second is particular to the enumeration of patriarchs named "Mark": the patriarch who passed away in 819 CE is identified as Mark I in some sources, but as Mark II in others.

CHAPTER 1

CHARTING THE COURSE

The world has thirty wonders,
twenty of which are in Egypt
– Ibn Zūlāq, *Faḍā'il miṣr*

Suddenly in the mid-seventh century, Byzantine and Sasanid armies found themselves reeling from disastrous military defeats and extensive territorial losses to an enemy hardly known to them. In rapid succession, Damascus, Ctesiphon, and Jerusalem surrendered, and in late November 641 CE Arab armies would boast of yet another major acquisition—Egypt. The conquest of the province, somberly dubbed "the Egyptian disaster" by Theophanes, constituted an enduring achievement for the nascent caliphate and an exasperating loss for the Byzantine Empire. Relatively peaceful, economically prosperous, and intellectually vibrant, Egypt was an ancient land punctuated by enigmatic monuments that linked it to the history and prophets of the monotheistic faiths through history and lore. By ushering in a new political order, the Arab conquest facilitated an unparalleled cultural metamorphosis in Egypt in which the Abrahamic religions, various "ethnicities," three distinct languages, and a host of classical, patristic, and Qur'ānic texts and ideas comingled. Incrementally, Egypt's Copto–Byzantine society transitioned into an Islamic one, often without contemporaries realizing the depth or ramifications of the developments they witnessed. As such, this study seeks to identify the aspects of hybridity, innovation, and continuity that characterize this transformative era, and to interpret their significance within the context of Egypt's history and that of the caliphate.

Scholars have traditionally identified 641 CE as a pivotal year demarcating the end of "Byzantine" and the beginning of "Islamic" Egypt. Nonetheless, while 641 may provide an accurate political marker, it proves inadequate, even misleading, when addressing almost every other aspect of historical inquiry, be it social, cultural, or intellectual. This has led to the rise of the more malleable designations of "late antique," "Byzantine," and "Early Islamic" Egypt.[1] Conceptually, the terms evoke very different cultural patterns: "late antique" and "Byzantine" suggest a Greco-Roman Christian society, while the third classification of "Early Islamic" demarcates an Arab Muslim one. Admittedly, the labels and chronological schemes employed are imperfect. Not only do they routinely overlap and are inconsistently applied by academics, but they are misleading. Much of what is deemed "late antique" persisted for centuries under Arab rule with little or no disguise, and throughout early "Islamic" Egypt Christians remained the best documented and the demographically dominant constituency. Flawed as they are, however, these designations facilitate a more nuanced discussion of cultural transformations. Ultimately, at the intersection of these conceptual frameworks and tentative nomenclature are old historical questions: which issues and accounts should one stress; when does nominal change translate into tangible evidence; and which catalysts brought about "significant" change?

The centuries under investigation, roughly the seventh through the tenth, have been surveyed by historians of the Late Roman Empire, the Mediterranean world, the early caliphate, Egypt, and the Coptic church,[2] though rarely have they served as the sole focus of study.[3] In part, this stems from the fragmentation rampant among scholars focused on the region. Late Roman historians largely discuss the Arab conquests as an historical appendix; those studying early

Islamic history have become somewhat cloistered due to unique historiographic concerns and are more concerned with developments east of Egypt, and scholarship on the Fāṭimids reflects but a passing interest in earlier developments and texts. These professional partitions only multiply as an individual scholar's disciplinary outlook, topical interests, and linguistic training are considered. The prevailing specialization hardly needs an apology,[4] though it has undoubtedly limited substantive cross-pollination. Arabization provides a salient example. Overlooking historiographic and methodological concerns for the moment, the topic has attracted papyrologists, historians of the Middle East (focusing on Islamic narratives), and specialists in Coptic Arabic literary and liturgical manuscripts. Despite addressing the same phenomenon, however, the findings of each bevy of specialists are seldom meaningfully informed by those of their peers.[5] Here, in an attempt to overcome such fissures, a deliberate attempt is made to situate old data in new and arguably more valid contexts, to traverse chronological and disciplinary boundaries, and to diversify the canon of studies and texts that inform the analysis of specific issues.

In striving toward these goals, however, several of the following discussions may first seem revisionist. Although unintentional, this proved unavoidable. The scholarship of the past century, while foundational to the present study, has sheltered and promulgated a pervasive nationalist reading that maintains the existence of an "authentic," distinct, and unalterable Egyptian political and cultural consciousness that has defied "foreign" intrusions.[6] This ideological perspective has infiltrated every aspect of historical inquiry; the historiography of the Arab conquest, that of Coptic literature, and the history of the Melkite community in Egypt have all been affected to one extent or another. Cognizant of the problem, contemporary scholars avoid such anachronistic concepts in their own research (with varying degrees of success), but they have implicitly accepted many of the nationalist-inspired suppositions and conclusions of earlier generations.[7] This has led to the persistence of a master narrative that is frequently at odds with what may be soundly deduced from the historical record; the subsequent discussions of the Arab conquest, its immediate aftermath, and the perceptions of the Greek language in post-conquest Egypt demonstrate as much.[8]

Before addressing these issues, however, this chapter will provide something of a textual and methodological orientation focused on the most pressing interpretive issues and problematic texts. It concludes with a discussion of the habitually distorted beliefs of the anti-Chalcedonians of Egypt, and the questions pertaining to the origins of their hierarchy and the extent of their demographic hold.

Sources and their Limitations

Egypt yields a wealth of historical sources, possessing unique qualities as well as methodological limitations. These "limits of abundance" are the focus here.[9] Narratives for the period surveyed demonstrate remarkable range and depth, though only a handful of writings, such as Ibn 'Abd al-Ḥakam's *Futūḥ miṣr* and the *History of the Patriarchs*, have (with good reason) attracted the greater part of scholarly attention. Nonetheless, there exists a much deeper reservoir of literary accounts than has been traditionally utilized. Critical editions and studies by specialists in an assortment of fields ranging from hagiography and apocrypha to liturgical and Arab Christian studies add breadth as well as substance to the historical record, and are incorporated here whenever possible.

Normative histories and chronicles, whether written by Christians or Muslims, share two significant characteristics. First, they are largely the selective writings of the urban (secular and religious) elites of the Delta. Early Arab historians in Egypt, such as Ibn 'Abd al-Ḥakam or al-Kindī, focused almost exclusively on the Muslim community.[10] Similarly, Christian authors, though more forthcoming in this respect, were equally particular, discussing Muslim governors, edicts, and sectarian incidents only as far as they had a direct bearing on their community. Second, the literature enshrines communal perspectives penned by later generations, who constructed, imagined, and employed the past in light of later developments or, more intentionally, to serve contemporary socio-political needs. This has long been argued for the early Islamic tradition; here, a similar, though not as distinct a pattern, is demonstrated among Christian sources as well.

Early Arabic sources present the greatest interpretive obstacles since they are plagued by a ubiquitous historiographic problem. Tersely stated, with the exception of the Qur'ān, the entirety of that literature circulated orally for the duration of Umayyad rule and, where Egyptian writings are concerned, well into the 'Abbāsid era.[11] Repeatedly, scholars have demonstrated that this corpus passed through various socio-political alignments, realignments, and ideologically inspired additions and omissions before it was ever written down.[12] This has led to highly polarized views as to the reliability of the early Islamic tradition,[13] which often (though fortunately not always) indulges in literary *topoi*, presents contradictory details, and fixates on anachronistic issues.[14] To compensate, the present study carefully weighs the sources in order to discern *topoi* as such, to read against the grain wherever possible, and to reinforce Islamic writings with Christian tracts and documentary papyri when feasible.

Among Christian writings, the *History of the Patriarchs of Alexandria* [HP] continues to reverberate on nearly every front, providing a deep reservoir of information not only for the history of the Coptic church, but for everything from taxation to theology and politics. Still, scholars often misuse this text. Historians of the Middle East tend to cite the HP when it corroborates information gleaned elsewhere, but promptly label it erroneous or partisan when it contradicts Arab Muslim sources. Similarly, in the (admittedly few) studies of the Melkite community in Egypt, information gleaned from the writings of Patriarch Eutychios (d. 940 CE) is read *prima facie* as more accurate than a history compiled by Copts.[15] In neither case, however, can readings from the HP be dismissed so blithely, especially since it preserves some of the earliest evidence for a host of individuals and events that transpired during the first three Islamic centuries.

The traditional attribution of the HP to Bishop Sawīrus ibn al-Muqaffa' (d. ca. 1000 CE) has proven erroneous in light of the crucial glosses on the composition of that work by Michael of Tinnīs

(d. 1056 CE) and Mawhūb ibn Manṣūr (ca. 1025–1100 CE).[16] Most decisive, however, has been Johannes den Heijer's pivotal study which proves that it was Mawhūb ibn Manṣūr who translated and redacted the *History*.[17] Overlooking the initial entries which were added later,[18] the first group of biographies—2, Anianos, to 24, Cyril I (d. 444 CE)—are heavily reliant upon the now fragmentary *Histories of the Holy Church*, which in its original form chronicled the patriarchates of Dioskoros I and Timothy II (d. 477 CE) as well. The *Histories* was composed during the last quarter of the fifth century, perhaps by a monk named Menas.[19] Early in the eighth century, Archdeacon Jirja (George) drafted the biographies spanning the patriarchates of Dioskoros I to Simon I (d. 701 CE). As with his successors, Jirja was well integrated into the ecclesiastical hierarchy; he was the spiritual son of John III (677–86 CE) and served as a scribe for Simon I.[20]

By the third-quarter of the eighth century, Deacon John (who later became a bishop) composed the third group of biographies, covering 705 to 768 CE—from Alexander II to Khaīl (Michael) I. The spiritual son of the famed Bishop Moses of Awsīm, Deacon John developed a close friendship with Khaīl I,[21] and at one point even shared a prison cell with that patriarch. Another John, a monk, wrote the fourth quire of biographies in the late ninth century, those of Mīnā I to Shinūda I (d. 880 CE). This John, "the Writer," functioned as a scribe to the last three patriarchs whose *Lives* he recorded, and likely relied on a lost *bios* written by a contemporary of Yusāb I (Joseph: 831–49 CE) for that patriarch's lengthy biography.[22] In the early 1050s CE, maintaining that no one had added to the biographies since John the Writer,[23] Bishop Michael of Tinnīs composed the next installment of biographies, those of Khaīl II to Shinūda II (d. 1046 CE). Bishop Michael's entries are extremely rich in content, well researched, and candid—at times, even scathing. A few decades later, his young contemporary Mawhūb ibn Manṣūr began to translate and redact the extant *Lives*, and he then appended the first biographies composed in Arabic, those of Khrisṭūdulūs and Kyrillus II (d. 1092 CE). After Mawhūb's death, Yūḥannā ibn Ṣā'īd al-Qulzūmī contributed the biography of Khaīl IV (d. 1102 CE).

Notably, while the biographies down to the late eleventh century were filtered through Mawhūb (an important fact), the HP enshrines many accounts of contemporaries and eyewitnesses,[24] and as Mark Swanson's recent study has amply demonstrated, each quire of biographies retains distinct thematic elements that betray its author's style and point of view.[25] Contributing to the HP's reliability is Mawhūb's sober understanding of his initial task as one of translation, not of "correction" or censorship. (If he had taken the opposite view, perhaps none of Michael of Tinnīs' critical biographies would have survived.) Certainly, this does not eliminate the perspectives of the original writers or Mawhūb's editorial hand, but it speaks to the integrity and competence of the primary redactor through whose eyes the modern historian reads the biographies.

Still, the HP requires a great deal of scrutiny. First, there are the textual variants between the two main recensions, which for convenience are identified here as the "primitive" (11th c., HP-P) and "vulgate" (13th c., HP-V).[26] The differences between the two versions are significant on occasion, but more often inconsequential. Typically, the Arabic diction of HP-V is more refined and laudatory. I have consulted both recensions, but cited or translated HP-P only where it significantly deviates from the far more accessible HP-V. There is also something to be said for the accordion-like structure of the work. Unless a biographer had access to older historical materials, the earliest entries within any given quire tend to be fairly terse in comparison with the latter biographies within the same grouping, which brim with rich details and anecdotal information.[27] Additionally, in chronicling the deeds of long-reposed patriarchs, some authors tended to record history as they saw fit. The 'Amr-Benjamin paradigm (defined by M. Swanson) provides a salient example.[28] While the biography of Patriarch Benjamin (622–61 CE) would appear to set a precedent for harmonious interactions between the Coptic hierarchy and Islamic administration immediately after the conquest, the discussions forwarded in Chapters Two and Three below would argue that the amicable relations described in that *Life* best resonate within the tenure of 'Abd al-'Azīz ibn Marwān (d. 705 CE)—after which Benjamin's biography was written—rather than the socio-political environment that prevailed in the early post-conquest decades. Arab Muslim scholars were certainly not the only ones tempted to record history in light of later developments, or with an eye toward their contemporary needs and expectations.

Coptic Arabic apocalyptic texts provide another important resource. Blinded by esoteric passages and repetitive motifs, however, scholars have until recently failed to discern the potential of this popular genre. Apocalyptic tracts certainly demand a judicious—even cynical—reading, but they intermittently preserve voices of dissent and document societal shifts and anxieties in an explicit manner reticent or entirely lacking in normative histories.[29] Most significant in this regard are the *Apocalypse of Athanasios*' sharp censure of the clergy of its day and the *Apocalypse of Samuel's* hyperbolic critique of social transformations within Egyptian society. Despite the stated monastic setting of that apocalypse, its themes and content (as with most of these "visions") resonate best among a predominantly urban lay audience.

Documentary texts for the period studied survive in Greek, Coptic, and Arabic papyri,[30] presenting historians with remarkable opportunities for research along with an assortment of challenges.[31] Papyri represent an egalitarian cross-section of society and are current with the events and issues they address, which often allows them to supplement and even correct narrative sources. Beyond the limitations associated with their state of preservation and the interpretive challenges they pose, however, such documents primarily reflect the environment of Upper Egypt and should be interpreted within the immediate vicinity of the village or region from which they hail.[32] Intrinsically, they provide particulars and the extent to which a text or dossier reflects universals, or societal norms, must not be automatically presumed. Here, while the survey of papyri for this study has not been exhaustive, all major publications and catalogues have been examined with regard to items spanning the sixth to the tenth centuries CE.

Literary and documentary sources pose antithetical challenges. Narrative texts often lack specificity and implicitly claim to represent the whole community when, in fact, they forward the perspectives of urban elites of the Delta, who had a distinct interest in how the past was framed and recalled. A documentary source, on the other hand, encapsulates the voice of an individual author almost at ground level, but it typically lacks orientation and context. Consequently, the extent to which any text—documentary or literary—reflects provincial norms, let alone society as a whole, is not immediately discernible. When literary and documentary sources are extant, the approach has been to interlace them while preferring the latter, an approach most evident in (and, arguably, best suited for) studies on taxation and land tenure.[33] Nonetheless, despite their perceived compatibility and ostensibly complimentary virtues, these two types of sources cannot readily or consistently supplement or correct one another—a problem that is somewhat mitigated during Late Antiquity.[34] Most normative histories stem from the Delta, where papyri that may function as a control to corroborate or contradict them are minimal at best. Conversely, Upper Egyptian papyri seldom have any local histories or chronicles to dispute, substantiate, or place them within a wider framework. A sagacious reading is crucial. Where narrative and documentary texts overlap,[35] both are strengthened, but when they differ, care must be taken before "correcting" the perspective of narrative sources.[36]

Throughout this study, several methodologies and intellectual frameworks have been referenced and employed in various capacities (and are alternatively vindicated or dismissed when appropriate), but they have been intentionally subordinated to texts. Far too often the reversal of that relationship has rendered historians into the unwilling scribes of self-fulfilling prophecies. The ensuing discussions that dismiss many of the conclusions reached under the influence of the nationalist paradigm, which seemed logical and self-evident to generations of scholars, proves as much.

Finally, one must note the impossibility of studying the Jewish community in Egypt during the early post-conquest centuries. Richly documented throughout Late Antiquity and especially from the late tenth century CE on, Egyptian Jews are marginally attested in the sources of the centuries under investigation.[37] This prevents even a cursory survey.[38] The general trajectories of that community likely paralleled those of other non-Muslim confessions, but such an assertion relies primarily on conjecture and probability rather than historical inquiry.

The Doctrinal Labyrinth

An historian who is unfamiliar with—or misconstrues—the religious traditions of the peoples he or she studies is missing, misinterpreting, or ignoring a stratum of every text read.[39] For Egypt, an immense bibliography may be compiled in which monophysitism—defined as the heretical belief that Jesus Christ had a single divine nature—underpins the conclusions of works that cut across disciplinary and topical boundaries. Seemingly anything and everything, from the very rise of Islam and the Arab conquest of Egypt[40] to religious conversions and distinctive features in medieval Coptic art,[41] can be explained more or less by the alleged doctrinal "corruption" of the Copts.[42] Moreover, monophysitism has been presented by some scholars as the cause, and by others as the result of the rise of an Egyptian "national" consciousness. Among the anti-Chalcedonian confessions, all have repeatedly maintained that they do not and have never accepted such a belief, which they have also historically condemned as heresy.[43] Nonetheless, the scholarly community has been averse to reassessing its understanding of doctrinal issues in Egypt,[44] and has largely ignored academic studies that seriously consider the anti-Chalcedonian perspective, though that is now changing.[45]

Since its publication, W.H.C. Frend's *The Rise of the Monophysite Movement* has dominated all discussions of the topic.[46] An immense work of scholarship, the book defines monophysitism as the belief that Jesus Christ had a single divine nature and then proceeds to discuss diverse groups (many of whom were marginal) under that umbrella.[47] Among those groups are the so-called "moderate Monophysites," the Jacobites of Egypt and Syria, who were the numerically dominant body. Several conceptual problems and incongruities promptly emerge, not least of which is that most of these "monophysites," even those branded as heretics by their own camp, never questioned the humanity of the incarnate Logos.[48]

Predominantly, the basic agreement among the "monophysites" was not a belief in a "single divine nature" (it is difficult to ascertain who actually espoused this amateurish doctrine),[49] but rather (1) rejection of the Council of Chalcedon, which they—to varying degrees—believed was susceptible to a "Nestorian" interpretation,[50] and (2) adherence to the Cyrillian terminology emphasizing the oneness of Christ through the formula "*of* two natures" (ἐκ δύο φύσεων) as opposite to the Chalcedonian "*in* two natures" (ἐν δύο φύσεσιν), which had Nestorian parallels (though pro-Chalcedonians use the phrase in a different theological context).[51]

The theological dispute was complicated by the use of terms that carried double connotations, leading to linguistic and theological confusion (the ecclesiastical politics involved are an altogether different issue).[52] For example, the anti-Chalcedonian "one *phusis*" (or "nature") may be understood as either "one person" or "one generic category" (either divinity or humanity);[53] similarly, the pro-Chalcedonian "in one *prosōpon*" may be understood as either "in one person" or "in a single facade".[54] "One person" is perfectly orthodox, while "one facade/guise" and "one generic category" are anathema to pro- and anti-Chalcedonians alike.

Significantly, in modern literature and traditional polemic, the so-called monophysites are defined as those who believe in a single *divine* nature; thus, *phusia* is consistently interpreted as a "generic category" rather than "individual." It is here that One Nature Christology can be authenticated as orthodox.[55] Nowhere in the literature of the Copts (or Syrians or Armenians, for that matter) is Jesus Christ defined as possessing a single "divine" nature.[56]

Consistently, each confession designated itself as "the orthodox." Pro-Chalcedonians labeled their opponents "monophysites," maligning them as those who believed in a single "divine" nature, while the anti-Chalcedonians labeled their opponents "dyophysite," that is, those who "split the one Christ into two".[57] Each constituency interpreted their opponent's terminology in accordance with their own definitions and theological framework rather than within the other's theological context. "Monophysitism" and even "dyophsitism," as defined in anti-Chalcedonian literature, are but straw-man doctrines intended to portray the Christology of the opposing faction as a blatant heresy that could be attacked at length with the most rudimentary of theological training.

In sum, the anti-Chalcedonians believed in a "single *divine* nature" just as fervently as the pro-Chalcedonians worshiped "two Christs". Contextually read, anti- and pro-Chalcedonian theologians aimed at stating the same belief. It is therefore nonsensical to discuss the "monophysites'" intrinsic inability to resist Islamic theology, or to interpret historical developments as consequences of theological error. In time, linguistic and theological confusion along with the complexities of ecclesiastical politics and social memory (particularly of periods of intolerance and persecution) forged contentious factions, though, on occasion, a more ecumenical spirit prevailed. After scrutinizing the beliefs and practices of the Melkites, pseudo-Sawīrus concluded his *Tartīb al-kahanūt* by praying:

> May the Lord God guide [the Copts] and [the Melkites] onto the path of salvation, and protect us and them from the punishment of the [final] judgment (*al-qiṣāṣ*). May he reconcile this schism of the One Holy Catholic and Apostolic Church, and reveal to us and to them any pitfalls on the path [of salvation by] revealing the truth while pushing darkness afar. Perpetually, may he keep Satan away from us and them through his grace, kindness, and benevolence, in the same manner as he had earlier healed our souls through the wounds of his Passion.... May the Lord God accept the deeds of both confessions.[58]

Hierarchies and Demographics

Finally, a brief note on hierarchies and demographics is in order. Several scholars have questioned the origins of the anti-Chalcedonian hierarchies and their demographic hold. To be sure, the question itself assumes a normative pro-Chalcedonian perspective that scrutinizes those who refused to accept the council while largely ignoring the plurality within pro-Chalcedonian ranks and the length of time it took for the Definition of Chalcedon to become the doctrinal standard.[59] It is a perspective predicated upon the premise that the anti-Chalcedonians were an aberration whose origins must be surmised. Conversely, if a normative anti-Chacedonian perspective and literature are considered, it would be the origins of the Melkite hierarchy in Egypt and Syria that would come into question. In either case, I am skeptical of the cogency of this approach, and the utility of structuring an historical analysis around these parameters. Here, it is taken for granted that the schism at Chalcedon resulted in the bifurcation of the Alexandrian hierarchy, and eventually led to the development of several splinter groups. Still, the dominant historiography points to the mid-sixth century, more specifically the failure of deliberations under Emperor Justinian and the career of Jacob Baradaeos, as the crucial juncture for the founding of an anti-Chalcedonian hierarchy. More recently, though with a slightly different focus, that date has been pushed even further for the Copts, proposing that the identity of that jurisdiction only coalesced under early Islamic rule.[60]

To be sure, the ecclesiastical landscape is easier to negotiate after the mid-sixth century than before. Nonetheless, lines were drawn in the immediate aftermath of Chalcedon:[61] the faithful were instructed as to where they could and could not partake of the sacraments; confessional hymns emerged; some bishops were hailed as orthodox while others were berated as heretics; and each faction formulated guidelines for accepting those who had belonged to the other confession.[62] Already by the late-fifth century in Egypt (cf. the career of Peter the Iberian), the *Histories of the Holy Church* distinctly articulated an anti-Chalcedonian awareness, tracing a patriarchal line of succession from Cyril I and Dioskoros I to Timothy II, the same figures from whom Damian I and Benjamin I claimed their descent long before the Arabs were on the scene.[63]

With regard to the issue of identity, one can convincingly argue that the character of the Copts or that of their church—or that of any group or institution for that matter—was radically different at any 200-year interval. In general, while the emerging historiography poses new questions and functions as a counterbalance to essentialist, totalizing, and popular ideals that conceive of a static Coptic identity that stems from "the Pharaohs" and persists into the present, it is, nonetheless, problematic on two fronts. First, it minimizes, even dissolves the discernible bonds of continuity—hierarchical, liturgical, theological, monastic, and communal—between the church of the Patristic era or, to be more specific, that led by Cyril of Alexandria, and the eighth-century hierarchies and confessions that claimed descent from it. The Coptic Alexander II and the Melkite Kosmas I were, indeed, legitimate successors to Athanasius and Cyril; they did not simply imagine themselves to have been, or surreptitiously attempt to pass themselves off as such. Additionally, the search for the genesis of a new Coptic ethos—a novel sense of self and other—or rather, the discernment of a new phase in an ever-evolving hybrid identity, is largely a function of the criteria one deems most valid. Research focused on legal literature will yield a different chronology than that concerned with the processes of Arabization or political ideology. These issues are repeatedly explored over the course of this study.

A related and equally problematic assertion maintains that the Coptic/anti-Chalcedonian population constituted a numerical minority until early Islamic rule.[64] Chapter Four does enumerate nine Christian jurisdictions on the eve of the conquest, most of whom eventually joined the Coptic church. In each case, however, even with the Melkites who never recognized the Coptic hierarchy, the extant evidence suggests that these confessions had an extremely limited reach beyond Alexandria and a meager following. For example, in the decades following the conquest, the Akephaloi dominated in a single village in the Delta, and had a constituency in one of the quarters of Babylon (Miṣr).[65] Similarly, the Barsanuphians, another alternative confession that could claim a following outside of Alexandria, were confined to specific villages in the eastern Delta. And judging by the accounts narrating their union with the Coptic hierarchy in the late eighth and early ninth centuries, they had but three bishops. By comparison, at that same juncture, the Melkites could boast a patriarch, several bishops, at least three monasteries, and well over a dozen churches, and the Copts could still convene the "Council of a Hundred [bishops]," though the actual number of bishops was likely closer to 70 bishops. (On these groups and figures, see Chapters Four, Five, and Ten.)

Significantly, in the sixth and seventh centuries only the anti-Chalcedonian Coptic hierarchy had roots throughout the branches of the Delta, Upper Egypt, Nubia, and Ethiopia. Moreover, the early caliphate only recognized the Coptic and Melkite confessions–that was not by accident. Finally, the total omission of the confessional squabbles and factionalism that dominate the sources of the Delta from Upper Egyptian papyri, while not definitive, bolsters the notion that the contentions of Lower Egypt were a world away from the *ṣaʿīd*. In this light, not only do the Copts emerge as the dominant constituency, but the Melkites come across as the second major Christian confession in Egypt. The traditional historiography—on *this* front—stands on a firm foundation.

CHAPTER 2

THE CONQUEST: EVENT, TEXT, AND MEMORY

Over the past few decades, historians have developed increasingly sophisticated strategies for reading the early Islamic historical tradition and, in particular, the *futūḥ* (conquest) accounts.[1] By identifying literary tropes and honing the skill and artistry of plaiting Arabic, Greek, and Syriac sources, modern scholarship has produced insightful narratives that have surpassed those advanced just a few generations earlier. Yet, despite increasing methodological rigor and the glaring significance of the Arab conquests as the pivotal transformative event since Constantine's conversion, what may be confidently narrated remains meager. Ostensibly, historians exploited fissures within the writings of Arab historians and proceeded to undermine them without providing a tangible alternative. In that light, the goal here is to develop a methodological strategy that facilitates a deeper understanding of the historical details, ideological grounding, and cultural significance of Egypt's *futūḥ* narratives.

The following analysis lacks a chronology of the conquest as such. To that end, A.J. Butler's *Arab Conquest of Egypt* and, more recently, L. Chagnon's *La conquête musulmane de l'Égypte*, provide the most plausible scenarios.[2] Rather, this discussion scrutinizes the interpretive prisms through which the conquest has been read and interpreted. Here, proceeding from old debates to new approaches, an introductory summary outlines the dominant interpretive paradigm, the abject failure of which is demonstrated through a parsing of the mutually exclusive traditions attributed to Patriarch Benjamin I (622–661 CE). Subsequently, the focus shifts to the catalytic role played by Egyptian elites (Melkites and Copts) in the unfolding of the conquest. Finally, building upon those two discussions, the last segment draws upon an interpretive framework based on Memory Studies and Textual Criticism to explore the highly selective ninth-century conquest memories shared by Copts and Muslims in light of the processes that informed the simultaneous suppression and guised expression of old, dangerous pre-conquest ideals.

The Master Narrative

As discussed in the previous chapter, the historiography of seventh- and eighth-century Egypt has been significantly distorted by a pervasive nationalist reading that has endured for a century. According to this interpretive scheme, the "nationalist" Copts, having been alienated from their Byzantine "oppressors" due to the Chalcedonian schism and the tyranny of "imperial" Byzantine landlords,[3] received Arab armies with open arms (or at least indifference), which, in turn, enabled Coptic notables and their church to share in the spoils of the Arab's victory.[4] Conversely, the "Greek" pro-Chalcedonians purportedly fought the Arabs to the bitter end.

In recent decades, historians have attempted to steer clear of this paradigm with little to no success. Academics have largely succeeded in purging such terms as "national," "colonial," and "imperial" from their prose—though some attempts to read pre-modern history in light of current theoretical frameworks threaten to repeat those old misleading binary perspectives under new, more sophisticated guises. Still, apart from coining new verbiage, much of the underlying interpretive apparatus has survived remarkably intact. P.M. Fraser had offered a succinct and still valid summary of the master narrative:

> The relative ease with which Egypt fell before the small Muslim forces was long explained as the result of the

> cooperation of the Monophysite population, which under the leadership of their patriarch, Benjamin I, could no longer brook the long-standing Melchite persecution ... This view was challenged in forceful terms by A.J. Butler, who regarded the Copts as having remained faithful to their imperial allegiance in spite of all their tribulation, *until after the surrender of Babylon or the capture of the Fayyūm*, when they saw that further resistance would be fruitless. They then collaborated with the invading forces. *Others have not been convinced by this argument, and indeed the evidence, in spite of all the confusion in either direction, seems to point to the traditional view.*[5]

Nonetheless, despite its tidiness, this paradigm falters in several respects. Conceptually, contemporary scholarship defines "nationalism" more narrowly than at mid-century, maintaining that a nationalist ideology as such did not exist in the Middle East prior to World War One, which renders the whole discussion of "nationalism" in seventh-century Egypt anachronistic.[6] Moreover, setting aside the current academic parameters for defining nationalism, there remains a fundamental incongruity between the particulars of the conquest and the now dominant interpretive schemes. Indeed, the sources consistently depict various divisions among the Egyptian populace, both commoners and notables. Quintessentially, however, time and again the fragmentation described in the earliest accounts fails to conform to the stereotypical religious or "ethnically"-inspired enclaves envisioned by medieval historians or modern scholarship. This is amply demonstrated by the subsequent discussions of Patriarch Benjamin's problematic historiography, and the overlooked, yet key role played by seventh-century notables in facilitating the conquest.

Depictions of Patriarch Benjamin

Patriarch Benjamin's involvement in the events culminating with the conquest of Egypt provides an essential grounding for the diverse interpretations of that event. Three views dominate: each concedes

Benjamin's self-imposed exile in 10/631 to flee from the Melkite patriarch-prefect Kyros, but diverge as to the date of his return and his general attitude toward the new Arab regime. In assessing the historicity of the patriarch's actions, however, two basic but crucial steps are necessary. First, the traditions must be examined in order of their antiquity; that, alone, allows for the discernment of an unmistakable pattern, which enables the dating of a significant historiographic shift. Subsequently, the reliability of each narrative must be individually appraised.

In that regard, one cluster of sources comprised of seventh and early eighth-century Egyptian writings—the HP's biography of Benjamin, the *Chronicle* of John of Nikiou, and the sermon *On Cana of Galilee*—dates Benjamin's return to Alexandria in 23/644, well after Arab armies had full control of Egypt, and specifically Alexandria.[7] Thus, the early Coptic tradition positively excludes the patriarch from participating in any aspect of the conquest.

A second tradition finds its justification in two ninth-century writings, Ibn 'Abd al-Ḥakam's *Futūḥ miṣr* and the *History of Dionysios* of Tel-Maḥrē (d. 230/845), as reconstructed from the Syrian *Chronicle of 1234*.[8] Both compilations maintain that 'Amr ibn al-'Āṣ contacted Benjamin at the onset of the campaign, and that the patriarch responded by instructing the Coptic population and hierarchy to aid the Arabs.[9] Here, Benjamin appears to have played a prominent role in the conquest from its inception. More recently, R. Hoyland introduced a third perspective that attempts to bridge the gap between the sources and the conflicting chronologies. He situates Benjamin's return to Alexandria in 23/644, but asserts that he actively aided Arab armies in their attempt to reclaim Alexandria after the revolt of Manuel the Eunuch in 25/646.[10]

Demonstrably, *Futūḥ miṣr* and the *History of Dionysios* sampled the same pool of traditions, and reflect the emergence of analogous historiographic impulses. Dionysios' *History* drew upon the prevailing traditions of its day along with the lost Syriac Common Source—an eighth-century Syriac recension of Arabic traditions.[11] Consequently, it transmits a number of the same *topoi* and historiographic sensibilities embedded in early Islamic literature and, thus, it poses analogous interpretive difficulties. A few decades after the Syrian patriarch composed his history, Ibn ʿAbd al-Ḥakam wrote *Futūḥ miṣr*, which canonized Egypt's conquest traditions. Hence, the two authors represent the crystallization of conquest narratives nearly two centuries after the historical event. Upon closer examination, *Futūḥ miṣr* and the *History of Dionysios* again betray their common outlook. In both, Patriarch Benjamin's purported actions adhere to A. Noth's Conquest of Cities *topos* so closely that, lacking any independent control or outside corroboration, the historicity of the accounts must remain suspect.[12]

Fundamentally, one seeks to identify the impulses that led ninth-century historians to depict Benjamin in the role of an ally to the Arab conquerors when the earliest narratives did not. In fact, several factors may account for this tendency. Textually, as noted in Butler's *Arab Conquest* and reiterated by various scholars since, *futūḥ* chronicles typically identify the Alexandrian Patriarch as *al-Muqawqas* rather than by name. The title originally identified Kyros, but the enigmatic moniker has led to confusion. More specifically, I believe that the misunderstanding stems from the Arabic sources' propensity to employ the term as a generic designation for the leader of Egypt's Christians without accounting for the pro- or anti-Chalcedonian confessions or their rival hierarchies. Read from a ninth-century perspective, the leader of Egypt's Christians was undoubtedly the Coptic Patriarch not his Melkite counterpart (see Chapter Four); this led to the inclination to identify Benjamin rather than Kyros as *al-Muqawqas*.[13]

Thematically, the depiction of bishops as lead negotiators with Arab generals is by no means foreign to conquest narratives. Syriac and Greek writings, which predate and supplement the extant Arabic chronicles, place great emphasis on Patriarch Sophronios' (634–8 CE) role in the surrender of the Holy City.[14] Still, while Sophronios negotiated with Arab armies in Jerusalem, the case for Benjamin fulfilling a similar role in Egypt cannot be demonstrated from the earliest accounts.

Historiographic sensibilities may have also led to the recasting of Patriarch Benjamin. Two new schools of thought were in play by the ninth century CE. Among Arab Muslim historians, Ibn 'Abd al-Ḥakam actively cultivated a theme of communal cooperation throughout his *Futūḥ miṣr*. In that context, he needed Benjamin—not Kyros—to have participated in the conquest. Where that impulse is lacking, as in the chronicles of Theophanes and Agapios (which had also utilized the Syriac Common Source), Kyros is the one depicted as the lead negotiator with the Arabs while Benjamin is completely omitted—this is likewise the tradition known to al-Balādhurī.[15] Ibn 'Abd al-Ḥakam's description of an alliance between Benjamin and Ibn al-'Āṣ provided an unmistakable precedent to his ninth-century readership, emphasizing cooperation between Coptic and Muslim leaders, and finds a parallel in the *History of the Patriarchs'* description of the initial meeting between the two figures.[16] Additionally, *Futūḥ miṣr* interprets the conquest, on the one hand, as an act of liberation from Byzantine tyranny (an aspect that was retained to an extent in the HP-Primitive) and, on the other, as the fulfillment of prophecies enumerated at the beginning of that history, where the Prophet of Islam purportedly stressed an ancestral link between Egyptians and Arabs and repeatedly prophesied that the *qibṭ* would aid the Arabs.[17] Ibn 'Abd al-Ḥakam positions Benjamin's role as a fulfillment of that prophecy.

A second, nearly contemporary, school of thought emerged among the Copts which promoted a new anti-Chalcedonian historiography that depicted Byzantine rule as a uniform period of oppression (see Chapter Nine). Regardless of the actual sentiments of the generation that lived through the military campaign—which, significantly, had protested persecution by the "heretics," rather than the "Romans" or "Byzantines"—[18] ninth-century anti-Chalcedonians believed that their ancestors sought "to make themselves free from [Byzantine] oppression,"[19] hence Benjamin's favorable depiction as a liberator in the Christian histories of that period and beyond. In sum, whether that recasting of Benjamin's role, which rendered him an agent of liberation from (presumed) Byzantine oppression and an ally to Arab armies, resulted from textual confusion, thematic borrowing, or adherence to new historiographic trends—or a convergence of these factors—this ninth-century tradition contradicts the earliest narratives in which the patriarch was no more than a passive bystander. Inexorably, these discrepancies prove invaluable in demonstrating the historicity of seventh-century sources.

On occasion, the HP lauds Egyptian resilience in opposing the Council of Chalcedon, which may be gleaned from an often-quoted passage:

> For the rest of the churches and monasteries that belonged to virgins and monks had been defiled by Herakleios when he forced the faith of Chalcedon upon them, *except for this single monastery* [of Metras]. For those who inhabited it were a mighty group of Egyptians, all of whom were locals (*wa jamīʿahum ahl*). Hence [Kyros] could not entice them.[20]

So much has been made of this brief passage to vindicate the existence of a "nationalist" Egyptian church.[21] Taken in the context of the arguments presented earlier in this chapter (and others in Chapter Nine), however, at best this gloss reflects a regional chauvinism similar to that found in the later *faḍāʾil* literature, but not a nationalist ideology. Significantly, even here, the central issue remains staunch opposition to Chalcedonian theology, not Byzantine rule as such. Moreover, if the passage is read literally through an ethnic lens, then one must believe that Kyros succeeded to entice all other monasteries because they presumably housed a mixed population of pro- and anti-Chalcedonian monks, or Coptic-speaking Egyptians and Greek-speaking Byzantines; neither scenario conforms to the historical situation. Arguably, if not an altogether later interpolation, the stated passage simply aimed to justify the prominence of the Monastery of Metras, which became Benjamin's patriarchal residence after his restoration.

Nonetheless, of significance here is that such regional sentiments did exist, at least in the mind of the author of the HP's biography of Benjamin, which was written in the early eighth century. Consequently, had the HP depicted Benjamin as a liberator who freed the Copts from Byzantine oppression, such a depiction would have been met with general approval, much as in the *History of*

Dionysios. Yet, the HP's narrative lies in direct opposition. By locating the patriarch in Upper Egypt until 644, the HP temporally and geographically isolates him from the conquest. Even in the subsequent dynamic that led to his restoration, Benjamin emerges in a passive role, as a lamentable figure at the mercy of 'Amr ibn al-'Āṣ and Shenoute the *dux* of Antinoë. The fact that the HP does not credit Benjamin with liberating his church, despite an impulse to bolster his role and persona, testifies of the account's antiquity and the moderation exercised by later redactors. Thus, on account of its early composition, its restrained efforts to glorify Benjamin's persona or actions vis-à-vis the conquest, and the lack of *topoi* from *futūḥ* narratives, the HP's account and chronology, as corroborated by the *Chronicle* of John of Nikiou and *On Cana of Galilee*, must take precedence over all others.

While the two sets of traditions discussed thus far focus on Benjamin's role (or lack thereof) at the outset of the conquest, a revisionist reading scrutinizes his subsequent actions. R. Hoyland's thesis, which maintains that Benjamin aided the Arabs after returning from exile, rests upon the following tradition preserved in *Futūḥ miṣr*: "There was in Alexandria a bishop of the Copts called Abba Benjamin. When he heard of the coming of 'Amr ibn al-'Āṣ to Egypt, he wrote to the Copts informing them that the Byzantines (*rūm*) would [soon] have *no rule and that their kingdom was at an end*, and he instructed them to receive 'Amr. And it is said that the Copts who were in Faramā (Pelusium) were *that day* helping 'Amr".[22] Whereas most scholars have accepted the chronological placement of this tradition at the inception of the conquest, Hoyland's reconstruction correctly maintains that the incident could not have occurred in late 639, as Ibn 'Abd al-Ḥakam maintains, while 'Amr and his army camped at the distant Faramā. Rather, assuming that the account retains a kernel of historical truth, Hoyland deduced that it: "should then be understood as referring to a measure taken by Benjamin during the Byzantine recapture of Alexandria in 646 to maintain the agreement concluded between himself and 'Amr in 644".[23] P.M. Fraser had also accepted the historicity of this tradition, though it is unclear whether he situated it in 18/639 or 25/646.[24] In general, this analysis reinforces A.J. Butler's basic premise that Coptic-Arab cooperation developed in the wake of the conquest, rather than prior; still, both interpretations cast Benjamin more or less in the above-mentioned mold of Sophronios.

As it stands, however, this *ḥadīth* defies historical reconstruction. Had it taken place in 18/639, Kyros rather than Benjamin would have been at Alexandria. Moreover, it is difficult to image how Benjamin, in Upper Egypt, would have heard of the Arabs' arrival, and believing that the Byzantine "kingdom was at an end," decided to issue and successfully disseminate an edict in support of the Arabs' campaign. Conversely, if the account is situated in 25/646 to accommodate the revisionist reading, then the narrative's geographic moorings must also be revised.[25] 'Amr would have hardly retreated to the distant Faramā (Egypt's outpost in the Sinai) to regroup and plan his recapture of Alexandria, and it is even less tenable to assume that Benjamin would have remained in Alexandria after the pro-Chalcedonians recaptured it. Regardless of how scholars modify or read the details of this tradition, its historicity remains insolvent as every scenario resolves one difficulty while generating another. The tradition's true merit may be best appreciated as a literary device, an ideological rather than a historical narrative that subtly, though brilliantly, promotes Ibn 'Abd al-Ḥakam's historiographic sensibilities and prerogatives:[26] the theme of communal cooperation, and his two-pronged interpretation of the conquest as the liberation of Egyptians and the fulfillment of prophecy for Muslims.

Moreover, this revisionist perspective, along with the preponderance of scholarly literature, assumes an air of cooperation between the Coptic hierarchy and the Arabs directly after the conquest, a highly doubtful premise in light of the subsequent discussion as well as that presented in the following chapter, which advances the thesis that secular elites, rather than the Coptic hierarchy, aided the Arab army and facilitated the conquest.

In sum, this analysis demonstrates the persistence of the crypto-nationalistic underpinnings of the hegemonic narrative, which have led to distorted, even contradictory readings of the historical record. In providing a historical assessment of Patriarch Benjamin's actual role in the conquest, and an evaluation of the relevant sources, it has delineated the contours of ninth-century Islamic and Christian (anti-Chalcedonian) historical writings. Scholars have long demonstrated the rise of a new historiography under early ʿAbbasid rule, but by limiting themselves to Arab Muslim authors they failed to discern a parallel development within Christian literature, which at once reflected the bourgeoning Islamic discourse while addressing strictly Christian concerns. Accounting for this nascent historiographic school is fundamental when reading the Christian texts of the seventh through the tenth centuries, as it facilitates a contrapuntal reading of an array of traditions whose historicity remains doubtful.

Conquest through Elites

In the early seventh century, while Islam was still confined to the Arabian Peninsula, secular elites demonstrated their strategic importance in waging military campaigns in Egypt. Generals Niketas and Bonosos, representing Herakleios and Phokas respectively, maneuvered and engaged one another with the assistance of local notables.[27] Bonosos' injunction to Paul of Samannūd to place his ships under the general's command is of particular interest as a generation later, ʿAmr ibn al-ʿĀṣ would echo a similar imperative to Apacyrus, pagarch of Dalās.[28] Significantly, in these incidents, the generals did not forcibly seize or sequester the necessary ships, but negotiated with their owners. John of Nikiou documented the multipurpose utility of these vessels. In addition to their use in transportation, during the Arab conquest soldiers constructed impromptu bridges by laying wooden planks across rafts lined up from one bank of the Nile to the other.[29] These bridges enabled Arab forces to cross the river, but additionally functioned as blockades that hampered the movement of Byzantine ships and soldiers.[30] Plainly, Arab and Byzantine generals depended upon the ships of Egyptian elites as part of their military strategies, and likely utilized them in other facets as well.[31]

Turning to the Arab conquest, scholarship assumes that the conquerors received an amicable reception from the Coptic populace, but to the contrary, the sources fail to depict a uniform reaction. In general, discerning the attitudes of Egyptians at that juncture, many of whom had already seen the Sasanians come and go just a decade prior, is but an exercise in conjecture. Far from being indifferent or sympathetic, a number of Egyptian villages fought against the invading armies, only the most troublesome of these encounters warranted mention in Arabic writings.[32]

Nonetheless, while some Egyptians resisted, others collaborated. Immediately following the signing of the first treaty at Babylon, Ibn 'Abd al-Ḥakam maintains that: "a group of Coptic notables went out with 'Amr; they fixed roads and repaired bridges for the [Muslims]. They [also opened] the markets and aided [the Muslims] who desired to kill the Byzantines (*rūm*)".[33] As proposed earlier in this chapter, Ibn 'Abd al-Ḥakam repeatedly stresses the theme of cooperation between Egyptians and Muslims; this is another example to consider in addition to his depiction of Benjamin's alleged endorsement of the conquest.[34] Yet, whereas the earlier example focused on elites, 'Amr and Benjamin, here the tradition functions as an exemplar for the populace, reiterating the same theme of communal cooperation. Similarly, Ibn 'Abd al-Ḥakam's above-referenced prophecy, stipulating that the *qibṭ* will be an aid to the Muslims, finds another, more literal fulfillment here.

Still, with regard to the issue of historicity, a fundamental distinction is that while Benjamin's predicament in exile prevented him from rendering aid or mounting resistance to the advancing Arabs, Egypt's landed elites were positioned to do just that. Such notables had tremendous resources at their disposal, but ostensibly came to terms with the advancing Arab armies rather than risking their personal safety and wealth. Conquest narratives and documentary papyri prove that such elites retained control of their estates and attained influential posts in the early Arab administration.[35]

While John of Nikiou and Ibn 'Abd al-Ḥakam narrate this collusion of elites, they fundamentally disagree as to the motivation behind the assistance rendered. In one incident, Ibn 'Abd al-Ḥakam states that Coptic notables accompanied the Arabs and aided them by supplying "all that they needed from food to fodder".[36] In commenting on what is likely to have been the same incident, John of Nikiou, acknowledging as much, adds that the assistance rendered was under duress; those who aided the Arabs were "under the constraint of an unceasing fear".[37]

Communal fragmentation and a diversity of responses again emerged during the Second Siege of Alexandria (25/646),[38] at the conclusion of which, a group of villagers purportedly complained that the rebels sustained themselves by pillaging their goods, which, according to the agreement they signed, were under 'Amr's protection.[39] Gracious, the Arab general compensated the farmers.[40] While the historicity of this whole *ḥadīth* remains suspect, in the context of the present discussion it conforms well to Ibn 'Abd al-Ḥakam's grand narrative of the conquest, while providing a blueprint of sorts outlining the reciprocal rights and liabilities of each community: Muslims had the prerogative to maintain security and to assure justice, while the cooperation and loyalty of *dhimmī*s was expected and rewarded. Moreover, the incident resonates well with the chaos described in John's *Chronicle* and the divided loyalties paradigm stressed here. While some took up arms and vehemently fought against the Arabs, others quickly came to terms with the new regime. Two aspects are clear: that Arab armies relied on the aid and resources of secular elites rather than clerics, and that even after the conquest loyalties in Egypt remained divided and demonstrably fickle.

With regard to Egyptian elites, the notables named in all extant narrative and documentary sources, with a singular exception, may be identified as Melkites. In fact, of the dozens of individuals that may be identified in historical narratives and administrative papyri immediately prior to, during, and in the decades *after* the conquest—primarily *duces*, generals, and pagarchs—only Shenoute the *dux* of Antinoë adhered to the anti-Chalcedonian confession, and he must have kept his religious preferences private.[41] All other elites were appointed and served under Kyros' administration and were no doubt Melkites, at least nominally, as was the norm since the mid-sixth century.[42] This was obvious enough to the pro-Chalcedonian patriarch Eutychios, who, in his *Naẓm al-jawhar*, clearly identifies the controlling elites at the time of the conquest as members of his own confession.[43]

But what would have motivated regional elites (pro- and anti-Chalcedonians) to aid the invading Arab generals against the empire with which they shared confessional and civic ties? First, it is difficult to discern if these elites viewed the Arabs as an invading army or a raiding force. Second, narrative and documentary sources demonstrate that upon assuming command, the Arabs handsomely rewarded elites who aided them by (re-)appointing many to influential post-conquest positions.[44] Third, the Arabs did not confiscate the personal estates or funds of these individuals as might be expected.[45] Hence, the preservation of personal wealth and status appear to have been the primary incentives for cooperation with Arab armies. Another possibility is that Monenergist and Monothelite controversies had divided the pro-Chalcedonian community in Egypt, as they had in Syria and Jerusalem.[46]

The evidence forwarded thus far for Coptic resistance and Melkite collaboration further erodes the politico-religious paradigm envisioned by current scholarship, and underscores the inadequacy of the prevailing master narrative. The simplistic depictions of the Copts as a separatist, distinct "other," or as complacent agents in their own conquest, along with the ideological portrayals of the Melkites as staunch loyalists, fail to withstand scrutiny. These caricatures are at best problematic, if not altogether untenable.

In sum, historians have tended to favor a few (and in light of this chapter, problematic) traditions that focused on the Coptic hierarchy's role in the conquest while overlooking the multitude of passages that narrate the vital role played by secular elites during that tumultuous juncture. When scrutinized, these accounts manifest the integral role of regional elites in facilitating the conquest of the province and the means by which the new Arab rulers rewarded them.

In the decades immediately following the Arab conquest, the plight of the anti-Chalcedonians surely improved, but this resulted from the lifting of prohibitions rather than the granting of new privileges. As demonstrated in the following chapter, the early

Islamic government exhibited a general indifference in its interactions with the Coptic church and populace, which was often harmful to that confession until the governorship of ʿAbd al-ʿAzīz ibn Marwān (65–86/685–705). It was only at that later juncture that the Coptic hierarchy was treated with deference.

False Memories and Suppressed Narratives

Whereas the above discussions tended to emphasize historicity over historiography, the remainder of this chapter reverses the trajectory by drawing upon two intellectual traditions. Form and Redaction Criticism have repeatedly proven their merit as vital methodological tools in reading the early Arabic historical tradition and in identifying the socio-political and religious factors that forged it.[47] Memory Studies provide a second stimulus, though admittedly, the subsequent analysis employs this term and its intellectual underpinnings rather conservatively.[48] Memory scholarship, whether in the context of the formation of social memory, culture, or identity, provides intriguing possibilities, but while the methodologies employed relate well to sociology, anthropology, post-colonial studies, and post-processual archeology, they present unresolved difficulties for those researching ancient or medieval civilizations.[49]

Still, a branch of that literature which problematizes the gulf between oral and written traditions proves of particular significance to historians. In that regard, Patrick Geary's approach in *Phantoms of Remembrance*, where he argues for a symbiotic relationship between word and text, provides an intellectual roadmap for further research. Tersely summarized, he argues that as oral traditions are recorded, the ensuing texts inevitably influence the content and contours of oral culture and communal memories, which, themselves, would be written down later still; hence, he establishes an organic relationship between the spoken word and written text through something of a feedback mechanism.[50] Geary's study sketches a methodological approach that may shed light on the evolution of *futūḥ* accounts. Inadvertently, however, his scheme has, in part, brought the study of memory ever so close to the repertoire of Redaction Criticism.[51] Still, the paradigm of memory proves particularly insightful in refining our understanding of certain processes that Redaction Criticism typically glosses over. Foremost, to the historian of the pre-modern world the significance of Memory Studies lies in conceiving of memory as a social process that engenders specific cultural—textual, oral, and physical (monumental or territorial)—renderings of the past, and in drawing attention to the mechanisms that enable the retention, reproduction, and proliferation of that same vision, at times in a non-linear fashion. Keeping these methodologies in mind, the focus now returns to the Arab conquest of Egypt.

As hitherto documented, while scholarly analyses of the conquest have reached considerable sophistication, the questions posed remain poorly constructed, and the answers strained. Conceptually, scholars continue to underestimate the chasm between seventh- and ninth-century texts, particularly where Christian sources are concerned. Here, it is argued that by the ninth century Copts and Muslims recalled their past with the aid of a series of false narratives and (imperfectly) suppressed historical memories. Repeatedly, these selective acts of remembrance and forgetfulness, or of suppression, betray themselves as agents of contemporary—that is, ʿAbbāsid—communal prerogatives; still, somehow an illicit set of memories reflecting pre-conquest sensibilities not only persisted but were articulated anew at that time. Above all, these memories and narratives functioned as strategies for negotiating communal interactions within a society where Christians numerically prevailed but Muslims dominated the socio-political discourse. To demonstrate the forces in play, two issues are addressed below: the general characteristics of the conquest as described by John of Nikiou and Ibn ʿAbd al-Ḥakam, and anti-Chalcedonian political ideology as reflected in Copto-Arabic apocalyptic tracts.

Conquest and Memory

When contrasting the seventh-century *Chronicle* of John of Nikiou with Ibn ʿAbd al-Ḥakam's ninth-century *Futūḥ miṣr*, several contradictory themes quickly emerge.[52] Certainly, the two writers interpreted the conquest according to diametrically opposed religious paradigms: John viewed it as a divine reprimand, while Ibn 'Abd al-Ḥakam conceived of the unfolding of the conquest as a manifestation of God's providence.[53] Beyond religious ideologies, however, throughout his description of the conquest John consistently depicted the inefficiency of the Byzantine army, the cowardice of soldiers, the betrayal of generals and elites, along with a host of military retreats, surrenders, and blunders.[54] He did cite examples of sectarian aggression, including several incidents of intra-communal violence in which the Arabs had no part.[55] In essence, however, John documented the failure of Byzantine forces to effectively respond to the Arab military threat,[56] and the violence that raged due to political chaos and the absence of civic leadership.[57]

Ibn 'Abd al-Ḥakam, on the other hand, was less interested in the Byzantine army as such, primarily using it as a foil in his narrative. In comparison to John's at times vivid descriptions of slaughter and mayhem (which are endemic of war),[58] Ibn 'Abd al-Ḥakam's conquest appears less bloody, particularly where the Copts are concerned. While sampling an assortment of *topoi*, Ibn 'Abd al-Ḥakam's carefully narrated accounts depict amicable interactions, even a symbiotic relationship, between Copts and Muslims, Egyptians and Arabs.[59] This is pivotal. Whereas John characterized the conquest as a barrage of Byzantine military failures and intra-communal unrest, Ibn 'Abd al-Ḥakam conceived of it as a monument to Islamic piety and a paradigm for inter-communal harmony, ultimately depicting it as an act of liberation rather than subjugation.[60] This particular theme of inter-communal cooperation is unique to Ibn 'Abd al-Ḥakam's work and does not appear in al-Balādhurī or al-Ṭabarī's description of the conquest of Egypt.

For its part, *Futūḥ miṣr* has enjoyed tremendous success. It is difficult to identify a single Arabic conquest tradition in later sources that is not dependent upon that work. Meanwhile, John's *Chronicle* faded into the periphery of manuscript depositories and historical writing. Thus, a narrative recounting military blunders, violence, and treachery was suppressed in favor of another that promoted several false memories—demonstrably so in the case of Patriarch Benjamin—but promoted communal cohesion and cooperation. One should hasten to emphasize that this disjointed historiography is not a reflection of a confessional bias; it is not that Christians and Muslims retained different versions of their past. To the contrary, while specifics vary, post-ninth century traditions from both communities reflect a remarkably similar outlook. Patriarch Eutychios' *Naẓm al-jawhar* (*Annals*) provides an interesting aside, where its organizational scheme is based on caliphal tenure.

Here, John's *Chronicle* may be read as the archetypal suppressed narrative. It preserved accounts that did not interest Christians or Muslims in the ninth century as it documents events better forgotten than remembered. In the ninth century, Muslims did not seek to emphasize the bloody nature of the conquest, and Christians did not wish to depict accounts of violence against Muslims, let alone sympathy toward the Byzantine empire.

Reading Bishop John's *Chronicle* as a suppressed narrative gains further nuance when one contrasts its importance to modern scholars and medieval historians. No serious academic dismisses John's work; rather, scholars only lament its manuscript tradition and state of preservation. As is well known, the section narrating the initial stages of the conquest is lost, and the *Chronicle* survives in a few Ethiopic manuscripts that reflect an Arabic translation based on a Coptic or possibly Greek original (cf. Chapter Five). Beyond the accident of preservation, however, the *Chronicle* did not enjoy wide circulation among medieval historians or readers. None of John's successors, be they Christians or Muslims, utilized his *Chronicle* or grafted any portion of it onto their historical compilations. Late antique and medieval historians alike routinely composed their narratives by freely adopting the writings of their predecessors. Bishop John himself had relied a great deal on the *Chronicle* of John Malalas (he must have been fluent in Greek); yet, no historian seems to have preserved the writings of the Bishop of Nikiou. John's *Chronicle* was best forgotten. Christian and Muslim communal prerogatives were best served by ninth-century texts rather than seventh-century memories.

Political Ideology and Memories

A discussion of political ideology further demonstrates the creation of narratives and the imperfect suppression of memories in ninth-century Egypt. Discussions of early Byzantine political ideology are few, and those that focus on anti-Chalcedonians are almost unique. By and large, scholars start from the problematic hypothesis, repeatedly criticized above, that the "monophysites" of Egypt and Syria were alienated from the Byzantine empire due to religious strife and, particularly in Egypt, a decade of persecution.

Chapter Nine investigates Coptic political ideology from the fifth through tenth centuries CE; two findings from that analysis have a bearing on the issue at hand and are tersely summarized here. First, in fifth- through seventh-century sources the Copts appear to have consistently regarded themselves as members of the Byzantine empire. While maintaining that the emperor was theologically in error (often through deception rather than conviction), anti-Chalcedonians upheld his divine mandate to rule. A second conclusion, which may be anticipated from this chapter, is that in the ninth century Coptic historiography begins to consistently portray Byzantine rule (451–641 CE) as a uniformly oppressive period. This perspective has dominated among the Copts ever since, and it is that which scholars have accepted and anachronistically projected back onto the seventh century, thus providing the foundation for the socio-religious thesis attributing the conquest to confessional strife and "ethnic" alienation.

In ninth-century Egypt, realizing that any identification with the Byzantine empire would have branded them a fifth column in Egyptian society, the Copts suppressed earlier narratives that presented a more balanced depiction of Byzantine rule; those were memories best forgotten. Rather, replicating the contours of the prevailing Islamic discourse, anti-Chalcedonian authors uniformly condemned Byzantine rule as tyrannical.[61]

Paradoxically, at that same juncture, while Christians and Muslims reimagined the conquest in a utilitarian manner that served their contemporary needs, parts of the suppressed seventh-century narrative reemerged in the Coptic literature of dissent: the Coptic Arabic apocalyptic tradition. Several texts are of interest;[62] here the tenth-century *Letter of Pisentios* will provide a pertinent, but by no means unique example. In the *Letter*, the Byzantine emperor, while remaining faithful to the Definition of Chalcedon, emerges as a messianic figure that defeats caliphal armies and reclaims Egypt as his rightful possession.[63] Consequently, the hitherto truncated Byzantine Empire regains its former glory and the Copts are *again* part of it. This tradition preserves the socio-historical remnants—the memories—of seventh-century Egyptians, which sit in sharp contrast to the newly constituted historiographies of the ninth century. The *Letter of Pisentios* forwards a vision of a victorious Byzantine emperor whose legitimacy is unquestioned, who maintains the territorial integrity of his empire, and who protects its subjects irrespective of confessional differences—all were tasks that seventh-century Byzantine emperors attempted but failed to achieve. Hence, in the ninth century suppressed memories conjured up a scandalous summary of pre-conquest anti-Chalcedonian political ideology.

Memory studies best resonate in this setting. Emergence of this pre-conquest perspective was not predicated upon a textual tradition; no late antique author or passage addresses the issue as such. Still, somehow old ideals and perspectives resurfaced. It should be noted that, at least in theory, the apocalyptic scheme envisioned in the *Letter of Pisentios* had several alternatives. The Emperor of Ethiopia also plays a prominent role in medieval Coptic Arabic apocalypses, yet the Copts did not replace the pro-Chalcedonian *basileus* with their coreligionist, the anti-Chalcedonian Ethiopian *Negus*. The resurgent memory had a historical basis; the Copts had been members of the Byzantine empire, not that of Axum.

The *Letter of Pisentios* continues. It prophesizes that only after the defeat of Muslim armies and the reconstitution of the Byzantine empire will the Chalcedonian schism finally cease. The prophecy maintains that at the end of an ordeal (based on 1 Kings 18:20–40), the Byzantine emperor will abandon the faith of Chalcedon and return to the "orthodox" fold. Another memory emerges here, encapsulating the hopes and aspirations of anti-Chalcedonians living during the sixth and seventh centuries;[64] again, they diametrically oppose the Copto-Islamic historiographic sensibilities of the ninth century. Yet, the outlook is unmistakable. Those were the sentiments earlier expressed by Severos of Antioch, who believed that he could lead Justinian to orthodoxy if only he could speak with the emperor in private;[65] those were the hopes of generations of anti-Chalcedonians living in the Byzantine empire who prayed to God to send them a "good emperor".[66]

Between Texts and Memories

This examination has challenged the master narrative of the Arab conquest of Egypt on several fronts. Whereas the dominant paradigm assumes a monolithic, objectively verifiable bias on behalf of Copts and Melkites (Copts supported Muslims, Melkites supported Byzantines),[67] the primary sources repeatedly protest. Demonstrably, the historicity of much of the extant evidence lies beyond the rehabilitation of modern scholarship and would only yield frustration if approached from a purely Rankian perspective. Nonetheless, it has been argued that any consideration of the conquest "as it was" must now devalue the alleged role of the Coptic hierarchy and focus more intently on the function of local elites irrespective of their confessional allegiance (a thesis further buttressed in the following chapter).

Repeatedly in this analysis, the ninth century CE emerges as a period of radical conceptual and historiographic shifts. Textually, ninth-century narratives have become the normative foundation for the conquest as described and interpreted from the medieval period until today. Nonetheless, if probed, these chronicles betray their allegiance to two ninth-century historiographic schools that recorded and manipulated history with an eye toward contemporary social needs. Muslim scholars filtered *futūḥ* traditions through several prisms, some literary, some legal, fiscal, and social. Hence, the dominant historical narrative, Ibn 'Abd al-Ḥakam's *Futūḥ miṣr*, which was copied by all later historians, carefully depicted the conquest in ideological terms that positively influenced later socio-political and communal interactions.

Similar patterns may be observed in Christian literature. As Islamic rule endured, Christians could not risk withholding their full support of the caliphate or positively depicting any aspect of Byzantine rule; these factors inevitably led to historiographic synergy.

Ninth-century Christian writers, clearly influenced by their Muslim colleagues and the increasingly uniform socio-political and literary environment they both shared, developed a new anti-Chalcedonian historiography that rendered Byzantine rule a monotonous era of oppression. Hence, regardless of religious affiliation, ninth- and tenth-century historians conceived of the conquest as a positive development, while earlier—at least for John of Nikiou and the anonymous author of the *Panegyric on the Three Holy Children*—the Copts (like the Byzantines) conceived of the fall of Egypt as a thoroughly negative event.[68] Ninth-century historiographic synergy and the need to establish a precedent for the political *status quo* led to Patriarch Benjamin's depictions as a liberator of his people and as an ally of Arab armies, which are without precedence in earlier narratives.

Nonetheless, ninth- and tenth-century literature also demonstrate the imperfect triumph of historiography over history as well as the resilience of communal memories. While Christians and Muslims documented and recalled the conquest in analogous terms, John of Nikiou's *Chronicle* and the Copto-Arabic apocalyptic tradition stood in defiance. By the ninth century, the *Chronicle* did not fit either constituency's histories or memories of the past. To the contrary, by depicting Arab violence against Egyptian and Christian resistance to Muslim armies, as well as their affinity for Byzantine political rule, that chronicle retained harmful memories that contradicted what later generations deemed "historical".[69] These traits, it is argued, contributed to the *Chronicle's* marginal status in medieval manuscript production and historical writings.

The ninth-century triumph of historiography over history was nearly complete, if it were not for the imperfect suppression of old memories. Without the aid of the written word—rather, in opposition to normative texts—dangerously subversive memories emerged. In prophetic guise, Coptic Arabic apocalypses favorably recalled pre-conquest norms and aspirations. Such tracts envisioned the reconstitution of a powerful Byzantine empire to which the Copts belonged despite religious schism, the victory of the *basileus* over the *khalīfa*, and the return of the Byzantine emperor to the orthodox—that is, the anti-Chalcedonian—fold.

CHAPTER 3

CHRISTIAN ELITES: THE DIALECTIC OF DUTY AND FAITH

In the aftermath of the conquest, Christian notables continued to exercise tremendous authority due to their personal wealth and administrative appointments. Socio-political elites typically belonged to one of three cohorts.[1] The most celebrated were the large landlords whose wealth attracted the attention of the government and the church. Often, high-ranking government officials similarly owned property and land, but they derived their influence from their prestigious posts. Until the 720s, such individuals could still attain appointments as pagarchs, but, notwithstanding a few exceptions, the most prestigious later appointments were as secretaries (*kuttāb/notarioi*). Most of these individuals came from urban regions, belonged to affluent families, and are documented in Christian narratives and papyrological records.[2] In addition, a third group of notables, discussed at greater length in Chapter Seven, is almost exclusively mentioned in documentary papyri. These were the village elites of the seventh and eighth centuries: the local *lashane* (ⲗⲁϣⲁⲛⲉ/μείζονες) and the Great Man (ⲠⲚⲞϬ ⲚⲢⲰⲘⲈ). Such individuals were neither as rich nor as influential as their urban counterparts, though on a local level they exercised wide-ranging jurisdiction and social clout. For the early Islamic centuries, the names and functions of Christian notables are especially difficult to discern. One is often left with disjointed information from which to attempt a historical reconstruction. Later Muslim and Christian historians, however, are more forthcoming in this regard.[3]

Here, the analysis focuses on the functions of Christian elites as a group and, where feasible, as individuals from the beginning of the seventh until the ninth century CE. The analysis stresses the dual functions performed by most of these individuals as government employees and delegates on one level, and advocates for their respective religious communities on another. In essence, the analysis examines the power dynamic among Egypt's Christian elites, the state of their religious communities, and the government's evolving strategies, which sought to efficiently administer the province.

Shenoute the *Dux* of Antinoë

The best documented and the only discernible anti-Chalcedonian notable in conquest literature is Shenoute "the faithful *dux*" of Antinoë. Conspicuously absent from Islamic narratives, he figures prominently in the *History of the Patriarchs* and Patriarch Benjamin's sermon *On Cana of Galilee*.[4] His disproportionate representation in these early narratives, however, likely contributed to the misleading impression that anti-Chalcedonians (church and notables) played a key role in governing Egypt for the new regime. To the contrary, not only is Shenoute the only anti-Chalcedonian figure identified in conquest narratives, but, as demonstrated below, pro-Chalcedonians staffed most positions within the early post-conquest administration. Still, as a prominent official and an advocate for his religious community, Shenoute provides a paradigmatic example of the diverse roles executed by Egyptian notables in the early decades of Arab rule.

It was Shenoute who first brought the plight of Patriarch Benjamin to the attention of 'Amr ibn al-'Āṣ, and made provisions for the patriarch's return. Later, the *dux* donated a large monetary gift to the patriarch for the rebuilding of the Church of St. Mark in Alexandria; as with Melkite notables, the invading forces did not sequester Shenoute's estate.[5] The HP depicts Shenoute as a member of 'Amr's personal entourage,[6] an influential guide intimately familiar with the geography and languages of the province. Throughout subsequent centuries, Christian elites, both Coptic and Melkite, played the two roles illustrated by *dux* Shenoute in evermore dynamic and complex fashions.

Early Post-Conquest Decades

The assumption that the Coptic hierarchy and population welcomed and aided the advancing Arabs as liberators, which was challenged in the previous chapter, led to another inference: that the Islamic government favored the Coptic church and utilized it to rule. The assumption is reflected in the erroneous observation: "in Egypt as late as 86/705 the Coptic Patriarch of Alexandria was the head (*mutawallī*) of the bureau of tax in money (*dīwān al-kharaj*); as such he was able to protect the interest of the church".[7] The assertion itself is based on a misreading of HP I.3: 302, the *mutawallī* was not the Coptic patriarch Alexander, but rather Athanasios the Syrian secretary who never held any ecclesiastical office.[8] The misreading itself is a trivial matter; more significant are the unquestioned scholarly assumptions that enabled such a misreading to go undetected, rendering it normative or even logical.[9]

In the immediate aftermath of the conquest, the Arabs did not focus on adjudicating between various Christian factions, but rather the establishment of an efficient bureaucracy,[10] an imperative that led to the rehiring of the bulk of the pre-conquest—predominantly Melkite—bureaucracy.[11] Thus, not only was the early Arab administration structurally similar to that of the Byzantines, but it even employed many of the same personnel. Indifference to sectarian issues led to renewed intolerance against the Coptic population and patriarchs, as government-employed Melkites used their civic appointments to further their confessional aims. That dynamic was reversed during the governorship of ʿAbd al-ʿAzīz ibn Marwān who was the first to treat the Copts with deference.

Reappointing pre-conquest personnel placed power back in the hands of Melkites, who maltreated Coptic patriarchs and appropriated Coptic churches (see Chapter Ten). Most intriguing were the actions of the Melkite Theodore, the governor of Alexandria, and his brother-in-law, Theophanes, the governor of Maryūṭ, who targeted Coptic patriarchs.[12] Theodore increased taxes on the Coptic church and confiscated the belongings of the Patriarch Agathon, while Theophanes' agitation led to the arrest and imprisonment of Patriarch John III.

The *Life of Isaac of Alexandria* provides a glimpse of the influence notables could exert in the early post-conquest decades and of the tenor of Coptic relations with the government. When Isaac decided to take monastic vows, his parents were so distraught by their son's decision that Patriarch Benjamin I: "fearing that they would inform the [civil] authority (ϯⲉⲝⲟⲩⲥⲓⲁ) and do evil to the holy place, sent a letter to Scetis so that [Isaac] would not be allowed west of the river".[13] The patriarch's fear was likely a response to the dismay of Isaac's prestigious, land-owning family.[14] This incident helps to gauge the relationship between the Coptic hierarchy and the Islamic government during the decades immediately following the conquest. Had Benjamin enjoyed the same affinity with ruling officials as many of his successors, he certainly would not have given this matter much thought. Furthermore, Benjamin's fears and actions would hardly be expected from someone who allegedly "handed over" the country to the Arabs and helped them rule.[15] Rather, the patriarch's reaction, along with the activities of the pro-Chalcedonian Theodore and Theophanes, are best interpreted within a socio-political matrix in which secular elites (irrespective of confessional affiliation), rather than religious leaders, commanded the attention of governing officials.

The Arab administration's ambivalent attitude toward the Coptic population persisted until the governorship of ʿAbd al-ʿAzīz ibn Marwān (65–86/685–705), who began courting the Coptic ecclesiastical hierarchy and notables. The only documented maltreatment of the Coptic hierarchy after that juncture came at the hands of Muslim officials, rather than Melkite elites. It was under ʿAbd al-ʿAzīz's watch that the Coptic churches appropriated by Theodore and Theophanes were returned, and a number of churches that had hitherto been in the possession of Melkite clergy fell into Coptic hands (see Chapter Ten).[16]

Diverse factors led to this policy shift. On a personal front, ʿAbd al-ʿAzīz's cordial attitude toward the Copts found expression through his interactions with their patriarchs, especially Isaac I, with whom he met regularly. Administratively, ʿAbd al-ʿAzīz also placed his confidence in two anti-Chalcedonian secretaries, Athanasios Bar Gūmōyē and Isaac (al-Shubrawī),[17] who became staunch advocates for the anti-Chalcedonian cause. Once in office, the two secretaries proceeded to return the above-referenced ecclesiastical properties confiscated by Theodore to the Copts.[18] Additionally, both secretaries served as advisors and confidants to the Coptic patriarchs who occupied the see during their tenure: John III, Isaac I, Simon I, and Alexander II.[19] On the political front, another contributing factor may have been the constant skirmishes between the Arab and Byzantine armies at that time.[20] Realizing that the vast majority of Egyptians recognized the Coptic hierarchy, ʿAbd al-ʿAzīz attempted to consolidate his rule and bolster his popularity by favoring that constituency; it is hard to justify his attitude if those affiliated with the Coptic Orthodox hierarchy were only a minority as is claimed by some scholars. In general, Coptic authors treat ʿAbd al-ʿAzīz quite favorably. Even an incident in which he imprisoned the Coptic patriarch and demolished crosses is shrugged off as nothing more than a misunderstanding.[21]

From ʿAbd al-ʿAzīz to the ʿAbbāsids

By 690 CE, a significant realignment took place. During the tenure of ʿAbd al-ʿAzīz ibn Marwān and his two anti-Chalcedonian secretaries, the Copts were treated favorably, marking the first instance since the conquest that the Islamic government demonstrated a religious bias. This new policy had several ramifications for the pro- and anti-Chalcedonian communities; nonetheless, one would be in error to interpret it in religious terms. It was but another chapter in the socio-political history of early Islamic Egypt, another means by which the Islamic government attempted to consolidate its hegemony over a predominantly non-Muslim, anti-Chalcedonian society. The policy shift likely contributed to the pattern of Institutional Conversions discussed in Chapter Four, though that process was already well underway.

The shift may have begun in the twilight of John III's patriarchate (57–66/677–86), though the dossier stemming from the brief patriarchate of Isaac I (67–70/686–9) provides conclusive proof. Of primary importance is the underappreciated Coptic *Life of Isaac of Alexandria*, which supersedes (chronologically and in importance) the patriarch's brief biography in the HP. This fascinating text provides an abundance of information regarding the actions and personalities of the two anti-Chalcedonian secretaries and ʿAbd al-ʿAzīz's amicable relationship with the Coptic patriarch. As a manifestation of these congenial sentiments, the governor often addressed Isaac as "patriarch," a new laudatory appellation in Egypt. In time that designation, which had been in use in other sees, become the normative title for the Bishop of Alexandria in Arabic literature, while "archbishop," still the normative title in seventh-century Egypt, continued to dominate in Coptic literature.[22] With regard to ʿAbd al-ʿAzīz's anti-Chalcedonian secretaries, the *Life* is particularly reverential to Isaac (not to be confused with the patriarch), who is portrayed as a living saint—one who was able to "boldly contemplate the light of the Lord".[23] Isaac was a strong advocate for his namesake from the outset. Directly following the monk Isaac's ordination as patriarch, "lord (ⲔⲨⲢⲒ[ⲞⲤ])" Isaac the secretary hosted "a great feast for the bishops and the clerics" in the patriarch's honor.[24]

Relations with the Syrian Athanasios, however, were initially strained and his goodwill had to be cultivated. The more senior of the two secretaries, Athanasios, may have favored George, the Alexandrian nominee who rivaled Isaac for the patriarchate,[25] but eventually the two men settled their differences. The account of their reconciliation offers a salient example of the means by which the Coptic church procured the aid of government-employed notables: "While they were on such good terms with each other," the *Life* recounts, "the archbishop spoke with Athanasios about the Evangelion in Alexandria so that he would take an interest in it . . .

[Athanasios then] rebuilt it and adorned it with great beauty".[26] For the remainder of his tenure, Athanasios became a patron of the Coptic church through his personal estate and, more importantly, through his administrative post and influence with 'Abd al-'Azīz.[27] The circumstances under which Athanasios (Ar. Ashnās/Athnās) left his post are not entirely clear. According to Arabic historians, 'Abdallāh ibn 'Abd al-Malik acrimoniously removed him from his post in 87/709, and replaced him with Ibn Yarbu' al-Fazarī.[28] Syrian and Coptic authors, however, provide a positive depiction of Athanasios' retirement from office.[29]

Sources for this early period document two means by which individuals secured administrative appointments. Attaining an elite education provided one method, evident in the early career of Patriarch Isaac. Although his father was not employed by the government, the family's wealth and connections enabled Isaac to receive a thorough education in Greek and Coptic.[30] As a young man, he became a secretary (*notarius*) to Menesōn, a blood relative employed as registrar (*chartularius*) to George, the prefect (*eparchos*) of Egypt.[31] Subsequently, on account of his talents, Isaac eventually became the Chief Secretary.[32]

The early career of Zacharias, the eighth-century Bishop of Sakhā (ordained ca. 700 CE), provides several parallels, though in this case Zacharias' father had worked for the *dīwān* prior to joining the Coptic clergy. As a young man, Zacharias also received a Hellenic education and subsequently relied upon his father's connections to secure an appointment as a secretary of the *dīwān*. Careers such as these were in all probability typical throughout early Islamic rule.[33] While education and familial connections proved instrumental in attaining employment, individual merit dictated advancement.

The *Life of Isaac* provides additional documentation in this regard. It states that Athanasios and Isaac managed the affairs of the government "together with their sons,"[34] and that under their guidance "the *Praetorium* was full of Christians".[35] In that *Life*, it is safe to assume that "Christians" referred only to anti-Chalcedonians. Thus, during the governorship of 'Abd al-'Azīz ibn Marwān, top administrative posts switched hands and were now staffed by anti-Chalcedonian personnel, who were aided, and eventually succeeded, by their sons and relatives. Such a pattern also prevailed among many Muslim bureaucratic families as well (see Chapter Seven).[36]

In the mid-ninth century CE, an analogous set of socio-religious circumstances prevailed. Maqāra ibn Yūsuf, secretary to the head of the *dīwān*, and Ibrahīm ibn Sawīrus, Superintendent of the Treasury, acted as guardians of Coptic interests in the government.[37] On several occasions, they interceded with the governor on behalf of the patriarch, and in one incident, the pious Ibrahīm anonymously paid the church's property taxes from his own funds.[38] Similar to the pattern attested in the careers of Isaac and Athanasios in the early eighth century, Ibrahīm and Maqāra likewise drew upon a large contingency of Christian secretaries.[39] Eventually, as part of the Caliph al-Mutawakkil's puritanical campaign, both secretaries were dismissed from their posts.[40] Patriarch Quzmā (851–58 CE) ordered churches and monasteries to pray for the two officials; meanwhile, his affairs were entrusted to the notables of Miṣr.[41] Maqāra died during this crisis, but Ibrahīm would return to his office and, again: "attended to the duties of the church and shouldered the affairs of the father, the patriarch, as he did for the bishops of the land of Egypt and the monasteries. He devoted himself to their causes and secured their necessities on account of his great love for Christ and *his position* among the officials (*wulāh*)".[42]

Eighth and Ninth Centuries CE

At the beginning of the eighth century, an anti-Chalcedonian notable, John of Ṣā convinced Qurra ibn Sharīk to double the tax (*jizya*) on heterodox communities. He and his entourage then toured the Delta, (re)baptizing monks and laymen according to the Coptic rite (see Chapter Four).[43] As an administrative elite who used his appointment for the benefit of his religious confession, John followed in the same pattern set by the above-named Coptic and Melkite personalities. His career proves that the Islamic government's deference toward anti-Chalcedonians outlived that policy's architect, 'Abd al-'Azīz ibn Marwān, though that attitude would quickly abate.

During the first half of the ninth century, Christian narrative sources provide a great deal of information regarding three notables in particular. Two anti-Chalcedonians, Maqāra ibn Sāth of Nabarūh and lord (*al-sayyid*) Isḥāq ibn Andunā,[44] exemplified the blurring of the lines between notables and clergy. The third prominent notable, Bukām of Būrah, was a pro-Chalcedonian.[45]

Maqāra belonged to the wealthiest family in the district of Samannūd. His parents had built the largest church in that city and dedicated it to their patron saint, Makarios the Great (their son's namesake).[46] Maqāra's wealth must have been immense. Although not employed by the government, he routinely interacted with ruling elites, who held him in high regard.[47] When he set out to request a reduction in his taxes, he did not bother to plead his case with local officials, but took his case directly to the caliph Hārūn al-Rashīd, who purportedly granted him an audience and agreed to reduce his taxes.[48] A philanthropist, the Coptic notable *par excellence*, the HP repeatedly lauds Maqāra's charitable deeds and credits him with building the Church of the Magdalene in Jerusalem for the orthodox (i.e. anti-Chalcedonians) and with placing his funds at the disposal of the Coptic hierarchy.[49] Maqāra's affluence and political connections enabled him to function as a liaison between church and government. Most prominently, he played the diplomat by facilitating a tense meeting between Patriarch Yaʿqūb and the governor, ʿAbd al-Azīz al-Jarawī,[50] by reassuring the patriarch: "[If need be] I would give all my money for you [as ransom], that you may suffer no grief".[51] Maqāra frequently visited the patriarch, and enjoyed a close relationship with him, becoming his spiritual son. Later, the patriarch retired to Nabarūh, where he eventually died.[52]

A near contemporary of Maqāra was the pro-Chalcedonian notable Bukām of Būrah, whose career is documented in the *Naẓm al-jawhar* of Eutychios.[53] Bukām's biography is striking in its proximity to that of Maqāra; the parallels are more than coincidental. Similar to Maqāra, the wealthy Bukām patronized churches in Egypt and Jerusalem, and had an audience with the caliph (at that time al-Ma'mūn, 198–218/813–33).[54] Bukām's son, Michael, would later become the Melkite patriarch of Alexandria.[55] Perhaps these individuals had parallel careers, but more likely, Eutychios drafted his tenth-century account of Bukām as a pro-Chalcedonian counterpart to the ninth-century account of Maqāra. Literary parallels and competition of this sort may be observed in other Coptic and Melkite historical accounts. Sometime after the end of Iconoclasm in Byzantium, both communities drafted confessional accounts attributing a prominent role in the Triumph of Orthodoxy to its respective sect.[56] Historically, it is at best improbable that either the Melkites or Copts of Egypt were even privy to the events at Constantinople as they unfolded, let alone were directly involved in that controversy.[57] Similarly, at a later juncture, each confession claimed sole responsibility for ending al-Ḥākim's persecution and the reversal of his oppressive policies.[58]

While most notables used their socio-political standing to serve their respective confession, not all had the best interest of their community at heart. In the early ninth century, upon the death of the Bishop of Fāw, the governor of Alexandria (*al-amīr al-wālī bī al-iskandariyya*),[59] Elias, accepted a bribe and consequently endorsed an unnamed candidate for the vacant bishopric. Far from a mere suggestion, the "nomination" reached Patriarch Yaʿqūb (819–30 CE) accompanied by a barrage of threats. Initially, the patriarch refused to yield to the strong-arm tactics, but his advisors pleaded with him to ordain the man "lest evil befall [him] and the church".[60] Patriarch Yaʿqūb ordained the man, who miraculously died en route to his new diocese.[61] Unquestionably, Christian notables on the government's payroll could be valuable allies as well as formidable adversaries to the ecclesiastical hierarchy.

Most striking, however, is an affluent Coptic notable living in the first half of the ninth century, Lord Isḥāq ibn Andunā, who almost single-handedly constitutes an exception to the pious-notable motif encountered so often in Christian Arabic writings.[62] Initially employed as the chief of the governor's *dīwān*, nothing suggests that he used his post to benefit the Coptic community. To the contrary, he utilized his personal fortune and the contacts he cultivated as a government official to bolster his defiant stance vis-à-vis the Coptic hierarchy. Isḥāq undermined the prerogatives and jurisdiction of the

Coptic Patriarch, whose position is typically regarded as unassailable, practically under early Islamic rule.

Due to his wealth and position, the Alexandrians nominated Isḥāq for patriarch.[63] Eventually, three bishops rejected his nomination citing that he was a married man who fathered several children (he does not appear to have separated from his wife). Nevertheless, what is noteworthy is that two bishops, Zacharias of Wasīm and Theodore of Miṣr, had supported his candidacy.[64] Bishop Theodore's endorsement should not be underestimated. Nominated by the Alexandrians and endorsed by the Bishop of Miṣr, the most influential bishop in Egypt after the patriarch, Isḥāq's chances of becoming patriarch were excellent. Ultimately, however, in the face of mounting opposition, Isḥāq withdrew his candidacy and the synod consecrated Yusāb I (Joseph, 215–35/830–49).

After his ordination, Patriarch Yusāb knew that he could not afford to make such an influential man his enemy; thus, upon their first encounter, the patriarch's comments had an unmistakable conciliatory tone: "My lord (*sayyidī*) Isḥāq, I have been longing for you and I have a strong affection for you. I want you to be equal to myself (*'adila nafsy*), and I would like you to be my deputy in all my affairs, and hold the patriarchal signet ring. So that all may know that you are my administrator in all matters, both ecclesiastical and civil".[65] Shortly after that meeting, Patriarch Yusāb ordained Isḥāq a deacon,[66] and subsequent to the death of Bishop Zacharias, he ordained him Bishop of Wasīm.[67]

As bishop, Isḥāq was anything but typical. Throughout his tenure, he deliberately (and blatantly) blocked the ordination of a bishop to the prestigious diocese of Miṣr, and positioned himself to control both dioceses: "and none could resist him because of the influence that his words had with the governors, his brethren, and his community".[68] Doubtless, this eloquent gloss sought to diplomatically convey that Patriarch Yusāb himself could not oppose Isḥāq, whose actions were overtly self-serving. After the diocese of Alexandria (that of the patriarch), the diocese of Miṣr was the most important in all of Egypt, arguably even more prominent than Alexandria by that juncture (see Chapter Ten). Already by the patriarchate of Mark II (799–819 CE), in addition to administering his diocese, the Bishop of Miṣr supervised all the affairs of the monasteries,[69] an administrative and prestigious responsibility that likely persisted during the patriarchate of Yusāb I. Furthermore, upon the passing of a patriarch, the Bishop of Miṣr acted as interim head of the church (current practice favors the longest serving bishop).[70] Control of the diocese of Miṣr surely increased Isḥāq's prestige and wealth.[71] The married notable and former financial minister failed in his bid for the patriarchate, but succeeded in attaining most of the trappings.

Upon Isḥāq's death, the diocese of Miṣr finally welcomed a new bishop, the deacon Wannā (Bannā), who was handpicked by "the chief men of Miṣr".[72] One of Isḥāq's sons, Apacyrus, succeeded his father as Bishop of Wasīm, but died shortly after his ordination.[73] At that point, another son, Theodore, wished to succeed his father and older brother in the same bishopric; the notion probably seemed natural to him, as practically a birthright. Patriarch Yusāb adamantly refused; unable to check the abuses of Isḥāq and Apacyrus, he desperately wanted to regain control. But the family's influence and wealth again prevailed. Theodore approached the governor, ʿAlī ibn Yaḥyā al-Armannī (during the caliphate of al-Muʿtaṣim), and secured his support through a bribe. Under pressure from the governor, Patriarch Yusāb eventually ordained Theodore a bishop.[74]

Lord Isḥāq ibn Andunā succeeded in establishing a veritable dynasty of wealthy bishops throughout the second half of the ninth century CE, who were not only largely independent of the patriarch but had him at their mercy. As laymen and clerics, Isḥāq and his sons defied the typical depiction of the pious Christian notable by consistently pursuing their personal interests and drawing upon their wealth and political influence to attain ecclesiastical offices that were probably little more than business ventures to them.

The account of Isḥāq and his children is almost unique. Subsequent notables encountered in the sources revert to a more pious mold. Under the Ṭūlūnids, Christian notables again resumed their indispensable role as liaisons between church and government. At one juncture, relations between Patriarch Khaīl III and Aḥmad ibn Ṭūlūn had deteriorated to such an extent that the governor imprisoned the patriarch. Nonetheless, Christian notables still retained a great deal of clout. Aḥmad ibn Ṭūlūn's secretaries, the brothers Mūsā and Abra'ām, pleaded for the release of the patriarch to no avail. Another Christian secretary, Yu'annīs, along with his son Maqāra, recruited a pious Muslim notable, Aḥmad ibn ʿAlī al-Mardānī, and with his aid were able to secure the release of Patriarch Khaīl for bail amounting to 20,000 *dīnār*s.[75]

Under the Fāṭimid and Ayyūbid dynasties the dominant pattern persisted. Early under Fāṭimid rule, Qishlām, a notable of Tinnīs, took a leading role in negotiating between the "ruffians" who took over the city and Fāṭimid officials.[76] Qishlām emerged as a communal, not just a sectarian leader. Other Christian notables may have functioned in a similar vein, but Qishlām provides the clearest example of such a bipartisan figure.

Generally, the best documented notables were independently wealthy or politically influential men. Nonetheless, a few women are also noted, though they remain marginal in the historical record. In the early tenth century CE, a certain Dīnah provided for Patriarch Mīnā II and his entourage for a full year while he resided in Maḥallat Danyāl, and the *History of the Churches and Monasteries of Egypt* (HCME) lauds another, anonymous, female patron.[77]

Observations

Throughout the early Islamic centuries, Coptic and Melkite notables played key roles as socio-political catalysts that facilitated interactions among the new Arab government and religious hierarchies. Government-employed elites, in particular, occupy a significant portion of the historical record and the above discussion. To their credit, these individuals succeeded in harmonizing duties which, from a modern perspective, seem incompatible if not contradictory. Their experience, language skills (especially in the post-conquest decades), and efficiency rendered them valuable assets to the Arab administration. To their religious communities, in addition to their often lauded roles as wealthy patrons, such individuals served as a diplomatic arm within the government. In the wake of the conquest, notables provided a vital link between the provincial administration and the ecclesiastical hierarchies to an extent that was unprecedented during Late Antiquity.

The governorship of ʿAbd al-ʿAzīz ibn Marwān marks the end of the Islamic government's initial indifference to Egypt's Christian factions, and the inauguration of a policy that favored the Copts. Nonetheless, the new orientation was short-lived; church and government relations were often fickle and would take successive turns from bad to worse, beginning with the tenure of Qurra ibn Sharīk through the end of Umayyad rule.

With regard to religious bias, Christian notables were the first to allow their confessional views to influence their political decisions. In the wake of the conquest, Melkite officials favored members of their own confession and oppressed the Copts financially and by annexing their properties; later, when Coptic notables gained the upper hand, they reciprocated. By the mid-eighth century, Christian notables had lost the preeminent status they enjoyed in the early post-conquest administration, and the days in which a Theophanes or Athanasios could claim a church at will were also long gone. Still, such individuals continued to exercise a great deal of authority and influence, and as demonstrated through the careers of Maqāra and Bukām, personal fortunes often proved as advantageous as governmental posts. In either case, the individual had direct access to the administrative establishment and the ecclesiastical hierarchy.

CHAPTER 4

RELIGIOUS CONVERSION AND SOCIAL COHESION

Since the dawn of the twentieth century, the topic of religious conversion has amassed an ever-increasing bibliography of historical, sociological, and psychological examinations.[1] With regard to Egypt, the existing literature addresses two distinct periods: the fourth and fifth centuries CE, when Christians emerged as the dominant political and demographic constituency, and the ninth and tenth centuries, when they no longer retained a numerical advantage. Assuming an uneventful era of Christian dominance, however, scholars have neglected the interim period spanning the fifth to the ninth centuries.[2] The following analysis addresses this omission by documenting the shifting patterns and trajectories of religious conversion from the Council of Chalcedon until the ninth century CE. Beyond stressing the socio-political factors that facilitated and hindered religious transitions, this discussion underscores the importance of scrutinizing the tenor of religious conversion, particularly during those centuries of neglected study, in order to gain a comprehensive, contextual understanding of the phenomenon.

A study of conversion and religious identity is of fundamental importance for the social history of Egypt under Arab rule since the prevailing cultural matrix defined an individual's social status, fiscal liability, and legal standing as a direct function of religious affiliation. Certainly, many individuals and families managed to circumvent (or perhaps transcend) the letter of the law and social restrictions; nonetheless, it is difficult to overestimate the social impact of religious identity on the daily life and historical narrative of individuals and communities living under caliphal rule.

Here, conversion signifies two types of transition that may be sudden or gradual. The first is what sociologists and historians of religion have termed Tradition Transition: conversion from one religious tradition to another, as in the case of a Buddhist who converts to Christianity. Institutional Conversion, on the other hand, describes a change from one faith community to another within the same religious tradition, as in the case of a Methodist who joins the Roman Catholic Church.[3] Less dramatic, the significance of this type of conversion, particularly between Copts and Melkites during the "middle ages," must not be underestimated. Modern ecumenism has all but eliminated the Chalcedonian schism, but historically, each faction regarded the other as a heretical sect best avoided and certainly condemned.

In highlighting patterns of religious conversion, this investigation does not intend to isolate the phenomenon from the topics discussed in other chapters, such as Arabization, taxation, and Arab immigration into the province, all of which are believed to be intertwined. A second supposition is that the aim here is to identify and analyze the extra-religious dynamics that facilitate the processes of conversion.[4] The plurality of the socio-political factors considered below, even over an extended period of time, does not in itself cause individuals to convert from one faith community to another. This is obvious in modern Egypt; thoroughly Arabized and Islamized, the country still retains the largest Christian community in the Middle East.

Below, after a terse survey of Christianity in Egypt up to the mid-fifth century, the analysis focuses on three overlapping periods of shifting religious affiliation that extend into the tenth century. Finally, it concludes by parsing the effects of religious conversion on the amalgamation and erosion of various confessions, and the socio-political factors that facilitated and hindered the process and act of conversion.

Origins to the Council of Chalcedon

On the eve of the Council of Chalcedon (451 CE), Christianity in Egypt had already experienced consecutive periods of growth and fragmentation. Traditions associated with Demetrios I (189–231 CE), believed to have been the first Alexandrian hierarch to appoint bishops for Egyptian cities,[5] provide the earliest evidence for expansion beyond that metropolis. It was possibly at that same juncture, or soon thereafter, that the third-century church began to evangelize the countryside, as indicated by the emergence of Coptic translations of the Greek scriptures.[6] These processes of expansion only intensified in the fourth and fifth centuries CE, during which Egyptians experienced a period of hyper-conversion. Some Jews and the staggering majority of Pagans from every cult and creed embraced Christianity. Beyond Egypt, Alexandria's jurisdiction eventually extended over the Pentapolis (in Libya), Ethiopia, and Nubia, a development that had mixed socio-political repercussions for the Coptic hierarchy under Islamic rule.[7] Conversion in fourth- and fifth-century Egypt has long been the subject of study and debate;[8] here, it is taken for granted that by the mid-fifth century, most Egyptians were at least nominally Christian and allied themselves with the hierarchy of the see of Alexandria over and against the alternative confessions that existed at that time.[9]

While the ever-expanding church became embroiled in conflicts with schismatics, "Pagans," and heretics, Alexandrian patriarchs successfully curtailed the number of potential religious rivals and institutions. In part, they accomplished this by (directly and implicitly) expanding their jurisdiction into rural districts and ingratiating themselves among monastic communities. This was a crucial development. Alexandrian patriarchs—whether Athanasios, Cyril, or Benjamin—did not take rural districts for granted. Hence, in times of controversy only a few sects, the Meletians being the most prominent (though, even then in a fairly limited capacity), had any support in the countryside or Upper Egypt. Third century developments also translated into a *de facto* primacy of the Bishop of Alexandria—officially recognized by the Sixth Canon of

Nicea—that was only challenged by schism during Late Antiquity and by a few powerful bishops under early Islamic rule. Alexandrian Popes reinforced their position by insisting to personally ordain all bishops within their jurisdiction.[10] Elsewhere, patriarchs and popes provided consent for the elevation of individuals to the episcopate, but did not necessarily participate in the actual ordination rite.

At the mid-fifth century CE, while Christianity enjoyed political and demographic dominance, a new age of conversion commenced in the immediate aftermath of the Council of Chalcedon (451 CE). Overnight, it would seem, the see splintered into warring factions that competed for imperial patronage and a public constituency. Religious fragmentation was nothing new to Egypt. Meletians, Arians, and Manicheans had long contended with the Alexandrian hierarchy, but in the mid-fifth century, the number of factions and the vindictiveness of the quarrels quickly escalated, though, as noted above and in Chapter One, their constituency appears to have been limited and largely restricted to specific districts in Alexandria and the Delta. After Chalcedon, in addition to the chief schism between pro- and anti-Chalcedonians, four other sects emerged: Eutychians/Phantasiasts,[11] Julianists/Gainites,[12] Akephaloi, and Barsanuphians.[13] Thus, on the eve of the Arab conquest, no less than nine factions claimed to be the true Church. Yet, by the ninth century CE, while some survived in name (and infamy),[14] the number of confessions narrowed to two: an anti-Chalcedonian majority that included Syrians, Nubians, and Armenians who were in communion with the Coptic church, and a numerically marginal, though historically significant, pro-Chalcedonian community.[15]

It is difficult to assess the tenor of interreligious conversion in any of its various forms during the Byzantine period in Egypt (ca. 451–640). The province lacks a counterpart to Cyril of Scythopolis' invaluable *Lives of the Monks of Palestine*, which sheds light on several important religious figures and developments in that region in the wake of Chalcedon. Secular and ecclesiastical histories, on the other hand, such as those of Evagrios and John Malalas, provide some insight, but they typically had a regional or imperial focus to which Egypt was seldom central. Moreover, in regard to religious conversion, the historians of that period elected to chronicle singular incidents that either entailed supernatural phenomena or had implicit political overtones.[16]

An interesting and valuable exception to the paucity of relevant Byzantine sources is provided by the fifth- and sixth-century Apions of the Oxyrhynchus nome. Most male members of this prestigious landowning family served in the government in some capacity. Apion I appears at the end of the fifth century as an anti-Chalcedonian, but he accepted the pro-Chalcedonian confession in 518 CE during the reign of Emperor Justin I, apparently for political pragmatism. No more than a few generations later, the Apion family returned to the anti-Chalcedonian fold.[17] The actions of the Apions likely paralleled those of other wealthy families who attempted to balance political ambitions with religious beliefs and imperial patronage. Their wavering allegiances were not likely induced by religious conviction, but rather political expediency. Less affluent families that did not entertain the possibility of appointment to high imperial offices, such as that of the famed Dioskoros of Aphrodito, simply held on to their faith and did not waver in their religious allegiances.[18]

By the early seventh century in Egypt, the Melkites, whose numbers were dwindling, experienced a resurgence under the charismatic leadership of Patriarch John the Almsgiver (610–19 CE),[19] who attracted converts from lay and clerical ranks. His *Life* provides a salient example of the process of conversion in his day: "The priests who adjured their heresy [i.e. the anti-Chalcedonian faith] and gave written declarations of their repentance ... were willingly received by John who made them members of the catholic church".[20] Lay conversion proceeded along similar lines. In the shadow of Chalcedon, both confessions routinely required written denouncements and statements of theological fealty from converts.[21] Outside of Egypt, the *Life* also credits two of Patriarch John's contemporaries, John Moschos and Sophronios (later, the Patriarch of Jerusalem) with "deliver[ing] many villages, and very many churches and monasteries" from the anti-Chalcedonians.[22]

Institutional Conversion to pro-Chalcedonian Christianity persisted in the second quarter of the seventh century due to the proselytizing efforts of John's successor, Kyros, the patriarch-prefect of Alexandria. Kyros' tenure and conciliatory efforts are complex and not entirely clear. Byzantine and Coptic traditions document that he attracted (or coerced) converts, but they agree on little else.[23] Early in his career in Alexandria, he reunited with some anti-Chalcedonian bishops and clergy under the banner of Monenergism. Adopted in June 633, this *Pact of Union* (or the *Nine Chapters*) was the latest of a series of conciliatory agreements sponsored and, at times, directly negotiated by the Emperor Herakleios and Patriarch Sergios of Constantinople.[24] Over the previous four years, similar accords were signed with the Armenians, West Syrians, and East Syrians, all with very mixed results.[25] Reporting on the *Pact*, Kyros enthusiastically wrote: "All the clergy of the Theodosian party *of this city* ... took part with us in the Holy Catholic Church, in the pure and holy mysteries".[26] Several anti-Chalcedonian bishops (including Victor of Fayyūm and Kyros of Nikiou) accepted the *Pact*, though there is no evidence as to the number of other bishops who joined them and the reach of this agreement beyond the city of Alexandria remains far from certain.[27] What is definite, however, is that the leader of the Theodosians, Benjamin, did not participate in these deliberations or recognize them, and, if history is any indicator, as goes the Coptic Patriarch so did his constituency. Deliberations with the other three major confessions were conducted with their patriarchs (or Catholicos); the Alexandrian *Pact* is the only agreement that did not include the head of the opposing party.

Yet, J. Meyendorff was very positive as to the outcome of the accord, arguing that the lack of Coptic evidence proves the success of the reunion.[28] Nonetheless, given the dearth of evidence at hand which Meyendorff notes, it is equally plausible that its omission was rather due to its marginality. The *Pact* certainly had some support, but demonstrably it was not universally adopted by pro- or anti-Chalcedonians. In fact, the most vehement opposition came from pro-Chalcedonian ranks—Patriarch Sophronios of Jerusalem's opposition was early, energetic, and constant—and within a few years the whole discussion shifted to Monothelitism and all the agreements signed with the Armenians, West Syrians, and East

Syrians were abandoned; only the Maronites upheld the doctrinal compromise.[29] Ultimately, the *Pact of Union* functioned in the same vein as the *Henotikon* of Zeno (482 CE), the "Second" *Henotikon* of Justin II (571 CE), the *Ekthesis* (638 CE), and the *Typos* (648 CE), as another failed attempt at conciliation which faltered on nearly every front.

Within the Coptic tradition, which confiscates all the above-mentioned theological declarations into the *Tome of Leo*, Kyros' tactics appear more violent and, oddly enough, more successful, though both impressions are deceptive. The *Life of Samuel of Qalamūn* (along with most hagiographic and historical writings) repeatedly portrays Kyros as a tyrant who coerced monks to convert by forcing them to subscribe: "to the defiled Tome of the impious Leo and celebrate the liturgy with him (ⲛ̄ϥ̄ⲧⲣⲉⲩⲥⲩⲛⲁⲅⲉ ϩⲛ̄ⲛⲉϥϭⲓϫ)".[30] Those who resisted were risking torture and death.[31] In general, a rhetoric of violence often appears in Coptic literature not only in association with heresy, but more specifically with the figure of Kyros; hence, the atrocities associated with him and the scale of the resulting conversions should be read with great reservation. (In pro-Chalcedonian literature, violence is likewise associated with heresy, though there the Copts are the perpetrators rather than the victims.) In any case, by whatever means Kyros succeeded in attracting converts, ultimately he failed to heal the schism but only succeeded in further fragmenting the pro- and anti-Chalcedonian confessions. Likewise, Coptic passages stressing Kyros' success need to be read with equal restraint. While most sources don't address the issue, two prominent references—a gloss in the HP (I.2:234), which has been discussed in a different context in Chapter Two, and another in the *Life of Samuel*—comment on Kyros' success, but both are problematic on at least two fronts. The two traditions are mutually exclusive, and emphasize Kyros' success only to bolster the standing of a particular monastic community and that of its ascetics: those of the Monastery of Metras in the case of the HP, and of the monks of the Qalamūn in the *Life of Samuel*.[32] In general, it is unclear if Kyros directly targeted monastics at all; his earlier conciliatory efforts only involved bishops.

Thus, while the fourth and fifth centuries were an era of tremendous expansion, Christianity in Egypt endured a prolonged phase of internal dissent from the mid-fifth century until the Arab conquest. It was a period of Institutional Conversion that engendered several contentious factions, and culminated with a surge among the Melkites of Egypt during the patriarchate of John the Almsgiver.

From the Conquest to the ʿAbbāsids

Early post-conquest conversions are seldom documented in the oldest Arabic chronicles.[33] Consequently, Christian texts necessarily provide the bulk of the evidence. Despite some deviations,[34] scholarly consensus still maintains that the ninth through tenth centuries constituted a period of rapid conversion.[35] Minimally, those centuries demarcate the demographic demise of the Christian community through conversion to Islam, and the reciprocal growth of the Muslim population, whose ranks were further supplemented by immigration from abroad.[36]

According to Ibn ʿAbd al-Ḥakam, the first Egyptian converts to Islam, Mariyya al-Qibṭiyya, the Prophet Muḥammad's concubine, and her sister Shīrīn, accepted Islam a little over a decade prior to the Arab conquest of the province.[37] Frequently cited, this tradition must be read with reservation. S. Bashear dated the traditions identifying Mariyya as a Copt to the beginning of the eighth century,[38] and in general, the earliest writings are not unequivocal as to her origins. Other factors further erode the historicity of the tradition. A primary point of contention is that the traditional pericope, preserved by Ibn ʿAbd al-Ḥakam and al-Balādhurī, maintains that the women were sent as gifts to the Prophet in response to a missive in which he prompted "al-Muqawqas" to accept Islam. Such invitations were purportedly sent by the Prophet Muḥammad to contemporary rulers, including the Byzantine, Sasanian, and Ethiopian emperors, and in all cases their historicity is doubtful.[39] Another problematic issue is that the names of the women involved are identical to those of the concubines of the Sasanian emperor Khusraw II Parvez (590–628 CE).[40] Furthermore,

Ibn ʿAbd al-Ḥakam's identification of Mariyya as a Copt resonates with the overarching themes of communal harmony and common ancestry which he actively cultivates throughout his narrative (discussed in Chapter Two). Finally, the name "Shīrīn" (or Sīrīn), popular in Persia, is unattested in the Greek and Coptic documents of this period. Setting aside the question of historicity, over the course of the first Islamic century, Mariyya and Shīrīn were not joined by many Egyptian converts.[41] This has been the scholarly consensus since D. Dennett's groundbreaking study and is supported by more recent papyrological investigations.[42]

Egyptian converts to Islam are attested early in the historical record. The late seventh-century *Chronicle* of John of Nikiou identifies several early converts and notes that: "many of the Egyptians who had been false Christians denied the holy orthodox faith and life-giving baptism, and embraced the religion of the Muslims".[43] Some of these individuals immediately found work as guides and translators for the advancing Arab armies,[44] and by the first quarter of the eighth century, the *Apocalypse of Athanasios* noted the swelling ranks of those who converted to Islam.[45] The importance of such Coptic-speaking *mawālī* likely increased after 99/718, when Muslim personnel replaced Christian village notables in assessing and collecting taxes.[46] *Mawālī* would have facilitated communication between Coptic villagers and the newly-appointed Arab officials.[47] Still, the thoroughness and aim of that reform must be questioned; as repeatedly demonstrated in documentary papyri, Christians remained profoundly involved in rural tax collection efforts through the Ottoman era.

In his *Futūḥ miṣr*, Ibn ʿAbd al-Ḥakam preserved isolated traditions pertaining to converts, including calls for conversion that were allegedly extended to entire villages; still, the historicity of such early attempts at proselytization has been rigorously challenged.[48] Most amusing is an account of a whimsical convert who converted back and forth between Christianity and Islam on several occasions.[49] More relevant, however, are the conflicting traditions Ibn ʿAbd al-Ḥakam retains regarding the collection of the poll tax (*jizya*) from converts and the discrepancies pertaining to the status of their land.[50]

Nonetheless, while these traditions are ostensibly early, their fiscal dimensions betray eighth- and ninth-century considerations.

In sum, while early narratives note converts to Islam, the documentation is thin, and the size of that nascent Egyptian-Muslim community must have remained negligible and socially marginal. Rather, throughout the first two Islamic centuries, Institutional Conversion persisted as the most dynamic facet of religious affiliation. The social, linguistic, religious, cultural, and even spatial chasm that existed between Arab and Egyptian communities throughout Umayyad rule was simply immense and seldom traversed.

Post-Conquest Christian Conversions

The Arab conquest incited an instantaneous shift in the direction and social dynamics of conversion. Two clear patterns emerge. The first is that Institutional Conversion to the Melkite community came to a sudden halt; incidents of conversion from Coptic to Melkite ranks in the wake of the conquest are extremely rare.[51] Doubtless, the new socio-political environment in which the pro-Chalcedonians lacked both a patriarch and Byzantine support advanced this dynamic.[52] A second pattern is that the Institutional Conversion evident under Byzantine rule persisted and even intensified throughout the early post-conquest centuries with one significant distinction: it reversed course. After the Arab conquest, Melkites and members of other Christian factions gravitated toward, and through diverse means joined, the Coptic church. Thus, while the first Islamic century lacked any significant number of Egyptian converts to Islam, it was a period of rampant Institutional Conversion in which the Coptic church consolidated its communal base and reaffirmed its hegemony over the Christians of Egypt, the bulk of the populace.

In the wake of the conquest, the Coptic church capitalized upon its newfound freedom by replenishing its hierarchy; significantly, Patriarch Agathon (661–77 CE) ordained a number of bishops to revitalize the church's ecclesiastical ranks.[53] The appointment of new bishops stabilized the dioceses of the see, which had been decimated for decades, particularly since the Persian occupation

(618–28 CE) and reinforced the church's infrastructure, which would absorb new converts. The ecclesiastical apparatus also proved advantageous to the nascent Arab government, which on occasion used it to disseminate its edicts[54] though, by and large, as repeatedly demonstrated in the previous chapters, the amicable relationship between the early Islamic government and the Coptic hierarchy has been grossly exaggerated.

The HP demonstrates well the shifting trajectory of conversion in Egypt. Immediately upon his return from exile in 23/644, the Coptic patriarch Benjamin drew: "to himself most of the people whom Herakleios, the heretical king, had led astray; for he induced them to the right faith by his gentleness, exhorting them with courtesy and consolation".[55] Episodes of Institutional Conversion punctuate the biographies of several of Benjamin's successors: Agathon I, John III, Isaac I, Khaīl I, and Mark II (d. 819 CE).[56]

The Coptic *Life of Isaac of Alexandria* provides another, more nuanced example. Similar to Benjamin and Agathon before him, the biography lauds Patriarch Isaac (686–89 CE) for leading a multitude from their: "heresies. . .some he baptized (ⲁϥϯⲱⲙⲥ ⲛⲱⲟⲩ); others he accepted when they anathematized their heresies by means of the grace with which God had favored him".[57] (Re)baptism is quite significant here. While confession sufficed for some, the insistence on rebaptizing others indicates membership in a heterodox group since infancy. Throughout these early post-conquest decades, the Coptic church assimilated various factions and, accordingly, had a different policy for dealing with each. Ultimately, the church gained scores of those who had accepted the pro-Chalcedonian confession decades earlier (and likely those who accepted that confession through the Monothelite and Monenergite compromises), along with many others who had been estranged possibly for centuries.

The Conversion incidents and patterns analyzed thus far—whether relative to Coptic patriarchs or the pro-Chalcedonian patriarch John the Almsgiver—highlight the role charismatic leaders played in attracting the laity of Egypt to their respective creeds.[58] Still, this means of conversion should not be overstated. It is significant; nonetheless, the HP by virtue of its very subject matter, reflects a specific, limited perspective. Although thinly documented, the scope and frequency of incidents in which individuals and even entire villages converted of their own volition without ecclesiastical prompting may have been much more prevalent and significant than the sources would indicate. Such was the case with several villages in the nomes of Agharwah and Sakhā, which recognized the Coptic hierarchy during the patriarchate of John III (d. 686),[59] and the village of Būkhabshā which converted in the mid-third/ninth century.[60]

At the beginning of the eighth century, a single man incited a wave of Institutional Conversion and demonstrated the influence of tangible incentives on religious affiliation. According to the HP, an anti-Chalcedonian notable, John of Ṣā,[61] convinced the governor Qurra ibn Sharīk to double taxes on all heterodox groups in Egypt. John and his entourage, which must have included clergy, traversed the Delta, from Ṣā to Banā, and from Rosetta to Damietta, "baptizing" laymen and monks of different sects.[62] Again, rebaptism indicates the conversion of individuals and families who had belonged to other factions since infancy. The efficacy of financial incentives for conversion would be again demonstrated under ʿAbbāsid rule.

Accommodating the clergy of rival Christian factions provided an additional means by which the Coptic church consolidated its hegemony and healed old schisms. Even amidst earnest deliberations, the ambiguous status of converting clergy posed a fundamental stumbling block, which led to the breakdown of negotiations between Patriarch Khaīl I (Michael, 744–68 CE) and his pro-Chalcedonian counterpart, Quzmān (727–68 CE), and was likely behind the deterioration of similar dialogues with the Julianists and Meletians.[63] At several junctures, however, compromises allowed for the (re)ordination of the clergy of schismatic sects after their formal reunion with the Coptic hierarchy.

The *Life of Isaac of Alexandria* may provide the first glimpse at this means of ecumenism. Iannē, a man of noble lineage (ΟΥΓΕΝΟϹ ϾϤϬΟϹΙ) who belonged to the Akephaloi, accepted the anti-Chalcedonian confession and became Isaac's spiritual brother.[64] In time, he took monastic vows, and was later elevated to the episcopate as Bishop John of Terenouti.[65] The episode remains shrouded in ambiguity.[66] It is not at all clear whether the two men befriended each other before or after Iannē left the Akephaloi, or if Iannē held any ecclesiastical rank while a member of that sect. It is possible that Iannē's ordination was negotiated beforehand, providing the first example of the means of ecumenism described here, though the issue will ultimately remain open.

Stronger support appears sixty years later. Already alluded to are the largely unsuccessful negotiations headed by Khaīl I in the mid-eighth century CE; those conciliatory efforts did bear some fruit, however. Constantine, the pro-Chalcedonian bishop of Miṣr, converted and accepted the anti-Chalcedonian hierarchy.[67] Most likely he was re-ordained a Coptic bishop, as this was the only stipulation made prior to his very dramatic, public conversion. Here, the silence of the HP as to Constantine's subsequent fate is laden with meaning.

Under ʿAbbāsid rule, heterodox factions became increasingly receptive to the ecumenical efforts of the Coptic church. Equally significant were the Coptic church's policies toward converting clergy which abated after Khaīl I. Perhaps his successors demonstrated greater tact or skill in such matters, though socio-political circumstances were probably a greater determinant of historical events than personal demeanor. ʿAbbāsid policies intermittently—and often irreversibly—situated non-Muslim communities in increasingly marginal socio-political roles. This likely motivated fringe groups to align themselves with the dominant Christian body.

The events surrounding the end of the Barsanuphian schism provide a salient example of the malleability of Coptic policies toward converting clergy. A faction of that sect had been reconciled late in the patriarchate of Khaīl I (d. 768 CE), primarily due to the efforts of John, the saintly Bishop of Samannūd,[68] but the schism persisted until the patriarchate of Mark II (799–819 CE).[69] At that juncture, immediately after the reunion, the Barsanuphian hierarchs, George and his biological son Abraham, were re-ordained as Coptic bishops. Again, this must have been one of the stipulations of the reconciliation agreement.[70] Contemporaries surely noted the peculiar nature of these ordinations. By the ninth century, the lifelong celibacy of bishops was increasingly a matter of concern.[71] Moreover, George and Abraham were consecrated bishops *before* there were dioceses for them to occupy; hence, eventually, Bishop George headed the diocese of Tunbudha and his son the Upper Egyptian diocese of Atripe.[72] Although not unique, this must have seemed highly irregular and wholly inconsistent with canon law and nearly contemporary parallels in which those promised elevation had to wait for a vacant diocese prior to their ordination.[73] Such concessions demonstrate the lengths to which the Coptic church was willing to negotiate with its rivals in the ninth century. Still, it was a shrewd move. The awkwardness of the arrangement died with the participants, and the compromise ended a schism that spanned centuries.

Significantly, Institutional Conversion persisted throughout the early post-conquest centuries. This was a pivotal period in which many pro-Chalcedonians, schismatics, and members of an assortment of heterodox factions accepted the leadership and creed of the Coptic hierarchy. The means of membership and reunion varied, but the multi-pronged dynamic led to the consolidation of Egyptian Christianity into a more unified and highly structured entity: a Coptic church that absorbed all of its Christian competitors save one, the Melkites.

From the ʿAbbāsids to the Tenth Century

Except for the fleeting reforms of ʿUmar II (99–101/717–20), Umayyad caliphs did not actively promote conversion to Islam.[74] To the contrary, they discriminated against non-Arab Muslims and unabashedly extracted the *jizya* from converts. Such deterrents to conversion endured until the very last days of Umayyad rule when the Egyptian governor, Ḥāfiṣ, declared that all converts would be exempt from the poll tax.[75] Twenty-four thousand men answered the invitation, some of whom even enlisted in the army (*iktatabū wa sarū min al-ʿaskariyyā*).[76] Thus, exempt from the *jizya*, these new converts also sought to receive *ʿaṭāʾ* (a military salary in this case). This is the first documented mass conversion to Islam in Egypt. Others would follow.[77] Within months, the ʿAbbāsids reinstituted the same policy and gained a number of converts at its implementation.[78] ʿAbbāsid rule ushered in a strong financial incentive to convert and, as in the above discussion of John of Ṣā, it proved effective.

Another incident of mass conversion, important symbolically rather than numerically, occurred in the early ninth century (ca. 194–6/809–11). A delegation representing *Ahl al-Ḥarās* (the Community of the village of *Ḥarās*) bribed the *qāḍī al-quḍāt* and asked him to certify their Arabic ancestry.[79] Most likely a nominal conversion, this incident demonstrates waning Christian conviction. While fourth- and fifth-century authors celebrated individuals who preferred torture and death to apostasy, and enthusiastically documented the wholesale conversion of villages to Christianity, five centuries later, the opposite was true.

Typically, records of conversion focus on males. The historical record is not forthcoming as to the fate of the wives and children of these men. Several questions arise. Did women sever their familial ties with male converts, or did the conversion of husbands and fathers translate into the conversion of wives and children? Or should one assume that converts were predominantly single men? There are no unequivocal answers to these questions, though the scraps gleaned from Egyptian texts suggest that the conversion of husbands and fathers served as catalysts for the subsequent conversions of their wives and children.[80]

Intermarriage between Muslims and Christians may have increased during the ninth century CE;[81] this is speculative, but likely. Marriage contracts in general, whether in Greek, Coptic, or Arabic, are notoriously scarce,[82] and often the names of the groom and bride fail to clearly identify the religious affiliation of the families involved.[83] Still, the few documentary examples that may be cited all date to the ninth century and beyond.[84] Nabia Abbott identified two papyri published by A. Grohmann (*P.Cair.Arab.* I.40 and I.43, dated 271/855 and 306/918) as examples of such unions. She observed that while the parties involved had Christian names, the contracts fail to designate them as such.[85] Consequently, Abbott inferred that the two papyri document rare examples of intermarriage in which at least one of the parties had recently converted to Islam. While certainly not implausible,[86] the two contracts in question likely involved Christians. They lack the polygamy and divorce clauses typically found in Islamic marriage contracts,[87] and neither contains the formulaic passages stipulating that the groom should care for his bride in accordance with the precepts of the Qur'ān and the *sunna* (e.g. *P.Cair.Arab.*I.42.5-6).

Still, examples of intermarriage during this period may be sought in *P.Cair.Arab.*I.38, I.41, and I.48 (dated 259/873, 279/892, and 233/847, respectively). The first is a marriage contract between Isma'īl, the *mawlā* of Aḥmad ibn Marwān al-Qurayshī, and 'Ā'yshā, daughter of Yūsuf, whose grandfather and *wālī* (according to the contract) was Ya'qūb ibn Isḥāq. Isma'īl's designation as a *mawlā* betrays his status as a recent convert to Islam.[88] It may have also been the case that 'Ā'yshā, whose patronymic may be either Christian or Muslim, was a recent convert. A second contract is between Ya'qūb ibn Isḥāq ibn Yaḥyā and Hanīdā, daughter of Sarī. While "Ya'qūb" and "Hanīdā" are nondescript, Sarī is Christian (cf. *P.Cair.Arab.* I.54.3). As for the contract, it is unambiguously Islamic, containing a polygamy clause (I.41.7-9) and instructions to follow the *sunna* (l.12-13). The third contract, drawn between Yunā (ⲒⲰϨⲀⲚⲚⲀ), daughter of Ḥalyṣ (ϨⲈⲖⲒⲤⲀⲒⲞⲤ or Ἐλισά), and Yazīd ibn Qāsim, plainly documents a mixed marriage.[89]

Overwhelmingly, conversions in the post-conquest era were ultimately voluntary, but a few were coerced. Four incidents loom large in Christian literature. The first occurred at the beginning of the second/eighth century. Governor al-Aṣbagh ibn 'Abd al-'Azīz detained and compelled many to convert to Islam: "among them Peter, governor of Upper Egypt, and his brother Theodore, and the son of Theophanes, governor of Maryūṭ, and a body of priests and laymen not to be numbered on account of their multitude".[90] For all the troubles al-Aṣbagh caused the Christians (which were considerable and included heavy taxation and mutilation),[91] he was not in office for more than a few months in 86/705,[92] and it may be assumed that the majority of his forced conversions were nominal and impermanent. A second incident transpired during the patriarchate of Yusāb I (Joseph, 830–49 CE). The governor kidnapped the Roman, Abyssinian, and Nubian servants of the Coptic patriarch and forced them to convert. The patriarch pleaded his case with the local *qāḍī* thus: "You know that none of your predecessors forced any one like these, who are Christians and the sons of Christians, to become Muslims".[93] While not completely unprecedented as Patriarch Yusāb alleged, forced conversion was practically unheard of until the middle of the ninth century CE. Finally, the third and fourth incidents are associated with the violent conversions extracted by al-Mutawakkil (also in the mid-ninth century) and the Fāṭimid al-Ḥākim bi Amr Allāh at the dawning of the eleventh century.[94]

Egyptian literary sources contain but a few references to Muslims who embraced Christianity. In one case, an anonymous man converted to Christianity after experiencing a miracle, but had to flee his home in fear for his life.[95] He, along with the few other converts on record during this early period, gravitated toward the monasteries of Wādī al-Naṭrūn (Scetis). A later witness to the same pattern may be found in the tenth century; immediately upon his conversion, Wāḍiḥ ibn Rajā was instructed to flee to the monasteries.[96] The flight of converts to Coptic monasteries was an open secret. When authorities sought out such individuals, they knew to seek them out in the Wādī.[97] By the thirteenth century, the monasteries sought out for refuge appear to have been those of the Red Sea. The novelty of a Muslim convert to Christianity is understandable considering the repercussions of apostasy,[98] but several imposing social barriers also hindered such an event. It would be safe to assume that the absolute majority of the early Muslim population never considered the possibility of conversion. The Arabic language, tribal solidarity, and acceptance of the message of Muḥammad comprised the basic tenets of Arab identity, and Coptic Christianity simply did not offer any of the three. Furthermore, for the better part of two centuries, most Christians and Muslims lived in insular communities that were geographically and linguistically distinct from one another.

A Prelude to Conversion

It is important to consider how new Muslims were perceived and functioned within their immediate environment and society at large. In general, Christians identified converts as insincere in their faith: individuals who succumbed to worldly enticement rather than religious conviction.[99] Historically, throughout Umayyad rule, apostates were scorned by their Christian neighbors, but a fundamental shift in social interactions and popular attitudes eventually unfolded and is best documented in the ninth and tenth centuries CE.

The early eighth-century *Life of Isaac of Alexandria* provides a paradigmatic example. A Christian "from the land of the Saracens," a relative of the governor ʿAbd al-ʿAzīz ibn Marwān and his brother the Caliph ʿAbd al-Malik, traveled to Egypt in search of a son who had converted to Islam.[100] Personal ambition may have motivated the young man. Related to the governor of Egypt and the caliph himself, it is likely that only his creed hindered his advancement in the Islamic administration. Eventually, the anonymous father found his son and attempted to persuade him to return to the faith of his ancestors. It is here that the story takes on wider implications. Upon the young man's refusal, the father solemnly disowned his son: "May your blood be upon your own head, my son; from this moment you are a stranger to me in this world and in {the world} to come".[101] The father disowned his son in a society that identified an individual first and foremost by his or her patronymic.

Despite its brevity, this is one of the earliest and certainly the fullest account of an individual's conversion to Islam in Egypt. Its inclusion in a patriarchal biography serves historical and ideological purposes, functioning as a pedagogical strategy educating Christians as to the gravity of conversion, an apostate's socio-religious standing, as well as appropriate familial sanction.[102] Concurrently, it may be understood as a deterrent measure, warning would-be converts of the dire consequences for such an act. Early converts to Islam had to endure an explicit and foreboding censure. Far from a purely religious (let alone personal) decision, religious conversion at that time constituted an act of social deviance that evoked the most stringent communal and familial reprimands.

The martyrdom of Dioskoros the neo-martyr, though likely not as early as the account preserved in the *Life of Isaac*, demonstrates the austerity and efficacy of familial sanctions.[103] An Alexandrian, Dioskoros had converted to Islam for undisclosed reasons. Upon hearing of this, his sister in Fayyūm wrote to him a letter of reproach: "I would have longed to hear of your death as a Christian—I would have rejoiced at that—rather than to hear that you left Christ your God." She then concluded: "Know that this letter is the last communication between you and I; from now on do not show me your face or write to me." The stringent letter prompted Dioskoros to put on the *zinnar* and to publicly apostatize, which led to his torture and eventual execution and burning.

Similar popular attitudes and societal censure still dominated in the mid-eighth century. After a failed attempt to usurp the patriarchate, a deacon Peter purportedly won favor with the Caliph Abū Jaʿfar al-Manṣūr (137–58/754–75), converted to Islam, and changed his name to Abū al-Khayr. After the caliph's death, however, Abū al-Khayr lost his prestigious appointment and decided to return to his former village: "as soon as his family, kinsmen, and acquaintances saw him, he was hated and detested among them". Later, in that same village, he died "a bitter death in *sin* and *poverty*;"[104] that is, he failed—perhaps even was punished—in this world and the next. Abū al-Khayr's decision to return to his hometown rather than to retire to a more hospitable location, such as an urban center, is puzzling. Perhaps he feared reprisal from the incoming administration, or he did not expect such a hostile reception at his village.[105] Whatever his motivation may have been, Abū al-Khayr's ostracism and biography served as a cautionary tale. The inclusion of this narrative in the HP is as much an attempt to dissuade potential converts, the ranks of whom had dramatically swelled under ʿAbbāsid rule, as it is an encapsulation of a historical event. Perhaps the very need to utilize such a moral tale, however, is more telling than the episode itself.[106]

Later, as conversion to Islam became more prevalent, social isolation and condemnation were not observed with such stringency. The *Apocalypse of Samuel* betrays a more lenient, perhaps even an altogether new dynamic, in interacting with converts. Written as a prophecy, this apocryphal tract laments that when individuals convert: "their siblings and relatives will not weep over them or be saddened, but they will be proud and will [continue to] eat and drink with them. Then they will envy and emulate them and blaspheme Christ as they did".[107] Allowing for a degree of embellishment, it is nonetheless evident that by the time the *Apocalypse of Samuel* was drafted, likely by the late tenth century CE, converts did not suffer the intense social isolation or communal censure Abū al-Khayr had to endure.

An increasingly tolerant attitude on behalf of the Christian population may be further illustrated by a contract involving the intermarried couple identified above: Yunā, daughter of Ḥalīṣ, and Yazīd ibn Qāsim (*P.Cair.Arab.*I.48). In *P.Cair.Arab.*I.56, dated 239/854 in Edfū, Yunā bought a house from her husband Yazīd (most likely in lieu of the remainder of her wedding gift, as Grohmann suggests). Among the witnesses were three Christians, one of whom, Moses, apparently could understand but not write Arabic; he signed in Coptic. Such interactions between converts to Islam and their Christian neighbors are indicative of social change, tolerance, and acceptance. The vehement social isolation that characterized the Coptic community's early response to Christian apostates subsided in favor of a disapproving though tolerant attitude. Converts were no longer shunned or ostracized and, thus, conversion was destigmatized in part.

Socio-Religious Catalysts

Several factors likely converged under ʿAbbāsid rule to alleviate communal censure and eventually facilitate large-scale Tradition Transition. On one front, as the ranks of converts grew, individuals were increasingly difficult to isolate and censure. They became a ubiquitous element to which the Christian population—no longer the absolute majority—became increasingly desensitized, and consequently, stringent social and familial sanctions abated. Hence, a new convert did not necessarily suffer isolation or ostracism from his or her preexisting social networks or environment, especially as these networks came to include lifelong Muslims. Islamic political hegemony coupled with the attitudes and policies of various governors may have also served as catalysts. For some, conversion provided a means for social mobility, while for others it secured an individual—and a family's—socio-political standing. Hence, each ʿAbbāsid *dhimmī*-purge of the bureaucracy, though usually short-lived, sparked waves of conversion among elites.

Socially, while conversion to Islam became increasingly less disadvantageous, ʿAbbāsid policies promoted an ideology that welcomed converts on an equal religious and social footing with other Muslims. Certainly, a segment within the Islamic community, particularly under Mamlūk rule, viewed converts askance, doubting their sincerity and motivation, but that does not seem to figure in the writings of the period surveyed.

Still, a number of other factors must be highlighted: the numerical increase of the Arab population, their settlement in or near Coptic villages, and their assumption of tax assessment and collection duties provided stimuli with wide-ranging social ramifications.[108] Once settled, Arab Muslims functioned as a potential socio-religious network for those contemplating conversion as well as a vital catalyst that accelerated the process of Arabization in a given region. Arab immigration to Egypt officially began in 100/719, when Qaysī tribesmen were purposefully settled in the province.[109] Unofficial waves of immigration, however, are well documented from the time of the conquest through the tenth century CE.[110] An almost simultaneous means by which Arabs settled in Coptic villages occurred in 99/718.[111] At that juncture, Muslim agents began to replace the local Christian notables who previously assessed and collected taxes on behalf of the government, functioning in a manner reminiscent of the *dihqāns*, or small landowners, of Iraq (cf. the *shahārija*).[112] While scholars postulate that these individuals did not initially reside in the villages to which they were assigned,[113] there is nonetheless evidence that some did relocate along with a contingent of *mawālī*.[114]

A lack of foresight on behalf of the Coptic hierarchy and stagnation in Christian religious education under the early ʿAbbāsids provided yet another catalyst that enabled a shift in societal attitudes and large-scale conversion. As that dynasty propagated its *daʿwā*, an egalitarian ethos among Muslims, and consolidated its political rule, it also reinstituted late Umayyad fiscal policies regarding converts. These new material incentives were coupled with sophisticated religious critiques by ʿAbbāsid scholars who were the first to present a formidable intellectual challenge to Christians and Jews.[115]

The Syrian fathers immediately perceived the threat these new ʿAbbāsid policies and religious critiques posed to their community and reacted promptly. Thus, early ʿAbbāsid rule has become synonymous with a literary surge in Syrian Christianity, which yielded both the first major translations of the Christian Scriptures into Arabic[116] and the first Arabic and bilingual (Syriac/Arabic) Christian apologetic tracts under Islamic rule.[117] By contrast, in Egypt, with the exception of a few anonymous hagiographic and apocryphal tracts, the first ʿAbbāsid century largely demarcates literary silence and stagnation. The volume of Coptic writings stemming from that period is meager, and it remained as such during the second century of ʿAbbāsid rule.[118] Throughout that period, the copying of older manuscripts persisted, but original composition languished and the literature that was composed circulated under the names of fourth- and fifth-century figures and typically did not address the historical context or developments within the church or community. Coptic apologetic and theological treatises analogous to those in Syria would have to wait two hundred years for Sawīrus ibn al-Muqaffaʿ to write—in Arabic—his *Tafsīr al-amānah* in the mid-tenth century CE.

Throughout this period, the most striking examples of Coptic original compositions were in the form of apocryphal literature that, if read as texts of social criticism and dissent (especially the third *Apocalypse of Athanasios* and the *Apocalypse of Samuel*), betray utter frustration at the lack of ecclesiastical instruction; indeed, one is struck by their sweeping condemnations of the corruption and ignorance of bishops, priests, deacons, and monks. The late tenth-century *Apocalypse of Samuel* goes on to cite ignorance and corruption as the underlying causes for conversion.[119] Further proof for the deterioration and dilution of religious conviction may be sought in the tenth-century *Kitāb miṣbāḥ al-ʿaql* and in two eleventh-century compositions, *Kitāb al-īḍāḥ* and the preface to the HP (both erroneously attributed to Bishop Sawīrus).[120] Several passages in *Kitāb al-īḍāḥ* are particularly striking, as the book itself constitutes one of the first attempts in centuries aimed at renewing Christian education. It spearheaded a new genre; as a catechetical tract, *Kitāb al-īḍāḥ* has no Coptic predecessor or peer. Hence, although a product of the eleventh century, the book addressed problems and corrected ideas that had festered for centuries.

It is difficult to gauge the lack of religious and theological sophistication that permeated the Christian populace during these crucial centuries of early ʿAbbāsid rule. The principle Christian source, the HP provides the perspective of clerical elites; consequently, its theological acumen doubtless surpassed that of the lay Copts. Indirectly, however, the compilation still contributes a great deal, particularly through the terse glosses it appends to the domestic heresies that plagued the Coptic church under Islamic rule.

In the middle of the ninth century, a heresy swept Upper Egypt espousing that the divinity of Christ died on the cross. A pervasive belief in such a nonsensical doctrine betrays a Christian population only marginally aware of normative Christian principles. Surprisingly, this doctrine found many adherents, including most bishops of the region.[121] Amazed at the popularity of this doctrine, Bishop Michael of Tinnīs, an astute cleric and the author of the pertinent section of the HP, could not help but note that: "the scantiness of the knowledge of their shepherds [the bishops of Upper Egypt] was manifest in those days." Eventually, the majority of Upper Egyptian bishops condemned the heresy,[122] but two staunch advocates preferred excommunication to changing their views.[123] Still, this was not the end of the tenacious heresy, which prompted a rare visit of a

Coptic Patriarch to Upper Egypt.[124] Similar proofs of theological and religious naïveté may be gleaned from the eleventh-century *Kitāb al-īḍāḥ*,[125] and the doctrines and controversies surrounding Murqus ibn al-Qunbar (late twelfth century CE).[126] Although confused with regard to a number of theological issues—a symptom of the endemic problem—Murqus rightly championed one orthodox doctrine, the need to confess before a priest, and for that he was excommunicated.[127]

Decline in Christian instruction provided a catalyst for the conversion of many to Islam. The scarcity of popular religious education, whether formal or informal, allowed the worldviews of Islam and Christianity to draw nigh to one another; the closer the proximity, the easier the act of conversion. Sociologists have acknowledged as much,[128] and M. Morony has already demonstrated the utility of this concept in his discussion of reinforcement in Iraq.[129] Without basic religious indoctrination, Christianity and Islam take on a similar guise; both espouse belief in one almighty God,[130] the Hebrew patriarchs and prophets, revealed scriptures, a final judgment, heaven and hell, angels and devils, a similar code of ethics, and analogous religious practices such as fasting and prayer.[131] The similarities are palpable in the nuance of the above-mentioned "Upper Egyptian heresy." Believing that the divinity of Jesus died on the Cross—implying his divinity was neither complete nor immortal—is certainly within proximity to the belief that he was but a divinely-inspired prophet. On occasion, the religious gulf that separated the faithful of the two communities could be traversed with a small leap.

An uninitiated parishioner faced with the option of conversion to Islam (which entailed exemption from the *jizya* and the possibility of social mobility) versus remaining Christian did not face much of a dilemma. For most converts, the foundation for their religious worldview did not change significantly. Here, social forces played a key role. While the cost of conversion to Islam in the form of social repercussions remained greater than the reward, an individual would not convert. Once the benefits of conversion equaled or outweighed adherence to Christianity, however, life as a Muslim became a viable, even lucrative option.[132] Conversion to Islam during this period provided a subconscious yet visible critique of Coptic society. Many individuals converted long before they ever recited the *shahādā*; the event must not be mistaken for the process.

The importance of this religious factor in the dialectic of conversion may be further appreciated through a comparison with the process as it unfolded in Anatolia, where Muslims (especially sufīs) actively proselytized.[133] The heterodox practices and ideas introduced by sufīs proved vital in forging a hybrid version of Islam that bridged the spiritual and theological gap between traditional beliefs and Islam, bringing them into a proximity that facilitated conversion. To the contrary, throughout the period under investigation, Muslims in Egypt did not proselytize among Christians.[134] The lack of religious indoctrination functioned in a similar manner by producing individuals whose worldview and concepts of the divine were so close to Islamic popular beliefs that conversion did not require any radical shift in paradigms; diluted Christian beliefs proved just as effective as a hybridized version of Islam.

The Bashmūr

Finally, a few words to address the one event that several medieval historians and modern scholars have cast as the turning point in the history of Egyptian Christianity: the ninth-century Bashmūric revolts.[135] Briefly, the Bashmūric revolts were the largest and most violent of the so-called "Coptic Revolts" which have been ideologically (even romantically) depicted as the last Coptic stance against the prevailing Arab-Muslim society. As the discussion in Chapter Six demonstrates, however, these revolts were far from the ideological uprisings imaged by later authors. The revolts are pivotal in illuminating a number of implicit socio-political developments, but their significance in regard to religious conversion has been greatly exaggerated.[136]

The mid-ninth century was, indeed, a watershed in Egyptian history, but for reasons that are quite distinct from the defeat of the Bashmūrites. By that juncture, the Muslim population had already increased exponentially; more significantly, the end of Bashmūric resistance coincided with the beginning of the above-mentioned shift in social attitudes toward converts. A particular socio-religious dynamic, independent of the revolts, had already been set in motion. In the eighth century, the *Apocalypse of Athanasios* rebuked the laity on their procrastination in attending church; the tenth-century *Apocalypse of Samuel*, on the other hand, while repeating the same reproach as a *topos*, appends allusions to churches that remained empty or in ruins (*kharāba*).[137] Egyptian Christianity, it seems, had been dealt the same blow it delivered to paganism in the fifth century.[138]

Observations

Far from a monotonous era of Christian dominance, distinct phases of religious conversion punctuated the transition from Late Antiquity to Early Islam, transforming the socio-religious landscape of Egypt. During the fourth and fifth centuries, many who had worshipped the Greco-Roman pantheon, ancient Egyptian deities, and Yahweh embraced a new religion: Christianity. A second phase, discernible from the Council of Chalcedon (451 CE) through the tenth century, prompted waves of Institutional Conversion that engendered several contentious communities within Egypt, but concluded with their absorption by the Coptic hierarchy. The Arab conquest proved a significant turning-point in that regard. In the wake of the conquest, successive waves of Institutional Conversion to anti-Chalcedonian ranks enabled the Coptic church to consolidate its hegemony over the Egyptian populace, particularly in the urban centers of the Delta. The Arab conquest also initiated an overlapping and ultimately open-ended era of conversion to Islam: Tradition Transition. Although 641 CE serves as the historical start of this third phase, it was with the rise of the ʿAbbāsids in 750 CE that it commenced in earnest. The mid-eighth century witnessed the first large-scale conversions to Islam and the beginning of the reciprocal demographic erosion of the Christian community.

Initially, it would appear that those most susceptible to conversion occupied the two extreme ends of the socio-political spectrum: society's riff-raff and its elites. One constituency sought to improve its lot, while the other strategically positioned itself to maintain its status and prestige.[139] For the general populace, it is readily apparent that the social dynamics of censure and tolerance affected the decision to convert as much as—if not more than—financial incentives and analogous beliefs, and that the combination of these factors provided an enticing formula for conversion.

In the ninth century, several factors converged to facilitate large-scale conversion to Islam. From an economic standpoint, the lure of exemption from the burdensome *jizya* was all too enticing. Some, viewing conversion as a strictly religious phenomenon, are disturbed by the very mention of fiscal incentives. As this chapter has repeatedly demonstrated, however, to many—though certainly not all—non-religious, social and fiscal factors influenced the process of conversion to the Coptic creed and the Islamic faith (cf. John of Ṣā and ʿAbbāsid policies). On the religious front, a decline in Christian education blurred the distinction between the worldviews of Islam and Christianity. Socially, among Christians, the harsh communal censure of converts evident in the seventh and eighth centuries had eroded by the ninth and tenth centuries CE, giving way to more tolerant attitudes. Conversely, among Muslims, ʿAbbāsid policies prompted the perception and acceptance of converts on an equal footing. Such synchronicity allowed Islam to provide a cultural and religious alternative to Egyptian Christians for which individuals would increasingly opt.[140]

Broadly speaking, converts tended to gravitate toward the religion of the dominant regime; that much was expected. What is of note, however, is that the examination of Institutional Conversion proved that that "regime" was not necessarily identical with political sovereigns but rather designates those with tangible social capital. It is no accident that the century and a half after the Arab conquest, when the Coptic hierarchy still retained a substantial presence and influence in the public sphere, constituted a period of conversion to

Coptic ranks—the primary institution to which the bulk of the populace had direct access.

Although the Coptic church's position began to erode in the second quarter of the eighth century, by that juncture it functioned as the primary advocate for the Christians of the province, a fact that no doubt reinforced the pattern of Institutional Conversion. An eighth-century "Meletian" was practically a non-entity. As far as the Muslim government was concerned, that individual belonged to *ahl al-dhimmā* for better or worse, but within the larger Christian community that individual was a marginalized *persona non grata*. In those early post-conquest centuries, accepting the anti-Chalcedonian hierarchy constituted the only logical step toward alignment with social power and mobility short of conversion to Islam.

Finally, it is evident that religious conversion had a direct bearing on social cohesion and the emergence of sectarian communities and identities. In the aftermath of the Arab conquest through the ninth century, Institutional Conversion led to the reconciliation of several minority Christian sects with the Coptic hierarchy, rendering it a more cohesive socio-religious unit. A similar effect emerged as a consequence of the ʿAbbāsid revolution, in which Muslim authorities patronized religious conversion with the ultimate aim of recruiting and consolidating a loyal constituency. The trajectories of conversion in these two examples were certainly different. In the first, fundamental Christian beliefs such as the divinity of Jesus and the Trinity were not abandoned, while in the second case converts adopted a new religious tradition altogether. In both cases, however, individuals gravitated toward the religion with the greatest socio-political capital and were consequently the cause of the growth and stability of that faith community.

CHAPTER 5

LANGUAGE, IDENTITY, AND ASSIMILATION

From the mid-fifth through the tenth century CE, the history of Egypt was primarily documented in three languages: Greek, Coptic, and Arabic. The only notable exceptions are a small number of surviving Latin papyri, and numerically negligible—though historically significant—Pahlavi (Middle Persian) texts.[1] Gradually under caliphal rule, Arabic replaced Coptic and Greek, first as the language of the administration and socio-political elites, and then as the mother-tongue of Christians and Jews. These are the two self-evident truths that every scholar recognizes; still, many issues pertaining to the utility and perception of language remain unsettled. Several factors contribute to the stalemate: the gap between papyrologists and historians; the accident of preservation; and the various degrees of maturity at which the fields of Greek, Coptic, and Arabic papyrology find themselves. Primarily, however, questions relating to language and culture have been unanswerable (or divisive) because of conflicting methodologies and academic presuppositions.

To be sure, the sources are often less than forthcoming. As discussed in Chapter One, normative literature typically reflects the urban perspectives of the Delta, and while documentary papyri provide representation of a wider cross-section of society, they predominantly reflect life in Upper Egypt and are plagued by the accident of preservation (not to mention physical deterioration). This dichotomy often leads to incompatible historical assessments that have forced scholars to choose sides. Studies of religious conversion, in which conclusions based on chronicles and histories are at odds with those derived from documentary papyri, illustrate this tendency.[2] Faced with this dilemma, historians have tended to favor one genre to the detriment of the other. Here, it is taken for granted that both are reliable historical witnesses, but only in relation to their geographic jurisdiction and the cogency of the questions posed.

Another hindrance is the manner in which scholars have framed their research. Complex socio-linguistic processes such as Arabization and religious conversion are not only multi-causal, but are temporally and geographically sensitive as well. The question of "when" must be answered concurrently with "where"? Nonetheless, while the lack of specificity in previous scholarship has contributed to conflicting historiographies, it is precisely here that historians become acutely aware of the limitations of their task, recognizing that the evidence at hand frequently falls short of definitively answering either question posed. Nonetheless, the questions must be posed, though care must be taken not to automatically project any conclusion reached onto the whole of Egypt, but rather to situate it within a chronological and geographical context whenever possible. The following analysis attempts to expand the range of sources hitherto surveyed in addressing these topics, and seeks to ask new questions of old data, arguing that the emerging patterns and conclusions better elucidate the dialectic among language, community, and identity. Still, the examination is particularly interested in how the three languages were perceived, and the social factors and mechanisms that facilitated and hindered the linguistic shift from Coptic and Greek to Arabic.

The Greek Language

From the Council of Chalcedon (451 CE) until the eighth century, Greek persisted as the dominant language of the administration.

Despite the increasingly prevalent use of Coptic and Arabic throughout the first Islamic century, Greek proved resilient and simply too ingrained in the administrative apparatus to be easily replaced. It took a caliphal decree to check the use of Greek by the administration, and decades for that mandate to be fully implemented.[3] Even a cosmetic alteration, such as removing Greek from the protocol of documents, took no less than thirty years to be fully realized.[4] Even among the conquering Arabs, a segment of that population and new converts exhibited fluency in Greek; Wardān, the *mawlā* of ʿAmr ibn al-ʿĀṣ, provides a salient example.[5] Coptic and Greek were more identifiable with the conquered population, and it should be taken for granted that all communication among the various communities, beginning with negotiations during the conquest period, proceeded in the Greek language, the one common medium.[6]

Among Muslims

For the greater part of the first Islamic century, Arabic played a supplementary role to Greek. It is commonly believed that Arabic translations were made of most (if not all) letters and decrees issued by the Arab government in the first half of the eighth century. K. Morimoto has challenged this assumption by citing a lack of documentary support,[7] noting that even records intended solely for the use of the Arab Muslim community, such as those of the early *dīwān*, were compiled in Greek, which is not surprising given that the registers were maintained by Egyptian scribes. Moreover, even when Arabic parallels are extant, as is the case with some of the early eighth-century correspondences between the governor Qurra ibn Sharīk and Basilios, the magistrate of Aphrodito/Jkōw, the Arabic versions usually post-date the Greek original—sometimes by as much as a full year. This underscores the extent to which the early Islamic bureaucracy relied upon the Greek language for its day-to-day activities.[8]

Still, the very existence of a dossier composed of Arabic translations of Greek papyri is puzzling and defies a simple explanation. Dispatching an Arabic letter to Aphrodito (where the document was found) seems meaningless and redundant. Nothing suggests that Basilios, to whom the letters were addressed, was bilingual. Thus, he could not have understood the Arabic correspondences, nor would he have needed to since a Greek version—a document he could actually read—preceded the Arabic version. The translations were possibly made in Aphrodito rather than sent from Fusṭāṭ, but then, in addition to the question of utility, another question of selection arises. The correspondences for which both Greek and Arabic versions exist are seldom noteworthy. Furthermore, it is not altogether clear why the Arabic versions were not dated the same as their Greek originals. Most likely the Arabic translations of the early eighth century were simply a half-hearted attempt to comply with the 705 CE mandate to Arabize the bureaucracy.

Away from urban centers, the use of Coptic as an administrative and legal language increased after the Arab conquest,[9] whereas its earlier use in official capacities had been rather marginal. An intriguing pattern may be observed throughout the second/eighth century, though it was by no means universal. Official correspondences addressed to the pagarch or *amīr* (even the governor in Fusṭāṭ) were often composed in Coptic,[10] while most correspondences between the governor and regional magistrates during that same period were issued in Greek, some accompanied or followed by an Arabic version.[11]

Among Melkites

Throughout the post-conquest period, pro-Chalcedonians were concentrated in a few urban centers in the Delta, especially Fusṭāṭ, Alexandria, and Būrah; Melkites remain unattested in Middle and Upper Egypt.[12] As with their Coptic and Jewish neighbors, the Melkites adopted the Arabic language relatively early as compared to rural populations. The extant writings indicate that the Melkites relied primarily on the Greek language;[13] the absolute lack of pro-Chalcedonian Coptic literature illustrates this point well. Nevertheless, this should not exclude the possibility that some members of that confession were fluent in the Coptic language.

It is an interesting facet of Melkite history in Egypt and Syria that the community came to terms with the Arabic language quite early, long before the Copts.[14] Melkites completed the earliest Arabic translations of the Christian scriptures, and could boast of the first Egyptian-Christian writer to compose in Arabic, Patriarch Saʿīd ibn Baṭrīq (877–940 CE).[15] Hence, the rants found in Coptic Arabic apocryphal tracts against the Arabic language do not have parallels in the few extant Egyptian-Melkite writings.[16] This was due to a dynamic (discussed below and in Chapter Twelve) in which tenth-century Copts, as opposed to their predecessors who lived under early Islamic rule, came to ideologically associate the Arabic language with Islam. The language came to signify a religious tradition rather than a political regime or a neutral means of communication—an unparalleled development in Melkite history. An onslaught of questions regarding the use and perception of the three languages by the pro-Chalcedonians of Egypt comes to mind, but, unfortunately, given the extreme paucity of sources the issue constitutes a historical dead end. The principal history of the Egyptian Melkite community throughout the early post-conquest centuries is the aforementioned tenth-century *Naẓm al-jawhar* of Eutychios, which fails to shed light on the perception or use of language in the preceding centuries.

Among Copts

It is taken for granted that Greek survived as the language of the early Islamic administration and among the pro-Chalcedonians of Egypt, but it is assumed to have been long in decline among the Coptic population—a ubiquitous claim that runs contrary to much of the available evidence. The nationalist-inspired sentiments rampant in the scholarship of the past century have severely distorted discussions of the perception and use of the Greek language by the anti-Chalcedonian community. The assumption, transparent in an article on Coptic literature,[17] is that the Council of Chalcedon (451) resulted in the: "detachment of most of the Egyptian church from the 'international' Christianity supported by the emperors of Byzantium". It further assumes that by the beginning of the sixth century: "Greek began to be perceived as the language of the oppressors and the patristic Greek ('international') culture was looked upon with suspicion as the vehicle of false dogmas and misleading historical information".[18] Moreover, beginning in the sixth century, Coptic literature is described as demonstrably more "nationalistic," as texts tended to be compose solely in the Coptic language and much of the subject matter seems Egyptian (e.g. John of Shmūn's encomiums on St. Mark and St. Antony).[19] This perspective has had significant political, theological, and linguistic ramifications, and has left a distinct mark on the historiography of Coptic literature and that of the Melkite community in Egypt.[20] The political implications of this thesis, especially in regard to the Arab conquest, have been addressed in Chapters Two and Three. Here, the focus turns to its linguistic and cultural ramifications, proposing that the normative historiography is in need of radical revision as it is selective by nature and fails to account for much of the historical record.

One of the foundations of the current paradigm is the assumption that the Council of Chalcedon initiated a religio-cultural chasm that resulted in the abandonment of the Greek language among the anti-Chalcedonian population. Tersely stated, the Copts perceived the Greek language as heretical and their own as orthodox. The literature of this period, however, often testifies in direct opposition to this assumption. First, it is difficult, if not impossible, to ascertain the original language of composition for the bulk of anti-Chalcedonian literature, particularly that of the Copts.[21] It would be hardly unique for a treatise composed in Greek to survive only in a Coptic translation, as with the Nag Hammadi Library and several Manichean writings.[22] Indeed, even though a large number of anti-Chalcedonian texts survive only in Coptic, scholarly consensus is that much of that corpus was likely composed in Greek.[23] It should also be noted that throughout the post-Chalcedonian period Coptic prose continued to be saturated with Greek loanwords even though perfectly acceptable and common Coptic equivalents were at hand. At the very least, anti-Chalcedonian writers were not hypersensitive to the Greek language as such.

Overwhelmingly, the argument for linguistic chauvinism, based as it is on Coptic literature, is only as effective as it is selective. The plurality of anti-Chalcedonian literature in Egypt stems from Greek originals or still survives in that language. The writings of Theodosios I (535-67 CE), the thirty-third Patriarch of Alexandria, may be singled out as a passing example. After the death of Severos of Antioch (538 CE), Theodosios became the theological voice of the anti-Chalcedonian population. Similar to Severos, he too composed his theological treatises in Greek, and similar to many of his predecessors, such as Cyril I and Dioskoros I, he did not demonstrate any competence in the Coptic language.[24] In this light, Patriarch Athanasios' bilingualism appears as an exception rather than the rule among Alexandrian hierarchs. Under Byzantine rule and into the ninth century, anti-Chalcedonian theology continued to be articulated in Greek, and was subsequently expressed in Arabic. Unlike Syriac, Coptic never developed into a medium in which strictly theological treatises were composed or translated.[25]

Another strategy to gauge the perception and usage of the Greek language among anti-Chalcedonians is to survey the educational background and literary output of Coptic patriarchs. Patriarch Damianos (569-605 CE) was an Alexandrian whose lost writings are known only by their Greek titles.[26] Patriarchs Anastasios (605-16 CE) and Andronikos (616-22 CE) similarly had strong ties to Alexandria and were fluent in Greek.[27] In the post-conquest period, Patriarch Isaac's (686-9 CE) education allowed him to secure an appointment as a government secretary, an occupation that demanded a high degree of Greek literacy at that date, and to devote himself to "the discourses of the teachers of the church," which, in a seventh-century context, likewise indicates Greek literacy.[28] Later, he composed festal letters for Patriarch John of Samannūd (677-86 CE);[29] these annual open letters were drafted in Greek until the ninth century (see below). As demonstrated in Chapter Three, a Hellenic education remained the norm among elite families through the seventh and into the early eight century.

Another aspect of the dominant historiography links creed and language with "ethnicity." The nondenominational nature of the Greek language, however, may still be observed a full century after the Arab conquest. For the duration of Umayyad rule, the Coptic church continued to employ the Greek language in official capacities. Two eighth-century public texts are definitive in this respect. One is the Greek Festal (or Paschal) Letter of Patriarch Alexander II (705-30 CE);[30] another is the Greek dedication of the Muʿallaqa Church, which has been definitively dated to 735 CE.[31] While the Festal Letter surely prompted Coptic translations, it is noteworthy that a century after the Arab conquest, Coptic bishops—the recipients of the missive—were themselves fluent in Greek or at least assisted by those who were. Moreover, the use of Greek as the sole language for the dedication of the prominent Church of al-Muʿallaqa underscores that language's official status and its favorable perception. It is evident that until the eighth century, the Coptic church employed the Greek language in official correspondences and public inscriptions and did not view it as the distinctive marker of a specific community or creed, much less as indicative of "heresy."

The Coptic church and hierarchy continued to utilize the Greek language well into the ʿAbbāsid period. When Patriarch Mark II (799-819 CE) sent his Synodal Letter to Syria, he entrusted it to a Coptic delegation headed by two bishops, Mark of Tinnīs and Mark of al-Faramā, along with his deacon, George, all of whom were fluent in the Greek language.[32] This is a significant event underscoring the survival of Greek among the Copts as a written and spoken language. Additionally, the incident demonstrates that throughout the first centuries under Islamic rule the anti-Chalcedonian patriarchates exchanged synodal letters (and presumably other official correspondences) in Greek: not in Coptic, Syriac, or Arabic.

The biography of Patriarch Yusāb I (Joseph, 830-49 CE) provides additional documentation.[33] As a youth, Yusāb—along with his peers, the so-called "Children of the Cell"—received a thorough education under the direction of a deacon described as "a learned man" in order to learn how to *write* in the Greek language.[34] Thus, by the ninth century, the hierarchy continued to actively cultivate Greek literacy among individuals groomed for the higher offices of the church.[35] Equally significant, fluency in the Greek language remained the distinguishing mark of a "learned man" in ninth-century anti-Chalcedonian Egypt, much as it had been throughout the preceding millennium. Clearly, the Coptic church did not discard or shun the Greek language after the Arab conquest, let alone after Chalcedon; rather, fluency in that tongue and the ability to teach it remained in demand well into the Islamic period. It would be a mistake to view the Melkite community as the sole guardians of the Greek language in Egypt.

Patriarch Yusāb was likely fluent in Arabic as well. This may be deduced from a heated exchange in which he freely conversed with a Muslim *qāḍī* without the aid of an interpreter.[36] It is here, in the mid-ninth century, that the three languages converge. The patriarch's mother tongue was likely Coptic,[37] yet fluency in Arabic, the official language of the administration and increasingly the dominant language in urban centers and among affluent Copts, was vital. Meanwhile, Greek remained essential to accessing theological and liturgical texts and communicating with the other anti-Chalcedonian sees, most notably Syria.[38] Patriarch Yusāb provides a significant historical marker. He was a true product of his time: a hybrid emerging from the intermingling of three languages and cultures. His successors, however, even those with comparable credentials, reflected a decidedly Arabic milieu and literary environment. The sources surveyed thus far argue for a favorable perception of the Greek language among secular and ecclesiastical elites who continued to perceive it as a token of status. The remainder of this section advocates for a similar perception among the Coptic faithful through the tenth century CE.

Assessing popular sentiments is infinitely more complicated than gauging official attitudes, but to that end liturgical manuscripts provide a hitherto underutilized resource.[39] A number of late all-Greek versions of the Coptic rite have been preserved, though they are few in number and their *Sitz im Leben* remains unexplored.[40] Some Greek elements have been retained in the Coptic Eucharistic liturgy, such as diaconal responses, a few congregational responses, and prayers such as *E Agape*. Several popular explanations rationalize this phenomenon, though none are especially convincing.[41] At any rate, these frozen lections should not be read as reliable indicators of attitudes toward the Greek language; at best, they prove tolerance (and, perhaps, antiquarianism). A more fruitful line of investigation explores the Greek liturgies and hymns that were employed by "medieval" Copts,[42] but care must be taken. While the modern Coptic Orthodox rite retains a number of popular Greek hymns (e.g. *E Parthenos*, *Christos Anesti*, and *Tenēn*), most were borrowed directly from the Greek Orthodox in the late eighteenth century and, later, as part of Patriarch Kyrillus IV's (1854-61 CE) reform movement.[43] Of greater relevance are the Greek liturgical texts preserved in eighth- through eleventh-century Sahidic manuscripts, which have fallen completely out of use.[44]

The amount, diversity, and late dates (most date to the tenth or eleventh centuries) of these hymns are of great significance. While a number of these Greek manuscripts contain Coptic translations, remarkably, many are only prefaced by Coptic rubrics, indicating that they were chanted in Greek.[45] Some Greek hymns were translated directly into Arabic, never passing through a Coptic phase.[46] Of these hymns, some, such as the anti-Chalcedonian version of the *Trisagion*, are not surprising to find,[47] though it is significant that the Copts continue to pray it in Greek until this very day. A tenth-century Greek hymn celebrating Patriarch Dioskoros I, the champion of Coptic Orthodoxy, provides an additional, more intriguing example.[48] Until the eleventh century CE, when Coptic liturgies and hymns were officially translated into Arabic, the faithful chanted their most distinctive prayers in the Greek language without any reservation.

A number of ninth- to eleventh-century liturgical manuscripts at the British Museum and the John Ryland's Library lead to an even more startling conclusion.[49] There, not only hymns but the liturgical prayers themselves are entirely in Greek while the rubrics are in Coptic. The late dates and Upper-Egyptian origins of these manuscripts preclude their use by the Melkite community, and the insertion of Coptic rubrics stresses that these manuscripts were indeed used (they were not idle manuscripts) and that the Christians who read them were primarily fluent in Coptic rather than Greek. This suggests that to one degree or another, Greek survived as a liturgical language among the Copts well into the Arabic period.[50]

Even the Gradual Psalm (the προκείμενον, which precedes the reading of the Gospel) in these manuscripts is often written in Greek and not necessarily followed by a Coptic translation.[51]

Demise of the Greek language in the Coptic liturgical rite was not a consequence of the schism at Chalcedon or the Arab conquest, but rather the tenth- through eleventh-century switch from the Sahidic dialect to the Bohairic dialect and Arabic. The earlier observation regarding the proliferation of Greek loanwords in Sahidic manuscripts holds true for Bohairic literature as well. Regardless of the genre, Bohairic literature retains a high frequency of Greek loanwords, hymns, and congregational responses.[52] Perhaps more than any other urban populace, the Alexandrians defiantly retained the liturgical use of the Greek language. By the mid-1300s CE, Ibn Sabbāʿ noted that immediately prior to patriarchal ordinations the Alexandrian clergy would secure a handwritten promise from the patriarch-elect: "not to change their Greek language (*lughatahum al-rūmiyya*), which they have retained since Mark the Evangelist".[53]

The above discussion demonstrates that the Copts did not view the Greek language as "heretical". Yet the language was certainly in decline due to several factors, the most fundamental of which is that the average Egyptian, typically a farmer, did not converse in the language, and after the early eighth century even elites began to gravitate toward learning Arabic, the new language of power and social mobility.[54] Additionally, a wave of conservatism swept through anti-Chalcedonian ranks.[55] This movement, however, focused on the content of literature rather than its language of composition. Many had come to believe that the scriptural and doctrinal commentaries of the Fathers sufficed, and warranted no further addition. In other words, what was of benefit—in Greek and Coptic translation or original composition—already existed,[56] which may, in part, explain why much of what was composed at that juncture circulated under the names of patristic figures. Rufus of Shotep and John of Shmūn challenged this outlook in the late sixth and early seventh centuries CE,[57] not so much by their choice of language as by the decision to compose new writings to be circulated under their own names.

Rufus memorized the Christian scriptures in Greek;[58] his choice to deliver the sermons, which comprised his biblical commentaries, in Coptic reflected his audience's comprehension of the language, not his distaste or distrust of Greek.[59] So much emphasis on nationalism has shrouded a very significant development in the history of post-Chalcedonian Coptic literature: for the first time biblical commentaries were composed in Coptic rather than translated from Greek.[60] Coptic clergy began to venture into a new genre that had been previously the domain of their Greek-writing counterparts; not even the towering Coptic literary and monastic figure Shenoute of Atripe (348-466 CE) had ventured in that direction. The tradition of drafting biblical commentaries in Coptic persisted until the twelfth century when Murqus ibn al-Qunbar translated his own writings from Coptic into Arabic.[61] Finally, a brief observation regarding the alleged emphasis on Egyptian subjects in sixth- and seventh-century literature. In general, that assertion relies heavily on the works of John of Shmūn. Nonetheless, John's writings must be considered alongside those of his Egyptian peers, such as Constantine of Asyūṭ, whose much larger literary corpus does not focus on Egyptian figures.[62]

During the post-conquest era, it is not surprising that Greek—the language of pro- and anti-Chalcedonian elites—gave way to Coptic and Arabic among the Christian populace. Since the Arabization of the bureaucracy in the early eighth century, the social and cultural status of that language had been in decline. Those who understood Greek were a shrinking minority, and those who could compose in it were fewer still. Reciprocally, Arabic emerged as the sole language of social mobility and, increasingly, of education and culture.

In sum, the nationalistic sentiments that have branded Greek as the "heretical" tongue of the Byzantine Melkites did not exist as such throughout the centuries surveyed. That perspective is but a cultural relic from a later period in which the Greek language was in decline among religious elites and marginalized in liturgical texts after centuries of widespread usage under Arab rule (see also Chapter Twelve). The hegemonic hold this anti-Greek perspective gained must also be interpreted in light of the ninth-century genesis of a decidedly anti-Byzantine Coptic historiography, addressed in Chapters Two and Nine. The recasting of Byzantine rule in Egypt as a period of persistent persecution and intolerance buttressed the new perception of Greek as a questionable tongue, but more importantly, of Coptic—increasingly Bohairic, not Sahidic—as the "language of our fathers," the ardent perspective voiced in *pseudo-Samuel*.

Until the tenth century, anti-Chalcedonians in Egypt perceived Greek as a vehicle for orthodoxy as well as heresy—two inherently theological categories. Under early Islamic rule, Greek dominated as the language of prestige and culture among socio-political elites, but it enjoyed a much longer tenure among ecclesiastics, who utilized it well into the ninth century in official capacities, such as issuing synodal letters, festal epistles, and commemorative inscriptions. The language also enjoyed a certain popular currency among the laity who prayed long liturgical passages, if not whole liturgies, in it. Significantly, at certain locations in Upper Egypt and Alexandria, Greek survived as the liturgical language of the anti-Chalcedonian Copts through Fāṭimid rule.

Bilingualism

In the early post-conquest decades, many individuals (including converts) gained employment as bilingual (Coptic/Arabic), and even trilingual translators.[63] Still, the transition from Coptic and Greek to Arabic, once initiated in a region, must have been quite rapid. Despite some partisan claims to the contrary, it is highly doubtful that Coptic/Arabic bilingualism prevailed in any region for an extended period of time.[64] As languages coexist, they cross-pollinate each other, and as the period of comingling is prolonged, the number and variety of loanwords increases. Coptic offers an excellent example of this phenomenon.[65] It contains a high percentage of loanwords that span the grammatical spectrum of the Greek language, from nouns to verbs and particles.[66] While the influence of Coptic on the Greek dialect used in Egypt was not as immense, it was still discernible, and it may have contributed to the "peculiar" Greek dialect of the Alexandrians.[67] This, however, resulted from centuries of coexistence.

In contrast, Coptic and colloquial Egyptian Arabic do not share many loanwords,[68] and the few terms that migrated are predominantly nouns; typically, nouns are the first category of words to cross over from one language community to another.[69] In all, these loanwords are common to all Egyptians. Arabophone Copts did not use any words that their Muslim neighbors would not have understood; nothing approaching Yiddish or Creole has ever existed in Egypt.[70] The lack of loanwords suggests the speed at which the linguistic transition unfolded. Fundamentally, the process of Arabization occurred in various locations at different junctures; once inaugurated, however, the transition was swift.

Early official contacts between Arab rulers and Christian subjects proceeded in Greek or through the aid of translators.[71] For commoners, a cooperative Coptic-speaker (convert, employee, or friend) often facilitated communication. While Arab Muslims on the whole did not demonstrate an interest in learning Coptic, documentary papyri provide some examples of Arab Muslim individuals who may have communicated with each other in that language (they do not appear to have been converts).[72] Conversely, an account in the HP implies that some Coptic clerics were conversant in Arabic at the dawning of the eighth century.[73] The biography of Alexander II provides a noteworthy gloss, recounting that al-Aṣbagh (d. 86/705) had befriended a deacon named Benjamin, who instructed him in the scriptures and the sacraments (*asrār*) of the Copts in Arabic.[74] Decades later, in a controversy over the ownership of an ecclesiastical complex, the Coptic hierarchy submitted its appeal to the Arab governor and judges in Coptic and Arabic, a translation that was most likely drafted by members of the clergy.[75] In another contentious episode, Patriarch Yusāb (830-49) spoke to Zacharias, Bishop of Buḥayra, in Coptic, while before a *qāḍī*. Some of the Muslim lawyers (*fuqahā'*) present understood the comment and translated it to the *qāḍī*. It is unclear if these lawyers were converts or Muslims who had learned Coptic.[76]

From Coptic and Greek to Arabic

Arabization is a multipronged socio-linguistic process indicative of a key cultural shift.[77] Although interpreted in a very different vein, this aspect figures prominently in the *Apocalypse of Samuel*, which consistently associates culture, religion, and language. The relation is tangible, though nonlinear. In Egypt (as opposed to Persia or Anatolia), religious conversion directly led to Arabization. Hence, it may be taken for granted that converts to Islam abandoned the use of the Coptic language within a generation. Most Coptic-speaking Muslims encountered in documentary texts were first-generation converts.[78] While the relationship between conversion and Arabization is direct, the reverse relationship was indirect. Fluency in the Arabic language eliminated the linguistic divide that separated Egyptians and Arabs and promoted interaction among the various religious communities. Thus, Arabization may be considered as an indirect catalyst for Tradition Transition; the *Apocalypse of Samuel*, albeit in hyperbolic prose, renders this relationship as explicit and direct. Still, Arabization in and of itself does not lead to conversion. The Christian population of Egypt has now survived longer using Arabic as a mother tongue than it has using either Greek or Coptic.

Before parsing the processes that led to the rise of Arabic as the dominant language in Egypt, it is perhaps best to begin by identifying those who conversed in it. Undoubtedly, the Arabs who immigrated to Egypt were fluent in the language. Converts (*mawālī*), who inevitably abandoned the use of Coptic, should be adjoined to this segment of the population. Islam was the religion of the Arabic Qur'ān, and to this day there is no trace of a Coptic translation of the Qur'ān, as there is in Syriac, Persian, and Berber.[79] Egyptian converts were religiously and socially motivated to learn Arabic rather than to continue using their mother tongue. Such individuals and families did not wish to present themselves as ex-Christians, but sought acceptance by their peers on an equal footing, as full members of the same religious community; linguistic conformity was a crucial means toward that end.[80] Of course, this did not mean that individual converts immediately discarded the Coptic language. Indeed, such individuals were often employed precisely because of their fluency in the language.[81] Nonetheless, the linguistic ramifications of conversion, if not evident with the first generation, were manifest in the second, doubtless giving rise to a dynamic similar to that found among modern immigrant communities where children tend to be far more fluent in the new language than their parents.[82] By the time a second generation—the children of converts—married and procreated, quite possibly with a spouse who only spoke Arabic, proficiency in the Coptic language would have been minimal at best.

It is reasonable to suppose that a Coptic-speaking family could become fluent, if not solely dependent, on Arabic within three generations, or roughly fifty years. Such a dynamic may be observed in a papyrus dated 220/835, which preserves a letter from Nuʿmān ibn Yazīd, ʿAlī, ʿAbdallāh, and al-ʿAbbās, the sons of Isḥāq ibn Damāna, to Thīdra (Theodoros), their employee.[83] "Isḥāq" was common to Christians and Muslims, but Damāna (Damianos/Damian) is clearly Christian; thus, the men were the descendants of a convert. Damāna, the grandfather, may have been the original convert, or perhaps it was their father Isḥāq. In either case, the three children had Arabic-Islamic names and were fluent in the Arabic language, as was the Christian guard, Thīdra, to whom the letter was addressed.

For such individuals, three factors facilitated the linguistic shift. The first was the lack of a pressing need to use Coptic in order to live as a Muslim in Egypt. Nuptial unions posed a second factor. Intermarriage between a convert and a life-long Muslim strongly predisposed the children of that union to learn Arabic. Finally, moving to an urban center or within proximity to a Muslim community, as was common for converts throughout the early Islamic period and beyond, would accelerate the process of language acquisition. Adults became more fluent in Arabic as they conducted business and formed new social networks, and children quickly acquired the language through peer interactions and, later, religious schools—the *kuttāb*.[84] Thus, it can be postulated that acts of religious conversion were succeeded by a proportionate (arguably exponential), though staggered, increase in the use of the Arabic language. Religious conversion resulted in irreversible linguistic and cultural shifts.

In addition to Muslims, immigrants, and converts, the 705 Arabizing edict led Christian elites to adopt the language and to teach it to their children as preparation for securing administrative appointments and the possibility of social mobility. Prevalence of this practice among Christians invoked the ire of the author of the *Apocalypse of Samuel*, who lamented: "Woe (*al-wayl*) to every Christian who teaches his son the language of *hijra* from his childhood and makes him forget the language of his ancestors".[85]

The analysis above yields two conclusions that may serve as givens for the remainder of this chapter: converts to Islam severed their connection with the Coptic language within three generations (if not less), and Christian elites along with their children acquired proficiency in the Arabic language during the first half of the eighth century. In all these cases, however, Arabization was limited to old socio-political elites and new Muslims living in urban centers and the Delta. The focus now turns to answering when, where, and (with more difficulty) why average Christians, those who did not need to learn Arabic, adopted the language.

The Delta

The linguistic shift in Lower Egypt can be gauged only through literary texts. Most Arab Muslim historians do not shed any light on this issue, and later Christian authors only lament the decaying state of the Coptic language, but fail to document the actual process. Moreover, the dearth of post-conquest papyrus documents from the Delta during the early Islamic centuries further limits the pool of possible sources;[86] thus, historians are left primarily with Christian literary and liturgical texts, studies of which are extremely lacking.

In his seminal study on the translation of Coptic ecclesiastical literature into Arabic, Samuel Rubenson distinguished three phases.[87] The first, starting roughly in the mid-tenth century CE, focused on translating liturgical and biblical manuscripts, especially lectionaries. Translations of some apocryphal, apocalyptic, and hagiographic texts were also completed, as were a few collections of ecclesiastical canons, such as *Jumlat al-qawānīn* by Abū Ṣulḥ Yūnus ibn ʿAbdallāh and the Copto-Arabic *Didaskalia Apostolorum.*[88] Patriarch Khrisṭūdulūs (Christodoulos, 1047-77 CE), himself highly proficient in Arabic, inaugurated the second stage of transition by sanctioning the first official Arabic translations of Coptic liturgies. Khrisṭūdulūs' *Canons* were likely the first Patriarchal documents officially issued in Arabic.[89] During this phase some dogmatic anthologies, such as *I'tirāf al-abā'* (*Faith of the Fathers*) were translated.[90] The HP (biographies 1-65) was also redacted and translated for the first time into Arabic by Mawhūb ibn Manṣūr ibn Mufarrij and his assistant Ḥabīb Mikhā'īl ibn Budayr al-Damanhūrī. Mawhūb's contribution to this composite work, the biographies of Khrisṭūdulūs and Kyrillus II (Cyril, d. 1092 CE), were the first biographies originally composed in Arabic.[91] In the third stage, Patriarch Gabriel Ibn Turayk (d. 1145 CE) limited the number of Eucharistic liturgies prayed by the Copts to the three that have survived until today, as translators continued to refine older Arabic translations as well as translate a host of hagiographic and homiletic literature that had hitherto remained in Coptic. Significantly, this is the period in which the normative Coptic Arabic recensions of the *Synaksār* (συναξάριον) and *Difnār* (ἀντιφωνάριον) emerged.[92] Although the *Difnār* drew upon older all-Coptic antecedent,[93] it would become a largely bilingual prayer book, no doubt reflecting the psychological outlook of Arabophone monastics who perceived themselves as the guardians of the Coptic language.[94] As for the *Synaksār*, its compilation was, among other things, an antiquarian enterprise: a process concerned with the translation, codification, and preservation of earlier traditions, at times to the detriment of historical accuracy.[95]

It is with this final stage—the best documented of the three—that the striking decline of the Coptic language, even among clerics, may be observed. In the second quarter of the thirteenth century,[96] Anba Yūḥannā al-Samannūdī used Arabic as the language of instruction in his *sullam* (*Ladder*, a wordlist) and *muqaddima* (*Introduction*, a Coptic grammar); Yuḥanna's contemporary, al-Asʿad ibn al-ʿAssāl, drafted analogous manuals. In all, Coptic Arabic scholars compiled language tools for the Sahidic and Bohairic dialects, as well as the Greek language.[97] This was a telling development: Coptic could only be taught to the Christians in Arabic and *through books* rather than social interactions or any sort of language immersion. Rubenson sums up the three stages thus: "If we may characterize the first period of translation as more popular and provisional, the second as one geared by necessity, then the third is a period of more scholarly work on sources".[98]

These three stages are in tune with the available manuscripts. How they reflect the process of Arabization, however, requires further comment. Understanding the initial phase of this scheme is crucial but, unfortunately, it is poorly documented and studied. Its significance is twofold. First, as essentially a grassroots movement born out of necessity, the first stage is a far better indicator of social transition than the latter stages, which were more concerned with uniformity and accuracy. Second, the translations of the first stage, liturgies and lectionaries, were predominantly public in nature: codices that were in use weekly, even daily. Conversely, while the translation and revision of such texts persisted during the latter stages, they also included compilations that were marginal to the religious life of an individual or parish. For example, the average person had no need of a manual of canon law. Even the institutional church, as long as it could still rely on those fluent in Coptic, had no pressing need to translate such works; still, the fact that at least two such anthologies were translated in the first stage is quite striking.[99]

Liturgical translations characteristic of the first stage were for the most part *ad hoc*, indicating that either the Coptic church's hierarchy was unaware of the need or, more likely, too conservative and slow to react. Patriarch Khrisṭūdulūs' "official" translation of the liturgy, while an important development, does not reveal much about the process of Arabization except that the hierarchy began to come to terms with it, perhaps giving in to popular demand. While Rubenson's three-stage description is essentially sound, it is clear that the first period is most telling about the process of Arabization, and that it is that stage—not the second—that should be described as "geared by necessity". The first and second stages can be delineated by a shift in the perspective of the ecclesiastical hierarchy, particularly with regard to the liturgical use of Arabic, which progressed from a popular movement to an officially sanctioned one. Furthermore, the latter two phases built upon the first by revising older translations, but more significantly by expanding the subject matter of the literature translated. Only after the most immediate need was met—that for liturgical and biblical translations—was attention, time, and effort spent in translating other Christian genres.

Liturgical manuscripts also provide a wealth of data, though the linguistic shift they signify assuredly postdated actual cultural change. Such texts are conservative by nature, and those of the tenth and eleventh centuries were embedded within a socio-religious matrix in which language became emblematic of community. Above, I argued that the Copts did not perceive the Greek language as indicative of heretical tendencies or of a particular community until the tenth century. At that same juncture, Arabic was rebranded as the distinctive marker of the Islamic religion and community. In hindsight, this seems obvious in Egypt, but initially, the association was not automatic. Prior to the tenth century, Christians who learned Arabic were not accused *prima facie* of becoming Muslims, or of abandoning their religious and cultural heritage—as is clear in several Coptic Arabic apocalypses. Earlier, the Copt's perception of the language appears to have been more neutral, similar to that of the Melkites in Egypt and abroad. I explore these ideological aspects of language use and perception at greater depth in Chapter Twelve. Here, it suffices that this identification of Arabic as the distinctive marker of Islam is clearly expressed in *pseudo-Samuel* and was retained in several other Coptic Arabic apocalypses. Such an amalgamation of language, community, and religion likely hindered the use of Arabic in church services and reinforced the liturgical use of Coptic.

Despite the scarcity of early Christian-Arabic sources from Egypt, the mid-tenth century emerges as a watershed. The necessity of using Arabic by the Coptic faithful could no longer be ignored, and despite its cultural—largely polemical—association with Islam, Arabic had to be used. Coptic was certainly in decline in Lower Egypt by that date. A missing piece of the puzzle is the rubrics of tenth-century liturgical manuscripts from the Delta. Unfortunately, the earliest extant Bohairic liturgical manuscripts are no older than the eleventh century, and those are few.[100] This scarcity is due, at least in part, to the burning of Christian manuscripts in the early eleventh century CE, during the height of al-Ḥākim's persecution.[101] As with papyri, the survival of liturgical manuscripts, which by their very nature are in constant use (and deterioration), is often a product of the accident of preservation.

The most telling of the available narratives from the Delta is the *Apocalypse of Samuel*. Dating this "prophecy" has eluded historians for generations.[102] Estimates have ranged anywhere from the first half of the eighth century—which is certainly inaccurate—to the eleventh century.[103] The late-tenth century CE, however, is conservatively the best estimate for its *Sitz im Leben* (even if this elusive tract was drafted later, the social context it describes can be accounted for by that juncture). Two factors establish this date. First, the *Apocalypse of Samuel* denounces the use of Arabic by clergy during the liturgy, a phenomenon that cannot be definitively dated until the first half of the tenth century (though an earlier date is possible). A second clue is the criticism leveled at Christians for giving Arabized names to their children; notably, the two distinguished tenth-century Christian literary figures, Saʿīd ibn Baṭrīq (ordained Eutychios) and Abū al-Bishr (ordained Sawīrus ibn al-Muqaffaʿ), had Arabized names. That trend is also well documented in tenth-century papyri from Upper Egypt (discussed in the last section below). In general, I find an early eleventh-century date problematic in that if the text had been composed during the turbulent reign of al-Ḥākim bi-Amr Allāh (387-411/997-1021), the most oppressive and violent period for Christians and Jews under early Islamic rule, one would expect the role of persecution to be more prominent; in fact, it is altogether lacking. Finally, it would appear that whoever penned the eleventh-century *Kitāb al-īḍāḥ* was familiar with that apocalypse; certainly both texts share analogous concerns.[104]

A sense of rapid social change may be discerned throughout that tract, much of which was unsettling to its author. Two trends are relevant to this discussion. The first is the abandonment of the Coptic language in favor of Arabic in the Coptic church and community,[105] which the apocalypse repeatedly describes in religious terms as a "sin".[106] Moreover, the writer condemns his contemporaries for ostentatiously teaching the Arabic language to their children and giving them Arabic names.[107] Use of Arabic among non-elite Christians prevailed to the extent that those who continued to speak Coptic were purportedly mocked by their Arabized Christian neighbors.[108] Behind this linguistic bias is the perception of the Coptic language as the cultural conduit and authenticating seal of Egyptian Christianity. As a corollary, *pseudo-Samuel* directly links the Arabic language and culture—albeit described in a pejorative manner—with Islam. This is most evident in the assertion that Christians used Arabic proudly: "to the extent that they do not know at all that they are Christians, but believe that they are *barbar*".[109]

The apocalypse further notes that sermons were no longer delivered since the people had "forgotten their language";[110] again, the Coptic language is positioned as the exclusive idiom of Christianity. Herein, however, lies an apparent contradiction: Coptic sermons are no longer intelligible, yet the clergy are simultaneously criticized for praying in Arabic. Perhaps the apocalypse did contradict itself, or one set of comments were a later interpolation. Another possibility is that language usage varied from one parish or region to another. Conservative parishes that exclusively used Coptic in the liturgy found it, nonetheless, futile (and increasingly impossible) to deliver sermons in that language. Finally, a third possibility is that "delivering" a sermon actually meant reading a patristic or popular homily of some sort.

The tenth century was a crucial time for the pervasive adoption of Arabic in the Delta. Already alluded to is the fact that the first prominent Arabic-Christian writers made their debut at that time: the Melkite patriarch Saʿīd ibn Baṭrīq (d. 328/940) and the Coptic bishop Sawīrus ibn al-Muqaffaʿ (d. ca. 390/1000). Both clerics were highly educated and noted writers in the Arabic language. Unlike the first generation of Arabic-Christian authors in Syria, however, neither composed works in any language other than Arabic, nor were any of their works translated into Greek or Coptic.[111] This was possibly due to their subject matter and audience,[112] but more likely this pattern reflects their social milieu. By the mid-tenth century CE, an irreversible moment had been reached. With very few exceptions,[113] none of the literary works composed by Egyptian Christians in Arabic were ever translated into other languages.

Two eleventh-century Christian Arabic texts, *Kitāb al-īḍāḥ* and the preface to the HP (both erroneously attributed to Sawīrus ibn al-Muqaffaʿ), provide additional evidence for the rapid decline of the Coptic language in the Delta.[114] These works positively link the Coptic language with Christianity proper, as in the *Apocalypse of Samuel*. *Kitāb al-īḍāḥ* alludes to the decline of Coptic in its introductory pages: "The reason behind the concealment of this mystery [of the Unity and Trinity of God] at this time from the believers is their intermixing with foreigners, and the loss of their original Coptic language through which they were instructed in their doctrine".[115] And again, later in the same work: "Recall, my beloved, that a multiplicity of views has spread among the Copts at this time. Each abides by a different belief and makes an infidel out of the other, and you are astonished and bewildered by this. Do not marvel. The reason for this is their ignorance of their language. For the Arabic language has overcome them. None of them know what is being read to them in church in Coptic. They hear but do not comprehend; because of this they have lost the knowledge of Christian doctrine".[116] Similarly, the Third Preface to the HP glosses Arabic as the language: "that is known by the people of this time throughout the districts of Egypt. For most do not understand Coptic or Greek".[117] The poignant comments of the fourteenth-century Bishop Athanasios of Qūṣ in his *Qilādat al-taḥrīr fī ʿilm al-tafsīr* are largely an echo of these earlier texts.[118]

The use and perception of the three languages of the Delta underwent several historical and, later, ideological shifts. Despite later perceptions, under Byzantine and early Islamic rule, Greek dominated as the language of erudition and orthodoxy for pro- and anti-Chalcedonians. It was not until later generations that the ideologically inspired antimonies—Greek/heretic versus Coptic/

orthodox—seemed logical. In time, as both languages were subverted by a dominant Arabic culture, a new binary relationship emerged; increasingly, Arabic became synonymous with Islam and Coptic with Christianity. The association coalesced at a time when Arabic and Islam dominated the public sphere and Coptic/Christian identity needed a firm anchor in the midst of a society in flux. Significantly, the dynamic that led to the nostalgic designation of the Coptic language as the authenticating emblem of identity, was largely a product of the period in which that language was in steep decline.

Finally, a few comments are warranted as to the significance of the eleven Coptic documents from the village of Teshlot in Middle Egypt, which have had a disproportionate effect on the study of Arabization. Eight individuals wrote these texts over the span of thirty-five years in the mid-eleventh century CE, from 420-55/1029-63.[119] The late date of the documents is interesting, but not altogether surprising. A fundamental premise of this chapter is that Arabization proceeded in various regions at different times.

Two observations help situate the Teshlot dossier. First, the contracts were by and large written and witnessed by Coptic deacons. The sixth contract is particularly illustrative. Four witnesses are identified as second generation deacons (lines 14, 17, 23, and 27), and two others (including Rafael, the owner of the document) were the sons of deacons. Long before the eleventh century, deacons took a prominent role in administrative and literary tasks, from drafting contracts and leases to copying literary manuscripts.[120] It is not surprising that such households retained a high degree of Coptic literacy. A second observation is that the last document is likely the key to placing the whole archive in context.

Contrary to the initial analysis, this Arabic letter is not directly related to the Coptic contracts.[121] Sūsinah (Soucine) received the Arabic letter from Buqṭur (Victor) and later wrote a separate Coptic letter to Rafael on the back of that document. Clearly Sūsinah was bilingual, but other Christians (specifically, Buqṭur) were more comfortable writing in Arabic than in Coptic. In this light, mid-eleventh century Teshlot may be understood as simply another Coptic village going through the process of Arabization, albeit later than many others. There is no reason to interpret its peculiarity as normative, especially since papyrological documents from roughly the same period demonstrate a much greater degree of Arabization and Islamization.[122]

Upper Egypt

A few brief observations on the unfolding of the process of Arabization in Upper Egypt draw this discussion to an end; a thorough analysis of the topic in the Ṣaʿīd remains elusive, though the accumulating body of scholarship will soon enable such a study. As discussed in Chapter One, the majority of narrative sources are grounded in the urban centers of the Delta. Thus, documentary papyri have a direct bearing on the historiography of Upper Egypt, and (arguably) exert an indirect influence on that of the Delta. It is inferred that the social processes evident in Upper Egypt likely occurred at an earlier date in the Delta, since it retained a much greater Arab-Muslim presence throughout the first centuries of Islamic rule. Thus, societal shifts evident in Upper Egyptian papyri likely set a date *terminus ante quem* for change in the Delta.

Al-Ashmūnayn yields extensive though somewhat elusive documentation. Some Arabic texts mention an interpreter or that the document was read in "the language of the Copts";[123] the majority, however, do not. Similarly, a few papyri stipulate that the contract "*fussir*,"[124] which may indicate that it was "explained" or "translated" to the parties involved: the Arabic verb carries both connotations.[125] More indicative of Arabic fluency, several ninth-century Arabic contracts involving Christians contain a standard clause stating that it was read to the relevant parties "word by word" and that they understood its ramifications, which indicates the Christian party's comprehension and likely verbal fluency in the Arabic language.[126] The clause is found in diverse documents regardless of the party's religious background.[127] What strengthens the case for widespread Arabization by the late-ninth and tenth centuries is increased documentation for Arabic-speaking Christians who do not appear to have worked for the government. In 241/855-6, writing in Arabic, Ṭanūs ibn Yuḥannis witnessed a contract (itself a rare act for a Christian),[128] and in several other 3-4/9-10th century documents, Christians personally witnessed or drafted contracts in Arabic.[129]

Eighth-century papyri from Akhmīm denote a population that remained predominantly Coptic-speaking. The pagarch/*amīr* Rashīd was clearly a Muslim, but he may have been competent in Coptic.[130] Nonetheless, interactions between Copts and Arabs required the assistance of translators.[131] Official letters and contracts are found in all three languages. *P.Ryl.Copt*.221 is a legal document in Sahidic and Greek, while the verso of *P.Ryl.Copt*.401 contains an Arabic list of Coptic taxpayers.[132] In general, Coptic dominated, as reflected in *P. Cair.Arab*.III.167, a lengthy tri-lingual declaration (ὁμολογία) addressed to Yazīd ibn ʿAbdallāh, the pagarch of Akhmīm, which contains 80 lines in Coptic, eleven in Greek, and only nine in Arabic (cf. *P.Clackson*.45). The individuals who signed were predominantly Christians, a number of them clergy or monks of some rank. Slightly later papyri, dated to the 2-3/8-9th centuries, provide evidence for conversion. Examples may be derived from personal correspondences such as *P.Ryl.Copt*.324, a Sahidic letter from Muḥammad to Victor, or *P.Ryl.Copt*.346, a letter from Iszem (Hishām) son of Bīlal to Severos son of Bane.

Arabic gains prominence in third/ninth- and fourth/tenth-century papyri, however. *P.Ryl.Copt*.236, though a Sahidic text, contains a high number of Arabic names and loanwords. Another papyri, *P.Ryl. Copt*.309, preserves an Arabic *jizya* receipt issued to ʿAbd al-Misīḥ (Χριστόδουλος) the brother of Abū Yumīn, by the scribe Bishay ibn Shinūda in 388/998. By the end of the tenth century, a linguistic shift had clearly taken place; the Christians of Akhmīm wrote in Arabic and had Arabized names.

The final aspect discussed here is the Arabization of Christian Greco-Coptic names. The origins of the phenomenon are extremely difficult to discern. Scores of popular names, such as "Saʿīd" and "ʿAbdallāh,"[133] as well as those of the Hebrew prophets, were used by Christians and Muslims alike. Such names are often vague indicators of religious affiliation. In the papyrological record, "Yūsuf"—lacking additional details—may have been an Arab Muslim, a convert to

Islam, a Christian with an Arabized name, or possibly Jewish. The issue is further complicated by the fact that proper names often reflect shades of Arabization. The vocalized difference between the Greco-Coptic "Markos" and the Arabic "Murqus" is very slight in comparison to the radical shift from "Christodoulos" to "ʿAbd al-Masīḥ." In general, widespread Arabization of names in Upper Egypt commenced in the mid-ninth century, and while the phenomenon was by no means universal,[134] such names were prevalent throughout the region by the end of the tenth century CE.[135]

CHAPTER 6

THE LONG EIGHTH CENTURY: A CULTURAL BRIDGE

In the decades following the Arab conquest, cultural continuity eclipsed radical political change. It was not until roughly the first quarter of the eighth century that the Marwānids initiated the first reforms with enduring ramifications. The significance of that era was not lost on the Christians of the region. Identifying the Byzantine Empire with the fourth kingdom in the Book of Daniel, many had interpreted the initial Arab conquests as an apocalyptic omen heralding the end of the world, but by the dawning of the eighth century the caliphate was grafted onto that very apocalyptic scheme. At that point, the Kingdom of the Arabs became synonymous with the fourth kingdom of Daniel.[1]

Some early eighth-century reforms yielded immediate tangible results, while others took well over a century for the full range of their ramifications to mature. A second watershed came at the mid-century mark with the rise of the ʿAbbāsids, who ushered in a new impetus for wide social and religious transformations. On every front, it would seem the seeds of permanent cultural change were sown within the span of a single extraordinary century.

Islamization

Arabization, Islamization, and religious conversion are three closely related yet distinct processes, whose proximity has led to a great deal of diversity and confusion in the manner in which each term has been defined and employed in academic literature. Some scholars employ Islamization as a synonym for religious conversion,[2] while others equate it with Arabization.[3] In this study, each designation is defined and analyzed separately. Religious conversion, in its diverse manifestations, has been addressed in Chapter Four, while Chapter Five parses various aspects of Arabization, which had been defined as a linguistic process.[4]

Here, Islamization is analyzed in light of a two-pronged definition. The first is the historical development and implementation of policies and practices that fostered a distinctly Islamic character and ethos throughout the caliphate. A second aspect is the interpretive strategies that facilitated the adoption and (re)framing of pre-Islamic ideals, views, and monuments, synchronizing them with Islamic history, legends, and beliefs. Thus, it is possible to speak of the Islamization of art, ancient Egyptian history and monuments,[5] as well as the historical figures, texts, and holy sites of the Judeo-Christian tradition.[6] Islamization proceeds hand in hand with religious conversion, but its influence reaches far beyond the Muslim community.

The ensuing discussion of Islamization begins by addressing two developments that brought about diverse fiscal and social distinctions: the articulation of the terms *kharāj* and *jizya*, and the ramifications of the *ṣulḥ*/*ʿanwa* debate. The focus then shifts to a number of edicts that served dual purposes by fostering an Islamic ethos throughout the caliphate while providing ideological legitimacy for the ruling regime.

Fiscal and Ideological Shifts

The first series of changes came about subtly, as a consequence of evolving fiscal policies and the recasting of historical traditions. The Qur'ān cites the *jizya* only once at the *ghazw* of Tabūk, the last campaign in which the Prophet Muḥammad participated: "Fight those who do not believe in God, nor the Last Day, nor forbid what God and his Messenger have forbidden, nor do they practice the religion of truth—that is, those who have been given the Book—until they pay the *jizya* out of hand as they are humbled" (or, "humiliated," *wa hum ṣaghirūn*, Q. 9:29). Most traditions that cite this verse emphasize the last clause,[7] and while several jurists stipulated that *dhimmīs* should not be mistreated while paying the *jizya*, others prescribe their abuse precisely to that moment.[8] Historically, it is difficult to account for a *jizya*, as defined in normative Islamic literature, in seventh-century Egypt. Even in the pertinent Qur'ānic verse, the payment does not resonate as a tax but, rather, as a punitive tribute, the humiliating nature of which motivated the Banū Taghlib, an Arab-Christian tribe, to negotiate with the Caliph ʿUmar to pay a double *ṣadaqa* rather than a *jizya*.[9]

The existence of a poll tax in Byzantine Egypt is currently dismissed, but it is clear that the Arabs levied such a tax on at least some provinces soon after the conquest.[10] Still, that early tariff must not be interpreted as the *jizya*; had the concept been as clear to the early Arabs as it was to their descendants, one would hardly expect the documentary and literary confusion between *kharāj* and *jizya* that permeates early papyri. Additionally, the rate of this early tax fluctuated from one individual to another, perhaps in a manner similar to that of a modern income tax.[11] In all, the taxpayers must have viewed this new *andrismos* as just another tax, devoid of religious connotations.

In the earliest papyri, *jizya* and *kharāj* were synonymous; unqualified, they simply denoted "taxes".[12] The initial means of assessing and collecting taxes, which focused on regions and villages rather than individuals, facilitated the ambiguity.[13] Governors issued demand notes (ἐντάγια) to villages, but then local officials assessed individual liability. In such instances, the distinction between land tax and poll tax (if it existed at all) was theoretical and devoid of any tangible meaning for the average individual. By the beginning of the eighth century CE, however, taxation began to be assessed on an individual basis throughout the province,[14] and what would become the normative definitions for the two terms began to be articulated. Both were taxes paid by non-Muslims; *kharāj* designated a land tax while *jizya* identified a poll tax levied on healthy adult males.[15] (Meanwhile, *ṣadaqa* became a mandatory tax on Muslims, collectable by the government.) It was then that the religious connotations of the *jizya* emerged; no longer a personal tax or tribute, as in the immediate aftermath of the conquest, it became a distinctly religious levy.[16] The emergence of this "classical" definition of *jizya* effectively changed the status of Egypt's Christians on a fundamental level that superseded the implications of the newly articulated *kharāj* tax. They were no longer simply taxpayers, but a distinct "other," liable for a specific tax due to their religious affiliation.

Recasting *ṣulḥ* (conciliation) and *ʿanwa* (hostility) traditions (ca. 96–122/715–41) proved to be another eighth-century development with far-reaching implications.[17] In the early post-conquest decades, oral traditions narrating the conquest of cities and other locals circulated, and that sufficed; there were no systematic attempts to compile detailed accounts of the military campaigns. This changed drastically in the early eighth century CE as novel fiscal and social dynamics led to ideological interest in the specifics of the *futūḥ* and the preservation of conquest narratives in general.

Fred Donner has persuasively argued that the resulting compilations were the product of three impulses.[18] For some, the accounts enabled certain prominent families and tribes to claim precedent and honor, important factors for a population whose ethos was still largely tribal (see Chapter Eight). For others, they functioned as a pious call to participate in the expansion of the caliphate by engaging in *jihād* or *ghazwa*. Finally, the chronicles justified Arab dominion by interpreting the conquests as an expression of Allāh's will and providence.[19] For their part, Christians agreed that the conquests were in accordance with God's will, but diverged in maintaining that they did not indicate his favor but rather his reprimand. For the Copts, the conquests were a chastisement stemming from their communal sins, and a punishment for those who accepted the Council of Chalcedon and persecuted the "orthodox".[20] As for the pro-Chalcedonians, the conquests were likewise interpreted in the light of God's chastisement, particularly as a consequence for the empire's flirtation with Monenergism and Monothelitism, which were officially condemned in the Sixth Ecumenical Council (680 CE).[21]

As the *futūḥ* genre began to coalesce early in the eighth century CE, fiscal policies prompted interest in the often lacking and confusing details of the conquests.[22] Specifically, the jurists of the early to mid-eighth century maintained that the tax levied on *kharāj* land and the ease with which its rate could fluctuate were a function of the manner in which a specific region came under Islamic rule.[23] Land acquired amicably through a *ṣulḥ* (treaty) was subject to the tax rate stipulated in that agreement (often a tenth of revenue, a *ʿushr*), the terms of which were inalienable. Territories conquered through military aggression, or *ʿanwa* (military conquest and/or without a treaty),[24] however, were considered *fay'* for the Muslim community.[25] Those districts could be taxed at the higher rate assessed on *kharāj* land, and their tax rate could be easily changed at the discretion of ruling authorities. The traditions synchronized—and manufactured—during this crucial period (700–40 CE) had tremendous fiscal and social ramifications.

With regard to Egypt and Iraq, the two most productive agricultural regions in the caliphate, the relevant Arabic narratives were first recorded in the ninth century CE and are permeated with contradictory claims regarding the circumstances of the conquests. It is not uncommon for a pericope stating that a specific town or region agreed to a *ṣulḥ* to be immediately succeeded by another claiming *ʿanwa*. Ibn ʿAbd al-Ḥakam's *Futūḥ miṣr* provides a number of relevant passages characteristically infused with chaos and contradictions.[26] The traditions run the gamut. Some narrate a *ṣulḥ* agreement complete with clauses guaranteeing an irrevocable tax rate, a list of witnesses, and individuals who possessed copies of the treaty, while others deny that such a contract ever existed.[27] To further complicate matters, seemingly reliable *asānīd* (chains of transmission) lend a guise of legitimacy to the mutually exclusive claims.

A. Noth and W. Schmucker have convincingly demonstrated that during the first thirty to forty years of the eighth century CE jurists revamped the earlier conquest traditions.[28] Accordingly, a number of regions—most prominently Egypt and Iraq—were defined *a priori* as conquered by *ʿanwa* despite several traditions to the contrary. Consequently, this allowed arable land to be taxed at the higher *kharāj* rate, and for that tax rate to fluctuate at the discretion, even whims, of governors.

Egyptian farmers were the first to feel the ramifications of this fiscal policy. Taxes were high and rates constantly in flux. This newfound flexibility in setting tax rates lies behind the popular tax revolts discussed below. Initially, redefining Egypt's status proved advantageous for the Muslim community; increased taxes translated into stable funds for the *ʿaṭāʾ* that supported the ever-swelling ranks of those named in the *dīwān* registers. Nonetheless, over the span of decades, the ramifications of the reform negatively impacted that community as well. Arab Muslims who had taken to agriculture under the Umayyads did not pay a land tax, but simply the *ʿushr*, which is obligatory for Muslim landowners.[29] Under the ʿAbbāsids, however, not only were they required to pay a land tax, but since the land had been defined as *ʿanwa*, they were liable for the higher tax rate and whimsical increases that Egyptian farmers had been subjected to since the early eighth century.[30]

Additionally, redrafting the province's historical traditions modified the status of Egyptians, since the same principles governing tax rates also dictated the standing of conquered peoples. A population that negotiated a *ṣulḥ* was subjected to the terms of that agreement, which usually stipulated a fixed tax rate in exchange for the protection of lives and properties. Conversely, individuals conquered through *ʿanwa* were not guaranteed anything: they were at the mercy of their conquerors with respect to their tax rate, person, land, and property. The difference was stark. In theory, those who produced a valid *ṣulḥ* agreement were free (*aḥrār*) to live as they pleased; they were explicitly not to be categorized or treated as spoils or slaves.[31] Those conquered through *ʿanwa*, however, were reckoned as slaves (*bi-manzilat al-ʿabīd*),[32] who could be sold or killed at will. Khalīfa ibn Khayyaṭ and al-Balādhurī retain a tradition according to which ʿAmr ibn al-ʿĀṣ summed up the rights of Egyptians thus: "No one among the *qibṭ* of Egypt has an *ʿahd* or *ʿaqd* with me. If I wish, I can kill [them], or sell [them], or take a fifth [of their possessions],[33] except for the people of Ṭarābulūs. They have an *ʿahd* that will be honored".[34] ʿAmr's words distinctly betray the concerns of later generations, but vividly illustrate the social ramifications of the *ṣulḥ/ʿanwa* traditions.

By modifying older traditions, jurists provided governors and caliphs with tremendous flexibility in dealings with conquered peoples and lands, but they soon ran against an obstacle of their own making. Strictly speaking, a *jizya* cannot be levied on slaves.[35] This quandary led to the development of a tradition claiming that the initial conquerors granted manumission to the populace as an act of clemency, which, in turn, legalized their taxation.

Dhimmī properties, particularly churches and monasteries, would become increasingly vulnerable as a result of this manipulation of traditions.[36] Defining Egypt as *ʿanwa* land eliminated *a priori* any agreements for the protection of ecclesiastical structures.[37] Although ultimately futile, Syrian Christians were able to thwart several Muslim attempts to confiscate the Church of St. John in Damascus by producing a vouchsafing agreement allegedly signed by Khālid ibn al-Walīd immediately after the conquest. Such events are unparalleled in Egypt. Already at the end of the eighth century CE, in his *Kitāb al-kharāj* Abū Yūsuf explicitly linked the legal standing of *dhimmī* places of worship to the (*ṣulḥ/ʿanwa*) status of the land they stood upon. Later, in the eleventh century, Abū Yūsuf's legal precedent, which had been intermittently enforced, was more strictly interpreted and subsequently amended to become much more stringent (see Chapter Ten).

Another shift, demonstrative of further deterioration in social categories and perceptions, may be observed in the terms used to identify non-Muslims. Within their own communities, Jews and Christians positively identified themselves as such. In the various genres of Arabic literature, however, the preferred terms for non-Muslims became *al-ʿajam* (pl. *aʿājim*; "foreigners") and *ahl al-dhimmā* ("Protected Community"); later, the derogatory *kuffār* ("infidels") was frequently used. The older and more congenial *ahl al-kitāb*

("People of the Book"), the only designation employed by the Qur'ān, was seldom used in contrast to the other terms.

The articulation and application of the normative definitions for *jizya* and *kharāj*, along with the recasting of the *ṣulḥ/ʿanwa* traditions, had tremendous fiscal and social ramifications for all Egyptians. Swiftly, these reforms transformed the province from a country of Arabs, Egyptians, Christians, Muslims, and Jews (among others), to one populated by Muslims and non-Muslims—categories defined solely by adherence to Islam (or the lack thereof). Furthermore, these designations were no longer mere labels indicative of religious or communal affiliation, but they denoted legal, social, and fiscal classifications that had a direct bearing on the rights and responsibilities of the individual.[38]

Legislating Reform

Beginning in the last decade of the seventh century, a series of legislative reforms and building programs combined to cultivate a distinctly Islamic identity within the former Byzantine and Sasanian territories.[39] These mandates reflect the Marwānid's centralizing agenda, which routinely intertwined ideology with pragmatism. Moreover, the politico-religious nature of these edicts added an air of piety and, hence, legitimacy to Marwānid caliphs in the face of their ʿAlid and Khārijī detractors.[40] ʿAbd al-Malik ibn Marwān (65-86/685–705) issued the earliest of these decrees, which were implemented in Egypt by his brother ʿAbd al-ʿAzīz, and subsequently by the caliph's own son and successor, ʿAbdallāh (85–90/704–9), who followed through with his father's policies.[41]

ʿAbd al-Malik's 75/694 monetary reform, which extended to weights and measures, spearheaded enduring reform.[42] In the decades after the conquests, the populations of the caliphate utilized the coins issued by the preceding empires, which were increasingly irregular as to weight and value. Early Arab attempts at minting coinage were marginal, somewhat eclectic, and regional, but ʿAbd al-Malik's comprehensive reform stabilized the economy and provided the eastern and western halves of the empire with standardized currency.[43] It was an act in which uniformity fostered a new sense of identity: a reform of substance as well as semblance.

On the eve of the reform in Egypt, the Byzantine golden solidus, along with silver (minted during the reign of Herakleios), bronze, and copper coinage were still in circulation.[44] The so-called Arab-Byzantine and Arab-Sasanian coins were minted during the initial phase of the reform, roughly 75–7/694–7.[45] As their nomenclature indicates, these hybrid coins were modeled after their more established predecessors. Hitherto, the solidus retained a large cross and the name of the Byzantine emperor. The newly minted coins removed the cross, substituted the name of the *amīr* for that of the emperor, and appended two Arabic phrases: *lā īlahā illā allāh*, "there is no God but Allāh," and *tayyib*, "good" or "valid".[46] They exhibited a variety of iconographic motifs, the most famous of which, the Standing Caliph pose, which depicts a standing figure unsheathing a sword, is now believed to represent the Prophet Muḥammad himself.[47] Al-Balādhurī retains a tradition in which this coin was presented to the surviving Companions of the Prophet in Medina, who summarily rejected it, presumably because of its iconic features.[48]

The Companions' reaction led to the second phase of the reform, forcing 'Abd al-Malik to mint the first "Islamic," that is decidedly epigraphic, coins: a major departure from established precedence.[49] Beginning in 77/697 and in 79/698, respectively, gold and silver coins were purely epigraphic in Egypt.[50] The obverse read, "There is no God but Allāh, One, without associates";[51] while the reverse stated, "Muḥammad is the Messenger of God".[52] The reform was thorough. Al-Balādhurī records that those who did not employ the official *sikka* (stamp used to mint coins) were severely punished.[53] Still, the actual process of exchanging the late antique coinage in circulation with the newly struck currency took some time to complete and in the bulk of the eighth-century papyri the solidus stands out as a common monetary unit.[54] By the late ninth century, however, finding a coin with a cross on it—a solidus—was tantamount to a miracle.[55] Under the Umayyads, Egyptian mints only struck silver and copper currency. Damascus minted the gold *dīnār* until 199/814, at which time it was first struck in Egypt, though an earlier date is possible.[56] Fusṭāṭ housed the most prominent mint in the province, but others are attested in Alexandria, Fayyūm, Atrīb, Ashmūn, and Faramā.[57]

Minting epigraphic coins was a significant step. Throughout the seventh century CE, late antique coinage provided an iconographic link to the Byzantine/Christian and Sasanian/Mazdean past, but the eighth century ushered in a ubiquitous and distinctly Islamic symbol of hegemony. Contemporary Christians did not welcome the innovation. Al-Balādhurī states that the new coins were unpopular among non-Muslims (*al-ʿajam*), though he does not elaborate on the reasons.[58] Al-Maqrīzī retains a more explicit tradition according to which the first epigraphic coins were rejected because they "did not have a cross".[59] Epigraphic currency provided a visible, tangible reminder of Islamic political control and proof of an ever-expanding Islamic cultural identity and influence.

The Marwānid's Islamizing agenda may also be observed in their extensive building program. Most notable among these are ʿAbd al-Malik's Dome of the Rock (*Qubbat al-Ṣakhra*)[60] and al-Walīd's *al-Masjid al-Aqṣa*.[61] The Dome of the Rock is perhaps the quintessential monument to interpret in light of the Islamization trend. Positioning the structure atop the ruins of the Second Temple visually and ideologically served as an unambiguous symbol of Islamic control of the Holy City.[62] And while its location proclaimed a link to Judaism, its inscriptions provide a critique of orthodox Christology.[63] The Qur'ānic verses inscribed in the monument reiterate the Islamic understanding of Jesus Christ: "The Messiah, Jesus, son of Mary, is only an apostle of God ... Believe therefore in God and his apostles, and say not, three" (Q. 4:169-71). The verse takes issue with the Christian Trinity. Another prominent inscription reads: "Say: he is God, the One; God the Eternal; he has not begotten nor was he begotten; and there is none comparable to him" (Q. 112). This seems to respond to a clause in the Nicean Creed: "Begotten not made, of one substance with the Father."

As these verses were inscribed onto the Dome of the Rock, similar slogans were placed at the entrance of Egyptian churches. The HP records that ʿAbd al-ʿAzīz issued an edict calling for the destruction of crosses and the placement of inscriptions at the entrances of churches reading: "Muḥammad is the great messenger of God, and Jesus also is a messenger of God. *But God is not begotten and does not beget*".[64] The "symbolic appropriation of land"[65] was also clear in Egypt through ʿAbd al-ʿAzīz and ʿAbdallāh's extensive building programs, where it included the expansion and building of several mosques.[66]

At the twilight of his caliphate, ʿAbd al-Malik issued an edict that established the Arabic language as the official language of the administration, replacing the regional languages used hitherto: Greek, Coptic, and Pahlavi. Immediately upon succeeding as caliph, ʿAbdallāh enacted his father's edict in 86/705.[67] This policy instigated a powerful social dynamic that enabled the Arabic language to permeate the whole of Egyptian society (see Chapter Five). Government employees, overwhelmingly non-Arabic-speaking Christians, were the first to feel the effects of the new policy, which was followed by several personnel changes. Ashnās (Athanasios Bar Gūmōyē),[68] head of the Egyptian *dīwān* under ʿAbd al-ʿAzīz ibn Marwān, was replaced by Ibn Yarbūʿ al-Fazārī from Ḥimṣ.[69] The shuffling of officials and the ensuing political ascent of the Qaysīs in Egypt (see Chapter Seven) resulted from the Caliph al-Walīd's preference for replacing Egypt's entrenched administrators, who were loyal to his (by then deceased) uncle and cousins, with his own appointees.

In 99/718 a second phase of administrative reforms commenced as Arabs began to replace local Coptic officials,[70] a shift that coincided with new tax assessment methods that focused on individuals rather than villages. The deliberate nature of the policy is clear: the first stage Arabized the administration, the second targeted the personnel (see Chapter Seven). Still, while the number of Arab Muslims at all levels of the bureaucracy dramatically increased during the first quarter of the eighth century, Christians and Jews continued to be gainfully employed in significant numbers.

Early Marwānid caliphs emphasized the Islamic identity of their government by sponsoring the Arabic language and a host of building programs. They also sought to enhance their reputation as pious rulers through a peculiar act with modern resonance: ʿAbd al-Malik ordered the slaughter of pigs, a decree which, according to Abū ʿUbayd al-Qāsim ibn Sallām, finds a precedent in an edict issued by ʿUmar ibn al-Khaṭṭāb (d. 644 CE).[71] While the command lacks overt political implications, it may be best interpreted in a religious or ideological context. For Muslims (and Jews), pork is *najis*, or impure,[72] though it was—and remains—perfectly acceptable for Egyptian Christians.[73] ʿAbd al-Malik's actions, deliberately echoing those of ʿUmar I, were meant to reinforce his image as a pious, even zealous caliph in the eyes of his Muslim detractors. Soldiers carried on a similar slaughter of pigs under al-Ḥākim bi Amr Allāh in the early fifth/eleventh century, and again in 568/1173 when, after sacking the city of Ibrīm in Nubia, seven hundred pigs were slaughtered.[74] Beyond its ideological implications, in ʿAbd al-Malik's case, the slaughter was but one aspect of the Islamic government's evolving concerns with the regulation and taxation (and occasional eradication) of wine and pigs.[75]

A later Marwānid caliph, Yazīd ibn ʿAbd al-Malik (101–5/720–4), prompted another wave of Islamizing legislation by ordering the destruction of "idols" (*aṣnām*) in 104/723.[76] It was the first Islamic edict of its kind, though not unique in the light of later history.[77] Al-Kindī specifically mentions the destruction of the statues in *ḥammām* Zabban ibn ʿAbd al-ʿAzīz, which was known as *ḥammām* Abī Murrā.[78] The idols in question were most likely Greco-Roman statuary used as decorative elements in public baths. Al-Kindī's example highlights an attack on late antique public art. Other sources, however, maintain that the edict, or at least its implementation, extended to Christian icons in the public domain and private possession. The edict has been often associated with the rise of the Iconoclastic Controversy in Byzantium, though the relation is problematic and likely erroneous.[79] Additionally, it should be noted that while the date of this iconoclastic edict and the second Egyptian revolt (discussed in the following section) may have coincided, there is no substantive link between the two events. By and large, the historical record suggests that the revolt was sparked by fiscal demands rather than religious policies.

Finally, some passages suggest that the Islamization trends ushered in during the eighth century heightened sensitivity toward the conduct of women in the public sphere.[80] Care must be taken since the evidence is so scarce, but al-Kindī records that a law issued in 99/718 banned women from frequenting the public baths, *ḥammamat*, of Egypt.[81] A late antique practice, apparently viewed with indifference up to that juncture, was condemned. Still, it is clear the practice persisted as later decrees would reissue the same prohibition.[82]

Islamization, as discussed here, is an ideological, and to a large extent, hegemonic program that affected every aspect of Egyptian culture along with the whole of the population: Muslims, Christians, and Jews. Arab Muslim ideology began to permeate the public sphere on nearly every facet; the dominant language, legal classifications, currency, and fiscal policies began to reflect a new social order.

Agrarian Revolts

Throughout the eighth and extending into the ninth century CE, a series of revolts plagued Egypt. With few exceptions,[83] scholars have focused on a limited number of these uprisings, the so-called "Coptic revolts," a counterproductive designation on several fronts. The double meaning of *qibṭ* (Egyptian/Christian), while often useful, is misleading when analyzing these disturbances. For some, "Coptic revolts" stood for a romanticized concept of Egyptian resistance to foreign occupation, while others interpreted them as a Christian political movement aimed at repelling Islamic rule.[84] Neither scenario has any historical merit. The histories and chronicles that document the revolts consistently employ *qibṭ* as a designation for "Egyptian"—an antonym to "Arab"—and describe them as reactions to economic exploitation rather than religious or political movements. The "Coptic" label also shrouds the fact that in several revolts, including the three largest and most violent uprisings, Arab

Muslims rioted alongside Egyptian Christians, which undermines the labeling of any revolt as "Coptic" or "Arab."

Eighth- and ninth-century insurrections are best interpreted within their socio-political environment without dwelling on the religious or "ethnic" affiliation of the rioters. The fiscal and juristic reforms discussed in the previous section were in the immediate background, particularly the development of what would become the normative meanings for *kharāj* and *jizya*.[85] As demonstrated by the studies of Gladys Frantz-Murphy, over the span of a century, the concept of *kharāj* underwent a number of refinements: it changed from a generic designation meaning "tax," to a land tax levied on non-Muslims, to a land tax paid by all landowners (irrespective of creed), and finally to a land tax payable only in cash.[86] Each new dimension translated into either a new tax, or a greater tax burden for some segment of the population. Below, the revolts are chronologically analyzed with regard to their political and fiscal roots along with their social ramifications; their military significance has been already addressed elsewhere.[87] Here, I argue that a close reading of these revolts provides some of the most salient indicators for the emergence of a new society in Islamic Egypt.

The first series of revolts coincided with the period during which jurists rewrote the conquest traditions, thereby defining Egypt as *'anwa* land,[88] which enabled officials to alter the tax rate at will. In this early period, it was Egyptians who were hardest hit by the revision. Arab farmers were still relatively few, and enjoyed exemption from any sort of land tax: under the Arabophile Umayyads, only the *'ushr* was expected of them. The first revolt (αντασρσία), which occurred in 78/697 or 93/712 in the Thebaid, is known only through a single papyrus.[89] The lack of documentation likely reflects the marginal nature of the incident. The second revolt, which normative literature enumerates as the first, occurred in 107/725,[90] shortly after 'Ubayd Allāh ibn al-Ḥabḥāb, the influential *ṣāḥib al-kharāj*, initiated a land survey and increased taxes.[91] The HP portrays him as a cruel magistrate who branded Christians as a means of identification and abused them as corvée laborers.[92] Consequently, a number of villages and all of the eastern Ḥawf (Delta) rebelled;

al-Maqrīzī includes Upper Egypt (*al-ṣaʿid*) among the regions that revolted. According to the HP, Muslims as well as Christians participated in the disturbance, which was quelled by *ahl al-dīwān.* [93]

This incident establishes a pattern prominent in a number of subsequent revolts, all of which were sparked by tax increases and suppressed by the *ahl al-dīwān*, the main military force in Egypt at the time. Initially, the *ahl al-dīwān* constituted the Arab army, but by the date of this revolt they had likely ceased functioning as a standing militia. They were mainly composed of Arabs who were paid *ʿaṭāʾ* (a stipend) in exchange for serving in the army when needed, similar to modern military reserves.[94] In its aftermath, the second revolt prompted an official immigration of 3000 Qaysī families to Egypt,[95] where they were settled throughout the eastern Ḥawf, establishing an Arab-Muslim presence in the region.[96] It would be nearly a century before that region would revolt again, and by then its demographic composition had radically shifted; those later rebels were predominantly Arab farmers.

The *ahl al-dīwān* likewise suppressed the third revolt, which was confined to Upper Egypt in 121/739–40.[97] Little is known about this revolt, whose only outstanding feature is that it may have been the only tax-based revolt to take place in that region. Later, two other disturbances shook Upper Egypt, but they were politically and ideologically motivated, and lie beyond the scope of the topic at hand.[98]

The fourth through sixth revolts are difficult to disentangle; they occurred within a span of eighteen months during one of the most turbulent political transitions in Egyptian history: the end of Umayyad and the beginning of ʿAbbāsid rule. Yuḥannis of Samannūd led the fourth revolt in 132/750, which appears to have been easily suppressed.[99] It was, nonetheless, opportunistic, capitalizing on the mobilization of 7,000 men from *ahl al-dīwān* against ʿAmr ibn Suḥayl ibn ʿAbd al-ʿAzīz ibn Marwān, the disenfranchised grandson of the late governor ʿAbd al-ʿAzīz, who, along with al-Dumaḥis ibn al-ʿAzīz al-Kinānī, led a raiding party throughout the Eastern Ḥawf.[100]

The fifth uprising occurred within the same year and involved Egyptians and Arabs. It originated in the Bashmūr, but quickly spread to other regions; the prevailing political chaos rendered it far more difficult to suppress than previous uprisings.[101] In the midst of this disturbance, Egyptians—especially the Bashmūrites—along with the Arabs of the Ḥawf, assisted the Khurāsāniyya against Umayyad troops (see Chapter Nine). The sixth revolt (135/752) parallels the fourth to a great extent; it took place in Samannūd under the leadership of an otherwise unknown individual named Abū Mīnā.[102] Similar to Yuḥannis' revolt, it was localized and thus easily suppressed.

The seventh revolt (150/767) constitutes a significant historical marker.[103] Initially, ʿAbbāsid rule in Egypt was relatively peaceful. As a means of ingratiating itself among the populace, the new regime extended tax breaks and exemptions to the factions that had supported its revolution, including the Arabs of the Ḥawf and the Christians of the Bashmūr.[104] But such tax policies could not be sustained. A fundamental tenet of the ʿAbbāsid *daʿwa* demanded equality among all Muslims. Thus, non-Arab Muslims had to be treated and paid as equals, and as massive numbers of previously unregistered *mawālī* and new converts were able to join government service, the *dīwān* registers swelled and the need for funds became acute.[105] Revenue had to increase; thus, the government raised taxes and doubled its efforts in extracting the *kharāj* tax even from populations that had enjoyed exemption, including the Arabs of the Ḥawf (who had been paying a structured *ṣadaqa/zakāt* since the 730s).[106] These new tax hikes along with the imposition of extraordinary duties sparked the seventh revolt,[107] in which the rebels targeted the governor Yazīd ibn Ḥātim, whom they blamed for the new policies. Ṣā was the epicenter, but the violence quickly spread to Barshūd (Bashmūr), Awsiyya, and Bujūm. The uprising began as a stereotypical incident; government agents (*ʿummāl*) were ousted and the governor responded by summoning the *ahl al-dīwān* and sending them to quell the disturbance. But on this occasion, the *ahl al-dīwān* were routed and returned to Fusṭāṭ in defeat.[108] For the first time, they proved to be an ineffective (and expensive) military force, which prompted a strategic shift. When the localized and relatively minor eighth revolt took place in Balhīb (156/773), it was not suppressed by *ahl al-dīwān* but by soldiers (*jund*).[109] The cause of this specific revolt remains obscure, but most likely it was tax related.[110] Professional armies suppressed disturbances in Egypt beginning with this incident.[111]

A new tax policy initiated by the governor Mūsā ibn Muṣʿab al-Khathʿamī instigated the ninth revolt in 168/784. Far from popular, many accused Mūsā of corruption and blamed him for doubling the land tax (*kharāj*) and introducing new duties on merchants (*ahl al-aswāq*) and the owners of pack animals (*dawābb*).[112] By that date, the government had already withdrawn the *kharāj*-exemption status from Arab farmers.[113] Thus, whoever tilled *kharāj* land, Christian or Muslim, was subject to the same tax rate. It is here, at this juncture, that a new Arab cultural identity may be discerned. Qaysī and Yamanī Arabs, who had long jostled for prominence in Egypt, set aside their tribal feuds and joined to form a united front behind a bipartisan leader, Muʿāwiya ibn Mālik ibn Ḍamḍam al-Judhāmī.[114] It would be a gross oversimplification to maintain that tribal feuds and identities ceased at that point, but, demonstrably, a new concept of self and community based on regional interest rather than tribal affiliation began to emerge. Nonetheless, the persistence of tribal loyalties aided the rebels, who were able to secure the backing of the *jund* of Fusṭāṭ, most of whom, it would appear, were locally recruited Arabs with ties to the farmers of the Ḥawf.[115] Unaware of the pact, Mūsā ibn Muṣʿab marched into battle, was abandoned by his troops, and was killed. The rebels won the day.

An increase in the *kharāj* tax, decreed by the governor Isḥāq ibn Sulaymān, sparked the tenth revolt in 178/793.[116] The Arabs of the Ḥawf again rebelled, but failed to rally support among the *jund* of Fusṭāṭ and, to their detriment, were met early in 179/794 by the Khurāsāniyya under the direction of the general Harthama ibn al-Aʿyan. The foreign troops had no tribal ties and lacked religious sympathies for the rebelling Arabs: Isḥāq had learned from Mūsā's mistake. By the end of the eighth century, all ties between the army and the Arab farmers of the Ḥawf were severed. Soon the makeup of the army would also change, and the emerging identity of the Arab tribes as settled *Egyptian* farmers would take hold.

Two important fiscal changes took place in the interim period. *Kharāj* was no longer assessed in kind (*ḍarība*),[117] but in cash, which translated into a tax increase for peasants since the price of their produce fluctuated. Still, the government accepted the tax in cash or in kind for another decade. The switchover may have been tied to an increase in flax farming and the reciprocal decrease in wheat cultivation.[118] (The export of Egyptian grain to Mecca and Medina had ceased by that point.) Second, as G. Frantz-Murphy's research has shown, two new terms were introduced to circumvent the problem of requiring Muslims to pay a *kharāj* (a *dhimmī* tax). Tax receipts from this period designated the *kharāj* paid by Muslims as "rent" (*kira'* or *ujra*),[119] while another semantic attempt emphasized that payments were due to "the Muslims' register" (*ṭubūl al-muslimīn*).[120] Regardless, the nominal changes did not affect the tax rate; the payment was the *kharāj* in all but name.

Al-Layth ibn al-Faḍl's land survey ignited the eleventh revolt in 186/801.[121] Surveyors were accused of using shortened measuring rods, thus assessing taxes over a larger area than that actually cultivated. Arab farmers from the Ḥawf took their grievance to the governor with no avail. Upon their revolt, they were met by an army of 4,000 soldiers, but the contest had mixed results. Al-Layth and his troops defeated the rebels, but the Ḥawf still refused to pay taxes. The governor then dispatched a letter to the Caliph Hārūn al-Rashīd stating that without reinforcements he would not be able to extract taxes from the region. One of al-Layth's secretaries, Maḥfūẓ ibn Sulaymān, seized this opportunity to assure the caliph that he would be able to collect the taxes "without whip or stick".[122] Subsequently, al-Rashīd relieved al-Layth of his duties and appointed Maḥfūẓ head of *dīwān al-kharāj*. Within that year, Maḥfūẓ fulfilled his promise to the caliph.

The twelfth revolt (191/806) took place during the governorship of al-Ḥusayn ibn Jamīl.[123] The Ḥawf again refused to pay taxes, and under the direction of Abū al-Nady *mawlā* Balī a thousand men from the region formed an impromptu raiding party. News of the riot reached the Caliph Hārūn al-Rashīd, who was now forced to send troops to quell the disturbance and collect taxes. In the next few years, several attempts were made to avert the increasingly frequent uprisings. In 192/807, the government attempted to coerce the Ḥawf tribes into compliance by imprisoning their leaders; two years later, it employed the novel approach of negotiating directly with them, which led to an agreement on a tax rate.[124] Here, it is imperative to note that the tribal leaders were addressed en block, not as individuals, or representatives of separate tribes; the nascent society that began to emerge in the 780s continued to coalesce. No sooner had the agreement been reached, however, than the thirteenth revolt erupted.[125] ʿUthmān ibn al-Mustanīr al-Judhamī led an insurgence centered at the towns of Tanū and Tumayy. Eventually, the governor, Ḥātim ibn Ḥarthama, defeated the rebels and brought back a hundred prisoners with him to Fusṭāṭ. ʿUthmān, however, had escaped.

Egyptians and Arabs both participated in the fourteenth revolt, which began in 196/811.[126] Politics and opportunism along with disgruntlement over taxes fueled the uprising, which commenced during the *fitna*: the civil war between the two sons of al-Rashīd, al-Amīn and al-Ma'mūn. Arabs in the Ḥawf and ʿUthmān ibn al-Mustanīr, who had led the thirteenth revolt a few years prior, favored the caliph al-Amīn, while the majority of the *jund* supported al-Ma'mūn. A period of anarchy ensued until the death of al-Amīn. The fifteenth revolt (198/813) was the last effort to resist al-Ma'mūn in Egypt, but when news of al-Amīn's death reached the rebels, they were disheartened and scattered; still, a Madlajā uprising near Alexandria had to be suppressed.[127]

The Copts at Sakhā initiated the sixteenth revolt in 203/818-19, but they were quickly joined by a massive number of Arabs from the tribe of Madlij: 80,000 according to al-Kindī.[128] Historically, this was a pivotal revolt which demonstrates that the interests of many Arab Muslims (Qaysīs and Yamanīs) and Egyptian Christians (the Copts) were now in sync.

In 214/829, an old issue, increased taxation, sparked the seventeenth revolt.[129] Ṣāliḥ ibn Shīrzad increased the *kharāj*, and oppressed (*ẓalam*) the populace. The whole of Lower Egypt revolted and soundly defeated the soldiers who were sent against them. The new governor, ʿĪsā ibn Yazīd al-Julūdī, inherited the uprising and maliciously suppressed it. Exacerbating the situation, after his victory, the governor punished the rioters by beheading some and crucifying others, no doubt to make an example. Such acts of brutality, however, backfired and likely sparked the next series of revolts that commenced in 215/830, the first of which, the eighteenth revolt, was suppressed by ʿĪsā ibn Manṣūr.[130]

A few months later, in 216/831, the largest and best documented of these insurrections began when "all the *qibṭ* and *ʿarab*" of the Delta revolted.[131] Al-Kindī and the HP trace the uprising back to the abuse farmers suffered at the hands of government agents. Shortly thereafter, the famed Persian general al-Afshīn, who had previously dispatched troops to the region, arrived at Fusṭāṭ. After allowing for the inundation of the Nile to subside, al-Afshīn and ʿĪsā ibn Manṣūr embarked upon a series of campaigns that effectively ended the rebellion, which had spread to various locations.[132] The last battle of the campaign took place in the Bashmūr.[133] Al-Afshīn delayed marching against that region and waited for the arrival of the Caliph al-Ma'mūn, who had traveled to Egypt, accompanied by the Syrian patriarch Dionysios of Tel-Maḥrē, to personally take command of the campaign. Upon their arrival, the Coptic patriarch Yusāb (Joseph) I joined the caliph and Patriarch Dionysios. As a last attempt, al-Ma'mūn sent the two non-Chalcedonian patriarchs to negotiate with the rebels, but their counsel was refused outright, and upon their return the caliph authorized al-Afshīn to begin his military campaign. A long battle ensued, concluding with a decisive victory for al-Afshīn: men were killed, women and children were exiled, and buildings were burnt to the ground.[134] Al-Maqrīzī designated this as the last of the "Coptic" revolts, which he glosses as the beginning of the demise of the Coptic community.

Within a year, all Arabs were dropped from the *dīwān* and their pensions ceased.[135] The soldiers who had brought about victory for al-Ma'mūn were Turks and Persians; the Arabs of the *dīwān* had outlived their usefulness and had already proven their inadequacy in the 150/767 revolt, and their treachery in 168/784. This sparked a revolt in which five hundred men led by Yaḥyā ibn al-Wazīr al-Jarawī attacked and killed the governor Kaydur. Yaḥyā and his followers believed that the *ʿaṭāʾ* they received as members of the *dīwān* was their inalienable "right and *fay*'" (this was, indeed, the perspective of earlier generations, but had long ceased to be the case).[136] Kaydur's son and successor, Muẓaffar, killed Yaḥyā and his followers, ending the circle of violence.[137]

Striving to be comprehensive, this account could be somewhat misleading. A number of these "revolts" may be more accurately described as regional riots. They were local disturbances of uncertain magnitude that were quickly and easily suppressed. In general, the most significant revolts occurred in the Delta, only one (perhaps two) extended into Upper Egypt. The sequence of defiance began with the refusal to pay taxes, escalated with the expulsion of government agents, and eventually culminated with open combat against local troops. The early revolts were all quelled by the *ahl al-dīwān*, but after their defeat in 150/767, professional soldiers took the lead in suppressing disturbances in the province.[138] Egyptians clearly took a prominent role in ten revolts, though that does not exclude their participation in a number of later uprisings, particularly those that were likewise incited by tax increases or land surveys.

A few revolts were opportunistic, taking advantage of chaotic political circumstances in Egypt. The fourth, fifth, and sixth revolts took place during the tumultuous period in which the ʿAbbāsids bested the Umayyads. It was a frenzied era of competing claims of legitimacy and widespread anarchy, well-illustrated by the long accounts preserved in the HP and al-Ṭabarī. Later, in the fifteenth revolt, all took advantage of the chaotic political environment caused by the *fitna*, which pitted several factions against one another while the Andalusians raided Alexandria.[139] This led to the fragmentation of Egypt into a patchwork of autonomous regions.[140] The eighteenth revolt also conformed to this pattern, though with notable exceptions.

None of these revolts were religiously or "ethnically" motivated. Rather, the sources explicitly state that Muslims and Christians were united in the second, fifth, sixth, seventh, fifteenth, and eighteenth revolts. The fifteenth is especially intriguing, as it was initiated by the Copts at Sakhā, but was quickly joined by the Banū Madlij.[141] The usual pattern was the reverse; that is, that Copts typically joined Arab revolts already in progress, as in the fifth, sixth, seventh, and eighteenth revolts.

The fact that most "Coptic" revolts predate "Arabic" uprisings is only a reflection of the Islamic government's shifting fiscal policies. Under Umayyad rule, Egyptian farmers were easily taxed and exploited. The status of the land they farmed was redefined, and they suffered the double burden of being non-Arabs and non-Muslims. Meanwhile, Arabs enjoyed the privilege their ancestry afforded them.[142] Government-sponsored immigration and the resettlement of Arabs in 109/728 changed the demographic composition of the Ḥawf and provided an important catalysis for momentous social transformations (see Chapter Eight). The Arab migrants were settled as farmers, a new lifestyle that the government subsidized through grants and tax exemptions.[143] Soon these new settlers would set the precedent for a new Arab-Muslim agrarian society.

Late eighth- and early ninth-century revolts document two pivotal socio-historical processes. First, they reflect the transformation of clannish Arab warriors into settled farmers who increasingly based their concepts of self and community on regionalism and common interest rather than tribal affiliation. Second, the revolts illustrate the melding of the hitherto distinct Egyptian and Arab populations. In the great revolts of 150/767, 203/818, and 217/832, Arabs and Egyptians—Muslims and Christians alike—rebelled against a common enemy: the tax collector. Mutual benefit, common regional interests, and new political realities engendered a novel society in Egypt that would gradually mature through linguistic and cultural uniformity.

The Shape and Meaning of Time

The processes of measuring and labeling time pertain to practical and ideological concerns that are intrinsically tied to a society's self-image and ethos. During the Middle Ages, Christians in Europe increasingly conceived of and enumerated time in reference to the birth of Jesus Christ.[144] Earlier, other Christians inaugurated their calendars by the Ascension, and others still by the date of the Resurrection.[145] As for Muslims, they quickly deemed the *hijra* as the pivotal transformative event in history and everything that preceded it as occurring in a less fortunate time,[146] an Age of Ignorance (*al-jāhiliyya*).[147] Parallels can be drawn from most ancient calendars and societies, including those of the Hebrew, Roman, Persian, Chinese, and Mayan peoples.[148]

Nonetheless, labeling and ordering time are two distinct enterprises. The measuring or reckoning of time is a project concerned with mathematics, astronomy, and establishing standard units: hours, days, weeks, months, and years. The ancient world never agreed as to the length of these measurements. For the Hebrews, a "week" spanned seven days, while it denoted ten for the Ancient Egyptians, and thirteen or even twenty days for the Mayans. Lack of agreement, however, was irrelevant so long as uniformity was maintained within a given society. The other process, the labeling of time, reflects ideological concerns and involves two basic tasks that may or may not be interdependent. One undertaking seeks to establish a date for year one, a consideration inevitably tied to cultural and religious priorities, as the general examples above demonstrate. A second undertaking is to label the system: to name the calendar. The seventh through ninth centuries CE inaugurated a period in which Christians and Muslims in Egypt explored various means of measuring and labeling time, considerations that reflected deep socio-cultural and religious transitions.

In the first Islamic century, the fifteen-year indiction cycle employed since ca. 312 CE was retained, but it lost momentum and favor.[149] As an emperor-centered system, it increasingly became anachronistic in a post-Byzantine environment. Nonetheless, the Arab administration and the Christian population employed this reckoning well into early ʿAbbāsid rule.[150] The system had always been awkward. The indiction years were numbered 1–15 with each fifteen-year set constituting a cycle, but the cycles themselves were not enumerated, causing problems in dating texts up to this very day. To alleviate the difficulty, three practices emerged. One supplemented the indiction with a *hijra* date,[151] though that practice lacked precision and widespread appeal.[152] Another appended the Era of Diocletian (1 = 284/5 CE), which had been in marginal use throughout the late antique period, to the indiction clause; a third practice relied exclusively on Diocletian's reckoning.[153] Similar to the older Egyptian calendar, the Era of Diocletian (ἀπο Διοκλητιανοῦ) was linear and based on the solar year.[154] By the eighth century, the Era of Diocletian enjoyed wide circulation,[155] especially among Christians, though often only the reckoning and not the designation or label was documented. It even made some modest headway among the Byzantines (outside of Egypt) and the Arabs.[156]

Christians and Muslims alike relied heavily upon the Coptic calendar, particularly in matters that required scheduled payments or farming.[157] The uniformity of this system (twelve 30-day months, followed by a "short month")[158] and its synchronicity with the agricultural cycle propelled the usage of its months,[159] which the Arabs identified as *ashhur al-ʿajam* ("months of the non-Muslims") or as *ashhur al-qibṭ* ("months of the Copts").[160] Conversely, Arabic months were used rather sparingly from the seventh through the tenth centuries CE. They were noted in official documents and set the rhythm for the Muslim community's religious observances,[161] but they do not seem to have prevailed in the mundane facets of daily life, though that would later change as demonstrated below.

Into the eleventh century, three date formulas dominated. A Coptic system cited the date of the Coptic month (e.g. 14th of Ṭūba) and the year of Diocletian. In the eighth and ninth centuries CE, the use of a Coptic date clause often sufficed even when both parties were Muslim.[162] An Arab-Islamic date clause, in comparison, specified the Arabic month and the (lunar) *hijra* year. The third formula was a hybrid system that documented the Coptic day/month and the *hijra* year.[163] Use of Coptic date clauses in isolation or in combination with *hijra* years prevailed in the eighth and ninth centuries, and appears to have been more common than the sole use of the *hijra* date. Some documents were double-dated by both complete Coptic (date, month, and Diocletianic year) and Islamic (date, Arabic month, and *hijra* year) clauses. While attested in documentary texts,[164] this double-dating system gained momentum in Christian narratives sources beginning in the tenth century.[165]

Three tenth-century ostraca from Idfū illustrate popular calendrical usage.[166] All were written by Arab Muslims and, according to the order of their publication, date to 289/902, 324/936, and 320/932. The first ostracon is dated according to the Islamic calendar. The second employed the above-mentioned hybrid system, documenting the Coptic month and *hijra* year. The third text is double dated by the Islamic and hybrid clauses: "Muḥarram, year three hundred and twenty; on Sunday Amshīr 3 year 320." The temporal and geographic proximity of these three ostraca demonstrate the flexibility used by average Egyptians until the first half of the tenth century CE: dating systems were used interchangeably, even redundantly. This variety and hybridity may be contrasted with the contemporary narrative sources, which usually limit themselves to either the Era of Diocletian (later dubbed that of the Martyrs) or that of the *hijra*. In addition to the systems already mentioned, a simplified formula only referenced the Coptic date and month, or just identified the name of the *lashane* of that year.[167]

Throughout the eighth and ninth centuries, religious affiliation alone did not predetermine the use of these chronological systems. Christians were familiar with the *hijra* calendar from official documents and often (though not always) from contracts that involved a Muslim party.[168] As for the Muslim population, it seems to have favored the hybrid system, and had no reservations in relying upon the Coptic calendar. This is well demonstrated by *P.Cair.Arab.* II.97, dated 356/967, which is an employment contract for a mosque attendant (*maʿsūl*), whose salary schedule was based on Coptic months.[169] This would radically change in the eleventh and twelfth centuries CE as the *hijra* calendar gained wider acceptance. Even among the Christians, it is not uncommon to find it the only calendar referenced.[170] Synchronizing all of these systems was a necessary but arduous task; al-Maqrīzī documents a number of these attempts, which had to be periodically repeated.[171]

The Meaning of Time

Turning from the reckoning of time to its labeling, throughout the eighth and ninth centuries Christians and Muslims struggled to find appropriate labels for the calendars they employed. This is difficult for modern individuals who essentially live in secular time to appreciate. For Christians, the major shift was the rebranding of the Era of Diocletian as that of the Martyrs. Among Muslims, *al-sana al-hijriyya* was firmly established, though the Fāṭimids would introduce two other calendars.

Under Umayyad rule, the Copts designated their calendar as the "Era of Diocletian." It was not until the late eighth and early ninth centuries CE that the "Era of the Martyrs" {ⲬⲢⲘ︦ᴾ: χρ(όνος) μ(α)ρ(τύρων)},[172] a designation that first appeared on Nubian tombstones, came into limited use.[173] Nonetheless, it was by no means universal.[174] The earliest literary references are much later still; they may be found in a colophon dated (578 AM) 861/2 CE and an inscription likely commissioned in late (575 AM) 859 CE.[175]

The HP also supports the mid-ninth century as the first period of significant recognition and popularity of the new designation, though the issue is complicated by that work's textual history. The biography of Patriarch Khaīl I (744–67 CE), written in the 770s, retains the earliest reference to the Era of the Martyrs in that work;[176] nonetheless, those glosses are almost certainly spurious. Both designations—that of "Diocletian" and that of the "Martyrs"—are attested in that biography,[177] and while it may have been drafted during a transitional period in which the two labels were used, it is much more likely that a later scribe changed the date clauses in that biography from the Era of Diocletian to that of the Martyrs but overlooked a gloss in what is one of the longest biographies in the whole compilation (it is difficult to imagine the reverse to have occurred). This would postpone the use of the designation until the next author of the HP, the monk dubbed John "the Writer," who wrote the biographies of the 47th through the 55th patriarchs in

865/6 CE: within just four years of the above-cited colophon and inscription. Indeed, the "Era of the Martyrs" designation is consistently used throughout John's biographies.[178] Still, adoption of the new designation was not commonplace until the eleventh century CE.[179] Even Eutychios (d. 940 CE), while citing a dozen calendars in his *Naẓm al-jawhar*, does not gloss the era of Martyrs at all, though he repeatedly referenced that of Diocletian.[180] As late as the fifteenth century CE, al-Maqrīzī noted that the Christians used both designations,[181] though the last attestations of the Era of Diocletian in documentary texts date to the mid-twelfth century.[182] Outside of the province, writing about concepts of time and the historical calendars and festivals observed by the populations of the caliphate circa 1000 CE, al-Bīrūnī knew the calendar of Diocletian well, but not that of the Martyrs.[183]

Dubbing the Era of Diocletian as that of the "Martyrs" led to absolute exclusivity: Muslims would not use that calendar. As an alternative, under the direction of the early Fāṭimids, *al-sana al-kharājiyya* ("the tax year") came into use.[184] It was an attempt to standardize taxation through the adoption of a uniform solar-based system (synchronous with the Coptic year and months), a Muslim equivalent to the Era of the Martyrs in all but name.[185] Among Christians, motivation for this christening of the calendar is much less obvious (and certainly much later) than is usually presumed. Diocletian's infamy as the "Slayer of the Martyrs" is omnipresent in Coptic texts,[186] as is the legacy of the martyrs in Egyptian literature and liturgies. Moreover, drawing upon the martyrs' legacy as a means of establishing continuity with the past or to legitimize a particular hierarchy is well documented in the context of the early fourth century, the early fifth century, and yet again under Ayyūbid and Mamlūk rule.[187] Impulse for the change could not have been the memory of Diocletian or that of the martyrs *per se*, but more likely stemmed from the historical situation of the Christian community. Several factors likely converged, prompting the shift. Significantly, the earliest literary references date near the end or immediately after the turbulent caliphate of al-Mutawakkil (847–61 CE), which was especially harsh for nearly all religious minorities.[188] A second watershed may be identified with the cruel reign of al-Ḥākim bi Amr Allāh (997–1021 CE). As noted above, while the new designation emerged in Egyptian papyri by the end of the eighth century and is documented in the historical writings of the mid-ninth century, it was not widely employed until the eleventh century, and later still in some locations.

The ideological renaming of the Era of Diocletian coincided with the emergence of a new Christian identity and self-image and a host of social transformations (see Chapters Two, Four, and Eight). The Islamizing trends discussed above, along with the increase of converts to Islam and large-scale Arabization, further accentuated the perception of religious affiliation as the dominant factor in identifying and conceiving of one's self and community. A contributing factor lies in the probability that by the eleventh century Christians no longer retained the numerical advantage they had enjoyed in Egypt since the late fourth century CE. The renaming was in part facilitated by the community coming to grips with its demographic decline and its marginalized legal, social, fiscal, and political standing. This growing *dhimmī*-Christian identity also fostered the obsession with the Coptic language evident in apocalyptic texts (see Chapters Five and Twelve).

A second factor that led to the popularity of the Era of the Martyrs has already been discussed in a different context. Chapters Two and Nine demonstrate that ninth-century Christian narratives had a distinctly different perception of Byzantine rule than earlier texts.[189] Beginning at that juncture, historians chronicled Byzantine rule as a monotonous period of Melkite oppression and persecution. Understandably, the Copts living in the troublesome decades of the early eleventh century began to discern a pattern of persecution in their history which they came to embrace as proof of their virtue and their status as a chosen people despite what may be interpreted as political failure. Their community became an embodiment of the Righteous Sufferer, surviving Roman persecution under Diocletian, Byzantine oppression under Marcian, Justinian, and Kyros, and Muslim intolerance under Qurra, Usama, Marwān II, al-Mutawakkil and al-Ḥākim. In this light, it was easy for the Copts to conceive of their whole history as one of martyrdom. It is against this background of the rise of a revised historiography of Byzantine rule, major irreversible demographic and cultural transformations, and the oppressive reigns of al-Mutawakkil and al-Ḥakim that the dominance of the Era of the Martyrs may be best understood.

Calendrical usage among Muslims also fluctuated, though later shifts appear to have been more practical rather than ideological. In the pre-Islamic era, Arabs in the peninsula did not assign a historical significance or an eschatological trajectory to time. This allowed for diverse calendarical systems to coexist. Years were named rather than enumerated. The descriptive labels used to identify specific years were intended to commemorate prominent events that transpired during that lunar cycle. Most famously, the Year of the Elephant (570/1 CE), the year of the birth of the Prophet Muḥammad, was the year in which the Kingdom of Axum used elephants in its campaign against Mecca.[190] Thus, a highly subjective system developed in which the same year could be identified by different designations at the four corners of the peninsula. By the second half of the first/seventh century, however, it is evident that the Muslim community recognized a lunar calendar commencing with the year 622 CE, though its designation was not always explicit. According to literary sources, the *hijra* reckoning was first introduced in 17/639 by the Caliph ʿUmar ibn al-Khaṭṭāb. Initially, he sought to inaugurate the calendar with the Prophet Muḥammad's birth, but ʿAlī ibn Abū Ṭālib convinced him to use the date of the *hijra* instead.[191] The lunar calendar was a carryover from the pagan past, but the choice to enumerate years beginning with the *hijra* was a purely ideological decision.

Still, the earliest attestation for the *hijra* calendar in a documentary text is to the year 29/650.[192] Frequently, the year was not qualified at all; the formula written by X in the month of Y (in the year) Z sufficed.[193] In Greek papyri, the expression is usually some form of κατ' Ἄραβας ἔτους,[194] or, as was the practice in Thebes, ἔτους Σαρακηνῶν.[195] By the tenth century CE, *al-sana al-hilāliyya* (apparently a synonym for both *al-sana al-hijriyya* and *al-ʿarabiyya*) also came into use.[196]

Calendrical usage throughout these centuries paralleled social and fiscal evolution. In the seventh century CE, Byzantine norms continued to dominate. Thus, the indiction system persisted, but as it became increasingly incompatible with socio-political realities, indigenous innovations and hybrids attempted to replace it. Eventually, an Arab-Muslim norm (the *hijra* calendar) would dominate even among Christians, though, certainly, the Coptic reckoning was never completely routed. Calendrical transitions under early Islamic rule unfolded through these three stages. This same evolutionary process may be charted in the discussions relating to Coptic law and the maturing and defining of various governmental posts, which are discussed in the following chapter.

CHAPTER 7

MUSLIM ELITES, URBAN ADMINISTRATION, AND RURAL JUSTICE

In the early post-conquest decades, the Arabs implemented a few reforms that streamlined and centralized the administration; nonetheless, much of the administrative apparatus remained intact along with the micro- and macro- mechanisms and institutions that maintained order and administered justice. This would incrementally change. At the highest tier, four offices would come to dominate the urban administration; three were appointed by the caliph, while the fourth was recruited locally. In the countryside, authority continued to be mediated through local officials and religious figures, but this dynamic began to shift in the early eighth century and seems to have been subverted by the tenth.

Below, in addition to delineating each office's duties, the subsequent analysis aims to explore the interpersonal tensions and considerations that manipulated the actions of office holders. The focus then shifts to the administrative dynasties that monopolized top governmental posts, and the rural officials with whom the average individual would have had contact and recourse. The final section problematizes the concept of communal autonomy, and stresses the informal means by which disputes were resolved and order maintained in rural districts.

The Administration

Four officeholders constituted the core of the provincial bureaucracy: *ṣāḥib al-ṣalāt* (Overseer of Prayer), *ṣāḥib al-kharāj* (Treasurer), *ṣāḥib al-shurṭa* (Chief of "Police"), and the *qāḍī*, (Judge).[1] The governor, *al-wālī* (also designated as *al-ḥākim* and *al-amīr*), was by definition *ṣāḥib al-ṣalāt*. Caliphs routinely appointed regional governors, though in times of rioting or civil unrest, local troops and generals assumed that prerogative. As the Overseer of Prayer, the governor delivered the Friday sermon (*al-khuṭba*), either in person or through a surrogate, in the name of the ruling caliph, a pious act that functioned as a tangible means by which caliphs proclaimed their hegemony and governors demonstrated their loyalty. The political nature of this act is best observed in times of transition or civil war when omission of the caliph's name, or its replacement by that of a rival or a usurper, constituted a public act of defiance and sedition. General Jawhar's conquest of Egypt in 969 CE provides a vivid example. Three days after he secured Fusṭāṭ, the *khuṭba* was delivered in the name of the Fāṭimid caliph al-Muʿizz rather than the ʿAbbāsid al-Muṭīʿ.

Centered at Fusṭāṭ, the governor served as the civil and military chief of the province, though there are scattered references suggesting that Upper and Lower Egypt may have had their own respective governors at various junctures. In turbulent periods of rioting or war, he would commission the local troops and often personally lead them into battle.[2] During peaceful times, the governor's duties took on a more civic character. He, with the aid of the *shurṭa*, focused on maintaining peace and stability, assured the smooth collection of taxes, and (especially under Umayyad rule) secured necessary supplies and personnel.[3] From the conquest through the early eighth century, governors often functioned in a manner reminiscent of the *qāḍī* (judge). Papyri spanning early and mid-Umayyad rule demonstrate this aspect well. At the request of a Muslim or Christian, governors routinely intervened in civil disputes by instructing regional magistrates to inquire into the grievance and report back as to the resolution of the affair.[4]

Egyptian governors of the first Islamic century often held jurisdiction beyond the borders of the province. Several individuals commissioned or personally led troops to expand the caliphate's western frontier. Such was the case with ʿAbdallāh ibn Saʿd ibn Abī Sarḥ,[5] who led incursions (*ghazawāt* or *gharāt*) on the western frontier and to the south into Nubia. Later, in 41/661, while governor of Egypt, ʿAmr ibn al-ʿĀṣ appointed ʿUqba ibn Nafiʿ over Ifrīqiya (Tunisia).[6] A decade later, after the founding of Qayrawān in 50/670, caliphs assumed the prerogative to appoint governors over that province, which in turn functioned as the new strategic and administrative center for operations on the western front.[7] At several junctures, governors of Egypt gained direct command over adjacent provinces. In 47/667, Maslama ibn Mukhallad was appointed over the *ṣalāt* and *kharāj* of Egypt and the Maghrib,[8] and in 133/750, Abū ʿAwn ʿAbd al-Malik ibn Yazīd controlled even more territories when he was appointed over the *ṣalāt* and *kharāj* of Egypt, Palestine, and Ifrīqiya.[9]

Repeatedly, the Umayyads found it convenient to appoint a governor over both *ṣalāt* and *kharāj*, though the ʿAbbāsids typically separated the two functions: giving the same individual the ability to command and pay soldiers is always dangerous.[10] When the office of *ṣāḥib al-kharāj* was not conferred upon the *wālī*, the caliph made a separate appointment. The officeholder (also called *al-ʿāmil*, from ἀμαλίτης) had great latitude in setting tax rates, along with numerous opportunities for personal gain. This is abundantly clear from an oft-quoted remark attributed to ʿAmr ibn al-ʿĀṣ. When the Caliph ʿUthmān removed ʿAmr from this post in 24/645, appointing him over the army (*ʿalā al-ḥarb*) and entrusting ʿAbdallāh ibn Saʿd over the *kharāj*, ʿAmr objected: "That would be as though I were holding the horns of a cow while another milked it".[11] ʿAmr knew full well that his new assignment would force him to undertake all the labor and risk, while depriving him of the rewards of the prosperous province he subdued.

As the *ṣāḥib al-kharāj* demonstrated competence and gained the trust of the caliph, he became a permanent fixture of the bureaucracy, providing stability and continuity in fiscal matters even in periods of political flux or discord. The career of ʿUbayd Allāh ibn al-Ḥabḥāb aptly demonstrates the prestige of this office. Shortly after his appointment in 105/724, during the governorship of al-Ḥurr ibn Yūsuf,[12] a feud erupted between the two officials. ʿUbayd Allāh pressed the caliph, who implicitly trusted him, to remove the *wālī*;[13] thus, al-Ḥurr was ousted and Ḥāfṣ ibn al-Walīd (earlier appointed by al-Ḥurr as *ṣāḥib al-shurṭa*) was appointed governor. Still, ʿUbayd Allāh was disgruntled; he sent another letter to the caliph protesting: "You have not deposed al-Ḥurr if you appoint Ḥāfṣ".[14] The caliph responded by promptly removing Ḥāfṣ, but rather than appointing another *wālī*, he opted to delegate that prerogative to ʿUbayd Allāh.

The career of ʿUbayd Allāh ibn al-Ḥabḥāb demonstrates the power wielded by a trusted *ṣāḥib al-kharāj* as well as the interpersonal dynamics that often caused administrative reorganization (even chaos) in early Islamic Egypt.[15] ʿUbyad Allāh served alongside four governors, two of whom were removed and another appointed at his sole discretion. This is perhaps the greatest testimony to the influence and attractiveness of the post.[16]

Appointing a general to the third post, that of *ṣāḥib al-shurṭa*, constituted the first formal act of an incoming governor, though, on occasion, that office and its responsibilities were appended to those of the governor or the *ṣāḥib al-kharāj*.[17] Prominent throughout the first four centuries of Islamic rule, this office was marginalized in subsequent eras.[18] Chiefly, it functioned as an extension of the governor's peacekeeping duties.[19] On at least six occasions, a *ṣāḥib al-shurṭa* eventually advanced to the governorship,[20] which is not surprising given that the officeholder functioned in a capacity similar to a lieutenant governor. When a governor traveled abroad or passed away, the *ṣāḥib al-shurṭa* temporarily assumed his responsibilities.[21] As with the office of *ṣāḥib al-kharāj*, individuals and even families would come to monopolize this post over successive gubernatorial administrations. Often translated as "police," the *shurṭa* had responsibilities and prerogatives atypical of any modern police force. They were, as E. Tyan had keenly observed, first and foremost a military regiment, whose agents had the right to pursue and detain suspects as well as to charge, judge, and punish offenders for civil, criminal, and moral crimes.[22] Consequently, the function and jurisdiction of the *shurṭa* overlapped with those of the *wālī* and the *qāḍī*, particularly under Umayyad rule. The day-to-day policing of rural districts remains little understood, though "soldiers"—some of whom were Christians—and prisons may be cited in Greek, Coptic, and Arabic papyri.[23]

The *ṣāḥib al-shurṭa*'s chief responsibility was to maintain order, though his exact jurisdiction fluctuated from one period to another. Primarily, the officeholder was charged with keeping the peace in urban centers, but if need be, he was expected to competently command an army.[24] Administratively, the *shurṭa* was divided into two divisions: *al-shurṭa al-'ulya* and *al-shurṭa al-asfal*, each responsible for its respective region of the Delta.[25] At one point, Alexandria had its own *ṣāḥib al-shurṭa*, though it is unclear how long that office persisted, or if it was replicated elsewhere in the province.[26]

A *wālī* and his *ṣāḥib al-shurṭa* shared a dynamic relationship influenced by several factors, not least of which was popularity among the local troops.[27] Typically, the *wālī* had complete control over this post, retaining and dismissing appointees at will (or whim);[28] reciprocally, the *ṣāḥib al-shurṭa* served as a loyal proponent and spokesman for the governor.[29] At several junctures, however, the prerogative to appoint and dismiss existed only in theory.[30] As a few clans, especially from the Fahm tribe, dominated this post in Egypt, the process became somewhat mechanical; governors came and went, but the same individual(s) were appointed and reappointed to the office. To some extent, this dynamic demonstrates the entrenched power of regional military elites in opposition to the authority of appointed officials, which were increasingly selected from abroad.

The importance of the office is especially evident in the careers of two individuals. Maslama ibn Mukhallad appointed ʿĀbis ibn Saʿīd al-Murādī as *ṣāḥib al-shurṭa* in 49/669, a post he occupied until his death in 78/697. ʿĀbis, who undoubtedly secured the allegiance of the troops of Fusṭāṭ, became a constant fixture serving alongside four governors: Maslama ibn Mukhallad al-Anṣārī, Saʿīd ibn Yazīd al-Azdī, ʿAbd al-Raḥmān ibn ʿUtba ibn Jaḥdam, and ʿAbd al-ʿAzīz ibn

Marwān. His tenure is also noteworthy in that for sixteen years (starting in 61/681) he was concurrently appointed over the *quḍāt*.[31] Other individuals combined these two responsibilities during their careers as well,[32] though ʿĀbis' tenure provides the greatest testimony for the blurring of lines between the functions and responsibilities of the *ṣāḥib al-shurṭa* and *al-qāḍī* under Umayyad rule.[33]

Another prominent officeholder, Ḥāfṣ ibn al-Walīd ibn Yūsuf al-Ḥaḍramī, served alongside two governors. A three-year appointment as *ṣāḥib al-shurṭa* provided Ḥāfṣ with the recognition that later enabled him to ingratiate himself into the position of *wālī* on three separate occasions: first, for a very short appointment in 108/727, then again in 124/742—an appointment that was conferred upon him by three successive caliphs—and, finally, he served a third term in 127/745.[34]

As may be discerned from the above discussion, the final post, the *qāḍī* (pl. *quḍāt*), took some time to mature.[35] Perennially translated as "judge," the *qāḍī*, strictly speaking, had jurisdiction only in religious matters, which in an Islamic context extends to issues of marriage and divorce, inheritance, and the administration of charitable foundations (*al-awqāf*). The office is portrayed as one that predated the rise of Islam (conflating it with the *ḥakam*). Hence, Kaʿb ibn Ḍinnā, appointed *qāḍī* for two months in 23/644, is said to have served in that same capacity during the *jāhiliyya*.[36] Still, Ibn ʿAbd al-Ḥakam and al-Kindī document officeholders only as far as the conquest.[37] Three phases of development are discernible.[38] From the conquests until the 720s CE, the *qāḍī* should be equated with his pre-Islamic counterpart, *al-ḥakam*, who functioned in the capacity of an arbitrator more than that of a judge *per se*.[39] During this initial phase, the officeholder functioned as a legal consultant or deputy (*nā'ib*) to the local governor (and on occasion, even to the *ṣāḥib al-shurṭa*), who often selected him from among the elders of the province. As a result, the *quḍāt* of this early period were dependent upon, and deferential to, local officials and concerns, but not necessarily to the Caliph's prerogatives.[40] During this early period, local custom (*'urf* or *'āda*) and a *qāḍī*'s opinion (*ra'y*) exercised the greatest influence.

Under the Umayyads, individuals appointed to the office were ordinarily selected from among the men of the province, chosen primarily for their sense of justice and religious piety.[41] Perhaps the most salient example is Sulaym ibn ʿIṭr, whose most outstanding quality as a judge was that he purportedly recited the whole Qur'ān three times every night.[42] Beginning in the late Umayyad period, however, increased specialization and, under the ʿAbbāsids, adherence to established schools of jurisprudence took precedence.

The last decades of Umayyad rule ushered in a second phase, the office of the *qāḍī* proper. Increasingly, officeholders were selected from abroad, and were either *fuqahā'* or specialists in *ḥadīth*.[43] This trend came to full maturity during the third phase, under the early ʿAbbāsids, when all *quḍāt* were specialists in *sharīʿa*, and appointed directly by the caliph not local governors. Consequently, the *quḍāt* increasingly focused on adherence to concepts of justice rather than local politics or a governor's will, though they still had to take the Caliph's prerogatives in mind. It was not until the fifth/eleventh century that the *qāḍī* became regarded as a representative of the community. As may be expected, increased specialization among the *quḍāt* paralleled the maturation of Islamic jurisprudence and the codification of *ḥadīth* literature.[44]

A *qāḍī* functioned as a judge, in a civic sense, as well as a religious scholar; he was an *ʿālim*, whose judgments, at least in theory, were not based on civil law or precedent but on the *sharīʿa* (a clear contrast to the first stage).[45] From the third/ninth century, Egyptian *quḍāt* adjudicated in accordance with the dominant schools of jurisprudence, most prominent among which in Egypt were the Mālikī and Shāfiʿī *madhhab*s.[46] The ʿAbbāsids were the first to appoint a Chief Justice, *qāḍī al-quḍāt*, for the caliphate,[47] an office later duplicated in Egypt by the Fāṭimids, under whom Egyptian jurists had recourse to their own Chief Justice independent of Baghdad.

The *qāḍī* would come to play a vital social role for all Egyptians: Muslim and Christian. Earlier, local bishops and *lashane* performed some duties of the office, particularly in judging or mediating among litigants (see the discussion of rural elites below). That said, one would be in error to carry the comparison too far. Bishops were bound by the Gospel and by local custom. (Unlike Syria, canon law does not seem to have played much of a role in Egypt during the first three centuries under Islamic rule.) The *quḍāt*, on the other hand, were increasingly bound by complex traditions of jurisprudence and schools of interpretation. Furthermore, their judgments were subject to an increasingly formal appeals process that would reach maturity in the Grievance (*maẓālim*) Courts of the ʿAbbāsids.[48] In theory, a bishop's judgment and punishment (especially excommunication) could be challenged in a bi-annual synod in Alexandria, but it is uncertain how long that practice was maintained or if such councils convened at all under Islamic rule.

In general, while these four corners of the provincial administration coalesced under Umayyad rule, they lacked a clear separation of duties. It was an era of official and *de facto* overlapping of responsibilities and functions, as is well illustrated by the duties of the *ṣāḥib al-shurṭa*, which encroached upon those of the *wālī* and the *qāḍī* into the second Islamic century. With the ʿAbbāsids came the maturing of these offices and a formal separation of duties, which was in part due to increased bureaucratic specialization and the founding of the major schools of jurisprudence.

Administrative Dynasties

Of the large number of individuals who served in one capacity or another in the bureaucracy, a few families were able to establish administrative dynasties that became increasingly nepotistic over time (see Chapter Three). Prominent families in the first/seventh century tended to come from (or identify with) the Yamanī faction; historically, many of the Arabs who accompanied ʿAmr ibn al-ʿĀṣ at the time of the conquest appear to have come from the southern region of the peninsula (the Egyptian pronunciation of the jīm as /g/ may attest to that). The Qays, though represented, were vastly outnumbered until the immigrations of the early second century. Internal feuding among leading Yamanī families and a political realignment orchestrated by the Caliph ʿAbdallāh provided an opportunity for the Qaysīs to exploit. Once they gained administrative appointments, the Qaysīs began to exercise a degree of political authority starkly disproportionate to their numerical strength in the province. Cognizant of this problem, they used their newly acquired clout, which was particularly prominent under the Caliph Hishām, to orchestrate a Qaysī immigration to Miṣr. Thus, their political might came to rest upon a more tenable demographic constituency.

Of the administrative dynasties that emerged, the first family of note belonged to the Tujīb tribe. Sulaymān ibn ʿAmr al-Tujībī, appointed over the *kharāj* in 35/655, was the first member of the family to hold office.[49] As may be inferred from the early date of Sulaymān's appointment, the Tujīb came to Egypt along with the initial wave of conquerors under ʿAmr ibn al-ʿĀṣ. Although the tribe's early history is obscure, some clans appear to have been adversely affected by the policies of the Caliph ʿUthmān.[50] Of the six hundred-man Egyptian delegation dispatched to Medina, which eventually assassinated the caliph, a Tujībī, Kinanā ibn Bishr ibn Salāman, led one hundred men.[51] Presumably, at that early date when tribal solidarity still dominated, all the men Kinanā led were Tujībīs. After the caliph's assassination, the clan became embroiled in the resulting feuds of the first *fitna*, which eventually led to the rise of the Umayyads.

Following this incident, several Tujībīs held posts under the Sufyānids and early Marwānids.[52] But by 90/709, some members of the family again felt disenfranchised when, in an attempt to rid the bureaucracy of all traces of his uncle's administration, the Caliph ʿAbdallāh ibn ʿAbd al-Malik ousted a number of Tujībīs and replaced them with Qaysīs. A few years later, the governor Qurra ibn Sharīk (himself a Qaysī) propagated the trend by appointing Qaysīs to prominent posts, thus sparking al-Muhajir ibn Abī al-Muthannī al-Tujībī's revolt in Alexandria.[53] Bloodily suppressed, the revolt no doubt left a blemish on the family's name. Nonetheless, various Tujībīs were still able to secure top administrative posts, though not for another decade.[54]

In the twilight of the first Islamic century, members of the Fahm clan, the chief representatives of the Qays in Egypt at that point, were appointed to the post of *ṣāḥib al-shurṭa*. The first, ʿAbd al-Aʿalī ibn Khālid ibn Thābit ibn Ẓaʿīn al-Fahmī, was appointed by ʿAbdallāh ibn ʿAbd al-Malik in the wake of the above-referenced administrative purge. He was reappointed to the post by a fellow Qaysī, Qurra ibn Sharīk. Later, when ʿAbd al-Aʿalī died in office, he was replaced by his cousin, ʿAbd al-Malik ibn Rifāʿa ibn Khālid ibn Thābit [ibn Ẓaʿīn] al-Fahmī.[55] In 96/715 ʿAbd al-Malik vacated his post to become the *wālī* and immediately appointed his brother, al-Walīd, as *ṣāḥib al-shurṭa*. Thus, between the two brothers, the Fahms—and by extension the Qaysīs—had control over the *ṣalāt*, the *kharāj* (ʿAbd al-Malik was appointed over both), and the *shurṭa* of Egypt. Qaysī domination was short-lived however. There might have been a falling out between the brothers, or the fact that a single Qaysī family dominated the administration may have attracted resentment. Whatever the cause, al-Walīd was relieved of his duties in 97/716 and ʿAbd al-Malik left office two years later in 99/718, but would serve a second term in 109/728.[56] Upon his death, the Caliph Hishām named ʿAbd al-Malik's brother, al-Walīd, as *wālī*,[57] and in keeping with the earlier pattern, he, too, appointed one relative after another as *ṣāḥib al-shurṭa*.[58] At the end of his tenure, al-Walīd yielded the governorship to another Fahmī, ʿAbd al-Raḥmān ibn Khālid ibn Musāfir al-Fahmī. And, predictably, a relative, ʿAbdallāh ibn Yasar al-Fahmī, was appointed *ṣāḥib al-shurṭa*.

The prominence of the Fahms coincided with ʿUbayd Allāh ibn al-Ḥabḥāb's tenure as *ṣāḥib al-kharāj*. Thus, while the Fahms controlled the offices of *wālī* and *ṣāḥib al-shurṭa*, a fellow Qaysī provided uninterrupted administration of the *dīwān*. During that juncture of Qaysī political dominance, ʿUbayd Allāh requested the immigration of Qaysī tribesmen to the province, thus bolstering their numerical strength in the province.

The practice of appointing family members to the post of *ṣāḥib al-shurṭa* had two inherent advantages. Obviously it cultivated family loyalty. Secondly, as mentioned above, the post provided the officeholder with public recognition and command of an armed force;

the officeholder had to be an individual whom the governor could trust implicitly. Hence, the phenomenon of appointing family members to this key (potentially dangerous) post may be viewed as an attempt at self-preservation as much as a demonstration of the normative nepotistic tendencies rampant in nearly all circles—political and religious—in Islamic Egypt.[59] As demonstrated in the earlier discussion of Christian elites, a similar pattern persisted at the lower ranks of the bureaucracy as familial ties and inter-personal networks enabled individual families to monopolize administrative posts.

Rural Elites

Outside the urban centers of the Delta, it is unlikely that the average individual ever came in direct contact with any of the officials mentioned above,[60] which constituted the top tier of an administrative bureaucracy that, until the early eighth century, oversaw five eparchies and nearly sixty pagarchies. The documentary papyri suggest that through the tenth century CE a typical villager would have been best acquainted with a handful of local officials.

Local Christian elites governed most villages and rural districts in Egypt for nearly eighty years after the conquest.[61] These individuals are identified in the papyri by several designations: ⲗⲁϣⲁⲛⲉ/μείζονες/*mazūt*, ⲁⲡⲉ, διοικητής, πρωτοκωμῆται/ⲡⲛⲟϭ ⲛ̄ⲣⲱⲙⲓ (likely village elders/leaders), and πρωτεύοντες.[62] The exact function of these rural elites is not entirely clear—mostly due to a lack of specialization—and, especially for purposes of tax assessment and collection, their roles often overlapped with the duties of several administratively appointed tax officials, such as the ζυγοστάτης (*al-qusṭāl*), ὑποδέκτης, ϣⲁⲗⲓⲟⲩ, and *al-jahbadh*,[63] many of whom were also Christians.[64] Villagers annually elected the *lashane* who could serve consecutive terms.[65] Typically, two individuals were appointed each term, but *P.KRU* 42, dated 725-6 CE, indicates that four individuals held the office in that year. Papyri and ostraca often depict such men in quasi-governmental roles, as "judges" and mediators among villagers.[66] Predominantly, these rural elites represented their villages (and, at times, nearby monasteries) to local magistrates and the governor, aided in assessing the tax liability of individual villagers, and oversaw the collection and payment of taxes to the *dīwān*.[67]

This began to change in 99/718 when Muslim agents began to replace local Coptic elites.[68] To gain insight into one of the aspects that motivated this transition, it is crucial to peruse the administrative papyri of the late seventh and early eighth century CE, in particular the Papas archive (*P.Apoll.*, ca. 660s CE) and the Aphrodito papyri (*P.Lond.*IV, ca. 710s CE).[69] In general, even a casual reading of *P.Apoll.* or *P.Lond.*IV cannot but emphasize the dysfunctional nature of the relationship between the provincial center and the periphery.[70] The Aphrodito correspondences—*P.Lond.* IV.1333 to 1406—from the governor (σύμβουλος) Qurra ibn Sharīk to Basilios the local magistrate (διοικήτη) are particularly revealing.[71] They provide a glimpse not only into the interactions of these two officials, but, more generally, of the difficulties the central government encountered in dealing with a provincial administrator over a seven-year period (89-95/708-14). A significant number of letters request the delivery of various items or back taxes, or the fulfillment of duties that were already long overdue despite repeated requests. Taxes in kind or in gold appear to have been consistently delayed or lacking.[72] Qurra found this particularly troubling: "the first duty of the official is the collection of public taxes".[73] Consequently, in the majority of the correspondence Qurra threatens Basilios with everything from the loss of his position, to physical harm and imprisonment for his dereliction of duties.[74] Yet, despite the menacing tone of many of the letters, the only recorded consequence inflicted upon Basilios was a single fine.

This is open to several interpretations. The first might be that Qurra's words were meant only to intimidate; still, Qurra's resolve should not be easily dismissed. When provoked, the governor did not hesitate to shed blood.[75] More likely, this reflects Qurra's inability to exert his will over long distances without great effort; the difficulties involved likely increased the farther south one traveled from Fusṭāṭ and the Delta. At a minimum, these letters demonstrate Basilios' ability to mitigate, perhaps even defy the governor at Fusṭāṭ. At most, they document an attitude of indifference on behalf of regional Christian magistrates vis-à-vis the central government.

Tax evasion, a persistent and well-documented phenomenon in Egypt under Roman, Byzantine, and Arab rule, figures prominently in these archives. This led the Arab regime to restrict movement in the countryside; hence, the populace had to secure "passports" whenever they traveled away from their districts.[76] In his day, Qurra attempted to address the problem by deputizing special agents to register tax fugitives and bring them, their families, and their possessions to justice.[77] The populace learned of the edicts through public readings in parish churches.[78] Whistle-blowers would be financially rewarded, while those who harbored fugitives were described as having disregard for their own lives, and warned that they would be so ill-treated that they would "envy the dead".[79] The problem Qurra faced was not simply that Basilios refused to cooperate, but that the villagers themselves defiantly concealed fugitives. Such insubordination does not appear to have been exclusive to Aphrodito, but was a widespread phenomenon, also documented in the Papas archive.

Given the likelihood that Qurra could not readily exercise his authority beyond the Delta, the widespread passive resistance evident in the fugitive problem, and the sloth with which Papas and, later, Basilios performed their duties, the Islamic government's 99/718 decision to replace Coptic village notables with Muslim agents (accompanied by a retinue of Arabs or *mawālī*) is hardly surprising. Muslim agents enabled the governor at Fusṭāṭ to exert his will in remote locations with little more than a letter. Hence, the collection and shipping of taxes in kind or coin would be more efficient, and tax fugitives would find it much more difficult to elude capture. In 99/718 the government took a pragmatic step toward tighter fiscal and administrative control of the province in response to non-compliant and passive-aggressive Coptic administrators. Implementation of this monumental policy further reinforced the centralizing policies inaugurated a few decades earlier by the Caliph ʿAbd al-Malik ibn Marwān. This reform constituted the first major administrative change in Egypt since the initial decades after the conquest; through its implementation the Arab-Muslim bureaucracy extended into all levels of the rural infrastructure and inevitably undermined the standing of local officials, such as the *lashane.*

Increasingly, as Islam spread, another official began to emerge prominently in the papyrological record, participating in a host of unofficial duties: the *mu'adhdhin*. In addition to his primary responsibility of reciting prayers and the Qur'ān at the local mosque, the *mu'adhdhin* appears in papyrus documents as a scribe as well as an official witness to contracts.[80] Significantly, the non-religious duties of the local *mu'adhdhin* closely resembled those of Christian priests and deacons from late antiquity through the eleventh century CE (as well as those of the *ape* and *lashane*).[81]

The history of rural elites is the history of an evolving administrative apparatus. Early governmental policies were fundamentally geared toward greater fiscal and administrative control of the province, which was initially achieved by reappointing pre-conquest personnel, then by favoring Coptic notables (see Chapter Three), and finally by replacing local Coptic officials with Arab Muslims. Each initiative served the same purposes: greater political centralization and tighter fiscal control of the province. The offices and personnel addressed thus far constituted a hybrid administrative infrastructure comprised of government-appointed and community-elected individuals, performing a host of official and unofficial duties. This provides an important backdrop for the following analysis, which is focused on governance and justice.

Legislative and Communal "Autonomy"

Within the spectrum of studies that examine the history and social interactions of Christians and Jews living under Islamic rule, there exists a limited but rich literature focused on the issues of legislative and communal autonomy.[82] For the most part, the conclusions of those who have carefully studied this topic, most notably Fattal and Edelby,[83] are overwhelmingly positive. Indeed, non-Muslim communities enjoyed a significant degree of autonomy under the early caliphate. Still, whereas Edelby, in particular, understood his work as an important first step, his conclusions have been read with an air of finality. Here, the aim is to refine the discussion, particularly in terms of the dominant methodology employed and the historical issues investigated.

Before introducing the methodological issues at hand, however, a few words on nomenclature are in order. The heading of this section needed to identify the issue addressed and the historiography engaged in accordance with established precedence, hence the use of "autonomy". Nonetheless, the term is regrettable. "Autonomy" presumes a degree of independence and self-governance never fully realized by any *dhimmī* community; additionally, the term promotes a conceptually flawed paradigm that presents society as a mosaic of communities where cultural boundaries and political status are distinct and clearly delineated, which was not the historical state of affairs.

Typically, the discussion of "autonomy" draws heavily upon texts and conclusions stemming from East and West Syrian canon law, which are then extrapolated to reflect practice in less-documented regions of the caliphate.[84] This is a logical, though not necessarily cogent methodological step. Here, the regional focus on Egypt aims at greater precision, but quickly encounters a lack of sources. Edelby had long noted this problem, but his analysis often interprets a general lack of historical data as the absence of evidence to the contrary.[85]

Nonetheless, superimposing the socio-political environment of the Syrian tradition, particularly that of the East Syrians, onto Egypt is a flawed enterprise. Since the late fifth century CE, Sasanid emperors had officially recognized the Church of the East and granted it a civil jurisdiction over its constituents. Thus, diverse communal issues, including marriage and inheritance, came under the control of the East Syrian ecclesiastical hierarchy. This important precedent is without parallel in Egypt.[86] Even in the midst of sectarian squabbles stemming from the Chalcedonian schism, the empire never recognized the Copts as a separate "other," nor did they conceive of themselves as such until the ninth century (see Chapters Two and Nine).

The exceptional status enjoyed by Syrian Christians (and Jews) under Sasanian rule engendered new communal prerogatives. Syrian hierarches felt obliged to provide concrete communal guidelines—nomocanons—that would maintain order; hence, the development of East and West Syrian legislative traditions. Both relied upon the so-called *Syro-Roman Lawbook* and a host of canon laws that were passed by regional synods throughout the late antique and early Islamic era.[87] Thus, despite the turmoil of the Arab conquests and the end of Sasanid rule, it would appear that, for the most part, Syrian Christians survived under early Islamic rule much as they did under late Sasanid Shahs.[88]

Again, Egypt lacks any parallels. From the mid-seventh century until the tenth—theoretically the greatest period of "autonomy" for the Copts—the ecclesiastical hierarchy did not compose a single nomocanon. The omission is glaring. Egyptian Christian literature lacks any early allusions to judicial or communal autonomy; canon laws did not address social concerns, Coptic patriarchs did not issue laws or edicts that pertained to the social welfare of their community, and aside from general manuals and works that focus on the whole caliphate, there is no trace of independent or distinct Christian or *dhimmī* courts in Egypt under early Islamic rule.

By the ninth century, while Syrian Christians could draw upon distinct nomocanons (*Synodicon*), the Copts lacked an officially sanctioned law code. It was not until the tenth century that compilations analogous to the *Synodicon* were first drafted, and even then, the more thorough collections, such as the *nomocanon* of Ibn Turayk and the *Majmu'* of al-Ṣafī ibn al-'Assāl, did not emerge until the twelfth and thirteenth centuries.[89] Significantly, lacking any Coptic antecedent or precedent to draw upon, Egyptian *nomocanons* were compiled by sampling four founts: patristic and pseudo-patristic canons, Byzantine law codes (particularly the *Ekloga*),[90] Talmudic, and Islamic law. Consequently, Egyptian *nomocanons* are somewhat artificial, encompassing laws and regulations that had never held sway in the province: for example, the regulations pertaining to the deaconesses, whose order never existed in Alexandria (or Rome) prior to the modern period.[91]

In sum, there is no positive proof to support the notion that the Coptic hierarchy held an official responsibility for the social or legislative life of its community from the seventh through the tenth centuries CE. The remainder of this study investigates the nature of the privileges extended to the Christian population of Egypt, the erosion thereof, and the communal mechanism for adjudication and recourse that sustained the population in the absence of community-sanctioned laws.

Origins and Erosion of "Autonomy"

Past scholarship has been fairly idealistic and, occasionally, anachronistic in its assessment of *dhimmī* communal autonomy. S.D. Goitein has explained the phenomenon as a reflection of the caliphate's minimalist approach to government. For his part, A. Fattal preferred to explore the issue in terms of *liberté* ("liberty" or "freedom") rather than "autonomy," which he believed stemmed from the Caliphate's legal understanding of *dhimmā* as a contractual agreement between Muslims and non-Muslims living in *dār al-Islam*. On the other hand, N. Edelby noted that communal autonomy was but a natural outgrowth of Islamic law. In Islam, the inexorable link between community, religion, and law, he argued, made it impossible for non-Muslims to live under the jurisdiction of the *Sharīʿa* without converting to Islam. He further reiterates that just as early Muslims did not force *dhimmīs* to convert to Islam, they would not have forced them to accept Islamic jurisprudence, which is predicated upon the Qur'ānic revelation. In this manner, Edelby argued for the existence of an uncompromised autonomy that persisted throughout the Umayyad period and under early ʿAbbasid rule. The historical and methodological problems embedded in that perspective are many. Minimally, the analysis is anachronistic in its understanding of seventh-century Islamic "law".

On the whole, the scholarship surveyed lacks a certain pragmatic element. Simply stated, the new conquerors were numerically marginal (initially, even insignificant) to the populations they governed. They lacked sufficient personnel, an infrastructure, and a sense of "law" that surpassed the concrete examples derived from

Qur'ānic passages or those that were normative within each tribe. In this light, the decision to grant communal autonomy to the numerical majority appears to have been born of necessity rather than a sense of piety or ideology. Similarly, this same dynamic forced the early conquerors to adopt Byzantine and Sasanian pre-conquest administrative bureaucracies, practices, and even personnel with minimal or no change. Thus, a unique period of *de facto* communal autonomy, stemming from necessity and the ambivalence of the first generation of conquerors toward the populations they governed, lasted in Egypt from the conquest until the caliphate of ʿAbd al-Malik ibn Marwān (685–705 CE). Incrementally thereafter, as the Islamic government and community consolidated their hegemonic hold on the province, the communal—and even religious—liberties enjoyed by non-Muslims steadily eroded.

The Islamic government's involvement in Coptic patriarchal elections marked the erosion of one aspect of communal autonomy (see Chapter Nine). The first elections under Islamic rule, those of Agathon I and John III, did not interest or involve the government.[92] It was with the election of Isaac I (686 CE) that the administration took an interest, and became actively involved in the process. After several delays, the governor ʿAbd al-ʿAzīz ibn Marwan summoned the entire electoral synod and the two leading candidates, and he: "ordered the elevation of Isaac, and this matter was from God".[93] With this incident, ʿAbd al-ʿAzīz set a precedent. Similar interference in electoral proceedings is documented in the election of Isaac's successor, Simon I, as well as a host of later patriarchs (see Chapter Ten).

A second reform, discussed earlier in this chapter, led to the erosion of the internal independence of Christian villages, not just ecclesiastical elites. For decades after the conquest, many villagers learned of their tax liability en bloc and internally levied taxes as they saw fit. In 99/718, however, an administrative reform replaced Coptic officials in rural districts with Muslim personnel, positioning the entire Egyptian countryside under much greater scrutiny.[94] This reform inevitably weakened local notables, such as the *lashane*, and eroded the independence that villages had enjoyed since the conquest (see Chapter Six).

Authority and Recourse in Coptic Villages

Having defined the period of the greatest degree of communal independence and the beginnings of its erosion, the focus now shifts to the social structures that maintained order in the late antique and early Islamic Egyptian village. The key to understanding the social dynamic that persisted from the sixth through the ninth centuries lies in studying a phenomenon that prevailed throughout that same period: a sharp decline in formal litigation. Under Byzantine rule, arbitration gained acceptance as a legitimate means for settling disputes; hence, documentation for official litigation declined sharply. By the ninth and tenth centuries CE, however, official lawsuits again prevailed.[95] This phenomenon, along with the intricacies of "Coptic law," has occupied scholars for over a century.[96]

In *Settling a Dispute*, T. Gagos and P. van Minnen proposed three explanations to account for the lack of litigation and the rise of this peculiar phenomenon.[97] They noted that private settlement provided a safe and inexpensive means of settling grievances compared to going to court, and that arbitration ensured minimal gain for the party with the weaker claim.[98] Alone, however, these two rationales cannot fully explain the trend since even litigants standing on a solid legal footing and of high social standing preferred to settle their disputes privately.[99] The third explanation, which the editors believe to have been the catalyst behind the phenomenon, is that decline in litigation was a direct result of the Christianization of Egypt. It is thus the: "New Testament influence (on) the moral universe of late antique Egyptians".[100]

While the factors mentioned thus far certainly played a role, arguably, the transfer of legal and moral authority from civil servants to Christian clergy and holy men constituted the imperative catalyst that led to a decline in litigation. This socio-religious shift provided for the development of social mechanisms that were equipped to replace political institutions. This was, indeed, a byproduct of the Christianization of Egypt, but more specifically, the genesis of a specific socio-political venue for the private adjudication of disputes. Christian clergy and holy men provided the population with a convenient and trusted means to redress social and economic grievances. They wielded a spiritual capital that readily translated into the social ability to persuade and coerce. Nonetheless, on occasion sincere religious beliefs also guided the resolution of disputes. In *P.Mon.Epiph.*264, a man unilaterally annulled a contract that he believed unfairly favored him, stating: "I have reflected, with God's guidance, that (this contract) is contrary to what is just".[101]

These rural loci of authority and recourse are readily enumerated in seventh- and eighth-century papyri. Although there are some examples of villagers taking their grievances to a regional *pagarch* or the governor at Fusṭāṭ, most disputes were addressed locally through the intervention of *lashane* (or *ape*) and/or religious figures.[102] Proceedings were typically informal, at times convened in the monastic cell of a trusted monk (as per *P.Mon.Epiph.*88, quoted below), but on occasion, the proceedings resembled a trial by jury, in which village notables and clergy heard the dispute.

*P.CLT.*1, a contract dated 70/689, provides a paradigmatic map for the perspectives of average individuals. Near the end of the document, the plaintiff swears: "Unto every holy magistrate, whether God-fearing bishop or God-fearing judge, who shall examine this document".[103] While the *dikastēs*, or judge, is most likely the *pagarch*[104]—which would indicate a formal means of resolving the grievance—it is clear that at the end of the seventh century CE, local officials (*lashane*), along with clergy and monks, collaborated to settle disputes.[105] The *lashane*, who were annually elected, boasted a consensus of support among the villagers, though they lacked an official means for enforcing agreements.[106] Bishops, on the other hand, while sharing the same limitation, had tremendous moral and spiritual clout, as long as villages remained predominantly Christian.

The above-mentioned contract includes punitive clauses for those who would challenge the agreement: "Above all, if one of my children or my heirs ... should dare [to transgress this agreement], primarily this one shall not benefit any thereby but first he shall be estranged from the holy oath that serves him, the Father and the Son and the Holy Spirit, and you shall subject him to the fearful tribunal of Christ to be judged for this action, and he shall suffer the lot of Ananias and Sapphira, and he shall suffer the lot of Judas".[107] The repercussions were spiritual and financial: penalties that the Christian clergy, particularly bishops and holy men, were in a unique position to inflict. Such attitudes survived into the late tenth century CE. In *P. Ryl.Copt.*267, from the tenth or eleventh century CE, a widow who had been a victim of theft had a suspect in mind and sought the aid of her local bishop, who adjured the suspect to confess his crime by threatening him with spiritual punishments that echo those just quoted.

Documents from the Monastery of Epiphanios at Thebes provide an especially rich illustration of this prevailing dynamic. Papyrus 88 describes the resolution of a dispute resolved through the aid of a monastic figure: "We went to law one with the other and we came to agreement one with the other, at the dwelling of Apa Elias, son of Kalapese; and he brought us to agreement one with the other, in everything that was between us ... I have no other business with thee. ... I, Jacob, [wrote with my] hand and do assent thereunto." Cooperation among official and informal loci of power characterized rural life in Egypt. *P.Mon.Epiph.*151 and 163 are noteworthy in this regard; they are letters from a *lashane* asking a monk to mediate in various disputes. Similar requests for the aid of Christian monks and clerics in resolving village quarrels are fairly common.[108] Significantly, some of these arbitration cessions were somewhat formal, with the cooperation of the litigants guaranteed in writing before the actual meeting (e.g. *O.Crum.* 43, 86, and 295).

Through the early Islamic centuries, monastics, priests, and deacons were routinely involved in recording and witnessing contracts, settlements, and agreements,[109] but by roughly the third/ninth century, clergy were seldom involved in such activities. (Although in some locals, such as Teshlot, the practice continued into the fifth/eleventh century.[110]) By that juncture, Islamic jurisprudence dictated the requirements of a valid contract, one which a Muslim *qāḍī* (or a local *shaykh*) would recognize as binding. Most importantly, contracts had to be written in Arabic and witnessed by Muslims.[111] This new dynamic functioned as a watershed that led to an increase in formal litigation. Proportionally, as Islamic jurisprudence matured and the demographic composition of the countryside began to shift due to Arab immigration and Christian conversion to Islam, the traditional mechanism that adjudicated disputes so efficiently during the seventh and eighth centuries—i.e. *lashane*, local bishop, and holy man—began to lose their social capital.

This trajectory may be traced in documentary papyri, which demonstrate the propensity of Coptic Christians to depend on Islamic jurisprudence even when—strictly speaking—they did not have to. All Arabic contracts, regardless of the religious affiliation of the parties involved, were drawn in accordance with the precepts of Islamic jurisprudence. *P.Cair.Arab.*I.54, 57, and 58 provide examples in which Christians entering into contracts with each other carefully drafted their contracts "in accordance to Islamic law".

Even Arabic-Christian marriage contracts conformed. The similarities between the marriage contracts of Christians and Muslims are astonishing (see Chapter Four). Christian contracts typically lacked the polygamy and divorce clauses found in their Muslim prototypes[112] and omit the instructions to the husband to care for his wife in accordance with the precepts of the Qur'ān and the *sunna* (e.g. *P.Cair.Arab.*I.42.5-6).[113] Apart from those brief omissions, however, the structure and phrasing of Christian and Muslim contracts are identical.

Urban Centers

Despite the fact that most narrative accounts (Christian and Muslim) were written within an urban milieu, the early texts provide precious little evidence as to how urban Christians resolved their quarrels. The issue is further complicated by the dearth of documentary papyri from the Delta for the seventh through tenth centuries. Still, a passage in al-Kindī's *Wulāt* suggests that Christians and Jews grew increasingly dependent upon Islamic courts under ʿAbbāsid rule.[114] A number of factors contributed to this trend, not least of which is that the government recognized the verdict of a *qāḍī* but not that of a bishop, as was the case under Byzantine rule.

Another catalyst is that Christian men had a distinct advantage in seeking a *qāḍī*'s judgment over that of a bishop's on a number of issues, particularly those relating to matters of inheritance and divorce.[115] Finally, communal law codes contained glaring omissions. Neither "Coptic law" nor the later Coptic Arabic *nomocanons* (if they were ever binding) provided anything resembling a comprehensive law code. Hence, much of what might be delegated today under criminal and business law fell within the purview of Islamic jurisprudence from a very early date.[116]

It is difficult to assess the importance and function of the *qāḍī* among urban Christians (or even Muslims) during the thinly documented Umayyad era, but it appears to have been marginal. Second/eighth- and third/ninth-century sources, however, quickly establish the social dominance and importance of Islamic jurisprudence. Al-Kindī provides cursory comments suggesting that Christians became increasingly dependent upon Muslim *quḍāt* over the course of the mid-eighth century; the period in which the office of *qāḍī* reached maturity. He states that after judging among Muslims inside the mosque, the late-Umayyad *qāḍī* Khayr ibn Nuʿaym (120-7/739-45) would sit at the door of the mosque to adjudicate among Christians and Jews.[117] Al-Kindī further stipulates that Khayr would accept the testimony of a "Christian against a Christian, a Jew against a Jew," and that he would inquire after acceptable concepts of justice (*ʿadala*) among the people of their religion. It is important to stress that the *qāḍī* was not adjudicating between members of different faiths or confessions as a neutral third party (as was the case in disputes over churches), but among members of the same religious confession. Thus, by the end of Umayyad rule, the *qāḍī* had become a fixture of Egyptian urban society, an authority in the eyes of Christians, Jews, and Muslims alike.

In subsequent decades, al-Kindī maintains that the *quḍāt* routinely designated a day at their private residence for Christians to seek their services, and by the end of the eighth century CE, Christians were allowed to enter the mosque to seek the advice of the *qāḍī*.[118] Within half a century, urban Christians went from settling their disputes in front of the mosque, to the private homes of *quḍāt*, to the inside of the mosque. The act of consulting a *qāḍī* quite possibly followed a parallel social trajectory among Christians, evolving from a seldom-used last resort,[119] to an acceptable (though clandestine) venture, to a socially normative means of securing justice in the ninth century, the same century in which "Coptic law" began to wane in rural districts.[120]

In sum, communal "autonomy" in Egypt must be addressed apart from other regions of the caliphate. Lacking precedence for self-governance or a distinct law code in the form of a *nomocanon* or the like, Egypt's Christians relied upon late Byzantine legal and social norms that favored informal mechanisms for adjudicating disputes. Increasingly, however, formal litigation, based on Islamic jurisprudence, became normative in all levels of Egyptian society.

Eighth- and ninth-century Egyptian papyri clearly demonstrate the propensity of Coptic Christians to depend on Islamic jurisprudence. All Arabic contracts, regardless of the religious affiliation of the parties involved, were drawn in accordance with the precepts of Islamic law.[121] The only major exceptions are found in Arabic-Christian marriage contracts, which, while omitting clauses pertaining to the keeping of concubines and abiding by the precepts of the Qur'ān and *sunna*, did not append any distinctly Christian verbiage.[122]

CHAPTER 8

METAMORPHOSIS OF THE MUSLIM COMMUNITY

The history of the early Muslim community in Egypt is complex in its narrative, contradictory in its trajectories, and daunting in its historiography.[1] All extant sources for the early period are extremely problematic or incomplete. Even the papyri, which have been used with such efficacy to reconstruct the early fiscal system and administrative apparatus, are often sketchy when pressed for details relating to social interactions, cultural perspectives, and institutions.[2] Nevertheless, there is much that can be gleaned from the historical record, such as it is.

Similar to the previous chapter, the Arab Muslim community is largely the focus here. These are twin chapters, analyzing and documenting analogous cultural transformations from the macro- and micro-perspectives. Hence, while Chapter Seven focused on the evolution of specific offices and the careers of individual administrators, the following discussion tracks larger cultural shifts as the Muslim community transitioned from a tribal society with a palpable martial ethic into agrarian communities. The initial focus is on the Arab community before and after the pivotal career of ʿUbayd Allāh ibn al-Ḥabḥāb (105-15/724-34), during which Arab Muslims first took to agriculture, ushering in a crucial catalyst for socio-political changes that undermined the bonds of tribal solidarity. The discussion then shifts to the new Egyptian society, which matured over the third/ninth and fourth/tenth centuries. Finally, a brief excursion aims to frame the contradictory traditions and activities of Arab pastoralists in Egypt during the early Islamic period.

The First Century

Arabs came to Egypt as merchants and travelers long before the dawning of Islam.[3] One tradition depicts ʿAmr ibn al-ʿĀṣ as one such merchant traveling to Egypt decades before the conquest.[4] It was not until 18/639, however, that the Arabs constituted a military threat to the province. The conquest took well over a year, in part due to the Nile's inundation, which halted Arab advancement for some months. By 20/641, after Alexandria's capitulation, the Arabs claimed Egypt as their domain and quickly moved to establish a military garrison, a *miṣr*, that came to function as a permanent command center: a new capital.

Alexandria was the natural choice. It was the most prestigious city in the newly conquered province, a seat of culture, learning, commerce, and the vanquished Byzantine army, but it would not be chosen. Arabic authors have long explained this oddity in light of a tradition maintaining that the Caliph ʿUmar ibn al-Khaṭṭāb felt uneasy about its location and commanded the conquering general, ʿAmr ibn al-ʿĀṣ, not to allow a body of water to separate the Muslim army from the Holy Cities of Mecca and Medina. This rationale is a topos attested in several other conquest accounts, but more likely Alexandria was passed over as the capital in light of pragmatic military and administrative concerns. Still, the city developed into a prominent frontier fortress that housed as much as a fourth of the Arab army at one point.[5] The city was well fortified, forcing the Byzantines (and later, the crusaders) to increasingly target the less formidable cities (and garrisons) of Dimyattā and Tinnīs. Alexandria also served as a major port of call for merchants from around the Mediterranean and the Islamic navy, which used its ports to equip the annual κοῦρσα/*cursus* (raids against the Byzantines).[6]

The alternative site for the capital rested farther up the Nile, on the east bank of the river, adjacent to the Roman fortress of Babylon

(*Qaṣr al-sham'*). There, ʿAmr pitched a tent (*fusṭāṭ*), which came to designate the new capital.[7] Strategically located at the apex of the Delta, near Memphis, the onetime capital of ancient Egypt, Fusṭāṭ quickly expanded into a sprawling metropolis, particularly under the Marwānids. Nonetheless, the old designation of "Babylon" persisted throughout Umayyad rule, particularly among the Christian population.[8] The construction of a *masjid*, a practical as well as a symbolic act, legitimized the founding of the new settlement.[9] Hence, *Masjid* ʿAmr, as it would be known, served as the geographical and political hub of the Muslim community in Egypt, functionally replacing the late antique *agora* and theater by serving as a meeting space for popular and official gatherings; additionally, it served as the court in which early *wulāt* and *quḍāt* held audience (see Chapter Seven).[10] For Muslims, the mosque quickly became a point of geographic orientation. In describing the *khiṭaṭ*, the land allotments on which the Arabs settled, Ibn ʿAbd al-Ḥakam uses the mosque as the point of orientation, the boundaries of the *khiṭaṭ* radiating out from it.[11] Until the 660s CE, Fusṭāṭ also served as the center of operations for the expanding western frontier of the Islamic empire.

Fusṭāṭ's political dominance remained unchallenged until the tenure of ʿAbd al-ʿAzīz ibn Marwān, who relocated the seat of government fourteen miles south to the town of Ḥulwān.[12] Sources vary as to the impetus for the move. Some note that ʿAbd al-ʿAzīz sought to avoid a plague (*ṭaʿun*) that ravaged Fusṭāṭ at that time (perhaps that mentioned in *P.CLT* 1). Other accounts maintain that the governor had an ailment, which his doctors advised would be less aggravated by the dry climate of Ḥulwān. Whatever the motivation may have been, the city served as the hub of the government for much of ʿAbd al-ʿAzīz's long tenure, but upon his death Fusṭāṭ regained its position as the administrative capital of the province. A subsequent challenge to Fusṭāṭ's prominence came with the ʿAbbāsids, who built a new garrison town adjacent to the city. ʿAskir, however, quickly lost its independent identity as it was physically and conceptually absorbed by the ever-expanding Fusṭāṭ. Not until the founding of Fāṭimid Cairo (*al-Qāhira*) did the preeminence of Fusṭāṭ begin to wane, but even then, that process took centuries, allowing for the two "cities" to incrementally merge into a single geographic entity.

Throughout the first Islamic century, Arabs in the Peninsula were encouraged to emigrate, to make a *hijra*, to *amṣār* (military garrisons) throughout the caliphate. The majority complied and became known as *muhājirūn*, or "emigrants": the designation applied earlier to the Meccan supporters of the Prophet Muḥammad who accompanied him to Medina. The esteem held for these later *muhājirūn* was proportional to the distance they had traveled: the farther the garrison they emigrated to, the more pious and devout they were believed to have been, and the higher the stipend they were allocated under the early *dīwān* system.[13] Conversely, those who remained in the peninsula, the *a'rāb*, were viewed as uncultured, uncivilized individuals and were discriminated against.[14]

In Egypt, most of these *muhājirūn*/μωαγαρίται flocked to the two main *amṣār* (garrison towns) of Fusṭāṭ and Alexandria and joined the army, *al-muqatilā*, or served as soldiers in the annual *cursus* against the Byzantines.[15] The rapid numerical increase of these immigrants may be surmised from the need to compile several editions of the *dīwān* registers throughout the first Islamic century.[16] As a member of the army, a typical soldier received two payments: a *'aṭā'*/ῥογά, payable in gold, and a *rizq*/ῥουζικόν, a wheat ration paid from the *embolē*, the Byzantine wheat tax that persisted throughout Umayyad rule.[17] Additional provisions were also provided for the army by way of *ad hoc* government requisitions (discussed in the following section).

While the Arabs served as soldiers on the ships of the *cursus*, Egyptians comprised the majority of sailors and rowers. Each village had to provide a prescribed number of men for this purpose,[18] which indicates that most were not chosen as much for their seamanship as for their strong backs. Villagers responded to naval conscription through the same internal mechanisms they utilized to assess tax liability (Chapter Seven), choosing from among themselves the individuals that would travel and fulfill the village's obligation. Although drafted rather than recruited, these men received a wage that was in turn extracted from their own villages.[19] Still, individuals did not aspire to naval service; it was a task best avoided. The punitive nature of the task may be deduced from the early eighth-century CE comments of governor Usāma, who threatened that if monks did not pay a prescribed sum, he would: "destroy the churches and turn them into ruins, and make [the monks] serve on board the ships of the fleet".[20] The conscription of Egyptians into the Islamic navy backfired at least once. Byzantine historians record an incident in 97/716 in which Egyptian sailors abandoned their ships during the *cursus* and proceeded to warn the Byzantine emperor of the imminent attack.[21]

Labor and Commodities

One of the aspects most clearly illustrated by the papyri of the early (*P.Apoll.*) and mid-Umayyad (*P.Lond.*IV) periods is a persistent shortage in skilled labor and, occasionally, of specific commodities.[22] On the whole, Arabs were apt soldiers, but lacked skills in important urban professions such as carpentry and shipbuilding. General requests for men sufficed for naval conscription, in which essentially any healthy male would do, but in nearly all other cases, government officials specified the type of skilled laborers required. Sawyers, caulkers, and carpenters were especially lacking and constantly in demand.[23]

Request letters indicated a prescribed number of artisans and specified that the village should also provide for their pay (ἀπαργυρισμός). Often, these notices forbade cash payments in lieu of service; the villages had to provide the artisan(s) requested.[24] Some of these skilled workers were sent to construct and repair ships at the docks of major port cities, such as Fusṭāṭ, Alexandria, and Clysma; others traveled to work on an assortment of Umayyad projects that included governmental palaces and mosques as far away as Jerusalem and Damascus.[25]

Requests for commodities followed a similar pattern.[26] The rigidity of the request, it may be inferred, coincided with the availability of the commodity in or around Fusṭāṭ and Alexandria. *P.Lond.*IV.1392 and 1397 provide vivid examples. Both request butter (βoύτυρov), but while 1392 stresses the need for the actual commodity, 1397 prefers a cash payment, likely indicating a surplus of the product in the Delta.[27] A similar pattern may be observed in *P.Lond.*IV.1335, which is concerned with grain (*embolē*) payments (cf. *P.Lond.*IV.1370, 1386, and 1404). This differs significantly from the impression one gets from the normative chronicles, according to which Egyptians as a whole had to provide an annual allotment of articles of clothing and supplies to the Muslim population. While the literary sources suggest that every village provided these supplies, the papyri suggest that supplies were requested as needed, their cost (at times) credited against the annual tax liability of the providing village.[28]

The Second and Third Centuries

The second Islamic century inaugurated what was tantamount to a social revolution in Egypt. A new wave of Arab immigration into the province provided the immediate stimulus.[29] This singular event and its repercussions, and not the chronological boundary (though the two dovetail nicely), delineate the next important developmental phase in the history of the Islamic community in the province.

By the second century, Arab immigration to Egypt was hardly new. As the *a'rāb/muhājirūn* dynamic, discussed above, matured, Arabs in the Peninsula believed that it was their religious and social duty to emigrate to one of the newly founded *amṣār* of the caliphate.[30] Consequently, Arabs immigrated to Egypt from the time of the conquest onward. Most notable among such immigrants were members of the Judhām and Quḍā'a tribes, a third of whom immigrated to Egypt.[31] Over the span of the first century, however, these tribesmen predominantly functioned as soldiers.[32] A major shift in this pattern occurred in 109/728, when the influential *ṣāḥib al-kharāj* 'Ubayd Allāh ibn al-Ḥabḥāb, a Qaysī, took advantage of his post, a close relationship with the Caliph Hishām, and a recent revolt to issue the novel request for the official relocation of Qaysī tribesmen to Egypt.[33] The caliph approved the request which brought 3,000

Qaysī families to settle in the eastern Ḥawf, where the earlier revolt had erupted (see Chapter Six).

This settlement shifted the balance of power in Egypt in several respects. One disruptive aspect was that the Qaysī-Yamanī disputes, which had plagued other regions of the caliphate, now found their way to Egypt.[34] More importantly, the new Qaysī immigrants were deliberately settled in the eastern Ḥawf and encouraged to engage in agriculture. They would serve as the nucleus of a rapidly expanding Arab agrarian population, which would shatter the hitherto normative profile that readily identified an Arab as a soldier. Furthermore, this migration inaugurated a socio-political dynamic that would have tremendous ramifications over the next century.[35]

Already by the early eighth century CE, ʿAbd al-Malik ibn Marwān had demilitarized most Arab populations and forged a standing army out of the Arabs of Syria, facilitating the subsequent migration of Arabs to Egypt not as soldiers but as farmers. A host of individuals and tribes had taken to agriculture during the first Islamic century, but their actions defied established custom and law. Priorities in the early period demanded that Arabs serve as soldiers, not farmers,[36] a fact abundantly documented in *kharāj* and *ḥadīth* manuals, in which the earliest traditions, which predate the first quarter of the eighth century, explicitly discourage farming and ban outright the purchase and cultivation of land by Muslims.[37] Later traditions, however, advocated not only the procurement of land, but its active maintenance and cultivation. In addition to purchasing land, *kharāj* manuals provide several other means for Muslims to acquire it. The methods include the occupation of unclaimed land for a period of three years, reclaiming "dead" (that is, unfertile) land, fencing in parcels, and appropriating the land of individuals who died in battle or could not pay the *kharāj* due.[38]

Similar concerns are narrated in traditions relating to water resources.[39] According to these, a field's water supply dictated its rate of taxation. Thus, land watered by a pre-existent means, used earlier by non-Muslims, was considered *kharāj*, but if an Arab farmer took the initiative to provide a new water supply, such as a well, his land would be taxed at the lower *ʿushr* rate. It is difficult to gauge the impact of these traditions in Egypt, where the land was considered *kharāj* by definition and the legal and fiscal ramifications of these traditions were likely inert; nonetheless, these traditions demonstrate the extent to which the Islamic government attempted to foster and subsidize agriculture among Muslims in the eighth century CE.

In general, the new immigrants brought the issue of land acquisition to the forefront; they were allocated unclaimed land exposed by the retreating Nile.[40] Although described in novel—almost miraculous—terms, this was an annual occurrence in the Delta. Each year, as the Nile retreated after its inundation, it exposed unclaimed land that neighboring villages allocated as arable parcels to their farmers. The novelty here lies not in the exposure of the land *per se*, but in its appropriation by the government.

The political might of these new immigrants remained dormant for another twenty years, but emerged dramatically in the late 740s CE. Qaysīs spearheaded Egyptian opposition to the Umayyads by providing the first individuals to accept the ʿAbbāsid *daʿwa*.[41] As such, they were handsomely rewarded during the tenure of Ṣāliḥ ibn ʿAlī, the first ʿAbbāsid governor of Egypt.[42] Before long, however, this new constituency proved to be a persistent nuisance and a threat to ʿAbbāsid hegemony as they joined with the Yamanīs, withheld taxes, and repeatedly revolted against the government (at times with the support of pastoral Arabs—*al-ʿurbān*—and Coptic farmers, as discussed in Chapter Six).

A New Society

Islamic society in Egypt changed radically within two centuries. Initially, it exhibited a palpable tribal ethic (*ʿaṣabīya* was alive and well) and appears to have been exclusively militaristic, but the Arabs would readily adopt, adapt, and innovate. The sources themselves provide an interesting mixture of idealism, much of which was projected back onto earlier generations by their descendants, and unflattering and contradictory facts. Often, the early conquerors are depicted as members of a pious, egalitarian society: a golden age that later generations supposed came to an end with the rise of the Umayyads.[43]

Nonetheless, if such an ideological bent ever existed (to the extent it is portrayed in normative literature), it surely survived alongside very human concerns and squabbles. The fact that Islamic society in Egypt during the first/seventh century remained fundamentally tribal needs little qualification. The *dīwān*, from its very structure to the means through which one enrolled in it, took for granted a population organized primarily along tribal lines.[44] Conversion practices under the Umayyads reinforced that social structure by mandating that an individual must convert "at the hands" of an Arab Muslim, who would serve as that individual's sponsor, or *wālī*. Subsequently, the convert would be integrated into his sponsor's clan and tribe by becoming a client, or *mawlā*; thus, conversion grafted an individual onto a tribe and allowed Egyptian converts to identify with a tribal structure that was fundamentally foreign to them, but still germane to Arab society.

The persistence of a tribal perspective in the early Islamic community may be further deduced from the settlement patterns of the early conquerors. The *khiṭaṭ* allocated in the wake of the conquest, whether in Fusṭāṭ, Alexandria, or elsewhere, were allocated to tribes, not individuals. In general, these new settlements were far from the utopian social experiment envisioned by some. Each tribe lived on its own parcel of land: a geographic manifestation of tribal affiliation.[45] As the population increased, tribes were forced to live side by side at the borders of their *khiṭaṭ*, sources mention this fact with a tone of dismay. At least initially, the tribes resisted intermingling. At times, intra-communal relations were tense and, in all, pragmatic tribal concerns set the agenda. Pre-Islamic feuds not only survived conversion to Islam, but also emigration to the new provinces where they were bloodily settled.[46] Even at times of prayer, many early Muslims prayed separately,[47] the segregation persisting not only along tribal lines, but "ethnic" groupings as well.[48]

A fundamental shift occurred during the second Islamic century, ushering in several social developments, many of which have been discussed at length in other chapters. Here, the aim is to bring the dispersed factors together. Already discussed were the ramifications of the Qays immigration to Egypt, which fundamentally shifted the balance of power in the province and, more importantly, altered the dominant profile for an Arab Muslim in Egypt. This settlement of Arabs as farmers constituted the single most important event after the conquest itself. Second, as the Arabs took to agriculture, their priorities and allegiances shifted. Chapter Six's discussion of agrarian revolts aptly demonstrates the development of this process. Even entrenched tribal feuds, such as those that existed between the Qaysīs and Yamanīs, diminished and were incrementally abandoned in order to present a united front against the government. Common agrarian and fiscal concerns forged new regional identities and the emergence of a new society that sought to transcend several dichotomies: Qaysī/Yamanī, Christian/Muslim, Arab/Egyptian, and Arab Muslim/*mawlā*.[49] By the mid-second/eighth century, one may discern the origins of a century-long process through which the Muslim population transformed from a population dominated by clan allegiance and a warrior ethic into agricultural communities in pursuit of regional interests. The change was irreversible; divorced from their earlier military responsibilities, which were increasingly entrusted to Turks, Persians, and Berbers, Arab Muslims had to adapt to new socio-political realities.[50]

Immigration provided another factor that led to the erosion of tribal society. Tribes often fragmented as clans settled in different districts and provinces; al-Maqrīzī's *Bayān* repeatedly demonstrates this pattern.[51] Since the first century, governors and caliphs had introduced a slew of reforms and projects aimed at undermining tribal cohesion by diverting authority from tribal leaders to government-appointed officials. To that end, the administration implemented innovative policies that sought to secure the loyalty of new Arab immigrants. One early means to that end was the appointment of an *'arīf* for each tribe.[52] His function, earlier designated to the tribal chief (*al-ra'īs*), resembled that of a census-taker. As a government employee, the *'arīf* recorded deaths and births within each clan, providing the bases for an individual's enrollment in the early *dīwān*, which—in its earliest manifestation—served as a revenue-sharing system. Other strategies, such as government-run inns and public *mawā'id* (banquets) were also employed.[53] These attempts met with some success, but until the end of the eighth century CE, tribal solidarity remained largely intact. This may be demonstrated from the revolts of that century; the rebelling Arabs were tribally organized, as were the soldiers who fought against them.[54]

The settlement of Arabs as agriculturalists constituted an essential step that promoted the creation of a new Arab Muslim society, and in time would foster Arabization and conversion trends throughout the Delta. ʿAbbāsid rule ushered in a vital catalyst that fostered the development of a new social matrix. That dynasty's socio-religious platform quickly began to displace the hitherto dominant profiles for Muslims and Arabs in the province. The earlier ethnocentricity of the Umayyads gave way to an ideological egalitarianism—often anachronistically projected onto the period of the conquest—in which adherence to the Islamic faith and personal piety alone, rather than "ethnic" or tribal affinity, dominated an individual's perception of self, along with their legal, social, and fiscal (tax) standing. While this ideological bent should not be overstressed (nor the Umayyad's contribution to ninth-century developments forgotten), early ʿAbbāsid rule did witness significant societal transformations resulting from both policy and happenstance. ʿAbbāsid religious and fiscal policies stimulated conversion (Chapter Four), which in turn allowed Muslim ranks in Egypt to swell, fundamentally altering the composition of the Islamic community in the province and accelerating the rate of Arabization among the Christian population at large (Chapter Five). This, along with the ever-expanding hold of Islamization as a hegemonic program extending to all Egyptians regardless of religious belief, helped to usher in an increasingly homogeneous culture.

By the mid- to late ninth century, urban society began to exhibit a new cultural identity: public space looked and sounded different. Distinguishing Arab from Egyptian or Muslim from Christian by appearance, dress, or speech alone became increasingly difficult. This new phenomenon triggered angst and fear of loss of identity in conservative circles among Muslims and Christians. Hence, the development of a host of strategies that sought to foster and preserve tangible socio-political markers and communal boundaries. Ironically, society was becoming at once homogeneous yet deeply sectarian.

The ensuing anxiety had multiple manifestations. Within the Muslim community, apprehension led to the implementation of various restrictions on *Ahl al-Kitāb*, the most pertinent of which (for this discussion) were a series of social restrictions, which were projected back to the time of the conquest in order to gain legitimacy. Over a number of centuries, the restrictions were codified and became known as *al-shūrat al-'Umariyya*, the so-called "Covenant of 'Umar," which remains problematic on several fronts. Attributed to Caliph 'Umar ibn al-Khaṭṭāb,[55] the Covenant's normative recension cannot date earlier than the late fourth/tenth century, though a number of its regulations can be dated much earlier.[56] In its mature form, the Covenant is beyond the scope of this study; still, a few comments are warranted regarding the *ghiyār*, the distinctive clothing regulations, and the riding provisions imposed on non-Muslims.[57]

Different versions of the clothing restrictions find their way into the historical narratives. The earliest stratum is vague: "Do not resemble Muslims in their dress" is the clause retained by Ibn 'Abd al-Ḥakam.[58] Often repeated, these regulations were inconsistently applied, sporadically enforced, and hardly prevailed aside from exceptional periods of intolerance (e.g. under al-Mutawakkil and al-Ḥākim bi Amr Allāh). Another set of regulations concerned with promoting visible communal markers instructed non-Muslims to ride only donkeys, to mount pack animals sidesaddle, and to dismount in the presence of Muslims.[59] Without delving too deeply into the specifics of these ordinances (collectively known as *dhull*—debasement—regulations), they clearly had two aims: the humiliation of *dhimmīs*, which was on occasion articulated as providing an incentive for conversion, and the construction of visible social distinctions and boundaries predicated upon religious affiliation. At their core, these regulations and conservative attitudes sought to engender socio-religious signifiers within the public sphere.

Christians shared the very same fear of losing their identity. This is abundantly clear in the *Apocalypse of Samuel* (discussed in Chapter Five). A critique of assimilation, this tract was addressed to the Christian community by an individual who believed that he lived during an age of transition that undermined the identity of the community. The text instructs the Christian laity not to assimilate to Muslim ways, not to converse in the Arabic language, and not to fraternize with Muslims or mimic them in their manners or customs: to maintain the distinguishing features that set the Copts apart within the public sphere.[60]

A dramatic transformation occurred during the third Islamic century. Not only was the size and demographic composition of the Islamic community constantly in flux, but, fundamentally, what it meant to be a Muslim rapidly changed as well. The initial identification of Islam with Arab warriors faded as individuals from diverse backgrounds accepted Islam and the Arabs slowly withdrew (and, on occasion, intentionally excised) from the army and took to agriculture and urban professions. Meanwhile, urban Christians began to adopt the Arabic language as the elite members of their community had done at the end of the first Islamic century. These socio-political transformations led to the creation of a new society in which religious and communal affiliation was no longer obvious and needed to be artificially induced.

Pastoral Arabs (*al-ʿurbān*)

Pastoralists lived on the periphery of Egyptian society and within early Islamic historical writings. Yet, at several junctures these itinerant populations positioned themselves at the center of historical events. A few scholars, most notably Abdel Hamid Saleh, analyzed the scant references that exist for the history of this population.[61] Saleh's seminal study, however, has two (understandable) drawbacks, which are typical of academic literature on this topic. First, it only surveys Arab Muslim authors, which, by virtue of the extant texts, translates into relying heavily upon Mamlūk historians, particularly al-Qalqashandī (d. 821/1418) and al-Maqrīzī (d. 845/1442).[62] These authors are late, and by their own admittance are quite incomplete with regard to the early centuries of Islam. Unfortunately, by the time the Arabs were interested in chronicling their genealogies, al-Ḥamdānī's *Ansāb* being the most significant attempt (d. 334/945), much had already been lost.[63] Another limitation is that throughout his work, Saleh employs "Bedouin" as a synonym for "Arab," a confusion that stems from the historical sources themselves. Consequently, he addresses a number of issues pertinent to the history of Arabs in Egypt, but not that of "Bedouins" *per se*, who are defined in this study as nomadic or pastoral Arabs. Here the methodological aim is to supplement the historical record by drawing on Christian writings, which on occasion predate the available Islamic texts by centuries, and by focusing exclusively upon pastoral Arab populations.

Pastoralists often served as agents of political instability, social disruption, exploitation, and a host of other criminal activities. This is hardly unique. Tensions between settled/agrarian and nomadic/pastoral populations have long been documented and analyzed.[64] In the first Islamic century, most Arabs were employed by the government in one capacity or another, the majority serving as soldiers (*muqatilā*). Still, as tribesmen, they continued to graze their horses and livestock during the annual *irtibā'*, a spring migration to a designated region of the province, the location of which would in time became hereditary.[65] Not all would return from this annual trip, however. Some settled and took to agriculture, an oft-maligned profession in the first Islamic century,[66] while others assumed—or, more likely, resumed—a pastoral lifestyle. This thinly documented population remained nomadic, pasturing herds in a seasonal migration pattern along which they traded their commodities with settled agricultural communities.[67]

Typically, such populations appear in the historical record as agents of social disruption and chaos. As individuals and groups, they engaged in various economic activities, many of which appear to have been of a marginal or illicit nature. Doubtless this impression is colored by the nature of the extant literature. The *'urbān* did not chronicle their own history, and are seldom attested in historical writings apart from the brief instances in which they led revolts or rioted. Their activities are otherwise undocumented, and were most likely benign and legal. Still, it would appear that when opportunities for mischief availed themselves, they were grasped.

For the most part, Bedouin raids, though destructive and violent, were sporadic and localized. Most incidents chronicled by Christians follow in the infamous tradition of barbarian raids on monasteries chronicled throughout Late Antiquity. Under Islamic rule, non-Muslim populations, such as the Beja/Blemmeys, also engaged in such raids.[68] As with all pastoral populations, the movements of nomadic Arabs were not random. Such tribes traveled along a seasonal route known to those who would be most affected by them, for better or worse. In the HP, the arrival of these pastoralists was often a cause for alarm.[69] On several occasions, particularly in the mid-ninth century, the *'urbān* targeted the vulnerable monasteries of Upper and Lower Egypt, killing monks, abusing nuns, robbing pilgrims, and stealing whatever they could.[70] It was during that tumultuous juncture that the Madlajā Arabs, who had settled near Alexandria shortly after the conquest, joined forces with the *'urbān* and seized control of the city and most of the eastern provinces.[71] Other major disruptions recorded in the mid-eleventh century under the Fāṭimids were subdued by the Armenian *wazīr* Badr al-Jamālī. Later still, under Mamlūk rule, the *'urbān* rioted under the leadership of al-Malik al-Nāṣir Yūsuf ibn al-ʿAzīz, who was killed by al-Ẓāhir Baybars.[72] The stereotypically negative evaluation of the *'urbān* may be soundly supported from the literary descriptions of these incidents.

As individuals, the marginality and transience of Bedouins afforded them anonymity that rendered them suitable agents for illicit activities, particularly as mercenaries for hire. On one occasion, the HP chronicles that the father of a Muslim convert to Christianity hired some *'urbān* to kill his son. In another incident, a group of *'urbān* seem to have taken the initiative (but were likely commissioned) to kill a Muslim with strong Christian sympathies, who may have converted in secret.[73] On yet another occasion, Bishop Khaīl (Michael) of Sakhā instructed some *'urbān* to stone a man who attempted to rape a nun (he was later excommunicated for ordering the attack).[74]

Still, the role of pastoralists was not always disruptive or illicit; the majority of their economic activities were legal, even beneficial. By the early third/ninth century, some Bedouin populations functioned as the guardians of Coptic monasteries and possibly their business partners. The genesis of this symbiotic relationship remains obscure. Some early, though inconclusive, traditions point to the eighth century, while unequivocal evidence dates to the ninth century. In an incident mentioned in the HP's biography of Ya'qūb I (Jacob, d. 215/830), a deacon accompanying the patriarch assaulted and killed a man in the Monastery of St. Makarios. When news of this incident reached the Madlajā Arabs, who are described as the watchmen (*ghufarā'*) of the monastery, they demanded to take the deacon into their custody. Later, they were appeased by a hefty ransom.[75] A further reference to *'urbān* who were employed (or functioned) as guardians of monasteries is found in the above-mentioned incident involving Bishop Khaīl.[76]

The most positive demonstration of the symbiotic relationship between monasteries and Bedouins may be observed at the height of al-Ḥākim bi Amr Allāh's persecution in the early fifth/eleventh century.[77] While churches all over Egypt were closed and some demolished, the monasteries of Wadī al-Naṭrūn (Scetis) were largely unaffected. The soldiers sent to destroy them were: "afraid of the Arabs who are in this mountain on account of their great number".[78] The HP supplements this with a divine rationale, stating that St. George frightened away al-Ḥākim's soldiers.[79] Significantly, a scribal note in a manuscript colophon from the Borgia collection dated 1014 CE confirms the status of Wadī al-Naṭrūn as a safe haven beyond al-Ḥākim's grasp.[80] In it, the scribe tersely narrates his flight from a monastery in Fayyūm due to al-Ḥākim's persecution, and that he found refuge at the Monastery of Saint Makarios. Thus, at the worst period of intolerance in Egypt since the Great Persecution at the dawn of the fourth century CE, the protection extended to Coptic monasteries by the *'urbān* transformed the hostile desert into a safe harbor: the only place where the faithful were able to receive communion over a three-year period.[81] Demonstrably, the *'urbān* constituted a dynamic population in Egypt whose actions and historiography were far more complex (and intriguing) than the normative literature would indicate.

CHAPTER 9

IDEOLOGIES AND JURISDICTIONS

In delineating the responsibilities of the Coptic patriarch, the HP enumerates three duties: "[First to] attend to the synodal letter [sent] to the Patriarch of Antioch; secondly, [to attend to] our relations with the Abyssinians and the Nubians; and thirdly the implementation of decrees issued by the governor (*malik*) of Egypt to him and the bishops".[1] These ecclesiastical and secular relations informed historical interactions and developments on many fronts. Below, the initial focus is on anti-Chalcedonian political ideology, a topic of great relevance but marginal scholarly interest. In that vein, the task is to answer a compound but basic question: how did the anti-Chalcedonian hierarchy and, with more difficulty, their constituency interpret Byzantine and Islamic political rule? The discussion then shifts to interactions among the Copts and the three anti-Chalcedonian sees of Antioch, Nubian, and Ethiopia. There is much to be gained in structuring the analysis in this manner. Analogous investigations have addressed Alexandrian relations with either Syria or the sub-Saharan kingdoms, and while that either/or approach is functional, it cannot help but obscure several aspects of the reciprocal relations involved. By juxtaposing interactions with the two regions, a clearer understanding of both sets of dynamics emerges. The analysis underscores a fascinating dichotomy. While Coptic relations with Nubia and Ethiopia seem paternal in demeanor and certainly more autocratic in tone than those with the sibling apostolic see of Antioch, it was, nonetheless, the sub-Saharan kingdoms that provided the Coptic hierarchy with political leverage vis-à-vis the Islamic government.

In all, the subsequent historiography teems with examples highlighting the intermingling of governmental prerogatives with ecclesiastical politics and considerations. Throughout, one quickly realizes that the cold language of jurisdiction and hierarchy often masked incredibly complex realities in which power and authority did not necessarily reside in the same hands.

Anti-Chalcedonian Political Ideology

From the Council of Chalcedon until the Arab conquest, political leaders were religiously at odds with the majority of the Egyptian population they governed, a discrepancy that would be maintained and accentuated under Islamic rule when, at least until the early eleventh century CE, a Muslim minority governed an overwhelmingly Christian province. Whether under Byzantine or Islamic rule, however, the majority of Egyptians—Christians and Jews—exhibited remarkably similar attitudes toward political leaders. Significantly, they maintained the belief that political sovereigns were divinely mandated to rule irrespective of their own religious beliefs. Here, the aim is two-fold: first to explore the various ideological conceptions of political authority among the Christian hierarchy and population, and subsequently to analyze the historical interactions between church and government. The exploration of popular sentiments is admittedly limited by the nature of the extant sources. Nonetheless, the lack of any political or religious motivation for the Egyptian revolts of the eighth and ninth centuries (discussed in Chapter Six),[2] coupled with the impression gained from documentary papyri analyzed below, largely reinforce the perspectives gleaned from the normative literature.

In the first half of the fourth century CE, the conversion of Emperor Constantine provided Eusebios of Caesarea with an opportunity to formulate a political ideology that would bring church and empire into harmony.[3] According to Eusebios, the empire would be best ruled by an autocrat whose monarchy over the *oikoumene* reflected God's sovereignty over the world;[4] he would be a "bishop" to those outside the church, and an orthodox protector and patron of the ecclesia. His synthesis was highly successful and persisted for well over a millennium in Byzantium, Ethiopia, and Russia, but it was an ideal that was especially short-lived in Egypt.[5] For the better part of the period stretching from the mid-fifth to mid-seventh centuries, anti-Chalcedonians in Egypt lived under the rule of pro-Chalcedonian emperors.[6] This should have caused a crisis in political ideology, but such a development never materialized. Throughout those centuries, no secession movement can be detected, no religiopolitical revolts are recorded, no one withheld taxes, and no one challenged the emperor's legitimacy. Most Egyptians disapproved of the emperors' theology (and, on occasion, their heavy-handed tactics), but never questioned their divine mandate to rule. In its most radical manifestation, the dominant Coptic response simply prayed to God to send "a good emperor".[7] Otherwise, anti-Chalcedonians continued to pray for emperors as if they were "orthodox,"[8] and recognized even as problematic a figure as Herakleios as "God-crowned".[9]

This premise is at odds with the thesis advanced by several scholars over the past century: namely that "Monophysitism" fueled an Egyptian "national" identity that aimed to (or, as some would have it, led to) a rejection of Byzantine "imperial" rule.[10] At its core, this thesis masquerades theological conflicts as political movements due to the lack of evidence of a truly political nature to support it. Whether under Byzantine or Islamic rule, the majority of the population was acquiescent; Christians, Muslims, and Jews in Egypt shared a worldview that consistently vested rulers with a guise of divine election irrespective of the individual ruler's piety or creed.[11]

West Syrian sentiments were analogous. J.J. van Ginkel's studies of the writings of John of Ephesos concluded that the West Syrians continued to view the emperor as divinely sanctioned, and that John's political ideology reflected those of Eusebios and Sokrates.[12] East Syrian perspectives, on the other hand, appear to have been more diverse, but, significantly, they developed within a fundamentally different religiopolitical context: East Syrians had long lived under Sasanid rule prior to that of the Arabs.[13] Van Ginkel's first conclusion finds many parallels in Coptic sources, where the normative literature often portrays pro-Chalcedonian emperors in a positive light. Their persecutions at times are attributed to malevolent advisors, rendering emperors victims of deceit rather than perpetrators of malice. There are two main exceptions to this general rule, the emperors Marcian and Justinian, who are generally portrayed as tyrants (Herakleios' depictions are quite diverse).[14] In Justinian's case, however, the reputation and adoration of "the faithful queen," the Empress Theodora, usually offset the emperor's impious image in anti-Chalcedonian literature.[15]

The second conclusion, however, requires additional comment. Van Ginkel's analysis places the Eusebian synthesis at the core of Christian political ideology, a justifiable, though incomplete assessment. Arguably, the Eusebian ideal, though of lasting influence, is not essential. Earlier, the Christians of the Roman Empire lived for three centuries under Pagan emperors, and farther east, Christians always lived under non-Christian rulers: first Sasanid, then Muslim.[16] Van Ginkel is accurate in discerning continuity of thought between Eusebios and his anti-Chalcedonian successors, who likewise believed that emperors were divinely elected. Nonetheless, this continuity was not solely due to Eusebios' influence (or limited to that constituency), but it was predicated upon the influence of the New Testament Scriptures, which enabled the Christians of the pre-Constantinian era and those living under Sasanian rule to serve as faithful subjects to non-Christian emperors.

Various New Testament passages (e.g. Mt. 22:21, Rom. 13:1–7, I Tim. 2:2, I Pet. 2:13-14, Tit. 3:1) are alluded to and directly quoted in anti-Chalcedonian literature.[17] These verses promoted the belief that government—all government—was sanctioned by God, and that a good Christian had to obey civil officials. This belief complemented the Eusebian ideal, was accentuated in the post-Chalcedonian period, and provided the basis for anti-Chalcedonian political ideology under Islamic rule.

Transitioning from Byzantine to Islamic rule did not require the majority of Christians (and presumably Jews) in Egypt to make a radical adjustment to their political ideology.[18] Under Byzantine rule, prayers were offered on behalf of the emperor;[19] similarly, praying for Muslim officials began shortly after the conquest.[20] During their first encounter, Patriarch Benjamin purportedly prayed for ʿAmr ibn al-ʿĀṣ (though I remain suspicious of the historicity of many of the details of that whole account);[21] similar actions are ascribed to Khaīl I, Mark II, Kyrillus II, and Zacharias I, all of whom prayed for Muslim dignitaries in person.[22] This attitude also found expression in the litanies prayed on behalf of ruling officials and in formulaic phrases, such as "may the Lord establish your kingdom," which are placed on the lips of average Christians as well as bishops and patriarchs in the presence of Muslim officials.[23] The duplicity of such comments has been assumed, but such cynicism need not prevail. Even in apocalyptic literature, where Christians could anonymously "speak their mind," the downfall of the caliphate is "prophesied" but not called for; that is, the population is not prompted to bring it about.

Popular Christian perceptions of Islamic rule do not seem to have deviated significantly from the impression gleaned from the normative literature. This is especially evident in the Balaʿizah documents, the non-literary papyri among which date from the late-seventh to the mid-eighth century CE. A formula found in *P.Bal.*103 is most illustrative: "As a security, therefore, for you I have [drawn up] this agreement for you to which we assent. We [swear by] the name of Almighty God and the health of our lords [who] rule over us at any time [that we will adhere] for you to the validity of this agreement." This Coptic contract echoes a Byzantine formula attested in the early seventh century,[24] and finds a number of parallels within the Balaʿizah documents and among other Coptic papyri of the same period, such as *P.KRU*.[25]

By documenting interactions among Christian parties, the Balaʿizah texts provide a rare glimpse at popular sentiments; there was no need to mention rulers at all, rather the traditional reference to their "health" is used as one of the guarantees of the contract.[26]

Comparable sentiments are found in other papyri, such as *P.CLT.*3, dated 744 or 759 CE, but such a petition was intended to be read by Muslim officials and, consequently, its sincerity may be suspect. That is not the case with the Balaʿizah, *P.Mon.Apollo*, or most of the *P.KRU* papyri, which were overwhelmingly the private documents of Christians and, arguably, provide better indicators of popular attitudes. Demonstrative of scribal continuity,[27] the retention of these formulas additionally underscores the lack of any strong anti-Islamic (religious or political) sentiments among the then predominantly Christian countryside.

Even more telling, while documentary sources routinely reference "the lords who rule over us," post-conquest papyri often qualified this standard clause by adding: "*at the command of God* Almighty," "who have power over us *from* God," and "*by the counsel* of God Almighty".[28] Regardless, of what Christians thought of Caliphal rule, they believed that the Arabs were legitimate sovereigns ruling by the permission of the Christian God—of course, that also left those rulers susceptible to his chastisement.

The late Otto Meinardus had established the basic interpretive framework for church-government interactions during the early Islamic period nearly fifty years ago.[29] More recently, Marlis Saleh and Mark N. Swanson, focusing on early relations and interactions through Fāṭimid rule, have added needed nuance and greater depth to his assessment.[30] Meinardus outlined three prevalent attitudes among the Copts: acceptance of Islamic rule as divinely mandated, opposition to Islamic rule, and mutual acceptance between church and government.[31]

Overwhelmingly, however, the first attitude—acceptance of Islamic rule as divinely sanctioned—informed all normative Coptic interactions with the government. Coptic opposition was seldom, and then only in response to specific injunctions. Patriarch Yusāb's statement encapsulates the church's basic policy: "I do not resist the command of the ruler (*malik*) . . . but only unjust orders".[32] Nowhere do Coptic authors challenge a Muslim governor or a caliph's mandate to rule. The few references of the sort stem from the writings of fourteenth-century Mamlūk historians, and were merely ascribed to

Christians. Such glosses betray a polemical, anti-Coptic agenda (exacerbated by the crusades) and should not be read as indicative of early or widespread attitudes.[33]

Divine sanction for Islamic rule underscores the historiography of the Arab conquest itself. As non-Muslim communities interpreted the Islamic conquests, they all agreed that the events they witnessed were in accordance with a divine plan.[34] None questioned God's sovereignty or control of historical events. For non-Muslims in particular, the conquests were but a divine reprimand brought about by heresy, and communal and individual offenses. Even when faced with severe government persecution and intolerance, this fundamental belief remained unaltered, as is abundantly clear in the HP's biography of Patriarch Zacharias.[35] Written by his contemporary, Bishop Michael of Tinnīs, the biography documents the plight of Christians and Jews under al-Ḥākim's oppressive rule. At no point does the biography question the legitimacy of the caliph or his government, but rather reverts to the socio-religious interpretation of calamites and persecutions as consequences of communal sin—as God's chastisement of his church:

> The leaders of the church previously sought out an individual in whom was learning and knowledge that they might make him a priest, if a number of trustworthy (individuals) testified to his continency and learning, from his childhood (upwards). Matters are (now) reversed; the intelligent scholar is of no account, especially if he were a poor man, but the ignorant and he who is without intelligence was honored and revered by them, *especially if he were rich, that they might advance him to an exalted rank among the ranks of the priests. For that reason, the hand of the Lord came down upon them and His wrath descended upon the church* by reason of his knowledge that we were unworthy to enter her door, as at the time when he caused his wrath to descend upon Jerusalem.[36]

The fact that the majority of historical literature (Christian and Muslim) stemming from this period represents shades of religious or "salvation" history, which chronicle the interactions of God with his community, is emblematic of the mentality of the age.[37] Throughout Late Antiquity and early Islamic rule, divine sanction and censure provided the grounding for all events and historical processes; human agency occupied but a secondary role to divine will.[38]

Caliphate and Patriarchate

Thus far, the focus has been on political ideology, an issue never explicitly articulated by anti-Chalcedonian writers under Byzantine or Islamic rule. The remainder of this section underscores the tenor of historical interactions between the Islamic government and the Coptic church.[39] Already discussed in Chapter Three is the government's initial ambivalence toward the Coptic church and the socio-political shift that commenced with the governorship of ʿAbd al-ʿAzīz ibn Marwān. Novel constraints, however, accompanied newfound liberties and access to power. One tactical aspect of this burgeoning relationship was the limitations placed on the Coptic patriarch's ability to communicate with Christians outside of Muslim-controlled lands (*dār al-Islām*), which are analyzed below in the section examining Coptic relations with Nubia and Antioch. Another aspect was the government's interference and oversight of patriarchal elections.

There is no indication that the first Coptic patriarchal elections under Islamic rule, those of Agathon and John III, interested or involved the government.[40] It was with the election of Isaac I (686 CE) that governmental involvement in the process is first attested. As the two finalists, George and Isaac, became entangled in a prolonged campaign for the patriarchal office, ʿAbd al-ʿAzīz summoned the two candidates along with their respective delegations and the entire electoral synod. Eventually, he "ordered the elevation of Isaac, and this matter was from God" (*amarā bi taqdīm Isḥāq wa kanā al-amr min Allāh*).[41] Hence, governmental interference in Isaac's elevation—an unprecedented act—was rationalized under the guise of divine providence. To avert controversy, the HP consistently presents Isaac as the legitimate successor by attributing his nomination to his predecessor, John III. Perhaps more sensitive to this issue, the Coptic *Life of Isaac* provides further sanction for his election. In that biography, while the bishops and notables deliberated, Isaac stood quietly under a lamp that suddenly broke and drenched him with oil: it was as though God personally anointed him.[42]

Similar meddling is evident in the election of Isaac's successor, Simon I. Upon electing John, hegumen of the Enaton (*dayr al-zujāj*), the electoral synod traveled to Fusṭāṭ (or possibly Ḥulwān) to seek ʿAbd al-ʿAzīz's approval. In the presence of the governor, however, one of the bishops nominated Simon, John's spiritual son. Perplexed, ʿAbd al-ʿAzīz asked the delegation to choose between the two candidates, but he was met with an ambiguous response that ultimately maintained that the decision belonged "to God and then to you".[43] Almost two centuries later, in a heated exchange with a *qāḍī*, Patriarch Yusāb echoed the same sentiments, stating that his mandate came "from God and the caliph".[44] The explicit context of that later incident was the legal recognition of Yusāb as Coptic patriarch; implicitly, however, this underscores the notion that divine will may be channeled through political leaders.

ʿAbd al-ʿAzīz essentially handpicked Simon, possibly selecting the candidate with marginal support to underscore his own authority. Perhaps, he even hoped that his actions would indebt the new patriarch to him. Certainly, Simon enjoyed a constituency among the individuals gathered before the governor, but so did John, who initially had unanimous support. Moreover, passing over a candidate in favor of his disciple must have seemed awkward at best, even insulting. As for the devout Simon, he appears to have been completely uninterested in ecclesiastical or secular politics. At no point did he seek ordination; even after his elevation, he remained ambivalent as to the duties of his office. Simon spent the majority of his patriarchate in seclusion at the Monastery of the Enaton, while day-to-day activities were initially delegated to hegumen John, who apparently remained Simon's spiritual father, and upon John's death to another John, the noted Bishop of Nikiou.[45] The patriarch's apathy and absence from the public sphere did not go unnoticed, but stirred up considerable resentment that culminated in an attempt on his life. Still, it may have been that ʿAbd al-ʿAzīz's blatant interference in Simon's election undermined his patriarchate. In that light, Simon's reclusive ways may reflect his failure to gain legitimacy in the eyes of a community that viewed direct government interference in patriarchal elections as unprecedented and unwelcome. This would better explain the enigmatic attempt at the patriarch's life.

With the elections of patriarchs Isaac and Simon, ʿAbd al-ʿAzīz set the precedent for government oversight of patriarchal elections. This protocol has been maintained ever since. A nominee for the patriarchal office required government approval: a practice that was becoming normative throughout the caliphate, not just in Egypt.[46] Still, few governors were as entrenched in the process as ʿAbd al-ʿAzīz. Securing government permission for the ordination of a new patriarch was often mechanical: the electoral synod paid a "fee" and the governor would issue an edict permitting the ordination and recognizing the new patriarch.[47]

Procuring government approval, however, did not guarantee ordination. An incident involving the wealthy notable Ibrāhīm ibn Bishr demonstrates the complexity of the dynamics involved.[48] After the death of Patriarch Fīlūtā'us (Philotheos, 1003 CE), a certain notable named Ibrāhīm secured governmental approval for his elevation as patriarch. The electoral synod, however, acted quickly and elevated Zacharias, the priest and steward of the Church of St. Michael in Alexandria. Upon discovering that another was elevated, Ibrāhīm developed a tremor (perhaps due to a stroke) that plagued him for the rest of his life. To appease Ibrāhīm, and prevent him from contesting his ordination or involving the civil administration, Patriarch Zacharias ordained the layman as hegumen, promised him a diocese,[49] and later fulfilled that pledge by ordaining Ibrāhīm Bishop of Upper Minūf.[50]

Throughout the centuries discussed, the Coptic populace and hierarchy were completely uninterested in political sovereignty. All of the revolts discussed in Chapter Six took place at a time when Christians vastly outnumbered Muslims; yet, the church never became combative or militant. Even when patriarchs were arrested or imprisoned, no riots or disturbances are recorded. To the contrary, at one juncture, as Patriarch Yusāb was being arrested, some tried to interfere but were sternly rebuked by the patriarch himself: "Do not restrain me! We do not resist the government".[51] Coptic literature consistently asserts that Muslim governors and administrators were legitimate agents through whom God expressed his will, and several are praised for their integrity and piety.[52] ʿAbdallāh ibn Ṭāhir may serve as a passing example; the HP describes him as "a good and merciful man in his religion," under whom "God subdued all rebels".[53]

The perception of the Arab administration as a legitimate successor to that of the Byzantines is best demonstrated in the HP's description of the rise of the ʿAbbāsids, who are described as crypto-Christian liberators based on a Constantinian model. At what is depicted as the first battle between Umayyad and ʿAbbāsid troops (though it may be better read as a version of the Battle at the Zab River), the ʿAbbāsids were greatly outnumbered and under-equipped, but as the fighting progressed, Abū Muslim: "saw the angel of the Lord, in his hand a golden lance with a cross at the top of it, and he saw all whom the cross approached fall dead".[54] Thus, Marwān II, the last Umayyad caliph, was put to flight and the ʿAbbāsids won the battle. Subsequently "Abū Muslim commanded his soldiers to make crosses of every kind and to place them before them, saying 'By this [sign] God has given us victory, and it has conquered the kingdom for us.'" Unable to pursue Marwān, who had burned auxiliary boats, Abū Muslim and ʿAbdallāh proceeded to: "put on black garments. They did not shave their heads or unite with their wives, but persisted in fasting and prayer for six months until God delivered their enemy into their hands".[55] Even the soldiers purportedly placed crosses of gold and silver on their horses, tents, and garments.[56] At a later juncture in that narrative, the ʿAbbāsids are said to have "loved the cross," while Marwān II hated it.[57] Upon his arrival in Egypt, Abū Muslim issued a command that echoed the description of the Tenth Plague in the Book of Exodus: "[Abū Muslim] called upon every man who is a Christian to fasten a cross of God of silver or copper upon his forehead or upon his garment, and upon the door of his house. And whoever did not do so was slain. So were any Muslims not wearing black [the color of the ʿAbbāsids]".[58] The HP further demonstrates divine approval of the Khurāsāniyya's mission by associating that army's arrival with a miraculous increase in the level of the Nile (see Chapter Eleven).[59] After securing their rule over Egypt, the Khurāsāniyya purportedly decreased taxes on anyone "wearing a cross," and released Patriarch Khaīl, who had been arrested by Marwān II.[60] Within a year, however, standard tax rates were restored, and then doubled the following year. Soon two ʿAbbāsid secretaries, ʿAṭā and Safī, oppressed the Christians: "the Khurāsāniyya (forgot) that it was [*the Christians'*] God who granted them sovereignty (*al-mulk*), and they rejected the holy cross which gave them victory".[61] Thus ends the HP's version of the rise of the ʿAbbāsids.

The narrative unabashedly draws upon Constantine's conversion. Most prominently, Abū Muslim is cast as a new Constantine: he sees a vision of a cross, holds the *labarum* (battle-standard) described by Eusebios,[62] commands his troops to fashion and adorn crosses, and defeats his enemies with the help of the Christian God. His comment, "By this [sign] God has given us victory" has the unmistakable ring of the Constantinian ἐν τοῦτο νικά/*hoc signo victor eris*; similarly, the command to fashion crosses out of precious metals echoes Constantine's instructions.[63]

Here, Muslim troops are explicitly depicted as liberators: protagonists bringing about the Christian God's will (a role that is distinctly at odds with their description as agents of divine chastisement in early Coptic descriptions of the Arab conquest). The account is saturated with confessional and apologetic implications. While Arab Muslim historians ascribed the ascent of the ʿAbbāsids to Allāh's will, the HP attributes their success to the Christian God. In Coptic eyes, whether the Muslims knew it or not, they ruled through the favor and by the permission of their God; thus, the ʿAbbāsids, like the Byzantine emperors before them, were legitimate rulers. Additionally, this account demonstrates that the Christians of that period identified with the normative ʿAbbāsid historiography of Umayyad rule (though possibly just with regard to Marwān's corruption), and that they continued to depend upon late antique narratives and models to interpret later events.

The Christian population and hierarchy's attitude toward political rebellion provides further insight into their perception of Islamic rule. As mentioned above, the Coptic hierarchy did not support any of the revolts discussed in Chapter Six, either directly or indirectly. To the contrary, they actively resisted them. Ibn ʿAbd al-Ḥakam preserves a tradition that after the second conquest of Alexandria (646 CE), the Egyptians who did not rebel stated, "God rejects whoever rebels".[64] The historicity of the tradition is doubtful; nonetheless, the attitude it reflects is congruent with the emerging pattern.

The normative Coptic attitude toward rebellion may be gleaned from the events surrounding the two major revolts of the Bashmūr in 748–50 and 830–32 CE. Of particular significance are the letters sent by Coptic patriarchs to the rebels of the Bashmūr during those uprisings. In both incidents, the rebels were instructed to "repent". The hierarchy adamantly depicted a divisive political act (incited by taxation) as a spiritual vice. The HP reinforces this attitude by interjecting biblical verses that stress the sacerdotal nature of rulers.[65] At the end of the Great Revolt of the ninth century, when the *Biyamā* (the rebels of the Bashmūr) were defeated, the HP interpreted their fall—the punishment for their "sin"—through the biblical lens of Psalm 78:61–62: "And he gave their strength into captivity, and their beauty into the enemy's hand. And he gave his people to the sword; and disdained his inheritance".[66]

The rebels of the Bashmūr stand out due to the frequency and length of their insurrections. Located in the heart of the Delta, the Bashmūr was primarily marshland, the difficulty of the terrain providing a natural barrier that aided in the region's defense and possibly encouraged its inhabitants to defy the government.[67] On several occasions, the population of the Bashmūr turned militant. Still, it must be reiterated, their revolts never harbored any religious chauvinism or political ambitions; rather, reflecting the dominant pattern, the revolts of the Bashmūr were clearly sparked by economic concerns.[68]

Eutychios provides additional details about these Bashmūrites. He records that the name of the inhabitants, *al-Biyamā*, was derived from the Coptic "Offspring of the Forty," *nasl al-arbaʿūn* (likely reading *Biyamā* as echoing ⲠⲀϨⲘⲈ). He then relates the story that as the Byzantines (*al-rūm*, which for Eutychios also designates pro-Chalcedonians) withdrew from the Delta during the Arab conquest, forty men remained behind in the Bashmūr, and that they were the ancestors of the *Biyamā*.[69] The etymology is more legendary than historical (common in this literature), yet it would illuminate the existence of something of a separatist identity among the *Biyamā*. If this was indeed the case, that is, if they believed that they were of a different stock and did not quite see themselves as "Copts" (perhaps they were Melkites), this would go a long way in explaining the repeated indifference they demonstrated toward the petitions of the Coptic patriarch Khaīl I at the end of Umayyad period and those forwarded by the Coptic and Syrian patriarchs during the *fitna* of the early 830s.[70]

The end of the Great Revolt in 832 CE proved catastrophic for the *Biyamā*. Many were killed, and all survivors, including women and children, were exiled to Baghdad. The region was then settled by a Muslim population, which, under Fāṭimid rule, would also revolt against the government.[71] Thus, by the end of the *fitna*, the *Biyamā* were eradicated from Egypt, but some later returned and resettled in the province.[72] Their legacy in Coptic history, however, would be permanently tarnished. Much of the HCME's account of the reign of Marwān II is borrowed directly from the HP's biography of Khaīl I. Yet, while the HP chronicled Marwān's exploitative and violent deeds,[73] it positively portrays the Bashmūrites as allies to the Khurāsāniyya who fought with them against Marwān's army.[74] In the HCME, however, they are maligned as his supporters.

The HCME smears the *Biyamā* at yet another juncture. It draws upon a story earlier chronicled in the HP, in which a group of soldiers captured a young virgin (*ṣabīya ʿadhrā'*) intending to violate her (she is anonymous in the HP, but named Fibrūniyā in the HCME).[75] Desiring to preserve her chastity, the woman convinced the leader of the soldiers that she possessed a magical ointment that renders human skin impenetrable to swords. To prove its veracity, she rubbed her neck with the oil and instructed one of the soldiers to strike her; thus, she tricked them so that "she might appear before Christ a pure virgin". The HP clearly identifies the perpetrators as Marwān's soldiers, while the HCME claims that they were Bashmūrites.[76]

Among the Copts, the lack of an explicit political ideology did not negate the existence of a *de facto* worldview that interpreted political rule. What is intriguing here is that the worldview that emerges from these writings contradicts what one would expect to find in light of the pervasive nationalist paradigm, which modern historians often take for granted. Until the ninth century CE, the anti-Chalcedonians of Egypt did not view the Byzantines as "occupiers" or the emperors as illegitimate: they were simply misguided rulers whom God appointed for his own purposes, often as a consequence to communal transgressions.[77] Emperors were to be prayed for, not fought against. Similarly, that same basic premise existed under Islamic rule: rulers were appointed by God and functioned as his implements regardless of their confessional or religious affiliation.

Relations with Antioch, Nubia, and Ethiopia

Beyond the borders of Egypt, Coptic interactions with Syrians, Nubians, and Ethiopians provide a fascinating chapter in the history of early Islamic Egypt. Significantly, what at first glance may seem a topic of intra-Christian relevance quickly reveals itself as an inter-communal dynamic in which Islamic rule played no small part as ideology, jurisdiction, theology, and politics constantly negotiated new parameters. Beyond sketching the late antique origins of Alexandrian interactions with Antioch, Nubia, and Ethiopia, the primary focus here is upon the manner in which these relationships interacted with new political realities over the first three Islamic centuries.[78] Relations with Antioch, which stretch back to the early Christian centuries, were strained in the late fourth and early fifth century CE due to the contentious ecclesiastical rivalries, but in the aftermath of the Council of Chalcedon, sibling rivalry matured into theological and factional solidarity as most of Egypt and (western)

Syria vehemently championed the anti-Chalcedonian cause. Of marginal political significance,[79] both sees liturgically maintained the sororal relationship as a reflection of the Christian unity to which they aspired.[80] Frequent contact also fostered productive cross-pollination.

Theologically, the two sees espoused the same faith, articulated by Severos of Antioch and Theodosios of Alexandria (in Greek) to a degree of sophistication and elegance that has been hitherto unequaled.[81] Their unity may be also discerned from the very labels they used as a means of self-identification. The anti-Chalcedonian population (Egyptian and Syrian) was at one time labeled "Severians," just as later they were called "Theodosians".[82] The most enduring designation, however, "Jacobites," which stems from the Syrian bishop of Edessa, Jacob Baradaeos (500–78 CE), was routinely employed by Coptic authors in their writings (though they clearly identified with Egypt, the Copts consistently conceived of themselves as members of an anti-Chacedonian federation). With the rise of Islam, these sees became increasingly isolated from the rest of Christendom and found themselves facing similar socio-political and religious challenges.[83] Their unity was further reinforced by the founding of the Syrian Monastery in Wādī al-Naṭrūn sometime in the eighth century CE, and subsequently by the immigration of Moses of Nisibis and his followers to that monastery in the tenth century.[84] This provided a permanent Syrian ecclesiastical presence in Egypt until the Early Modern Period. It is quite possible that much of the Syrian influence on the Coptic church came by way of the intermingling of Syrian monks with their Egyptian coreligionists in the Wādī al-Naṭrūn—the spiritual hub of Coptic Christianity under Islamic rule until the fourteenth century.

The Coptic and Syrian hierarchies alike placed a premium on maintaining theological harmony and eucharistic fellowship. Drafting a synodal letter to the sibling see constituted one of the first official duties performed by an incoming patriarch in either jurisdiction.[85] (There is no proof that the Coptic patriarch sent such an official declaration to Nubia or Ethiopia, but it is likely.[86]) Typically, a clerical delegation delivered the letter, which provided an opportunity for face-to-face interactions.[87] Patriarchs of the two sees rarely met in person, though a notable exception occurred in the second quarter of the ninth century when the Syrian patriarch Dionysios of Tel-Maḥrē accompanied the Caliph al-Ma'mūn to Egypt.[88] Syrians were an important minority in Egypt throughout the period surveyed,[89] and over the centuries the Copts have had four patriarchs of Syrian descent.[90] For the most part, the sibling sees enjoyed an enduring, affable relationship, notwithstanding a few periods of discord.[91]

Reciprocal influences are evident, though difficult to disentangle.[92] There are, however, three areas where Syrian influence on Coptic Christianity may be clearly discerned. One is in the domain of theological terminology. As discussed in Chapter Five, the Syrians began the process of Arabization two centuries before the Copts. Thus, it is not surprising that once the process began in Egypt, the Egyptians borrowed many ecclesiastical terms from Syria. Some of these terms are of Syriac origin.[93] Others are of Greek origin, though their Arabic form betrays a Syriac conduit.[94] Others, still, are words common to Syriac and Arabic, but whose lexical—Christian—meaning was most likely coined in Syria.[95]

Beyond terminology, the first Copto-Arabic theologians were intimately familiar with the Arabic writings of their Syrian counterparts.[96] The theological dialogue with Islam began in Syria shortly after the 'Abbāsid revolution, and while it took longer for the official discourse to begin in Egypt, once inaugurated, it drew inspiration from the Syrian archetypes in both form and content.[97]

Liturgical celebrations and observances provided a third aspect of Coptic-Syrian relations. This is evident on several fronts, including literature and legends (such as that of Joseph of Arimathea),[98] as well as the adoption of fasts, such as those of Nineveh and Herakleios.[99] The Syrian Fraction, one of the liturgical prayers of the Coptic liturgy, provides a key passage that emphasizes the Christology of the anti-Chalcedonians: "Thus, truly did the Logos of God suffer in the flesh and was sacrificed and broken on the Cross. His soul parted from his body, while his divinity in no way parted either from his soul or from his body ... One is Emmanuel who cannot be divided after the union; there is no division into two natures. Thus we believe, thus we confess, and thus we affirm that this Body belongs to this Blood, and this Blood belongs to this Body".[100] Theological unity, analogous liturgical observations, and comparable socio-political circumstances fostered a sense of solidarity between these sibling sees that has endured into the present.

Coptic Relations with Nubia and Ethiopia

The second relationship, that between the Coptic church and hierarchy and the southern kingdoms of Nubia and Ethiopia, seems less symmetrical, though it had overt political implications unparalleled in Syrian-Coptic relations. Extensive Coptic influence on Nubia and Ethiopia is especially prominent in literature and liturgy. The southern kingdoms' influence on Coptic Christianity, however, was minimal. Their most enduring contribution was the renaming of the "Era of Diocletian" as that "of the Martyrs," an appellation that originated in Nubia in the late eighth century (see Chapter Six).

In the fourth and sixth centuries, anti-Chalcedonian missionaries travelled south of Aswān, eventually rendering the whole region religiously (and, in a roundabout manner, politically) dependent upon the Alexandrian hierarchy.[101] Despite what would seem a logical and geographic necessity, Ethiopia (Abyssinia/*al-Ḥabashā*) converted to Christianity almost two centuries prior to Nubia. As the traditional historiography narrates, in the first half of the fourth century CE, two Syrians, Frumentios (later Salama I) and Edesios of Tyre, were taken as prisoners to Ethiopia.[102] Convinced that the Ethiopians needed to hear the message of the gospel, upon his release Frumentios traveled to Alexandria and asked Archbishop Athanasios to send missionaries to the region. Athanasios responded by ordaining Frumentios a bishop (ca. 350 CE) and commissioning him to evangelize the region he had championed. By the end of that century, a Christian kingdom was established with a capital at Axum. A second phase of evangelism commenced in the late fifth century with the arrival (from Syria) of the Nine Saints and the *Ṣadqan*, or the

"Righteous Ones," a band of evangelizing ascetics who were eventually martyred by Pagan tribes (though it is difficult to discern history from legend where they are concerned).

Christianized prior to the schism of Chalcedon, in theory Ethiopia could have followed either hierarchy, Coptic or Melkite. Nonetheless, along with most of the Egyptian populace, it elected to follow the anti-Chalcedonian hierarchy. In time, the *Abunate* of Ethiopia would become nearly autonomous; its metropolitan, the *Abun*, was an Egyptian ordained in Egypt and subsequently sent to Ethiopia. All lower clergy, however, including the *echage* (the *de facto* head of the Ethiopian church), were native to the region. By and large, Ethiopia administered its own affairs well into the modern period before it became an autocephalous patriarchate.[103]

Systematic evangelizing efforts commenced in Nubia during the sixth century CE.[104] At that time, the region was home to three independent kingdoms: Nobadia in the North, Alwa in the South, and Makouria in between. Julian, an anti-Chalcedonian priest, was the first missionary of note. He arrived in the kingdom of Nobadia in circa 543 CE and remained there for two years;[105] then, Theodore, Bishop of Philae, continued Julian's efforts until 551 CE. Still, the most important phase of evangelism did not commence until the 560s CE, when the Emperor Justinian (or rather the Empress Theodora) sent Longinos to the kingdom of Nobadia,[106] where, prior to his departure in 569 CE, he baptized the royal household, ordained clergy, and built the first church in the region. Longinos returned to Nubia nine years later when the King of Alwa, an ally of the Nobadian king, requested that Longinos himself should evangelize Alwa's kingdom. Thus, by 580 CE, the Nubian kingdoms of Nobadia and Alwa had converted to anti-Chalcedonian Christianity at a phenomenal rate.[107]

The central kingdom of Makouria, which was often hostile to Nobadia and Alwa, initially accepted pro-Chalcedonian Christianity, though that would prove temporary. By the mid-seventh century CE, Makouria had conquered Nobadia, but while it dominated militarily, Nobadia triumphed religiously. Hence, the newly expanded kingdom, with its capital at Old Dongola, recognized the anti-

Chalcedonian hierarchy, indicating that that confession had set strong roots in the region by that date.[108] Thus, by the late seventh century CE, all of Nubia and Ethiopia adhered to the anti-Chalcedonian creed.[109] Northern Nubia, though no longer independent, retained its old designations of Nobadia and (later) Maris. For Arab historians, *al-nūba* usually identified only the northern-most province of the kingdom of Makouria.[110]

Unlike the semi-autonomous Ethiopia, Nubia was administered in a manner reminiscent of a Coptic diocese that was led by an Egyptian metropolitan.[111] Geographic proximity and the significant number of Egyptians who lived and traveled to Nubia further facilitated contact.[112] Hence, it was in Nubia, even more than Ethiopia, that Coptic influence is strikingly evident in language, art, and liturgical texts.[113] Nubia would remain predominantly Christian until the first half of the fifteenth century CE, though by 1323 CE the King of Makouria had converted to Islam.[114] The last point of contact with the Coptic church occurred in 1372 CE, when a certain Timothy, ordained Bishop of Qasr Ibrīm (Phrim), died en route to his new diocese.[115]

As Muslim armies swept over the region in the mid-seventh century, they embarked upon several campaigns aimed at expanding Arab rule beyond Aswān.[116] None were successful. In 31/652, under the command of ʿAbdallāh ibn Saʿd ibn Abī Sarḥ, the Arabs and Nubians reached an agreement in the ambiguous *baqṭ* (πάκτον), whose stipulations became increasingly explicit in later accounts.[117] Fundamentally, the treaty called for the cessation of hostilities and a gift exchange of Egyptian commodities for Nubian slaves. Beginning in the second/eighth century, the nature of the treaty itself, whether it was a *ʿahd*, *mithāq*, or *sūlḥ*, came under great scrutiny since the distinctions acquired explicit political and economic ramifications.[118] Eventually, a consensus, manipulated by political expediency rather than historicity, maintained that the agreement was but a *hudnat amān*, or "truce of security," and not an immutable treaty.[119] This allowed for the possibility of renewed hostilities against the Nubians at a later date, and provided a sanction for the enslavement and trade of Nubians throughout Egypt and the caliphate. Bolstered by demographic growth and military dominance, over the succeeding centuries the Islamic government increasingly described the *baqṭ* as a Nubian tribute paid to Egyptians rather than a good faith exchange between equals, which the earliest evidence—fragmentary as it is—presupposes.[120]

In general, the caliphate's failure to press beyond Aswan and the recognition of a border with the southern kingdoms engendered a fascinating dynamic. While Egypt's Christians lived under direct Islamic rule, Nubia and Ethiopia remained free Christian kingdoms jurisdictionally dependent upon the Coptic church to provide their highest ranking cleric, who crowned their kings and subsequently ordained them priests. Early caliphs and governors viewed this relationship with suspicion, but eventually came to regard it as advantageous. Thus, the government took an active interest, at times even a direct role, in maintaining Coptic relations with the sub-Saharan kingdoms. Hence, the Coptic hierarchy, Islamic government, Nubia, and Ethiopia found themselves negotiating an ever-elaborate choreography among political and religious jurisdictions and interests.

Coptic relations with Nubia and Ethiopia were not politically contentious until the end of the seventh century. According to the HP, Patriarch Isaac (686–9 CE) wrote letters to the warring kings of Nubia and "Maurōtania" commanding them to cease their hostilities.[121] The Coptic *Life of Isaac of Alexandria* adds that the king of Makouria and the king of Maurōtania were at odds with each other and with the Muslims, with whom the king of Makouria had not signed a treaty.[122] Consequently, when news of Isaac's communication reached the governor ʿAbd al-ʿAzīz ibn Marwān, his officials described the situation thus: "The king of Makouria has sent messengers with letters to abba Isaac the archbishop so that he will appoint a bishop for them whom they may take [back] to their own country. And not only this, but he has also sent [a message] to the king of Maurōtania counseling him to make peace with our enemy, the king of Makouria. If this happens, king, they will be of one mind, and will rise up against us and make war on us".[123] The governor was furious with the patriarch, whom he accused of conspiring with foreign rulers. Eventually, ʿAbd al-ʿAzīz's anti-Chalcedonian secretaries intervened and defused the tense situation.[124]

It is highly unlikely that this was the first communication between the Coptic hierarchy and the southern kingdoms under Islamic rule, but animosity between Arab-controlled Egypt and the adjacent kingdoms, along with ʿAbd al-ʿAzīz's attempt to assert his control over Egypt, brought the issue to the forefront. Fear that the Coptic patriarch would call upon the Nubians and Ethiopians to take up arms, or to divert the flow of the Nile, were genuine threats in the minds of government officials.[125] Arab insecurities were no doubt fueled by the fact that at the end of the seventh century, they remained a small minority vastly outnumbered by the Christian population they ruled, and that hitherto only the Nubians had successfully halted the advancement of a Arab army; the victory of Charles Martel at the Battle of Tours (732 CE) was still over forty years away.

Communication between Coptic patriarchs and Christians outside *dār al-Islām* continued to be a sensitive issue; consequently, interactions with Nubia and Ethiopia were always much more problematic than with Syria. Even by the mid-third/ninth century, a time when Muslims constituted a sizable minority in Egypt, unfounded accusations leveled at Patriarch Yusāb, alleging that he "writes letters to the princes of the Romans, and they send him a great deal of money," were enough to imprison and fine him.[126]

The repercussions of the above-mentioned incident involving Isaac I were felt almost immediately. An "Indian" priest approached Isaac's successor, Simon I, and asked him to ordain a bishop for his kingdom.[127] Simon refused, stating: "I cannot ordain a bishop for you without the command (*amr*) of the governor (*amīr*) who is in charge of Egypt. Go to him, inform him of your need, and if he commands me (*amaranī*), I will grant your request".[128] Coptic patriarchs had always acted autonomously and with impunity, but now new limitations on their sovereignty, unattested under Byzantine rule, were recognized.

The incident involving the Indian—or more likely, Ethiopian—priest did not end with that brief exchange. Seemingly unaware of the various Christian factions in Egypt (or perhaps simply unrelenting in his mission), the priest approached the Gainites, who ordained a bishop and two priests to accompany him back to his country. Nonetheless, the four men were detained at the Egyptian border, and assuming that the Coptic patriarch had secretly ordained the men, the Caliph ʿAbd al-Malik sent them back to his brother ʿAbd al-ʿAzīz with a castigative note: "It is as though you do not know what is happening in your (own) territories. For the patriarch of the Christians who resides in Alexandria has divulged (*anfaz*) the affairs of Egypt to India".[129] Clearly, the caliph and ʿAbd al-ʿAzīz viewed the Christian hierarchy as a potential fifth column that could rally (or support) outside forces against the Islamic regime. Due to this sensitivity, Nubian and Ethiopian requests for new bishops or metropolitans were usually sent to the governor of Egypt and not directly to the Coptic patriarch. It has been suggested that this practice commenced as a means of showing respect to the patriarch,[130] but more likely, political realities governed the logistics of communication. It was advantageous for the southern kingdoms and the Coptic patriarch to voluntarily divulge their communications to Muslim officials.

The Copts were not the only group rebuked for alleged communication with outsiders. In one incident, the Coptic bishop Pachomios unscrupulously used the government's paranoia to his advantage by falsely accusing the Melkite patriarch of spying on behalf of the Byzantines. The governor reacted by arresting the Melkite patriarch and mutilating him by severing two of his fingers. Only then did he permit the Copts to elect a new patriarch, a request he had previously denied.[131] Such sensitivities prevailed in Syria as well.[132]

At one period of instability, Muslim fears of a Nubian attack were realized. Late in the Umayyad period, Patriarch Khaīl I was imprisoned by the governor, ʿAbd al-Malik ibn Marwān ibn Mūsā, for communicating with the Nubians.[133] Informed of the patriarch's imprisonment, Kyriakos, the King of Dongola, marched on Egypt:

"with a great army including a hundred thousand horsemen, a hundred thousand horses, and a hundred thousand camels. . . . And when they approached Miṣr to capture it, they encamped at the pool known to this day as the "Pool of the Ethiopians." They plundered, slew, and imprisoned the Muslims [there], as they had done with the Muslims of Upper Egypt".[134] The governor quickly released Patriarch Khaīl and asked him to write a letter to pacify the Nubians. It was at that juncture that the HP clearly spells out (for the benefit of the administration) the relationship between the Coptic patriarch and the southern kingdoms: "[Kyriakos] is under the jurisdiction of Mark the Evangelist. For the patriarch of the Jacobites in Egypt exercises authority over him and all the kings of the Abyssinians and the Nubians, and he has in his country an orthodox bishop whom the patriarch ordains as metropolitan, and who ordains for the king the bishops and priests in that land".[135] The HP confounds the description somewhat. The relationship described here is better suited for Nubia rather than Ethiopia; nonetheless, the target audience—governing elites—received the message. Later, during the turbulent reign of al-Ḥākim, it was deemed necessary to reiterate these same sentiments.[136]

Some scholars have challenged the historicity of Kyriakos' invasion.[137] Doubtless the account retains a degree of embellishment in describing the size of the army and the distance the Nubians allegedly traveled north into Egypt, but there is no reason to completely dismiss the incident, which is corroborated by Ibn ʿAbd al-Ḥakam's *Futūḥ miṣr*, albeit lacking in detail.[138] For well over a decade prior to this incident (and intermittently thereafter), Nubian and Egyptian forces skirmished in Upper Egypt.[139] Moreover, the event should be interpreted against the backdrop of the twilight of Umayyad rule and the rampant chaos that prevailed throughout Egypt at that juncture.

This political dynamic saved the life of Patriarch Khaīl on yet another occasion. With the Khurāsāniyya in pursuit, Marwān II contemplated executing the patriarch, whom he had imprisoned. But then his son ʿAbdallāh pleaded for his father's clemency (the HP consistently portrays him as compassionate toward Christians).

ʿAbdallāh reasoned with his father: "We are surrounded by our enemies and we may need to escape to *bilād al-sūdān*. If you kill [the patriarch] we will not find refuge, but [the Nubians] will also attack us".[140] The insight proved valid. Marwān II was killed in Upper Egypt, but his two sons, ʿAbdallāh and ʿUbayd Allāh, escaped to Nubia.[141] Neither was allowed to remain for long, but they were treated kindly for the duration of their stay.[142]

Less than a century later, the dynamic among the Islamic government, the Coptic church, and the southern kingdoms had a markedly different political tinge. After the *fitna* of the early ninth century CE, Muslim officials prompted the Coptic patriarch Yusāb to send a letter to the Nubians, who were fourteen years in arrears in fulfilling the *baqṭ*. The patriarch opened his missive by emphasizing "the kind treatment" he had received from the governing officials,[143] and then proceeded to remind the Nubians of their obligations: "It is now proper, my beloved, that you should fulfill your [*baqṭ*] obligation to these kings [of the Arabs]".[144] The patriarch's efforts were successful. George, the son of the Nubian king Zakariyya ibn Yaḥnnis, traveled to Egypt and continued on to Baghdad, where he met with the Caliph al-Muʿtaṣim[145] and negotiated for the *baqṭ* to be fulfilled every three years rather than annually.[146]

The above-mentioned incident involving Patriarch Yusāb constitutes a significant turning point. Beginning in the second quarter of the ninth century CE, the government increasingly perceived the Coptic patriarch's relationship with the southern kingdoms as an asset rather than a liability. Fāṭimid policies underscored this view. In the sixth/twelfth century, when Ethiopia requested the consecration of ten bishops, which would have rendered it autocephalous, Patriarch Gabriel II refused to honor the request (which reached him via the Fāṭimid *imām* al-Ḥāfiẓ). He explained to the *imām* that by granting the request, the Coptic patriarch would no longer have any influence over the region. Immediately, al-Ḥāfiẓ ordered the drafting of a letter denying the Ethiopians' request.[147] The Islamic government clearly had a stake in keeping Ethiopia dependent upon the Coptic hierarchy. Still, Coptic involvement in the politics of the *baqṭ* was not always beneficial. In the mid-eleventh century, when the Nubians refused to honor the agreement, Patriarch Khrisṭūdulūs was accused of inciting the Nubian's noncompliance; though arrested and fined, he was later exonerated.[148] In general, the Coptic patriarch provided a ready scapegoat for any Egyptian problems with the Nubians.

Religiopolitical interactions with Nubian and Ethiopian kings were far from one-sided. These kings were dependent upon Coptic patriarchs for the bishops that guided their people and presided over their crowning and subsequent ordinations.[149] As discussed above, on a few occasions southern kings took up arms (or threatened to do so) on behalf of the patriarch, and in other instances they helped to alleviate his financial burden.[150] Such generosity endowed these monarchs with an intangible capital that allowed them to manipulate Coptic ecclesiastical dignitaries into doing their bidding, an unmistakable dynamic, particularly on two occasions in which Nubian kings tried to oust their bishop in favor of a handpicked candidate, an act that required the sanction and cooperation of the Coptic hierarchy.

In the 740s CE, King Ibrāhīm quarreled with Bishop Kyriakos (not to be confused with the above-mentioned King Kyriakos who succeeded Ibrāhīm). He sent a letter to Patriarch Khaīl threatening: "If you do not excommunicate (*taqṭāʿ*) Kyriakos, I will make my whole country worship idols".[151] Bishop Kyriakos traveled to Egypt, along with a certain John whom the king selected as his new bishop. To discuss the matter, Patriarch Khaīl convened a council, which eventually decided that Kyriakos would remain at a monastery in Egypt and that John would be ordained a bishop and sent back to Old Dongola. The decrees of the council were quite peculiar. No explicit charges were brought against the bishop, which would render Kyriakos' removal and the ordination of another bishop over his diocese in direct violation of a slew of canon laws. The HP skirts the canonical problem by asserting that the bishop was not excommunicated, but simply removed because of an unjust king. Nonetheless, no one objected too strenuously; Bishop Kyriakos refused to remain in Egypt and lived out his remaining days in a Nubian monastery, and the King of Dongola received John, his handpicked candidate.[152] The only repercussions were divine; the Nubians are said to have experienced a great drought and a plague due to the injustice perpetrated upon their bishop. A much more convoluted and prolonged ordeal in which the three jurisdictions and prerogatives intersected took place in the early tenth century, beginning with the patriarchate of Quzmān III (920–32 CE) and lasting until that of Philotheos (979-1003 CE).[153] There the appointment and dismissal of bishops and emperors demarcated political considerations, evident in the HP only in part.

Relations between the Copts and their coreligionists were symbiotic, but clearly relations with the southern kingdoms under Islamic rule exhibited an unprecedented political dimension. Both profited. The dynamic enhanced the prestige of the Coptic patriarch among his people and in the eyes of ruling Muslim elites, while enabling Nubian and Ethiopian kings to bolster the sacred nature of their throne and, on occasion, to successfully coerce Coptic patriarchs to do their bidding.

CHAPTER 10

A CHURCH AND COMMUNITY IN TRANSITION

The volume and nature of the extant sources allow for the study of the Coptic church and community at greater depth than any other contemporary institution or faction. Of the plethora of issues that may be addressed, I have chosen to focus here on three dynamics that resulted from or were acutely impacted by the Arab conquest: a novel discussion of the diocese of Alexandria's declining role in ecclesiastical affairs, the evolving roles of the Coptic hierarchy under early Islamic rule, and the contentious history of the acquisition and construction of churches. Squabbles over the ownership of ecclesiastical properties intensified in the wake of the Chalcedonian schism, particularly during the reign of Emperor Justinian, and were further complicated by the Arab conquest, while the other topics were engendered by that event.

Alexandria's Politico-religious Decline

Alexandria served as the spiritual hub of Egyptian Christianity throughout Late Antiquity, producing some of the greatest theological minds of the era,[1] but that began to change under early Islamic rule. While the city retained its cosmopolitanism and continued to function as a major port of call for merchants and the caliphal navy,[2] it was no longer preeminent as political and social weight shifted to the new nerve-center, Fusṭāṭ (and later, Cairo). This dilution of Alexandria's influence in secular affairs fostered a parallel decline in the ecclesiastical sphere. Over the course of a few decades, new centers of influence began to emerge and competed with the old capital. The struggle lasted for centuries and had several manifestations, the earliest of which may be traced to the late seventh century CE, and all of which came to a sudden halt in the mid-twelfth century CE, when the Coptic patriarchate officially relocated to Cairo.[3] Five historical developments are outlined here; three pertain to patriarchal elections and dovetail somewhat. The itinerancy of the patriarchal residence and the rise of multiple centers of influence, the fourth and fifth repercussions, stem from the same dynamics as the other three, but are better framed as parallel rather than dependent developments. All five historical trends demonstrate the progressive calcification of the new centers of socioreligious authority that challenged Alexandria's supremacy.

The first center of influence emerged during the tenure of ʿAbd al-ʿAzīz ibn Marwān (d. 86/705). His involvement in patriarchal elections (see Chapters Seven, Nine, and the next section below) transformed Fusṭāṭ and Ḥulwān into new centers of influence virtually overnight. His tenure provides the genesis of two congruent narratives: one of the slow demise of Alexandria in the ecclesiastical domain, and another of the reciprocal growth of Fusṭāṭ's influence. As the details in the election proceedings for Isaac I and Simon I demonstrate, decisions made in Alexandria were no longer binding, but were liable to be overturned at the new capital. To some extent, the emergence of Fusṭāṭ as a center of ecclesiastical influence simply reflected new political realities, but it led to a shift in ecclesiastical politics that became increasingly explicit in subsequent patriarchal elections. Gradually (and irrevocably), ecclesiastical affairs had to take the new capital and its clergy into consideration. As for Ḥulwān, its prominence lasted only as long as ʿAbd al-ʿAzīz's governorship.[4] Soon the churches and clergy of Fusṭāṭ (especially those of the churches of al-Muʿallaqa, Abū Sarja, and the Virgin at Ḥārat al-Rūm) would play an increasingly prominent role in patriarchal elections and would constitute one of the most influential factions within the

Coptic church. Although addressing a later period, the HP makes this new dynamic explicit: "[The diocese of Cairo] does not follow the same course as the other southern and northern sees, because in it are the archons of Cairo and its leaders and the Coptic notables and chiefs who are the scribes of the state and their servants of the kingdom. In addition, their bishop must at all times be present in attendance on the reigning king".[5] Fusṭāṭ was the first center to emerge, but others would soon follow.

As the Bishop of Alexandria, one would expect the Coptic Patriarch to reside and spend most of his tenure in that city,[6] but under Islamic rule, while he was certainly free to remain there, a new sociopolitical environment prevented most patriarchs from remaining long within their diocese. Simply stated, the new governmental apparatus was centered at Fusṭāṭ (and later Cairo), not Alexandria; this posed a geographical chasm that had to be breached. Officially, the seat of the patriarch moved to Cairo in 1131 CE, under Fāṭimid rule, a process that began with Kyrillus II (Cyril, 1078–92 CE).[7] This is quite misleading, however. Already by the late seventh century CE, Coptic patriarchs spent a great deal of time in and around Fusṭāṭ.[8] Again, the governorship of ʿAbd al-ʿAzīz is of central importance. When the governor moved to Ḥulwān, he asked the Coptic Patriarch and bishops to accompany him to his new capital, and they consented. The need to keep Coptic patriarchs, who were recognized as the leading (though certainly not the sole) spokesmen for their communities, in contact with government officials posed a geographic challenge and initiated what might be termed a second itinerant phase for the patriarchate. Earlier, due to the turmoil generated by the Council of Chalcedon, Coptic patriarchs were often forced to reside outside of Alexandria. During the post-conquest period, a second itinerant phase commenced, but at that juncture it was the result of necessity (and choice) rather than compulsion.

Most Coptic patriarchs living during the second half of Umayyad rule did not take up residence in Alexandria, a pattern that persisted under early ʿAbbāsid rule as well. In the mid-eighth century, shortly after ʿAbbāsid control extended to Egypt, Patriarch Khaīl I moved to the political capital.[9] At an uncertain date, the Melkite patriarch also relocated to the vicinity of Fusṭāṭ, taking residence at the Monastery of al-Quṣayr at the Muqaṭṭam Mountain.[10] Most of Patriarch Khaīl's successors lived outside Alexandria, usually near Fusṭāṭ, an observation buttressed by the patriarchal biographies themselves, which describe events occurring in the heart of the Delta, not Alexandria.[11] This pattern may be observed directly and indirectly. By way of example, in the mid-third/ninth century, Patriarch Yusāb traveled to Alexandria to meet a delegation from the Church of Antioch,[12] and after his death his body was taken to that city for burial.[13] Rarely, however, did patriarchs actually reside in the capital proper (the fact that Fusṭāṭ had its own bishop at that time, and for centuries thereafter, complicated the issue).

In addition to Fusṭāṭ and Ḥulwān, a number of other locations served as patriarchal residences at one time or another until the twelfth century. These included: Damīrah, Mamṭarūn, Wādī al-Naṭrūn/Habīb, Maḥalāt Danyāl (where the *mayrūn* was once consecrated), and Damrū.[14] Ironically, serving as a patriarchal residence did not guarantee that a local would emerge as a center of influence. Even though Fusṭāṭ and Wādī al-Naṭrūn developed into such epicenters, they did so irrespective of serving as patriarchal residences. This second itinerant phase—the second effect of the Arab conquest on Alexandrian Christianity—came to an end in the mid-twelfth century with the patriarch's permanent relocation to Cairo.

A third repercussion manifested in the itinerancy of the electoral synod. Initially, the synod consistently convened in Alexandria, but as Fusṭāṭ (and Cairo) progressively eclipsed Alexandria's dominance, the council increasingly assembled there. On several occasions in the eighth century CE, the electoral delegation first assembled at Fusṭāṭ, elected a nominee, secured government approval, and then traveled to Alexandria to ordain the new patriarch.[15] By 978 CE, the procedure of assembling at Fusṭāṭ could pass for established "custom,"[16] though the historical record is not altogether conclusive in that regard; at other junctures, the electoral college met at the Monastery of St. Makarios,[17] the Church of Abū Sarja (St. Sergios), and al-Muʿallaqa.[18] As opposed to the patriarchal residences, which did not develop into centers of influence, hosting the electoral synod reflected a location's prominence or, rather, that of the conglomerate of clergy and lay notables associated with it.

A fourth manifestation of the newfound clout of these new centers may be observed (implicitly and explicitly) in the debates surrounding the right to elect new patriarchs, which is addressed in greater detail below. Here a bare summary will suffice. By the mid-eighth century, the Alexandrian prerogative to elect patriarchal candidates met with stiff opposition; Alexandria's clergy and notables/*arākhina* had to share that right. The history of patriarchal elections from the mid-eighth until the early tenth century is convoluted. Elections were contentious events in which various coalitions claimed exclusive rights of election and promoted their own agendas and candidates.[19]

Generally speaking, the composition of electoral synods was representational. The biography of Patriarch Afrahām provides a typical breakdown: "The bishops of the land of Miṣr from the Rīf and from the two Ṣaʿīds, the secretaries (*kuttāb*) of Miṣr, and the priests of Alexandria assembled".[20] Thus, clergy of every rank and several dioceses, as well as lay notables, participated. By the tenth century CE, the dominant factions reached a compromise, and a clear pattern emerged: the Alexandrians (clergy and notables) would elect the patriarch, leaving those of Fusṭāṭ, Cairo, and the monasteries of Wādī al-Naṭrūn to choose his successor. Implicit in the arrangement was that the candidate had to be acceptable to the non-electoral party. The first clear attestation of this practice survives in the biography of Zacharias I (elected in 1004 CE), though it claimed the practice as an established custom: "since it was *the turn* of the Alexandrians *this time* to appoint the patriarch, and the council was in Alexandria".[21] The next biography, that of Shinūda II, does not explicitly note the practice, but the pattern is implicit: the electoral synod convened in the Monastery of St. Makarios and Cairene notables orchestrated the proceedings. After Shinūda's death, the Alexandrians elected his successor, Khrisṭūdulūs.[22] The biography of the subsequent patriarch, Kyrillus II, provides another overt reference and confirms the pattern: "It was the turn of the priest and the *archons* of Cairo and the monks of the Monastery of Abba Makarios to appoint the patriarch".[23] The biography of the succeeding patriarch, Khaīl IV, likewise contains an explicit passage and conforms to the established pattern.[24] The competing centers had found a means of coexisting: they alternated in electing patriarchs, with the non-electoral party possessing a *de facto* veto over the candidate.

As the oscillating pattern between Alexandria and Cairo coalesced, the main centers of socio-religious influence and power clearly emerged. They were: the clergy and notables of Alexandria, those of Cairo and Fusṭāṭ, as represented by the clergy of Abū Sarja and those of al-Muʿallaqa (who often quarreled among themselves), and the monks of Wādī al-Naṭrūn, who were usually, though not exclusively, represented by the monks of the Monastery of St. Makarios. It is certainly no accident that the next anomaly is concerned with these same centers.

The fifth manifestation, which most clearly reflects the socio-political dynamics of that era, was the controversial practice of multiple patriarchal ordinations.[25] Theologically, the proceedings were in error. Ordination to a clerical rank should be performed only once; still, multiple ordinations do not nullify a clerical rank or office. That said, the practice should be interpreted against the backdrop of ecclesiastical politics and the rise of competing centers of authority—not theology.

The ordination of Patriarch Kyrillus II provides a sketch of the typical pattern. Upon his election, members of the electoral synod traveled to his cell in the Monastery of St. Makarios: "took him by force, clothed him with the robe, and *named him* Kyrillus".[26] They then: "journeyed with him to Alexandria and consecrated him (*karrazuh*) in it on the twenty-second of (the month of) Baramhāt (in the) year 794 of the Martyrs" (18 March 1078).[27] He then traveled to the Church of al-Muʿallaqa in Fusṭāṭ and "was consecrated (*kurraz*) in it". A few days later, he departed for the nearby Church of the Virgin in Ḥārat al-Rūm and "was consecrated (*kurraz*) in it".[28] Strikingly similar descriptions are found in the ordination rites for Makarios I (932 CE), Shinūda II (1032 CE), Khrisṭūdulūs (1047 CE), Kyrillus II (1078 CE), Khaīl IV (1092 CE), Makarios II (1102 CE), and Gabriel II (1131 CE).[29] The ordination of Shinūda II is consistently cited as the first attestation of this practice;[30] nonetheless, the biography of Makarios I provides the oldest testimony, pushing the dating of this practice back a century. Even there, however, the practice emerges as established tradition: "When [Makarios] had been consecrated in Alexandria *and* at the Monastery of Abba Makarios *and* in Miṣr *according to the custom* (*ʿalā al-ʿadā*)".[31] Although the biographies that immediately follow Makarios' are not definitive they certainly do not rule out the practice,[32] and the pattern is well documented from the elevation of Shinūda II (1032 CE), in an account written by his contemporary Bishop Michael of Tinnīs, through that of Gabriel II (1131 CE).

In all instances, patriarchs were repeatedly ordained in three to five locations. The Arabic verb *kurraz*, "consecrated," (or a cognate) is often employed to describe the proceedings. The theological awkwardness of this practice did not escape the modern translators of HP II.2, who identify one ritual as a "consecration," while rendering all others "proclamations". In HP II.3, the translators followed a different strategy, consistently rendering the verb as "consecrate" in each instance, but the footnotes betray their wariness.

Nonetheless, the case for multiple ordinations is exceptionally strong and, in general, the practice appears to have been far more prevalent than is hitherto acknowledged. First, it is attested during the Byzantine era, and under Islamic rule among the Copts, Syrians, and Melkites, for patriarchs as well as bishops.[33] Second, the majority of the biographies documenting the practice are among the most historically credible witnesses in the HP. They were written by contemporaries who attended the rites and had firsthand knowledge of the events and personalities they described.[34] By way of example, Michael of Tinnīs wrote the biography of Shinūda II; he was that patriarch's secretary prior to his own elevation to the episcopacy. The biographies of Khrisṭūdulūs and Kyrillus II were written by their contemporary Mawhūb ibn Manṣūr, and that of Khaīl IV was recorded by Yūḥannā ibn Sāʿīd al-Qulzūmī. Third, the coherence in Mawhūb's translation of Bishop Michael's biographies (HP II.2 was originally written in Coptic) reflects his repetitive use of the term ⲦⲰϢ/ⲐⲰϢ (or a cognate), which Mawhūb rendered repeatedly and consistently as *kurraz*. Mawhūb was fully bilingual and not theologically naive;[35] had the Coptic text (or the rituals he personally witnessed) given a sense appreciably different from the Arabic, such as the difference between "ordination" and "proclamation," it must be assumed that his translation would have reflected the distinction. At any rate, the consistency of the term is evident in most of the later biographies, all of which were originally composed in Arabic by contemporaries of great learning.

One interpretation of such events, apparent in the English translation of HP II.2, is that there was only one actual consecration (presumably at Alexandria),[36] while the others were "proclamations," or as they are known today, "enthronements": ritualized celebrations conducted when a bishop first travels to his diocese after ordination. The sources, nonetheless, remain sharply at odds with this interpretation. First, all the documented instances of this practice took place at a time when the diocese of Miṣr had its own bishop. It would not make sense to "enthrone" a patriarch in another's diocese, nor would it make sense to "enthrone" the patriarch at several other locations in which he did not reside or have direct ecclesiastical jurisdiction. Second, as discussed above, the verbiage used in each instance is fairly consistent in describing each proceeding as a "consecration." Moreover, even if the reading of "proclamation" were taken as correct for argument's sake, it would raise more questions than it would answer. In most instances, the consecration in Alexandria was second or third in line. To regard the first or second event as an "enthronement" is illogical since, according to that line of thinking, the candidate would not yet have been ordained. Further, the issue of how to interpret the fourth or fifth events would be still unresolved. Finally, it is clear that ecclesiastical figures, likely realizing the theological awkwardness of the practice, tried to end it by the twelfth century. Thus, the consecration rites as described in the biography of Gabriel II (1131 CE) are decidedly different. The narrative unobtrusively depicts a fragmented ritual in which the candidate still traveled to four centers, but the consecration proceeded in a piece-meal fashion as an attempt to avoid the questionable duplication of the rite. The rite proceeded as thus: (1)

Gabriel was anointed (*dhahnūh*) in al-Muʿallaqa; (2) in Alexandria he was elevated (*awsamūh*) patriarch; (3) he then returned to al-Muʿallaqa, where he was clothed in monastic attire including the *schema*; (4) returning to Alexandria, he was consecrated (*kurraz*) there; and (5) he then went to the Monastery of St. Makarios in order to "complete his consecration" (*yakmal takrīzahu*).[37] This circumvented any theological awkwardness, while preserving each center's prestige. It is of great significance that this implicit reform coincides *exactly* with the end of the second itinerant phase of the patriarchate and the patriarchal residence's permanent relocation to Fāṭimid Cairo.[38]

The five historical trends highlighted above (rise of new centers of influence, itinerancy of the patriarchal residence, itinerancy of the electoral synod, sharing electoral duties, and multiple ordinations) resulted from the same stimulus: the decline of Alexandria in political and ecclesiastical affairs and the novel socio-political dynamics inaugurated by Arab rule. Significantly, all five developments came to an abrupt end in the mid-twelfth century CE. When the patriarch officially relocated to Cairo, the ecclesiastical and political domains again converged in one city, as they had in late antique Alexandria. Thus, the second itinerant phase of the patriarchate ended. With the new official status of Cairo as a patriarchal seat, no other center could claim dominance. Subsequent to this event, the electoral synod met regularly in Cairo, although consecrations were performed in Alexandria for another two centuries (doubtless for symbolic reasons). References to the Alexandrian/Cairene practice of nominating alternating candidates for the patriarchal office ceased, as did the practice of multiple ordinations. All of Gabriel II's successors have only one ordination.[39] Also significant is the absence of any mention of an "enthronement" for any of them. As the head of both dioceses, Fusṭāṭ/Cairo and Alexandria, it would not have been odd for the patriarch to have been ordained in one diocese and enthroned in the other. Nonetheless, the fact that only nondescript festivities are described without noting an official "enthronement" calls into question whether "enthronements" were practiced during these centuries at all.[40]

Beyond the topic at hand, this discussion underscores the importance of early Coptic Arabic sources for the study of the Coptic church through the twelfth century (much as those in other chapters have highlighted the same pattern with regard to Islamic history). Here, early texts provide an essential grounding for the interpretive framework used in analyzing the five above-mentioned developments, which previous scholarship, often addressing them in isolation and relying exclusively on later authors, had erroneously interpreted as outgrowths of Fāṭimid policies. Fāṭimid rule witnessed the fruition of processes and dynamics that were set into motion centuries prior to Jawhar's conquest of the province.

The Hierarchy

Bishops, priests, and deacons constitute the three dominant ranks of the clergy.[41] As may be expected, deacons and priests are well represented in literary and documentary texts, while bishops and patriarchs are best attested in normative literature. Here the aim is to trace the changing functions and responsibilities of these three ranks under Islamic rule.

Archdeacons and deacons distinguish themselves as some of the most educated members of the clergy,[42] who often were employed or functioned as scribes and financial administrators of various church properties.[43] Literary sources, predominantly reflecting the higher ecclesiastical circles of the Delta, frequently depict deacons as personal assistants to bishops and patriarchs.[44] Some even wrote the patriarchal biographies that were included in the HP: Deacons Jirja and Mawhūb ibn Manṣūr provide the most illustrious examples.[45] Deacons were routinely nominated and elevated to the rank of bishop or patriarch,[46] though their ordination as presbyters, while certainly documented, does not appear to have been as prevalent (or automatic) as in the modern period.[47] Most deacons held secular occupations in addition to their ecclesiastical duties (not uncommon among priests as well),[48] which enabled some to become wealthy patrons of churches.[49] In ecclesiastical Arabic, the term *kāhin* at times applied to deacons as well as priests.[50]

Until the tenth century, deacons exercised an immense degree of authority, equaling, on occasion even surpassing, that of priests. In several instances, deacons had charge of prominent churches, which undoubtedly had a large retinue of clergy attached. They also routinely served as stewards of ecclesiastical and monastic properties.[51] Such were the responsibilities of Deacon Mark of the Church of St. Menas and Deacon George: "one of the chief clerics of Alexandria and steward of the church of Alexandria".[52] Later, Archdeacon Simon also served in the same capacity as did the anonymous ("disobedient") archdeacon who served during the Patriarchate of Yaʿqūb I (819–30).[53]

Above all, one incident underscores the influence exercised by an archdeacon in the early post-conquest period. In selecting a successor to John III: "The bishops assembled under the leadership of Gregory bishop of al-Kaïs, Yaʿqūb bishop of Arwāṭ, John bishop of Nikiou, and a body of bishops and of the Christian laity. They consulted with the clergy of Alexandria, and they included with them the leading secretary (*al-kātib al-mutawallī*); and they agreed to nominate the deacon George of Sakhā".[54] On the following day, however, as this illustrious group was on its way to ordain George, Mark the Archdeacon of Alexandria stopped them and protested: "If you will not come to the church on Sunday, according to the custom prescribed by the canons, when all the people of the city shall be assembled, I will not assist in the ordination of this man [George]".[55] The archdeacon's threat halted the proceedings, and eventually the monk Isaac, not George, was appointed patriarch. The rite of consecration required the participation of the archdeacon, and the assembled bishops and clergy (who certainly knew beforehand that Sunday was the canonical day for episcopal ordinations) could not circumvent his participation.[56]

Liturgically, deacons of this period exercised their office in much the same manner as their late antique counterparts: a deacon read the Gospel, even in the presence of the patriarch,[57] he gave communion to the congregation from the chalice,[58] and partook of the *Isbādīqun*.[59] Traditionally, the deacon stood in the east (facing the congregation), opposite the priest.[60] The liturgical role of deacons included the offering of incense and the pronouncement of responses, prayers, and commands such as, "The holies are for the holy," "One is the holy Father,..." and "Go in peace. The peace of God be with you," all of which were later, as is still the case today, appropriated by priests and bishops.[61] The liturgical shift is evident when comparing the Coptic and Arabic recensions of the *Apocalypse of Athanasios*. Section 4.3 of that tract glosses the concluding directive, "Go in Peace," but while the Coptic version (composed ca. 720s CE) states that the deacon issued this parting command, the Arabic recension (ca. tenth century), reflecting contemporary practice, places the statement on the lips of the priest.[62] Ultimately, this is but another chapter in the history of the deteriorating liturgical duties of the deacon in Egypt. Still, it would appear that the order was in greater decline among the Melkites than the Copts. By the fourteenth century, al-Makīn the Younger denounced the Melkite practice of celebrating the Eucharist without a deacon and ordaining children to the office.[63] Among the Copts, deterioration is documented in the *al-Jawhara al-nafīsa*, where deacons are described as the "servants of priests," not of the bishop, as is clear from New Testament and patristic literature, though *Tartīb al-kahanūt* is more traditional on that front, describing the deacon as "a partner to the priest in the liturgy,"[64] which is consistent with the liturgical act of sharing the *Isbādīqun*.

Priests (and archpriests) are frequently referenced, though individual presbyters are rarely identified by name, in normative texts such as the HP;[65] most of the exceptions in that regard are comprised of priests who were subsequently ordained bishops or patriarchs.[66] As a cohort, the Clergy of Alexandria exercised disproportionate influence. In a fourth-century letter, St. Jerome stated that the Alexandrian clergy elected the patriarch.[67] By the late seventh century CE, in electing Isaac I (in 686 CE), the approval of Alexandria's clergy still remained a priority. Upon Patriarch Isaac's death in 689 CE, however, the two most prominent churches in Alexandria quarreled: "a dispute took place between the clergy of Saint Mark the Evangelist and the clergy of the Church of the Angelion".[68] The clerics feuded as to who should succeed Isaac, but it would appear that patriarchal elections remained an Alexandrian prerogative through the mid-eighth century.

Fifty years later, socio-religious dynamics had a distinctly different tinge. In the 744 CE election of Khaīl I, the clergy of Alexandria traveled to Miṣr in order to deliberate.[69] Still, while Alexandria no longer functioned as the center of ecclesiastical affairs, the clergy of that city maintained an increasingly anachronistic monopoly over the proceedings of patriarchal elections. The Archpriest of Alexandria, representing the clergy of the city, declared: "This matter [namely, the election of the patriarch] is our prerogative, not that of the bishops. They are only to lay hands (*waḍ' al-yad*) [upon the candidate]; we are the ones who elect the patriarch".[70] In response to this bold statement, Bishop Abraham of Fayyūm retorted: "Your bishops also may propose to you an individual whom they choose, and if you choose one who is worthy, we will ordain him; if not, we will not ordain him".[71] Significantly, the bishop did not challenge the Alexandrian clergy's entitlement to elect the patriarch, but simply affirmed the episcopal right to refuse ordination. Thus, while the Alexandrian clergy (and notables) chose a successor, the bishops had veto power over the candidate.[72]

Nonetheless, while the prerogatives of Alexandrian's clergy were acknowledged, they rested upon a contestable premise that was quickly challenged. The precipitating incident is treated somewhat comically in the HP; nonetheless, the 744 CE electoral proceedings initiated a new dynamic. After a prolonged stalemate, the old and infirm Bishop Moses of Wasīm (who had to be physically carried to the proceedings) stood up, and with his staff in hand chased the Alexandrian clergy out of the Church of St. Shinūda at Miṣr, where the synod had convened. Whatever may have actually occurred, in the election of Khaīl I bishops gained the right to actively participate in the electoral process, not just to ordain candidates.[73] Still, the clergy of Alexandria retained a great deal of clout.

Bishops and patriarchs are frequently cited in the literary sources of the Delta.[74] For the most part, little is known of Upper Egyptian bishops beyond some of their names and when they were active, the most notable exceptions being Bishops Pesynthios of Koptos (Qifṭ) and Abraham of Hermonthis (Armant).[75] Generally, bishops came from monastic ranks, though exceptions are not hard to come by.[76] Until the twelfth century CE, the ordination of widowers to the episcopacy (even those who had fathered children) was not uncommon.[77] Additionally, a number of laymen (mainly notables), along with urban deacons and priests, were nominated and elevated to the episcopal and patriarchal offices.[78] Until the past century, Coptic bishops were explicitly excluded from consideration for the patriarchate, the Bishopric of Alexandria. This issue even led to a schism between the Coptic and Syrian churches in the mid-eighth century, when Patriarch Khaīl I adamantly maintained that no bishop should ever become patriarch as was the case with his Syrian counterpart, Patriarch Isaac, who had served as the Bishop of Ḥarrān.[79] The schism ended after the death of both prelates.

Bishops attained their rank through varied means: a reputation for virtue and holiness propelled some to the office, a few were subject to a vote and elected from within the diocese they would head,[80] several were handpicked by their predecessor,[81] others were elected through miraculous means, while others still simply bought the office through simony or government interference.[82] In most cases, the consent of parishioners was obtained implicitly or explicitly,[83] and adhering to early Alexandrian practice, the patriarch (accompanied by at least two other bishops) ordained all bishops in the province.[84] Still, once ordained, a bishop had a jurisdiction over his diocese that no other, including the patriarch, could share in or challenge.[85]

Episcopal names were at times retained in dioceses, a pious practice that inhibits the historical identification of individual bishops and their accomplishments.[86] In total, the number of bishops (and diocese) throughout the period surveyed was roughly sixty,[87] though in the tenth century CE, due to depopulation (and possibly conversion of Islam), a number of dioceses merged.[88] The affluence of bishops fluctuated greatly. The mid-eighth-century Bishop Abraham of Fayyūm had jurisdiction over thirty-five monasteries and could draw upon tremendous resources,[89] while others, such as Bishop Shamūl, were "poor, in want of sustenance from day to day".[90]

The early eighth-century *Life of Isaac of Alexandria* describes two main organizational divisions: John, Bishop of Pshati, represented the bishops of Upper Egypt, while Gregory, Bishop of al-Kaïs, represented those of Lower Egypt.[91] By the end of the eighth century CE, however, the Bishop of Miṣr emerged as the most important ecclesiastical figure after the patriarch, a distinction that persisted until the twelfth century CE (when the patriarch annexed that diocese). In the absence of a patriarch, the Bishop of Miṣr took a leading role as documented in the tenure of Bishop Michael of Miṣr, to whom all looked for leadership after the death of John IV.[92] By the late seventh century CE, the Bishop of Miṣr attained jurisdiction over all monasteries.[93] Still, it remains unclear what that actually entailed, and it is likely that his prerogative only extended to the collection of taxes on monastic properties, which, by the mid-eighth century CE, had to be paid in Fusṭāṭ rather than Alexandria.

Those who were elevated to the patriarchate during the period surveyed came from a diversity of backgrounds, though not one of them was a bishop; they included laymen (Afrahām and Murqus III) and a monk who had led a spiritual, or chaste, marriage prior to joining a monastery (Mīnā II). Still, most patriarchs came from a more traditional monastic background. Over time, the titles for the officeholder became more elaborate: "bishop" gave way to "archbishop," and by the end of the seventh century, the title of "patriarch," used earlier in other provinces, was increasingly prevalent in Egypt.[94] To these, *papas*, "Pope," must be added. First applied to Bishop Heraklas (d. 249 CE), the title is certainly one of the oldest designations for the Alexandrian prelate (used once in the fourth century, the bishops of Rome did not routinely use the title until the sixth century). Still, despite experiencing a tremendous resurgence among contemporary Copts, in all pre-modern texts "archbishop" and "patriarch" dominate. In part, this was due to the ubiquitous application of the Greek *papa(s)* to lower clergy, especially parish and monastic priests.[95] The modern *abūna*, literally "our father," the normative designation for a Coptic priest, is no doubt a carryover from this earlier usage (cf. the Coptic *neiōt* in *P.Mon.Apollo*).

When electing a patriarch, a "fee" was routinely paid to the governor, who reciprocated by permitting the convening of the electoral synod and the subsequent consecration of a new patriarch (in some cases the fee was paid after the selection was made). On occasion, however, avaricious governors demanded exorbitant payments and delayed electoral proceedings for months, even years, until their demands were met.[96] Inevitably, the importance of the post, and that of the episcopacy in general, induced many governors to meddle both directly and circuitously in ecclesiastical affairs, leading to an assortment of abuses. Some individuals seeking ordination to various ranks or appointment to a specific bishopric or the patriarchate first sought the support of the governor, rather than that of the patriarch or bishops. Kyrillus III secured his ordination to the patriarchate through such means, but the problem was endemic; he was but one of a host of individuals who attained ecclesiastical ranks due to temporal maneuvering rather than spiritual merit.[97]

Two assistants,[98] often called "sons" or "disciples,"[99] usually accompanied bishops and patriarchs. Upon the death of a patriarch (or bishop), his disciples were often among those nominated to replace him.[100] As part of their annual routine, patriarchs spent the Forty Days of Lent in monastic retreat. Initially, they journeyed to the Enaton, but by the eighth century CE, the destination had shifted to the Monastery of St. Makarios.[101]

Under Islamic rule, the patriarch's political role reached an unprecedented level—a development with mixed results and ramifications. Perceived as the guardian and spokesman of his community,[102] governors often held the Coptic Patriarch responsible for events well beyond his control (e.g. riots, or problems with Nubia).[103] This should not overshadow the important, even vital, role played by Christian magistrates and notables (discussed in Chapter Three), but while magistrates came and went, the patriarchal office was constant. The authority wielded by Coptic patriarchs under Islamic rule was succinctly summarized in the heated response of Patriarch Yusāb to the *qāḍī* Muḥammad ibn ʿAbdallāh: "You say these words to these bishops who have no authority over me. Whereas my authority over them is from God and from the caliph, and the execution of my sentence takes place among my people and my flock".[104]

Most patriarchs enjoyed tremendous popular support by virtue of their office, and many, such as Khaīl I, gained a reputation for holiness. Even prior to his ordination, an enthusiastic crowd mobbed the patriarch-elect and tore off portions of his clothing to keep as a blessing, and for much of his tenure Christians and Muslims sought after his prayers and advice.[105] The holiness and sanctity of patriarchs is a prevalent theme in the HP, which often, though by no means exclusively, delves into hagiography.[106] Still, less than flattering depictions are also attested, particularly in the biographies drafted by Bishop Michael of Tinnīs and the lengthy account focused on Kyrillus III.

Two internal threats attempted to undermine the position of the Bishop of Alexandria as Patriarch—the ecclesiastical leader of Coptic Christianity—in the ninth century. Isḥāq ibn Andūna posed the first, indirect challenge (see Chapter Three). While Bishop of Wasīm, he successfully prevented the election of a bishop for Fusṭāṭ, and for the duration of his tenure controlled both bishoprics in direct defiance of Patriarch Yusāb. A second, more direct, confrontation came in the mid-ninth century CE, when Bannā, the Bishop of Miṣr, tried to usurp the patriarchate with the help of the *qāḍī* Muḥammad ibn ʿAbdallāh.[107] Five bishops sided with the *qāḍī* and recognized Bannā as their new leader (only three are required to elevate a patriarch).[108] If it had not been for the caliph's endorsement of Patriarch Yusāb, Bannā would have been able to enforce the *qāḍī*'s judgment and become *de facto* patriarch.[109]

During this transitional period, clergy had to quickly adapt and interact with new socio-political realities and new religious sensibilities. Deacons suffered the most as their office, still prestigious and influential in the ninth century, slowly deteriorated administratively and liturgically. Alexandrian priests lost some of their influence, particularly in regard to the monopoly they enjoyed over patriarchal elections, but they still retained a great deal of clout and a disproportionate influence over the see. Additionally, as Coptic patriarchs came to routinely reside outside of the city, the

Alexandrians developed something of a *de facto* autonomy. The irony is often palpable in later writings. As Bishop of Alexandria, the patriarch should have exercised absolute control over the clergy of his city, yet the itinerancy of the patriarchal residence fostered a sense of alienation that rendered them the very lot that he could control the least. Additionally, it may be argued that the Alexandrian clergy constituted the root cause of a great deal of corruption. Much of the rampant simony documented under Islamic rule may be directly linked to the financial demands they imposed on Coptic patriarchs.[110] Certainly, the festering problem was multi-causal, but the demands of the Alexandrian clergy undoubtedly played a significant role.

Under Islamic rule, the reach of the patriarchal office increased. Having survived two challenges in the ninth century, the Bishop of Alexandria's prerogative as patriarch became deeply entrenched. In due course, Coptic patriarchs gained control of the bishopric of Cairo/Miṣr over the objections of contemporaries who clearly understood the ecclesiological problem that would emerge once a bishop, even a patriarch, had jurisdiction over two dioceses.[111] Oddly enough, it was under Islamic rule that the patriarchal office regained the socio-political clout it enjoyed prior to the Chalcedonian schism. More often than not, patriarchs once again enjoyed the support of civil officials and directly communicated with them.

Status of Churches: Theory and Practice

A significant aspect of the Christianization of Egypt proceeded through the dissemination of Christian ideology and symbols in the public sphere. In part, this Christianization of space proceeded through the construction of churches, cathedrals, martyria, and monasteries, along with the closing and destruction of pagan temples and the conversion of some into churches and monasteries.[112] On one such occasion, the fifth-century Abbot Shenoute of Atripe (348–466 CE) enthusiastically proclaimed: "At the site of a shrine to an unclean spirit, it will henceforth be a shrine to the Holy Spirit. And at the site of sacrificing to Satan and worshipping and fearing him, Christ will henceforth be served therein, and he will be worshipped, bowed down to and feared. And where there are blasphemings, it is blessings and hymns that will henceforth be therein".[113]

Ecclesiastical structures would quickly dominate the landscape of late antique Egypt. Muslims would inherit that same landscape and Islamize it in a similar manner to that just described: some churches were destroyed, others were converted into mosques, while the construction of new churches (in time) was severely restricted as new mosques came to dominate the landscape. The transformation proceeded slowly, but by the late fourth/tenth century churches and mosques punctuated the topography of the province. Below, the initial analysis focuses on the means by which ecclesiastical properties changed hands, particularly under early Islamic rule. It problematizes the prevalent notion that the Arab government simply handed over properties to the Copts. Subsequently, the focus shifts to the building programs initiated by Christians, and the resistance they did and did not encounter during the first few centuries under Islamic rule. Indirectly, the emerging historiography may function as a valuable litmus test to gauge governmental and popular attitudes toward *dhimmīs* at various junctures. A related issue, intra-Christian sectarian and ideological debates surrounding the ownership of ecclesiastical properties, is addressed in the following chapter. Before proceeding, it must be noted that due to the nature of the extant sources, the following discussion is most relevant to the Delta: the situation in Upper Egypt may have been substantially different.

Earliest Interactions

Squabbles over ecclesiastical properties have a long history in Egypt. In the aftermath of the Council of Chalcedon, anti- and pro-Chalcedonians claimed and reclaimed several churches and monasteries.[114] Patriarch Eutychios noted that during the reign of Emperor Justinian, the Melkite patriarch-prefect Apollinarios reclaimed many of the churches that had been taken over by the anti-Chalcedonians.[115] Similar actions are ascribed to another Melkite patriarch-prefect, Kyros, in the decade prior to the Arab conquest, and to Melkite notables in the decades immediately following that event.[116]

In the post-conquest period, the traditional perspective, documented by only a few "medieval" authors but dominant in all secondary literature, is that once the Arabs gained control of Egypt they immediately handed over all churches to the anti-Chalcedonians.[117] This erroneous belief adopts a normative perspective of a later period and conflates two questions. First, how did anti-Chalcedonians gain control of churches in the wake of the Arab conquest; second, if the Islamic government played a role in the Coptic acquisition of churches, when, where, and how did it do so?

A major obstacle in addressing the first question is the nature of the extant evidence. Byzantine and Coptic authors do not provide anything resembling a catalogue of the properties owned by either faction, a problem underscored by the nagging and ultimately unanswerable question of the size and demographic distribution of the pro-Chalcedonian community in urban and rural regions during the Byzantine period. Post-conquest literature is equally vague, but consistently depicts the Melkites as an urban minority, with concentrations in Alexandria, Fusṭāṭ, Ḥulwān, and al-Būrah.[118]

It is highly unlikely that rural churches and those in areas heavily populated by anti-Chalcedonians exchanged hands at all during the century preceding the Arab conquest. More problematic, however, are the churches of Alexandria. Under Kyros, all anti-Chalcedonian churches were confiscated and their clergy expelled from the city; this was the enforcement of a law that had been hitherto intermittently enforced in Alexandria since the mid-sixth century.[119] The early career of Patriarch Agathon demonstrates the effects of this edict. While still a priest in the 630s, he criss-crossed Alexandria disguised as a carpenter to dispense communion to the anti-Chalcedonians of the city.[120] The means by which the Copts attained churches in Alexandria likely varied, but the process was likely facilitated by the lack of Byzanitien interference and the shrinking ranks of the Melkites in Egypt.

Intra-communal conversion (see Chapter Four) provided another means for the *de facto* acquisition of ecclesiastical properties. Early in the seventh century, the number of pro-Chalcedonian churches (and convert clergy) in Alexandria increased as much as tenfold under the saintly Melkite patriarch John the Almsgiver.[121] Later, after the Arab conquest, the pattern reversed course and conversion trends favored the anti-Chalcedonians.[122] A prominent example of such an acquisition is documented in the biography of Mark II (d. 819 CE), which cites the reconsecration of a formerly Barsanuphian church.[123]

As to the second issue, that of government interference in the process of church acquisition, it must be noted that the prevailing consensus, that the government simply allotted churches to the Copts, stems from the nationalist paradigm scrutinized in Chapters Two, Three, and Five. To reiterate one conclusion from those discussions, the Arab conquerors treated the Coptic church and hierarchy with ambivalence until the governorship of ʿAbd al-ʿAzīz ibn Marwān (d. 705 CE). With regard to the ownership of churches, a similar conclusion may be reached. While anti-Chalcedonians attained great liberty to build and restore churches in the wake of the conquest, they do not appear to have been simply "given" churches. Prior to the tenure of ʿAbd al-ʿAzīz, it is highly unlikely that the government played any role in the procurement of churches by either side. Hitherto, most Christians in positions of influence tended to be Melkites, who often wrought havoc upon the Coptic hierarchy and populace. Doubtless, Copts appropriated newly abandoned churches, and clearly began to build new ones. What is surprising, however, is that the only documented instances of church acquisition in the immediate wake of the conquest are by Melkites who confiscated Coptic churches.[124]

In general, the best assessment of the Islamic government's initial policy regarding ecclesiastical properties is found in the Syrian *Chronicle of 1234*: "For at the time when they were conquered and made subject to the Arabs the cities agreed to terms of surrender, under which each confession had assigned to it those temples (*hayklē*), which were found in its possession".[125] The government's early ambivalence toward confessional issues and affinity for the pre-conquest *status quo* are succinctly summarized here (also demonstrated in Chapter Three). This policy prevailed in Syria, but it was not strictly adhered to in Egypt, otherwise the Copts would not have had a single church in Alexandria. Still, in Egypt where the majority professed the anti-Chalcedonian creed, strict adherence would have been impossible to enforce.

Melkites held on to a significant number of ecclesiastical properties in Alexandria until the twilight of John III's patriarchate (ca. 685–6 CE),[126] but during the tenure of ʿAbd al-ʿAzīz the Copts gained strong governmental allies in the person of the governor and his anti-Chalcedonian secretaries, Athanasios and Isaac.[127] And while the governor sought to strike a balance by permitting pro- and anti-Chalcedonians to construct new churches,[128] the influence of Athanasios and Isaac should not be underestimated. The *Naẓm al-jawhar* of the pro-Chalcedonian patriarch Eutychios retains a telling passage. After his ordination, Quzmān, the Melkite patriarch of Alexandria (727–68 CE), asked the Caliph Hishām to return "the churches that the Jacobites had taken over *with the help of a group of secretaries* (*kuttāb*)".[129]

Building Codes

By the eleventh century CE, a consensus among Muslim scholars held that only those churches and synagogues that existed at the time of the conquest had a legal standing, and that no others should have been built, particularly in *ʿanwa* land.[130] The pertinent regulations were formulized in the so-called *Covenant of ʿUmar*, which is a later document that certainly does not predate the ʿAbbāsids. The earliest conquest narratives do not regulate the construction or maintenance of ecclesiastical properties,[131] but incremental regulations were invented, amended, and anachronistically dated to the period of the conquest: *nuqūs* were not to be struck,[132] churches were not to be higher than adjacent mosques, and then they were not to be higher than the adjacent dwellings of Muslims. Historically, most of these regulations—if they existed at all—had little to no effect on the Christian community over the first two centuries of Islamic rule. Even after regulations were on the books, strict enforcement of ecclesiastical building codes proved sporadic and short-lived until the early eleventh century CE.[133] Although the Fāṭimids were typically tolerant in this regard,[134] al-Ḥākim bi Amr Allāh's two decades of persecution radically altered the prevailing *status quo*, and increasingly stringent attitudes and regulations would follow under Ayyūbid and Mamlūk rule (certainly the Crusades contributed to the dynamic).[135]

Many Coptic churches and monasteries were destroyed or abandoned at the onset of the Persian occupation of Egypt (618–29 CE), and during the subsequent Byzantine recovery (629–39 CE) anti-Chalcedonians were not allowed to restore their churches. Thus, once Arab rule afforded them that opportunity, the Copts immediately engaged in the restoration of their churches and monasteries. Wealthy patrons took the lead,[136] though a few patriarchs, above all, John IV (d. 799 CE), began massive building programs on their own initiative.

In the wake of the conquest, Patriarch Benjamin I (aided by the donation provided by *dux* Shenoute) restored the Church of St. Mark in Alexandria, consecrated a new church at the Monastery of St. Makarios, and initiated similar projects elsewhere.[137] Construction and restoration projects continued throughout the first/seventh century under Benjamin's immediate successors: Agathon, John III, Isaac I, and Simon I.[138] Early ecclesiastical building projects were widespread and apparently unchecked by the nascent government. Ibn ʿAbd al-Ḥakam and the HCME date the first church built in Fusṭāṭ Miṣr after the conquest to the governorship of Maslamā ibn Mukhallad al-Anṣārī (47–68/667–87).[139] Early Umayyad caliphs and governors were generally very accommodating or, likely, altogether indifferent to the issue of ecclesiastical building projects. This is well illustrated by ʿAbd al-ʿAzīz ibn Marwān's instructions to Patriarch Isaac I to build two churches at Ḥulwān, a request he reiterated to Simon I.[140] Liberal-minded in this regard, ʿAbd al-ʿAzīz also accommodated the requests of his pro- and anti-Chalcedonian secretaries and employees for the construction of churches.[141]

While the decades stretching from the conquest through the tenure of ʿAbd al-ʿAzīz appear to have been an age of unchecked construction and repair, change was soon on the horizon. An initial shift first appeared during the governorship of Qurra ibn Sharīk (90–6/709–15), who confiscated gold and silver liturgical vessels along with the colored pillars and marble of churches;[142] ultimately, this was but a short-lived edict, however. Another significant, though perhaps misleading incident, occurred in 117/736. When the governor al-Walīd ibn Rifāʿa permitted the Copts to build the Church of Abū Mīnā at al-Ḥamrā', Wuhayb al-Yaḥṣubī led a revolt against him.[143] The insurrection may have been in reaction to the construction of a church, but more likely that was but a pretext for Yamanī factions to revolt against a Qaysī governor a few years after the Qaysī minority monopolized the top administrative posts in the province (see Chapter Seven).[144] Still, this provides the first Egyptian incident in which the building of a church developed into a contentious issue. By the late Umayyad period, restoration and construction projects persisted, but officials had to be bribed.[145]

Government policies continued to fluctuate under the ʿAbbāsids. Some churches and monasteries were destroyed during the violent events that led to the rise of that dynasty, though that was exceptional.[146] Similar to the early Umayyads, the early ʿAbbāsids exhibited a libertarian mindset, particularly where ecclesiastical projects were concerned. Patriarch John IV's tenure (158–84/775–99) is particularly noteworthy in this regard. He inaugurated a massive building program that included the construction of a new patriarchal residence and new parishes in Alexandria, and the adornment of existing churches.[147] The initiative also prompted proactive (even aggressive) attempts at procuring relics to sanctify the new structures.[148] Funding for these projects came from the faithful as well as wealthy patrons.[149]

Such a pitch of activity was bound to attract attention, however. The HP records that the pro-Chalcedonian patriarch, purportedly out of jealously, accused Patriarch John of illegally occupying government properties and turning them into churches. The allegation apparently carried some weight, or at least succeeded as an extortion ploy: the patriarch paid a heavy fine.[150] By the end of John's tenure, Hārūn al-Rashīd issued an edict calling for the destruction of churches built after the conquest, a command the local governor immediately implemented by destroying churches in and around

Fusṭāṭ. Soon after these events, the governor and the patriarch died.[151] John's successor, Mark II, fulfilling a prophecy foretold in the HP, rebuilt the churches that were destroyed and continued his predecessor's building program.[152] Throughout Patriarch Mark's tenure, the major restriction curtailing new construction was not Islamic law or regulations, but rather the interference of other Christian factions. When asked by a notable to build a church in the midst of the city, the patriarch replied: "You know the jealousy of these neighbors of yours. When we begin the work they will present petitions to the governor against us and complain about us; and so we shall fall into trials such as we endured during the building of the church of Michael the Angel [during the patriarchate of John IV]".[153] This intense intra-communal rivalry may be read as a commentary on the prevailing attitudes: as long as no one objected too strenuously, building projects proceeded unhampered by governmental regulations. Significantly, at least at that juncture, those who objected were fellow Christians rather than Muslims, but that would soon change.

Despite the lack of collegiality among the Christian factions, all benefited from the government's *laissez faire* attitude. Frequently during the first few centuries of Islamic rule, the initiative of an affluent patron, such as the Coptic Maqāra of Nabarūh or the Melkite Bukām, could result in the erection of a new church.[154] This remarkable period of building activity continued through the early ninth century under patriarchs Yaʿqūb I and Yusāb I, but the feverish pace abated.[155] By the patriarchate of Yusāb I, new construction projects were few and restoration projects were primarily due to a briefly-enforced, though destructive edict through which the government (again) confiscated the pillars and marble of churches.[156] Patriarch Yusāb also renovated the Hanging Church of Fusṭāṭ, al-Muʿallaqa, which had been destroyed in order to pressure the patriarch into ordaining Theodore, the son of Isḥāq ibn Andūna, a bishop for Wasīm—an ultimately successful ploy.[157]

The status of churches built after the Arab conquest was not of serious concern until the very end of the eighth century, when the Caliph Hārūn al-Rashīd (170–94/786–809) issued the above-referenced edict calling for the destruction of all such buildings.[158] At that juncture the pattern so prevalent in the history of Coptic churches in Egypt became pronounced: churches demolished under one governor were rebuilt during the tenure of his successor or, as was the case under al-Ḥākim bi Amr Allāh, by the same administration that had ordered their destruction.[159] Here, the structures destroyed by the governor ʿAlī ibn Sulaymān, who enforced al-Rashīd's edict, were restored under his successor, Mūsā ibn ʿĪsā ibn Mūsā, over the objections of those who (correctly) maintained that the demolished churches had been constructed in the post-conquest period.[160] The mid-ninth century proved to be a turbulent juncture, during which revolts in Alexandra combined with the harsh policies of Caliph al-Mutawakkil (233–47/847–61) to bring about general instability within the Coptic community, the abandonment of monasteries (due to raids by *'urbān*, see Chapter Eight), and the closing of churches by edict.[161] Significantly, none of these edicts or acts of vandalism targeted monasteries, several of which were built well after the conquest; they were likely overlooked on account of their remoteness.

Ecclesiastical building projects continued under the Fāṭimids, whose policies were in many ways fairly liberal, with the one major exception of the devastating reign of al-Ḥākim bi Amr Allāh.[162] Overall, building restrictions were not adhered to with any consistency,[163] but while the government exhibited a fickle, though predominantly lax attitude, legal precedent had been set since the days of Hārūn al-Rashīd, and it would appear that popular sentiments followed suit and were becoming increasingly rigid. This may be deduced from the events surrounding the restoration of churches during the caliphate of al-Muʿizz in Egypt (973–5 CE).

According to the HP, after gaining the caliph's admiration,[164] Christians were allowed to restore their churches in Fusṭāṭ and Alexandria, along with "all the churches that were in need of restoration".[165] Of interest, however, is the resistance encountered in restoring the Church of St. Merkourios in Fusṭāṭ.[166] The church had been in ruins for some time and Muslim merchants had used it as a storehouse for sugarcane, an important cash crop in Egypt at that time. Initially, the merchants objected to losing their warehouse, but when the patriarch brought the matter to the attention of the caliph, he sent troops to begin the rebuilding process. Intimidated by the soldiers, the merchants surrendered their claim, but then a local—presumably *sunnī*—*mu'adhdhin* threw himself into the foundation (the church appears to have been completely rebuilt) and proclaimed: "I desire to die today for the name of Allāh [rather than] let anyone [re]build this church".[167] Annoyed, the *imām* ordered the completion of the foundation, and the soldiers resumed their work. If not for the intervention of Patriarch Afrahām, the *mu'adhdhin* would have been entombed in the foundation of the church.

It is difficult to discern whether the situation would have deteriorated to the extent that it did had the merchants not objected to the renovation of the church, or had the *imām* not reacted by sending Muslim soldiers to rebuild a church, thereby causing a spectacle and arousing the curiosity and religious fervor of onlookers. As mentioned above, the early Fāṭimids were largely disinterested in the strict enforcement of religious building codes. Demonstrably, however, public sentiments regarding the restoration and construction of *dhimmī* properties were easily swayed and increasingly conservative.

In sum, the Islamic government and populace exhibited a liberal attitude toward the construction of ecclesiastical buildings, particularly during the first seventy years of Islamic rule, and the first fifty years under the ʿAbbāsids. Nothing approaching the austerity of the *Covenant of ʿUmar* can be cited: only bits and pieces of regulation and sporadic enforcement are evident in the historical record. Furthermore, on the occasions when churches were destroyed, they were usually restored in a matter of years (if not months), often regardless of the church's actual antiquity. This heterogeneous, predominantly moderate attitude began to succumb to an increasingly stringent and juristic line of thinking in the third/ninth century, which took its cues from the developing schools of Islamic Jurisprudence.

Beginning in the late fourth/tenth century, however, the ramifications of the *ṣulḥ/ʿanwa* debate, discussed in Chapter Six, came to dominate discussions relating to the construction and repair of *dhimmī* properties. Hārūn al-Rashīd (d. 194/809) had set the legal precedent, which called for the destruction of *dhimmī* properties constructed in *'anwa* land after the conquest—a sporadically enforced edict. Not until the late fourth/tenth century did more consistent enforcement emerge. In the spirit of al-Rashīd's edict, *dhimmī* properties constructed after the conquest were condemned, but the wording of later laws became increasingly stringent. According to ninth-century regulations, the restoration of *dhimmī* properties that predated the conquests was the prerogative of their owners. To the contrary, eleventh- through thirteenth-century legislation eroded that legal right by mandating that *dhimmī*s had to seek permission to restore their places of worship, even if they were built before the conquest. By the thirteenth century CE, legal *fatwa*s reiterated the same principle but added that officials should not feel compelled to grant such requests; approval for restoration projects was deemed to be at the sole discretion of the government.

Moreover, as the antiquity of ecclesiastical structures became a contentious issue, another development soon followed. Throughout the ninth century CE, "antiquity" often rested upon Christian claims and, especially in the case of large or well-known churches and monasteries, the typical *qāḍī* did not press the issue. Increasingly, however, the antiquity of ecclesiastical buildings in need of repair had to be "proven": a burden that was seldom met to the satisfaction of later jurists. This inflexibility with regard to *dhimmī* places of worship may be first observed in the late fourth/tenth century, but it reached its most austere articulation under Ibn Taymiyya (d. 1328 CE), who essentially held that the very existence of these buildings rested on the goodwill of Muslims, and that *dhimmīs* had no inherent right vis-à-vis the restoration (let alone the construction) of such buildings.[168] Nonetheless, while the spirit and letter of the law grew increasingly rigid, historically, Egyptian jurists and officials were often more generous in permitting construction activities than a strict interpretation would allow: some were motivated by their piety, others by greed. Ultimately, however, many ecclesiastical buildings simply fell out of use, lacking patrons to rebuild them or congregants to fill them.

CHAPTER 11

POLEMICS AND THE CONSTRUCTION OF COMMUNAL IDENTITIES

Pagans, Jews, and Christians exchanged religious polemics throughout Late Antiquity.[1] In the mid-fifth century, as Christianity eclipsed paganism on nearly every front, the Chalcedonian schism fragmented the eastern empire into pro- and anti-Chalcedonian factions, and later, with the emergence of Islam in the mid-seventh century, yet another interlocutor joined the debate. Hence, while the monotheistic religions dominated the Egyptian landscape, four prominent communities—Jewish, Muslim, Coptic, and Melkite—explicitly claimed to be the legitimate descendants of Abraham.[2]

Fundamentally, these communities share several ideals predicated upon a staunch belief in the existence of a single almighty deity who first revealed himself and his will to Abraham.[3] Similarly, they venerate a number of common religious Figures (e.g. Moses) and uphold analogous beliefs in the existence of angels and demons, and the importance of fasting and prayer. Shared beliefs united the adherents of the three faiths, while competing claims of election and exclusivity pitted them against one another.[4] Earlier, Christians were able to promptly repudiate pagan beliefs as a set of nonsensical doctrines inspired by superstition or the trickery of demons, but the claims of another Abrahamic religion could not be dismissed so blithely; such claims required correction, amendment, and refutation. To that end, each faith community compiled vigorous apologetic and polemical critiques that scrutinized the others' scriptures and religious claims while reaffirming their own.

Polemical discourses assumed many manifestations. Some took the form of impromptu oral debates among religious elites,[5] while others were expressed in sophisticated treatises.[6] A middle stratum may be observed in popular catechetical manuals, such as *Kitāb al-īḍāḥ* and *Kitāb al-muʿallim wa al-tilmīdh*.[7] Didactic in nature, and certainly lacking the sophistication of *Kalām* literature, these works often reinforced confessional beliefs and identity through a mixture of apologetic and polemical arguments.[8] Also included within this stratum are Egyptian pseudo-debate texts, such as pseudo-John III's *Questions of Theodore*, which have survived in Sahidic and Bohairic Coptic as well as Arabic.[9] Here the analysis explores yet another manifestation, that of communal or popular polemics: the community-defining narratives, practices, and rituals that informed concepts of "self" (individual and communal) and "other." The average individual consciously engaged in these strategies through the recitation of seemingly benign stories, and subconsciously through the observance of socio-religious celebrations and practices.

The popular nature of some of the accounts discussed below has veiled their apologetic and polemical undertones.[10] Nonetheless, a paucity of sophistication should not be equated with lack of efficacy. "Real" apologetic literature, such as the authentic writings of Theodore Abū Qurra or Sawīrus ibn al-Muqaffaʿ, is extremely elitist.[11] Those tracts circulated among the select few and demanded a high degree of literacy, a thorough knowledge of the scriptures of the three traditions, and an astute mind. They were the possession and tools of an elite minority, while communal polemics were intrinsically egalitarian.

Additionally, there is something to be said for the success of this polemical form. While erudite polemics and apologetics continue to occupy a few specialists, communal polemics, though seldom recognized as such, have enjoyed tremendous mass appeal and persist even today as living traditions. This aspect may be inadvertently masked by the subsequent discussion, grounded as it is in written sources; nonetheless, the narratives and practices discussed in this chapter have survived and continue to permeate the fabric of society through ritual performance and oral recitations. S.H. Leeder provides irrefutable proof of this fact. Early in the twentieth century, he unknowingly recorded several of the stories and sectarian claims addressed below not based on any textual evidence, but rather by drawing upon what he perceived as the quaint stories of the "natives".[12]

The following analysis touches on several themes and issues. It describes the means by which Muslims sought to validate their religious claims, often by mimicking the strategies of their predecessors and interlocutors. Moreover, it challenges the normative historiography of "non-Muslim" communities, which are typically analyzed through a passive paradigm. In the mainstream of academic literature, the distinguishing features of Christian and Jewish communities under Islamic rule often seem external, even generic. Ostensibly, they are but reflections of caliphal hegemony (as *dhimmīs* were categorized and marginalized socially, politically, and legally) rather than the result of any internal dynamics. Here, the analysis provides glimpses at the workings of a socio-historical dialectic through which all parties—Muslim, Christian, and Jewish—endeavored to construct positive identities that were much richer than the labels attributed to them by others. The following two-pronged discussion initially delves into the intra-Christian polemics exchanged between Copts and Melkites as each community attempted to differentiate itself from the other. The second half of the chapter turns to interreligious polemics among Copts, Melkites, Muslims, and Jews.

Intra-Christian Polemics

Christians have historically asserted the existence of an organic relationship between the veracity of theological belief and the efficacy and form of worship; proper worship leads to and reflects sound doctrine (lex orandi, *lex credendi*).[13] Thus, anti- and pro-Chalcedonians conscientiously maintained their liturgical practices and communal observances, but quickly discovered that they worshiped in nearly an identical manner. As discussed in Chapter Five, until the ninth century CE, both confessions used the Greek language liturgically, venerated the same saints,[14] frequented the same shrines, recited the same prayers (with a few notable exceptions),[15] and observed the same fasts. But if one were necessarily orthodox and the other heretical, how could they observe the same liturgical worship and communal practices? Lex orandi, *lex credendi* required a tangible, practical manifestation beyond an intellectual or theological articulation. Some markers, such as the two versions of the Liturgical Trisagion, emerged in the immediate aftermath of the Chalcedonian schism, but additional signifiers took centuries to develop. While dating some of the accounts and practices discussed here remains tentative, the fact remains that both confessions developed distinctive liturgical and communal practices under early Islamic rule that were much more radical than those documented in the Byzantine era.

Fasting and Feasting

Communal practice is arguably the foremost component of collective identity, and is the means by which an individual expresses his or her affiliation. By the end of the tenth century CE, two new fasts, one in imitation of the Rogation of the Ninevites and another associated with Emperor Herakleios, became ingrained in the Coptic liturgical cycle, but were rejected by the Melkite confession. In time, the acceptance and rejection of these new fasts demarcated confessional allegiance, but their very adoption posed a fascinating dilemma. While the Copts maintained the devout practices to reinforce their unity with Syria and, subsequently, to better delineate confessional boundaries between themselves and the Melkites, they nonetheless desired to maintain the authenticating seal of antiquity. Thus, novel practices masqueraded as ancient traditions.

The three-day Fast of Nineveh, which commemorates the Rogation of the Ninevites (Jonah 3:5–10), is observed three weeks prior to the start of Lent proper (two weeks before the Fast of

Herakleios). The Copts adopted the fast from the Syrian church, likely during the patriarchate of Afrahām ibn Zarʿah (975–8 CE), himself a Syrian.[16] Nonetheless, the earliest biographies, Patriarch Afrahām's *sīra* in the HP and the anonymous *Life of Afrahām*, lack any references to the fast, which originated in the Church of the East among the so-called "Nestorians".[17] Sabhrīshōʿ, the Metropolitan of Bēth Garmē, had inaugurated the observance when he called for a three-day fast in the midst of a plague epidemic in the early seventh century CE.[18] Of East Syrian origins, the observance made its way into West Syrian (anti-Chalcedonian) practice and by the late tenth century, the Copts adopted the fast and characteristically passed it on to the Ethiopians. The association with Patriarch Afrahām, while possible, is tenuous; in general, there has always been a great deal of secular and ecclesiastical contact between Syria and Egypt (see Chapter Nine).

This new fast quickly developed into a distinctive marker of the anti-Chalcedonian confession. Not only did Melkites question its legitimacy and refuse to observe it, they went as far as initiating an anti-fast. Thus, during the week the Copts observed the Fast of Nineveh, the Melkites did not fast at all, not even on the canonical days of Wednesday and Friday.[19] Consequently, fasting and feasting developed into distinctive markers of confessional boundaries and communal identities.

Historically more problematic, the "Fast" or "Week of Herakleios," which is a week-long fast adjoined to the start of Lent proper, functioned in an analogous manner. Currently identified as the "Week of Preparation" in the Coptic Orthodox Church,[20] this fast purportedly commenced shortly after Emperor Herakleios' 629 CE reconquest of Jerusalem. I have addressed this observance, along with the evolution of Lent in Alexandria, at length elsewhere.[21] Here a mere summary would suffice.

In general, the duration of Lent fluctuated greatly in the ante-Nicean period, and throughout the fourth and fifth centuries, three-, six-, seven-, and eight-week Lenten cycles are documented all over the empire.[22] Determining the length of Lent in Egypt prior to the fourth century is extremely difficult, and in the main an observance of a six-day fast likely prevailed in the third century. By the 330s, Patriarch Athanasios (326–73 CE), introduced a six-week Lenten observance that included Holy Week;[23] this became the norm in the province, documented as late as 596 CE.[24]

Sometime in the mid- to late-seventh century,[25] however, the Copts appended two weeks to their Lent by adopting the Week of Herakleios and by separating Lent from Holy Week. Hence the development of the eight-week cycle observed by the Coptic Orthodox until today. (This likely mirrored what had already developed into normative West Syrian practice.) As for the pro-Chalcedonians of Egypt, they too separated Lent from Holy Week, but the observance of the Week of Herakleios, after a period of fluctuation, was eventually rejected and condemned.

Appending this extra week of fasting had great confessional ramifications. Similar to the Fast of Nineveh, the observance and rejection of the Fast of Herakleios demarcated confessional boundaries by the tenth century CE. Hence while the Copts observed that extra week with all the austerity and solemnity of Lent, the Melkite clergy delivered sermons condemning that rogation, turning it into an anti-fast, during which no fasting was allowed even on Wednesday and Friday.

In the thirteenth century, al-Ṣafī ibn al-ʿAssāl casually glossed the Week of Herakleios, *jumʿāt Harqil*, as the Prelude to Lent (*muqaddimāt al-ṣawm al-kabīr*),[26] a designation that must have resonated with his readership. Later, al-Makīn (the Younger) and Abū al-Barakāt ibn Kabar contested the tradition attributing the fast to the actions of the Emperor Herakleios, arguing that Demetrios of Alexandria (d. 232 CE) and the Council of Nicea (325 CE) approved the additional week's fast. Thus, not only was that week's fast canonical, but it was the Melkites, not the Copts, who had transgressed patristic tradition by not observing it.[27]

Nomocanons added legitimacy to the antithetical confessional and polemical observances; hence, any transgression of these communal markers of abstinence and indulgence constituted an act of sacrilege.[28] As much may be gleaned from the indictment of Abū Yāsir the Priest, but is blatant in the condemnation of another Coptic presbyter, Murqus ibn al-Qunbar (d. ca. 1200), who: "abrogated the three days of the Fast of Nineveh and the first week of the Fast, *according to the rule of the Melkites*, and he allowed meat and milk to be eaten during the Week of Nineveh on the two days of Wednesday and Friday".[29]

Liturgical and Calendrical Practices

Fasts and anti-fasts were but one aspect of a slew of liturgical and calendrical strategies employed by the two dominant Christian denominations to delineate confessional boundaries and construct distinctive sectarian identities. Writing his *Mukhtaṣar al-bayān* near the end of the fourteenth century, al-Makīn the Younger compiled a list of fourteen Melkite "deviations":[30] the piercing of the oblation with a knife (*ḥarba*) during the liturgy, conducting marriage ceremonies in private homes, baking oblations in public ovens, the public (ritualistic) cursing of those who fast the first week of Lent (that of Herakleios), not reading the Gospel on Sunday nights or over the baptistery,[31] entering the church with shoes, entering the sanctuary (*haykal*) with shoes,[32] permitting the priest to pray a liturgy without a deacon, infrequent communion, preserving the oblation of Maundy Thursday for the whole year in churches and private homes, blowing in each other's faces on the Eve of Good Friday (i.e. Thursday night),[33] not fasting the first week of Lent (i.e. the week of Preparation/Herakleios), not fasting at all—even on Wednesdays and Fridays—during the Fast of Nineveh, and forbidding marriage for the fourth and fifth degrees of kinship. Of the fourteen "deviations," two are concerned with the Fast of Herakleios, a third with the Fast of Nineveh, and all pertain to communal practices, not doctrine. Ironically, a number of these deviations, such as the celebration of weddings at private homes and preserving the sacrament, are historically attested in the Coptic church at several junctures.[34]

Debates between the two factions influenced calendrical computations as well. The "correct" means of calculating certain feast days, especially Nativity and the "floating" feast of Easter, became subjects of great discord, even among members of the same confession.[35] In all, the overriding emphasis was not on mathematical accuracy or adherence to astronomic cycles, though they were certainly a consideration, but the justification of communal norms and the propagation of polemical and apologetic tropes; a fact abundantly demonstrated by the dizzying arguments and computations in Abū Shākir's *Chronography*, which often lack scientific parameters.[36] In the Middle Ages, calendrical computations among all religious communities were not simply a "scientific" enterprise,[37] but had their roots in apologetics and polemics.[38]

Ownership of Churches and Legacies

Christian disputes with Muslim authorities over the construction and restoration of ecclesiastical properties (discussed in Chapter Ten) were only one aspect of the debates surrounding these structures. Among themselves, Christians engaged in passionate quarrels over the ownership of prominent sites. These debates addressed the possession of buildings and the indirect procurement of revenue streams (through *awqāf*, the fulfillment of religious vows, and gifts by pilgrims), but even more so, at least in the literary sources, the debates parsed ownership of the past, and particularly heirship to the pre-Chalcedonian Fathers of the Church. These feuds over buildings were yet another component of the confessional polemics that ultimately informed individual and communal identities.[39]

Medieval controversies over the ownership of churches in Egypt commenced with the ordination of the Melkite patriarch Quzmān (Kosmas, 727–68 CE),[40] who, immediately after his ordination, asked the Caliph Hishām to return: "the churches that the Jacobites had taken over with the help of a group of secretaries (*kuttāb*)".[41] Later, upon his arrival in Egypt, he led the Melkites in an attempt to acquire the prestigious Church of St. Menas at Maryūṭ,[42] which had long functioned as a major center for the veneration of perhaps the most popular martyr in the Egyptian church. Additionally, it eventually served as the site of a sizable monastic complex, and controlled vast tracts of land in the form of religious endowments (*awqāf*). All these attributes rendered the complex one of the most important religious and economic sites in Egypt.[43]

According to the HP, Patriarch Quzmān addressed his petition to the last Umayyad Caliph, Marwān II, who in turn instructed the governor, ʿAbd al-Malik ibn Mūsā ibn Naṣīr, to sort through the competing claims of ownership. ʿAbd al-Malik summoned patriarchs Khaīl (Michael) and Quzmān, and instructed them to submit their claims in writing. He then assigned two men to oversee the matter.[44] Nonetheless, despite the stronger claim made by Patriarch Khaīl (according to the HP), ʿĪsā ibn ʿĀmir delayed ruling in the lawsuit on account of a bribe he had received. Eventually, Coptic protests led to ʿĪsā's dismissal and replacement with Abū al-Ḥusayn, who ruled in favor of the anti-Chalcedonians.[45]

The account provides only one perspective, and teems with a polemical agenda that shrouds the actual proceedings, but there is no doubt as to the resolution of the affair: the Church of St. Menas remained in Coptic hands. Most intriguing, however, are the arguments presented for the rightful ownership of this complex. A summary is placed on the lips of Patriarch Khaīl: "It was *my father* Theophilos and Timothy his successor who built [that church]".[46] Again, in a brief exchange between Abū al-Ḥusayn and the two patriarchs, the same perspective emerges: "'Do you abide by the faith of Yaʿqūb (James) the bishop of Jerusalem, one of the disciples of the Lord Christ?' [Khaīl replied] 'I do.' Then (Abū al-Ḥusayn) turned to the other and said, 'Tell me, elder (*shaykh*), who is your father and what is your creed?' The Melkite patriarch said, 'I abide by the faith of king Marcian.'"[47] This debate did not just address buildings, but heirship and identity. Ownership of ecclesiastical properties rightfully belonged to the legitimate heirs and successors to the Apostles and the patristic fathers, the undisputed pre-Chalcedonian patriarchs from whom both confessions could legitimately claim descent.

An invariable theme is discernible: the true heirs of the undisputed fathers, Theophilos, Timothy I, Athanasios, and Cyril, "whose writings are placed in all the orthodox churches of the world,"[48] are the Copts. The Melkites, on the other hand, are presented as a fifth-century innovation, though of course the Melkites saw the issue the other way around.[49] Beyond attaining tangible assets, debates over churches provided an opportunity for each faction to reaffirm its historiography and claim heirship to the undisputed Alexandrian fathers, and, hence, reassert its monopoly on orthodox doctrine and legitimate Apostolic Succession.[50]

The issues discussed here (the observance of fasts, calendrical computations, and heirship) are certainly concerned with pious sensibilities and socioreligious and political aims, but they were also fundamental constituents of sectarian identities. They functioned as personal and communal signifiers of orthodoxy, even legitimacy. Furthermore, it is evident that, far from being passive agents in a society defined by Islamic institutions and jurisprudence, Christian communities actively engaged in constructing positive identities. In their self-perception, Copts and Melkites were not "non-Muslims," *dhimmīs*, or *'ajam*, but rather the "orthodox" in the literal rendering of the term: those upholding correct (*orthos*) doctrine/worship (*doxa*).

Interreligious Polemics

Intra-Christian strategies of distinction comprised only one aspect of communal polemics, which transcended confessional boundaries by targeting all "other". Interreligious polemics were even more prominent, especially between the two dominant communities, the Copts and Muslims, though Jews and Melkites were certainly represented.[51] Two sets of narratives are discussed in this section: one cohort focuses on a Nile topos documented over the span of fifteen hundred years, while the other is comprised of the various recensions of the miracle of the moving of al-Muqaṭṭam Mountain.

Control of the Nile

"The River" in Egyptian literature hardly needs qualification.[52] In ancient times, the Egyptians believed that Osiris controlled the Nile, and they worshipped its inundation in the form of the god Ḥapy.[53] Under Hellenic and Roman rule, several cults venerated the river; later, Christians and Muslims blessed and prayed for it.[54] Ancient and Medieval authorities agree that an optimal inundation measured "sixteen cubits," or roughly eight and a half meters.[55] Any significant deviation from that hallowed mark resulted in anxiety, famine, and death, not to mention a significant loss of tax revenue.

In Late Antiquity, Christians and Jews believed that the Nile was one of the rivers of the Garden of Eden (cf. Gen. 1:11–14),[56] a tradition that Muslims adopted and augmented by identifying it as the river of honey in heaven.[57] In the fourth century CE, several Coptic holy men were associated with the river. Abba Aaron repeatedly controlled the Nile's flooding through his prayers,[58] while Paul the Hermit prayed: "the Lord may bring . . . the flood of the Nile in its due season".[59] Above all, the archangel Michael emerges as the principal intercessor of the Egyptians before the: "Lord concerning the waters of the river, until He increases it . . . to its measures every year".[60] The same belief persisted under Islamic rule.

Until the building of the Aswān Dam in the 1960s, the river's inundation set the rhythm of life in the country. As the quintessential element for life in the vast desert that is Egypt, it is not surprising that divine manipulation of the Nile developed into a topos of interreligious polemics. More specifically, each faction argued that its God and community controlled this vital resource, a proclamation that ultimately addressed questions of religious truth and proper worship, as well as a host of socio-political considerations. For Christians, sovereignty over the river proved the efficacy of their creed at a time of political and, increasingly, social subjugation to non-believers. As for Muslims, as Islamic sources are quick to point out, ascendency over the river proved that Islam triumphed over all that had preceded it.

A terse reference in the *Naẓm al-jawhar* of Eutychios helps to set the stage. It reads: "In the second year of the caliphate of al-Muktafī, which is 290 AH [/903 CE], the Nile of Egypt reached thirteen cubits and two measures. Muslims, Christians, and Jews went out to the river and prayed for water, but the water did not increase beyond what we mentioned. And the water subsided".[61] Eutychios' account is lackluster compared to those of the Copts and Muslims. Its significance lies in confirming the basic historical framework for the incidents discussed here. In times of a low Nile (among other catastrophes), members of the three religious communities would indeed congregate by the river and pray.[62]

Dominion over the Nile was expressed through a cluster of analogous narratives, which find their archetype in a passage from Eusebios's *Life of Constantine*:

> To those in Egypt and especially Alexandria, who had a custom of worshipping their river through the offices of effeminate men (δε' ἀνδρῶν ἐκτεθηλυμμένων), another law was sent out, declaring that the whole class of homosexuals (ἀνδρογύνων γένος) should be abolished as a thing depraved, and that it was unlawful for those infected with this gross indecency to be seen anywhere. Whereas the superstitious supposed that the river would no longer flow for them in its customary way, God cooperated with the Emperor's law by achieving quite the opposite of what they expected. For although those who defiled the cities by their abominable practice were no more, the river, as though the land had been cleared for it, flowed as never before, and rose in abundant flood to overflow all the arable land, by its action teaching the senseless that one should reject polluted men and attribute the cause of prosperity to the sole giver of all good.[63]

Pagan control of the river challenged the Christian affirmation that Pagans worshipped the work of their hands or demons; it also undermined the doctrine of the Christian God as all-governing (*pantokratōr*). This miracle succinctly addresses these concerns by maintaining that even though Pagans were prevented from performing their rites, the river "flowed as never before". Thus, true sovereignty rested in the hands of the Christian God.

Echoes of this account reverberated for well over a millennium. Details certainly varied, but all later versions share structural similarities: two (or more) religious communities quarrel over divine control of the Nile, the antagonists threaten that the river would not rise if not for their rites and prayers, the undeterred protagonists faithfully prevent them nonetheless, subsequently the river still rises, and the inundation is interpreted as a supernatural phenomenon, proving the bankruptcy of the antagonists' religion and the veracity of the protagonist's God. Pagans are clearly the antagonists in the Eusebian exemplar, a role that would be played in succession by Christians, Jews, and Muslims in each other's versions of this topos.

The earliest attestation under Islamic rule is situated in the mid-eighth century CE, shortly after the ʿAbbāsids bested the Umayyads.[64] The HP maintains that (the Christian) God held back the waters of the river due to the wickedness of ʿAṭā ibn Shurāḥbīl and al-Ṣāfī, the secretaries of the governor Abū al-ʿAwn.[65] Seeking divine compassion, several Coptic bishops joined Patriarch Khaīl I in prayer at Miṣr on the seventeenth of the Coptic month of Tūt—the Feast of the Cross, the traditional highpoint of the inundation. The clergy and faithful of the city walked in procession from Fusṭāṭ to the Church of St. Peter (which had part of its foundation in the river), carrying gospels and crosses, and burning incense.[66] The patriarch and Abba Menas, bishop of Memphis, prayed while the faithful chanted *kyrie eleison* ("Lord have mercy"). By nine in the morning, Muslims and Jews observed the spectacle and went to investigate only to witness that the river had miraculously increased by a cubit. Alarmed by the news of this phenomenon, Abū al-ʿAwn summoned his troops and went to the bank of the river desiring "to know which of the religions is *the true one*".[67] He then instructed the Muslims of Fusṭāṭ to congregate at the mountain east of Miṣr (most likely al-Muqaṭṭam, a holy locus for Muslims, see below), and persevere in prayer from midnight until ten o'clock in the morning.[68] Despite their fervent prayers, however, the level of the Nile decreased by a cubit. The following day, Muslims again gathered at the base of the mountain to pray, but this time they were accompanied by Jews and Samaritans. That day, the Nile was unaffected. Abū al-ʿAwn forbade anyone from praying at the mountain on the fourth day. The population complied with the order, and the level of the Nile held steady. Finally, in desperation, Abū al-ʿAwn asked the Christians of Fusṭāṭ and Abba Moses, the saintly Bishop of Wasīm, to pray.[69] The hierarch followed suit and by the end of the day the river rose three cubits, thus reaching the hallowed sixteen-cubit mark. Purportedly, the miracle prompted the governor to treat the Copts leniently and to decrease their taxes.

As written, the polemical account pits the three major traditions against one another; or more accurately, pits Judaism and Islam against Christianity. The HP is explicit: God performed the miracle to "prove the truth of the Christian religion".[70] And, as summarized above, only Christian prayers were effective, while the prayers of Muslims and Jews went unanswered or were even counterproductive. Interestingly, Jews fared better than Muslims in this recension.

In the ninth century, Ibn ʿAbd al-Ḥakam forwarded a Muslim counter-narrative. He maintains that after the conquest of Egypt, ʿAmr ibn al-ʿĀṣ learned that annually, on the twelfth of the Coptic month of Ba'ūna (the commemoration of the Archangel Michael), the *qibṭ* selected a maiden and threw her into the river, presumably killing her.[71] Immediately, ʿAmr prohibited the practice and exclaimed: "This shall not continue under Islam[ic rule], for Islam destroys (*yahdim*) whatever [superstition] preceded it".[72] Without performing the necessary rite, however, the river did not rise for three months. Perplexed, ʿAmr wrote a letter to the Caliph ʿUmar, who responded by sending the governor a folded note (*biṭaqā*) with instructions to throw it into the river. The note read: "From ʿUmar, Commander of the Faithful, to the Nile of the Egyptians. As for what follows, if you increase by your own accord, do not increase; but if the one God, the Almighty (*al-qahhār*), is the one who increases you, we ask the one God, the Almighty, to increase you".[73] ʿAmr threw the note into the river a day before the Feast of the Cross (17th of Tūt), and overnight the Nile reached sixteen cubits.

Ibn ʿAbd al-Ḥakam then proceeded to recount an analogous miracle. He states that during a similar season of low flooding, the Prophet Moses prayed to God and the Nile miraculously increased to its optimum height: "Thus, God in his might (*ṭaul*) answered (*istajāb*) ʿUmar ibn al-Khaṭṭāb as he answered his prophet Moses".[74] In the first of these accounts, Ibn ʿAbd al-Ḥakam wrestled away control of the Nile from the Copts and placed it squarely in the hands of Allāh.[75] In the second, he aligned ʿUmar I with Moses, decisively situating Islam in succession to the Hebrew prophets. This manifests another aspect of communal polemics: whereas Copts and Melkites fought over heirship to the pre-Chalcedonian fathers, Christians and Muslims waged similar battles over legitimate succession to the Hebrew prophets.[76]

By the thirteenth and fourteenth centuries CE, Christians and Muslims were heavily invested in these polemics of the Nile. Over the preceding centuries, the Christian blessing of the river transformed from a confessional act into a cultural spectacle in the form of *'Īd al-shahīd*, "Feast of the Martyr," which was celebrated in Shubra (or Shabra) on the eighth of the Coptic month of Bashans (May 16th).[77] Al-Maqrīzī describes this celebration in some detail. He states: "They claim that the Nile of Egypt will not increase annually until the Christians (*naṣarā*) throw in it a wooden box containing [a relic]—the finger of one of their saints".[78] The feast was celebrated by all the inhabitants of Cairo and the surrounding districts.[79] Muslims and Christians alike would pitch their tents on the banks of the river, while singers and various entertainers amused the sizable crowd over the course of the three-day festival. Al-Maqrīzī also documented the tremendous volume of wine consumed over the course of the celebration, and the debauchery that accompanied it.

Observed under the guise of a religious ritual, the atmosphere of the celebration seems to have been exceptionally secular, much like a modern Egyptian *mawlid* (less the public consumption of wine). This is underscored by the fact that the patron "martyr" of the feast, John of Sanhūt, a relatively obscure figure, is hardly ever mentioned. This led to widespread confusion in the thirteenth and fourteenth centuries when the feast was erroneously attributed to a Coptic neo-martyr, John of Phanijōit,[80] an early thirteenth-century CE convert to Islam who, after marrying a Muslim woman, publicly apostatized and was subsequently executed.[81]

The annual celebration lasted until 702/1303 when the Sultan al-Nāṣir Muḥammad ibn Qalāwūn and the *amīr* Rukn al-Dawla Baybars al-Jāshankīr brought the festivities to an end. Despondent, the Copts sought out Baybars' secretary, al-Tāj ibn Sa'īd al-Dawla (d. 709/1309), and pleaded with him to intercede in the matter. Cautiously, the Christian secretary reminded Baybars that the revenue generated by the festival paid for much of the taxes of Shubra, and added: "as long as the feast (*'īd*) was not observed, the Nile will never rise".[82] Reminiscent of Constantine and 'Amr's responses, Baybars boldly retorted: "If the Nile will not rise without this relic let it not rise, but if God—glory be to him (*subḥānahu*)—controls it, then let us make liars out of the Christians".[83] Observance of the feast ceased until 738/1338, when officials restored it essentially for its entertainment (*nuzha*) value, though fiscal considerations likely played a role as well. Annual celebrations persisted until 755/1354, when the Mamluks embarked upon a devastating campaign of intolerance that resulted in the destruction of churches, and the widespread confiscation of ecclesiastical properties and endowments (*awqāf*).[84] At that juncture, a mob targeted the church at Shubra Khayma, seized the relic, burnt it in the town square (*mīdān*), and later threw the ashes into the Nile to ensure that the Christians could not keep them.

For Christians, *'Īd al-shahīd* explicitly affirmed Coptic claims of dominion over the river (and by extension, of the validity of their creed and the significance of their community to Egyptian society), and it was for that reason halted and subsequently eradicated by Muslim authorities. It is difficult to ascertain the perspective of the thousands of Muslims who participated in the three-day festivities. Al-Maqrīzī suggests they were primarily motivated by the lure of entertainment and wine, but surely they must have known of the Copts' claims. The practice of blessing the Nile certainly did not cease with the demise of *'Īd al-Shahīd*, nor was it the only ritual to that effect. Much of the festivities and religious undertones had parallels with other Nile festivals, such as *Takhīq al-miqyās*, *Laylat al-nuqta*, and *Wafa' al-nīl*;[85] significantly, Muslim religious dignitaries had a leading role in those celebrations.[86] Even largely secular festivals, such as *Jabr al-khalīj* (the Opening of the Canal), increasingly gained a religious aura as time went on.[87] All these celebrations reinforced the same basic principle: the populace still believed that a successful inundation required divine intervention, they simply disagreed as to whose God—and community—should be adjured.

Still, the topos lived on. Divine control of the river through the agency of the Copts is attested in the HP and the current ecclesiastical version of the *Synaxarion* as late as the patriarchate of Buṭrus VII (Peter, 1809–52 CE).[88] The HP's recension is especially noteworthy for its polemical tone:

> And among these [miracles] (was) that the Nile did not increase in a certain year to its measure, and the people were afraid of a calamity of dearth and the misfortune of famine, and they sought aid from the pasha, entreating him that he should command the spiritual leaders, that they should raise supplications and prayers on account of the Nile, so that God might bless its waters and irrigate the land, and he complied. The Muslims assembled first for prayer, then the Jews, then the Greeks, then the Syrians, then the Catholics (*al-ifranj*),[89] but the river did not change from its place. Then the government asked Father Peter to do according to what the rest of the denominations had done. He sent for a group of clerics and a company of the bishops, and he went forth with them to the bank of the river, and celebrated the offering of the mystery of the Eucharist. He then concluded and washed the vessels of the service, and cast their water with a blessed oblation [an *antidoron* (Ar. *qurbānat al-barakā*)] into the river. And its waves were immediately agitated, and they were troubled, and they boiled up as a cauldron boils, and they overflowed. And the disciples of the patriarch hastened to take away the vessels of the celebration, and scarcely had they finished this when the water overtook them. The dignity of the patriarch and his denomination became great with the pasha, and [Patriarch Buṭrus] increased in their esteem.

While remaining faithful to the old topos, this recension reflects new sociopolitical realities. The basic outline and central thesis are maintained: God hears the prayers of the Copts over all others. What is fascinating here is the explicit enumeration of the "other" in a list that reflects the competing communities recognized by the Ottoman *millet* system.

Despite differences in detail, Christian and Muslim versions of the Nile topos function in a remarkably similar manner and achieve identical goals by attributing dominion over the river to their respective confession (their audience), while disenfranchising other religious sects from divine grace and, hence, legitimacy. Finally, the accounts highlight the potency of the "holy man" of the respective tradition, though certainly the holy men of these examples do not conform to the typical profile.[90]

Moving the Muqaṭṭam

The miracle of al-Muqaṭṭam provides a vivid recounting of a clash among the three faith communities.[91] It is perhaps the most persistent and successful of popular narrative; even today, every Coptic child knows of the day when prayer moved a mountain. The account has shaped Coptic consciousness over the past millennium, and is annually commemorated by a uniquely Coptic observance: a three-day fast adjoined to the Fast of the Nativity.[92] Still, while modern renderings have eliminated many blatantly antagonistic barbs, choosing rather to focus on the pious patriarch and the underlying spiritual message, the initial descriptions of the miracle exhibited several polemical features that were honed in some "medieval" recensions of the story.

The miracle is situated within the caliphate of al-Muʿizz (d. 975 CE),[93] who gained renown for presiding over debates among religious scholars in his court.[94] The leading Coptic figure in these deliberations was not Patriarch Afrahām, but the learned Bishop of al-Ashmūnayn, Sawīrus ibn al-Muqaffaʿ, who had been employed as a government secretary prior to becoming a monk and, later, a bishop.[95] The HP forwards the normative recension of the event as the last of three incidents involving the bishop, all of which clearly fit within the parameters of community polemics. None of these stories demonstrate Sawīrus' skills as a Christian theologian or apologist, preferring instead to depict non-Christians as caricatures who are easily overcome or caught off guard by the bishop's quips. Still, the scriptural underpinnings of the second and third episodes are noteworthy. At their core, these narratives reflect the scriptural diatribes rampant among the three faith communities; the third incident in particular, the Miracle of the Muqaṭṭam, presents an apology for the Christian sacred writ. This is a crucial aspect that has been eclipsed by the miraculous elements that dominate the oral performances and written recensions of the miracle.

A Muslim dignitary provoked the first incident. While Sawīrus casually conversed with the *qāḍī al-quḍāt*, a dog passed by.[96] The *qāḍī* then asked the bishop a vexing question: "What do you say, Sawīrus, is this dog Christian or Muslim?" Forced to either insult his illustrious host or his own creed, Sawīrus reminded the *qāḍī* that it was Friday, a day on which Christians did not consume meat but broke their fast with wine, whereas Muslims consumed meat but not wine. Sawīrus proceeded to suggest that a piece of meat and some wine be placed in front of the dog, which would then voluntarily divulge its religious persuasion. When the Muslims heard this: "they marveled at [Sawīrus'] wisdom and at the efficacy of his answer, and they departed from him".[97]

The second account, which instigated the moving of the mountain, involved a would-be debate between Bishop Sawīrus, Mūsā al-Yahūdī (Moses the Jew), and the influential *wazīr* Yaʿqūb ibn Killis, a convert to Islam who is consistently depicted in Coptic Arabic sources as a nominal Muslim who harbored strong Jewish sympathies.[98] In the palace, as the participants gathered and the debate was about to begin, Sawīrus declared that he would not address his Jewish opponent. He argued that it was improper to debate a Jew in front of the *imām*, as a Jew is more ignorant than an ox. When Mūsā objected, Sawīrus replied: "It is not I (who) bear witness against you, Jew, with regard to ignorance, but. . . . it is Isaiah who states in the beginning of his book concerning God: 'the ox has known its owner, and the donkey has known the manger of its master, but Israel has not known me'" (Is. 1:3).[99] The bishop then argued that since God had testified that animals are more rational than Jews, it would be improper to debate a Jew before the *imām*; thus, the debate ended before it began.[100]

An abrupt shift follows. Although it was Bishop Sawīrus who insulted the Jewish delegation and took the leading role in all interreligious debates (even in the presence of the patriarch), the ire of that party targeted Patriarch Afrahām. This is the precipitating event, which provides the immediate context for the Miracle of the Mountain. Attacked by a verse from the Hebrew Scriptures, Mūsā sought to reciprocate with an attack based on the New Testament. He pointed out to al-Muʿizz that the Christian scriptures state: "If you have faith the size of a mustard seed, you will say to this mountain, 'Move from here to there,' and it will move" (Matt. 17:20; Mk. 11:23). Mūsā then demanded that the Christians prove the veracity of this verse or else they would be liars deserving of punishment. This is an important element often overshadowed by the subsequent miracle. Essentially, Mūsā called into question the legitimacy of the Christian Scriptures, a frequent challenge that Christians had to address vis-à-vis their Jewish and Muslim interlocutors.

In response, the *imām* summoned the patriarch, authenticated the verse, and then informed him that unless he witnessed the mountain move, he would order the execution of all Christians in his domain. Despondent, the patriarch asked for a three-day reprieve, in which he called for a fast that he himself observed with local clergy in the Church of al-Muʿallaqa. On the third night, the patriarch had a vision in which the Virgin Mary consoled him and prophesied that a miracle would be performed by a one-eyed tanner carrying a water pitcher.[101] The patriarch then searched for that man, and upon finding him and discovering his virtuous way of life, shared the Virgin's message with him. Reluctantly, the tanner agreed to help, but only if he could stand with the laity so as to conceal his identity.

On the morning of the fourth day, the patriarch sent word to al-Muʿizz to assemble his entourage along with his two Jewish advisors at the base of the mountain. The choice to meet at the eastern mountain, at times explicitly identified as the Muqaṭṭam, was not random, but was religiously significant, even polemical. Long before the tenth century, Muslims in Egypt had come to recognize that mountain as a sacred site.[102] Hence, the location chosen to prove the veracity of the New Testament scriptures was far from neutral, but rather a landmark imbued with religious meaning—an Islamic locus that, in theory, should have been invulnerable to Christian prayers.

Similar to opposing armies before a battle, a delegation of Muslims and Jews led by al-Muʿizz stood to one side, while the Copts stood to the other with the patriarch at the front and the tanner positioned right behind him among the laity. The Christians then chanted *kyrie eleison*, and performed a prostration. As they rose, they made the sign of the cross and the mountain "was lifted up from the ground." They performed three prostrations, and each time the mountain moved. Awestruck, the *imām* shouted to the patriarch: "Enough, patriarch! I have recognized, indeed, *the soundness of your faith*".[103] The caliph greatly honored the patriarch and promptly granted permission to rebuild the churches of Egypt, most prominently the churches of St. Merkurios at Miṣr and al-Muʿallaqa. Thus ends the HP's account.

The narrative gained a further polemical coloring in the anonymous *Life of Afrahām* and the HCME, which fully integrated the Jewish community into the account (not just the two secretaries).[104] In those texts, Muslims and then Jews prayed first with no effect, but when the Copts called out to God, the mountain moved. In the HCME, the historical setting also shifts to the court of al-Muʿizz's successor, al-ʿAzīz (365–86/975–96).

A fourth version, preserved in the *Synaxarion* (Kyahk 6), is largely a summary of that found in the HP, with some notable deviations. It maintains that Bishop Sawīrus and the patriarch debated the Jewish delegation at court and defeated (lit. "embarrassed") it, but then the recension proceeds to depict the famous Ibn Killis as the primary antagonist rather than his less renowned companion, Mūsā. The most prominent late development was the claim that as a consequence of the miracle he witnessed, al-Muʿizz converted to Christianity and was baptized.[105] In the current ecclesiastical version of the *Synaxarion*, the incident is imbued with additional details: the mountain is clearly identified as al-Muqaṭṭam (not just the eastern mountain as in the HP),[106] and the hitherto anonymous miracle-worker is identified as St. Simon, who currently enjoys a great deal of popularity among the Copts.[107] Finally, in addition to moving up and down with each prostration, the mountain is said to have retreated when the Christians advanced toward it.[108]

The account illustrates a number of polemical topoi, such as Jews conspiring against Christians at court and the superiority of the Christian holy man (the tanner and Afrahām). Foremost, however, moving al-Muqaṭṭam is an apology for the Christian scriptures, the alleged interpolation of which is a standard feature of religious polemics. To its target audience, the miracle rebuffed Jewish and Muslim scriptural polemics and critiques by proving the authenticity and power of the Christian scriptures through a popular medium whose efficacy resonates well beyond the persuasion of logical arguments or the eloquence of the most skillful orator.

Observations

Whether intra- or inter-religious, communal polemics demonstrated to the faith community its inherent orthodoxy that God favored a specific community and no other, thus, securing the loyalty of the individual to a confessional ideal and a sectarian disposition. These deceptively simple stories and ostensibly benign, even pious practices and rituals resided at the core of communal identities and the individual's self-image in Islamic Egypt. Beyond theological and intellectual justifications of one's creed or community, these strategies negotiated "self" and "other" in relation to tangible markers through the aid of text, orality, and ritual performance. Communal polemics favored concrete topics: fasting and feasting, the inundation of the Nile, and the power of the miraculous, which the adherents of all three faiths believed was just beyond the facade of mundane reality.

These stories presented divine providence as a living reality rather than a historical relic; nonetheless, while religious in character, these narratives and practices betray a vigorous socio-political dimension. To Muslims, these accounts reinforced and legitimized their political domination and cultural hegemony by assuring the average Muslim living in the "Middle Ages" that Allāh did not just act on behalf of his *umma* centuries prior, during the age of conquests, but that he continued to intervene on their behalf. For the Copts, intra-religious polemics ensured that they maintained the right (orthodox) version of Christianity, and consequently of the soundness of their Apostolic Succession and the efficacy of their sacraments. Ultimately, these accounts ensured the Muslim community of God's favor as demonstrated by political success, while they assured the Christians of the veracity of their creed in spite of political failure.

CHAPTER 12

WEBS OF SIGNIFICANCE

Clifford Geertz began his analysis of culture by quoting and expanding upon an axiom forwarded by Max Weber asserting that humanity is suspended in "webs of significance" of its own making.[1] Reflecting upon Egyptian history throughout the transitional period surveyed, this chapter identifies the trajectories and intersections of these "webs" and the interpretive processes by which individuals and communities deduced meaning and identity from them over time.

Language

Few aspects of culture facilitate immediate access to identity and community, real or imagined, as promptly as language. Coptic Arabic apocalypses often belabor this point, but in so doing they betray a specific cultural milieu. Beginning in the tenth century, the Copts adopted an idealistic tripartite division of language and creed: Coptic/orthodox, Greek/heretical, Arabic/Islamic. The rise of a new Coptic historiography of Byzantine rule, a decline in the use of Greek and Coptic in urban centers, and the proliferation of the Arabic language and Islamic religion converged at that juncture to legitimize these binary pairings, rendering them seemingly inalienable and self-evident (see Chapters Two, Four, Five, and Nine).

Ideologically inspired, these pairings fail to withstand scrutiny in light of the historical record. Through the ninth century, the Coptic hierarchy utilized Greek as an official language of the see and actively cultivated its acquisition among ecclesiastical elites. Even the laity at that time continued to perceive fluency in Greek as a mark of elite status, and did not question hearing, reciting, or praying large portions of their liturgical tradition in that language. The Copts' perception of the Greek language did not change in the aftermath of the Chalcedonian schism or the Arab conquest, but only after they no longer had need of it. By the tenth century, it had long ceased functioning as the language of the administration, social mobility, or education; even the theology of Copts and Melkites was by then composed and debated in Arabic. In the tenth century, Bohairic translations of liturgical and literary texts, many of which are no older than Arabic versions, and some in fact based on Arabic antecedents, began to be recognized as the sanctioned versions and, in time, were perceived as the "originals."

Initially, correlating Arabic with Islam may not seem an ideological pairing. It was after all Arab Muslims who conquered Egypt and constituted the ruling elite. Still, in its tenth-century setting the association implicitly reflected an ideological premise. Hitherto, Christians who adopted the Arabic language—initially officials and government personnel, then the urban populace—were not accused *prima facie* of abandoning their Christian faith or becoming "Muslims." Such sentiments emerged in the late tenth century, at a time when Arabic began to dominate among Christians, who were inundated with socio-political changes on nearly every front.

Language has at times been distinguished as the quintessential aspect of culture. Certainly, in mixed company few factors delineate boundaries or cultivate alliances as quickly as language. Still, however one envisions the relationship between language and culture—whether language is a conduit, matrix, or progenitor of culture—it may be the case that language only assumes the role of a cultural signifier, as opposed to transmitter, in its decline. A living language is but a ubiquitous element expressing multiple cultures; languages that are in decline or dying, however, especially those whose adherents share another ubiquitous element (the Christian faith in this case), conveniently lend themselves as cultural and communal markers. At an earlier historical juncture in Egyptian history, Pagans, Meletians, Manicheans, and Gnostics employed the Coptic language alongside their Christian neighbors. The very fact that contentious communities envisioned and expressed their identities through the same language prevented it from demarcating any one of them. Later, by the tenth century, as diverse factions consolidated by joining the Coptic confession and the Arabic language began to dominate urban life, the Coptic language transformed from a medium of communication into a symbol of identification and demarcation, a unique marker for the anti-Chalcedonian confession in Egypt (Chapters Four and Five).

Reciprocally, the Greek language, which had hitherto functioned as a conduit for both orthodoxy and heresy and permeated the "Coptic" liturgy, was cast in a disparaging light by the Copts. Thus, the historical legacy of the Coptic language, a language equally employed by pagans, schismatics, and heretics, as well as the orthodox, was abandoned in light of its pious, ideological reminting as the "language in which the Holy Spirit spoke". Manifestly, popular Coptic sentiments suppressed one language's longstanding association with Alexandrian anti-Chalcedonian orthodoxy, while omitting the other's colorful past.

In tenth-century Egypt, language functioned as one of several ideologically conditioned strategies aimed at delineating clear boundaries within a social milieu that increasingly lacked visible markers (Chapter Eight). In that light, the development of Coptic as a liturgical language takes on new significance. Rather than an inevitable development or a devout penchant toward antiquarianism, liturgical use of the language reflects a historically dependent phenomenon. The ubiquitous nature of liturgical celebrations has obfuscated their importance, rendering them as white noise, which inevitably leads to their omission from discussions of culture and identity. Nonetheless, it was through liturgical recitations that the above-mentioned ideologically-inspired binary relationships began to take on ontological significance. As the Copts increasingly recited their rites in Coptic rather than Greek, they affirmed their hegemonic narrative of the ideological three-fold division of language and creed, by which they identified themselves among the adherents of the Abrahamic traditions with whom they shared the public sphere and a host of religious claims and practices. It was in the act of praying a liturgy in Coptic that the *qibṭ* became truly "other": a spatial, creedal, and linguistic other, a distinct community. Socially, the communal boundaries erected through *jizya*, law, custom, discriminatory edicts, and narrative were reinforced, arguably even embraced, through the transmutation of Coptic from a living language into a liturgical one (Chapters Five, Six, Seven, and Eleven). Allegedly achieved through compulsion, the language shift in Egypt was voluntary. Coptic Arabic apocalypses, along with a number of eleventh- and twelfth-century Christian sources, lament the deliberate acceptance of the Arabic language by the Copts. And while the historical record documents a host of discriminatory policies and periods of intolerance, in all accounts officials targeted the wealth and the religion of the Copts, not their language.

Late Antiquity

Throughout the early Islamic centuries, Christians and Muslims reimagined Late Antiquity in accordance with their immediate needs (Chapters Two, Five, Six, Nine, and Eleven). Christians, in particular, remained ever-mindful of the era: the patristic fathers, the Ecumenical Councils, the schism of Chalcedon and the subsequent turmoil all date to that paradigmatic period. Today, the era remains prominent among the Copts, whose communal memory begins with Saint Mark in Alexandria, proceeds to the age of martyrdom under Diocletian, waxes nostalgic over the patristic and monastic fathers (especially Athanasios and Cyril), notes Chalcedon and the Arab conquest, and then jumps to Pope Kyrillus VI (d. 1971).

Christians maintained the historical, dogmatic, and ideological significance of Late Antiquity on several fronts. Nicea's fundamental importance to Christian orthodoxy reverberates throughout Coptic and Melkite theological declarations, and provides an essential grounding for the attempts of twelfth- and thirteenth-century Coptic Arabic scholars who attempted to validate the observance of the

Week of Herakleios by linking it to the Council of Nicea and Patriarch Demetrios (Chapter Eleven).

Beyond anchoring later traditions, Christians continued to draw upon late antique models to interpret their history under Islamic rule. The HP's description of the ʿAbbāsid conquest proves as much, hence Abū Muslim's guise as a latter-day Constantine and the depiction of the Khurāsāniyya as crypto-Christian liberators (Chapter Nine). Late antique tropes and popular beliefs translated well into Arabic and flourished among Christians and Muslims. Hence, the fourth-century Nile topos not only survived the conquest, but was adopted by Christians and Muslims and persisted until the nineteenth century (Chapter Eleven).

Ideologically, Muslims minimized the significance of Late Antiquity, which belonged to the Age of Ignorance (*al-Jahiliyya*), but they were, nonetheless, directly affected by it. The greatest Islamic encounter with Late Antiquity came by way of grafting late antique, biblical, and Hellenic figures, events, texts, and monuments onto Islamized narratives that positioned Islam at the center of history rather than as a later development. Much of what Egyptian Muslims took for granted was predicated upon late antique models and standards, from the basic rhythm of life in the province, to the origins of communal celebrations, and even local assumptions and beliefs about everything from Pharaonic monuments to medicine and magic (Chapters Six and Eleven). Hence, the Great Pyramids became synonymous with the granaries of Joseph, and the shrines associated with the journey of the Holy Family in Egypt became important pilgrimage centers for Muslims, as they continued to be for Christians. Late Antiquity survived, albeit in an Islamic guise, a fact copiously documented in such texts as *Faḍā'il miṣr* and *Futūḥ al-bahnasā*.

Futūḥ

The Arab conquest proved seminal on three fronts (Chapters Two and Nine): the historical, the historiographic, and the ideological. Regrettably, aside from underscoring general (even generic) trajectories and an obvious conclusion, much of the specifics of the conquest lie beyond the reach of the modern historian. Specifics were shuffled, abandoned, and invented with the rise of every historiographic impulse that sought to explore the meaning of the conquest for the generations that lived in its shadow.

On the eve of the conquest, it has been argued that while the Egyptian populace was deeply divided, the charted fissures do not conform to the stereotypical "ethnic" or confessional factions that seemed logical or justifiable to ninth- and tenth-century historians, or to the scholarship that is based on their writings. The earliest stratum of historical evidence depicts the conquest unfolding with the aid of Coptic and Melkite secular elites rather than the Coptic hierarchy (Chapters Two, Three, and Nine). Fundamentally, the alleged support of Patriarch Benjamin rests on tenuous historical grounds and remains irreconcilable with the earliest accounts and the Islamic government's early ambivalence toward the Coptic hierarchy. This early indifference negates the supposition that the Islamic government simply "gave" ecclesiastical properties to the Coptic church immediately after the conquest, or that it relied upon that institution to govern or tax the province (Chapters Three, Eight, and Ten).

Within two centuries of the conquest, distinct narratives emerged among Christians and Muslims which catered to communal priorities and sought to provide an antecedent for inter-communal harmony and cohesion. Demonstrably, each community employed its respective historiography in a hegemonic program that supplanted historical details in order to perpetuate an idealized version of the past.

These historiographies provide fascinating illustrations of the various means through which Christians and Muslims constructed their historical memories. Certainly the descriptions are often formulaic, especially among Arab historians, but behind the topoi lies the firm belief of later generations that the traditions they recorded and the events they narrated must have transpired in a particular manner: instructions must have come from the caliph, Arab troops must have conducted themselves honorably, and the "oppressed" populations must have cooperated and welcomed the Arabs as liberators. Recent scholarship would prove these ostensibly logical conclusions to be at best incomplete assessments and often distortions and fabrications.

Equally important is the idealism that saturates *futūḥ* accounts, which is typically absent from early non-Muslim writings (Chapters Three and Eight). While retaining a blatant historical orientation, the literature is equally concerned with addressing contemporary needs and the Muslim community's perception of its "founding fathers"—men who are consistently portrayed as fearless, pious warriors. Among Muslims, the conquest era embodied an egalitarian ethos that purportedly ended with the ascent of the Umayyads—another ideological premise (Chapters Seven and Eight). Significantly, the bulk of *futūḥ* literature describes events that transpired during the age of *al-Rashidūn*, the Rightly Guided Caliphs. As such, they were embroidered with all the trappings of vignettes befitting the Golden Age of Islam.

Futūḥ accounts may be also read as theological documents. Often one has to squint to see that angle, but not much more than in the biblical books of Chronicles or Kings. To Muslim eyes, the *futūḥ* genre chronicles an intense period in which God constantly intervened in human history (an enduring act, as the narratives in Chapter Eleven argue). Obsessively, Muslim chroniclers stress God's role. He conquers, literally "opens" (*yaftaḥ*), and Muslims simply walk through and take possession of the land: a sequence and an ideology repeatedly attested in the Historical Books of the Judeo-Christian scriptures. By presenting the conquests as a "miracle," a divine act, Arab historians sought to indirectly confirm the veracity of the Prophet Muḥammad's message, and succeeded in infusing political events with a divine aura of inevitability that still hampers historical discussions of the conquests until today.

As for Christian writings, in addition to providing an important corollary and a control for Islamic narratives, Christian historiographies of the conquest demonstrate a ninth-century dawning of new Coptic sensibilities. Here, too, the sources provide a sketch of a community reimagining its past. Congruent with the ninth-century invention of Patriarch Benjamin's leading role in the conquest was a historiographic shift in the Coptic community's historical memory

(Chapters Two and Nine). Writing after centuries of caliphal rule, and influenced by normative Islamic historiography, ninth- and tenth-century Copts began to conceive of Byzantine rule as an incessant reign of oppression and tyranny, a perception that cannot be substantiated from earlier writings. A highly selective interpretation of nearly two hundred years of Byzantine rule in Egypt (451–641 CE) emerged in the ninth century and has hitherto prevailed among the Copts (Chapters Two, Five, and Nine).

Similar to their Muslim counterparts, later Christian writings focused on early Islamic rule must not be read as indicative of historical attitudes, but rather as the revisionist perspectives of later generations who reflected on the Byzantine era after centuries of Arab rule. Until the conquest, the Copts viewed the Byzantine emperor as a legitimate sovereign and remained faithful subjects. But to articulate such early attitudes under Islamic rule was dangerous and somewhat antithetical to the normative belief that political rulers were divinely appointed; still, such early views surreptitiously remerged in Coptic Arabic apocalyptic tracts (Chapters Two and Nine). Ninth-century Christians imagined what the attitudes of their predecessors *must have* been: the parallels to ninth-century Islamic historiography are striking.

Community

In a little over two centuries, a segregated Arab Muslim community dominated by tribal loyalty and a martial ethic transformed into an agrarian and urban populace comprised of an array of "ethnic" groups which were increasingly motivated by regional interests. The first quarter of the eighth century CE proved crucial to this metamorphosis. Marwānid policies, ushering in the majority of Islamizing trends discussed in Chapter Six, allowed all Egyptians—Muslims, Christians, and Jews—to incrementally participate in a material and intellectual culture that was no longer defined by Christianity or classical learning, but rather a new cultural hybrid that grafted those older elements onto a society dominated by a new language and religion.

ʿUbyad Allāh ibn al-Ḥabḥāb's early eighth-century settlement of Qaysī tribesmen in the Delta provided a momentous catalyst for the evolution of the Muslim community, establishing an agrarian precedent for subsequent immigrants who could no longer enroll in the *dīwān*, and for old settlers who were phased out of the army (Chapters Five, Six, Seven, and Eight). Settled in the heart of the Delta, these new farmers facilitated the processes of religious conversion and Arabization among the Christians of the Delta, spreading Islamic culture and society well beyond the *amṣār* or urban centers (Chapters Four and Six). That historic settlement also provided the Qays with an essential demographic constituency to buttress the disproportionate political authority they had skillfully acquired in the province just a few decades prior (Chapters Seven and Eight).

Over the course of the eighth century, new socio-political developments prompted significant shifts within Arab Muslim society. Increasingly disenfranchised from ruling circles and progressively alienated from the rank and file of the army, Arab Muslims began to conceptualize their identity anew and to reevaluate their priorities. An early manifestation of this trend appeared in the neo-tribalism of the Qaysī-Yamanī disputes in Egypt, but is unmistakable in the details of the later agrarian revolts of the ninth century and the contours of the new society that may be distinctly observed in the tenth. Ultimately, regional rather than tribal interests would prevail (Chapters Six, Seven, and Eight).

A new regime, the ʿAbbāsids, ushered in an imperative for cultural transformations. Founded over an Umayyad infrastructure, the new dynasty's ideological underpinnings, fiscal policies, and emphasis on intellectual rigor changed much within *Dar al-Islam*. Jurisprudence began to coalesce into a bulwark that provided for a less malleable society, contributing to the demise of the unofficial means of social organization and conflict resolution hitherto documented in rural villages (Chapters Four, Seven, and Eight). Even more significantly, as fiscal policies shifted and Muslims began to accept converts on an equal footing, their ranks began to swell, encompassing a wide array of individuals from various "ethnic" backgrounds and occupations.

Conversely, "Arab Muslim," increasingly detached from tribal affiliation, came to encompass any Arabic-speaking Muslim. This newly-constructed, highly diverse Islamic community in Egypt further distinguished itself by adhering to a distinct calendar, newly codified schools of Islamic Jurisprudence (particularly those of the Shafiʿīs and Malikīs, but a few domestic schools also developed), and the redrafting of old narratives and ideas to better resonate within a new socio-political milieu and Islam's hegemonic cultural discourse (Chapters Six, Eight, and Eleven).

Among Christians, the bonds that united them as a faith community (the divinity of Jesus, sacraments, saints, etc.) were often overshadowed by internal strife among the pro- and anti-Chalcedonian factions, who forged sectarian identities through the adoption of distinctive, often antithetical, communal and liturgical observances. On a wide range of subjects and through a plethora of means, these communities debated theology, right practice, and legitimate apostolic succession as each claimed exclusive descent from the fathers of the fourth and fifth centuries, the undisputed bastions of orthodoxy, and maintained that those hallowed figures aligned themselves with one faction and opposed the other (Chapters Four, Ten, and Eleven).

In the aftermath of the conquest, the fate of the two major Christian confessions was anything but certain. If one were to focus exclusively on the first few decades of Islamic rule, it would appear that intra-communal relations had hardly changed. Melkites monopolized administrative posts and continued to serve their confession by sequestering Coptic churches and posing difficulties for the Coptic community and hierarchy whenever possible (Chapters Three, Four, and Ten). Fundamentally, however, the dominance of Melkites in post-conquest Egypt was short-lived. By the late 680s, the Islamic government had recognized the numerical superiority of the anti-Chalcedonians and began to accommodate them. Moreover, much of the early Islamic government's policies in Egypt were a reflection of interpersonal relationships. Governmental and communal prerogatives were negotiated through encounters among governors, notables, and patriarchs; the absence of a Melkite patriarch in Egypt for the first Islamic century was a distinct disadvantage. Demonstrably, the Egyptian Melkite community lost the advances it gained in the first half of the seventh century (Chapters Three, Four, and Ten). Under Islamic rule, the Melkites are consistently documented as an urban minority that never expanded into the countryside. Significantly, this was not purely a function of language. As repeatedly demonstrated, the Greek language dominated the liturgical celebrations of the Copts and was regarded as the proper medium for theological reflection and a language of prestige until the ninth century and, arguably, long after.

Under early Islamic rule, unhindered by Byzantine constraints, the Coptic church and community reconciled schismatic and heretical groups, and expanded its hierarchical infrastructures (Chapters Three, Four, Nine, and Ten). (It is difficult to imagine the unfolding of this process in this fashion had the Copts not been the majority.) Still, while those processes persisted under the early ʿAbbāsids, they would be overshadowed by the ever-increasing tide of conversion to Islam. By the late tenth century, when the Coptic church began to tackle the intellectual and practical factors that led to conversion, significant time and numbers had been lost.

Society

From the Arab conquest until the early ninth century CE, Egyptian society subsisted as a cultural mosaic delineated by linguistic, social, and religious boundaries. This began to change in the late eighth century CE, and the new dynamic gained momentum in the ninth. A nascent, homogeneous culture first appeared in urban centers and progressively spread to rural areas. Irrespective of creed, litigants sought the judgment of the same *quḍāt*, spoke the same language, had similar-sounding names, and wore analogous clothing (Chapters Five and Eight). The spatial and cultural barriers that dominated in the seventh century were overcome. Apart from the strictly religious dimension of confessional observances, Christians and Muslims intermingled and celebrated some feasts, such as those of *ʿĪd al-Shahīd* and *ʿĪd al-Ghiṭās*, in remarkably similar fashions (Chapter

Eleven), a pattern that is replicated in Islamic *mawlid*s as well. Beyond these large social gatherings, however, the same patterns emerge on the much smaller scale of private celebrations. The late twelfth-century HCME relates: "At the weddings and other celebrations of the Muslims the Christians are present, and chant in the Sahidic dialect of Coptic, and walk before the bridegroom through the market-places and streets; and this has become a recognized custom with them, [and has continued] up to our own day".[2] Harmonious interactions between Christians and Muslims are often documented in the papyri. Personal letters, which lack the formulae and formality of contracts, reflect integrated communities in which religious and even linguistic barriers were overcome and certainly were not as divisive as they appear during periods of strife. *P.Khalili*.I.21 (*P.Khalili*.II.38) is a second/eighth-century letter from Ibn Muḥammad to Amīna bint Asad which concludes thus: "Give my best wishes to Palekhem (Παλαχῆμις) and to Abū Hasan and Abū Qiril (Κίριλλος) and his family." Arguably, such personal correspondences are the best indicators of day-to-day interactions.

The seeds for this new integrated society were sown in the late eighth century, as demonstrated by the discussions of Arab immigration into Egypt and agrarian revolts, and matured over the ninth and tenth centuries, influencing historical developments and engendering new socio-political constructs and perspectives (Chapters Six, Seven, and Eight). At that juncture, tribal solidarity, already undermined through various means, progressively yielded to a new identity based on regionalism and common economic and agrarian interests. For the first time, Qaysī and Yamanī, Muslim and Christian, shared common interests, participated in the same revolts, and structured a decidedly new social order (Chapters Five, Six, Seven, and Eight).

Paradoxically, this nascent cultural uniformity offset an intrinsic inequality. Here lies the dichotomy inherent in Egyptian society (Chapters Five, Six, and Nine): a society at once homogeneous yet deeply sectarian. While many names and *kunya*s were ambiguous, others were clearly indicative of religious affiliation (e.g. Muḥammad and ʿAbd al-Masīḥ). Sectarian identities were occasionally reinforced by government intolerance, discriminatory edicts, and a few brief periods of direct persecution of Christian bureaucrats and elites (Chapters Four, Five, and Eight), but on the whole, they were constructed through internal and external mechanisms. Externally, government-imposed regulations fostered distinctive identities through the employment of different law codes for *dhimmī*s and the levying and collection of the *jizya*. For various crimes against Muslims (especially relating to murder and rape), Christian and Jewish offenders were punished more severely than an equally culpable Muslim, and the *diyya* (blood money/ransom) demanded for the murder of a *dhimmī* was half that of a Muslim's.[3] Internally, each community developed and perpetuated distinctive customs, practices (e.g. tattooing for the Copts), calendars, and narratives that imbued it with particular symbols of affiliation and a communal ethos (Chapters Five, Six, and Eleven). Some of these identity-forming strategies were structural, while others were dependent; in all, this paradox, this tension between collective and sectarian identities, remained at the crux of the social history of Egypt.

By the late ninth century, urban Muslims and Christians interacted on a regular basis and, to the alarm and dismay of traditionalists on both sides, began to resemble each other even in dress and mannerisms; one could no longer visually distinguish Arab from Egyptian, Christian from Muslim (Chapter Eight). This lack of difference disturbed conservatives and led to parallel, even ironic developments. The Christian author of the *Apocalypse of Samuel* had much more in common with the Muslim jurists who drafted the *ghiyār* (clothing) legislation than he realized or would have cared to admit. All were threatened by the emergence of a new society in which one could not readily discern another's communal or religious identity: a fear of a rampant assimilation that would eclipse their "authentic" identities. Consequently, the authors of *pseudo-Samuel* and the *ghiyār* regulations attempted to construct visible identifiers and erect communal boundaries that reflected latent religious, fiscal, and legal distinctions.

The conflicting color codes of the *ghiyār* regulations demonstrate as much: the color itself was irrelevant.[4] These regulations were primarily concerned with constructing difference by fostering ciphers of status and religious affiliation. In the *Apocalypse of Samuel*, the Coptic language served as an analogous signifier of creed and community; it was no longer simply a means of communication, but increasingly a symbol of affiliation. Whether through distinctive attire or the spoken word, diverse factions sought to disrupt the homogenizing effects of urban life: the assimilation and hybridity that naturally result from sharing the same public space and language.

Modern Historiography

Repeatedly, this study has underscored the crucial importance of studying the history and historiography of the first Islamic centuries, not just in and of themselves but as a fundamental prelude for an understanding of later developments. Chapters Nine, Ten, and Eleven discuss several topics that earlier scholarship interpreted as Fāṭimid achievements, but which have now proven to have had strong roots stretching back to early Islamic rule, if not the Byzantine era.

Pre-modern Middle Eastern history has far too often been analyzed through the lenses of Arab "ethnicity" and confessional creeds. These lenses are not inherently distorted; each is as valid as any other filter used to engage primary sources. Rather, the problem lies in the insistence on their overarching, even singular importance. At different junctures, I argued that common socioeconomic interests outweighed the importance of tribal solidarity or religious affiliation. Discussions of the social ramifications of agrarian revolts, calendrical usage, and the symbiotic relationship that developed between Coptic monasteries and pastoral Arabs all underscore this interpretive approach (Chapters Six and Eight).

With regard to the historiography of the Coptic church and community, this monograph stresses the need to reevaluate the criteria upon which the status of that confession has been characterized. Traditionally, the welfare of the Copts has been gauged in relation to the austerity of the Islamic government's policies toward *dhimmīs*, but other criteria must now be examined. By way of example, according to the traditional standards the Patriarchate of John IV (775–99 CE) would appear as an age of prosperity that witnessed the development of a massive ecclesiastical building program, the procurement of relics, and inter-communal harmony. Nonetheless, that patriarchate should also be juxtaposed against the backdrop of group conversions to Islam (such as that of *Ahl al-Ḥarās*, discussed in Chapter Four), the lack of any significant attempts at the advancement or even the regurgitation of the "ecclesiastical sciences," and the proliferation of the gangrene of simony (Chapters Four, Five, and Ten). These factors were at least as destructive as the intermittent periods of governmental oppression or sectarian strife (Chapters Six and Eleven), and arguably they were much more detrimental to the long-term welfare of that community.

Squarely based upon the developments of those early centuries, the era spanning the tenth through the thirteenth centuries would prove of central importance to the Coptic church for seemingly contradictory reasons. That was the formative period for the type of Coptic Christianity that has survived today. Certainly, there is a plethora of tangible and ethereal differences between the late antique, medieval, and modern Coptic church; nonetheless, a modern Copt would more easily identify with the liturgical and religious celebrations and biblical exegesis of the Arabic ear much more readily than with those of the fourth-, sixth-, or even eighth-century church. Over those few centuries, the Copts lived through a golden age of Coptic Arabic literature, in which, as Sidney Griffith observed, they composed more Arabic Christian literature than all of their Christian peers combined. Nonetheless, two trends began to dominate the Copts' self-image from that time on: nostalgia for an imagined past, predicated upon ninth- and tenth-century antecedents, and a selective antiquarianism.

The pervasive adoption of the Era of the Martyrs signaled the mood of the age (Chapter Six). In the shadow of the intolerant regimes of al-Mutawakkil (when the designation was first employed in literary texts) and that of al-Ḥākim (after which it prevailed), Coptic narratives were drafted in a historical present that contested the notion that the Age of Martyrdom had ended. This selective antiquarianism (at times rendered all too real through the infrequent, though nonetheless historical bouts of government intolerance and accounts of neo-martyrdom) demarcates a significant conceptual shift.[5] Copts began to live in an age of martyrs, which, strictly speaking, existed over seven hundred years prior. A parallel development, the compilation of the Coptic Arabic *Synaxarion* (and to a lesser extent, the *Difnār*), reinforced this perspective by encapsulating and unabashedly promoting a specific vision of the past. "On *this* day" (*fī hadhā al-yawm*), the introductory formula of every entry in that compilation, elided present and past, the then and now. Coptic Christians would live in the Era of Martyrs, and at every liturgical observance a condensed, selective vision of the past, which emphasized martyrdom and persecution under Roman, Byzantine, and Muslim rulers (along with commemorations of saints and patriarchs), would be *re*presented—that is, "made present again". The Copts had, on the one hand, come to define themselves through persecution and perseverance, and on the other, sought refuge in their hallowed past at a time of increasingly demographic and political marginalization. The irony, of course, is that these processes were ongoing during the Golden Age of Coptic Arabic literature.

As for the early Muslim community, it proved resilient and highly malleable as individuals quickly adapted to professions and political circumstances that their grandfathers could have hardly imagined. Within roughly a century, merchants became soldiers, and then soldiers took to agriculture along with urban trades and professions. By the ninth century, as Persians, Armenians, and various Turkomen came to dominate the army and the administrative apparatus, most Arabs gradually accepted their position among the populace rather than within the political establishment. Repeatedly, the discussions above, particularly those focused on conversion, agrarian revolts, interactions with Coptic monasteries, and tensions among ruling elites, have traced the demilitarization of the Arab Muslim community, and have challenged its normative, monolithic descriptions (Chapters Four, Six, Seven, and Eight). Nonetheless, one is besieged by tantalizing but inconclusive tidbits, such as Ibn

Yūnus' reference to an Egyptian recension of the Qur'ān, which point to a much more diverse community than hitherto described or imagined.[6] Inevitably, a slew of unanswerable questions come to mind: the actual size of the Muslim community at any historical juncture is a matter for speculation; religious diversity remains an open question; and the means by which Egyptian Muslims conceived of and presented themselves as a distinct community from their Syrian or Iraqi peers remains faint, though that question becomes easier to answer after the tenth century.

Finally, as pertains to sectarian history, it is imperative that the confessional and communal histories of Jews, Christians, and Muslims not neglect the sociohistorical matrix in which the three factions were embedded, their reciprocal influences on each other's communities, and the extra-communal factors that enabled some individuals and families to have a closer affinity with each another than with peers within their own religious community. Several discussions, particularly those of the *'urbān* and the Nile topos, prove useful in demonstrating the existence, efficacy, and transformative effects of an ongoing dialectic in which members of the three faiths positioned themselves as active participants (Chapters Eight and Eleven). Nonetheless, historians continue to slip (often inadvertently) into old paradigms by studying Christians and Jews as simply "non-Muslims," and focusing on the Islamic community as if it were *sui generis*: originating and existing in a spatial, intellectual, and communal vacuum. Demonstrably, Christian and Jewish communities were far from "fossilized" or passive societal "dead weight," as one prominent historian had labeled them.[7] Similarly, much of what Egyptian Muslims have taken for granted was borrowed from or developed through the mediation of, and various encounters with, their neighbors. On every front, historians must trace the mechanisms by which Muslims, Christians, and Jews interacted with one another—as individuals and as communities—and influenced each other's lives, practices, and stories.

NOTES

Nomenclature and Conventions

1. Few Arabs lived in Egypt prior to the conquest. Some literature speaks of "Coptic Muslims," which was at times employed as an epithet. Certainly, many Muslims were Egyptians or came to conceive of themselves as such, though I am unaware of any Egyptian Muslims who referred to themselves as "Copts" during the early centuries surveyed here.
2. To rephrase a definition articulated by David W. Johnson, "Anti-Chalcedonian Polemics in Coptic Texts, 451–641," in *The Roots of Egyptian Christianity*, ed. B.A. Pearson and J.E. Goehring (Philadelphia, 1989), 219.

Chapter 1 Introduction

1. See Peter Brown, *The World of Late Antiquity, AD 150–750* (New York, 1971; 1989); A. Kazhadan and A. Cutler, "Continuity and Discontinuity in Byzantine History," *Byzantion* 52 (1982), 429–78; Frank Clover and R. Stephen Humphreys, "Toward a Definition of Late Antiquity," in *Tradition and Innovation in Late Antiquity*, ed. idem (Madison, 1989), 3–19; Jairus Banaji, *Agrarian Change in Late Antiquity: Gold, Labor and Aristocratic Dominance* (Oxford, 2001), App. 5; Joel Walker, "The Limits of Late Antiquity: Philosophy between Rome and Iran," *Ancient World* 33 (2002), 45–69; Roger S. Bagnall, "Periodizing when you don't have to: the Concept of late antiquity in Egypt," in *Gab es eine Spätantike?* (Frankfurt am Main, 2003), 39–49; also see the articles published in Tomas Hägg, ed., *Symbolae Osloenses* 72 (1997), 5–90; and the *Journal of Late Antiquity* 1.1 (2008).
2. E.g. A. Cameron, B. Ward-Perkins, and M. Whitby, eds., *The Cambridge Ancient History*, vol. 14, *Late Antiquity: Empire and Successors AD 425–600* (Cambridge,

2000); A.H.M. Jones, *The Later Roman Empire*, 2 vols. (Baltimore, 1986); John Meyendorff, *Imperial Unity and Christian Divisions* (Crestwood, 1989); Hugh Kennedy, *The Prophet and the Age of the Caliphates*, 2nd ed. (London, 2004); Marshall G.S. Hodgson, *The Venture of Islam*, vol. 1 (Chicago, 1974); Carl F. Petry, ed., *The Cambridge History of Egypt*, vol. 1 (Cambridge, 1998); Aziz S. Atiya, *A History of Eastern Christianity* (London, 1968; 1980); Otto F.A. Meinardus, *Two Thousand Years of Coptic Christianity* (Cairo, 1999); idem, *Christian Egypt: Ancient and Modern*, 2nd rev. ed. (Cairo, 1977); Chris Wickham, *Framing the Early Middle Ages: Europe and the Mediterranean, 400–800*, New Edition (Oxford, 2007); R.S. Bagnall, ed., *Egypt in the Byzantine World, 300–700* (Cambridge, 2007).

3. This period was discussed in Arietta Papaconstantinou, "Historiography, Hagiography, and the Making of the Coptic "Church of the Martyrs" in Early Islamic Egypt," DOP 60 (2006), 65–86, though this monograph reaches very different conclusions from those presented in that study; e.g. the end of this chapter, and chapters Four, Six, and Twelve.
4. Martin Krause, "The Importance of Wadi al-Natrun for Coptology," in *Christianity and Monasticism in Wadi al-Natrun*, ed. Maged S.A. Mikhail and Mark Moussa (Cairo, 2009), notes Walter E. Crum's mastery of the various branches of Coptic Studies as a now impossible goal.
5. See Timothy D. Barnes, "Late Antiquity and Early Islam: A Review Essay," *al-Masāq* 9 (1996–97), 194.
6. E.g. Johannes Leipoldt, *Schenute von Atripe und die Entstehung des national ägyptischen Christentums* (Leipzig, 1903); E.L. Woodward, *Christianity and Nationalism in the Late Roman Empire* (London, 1916); J.G. Milne, "Egyptian Nationalism under Greek and Roman Rule," *Journal of Egyptian Archaeology* 14 (1928), 226–34; E.R. Hardy, *Christian Egypt: Church and People, Christianity and Nationalism in the Patriarchate of Alexandria* (New York, 1952); Christopher Steed, *History of the Church in Africa* (Cambridge, 2000). Important critiques, which still retained some aspects of the nationalist reading, include A.H.M. Jones, "Were Ancient Heresies National or Social Movements in Disguise?" *Journal of Theological Studies* n.s. 11 (1959), 280–98; C.D.G. Müller, *Geschichte der orientalischen Nationalkirchen* (Göttingen, 1981); W.H.C. Frend, "Nationalism as a Factor in Anti-Chalcedonian Feeling in Egypt," in *Religion and National Identity*, ed. S. Mews (Oxford, 1982). More thorough critiques were forwarded by F. Winkelmann, "Ägypten und Byzanz vor der arabischen Eroberung," *Byzantinoslavica* 40 (1979), 161–82; and W. Wipszycha, "Le Nationalisme a-t-il Existe Dans l'Égypte Byzantine?" JJP 22 (1992), 83–128.
7. "Nationalism" in the Middle East, as it is academically defined and studied, was a product of the First World War. See Benedict R. O'G. Anderson, *Imagined Communities: Reflections on the Origin and Spread of Nationalism* (London, 1983); Anthony D. Smith, *National Identity* (London, 1991); idem, *Nationalism: Theory, Ideology, History* (Cambridge, 2001).
8. See chapters Two, Three, and Five.

9 The term is Roger Bagnall's (*Egypt in Late Antiquity* (Princeton, 1995), 4). On the sources, see James Howard-Johnston, *Witnesses to a World Crisis: Historians and Histories of the Middle East in the Seventh Century* (Oxford, 2010); Maged S.A. Mikhail, "An Orientation to the Sources and Study of Early Islamic Egypt (641–868)," *History Compass* 8.8 (2010), 929–50; CMR vols. 1 and 2; Harald Suermann, "Copts and the Islam of the Seventh Century," in *The Encounter of Eastern Christianity with Early Islam*, ed. E. Grypeou, M. Swanson and D. Thomas (Leiden, 2006); Robert G. Hoyland, *Seeing Islam as Others Saw It: A Survey and Evaluation of Christian, Jewish and Zoroastrian Writings on Early Islam*, SLAEI 13 (Princeton, 1997).

10. Exceptions abound in later literature: e.g. al-Mas'ūdī's *Murūj al-dhahab*; al-Maqrīzī's *khiṭaṭ* (14th c.), especially his *Dhikr qibṭ miṣr*; C.E. Bosworth, "Christian and Jewish religious Dignitaries in Mamlūk Egypt and Syria: Qalqashandī's Information on their Hierarchy, Titulature, and Appointment," IJMES 3 (1972), 59–72; repr. in his *Medieval Arabic Culture and Administration* (Brookfield, 1982).

11. Ibn 'Abd al-Ḥakam's (d. 257/871) writings are among the earliest in the province.

12. Gregor Schoeler, *The Oral and the Written in Early Islam*, ed. J.E. Montgomery, trans. Uwe Vagelpohl (London, 2006); Albrecht Noth, *The Early Arabic Historical Tradition: A Source-Critical Study*, 2nd rev. ed. with L.I. Conrad, trans. M. Bonner (Princeton, 1994); Michael Cook, "The Opponents of the Writing of Tradition in Early Islam," *Arabica* 44 (1997), 437–530; idem, *Studies in the Origins of Early Islamic Culture and Tradition* (Brookfield, 2004); Suliman Bashear, *Arabs and Others in Early Islam*, SLAEI 8 (Princeton, 1997); Chase F. Robinson, "Conquest of Khūzistān: A Historiographical Reassessment," BSOAS 67 (2004), 14–39; L.I. Conrad, "The Conquest of Arwād: A Source-Critical Study in the Historiography of the Early Medieval Near East," in *The Byzantine and Early Islamic Near East, I: Problems in the Literary Source Material*, ed. A. Cameron and L.I. Conrad (Princeton, 1992), 317–401.

13. Chase F. Robinson, *Islamic Historiography* (Cambridge, 2003); Fred M. Donner, *Narratives of Islamic Origins: The Beginnings of Islamic Historical Writing*, SLAEI 14 (Princeton, 1998); 'Abd al-'Aziz Duri, *The Rise of Historical Writing Among the Arabs*, trans. L.I. Conrad (Princeton, 1983). The most critical approaches have been those of John Wansbrough, *The Sectarian Milieu: Content and Composition of Islamic Salvation History* (Oxford, 1978); Patricia Crone and Michael Cook, *Hagarism: The Making of the Islamic World* (Cambridge, 1977); Patricia Crone, *Meccan Trade and the Rise of Islam* (Princeton, 1987). Much more conservative is Tarif Khalidi's *Arabic Historical Thought in the Classical Period* (New York, 1994).

14. Discussed in A. Noth's *Early Arabic Historical Tradition*.

15. E.g. Stanley H. Skreslet II, "The Greeks in Medieval Islamic Egypt: A Melkite Dhimmi Community under the Patriarch of Alexandria (640–1095)" (Ph.D. diss., Yale University, 1987).

16. Bishop Michael of Tinnīs states: "I found what the biographies ... adopted by the Church from the time of the saintly father [Mark], the Evangelist ... down to the time of father Abba Shenoute who is the fifty-fifth [d. 880 CE] ... After him, down to the time of Abba Shenoute the sixty-fifth [d. 1046 CE] ... *nothing was written of the biographies*." (HP II.2:102/133v, my emphasis). In HP II.3:260/162v, Mawhūb confirmed Bishop Michael' authorship of the ten biographies from Khaīl III (Michael) to Shinūda II. He does not mention Sawīrus at all. Moreover, Abū al-Barakāt ibn Kabar (d. 1324 CE), does not list this major work among Sawīrus' known writings.
17. J. den Heijer, *Mawhub ibn Mansur ibn Mufarriğ et l'historiographie copte-arabe. Étude sur la composition de l'Histoire des Patriarches d'Alexandrie* (Louvain, 1989); idem, "Coptic Historiography in the Fāṭimid, Ayyūbid, and Early Mamlūk Periods," *Medieval Encounters* 2 (1996), 67–98. Building on David W. Johnson, "Further Fragments of a Coptic History of the Church: Cambridge OR. 1699 R," *Enchoria* 6 (1976), 7–17; idem, "Further Remarks on the Arabic History of the Patriarchs of Alexandria," *Oriens Christianus* 61 (1977), 103–16; H. Brakmann, "Eine oder zwei koptische Kirchengeschichten," *Muséon* 87 (1974), 129–42; Tito Orlandi, *Storia della Chiesa di Alessandria*, 2 vols. (Milan, 1968–1970).
18. The initial entries are *On the Priesthood of Christ*, *Life of Saint Mark*, and *Martyrdom of Saint Mark*. Den Heijer, *Mawhub*, 127–8. For the *Life of St. Mark*, see Allen Dwight Callahan, "The *Acts of Saint Mark*: And Introduction and Translation," *Coptic Church Review* 14 (1993), 2–10; idem, "The *Acts of Mark*: Tradition, Transmission, and Translation of the Arabic Version," in *The Apocryphal Acts of the Apostles*, ed. F. Bovon, A.G. Brock and C.R. Matthews (Cambridge, 1999).
19. HP I.2:180; Tito Orlandi, "The Coptic Ecclesiastical History: A Survey," in *The World of Early Egyptian Christianity: Language, Literature, and Social Context*, ed. J.E. Goehring and J.A. Timbie (Washington D.C, 2007).
20. He was also the spiritual father of the Coptic patriarch Kosmas (730–1 CE).
21. HP I.3:433.For the earlier section see HP I.3:344–5.
22. See HP I.4:646, 648.
23. See n. 16, above, which positively excludes Bishop Sawīrus' authorship.
24. E.g. HP I.3:397, 274: "And the writer of this history [of John III] was with him, for he was his spiritual son." HP I.4:536: "from reliable and trustworthy persons, who were constantly ministering to our holy fathers we have heard the narratives which we are relating in part." HP I.4:646, 648 and 659: "such were the events which I witnessed with my own eyes."
25. Mark N. Swanson, *The Coptic Papacy in Islamic Egypt 641–1517* (Cairo, 2010), chs. 1–3.
26. See Abbreviations and Bibliography for references to both recensions; the primitive recension has been published in part. Another work by the same title, the *History of the Patriarchs* (*Tarīkh al-abā'*) of Pseudo-Yusāb of Fuwwā, has a limited bearing on the period at hand.

27. Only four patriarchs visited Upper Egypt in the first two Islamic centuries: Benjamin I, Alexander II, Khaīl I, and Patriarch Ya'qūb. See Benjamin, *On Cana of Galilee*, 29v, 30r; HP I.3:313, 393; I.4:568–9.
28. M.N. Swanson, *Coptic Papacy*, 4–7; cf. Johannes den Heijer, "La conquête arabe vue par les historiens coptes," in *Valeur et distance: Identités et sociétés en Égypte*, ed. C. Décobert (Paris, 2000), 227–45.
29. Paul J. Alexander, "Medieval Apocalypses as Historical Sources," *American Historical Review* 73.4 (1968), 997–1018; repr. idem, *Religious and Political History and Thought in the Byzantine Empire* (London, 1978); Hans D. Betz, "On the Problem of the Religio-Historical Understanding of Apocalypticism," *Journal for Theology and the Church* 6 (1969), 134–56; J. van Lent, "The Nineteenth Muslim Kings in Coptic Apocalypses," *Parole de l'Orient* 25 (2000), 643–93.
30. See Roger S. Bagnall, ed., *The Oxford Handbook of Papyrology* (Oxford, 2009); idem, *Reading Papyri, Writing Ancient History* (London, 1995); Adam Gacek, *The Arabic manuscript Tradition: A Glossary of Technical Terms and Bibliography* (Leiden, 2001); and his *Supplement* (Leiden, 2008); A. Grohmann, *From the World of Arabic Papyri*; idem, Handbuch der Orientalistik 1:1–2 I. *Arabische Chronologie*, II. *Arabische papyruskunde* (Leiden, 1966); *Chrest.Khoury*.I and II. A periodically updated checklist of published papyri is posted at <http://scriptorium.lib.duke.edu/papyrus/texts/clist_papyri.html>. For Arabic papyri, see John F. Oates and Petra M. Sijpesteijn <www.ori.unizh.ch/isap/isapchecklist.html>; also <www.papyri.info>. The most accessible papyrological studies are Roger S. Bagnall's *Egypt in Late Antiquity*; Terry G. Wilfong's *Women of Jeme: Lives in a Coptic Town in Late Antique Egypt* (Ann Arbor, 2002); and L.S.B. MacCoull's *Coptic Legal Documents: Law as Vernacular Text and Experience in Late Antique Egypt* (Turnhout, 2009).
31. See George T. Scanlon, Review of *Papyrology and the History of Early Islamic Egypt*, edited by Petra M. Sijpesteijn and Lennart Sundelin, *Journal of Islamic Studies* 7.1 (2006), 78–9; cf. C. Décobert, "Sur L'Arabisation et L'Islamisation," and G. Frantz-Murphy, "Conversion in Early Islamic Egypt."
32. Cf. the depictions of Oxyrhynchus and Aphrodito in Giovanni R. Ruffini's, *Social Networks in Byzantine Egypt* (Cambridge, 2008). Papyrological sources allow for the construction of micro-histories such as T.G. Wilfong's *Women of Jeme* and L.S.B. MacCoull's *Dioscorus of Aphrodito* (Berkeley, 1988). Still, the few deposits that allow for such in-depth studies tend to belong to individuals or families (almost always living in Upper Egypt); thus, the degree to which such studies reflect societal norms must always remain suspect.
33. Jørgen Bæk Simonsen, *Studies in the Genesis and Early Development of the Caliphal Taxation System* (Copenhagen, 1988), 85–6, 98–9, 101, 115, 122, 129–30; has demonstrated the incompatibility of the two types of sources in studying the first eighty years of taxation in Egypt; cf. the methodological approach of Wadād al-Qāḍī in "The Salaries of Judges in Early Islam: The Evidence of the Documentary and Literary Sources," JNES 68 (2009), 9–30.

34. It is possible to supplement late antique narrative sources with papyri, hagiographic, and homiletic literature; e.g. Paphnutios' *Histories of the Monks of Upper Egypt*. For the seventh through the tenth centuries, however, most secular and religious texts also stem from the Delta.
35. see Wadād al-Qāḍī, "An Umayyad Papyrus in al-Kindī's *Kitāb al-Quḍāt*," *Der Islam* 84 (2007), 200–45; Frank R. Trombley, "The Documentary Background to the *History of the Patriarchs* of Ps.-Sawīrus ibn al-Muqaffa' ca. 750–969 CE," in *From al-Andalus to Khurasan: Documents from the Medieval Muslim World*, ed. P.M. Sijpesteijn, L. Sundelin, S.T. Tovar, A. Zomeño (Leiden, 2007).
36. Historians of the Fāṭimid era and the Jewish community possess documentary texts—thanks to the Cairo Geniza archive—and narrative sources from the same region, time, and community. Yet reconciling the historical data has often proven rather prickly, occupying generations of specialists, as the protracted academic debates surrounding the origins of the office of Head of the Jews demonstrate. See the historiographic survey in Mark Cohen's *Jewish Self-Government in Medieval Egypt* (Princeton, 1980).
37. Most notably, S.D. Goitein's *A Mediterranean Society*, 6 vols. (Berkeley, 1967–1993); see the Bibliography of the Genizah Collection <www.lib.cam.ac.uk/Taylor-Schechter/Bibliography.html>.
38. Even Moshe Gil's massive *Jews in Islamic Countries in the Middle Ages* (Leiden, 2004) fails to shed any direct light on the history of the Jewish community in Egypt during these centuries. For a general survey, consult Norman A. Stillman, "The non-Muslim Communities: the Jewish Community," in *The Cambridge History of Egypt*, ed. C.F. Petry.
39. Cf. A. Cameron, "The Eastern Provinces in the Seventh Century A.D. Hellenism and the Emergence of Islam," in *Hellenismos: Quelques jalons pour une histoire de l'identité grecque*, ed. S. Said (Leiden, 1991), 290–1.
40. H. Grégoire, "Mahomet et le Monophysisme," in *Études sur l'histoire et sur l'art de Byzance* (Mélanges Chales Diehl), 2 vols. (Paris, 1930), I:107–19.
41. Some scholars maintain that "Monophysitism" could not resist the simplicity and rationality of Islamic doctrine; others highlight the alleged political alienation of the "Monophysites" as an essential catalyst for the conquest—a prevalent assumption. At best, in her *Mediterranean World in Late Antiquity* (London, 1993), Averil Cameron has noted the existence of several other factors that facilitated the conquests, but she did not challenge the validity of that supposition (see pgs. 176, 189–91)—here, see chapters Two, There, and Nine. That book's assessment of Monophysitism (pgs. 23–4, 66) is fairly traditional, though its description of Severos of Antioch as an "extreme Monophysite" (pg. 24) is an overstatement better suited for the Akephaloi or Julian of Halikarnassos.
42. E.g. Elizabeth S. Bolman, "The Coptic *Galaktotrophousa* Revisited," in *Coptic Studies*, ed. Immerzeel and Van der Vliet, 2:1173–84, at 1177 and 1181; and G.R.D. King's "Islam, Iconoclasm, and the Declaration of Doctrine," BSOAS 48.2 (1985), 267–77. King repeatedly alludes to a conclusion made explicit on

page 272. Namely, that Near Eastern churches and chapels adorned with crosses, rather than crucifixes, betray "Monophysite patronage," a conclusion predicated upon the assumption that "Monophysites" would object to portraying the humanity of Jesus Christ, which existence they deny. That conclusion is problematic. Most of the evidence, which is slim as King admits, predates the seventh century when crucifixes in general are seldom attested: cf. K. Weitzmann, ed., *Age of Spirituality: A Symposium* (New York, 1979; Princeton, 1980). Second, King's article, itself, cites acts of vandalism and iconoclasm perpetuated against "Monophysite" icons, at least one of which depicted "the Virgin and Jesus" (pg. 270). Finally, the so-called "Monophysites" never hesitated in liturgically expressing Christ's bodily death and resurrection: explicit in the anti-Chalcedonian version of the *Trisagion*: "holy God, holy Mighty, holy Immortal, who was born of the Virgin .... who was crucified .... who is raised from the dead and ascended into heaven ..." See, *Letter of Alexander II*; Grillmeier, *Christ in Christian Tradition*, II.4: 234–57.

43. F. Nau challenged the association between Egyptian Christianity and "monophysitism" over a century ago: "Dans quelle mesure les Jacobites sont-ils Monophysites?" ROC 10 (1905), 113–34.
44. Even in the *Cambridge History of Egypt*, vol. 1, the "Monophysite" designation is still taken for granted. In his "The non-Muslim Communities: Christian communities," T.G. Wilfong describes the Monophysite controversy as: "Ostensibly a dispute over whether Christ had both a divine and human nature, or just *a single divine nature* .... the majority of Egyptians, preferred the Monophysite doctrine of Christ having *a single divine nature*" (pg. 177)—my emphasis.
45. V.C. Samuel, *The Council of Chalcedon Re-Examined* (Madras, 1977; 2001); Karekin Sarkissian (Garegin II), *The Council of Chalcedon and the Armenian Church*, 3rd impression (Antelias, 1984); Iain Torrance, *Christology after Chalcedon* (Cambridge, 1988; 1998); Stephen J. Davis, *Coptic Christology in Practice: Incarnation and Divine Participation in Late Antique and Medieval Egypt* (Oxford, 2008).
46. W.H.C. Frend, *The Rise of the Monophysite Movement*, 2nd rev. ed. (Cambridge, 1979). Frend's "Monophysitism" (*CoptEncyc* 5:1669–78) simply reiterates the perspectives of his book without any critical reflection. On Chalcedon, also see R.V. Sellers, *The Council of Chalcedon* (London, 1961); A. Grillmeier and H. Bacht, eds., *Das Konzil von Chalkedon*, 3 vols. (Würzburg, 1951–54; 1979); J. Oort and J. Roldanus, eds., *Chalkedon: Geschichte und Aktualität* (Louvain, 1998); Patrick T.R. Gray, "the Legacy of Chalcedon: Christological Problems and their Significance," in *Cambridge Companion to the Age of Justinian*, ed. M. Maas (Cambridge, 2005); Geoffrey de Ste. Croix, *Christian Persecution, Martyrdom, and Orthodoxy*, ed. M. Whitby and J. Streeter (Oxford, 2006), ch. 6.
47. It also forwards a politically determinative analysis that repeatedly interprets theological disputes and schisms as manifestations of political and "national" ideologies.

48. E.g. the Julianists, followers of Julian of Halikarnassos (d. after 518 CE), advocated the full humanity of Christ, but maintained that it was consubstantial with that of the prelapsarian Adam. Among the anti-Chalcedonian, he was opposed by patriarchs Severos of Antioch and Theodosios of Alexandria. See Zachariah of Mitylene, *Chronicle*, 9.9–13; Grillmeier, *Christ in Christian Tradition*, II.2:79–89, 93–111; II.4:45–59.
49. Eutyches, the aged (or senile) abbot never stated his Christological position consistently. His theology has been condemned by pro- and anti-Chalcedonians since the mid-fifth century: Timothy Ailuros, *Letters*; John of Nikiou, *Chronicle*, §88.22—"Eutyches the Nestorian." "Eutychian" developed into a slur used to defame opponents.
50. This is the traditional depiction, but the evidence strongly suggests that the Church of the East—the so-called "Nestorians"—were not Nestorian. A vital point is how *hypostasis* and *prosōpon* were defined in each theological system: see Sebastian P. Brock, "The Christology of the Church of the East in the Synods of the fifth to early seventh century," in *Aksum-Thyateira: A Festschrift for Archbishop Methodios*, ed. G. Dragas (Athens, 1985), 125–42; repr. idem, *Studies in Syriac Christianity* (Aldershot, 1992), XII; idem, "The 'Nestorian Church:' A Lamentable Misnomer," *The Bulletin of the John Rylands Library Manchester* 78.3 (1996), 23–35; idem, "'About Heresies and the Syllabus Errorum of Pope Shenuda III': Some Comments on the Recent Article by Professor Meinardus," *Coptic Church Review* 23.4 (2002), 98–102.
51. The emergence of neo-Chalcedonianism in the mid-sixth century CE positively excluded the possibility of a "Nestorian" reading: see Constantinople II, esp. Canon 9; Patrick T.R. Gray, *The Defense of Chalcedon in the East (451–553)* (Leiden, 1979); idem, "Neo-Chalcedonianism and the Tradition: From Patristic to Byzantine Theology," *Byzantinische Forschungen* 8 (1982), 61–70; J. Meyendorff, *Christ in Eastern Christian Thought*, 2nd ed. (Crestwood, 1975); C. Moeller, "Le chalcédonisme et le néo-chalcédonisme," in *Chalkedon*, ed. Grillmeier and Bacht, I:637–720; Karl-Heinz Uthemann, "Definitionen und Paradigmen in der Rezeption des Dogmas von Chalkedon bis in die Zeit Kaiser Justinians," in *Chalkedon*, ed. Oort and Roldanus; Grillmeier, *Christ in Christian Tradition*, II.2. Since pro-Chalcedonians and "Nestorians" spoke of "two natures" confusion naturally ensued; hence, the frequent denouncement of pro-Chalcedons as "Nestorians,"—those who "divide the one Son of God into two"—in anti-Chalcedonian sources: HP I.2:180, cf. 182, 188; I.3:379; I.4:627, 628; John of Nikiou, *Chronicle*, §§89, 90, 92, 120.56, 123.4–5; Michael the Syrian, *Chronicle*, §11.18; cf. Theophanes, *Chronicle*, AM 6121 (628/9 CE).
52. See Kenneth P. Wesche's Introduction to *On the Person of Christ: The Christology of Emperor Justinian* (New York, 1991); cf. Kallistos Ware, Review of *The Rise of the Monophysite Movement*, by W.H.C. Frend, *The English Historical Review* 91 (1976), 354–56. Grillmeier, *Christ in Christian Tradition*, I.478–83; Jaroslav Pelikan, *The Christian Tradition*, vol. 1, *The Emergence of the Catholic Tradition*

(100–600) (Chicago, 1971), 211–25, 266–77. Thus, the Cyrillian "one nature out of two," regarded as orthodox by all normative Christians, can be read in accordance with the double connotations: "one *individual* out of two *generic categories* (i.e. humanity and divinity)."

53. See Grillmeier, *Christ in Christian Tradition*, I.333–40, 478–83; II.4:57, 254; V.C. Samuel, "One Incarnate Nature of God the Word," *Greek Orthodox Theological Review* 10 (1964/65), 37–53.
54. *Prosōpon* appears 76 times in the New Testament, but it can be read as "person" in only seven instances: Walter Bauer, *A Greek-English Lexicon of the New Testament and Other Early Christian Literature*, 3rd rev., ed. W.F. Arndt and F.W. Gingrich (Chicago, 2000), s.v. πρόσωπον.
55. Constantine, a Melkite bishop who joined the Coptic church in the eighth century, stated: "One union, one God, one Lord, *one nature, namely the Lord Jesus Christ*" (HP I.3:381, my emphasis). Clearly "one nature" is understood here as a single subject or individual; cf. *Panegyric on Apollo*, §8 (pgs. 11.25–12.7). This is reiterated in Shinūda I's Festal Letter quoted in HP II.1:28/118r, which articulates Coptic objections (and misunderstandings) of pro-Chalcedonian theology.
56. Both confessions agreed that the natures remained, according to the Cyrillian-inspired formula, "without confusion, change, division, or separation." Cf. Cyril's *First Letter to Succensus* (§6) and the *Definition of Chalcedon*.
57. Thus, they interpreted "two *phusis*" as "two individuals." The above-referenced Bishop Constantine (n. 55) allegedly criticized the Melkites' insistence on "two natures" since it adds "a fourth person to the trinity"; this was essentially the same charge leveled earlier at Nestorios and his followers (HP I.3:374).
58. Pseudo-Sawīrus, *Tartīb al-kahanūt*, ch. 21.pg. 59.
59. Richard Price, "The Development of a Chalcedonian Identity in Byzantium," *Church History and Religious Culture* 89 (2009), 307–25.
60. A. Papaconstantinou, "Historiography;" cf. Sidney H. Griffith, *Church in the Shadow of the Mosque: Christians and Muslims in the World of Islam* (Princeton, 2008), ch. 6—though I read Griffith in a different light; J. Zaborowski, "Coptic Christianity," in *Wiley-Blackwell Companion to African Religions*, ed. E.K. Bongmba (Malden, 2012). This historiography parallels and, on occasion, is directly influenced by scholarship focused on the development of Melkite identity in Syria and Jerusalem under Islamic rule; nonetheless, the situation for the Copts differed significantly in several respects.
61. Lucas van Rompay, review of *Severus of Antioch*, by Pauline Allen and C.T.R. Hayward, *Hugoye: Journal of Syriac Studies* 8.2 (2005) <www.bethmardutho.org/index.php/hugoye/volume-index.html>
62. Timothy Ailuros, *Letters*, 362; John Malalas, *Chronicle*, 16.19 (Gr. 407–8), 17.6 (Gr. 412); 18.64 (Gr. 468); Theophanes, *Chronicle*, AM 5949 (456/7 CE), AM 5950 (457/8 CE), AM 6003 (510/11 CE), AM 6005 (512/13 CE); also see Chapters Four and Five (esp. n. 47).

63. Patriarch Benjamin, *On Cana of Galilee*, fol. 9v; ibid. *Sixteenth Festal Letter*; Damian's synodal letter in H.G. Evelyn White, *The Monasteries of the Wâdi 'n Natrûn*, ed. Walter Hauser, 3 vols. (New York, 1926–1933; 1973), II: 331–37; Michael the Syrian, *Chronicle*, II: 325–32; T. Orlandi, "Coptic Ecclesiastical History," in *World of Early Egyptian Christianity*, ed. Goehring and Timbie.
64. E.g. J.J. van Ginkel, "John of Ephesus: A Monophysite Historian in Sixth-Century Byzantium" (Ph.D. Diss., University of Groningen, 1963), 166; A. Papaconstantinou, "Historiography."
65. *Life of Isaac of Alexandria*, 59, 72, Bell 65, 70; HP I.4:529. Only one bishop may be identified for them at that time.

Chapter 2 The Conquest: Event, Text, And Memory

1. See Chapter One. On the conquests and their immediate aftermath, see Fred M. Donner, *The Early Islamic Conquests* (Princeton, 1981); idem, "The Islamic Conquests," in *A Companion to the History of the Middle East*, ed. Y.M. Choueiri (Massachusetts, 2005); idem, ed., *The Expansion of the Early Islamic State* (Burlington, 2008); Michael G. Morony, *Iraq after the Muslim Conquest* (Princeton, 1984); Walter E. Kaegi, *Byzantium and the Early Islamic Conquests* (Cambridge, 1992); Robert Schick, *The Christian Communities of Palestine from Byzantine to Islamic Rule: A Historical and Archaeological Study*, SLAEI 2 (Princeton, 1996); R.G. Hoyland, *Seeing Islam*; Jamsheed K. Choksy, *Conflict and Cooperation: Zoroastrian Subalterns and Muslim Elites in Medieval Iranian Society* (New York, 1997); Chase F. Robinson, *Empire and Elites after the Muslim Conquest* (Cambridge, 2000); Hugh Kennedy, *The Great Arab Conquests* (Philadelphia, 2007); Parvaneh Pourshariati, *Decline and Fall of the Sasanian Empire: The Sasanian-Parthian Confederacy and the Arab Conquest of Iran* (London, 2008).
2. See the upcoming study by Phil Booth. Alfred J. Butler, *The Arab Conquest of Egypt and the Last Thirty Years of the Roman Dominion*, 2nd ed., P.M. Fraser (Oxford, 1978; 1998); Louis Chagnon, *La conquête musulmane de l'Égypte (639–646)* (Paris, 2008). Also see, Robert Brunschvig, "Ibn Abd al-Hakam et la conquête de l'Afrique du Nord par les arabes," *Annales de l'Institut d'Études orientales* 6 (1942–47), 108–55; repr. idem, *Etudes sur l'Islam classique et l'Afrique du Nord* (London, 1986); trans. in *Expansion of the Early Islamic State*, ed. F.M. Donner; P.M. Fraser, "Arab Conquest of Egypt," *CoptEncyc* 1:183–89; Alexander D. Beihammer, *Quellenkritische Untersuchungen zu den ägyptischen Kapitulationsverträgen der Jahre 640–646* (Vienna, 2000); Petra Sijpesteijn, "The Arab Conquest of Egypt and the Beginning of Muslim Rule," in *Egypt in the Byzantine world*, ed. R.S. Bagnall; eodem, "New Rule over Old Structures: Egypt after the Muslim Conquest," in *Regime Change in the Ancient Near East and Egypt*, ed. H. Crawford (Oxford, 2007).
3. See Chapter One, n. 6.

4. This ubiquitous thesis has several ramifications, affecting studies ranging from the historiography of Coptic literature to the use and perception of the Greek and Coptic languages in Egypt. See Chapters Three, Five, and Nine below.
5. P.M. Fraser, "Arab Conquest of Egypt," *CoptEncyc* 1:188—my emphasis. The initial Arab army of 4,000 eventually increased to 12,000 soldiers. These numbers should not be accepted at face value. Figures in pre-modern sources should always be read with skepticism. Here, Islamic authors had an additional implicit motive to minimize the number of conquerors: the smaller the advancing army, the greater God's role in the conquest. Cf. n. 32 below.
6. B. Anderson, *Imagined Communities*; A.D. Smith, *Nationalism*.
7. HP I.2:232; John of Nikiou, *Chronicle*, §121.1; Mikhail, trans., Introduction to Benjamin, *On Cana of Galilee*. The HP's biography of Benjamin is based on an early eighth-century composition, though, as J. den Heijer has pointed out (in "La conquête arabe"), the tenor of the HP's Primitive and Vulgate recensions do differ in this regard. (Pseudo-) Agathon's *Book of Consecration*, is not helpful in providing a chronology.
8. See Bibliography for editions and translations.
9. Ibn ʿAbd al-Ḥakam, *Futūḥ*, 58–9; *Chronicle of 1234/History of Dionysios*, I.251–3; Palmer, §§69–71; cf. Michael the Syrian, *Chronicle*, II.412.
10. R.G. Hoyland, *Seeing Islam*, 132–5; Fraser, "Arab Conquest," 188.
11. Used by Theophanes, Agapios, and Dionysios of Tel-Maḥrē, it subsequently filtered down into later works such as *Chronicle of 1234* and the *Chronicle* of Michael the Syrian. See, Lawrence I. Conrad, "Theophanes and the Arabic Historical Tradition: Some Indications of Intercultural Transmission," *Byzantinische Forschungen* 15 (1990), 1–44; idem, "The Conquest of Arwād," esp. 322–38; Beihammer, *Quellenkritische*, 20–29; R.G. Hoyland, *Seeing Islam*, 400–9.
12. A. Noth (*Early Arabic Historical Tradition*, 19–20, 167) observed that conquest narratives were highly repetitive and adhered to various literary motifs, a specific set of which is endemic in the descriptions of the conquest of cities. These clichés undermine the historicity of any single conquest narrative; hence, the need for outside corroboration, which is a criterion that is entirely lacking here.
13. See Ibn al-Kindī, *Faḍā'il miṣr*, 202, cf. 206; al-Masʿūdī, *Murūj al-dhahab*, II.412; A. Butler, *Arab Conquest*, Appendix C, pgs. 508–26; S. Lane-Poole, *A History of Egypt*, 2, 5. Typical of the early Arabic historical tradition, *Futūḥ miṣr* is hopelessly confused as to the Christian dignitaries it describes; e.g. contrast Ibn ʿAbd al-Ḥakam and al-Ṭabarī's treatment of *al-Muqawkas*.
14. Theophanes, *Chronicle*, AM 6127 (634/5 CE); Agapios, *Kitāb al-ʿunwān*, 215; R.G. Hoyland, *Seeing Islam*, 67–73; Daniel J. Sahas, "The Face to Face Encounter between Patriarch Sophronius of Jerusalem and the Caliph ʿUmar ibn al-Khaṭṭab: Friends or Foes?" in *Encounter of Eastern Christianity*, ed. E. Grypeou *et al.*

15. Agapios, *Kitāb al-ʿunwan*, 211–2; only Kyros is mentioned in al-Balādhurī's *Futūḥ*, 215, 218, 220–1.
16. That biography was composed in the early decades of the 700s CE.
17. C.F. Robinson (*Empire and Elites*, ch. 1) provides an essential discussion of the function of conquest narratives in establishing precedence for communal cooperation in Iraq. In HP-Primitive (Seybold 1912, pg. 99), the "king" of the Arab's dispatched troops to Egypt upon learning of Benjamin's hardships; see J. den Heijer, "La conquête arabe."
18. E.g. (Pseudo-) Agathon, *Book of Consecration*, 80, 82.
19. *Chronicle of 1234/History of Dionysios*, I:253; Palmer, §70. See also Chapter Nine, below.
20. HP-Primitive (Seybold, 1912), 101–2, my translation and emphasis; cf. vulgate recension, HP I.2:234, 229. This may reflect Herakleios' conciliatory efforts, though the comments are doubtless exaggerated. The reach of the reunions of the 630s *throughout* the Delta and into Upper Egypt is questionable and unlikely; see Chapter Four.
21. E.g. W.H.C. Frend, "Nationalism as a Factor," 21; idem, *Monophysite Movement*, 73–4.
22. Ibn ʿAbd al-Ḥakam, *Futūḥ*, 58, my emphasis; Hoyland, *Seeing Islam*, 134. The wording of the tradition resonates well with ninth-century Islamic historiography, not Benjamin's seventh-century *Sitz im Lebens*.
23. Hoyland, *Seeing Islam*, 135. Butler (*Arab Conquest*, 471, 476–9) makes a similar argument for another contentious account.
24. Fraser, "Arab Conquest," 188.
25. The chronology of conquest narratives is extremely precarious: Noth, *Early Arabic Historical Tradition*, 15–16, 41, 58; Donner, *Early Islamic Conquests*, 128.
26. This may be read as an aspect of the ʿAmr-Benjamin paradigm discussed by Mark Swanson; see ch. 1.
27. John of Nikiou, *Chronicle*, §107.45–6; cf. §108.13–4 with §107.48; Walter E. Kaegi, *Heraclius: Emperor of Byzantium* (Cambridge, 2003), 43–5.
28. Cf. John of Nikiou, *Chronicle*, §107.48 with §113.1. "ʿAmr sent to Abākīrī of the city of Dalās requesting him to bring the ships of Rīf in order to transport to the east bank of the river the Ishmaelites who were upon the west." A.J. Butler (*Arab Conquest*, n. 235) identified Abākīrī as Apacyrus, Pagarch of Heracleopolis Magna.
29. John of Nikiou, *Chronicle*, §113.2; cf. al-Maqrīzī, *Khiṭaṭ*, I.163.19–20. Prefect George was commanded to construct a bridge over the river near the city of Qaliyūb for ʿAmr.
30. John of Nikiou, *Chronicle*, §113.2–3. Two instances are mentioned; in the second the bridge functioned as a barrier preventing the passage of ships to Nikiou, Alexandria, and Upper Egypt. For the strategic role of the river and its inundation in an earlier period, see Danielle Bonneau, *La crue du Nil, divinité égyptienne, à travers mille ans d'histoire (332 av.-641 ap. J.-C.)* (Paris, 1964), 74–83.

31. In general, see W.E. Kaegi's *Byzantium and the Early Islamic Conquests*. Even after the conquest, renting private ships for government purposes was not uncommon; see *P.Lond*.IV.1448 and Bell's Introduction to that volume (pg. xxv).
32. Ibn ʿAbd al-Ḥakam, *Futūḥ*, 83, 84, 87; al-Balādhurī, *Futūḥ*, 215, 220. The inhabitants of Balhīb, Sulṭās, Qarṭasa, and Sakhā were exiled by ʿAmr, but were later returned under duress from the Caliph ʿUmar. John of Nikiou (*Chronicle*, §115.1–2) states that the Arabs marched unsuccessfully against Sakhā and Tūkū-Dāmsis—probably Tūkh [Mazīd] and [Mit] Dasīs as Butler suggested (*Arab Conquest*, 297, n. 2). Although late, the very beginning of *Futūḥ al-Bahnasā* (pg. 190) states that 5000 Muslims were killed at the conquest of that city alone.
33. Ibn ʿAbd al-Ḥakam, *Futūḥ*, 73. Also John of Nikiou, *Chronicle*, §113.2: ʿAmr "sent orders to the prefect George to construct for him a bridge on the river of the city Qaliyūb with a view to the capture of all the cities of Misr, and likewise of Athrīb and Kuerdīs. And people began to help the Moslems." In both accounts, the aid rendered was at the behest of notables. It is conceivable that "people" here is no more than those who were already employed by notables.
34. Ibn ʿAbd al-Ḥakam, *Futūḥ*, 3, also 2–5, 163; HCME 28a–29a, 97–100; cf. HP I.2:230; Abū Yūsuf, *Kharāj*, 138–9; Abū ʿUbayd, *Amwāl*, §376. Al-Balādhurī (*Futūḥ*, 219) records some of Muḥammad's instructions regarding the *qibṭ*, but the theme of Copts helping Muslims is absent.
35. On elites in the post-conquest decades, see; Simonsen, *Caliphal Taxation*, 117–21; J. Banaji, *Agriarin Change*, 152–9, App. 3; P.M. Sijpesteijn, "Shaping a Muslim State," 81–6. Similar patterns may be observed in Syria and Iraq.
36. Ibn ʿAbd al-Ḥakam, *Futūḥ*, 74.
37. John of Nikiou, *Chronicle*, §120.30–1; cf. 121.5, where aid was rendered to the Arabs "to prevent their destruction of the city."
38. Ibn ʿAbd al-Ḥakam, *Futūḥ*, 175–7; al-Balādhurī, *Futūḥ*, 221; al-Kindī, *Wulāt*, 11; Eutychios, *Naẓm al-jawhar*, II.32.
39. Agreements are cited in John of Nikiou, *Chronicle*, §120.18–21; Ibn ʿAbd al-Ḥakam, *Futūḥ*, 151–2.
40. Ibn ʿAbd al-Ḥakam, *Futūḥ*, 176.
41. Cf. Prosopography of the Byzantine World <www.pbw.kcl.ac.uk>.
42. Theophanes, *Chronicle*, AM 6022 (529/30 CE).
43. Eutychios typically employs "*rūm*" to denote pro-Chalcedonians. In *Naẓm al-jawhar*, II.22, he states that pro-Chalcedonian (*rūm*) notables accompanied Kyros as he fled from Babylon. Similar usage is found in eighth-century texts; see HP I.3:373. Ibn ʿAbd al-Ḥakam's usage is not always consistent, however. Kyros' persecution of anti-Chalcedonians had resumed upon his return to Alexandria—in the midst of the tumultuous events of the conquest (John of Nikiou, *Chronicle*, §116.14).
44. See the following chapter.

45. John of Nikiou, *Chronicle*, §§113.4, 115.7. Shenoute of Antinoë's estate was not confiscated; he donated a large sum of gold to Patriarch Benjamin to rebuild the Church of St. Mark (HP I.2:236).
46. Cyril Hovorun, *Will, Action and Freedom: Christological Controversies in the Seventh Century* (Brill, 2008); also see Chapter Four below.
47. Both Albrecht Noth (*Early Arabic Historical Tradition*) and Chase Robinson (*Empire and Elites*) have employed these methodologies with great success in their reading of the early Arabic tradition.
48. The foundational monograph is Maurice Halbwachs, *On Collective Memory* (Chicago, 1992; 1925). Also see, Pierre Nora, ed., *Realms of Memory: Rethinking the French Past*, 3 vols., A. Goldhammer trans. (New York, 1996–98), a translation of his *Les lieux de memoire* (1984–92); David Lowenthal, *The Past is a Foreign Country* (Cambridge, 1985); Paul Connerton, *How Societies Remember* (Cambridge, 1989); James Fentress and Chris Wickham, *Social Memory* (Oxford, 1992); Patrick J. Geary, *Phantoms of Remembrance: Memory and Oblivion at the End of the First Millennium* (Princeton, 1996); James V. Wertsch, *Voices of Collective Remembering* (Cambridge, 2002); Susannah Radstone and Bill Schwarz, eds., *Memory: Histories, Theories, Debates* (New York, 2010), esp. chs. 1, 2, 3, 5, and 19; Jeffrey Olick and Joyce Robbins, "Social Memory Studies: from 'Collective Memory' to the Historical Sociology of Mnemonic Practices," *Annual Review of Sociology* 24 (1998), 105–140; Kerwin Lee Klein, "On the Emergence of Memory in Historical Discourse," *Representations* 69 (2000), 127–50.
49. Critical reflections are forwarded in David Berliner, "The Abuses of Memory: Reflections on the Memory Boom in Anthropology," *Anthropological Quarterly* (2005), 197–211; Charles Golden, "Where Does Memory Reside, and Why Isn't It History?" *American Anthropologist* 107.2 (2005), 270–4.
50. P. Geary, *Phantoms*, 11. Geary observes: "books form an essential physical extension of memory" (pg. 28). His focus on eleventh-century Europe is also of interest. It was a juncture in which a predominantly oral culture changed into one that utilized word and text, a process that retains great resonance in the context of the first ʿAbbāsid century.
51. In both methodologies, scholars begin with a later "text," which preserves a specific historical object (person, idea, or narrative) in the written record. They then provide a theoretical model as to how that same object appeared at an earlier temporal juncture. To accomplish that goal, redaction critics and historians of memory scrutinize incongruities in the extant (later) narrative, which they read as remnants of the earlier version of the historical object. These remnants in turn become the nuclei for the hypothetical reconstruction of the earlier version of the said texts and memories. Thus, New Testament scholars discuss the Q Community, Medievalists analyze tenth-century Europe, and scholars of the Middle East discuss the shape, content, and development of *hadīth* and *maghazī* in the 720s. All are hypothetical reconstructions of historical objects based on a deconstruction of those same objects as they appear in later texts.

52. Beyond its archaic elements, the *Chronicle* forwards a relatively sober treatment of confessional issues. This is evident in its evenhanded—on occasion, even sympathetic—portrayal of Patriarch Kyros (§§120.36–7, 120.66–8); a unique account in Coptic literature. Moreover, John interpreted the conquest as a consequence of Melkite doctrine and persecution, as well as a reprimand for the sins of the Coptic community—an often overlooked aspect—but he does not blame Melkite generals or personnel.
53. R.G. Hoyland, *Seeing Islam*; Alan M. Guenther, "The Christian Experience and Interpretation of the Early Muslim Conquest and Rule," *Islam and Christian-Muslim Relations* 10.3 (1999), 363–78; John C. Lamoreaux, "Early Eastern Christian Responses to Islam," in *Medieval Christian Perceptions of Islam*, ed. J.V. Tolan (New York, 1996; 2000).
54. E.g. the conquests of Fayyūm (John of Nikiou, *Chronicle*, §111.4–16) and Nikiou (§118.8, 11, 13).
55. There may be a single exception, but it is not unequivocal. John of Nikiou, *Chronicle*, §115.11, states: "and they put to the sword all the Roman soldiers whom they encountered." Kennedy (*Arab Conquest*, 167), reads the first pronoun, "they," as signifying the inhabitants of the city, but in the context of the paragraph the pronoun may apply to either the inhabitants of the city or, more likely, its Muslim conquerors. Contextually, John attributes several massacres to Arab armies including one at Fayyūm, which is referenced in the sentence preceding the one containing the ambiguous pronoun.
56. John of Nikiou, *Chronicle*, §§112.11–12; 114.3; 114.10; 115.10; 118.6–7; 119.6, 9; 119.10.
57. John of Nikiou, *Chronicle*, §§116.10–12; 116.14; 117.5–6; 119.15–17. This last account describes a religious riot that broke out in the midst of the tumult of the conquest. At times, the Egyptians were too busy fighting amongst themselves to serve as either allies or foes to the advancing Arab armies. Also see the riots between the Egyptians who wanted to help the Byzantines and those who wanted to help the Muslims (*Chronicle*, §§119.1–2, 5–6, 120.4).
58. Cf. Sebeos' *History*, ch. 52 (pgs. 150, 153); also D.J. Constantelos, "The Moslem Conquests of the Near East as Revealed in the Greek Sources of the Seventh and Eighth Centuries," *Byzantion* 42 (1972), 325–57.
59. The two populations were linguistically and geographically segregated for much of Umayyad rule.
60. Ibn ʿAbd al-Ḥakam, *Futūḥ*, 72–4.
61. Chapter Five addresses the linguistic undertones of this new historiography.
62. See [*Third*] *Apocalypse of Athanasius* (composed early 8th c.); and the *Apocalypse of Samuel* (late 10th early 11th c.); CMR 1: 274–80; 2:742–52.
63. Although he does not survey the Copto-Arabic evidence, see Paul J. Alexander, "The Medieval Legend of the Last Roman Emperor and Its Messianic Origin," *Journal of the Warburg and Courtauld Institutes* 41 (1978), 1–15; idem, *The Byzantine Apocalyptic Tradition*, ed. D. deF. Abrahamse (Berkeley, 1985), 151–84; Francisco Javier Martinez, "The King of Rum and the King of

Ethiopia in Medieval Apocalyptic Texts from Egypt," *Coptic Studies: Acts of the Third International Congress of Coptic Studies*, ed. W. Godlewski (Warsaw, 1990); J. van Lent, "Nineteenth Muslim Kings;" L.S.B. MacCoull, "The *Apocalypse of Pseudo-Pesynthеus*: Coptic Protest Under Islamic Rule," *Coptic Church Review* 9.1 (1988), 17–22.

64. *Letter of Pisentios*, 310–11.
65. HP I.2:188.
66. In the sixth century, the population prayed God: "Give us a good emperor like Anastasios or else remove the emperor Justin *whom you have given us*" (John of Nikiou, *Chronicle*, §90.20, my emphasis).
67. Assumed in much of John C. Lamoreaux's "Early Eastern Christian Responses to Islam."
68. John of Nikiou, *Chronicle*, §121.7–8; Pseudo-Theophilos, *Sermon on the Three Youth*, 99–100; H. Suermann, "Copts and the Islam of the Seventh Century," in *The Encounter of Eastern Christianity with Early Islam*, ed. E. Grypeou *et al.*; idem, "Koptische Texte zur arabischen Eroberung Ägyptens und der Umayyadenherrschaft," *Journal of Coptic Studies* 4 (2002), 167–86.
69. E.g. at Nikiou, Arab armies are described as having "put to the sword all whom they found in the streets and in the churches, men, women, and infants, and they showed mercy to none" (*Chronicle*, §118.8; cf. §118.11, 13, and 111.4–16).

Chapter 3 Christian Elites: The Dialectic of Duty and Faith

1. Cf. Boaz Shoshan's "The 'Politics of Notables' in Medieval Islam," *Asian and African Studies* 20 (1986), 179–215, provides several important observations, though its conceptual framework is awkward if applied to this early period.
2. Notable exceptions, such as the Apion family, are well documented in fifth and six-century papyri—e.g. *P.Oxy.*I.130, 133–9, and *P.Oxy.*XVI; see below, Chapter Four, ns. 17 and 18. Athanasios, ʿAbd al-ʿAzīz ibn Marwān's secretary, is attested in Islamic as well as Christian narrative and documentary sources. He is discussed below.
3. Later documentation is richer thanks in large part to the HCME, but later Islamic sources are also more forthcoming. Colophons provide an additional (seldom exploited) resource, which typically cite the notable who commissioned the work. See D.S. Richards, "The Coptic Bureaucracy under the Mamlūks," in *Colloque International sur l'Histoire du Caire*, ed. A. Raymond *et al.* (Cairo, 1972), 373–81; C.E. Bosworth, "Christian and Jewish religious Dignitaries;" Marlis J. Saleh, "Government Relations with the Coptic Community in Egypt During the Fātimid Period (358–567/969–1171)" (Ph.D. dissertation, University of Chicago, 1995), esp. ch. 4; S. Khalil Samir, "The Role of Christians in the Fātimid Government Services of Egypt to the Reign of al-Hāfiz," *Medieval Encounters* 2.3 (1996), 177–92; Carl F. Petry, "Copts in Late Medieval Egypt,"

CoptEncyc 2:618–35; Louis Cheïkho, *Les Savants arabes chrétiens en Islam 622–1300*, ed. C. Hechaïme (Lebanon, 1983) and idem, *Les vizirs et secrétaires arabes chrétiens en Islam 622–1517*, ed. C. Hechaïme (Lebanon, 1987), both are in Arabic.

4. He is not listed in Cheïkho, *Les Vizirs*; see Benjamin, *On Cana of Galilee*, 23r–24r.
5. HP I.2:231–2; cf. John of Nikiou, *Chronicle*, §121.1. See the previous chapter.
6. See HP I.2:233–5; here, Shenoute plays the same role as Patriarch Sophronios in Jerusalem.
7. Gladys Frantz-Murphy's Introduction in *CPR* XXI, pg. 25; eodem, "The Economics of State Formation in Early Islamic Egypt," in *From al-Andalus to Khurasan*, eds. P.M. Sijpesteijn *et al.*, 101, 103. The misreading appears to be in the intellectual framework of eodem, "Conversion in Early Islamic Egypt."
8. Athanasios replaced Theodore, a pro-Chalcedonian who had raised taxes on the Coptic church.
9. The same view is maintained in M. Saleh, "Government Relations," 265: "The situation of the Copts immediately following the conquest was indeed quite favorable."
10. The same was true in Iraq, see Michael G. Morony, "Religious Communities in Late Sasanian and Early Muslim Iraq," JESHO 17 (1974), 119–20; repr. R. Hoyland ed., *Muslims and Others*, ch. 1.
11. See P. Sijpesteijn, "New Rule over Old Structures;" ʿAbd al-Munʿim Mukhtār, "On the Survival of the Byzantine Administration in Egypt During the First Century of the Arab Rule," *Acta Orientalia Academiae Scientiarum Hungaricae* 27.3 (1973), 309–19. Three notables are especially prominent in the earliest narrative sources: Shenoute Prefect of al-Rīf (Cheïkho, *Les Vizirs*, 277, cf. *CPR* XXX), Philoxenos the Prefect of Arcadia (Cheïkho, 340); Menas Governor of Lower Egypt (Cheïkho, 372). John of Damiatta (Yuḥanna al-Dimyāṭī) replaced Menas. Similar to the other three, John had cooperated with the Muslims during the conquest (John of Nikiou, *Chronicle*, §121.4–6; Cheïkho, 399); cf. John of Nikiou, *Chronicle*, §§120.29, 121.3, 6.
12. HP I.3:259–260, 264, 267–8, 272. Patriarch Agathon was forced to work in the naval shipyard (HP I.4:486). Theodore appears in *P.Lond*.IV.1392.13, dated 710–11 CE. He is listed in Cheïkho, *Les Vizirs*, 227, Theophanes is not. On the confiscation of churches, see Chapter Ten below.
13. *Life of Isaac*, 19, Bell 48. Benjamin is not directly named in the account.
14. On Isaac's prestigious family, see *Life of Isaac*, 7, 22, 27; Bell 44, 50, 52; cf. Isaac's instructions to his parents: "I beseech you, my parents, do not rest your hearts on these unstable riches, and do not pride yourselves in the abundance of your goods" (*Life*, 24–5, Bell, 51). D. Bell interpreted the patriarch's fear as an indication that parents who disagreed with their son's decision for a monastic vocation had recourse to the government (*Life of Isaac*, Bell, 80 n. 29).
15. No sort of "repayment" was made to Benjamin or the Coptic church in the first decades of Arab rule, while it is abundantly clear both in Egypt and elsewhere

that the Arabs handsomely rewarded those who cooperated with them; see Eutychios, *Naẓm al-jawhar*, II.5, 14–6, 62, 69; Cheïkho, *Les Vizirs*, 57, 58, 59.

16. HP I.3:373, 377; Eutychios, *Naẓm al-jawhar*, II.45–46; *Chronicle of 1234/History of Dionysios*, I.253, Palmer §70. These authors trace the Copt's acquisition of churches to the time of the conquest. It is argued here that this did not occur until the reign of ʿAbd al-ʿAzīz ibn Marwān (see Chapter Ten).
17. Cheïkho, *Les Vizirs*, 171, cf. 172, 179. For Athanasios, see *Chronicle of 1234/History of Dionysios*, I.294–95, Palmer, §132–4. Most of the information on Isaac the secretary is derived from the hagiographic *Life of {Patriarch} Isaac of Alexandria*. Both secretaries are repeatedly mentioned in *P.Lond.*IV.1412; also see *P.Lond.*IV.1413. The identification of Isaac as Isaac al-Shubrawī is likely, but not certain.
18. HP I.3:266. Possibly the same Theodore mentioned by John of Nikiou, *Chronicle*, §121.3, 5. This is clear in the HP, and is alluded to by the pro-Chalcedonian patriarch Eutychios (*Naẓm al-jawhar*, II.45).
19. HP I.3:266, 270–1, 286, 302. Also see the references below to the *Life of Isaac of Alexandria*.
20. HP I.3:267.
21. Initially, he treated Christians harshly: "when he first came to Egypt, he had tried to do evil to the churches—he had broken the crosses and done great evil to the archbishop—but God, who had punished Pharaoh of old, also put fear into this other in a dream, saying, 'Be careful how you treat the archbishop,' and he came to love him as an angel of God" (*Life of Isaac*, 49–50, Bell 61).
22. *Life of Isaac*, 68, 78; Bell 68, 72. Only ʿAbd al-ʿAzīz called Isaac "patriarch," the *Life* consistently refers to him as "archbishop;" similarly it designates the office as the "archiepiscopate," not the "patriarchate" (51, Bell 61). Seventh-century papyri employ both "archbishop" and "patriarch" (see *P.Mon.Epiph.*131, 133, 143). In this *Life* the term is treated as a pious novelty in Egypt, see R.S. Bagnall, *Egypt in Late Antiquity*, n.146, on the early history of the title. Among a host of other problems, the popular English translation of the current Coptic Arabic *Synaxarion* freely and randomly translates "patriarch" as "pope."
23. *Life of Isaac*, 38, Bell 56. ϢⲀⲦⲈϤⲈⲢⲐⲈⲰⲢⲒⲚ ⲘⲠⲒⲞⲨⲰⲒⲚⲒ ⲚⲦⲈ Ⲡⲟ̅ⲥ̅ ϦⲈⲚ ⲞⲨⲘⲈⲦϪⲰⲢⲒ.
24. *Life of Isaac*, 53, Bell 62.
25. *Life of Isaac*, 61, Bell 65, "for truly, the power lay in his hands." In *P.Lond.*IV.1447.137–9 Athanasios had twice as many notaries under him than Isaac. Cf. Kosei Morimoto, "The *Diwāns* as Registers of the Arab Stipendiaries in Early Islamic Egypt," *Itinéraires d'Orient. Hommages à Claude Cahen.* Res Orientales 6 (1994), 361–4. Athanasios' immense wealth is described in some detail in the *Chronicle of 1234/History of Dionysios*, I.295, Palmer, §133. On George, the would-be patriarch, see *Life of Isaac*, 61 & 64, Bell 65 & 67.
26. *Life of Isaac*, 65, Bell 67.
27. HP I.3:302; Eutychios, *Naẓm al-jawhar*, II.41.
28. Kindī, *Wulāt*, 59.

29. *Chronicle of 1234/History of Dionysios*, I:295, Palmer, §134; HP I.3:308.
30. *Life of Isaac*, 8, Bell 44. Isaac was employed as a *notarius* prior to the Arabization of the bureaucracy in 705 CE, had knowledge of the fathers (*Life*, 28, Bell 52), and composed Pascal letters (*Life*, 36, Bell 55), which at least until the time of his successor, Alexander II (705–30), were still composed and disseminated in Greek (see the *Letter of Alexander II*). See Chapter Five below.
31. *Life of Isaac*, 9, Bell 44. On these offices, see Intro. *P.Lond.*IV (pg. xxi).
32. *Life of Isaac*, 11, Bell 45.
33. *Synaxarion*, Amshīr 21. Familial succession dominated the civil and ecclesiastical spheres. See *P.Lond.*IV.1592 and W.E. Crum's *Introduction*, xlvi. In the late seventh century, Theodore the pro-Chalcedonian governor of Alexandria was succeeded by his son (HP I.3:264); cf. Chapter Seven.
34. *P.Lond.*IV.1447.144, identifies one son, "Stephanos Athanasios the illustrious chartularios" (Morimoto, "*Diwāns* as Registers," n. 48). According to *Chronicle of 1234/History of Dionysius* (I.294, Palmer, §132) Athanasios' oldest son, Peter, traveled to Edessa to manage his father's estate.
35. *Life of Isaac*, 49, Bell 61.
36. Additionally, after the death of Patriarch Simon, Athanasios and a group of secretaries (*kuttāb*) sought permission from the governor to allow Gregory bishop of Kaïs to travel to Alexandria, act as interim patriarch, and attend to the affairs of the church until a new patriarch was elected. ʿAbd al-ʿAziz granted their request (HP I.3:303). Early in the eighth century, anti-Chalcedonian secretaries constituted a powerful lobby.
37. HP II.1:4–8/113r-114r.
38. HP II.1:4–5/113r-v. At another incident, notables pooled their funds and bailed Patriarch Shinūda II out of jail (HP II.1:96/132v).
39. HP II.1:5/113v, "There was, by the grace of God, a body of the faithful which was in charge of the *dīwān* of the Sulṭān, and all of them devoted themselves to the Church earnestly and assiduously because of their faith. They procured tranquility for the patriarch, the church and the faithful."
40. They were dismissed by a new governor appointed by al-Mutawakkil, described as "a man who is not a Christian, but a Pharisee, named *al-ghayr* ʿAbd al-Masīḥ [i.e. "one who is not a servant of Christ"]." He may have been a convert to Islam, though the odd construction (using *ghayr*) is used to describe a monk and a deacon in the biography of Shinūda II who had not converted but behaved inappropriately. The awkward moniker likely reflects a literal Arabic rendering of a Coptic (or Greek) construction.
41. HP II.1:16/115v-116r.
42. HP II.1:17/116r, my translation and emphasis.
43. HPI.3:316–7; he is not mentioned in Cheïkho's *Les Vizirs*.
44. Located five miles northwest of al-Manṣūrah: Timm, *Christlich-Koptische*, 4:1718–9; Randall Stewart, "Nabarūh," *CoptEncyc* 6:1769. For Isaac, see Cheïkho, *Les Vizirs*, 20, 176. It is likely that both entries refer to the same individual. Entry 176 is misleading; the events surrounding Isḥāq took place

during the tenure of Patriarch Yusāb (Joseph) I not Mark II. Cheïkho's references to Bishop Isidhūrus' *al-Kharrīda al-nafīsa fī tarīkh al-kanīsa* [*Precious Pearls in the History of the Church*] (Cairo, 1883; 1964; 1991) should read "pg. 170."

45. Cheïkho, *Les Vizirs*, 218.
46. HP I.4:548. Their son, however, had St. Theodore as his patron saint (HP I.4:575–6).
47. HP I.4:547–8. Here Maqāra procured a letter of safety and assurance for the patriarch from the governor.
48. HP I.4:576–7.
49. HP I.4:574–5.
50. HP I.4:571–2. The patriarch had refused the governor's demanded for an unnamed individual to be ordained a bishop. The irate governor, ʿAbd al-ʿAzīz al-Jarawī, convened this meeting, which the patriarch was reluctant to attend.
51. HP I.4:572.
52. In HP I.4:574 Maqāra's young son died and the patriarch miraculously revived him.
53. Located just west of Dumyāṭ; Timm, *Christlich-Koptische*, 1:448; Randall Stewart, "Būrah," *CoptEncyc* 2:425.
54. Cf. HP I.4:574–5 with Eutychios, *Naẓm al-jawhar*, II.55, 58; and HP I.4:576–7 with *Naẓm al-jawhar*, II.58.
55. S.H. Skreslet, "Greeks in Medieval Islamic Egypt," 147, 149–51.
56. Maqrīzī, *Khiṭaṭ*, IV.1004, documents a tradition in which the Copts brought the controversy to an end.
57. See Sidney H. Griffith, "Theodore Abu Qurra's Arabic Tract on the Christian Practice of Venerating Images," JAOS 105.1 (1985), 53–73.
58. Discussed in Saleh, "Government Relations," 87–8.
59. Probably Ilyās ibn Yazīd, appointed governor and head of *al-kharāj* by ʿAbdallāh ibn Ṭāhir (HP I.4:581).
60. HP I.4:584.
61. HP I.4:584–5.
62. HP I.4:591: "a man of family and wealth; and he and his kinsmen possessed gold and silver."
63. This section of the HP is very critical of Alexandrians: see HP I.4:562, 591.
64. HP I.4:592.
65. HP I.4:610–11, my translation.
66. HP I.4:611: ordained in the Church of "Our Lady at Miṣr in the Fort of al-Shamʿ [in Babylon]."
67. HP I.4:616.
68. HP I.4:616.
69. HP I.4:519. Bishop John of Nikiou, famous for his *Chronicle*, was appointed administrator of the monasteries in 696 CE, but was later deposed for permitting the brutal beating of a monk who raped a virgin. The monk later died.

70. HP I.4:517–8. Gregory bishop of Kaïs took on that responsibility early in the eighth century CE, (HP I.3:302–3).
71. A variant (E) in the HP states, "Isḥāq the archon" was ordained.
72. HP I.4:633. Bannā (possibly "Yannā" or "Wannā"— likely a pseudonym; cf. S. Khalil Samir, "Yannah, dans l'onomastique arabo-copte," OCP 45 (1979), 166–70) caused as much trouble for the patriarch as Isḥāq. With the help of a *qāḍī*, he tried to wrestle away effective control of the see of Alexandria from Patriarch Yusāb. See HP I.4:637–40, 657, and Chapter Ten below.
73. HP I.4:633.
74. HP I.4:633–5.
75. HP II.2:105–7/134r-v. Aḥmad "had the custom, when he went out very early, not to answer anyone or to listen to his words until he had been to the mosque and had made five prostrations in it."
76. HP II.2:132–3/139v.
77. HP II.2:134/140r; HCME 102b, 279–80.

Chapter 4 Religious Conversion and Social Cohesion

1. From W. James' *The Varieties of Religious Experience* (New York, 1902) and Max Weber's *The Sociology of Religion* (Boston, 1993; 1922), to the more recent works of Rodney Stark, *The Rise of Christianity* (Princeton, 1996); Rodney Stark and Roger Finke, *Acts of Faith: Explaining the Human Side of Religion* (Berkeley, 2000), ch. 5; Kenneth Mills and Anthony Grafton, eds., *Conversion in Late Antiquity and the Early Middle Ages: Seeing and Believing* (Rochester, 2003); J.N. Bremmer, W.J. van Bekkum and A.L. Molendijk, eds., *Cultures of Conversion* (Louvain, 2006); Steve Bruce, "Sociology of Conversion: The Last Twenty-Five Years," in *Paradigms, Poetics, and Politics of Conversion*, ed. J.N. Bremmer, W.J. van Bekkum, A.L. Molendijk (Louvain, 2006), 1–11. Lewis R. Rambo and Charles E. Farhadian survey the academic approaches in "Conversion," ed. L. Jones, *Encyclopedia of Religion*, 2nd ed. (Detroit, 2005) 3:1969–74.
2. An exception is Daniel Dennett's *Conversion and the Poll Tax in Early Islam* (Cambridge, 1950), though it does not address conversion so much as the lack thereof.
3. Stark and Fink labeled this, "reaffiliation." One may also think of inter- and intra-communal conversion. I prefer and have adopted—with modifications—Lewis R. Rambo's definition in "Conversion," *The Encyclopedia of Religion*, ed. M. Eliade (New York, 1987), 4:73–9; idem, *Understanding Religious Conversion* (New Haven, 1993).
4. "Religious" motivation must be maintained as *an* (and, for some, *the*) impetus for conversion.
5. HP I.1:56–75; HCME 23b, 84; Eutychios, *Naẓm al-jawhar*, 104; W.C. Griggs, *Early Egyptian Christianity* (Leiden, 1990), ch. 2–3; Stephen J. Davis, *The Early Coptic Papacy: The Egyptian Church and its Leadership in Late Antiquity*

(Cairo, 2004), 22–8, 135–6. On Demetrios' historical and hagiographic legacy, see Maged S.A. Mikhail, "Demetrios of Alexandria" (*forthcoming*). The tradition identifying him as the first to ordain bishops for Egyptian dates to the tenth century. Still, it is not implausible.

6. Bruce Metzger, "New Testament, Coptic Versions," *CoptEncyc* 6:1787–9; idem, *The Early Versions of the New Testament* (Oxford, 1977), 99–152.
7. A. Grillmeier with T. Hainthaler, *Christ in Christian Tradition*, II.4: 295–304; and Chapter Nine below.
8. E.g. R. MacMullen, *Christianizing the Roman Empire* (New Haven, 1984); R.S. Bagnall, "Religious Conversion and Onomastic Change in Early Byzantine Egypt," *Bulletin of the American Society of Papyrologists* 19 (1982), 105–24; idem, "Conversion and Onomastics: A Reply," ZPE 69 (1987) 243–50; Ewa Wipszycka, "La christianisation de l'Égypte aux IV-VI siècles: Aspects sociaux et ethniques," *Aegyptus* 68 (1988), 117–65.
9. The most prominent groups were the Meletians, Arians, and Manicheans. Paganism also survived through the sixth century (see n. 14 below); see Moses of Abydos, *Dossier*; Paphnutios, *Histories of the Monks*.
10. T.A. Kane, *The Jurisdiction of the Patriarchs of the Major Sees in Antiquity and in the Middle Ages* (Washington, 1949); Ewa Wipszycka, "The Institutional Church," in *Egypt in the Byzantine World*, ed. R.S. Bagnall. Even a patriarch had to be accompanied by at least two bishops (Nicea, Canon 4). There were a few historical exceptions to this general rule.
11. In fifth-century anti-Chalcedonian literature, "Phantasiasts" (φαντασιασταί) often referenced those who believed that the body of Christ was uncreated, and thus not consubstantial with that of humanity. See Timothy Ailuros, *Letters*, 367, 369.
12. For Julian of Halikarnassos, see HP I.2:189–90; A. Grillmeier with T. Hainthaler, *Christ in Christian Tradition*, II.2: 79–111. On Gaianos, see HP I.2:192, 197–8; John of Nikiou, *Chronicle*, 145 ch. 92; Grillmeier and Hainthaler, *Christ in Christian Tradition*, II.4:45–52.
13. The Basanuphians split from the Akephaloi in the latter half of the sixth century (HP I.2:182–3, 211).
14. The farther removed a text is from the fourth and fifth centuries CE, the more problematic it is to connect individuals labeled "Manicheans," "Melitians," or "Arians," with the doctrinal views traditionally ascribed to them: Benjamin, *On Cana of Galilee* (Mikhail pg. 85 n.121); *Chronicle of Zuqnīn*, 91; Ilse Rochow, "Zum Fortleben des Manichaismus im Byzantinischen Reich nach Justinian I," *Byzantinoslavica* 40 (1979), 13–21. Cf. under Islamic rule, see HP II.2:169/146v, 185–6/149v, cf. 199/151v; Frank Griffel, "Toleration and Exclusion: al-Shāfiʿī and al-Ghazālī on the Treatment of Apostates," BSOAS 64 (2001), 339–54.
15. The numerical dominance of the Coptic anti-Chalcedonians (those recognizing the orthodoxy of Dioskoros and Theodosios of Alexandria) is addressed at the end of Chapter One.

16. *Chronicon Paschale*, 467, 522, 528, 530; *Chronicle of Zuqnīn*, 74, 75; John Malalas, *Chronicle*, Dindorf 412–3 (17.9); 429 (18.9); 431–2 (18.14); 433–4 (18.15); 456–7 (18.56); Theophanes, *Chronicle*, AM 6015 (522/3 CE) and AM 6020 (527/8 CE); Nikephoros, *Short History*, §9; John of Nikiou, *Chronicle*, §§ 88.7–11; 90.42–6; 90.52; 90.66; 90.70; 91.9; 95.23; 96.1–6; 98.2; 120.47, 49.
17. Theophanes, *Chronicle*, AM 5997 (504/5 CE), AM 5998 (505/6 CE), AM 6011 (518/9 CE). Discussions of the Apions usually focus on their estates and economic activities. See E.R. Hardy, *The Large Estates of Byzantine Egypt* (New York, 1968; 1931), 25–37; Germaine Roullard, *La vie rurale dans l'Empire byzantine* (Paris, 1953); Jean Gascou, "Les Grands Domaines, la Cité et l'État en Égypte Byzantine," *Travaux et Mémoires* 9 (1985), 1–89; J. Banaji, *Agrarian Change in Late Antiquity*; G.R. Ruffini, *Social Networks in Byzantine Egypt*; Peter Sarris, *Economy and Society in the Age of Justinian* (Cambridge, 2006); C. Wickham, *Framing the Early Middle Ages*, 245–9.
18. MacCoull's *Dioscorus of Aphrodito*; Jean-Luc Fournet, ed., *Les archives de Dioscore d'Aphrodité cent ans après leur découverte* (Paris, 2008); C. Wickham, *Framing the Early Middle Ages*, 412–4.
19. John the Almsgiver found seven Chalcedonian churches upon his arrived at Alexandria, they purportedly increased to seventy; Anonymous, *Life of John the Almsgiver*, Delehaye 5.8–12, Dawes and Baynes, 201.
20. Anonymous, *Life of John the Almsgiver*, Delehaye 5.28–30. Τοὺς ἐξ αἱρέσεων δέ τινων ἐπιστρέφοντας κληρικούς, διδόντας λιβέλλους μεταμελείας καὶ τὸ τῆς ὀρθοδόξου πίστεως.
21. Both Timothy Ailuros (458–80 CE), the anti-Chalcedonian patriarch of Alexandria, and John the Almsgiver required them: Timothy Ailuros, *Letters*, 362; Anonymous, *Life of John the Almsgiver*, §5, cf. §12.
22. Leontios, *Life of John the Almsgiver*, Festugière 33.10, Dawes/Baynes §32: πολλὰς μὲν κώμας, πλείστας δὲ ἐκκλησίας, ὡσαύτως καὶ μοναστήρια.
23. I am thankful to Phil Booth and Marek Jankowiak for a valuable discussion of this reunion attempt.
24. C. Hovorun, *Will, Action and Freedom*, 67–72; P. Allen and B. Neil, ed./trans., *Maximus the Confessor and his Companions: Documents from Exile* (Oxford, 2002), 6–15; J. Meyendorff, *Imperial unity*, 240–8; J. Duffy and J. Parker, ed./trans., *The Synodicon Vetus* (Washington, 1979), no. 130.
25. C. Hovorun, *Will, Action and Freedom*, 63–66; J. Meyendorff, *Imperial unity*, 342–44. In the mid-650s, Emperor Constans attempted another reunion with the Armenians under Catholicos Nersēs (Sebios, *History*, ch. 49).
26. C. Hovorun, *Will, Action and Freedom*, 67, n. 78; K.J. von Hefele, *A history of the Councils of the Church*, vol. 5 (Edinburgh, 1895), 18, my emphasis.
27. *Life of Samuel*, Cop. 9, Eng. 83; Benjamin, *On Cana of Galilee*, 12v; HP I.2:227. (Pseudo-)Agathon, *Book of Consecration*, 106, only mentions Kyros' successor, Basilios of Nikiou. See also C. Hovorun, *Will, Action and Freedom*, 68.
28. J. Meyendorff, *Imperial unity*, 347, 351.

29. C. Hovorun, *Will, Action and Freedom*, 59, 68–70; Allen and Neil, *Maximus the Confessor*, 12.
30. *Life of Samuel* (of Qalamūn), Cop. 9, Eng. 83. The Syrian *Chronicle of 819* states that in 598 CE (910 AG), "Domitian, the Chalcedonian bishop, came and persecuted the faithful, forcing them to receive communion from him." Communion was the true mark of unity. John the Almsgiver gave explicit instructions to his followers never to receive communion in anti-Chalcedonian churches; Leontios, *Life of John the Almsgiver*, §42.
31. *Life of Samuel*, Cop. 7, 10, 11, Eng. 80–1, 84, 85; *Life of Isaac*, 17, Bell 47; HP I.2:227–8; (Pseudo-) Agathon, *Book of Consecration*, 80–82, 106–10.
32. See Chapter Two, n. 20. On the *Life*'s attempt to increase the prestige of the Monastery at Qalamūn, see *Life of Samuel*, §7, and Jason R. Zaborowski, "Egyptian Christians Implicating Chalcedonians in the Arab Takeover of Egypt: The Arabic Apocalypse of Samuel of Qalamūn," *OrChr* 87 (2003), 103–7. The *Life of Isaac of Alexandria* only notes a priest named Joseph who is said to have been beaten in Kyros' court (Coptic 17, Bell pg. 47). Pseudo-Agathon's *Book of Consecration* notes the hardship under Kyros (pgs. 108, 110), but does not reference conversions. Significantly, there, the bishop of Nikiou is Basilios—not Victor (pgs. 106, 112, 128).
33. See Richard W. Bulliet, "Conversion Stories in Early Islam," in *Conversion and Continuity*, ed. M. Gervers and R.J. Bikhazi (Toronto, 1990). Ibn ʿAbd al-Ḥakam's often misconstrued comment—"We do not know of any group that has converted (*aslamat*) in a single hour as did the Copts" (*Futūḥ*, 5)—is in the context of Egyptians converting to the religion of Moses in Ancient Egypt *not* the ninth-century. See Yohanan Friedmann, "A Note on the Conversion of Egypt to Islam," JSAI 3 (1981–82), 238–40.
34. John Iskander ("Islamization in Medieval Egypt," *Medieval Encounters* 4.3 (1998), 219–27) places the bulk of conversion under the Fāṭimids and Ayyubids. J.M. Mouton dates significant conversion later still ("L'Islamisation de l'Égypte au moyen âge," in *Chrétiens du monde arabe*, ed. B. Heyberger (Paris, 2003), 110–23). On the other end of the spectrum, Saun O'Sullivan ("Coptic Conversion and the Islamization of Egypt," *Mamluk Studies Review* 10.2 (2006), 65–79) contends for mass conversion during the first centuries of Islam (also Y. Courbage and P. Fargues, *Christians and Jews under Islam*, trans. J. Mabro (London, 1997), ch. 1). Beyond contradicting—without invalidating—the bulk of earlier scholarship, that study reads the early tradition at face value without heading its endemic historiographic problems. Finally, Petra M. Sijpesteijn ("Shaping a Muslim State: Papyri Related to an Eighth-Century Egyptian Official" (Ph.D. diss., Princeton University, 2004), esp. ch. 2), repeatedly alludes to the introduction of strict taxation in the second quarter of the eighth century to the Islamic government's need to raise revenue due to increased conversion. Nonetheless, there is a host of other considerations could account for the pattern: e.g. the expansion phase of the early caliphate had effectively ceased by 712, the size of the bureaucracy and its rate of increase at

any juncture is a matter of speculation, as is the extent of inefficiency and corruption—to name but a few possible stimuli for the new, more rigid tax practices.

35. See Michael G. Morony's survey in "The Age of Conversions: A Reassessment," in *Conversion and Continuity*, ed. Grevers and Bikhazi. By the ninth century CE, Egypt experienced a demographic increase that coincided with a dramatic swell in agricultural productivity. See C. Issawi, "Area and Population," in *Islamic Middle East, 700–1900: Studies in Economic and Social History*, ed. A.L. Udovitch (Princeton, 1981); Andrew Watson, *Agricultural Innovation in the Early Islamic World* (Cambridge, 1983).
36. This is impossible to quantify. Only official waves of immigration were documented, and polygamy likely increased the Arabs' birthrate as compared with their Christian neighbors. See C. Issawi, "Area and Population," and B.F. Musallam's "Birth Control and Middle Eastern History," both in *Islamic Middle East*, ed. A.L. Udovitch; cf. Wadād al-Qāḍī, "Population Census and Land Surveys under the Umayyads (41–132/661–75)," *Der Islam* 83 (2006), 341–416.
37. Ibn ʿAbd al-Ḥakam, *Futūḥ*, 49; Ibn al-Kindī, *Faḍā'il miṣr*, 186; al-Yaʿqūbī, *Ta'rīkh*, II.93, 95–6; al-Maqrīzī, *Khiṭaṭ*, I.78–81. Mariyya purportedly died in 15/636, and was prayed over by the Caliph ʿUmar ibn al-Khaṭṭāb. Caliph Muʿawiya granted tax relief to her former village (Ibn ʿAbd al-Ḥakam, *Futūḥ*, 52–3; al-Maqrīzī, *Khiṭaṭ*, I.81), and, later, her alleged home in Anṣina became a mosque (HCME 86b, 244).
38. S. Bashear, *Arabs and Others*, 70; more generally, see pgs. 68–70 and 122.
39. See A. Noth, *Early Arabic Historical Tradition*. Some of the later invitations may be historical however; see Sebeos, *History*, ch. 50 (pg. 144) and J. Howard-Johnston's commentary on that passage.
40. Sebeos, *History*, 4; Firdawsī, *Shāhnāma*, 34.5, 37.3, 38.2–3, 5, 11, and 39 (D. Davis, trans., *Shahnameh: The Persian Book of Kings* (New York, 2006), *passim* pgs. 783–831); F.E. Peters, *Allah's Commonwealth* (New York, 1973), 33; Shīrīn was a Persian (possibly Armenian) Christian, while Mariyya was allegedly the daughter of the Byzantine Emperor Maurice. A recent study asserts that while Shīrīn was a historical queen of the Sasanid empire (see Sebeos, *History*, 85, 151; chs. 13, 46) the entire account of Mariyya is more myth than fact; see Wilhelm Baum, *Shirin, Christian Queen, Myth of Love* (New Jersey, 2004).
41. Most significant: Dennett, *Conversion and the Poll Tax*; Ira M. Lapidus, "The Conversion of Egypt to Islam," *Israel Oriental Studies* 2 (1972), 248–62; R.W. Bulliet, *Conversion to Islam in the Medieval Period* (Cambridge, 1979); M. Gervers and R.J. Bikhazi, *Conversion and Continuity*; G. Frantz-Murphy, "Conversion in Early Islamic Egypt: The Economic Factor," in *Documents de l'Islam Médiéval: Nouvelle Perspectives de Recherche*, ed. Y. Ragib (Cairo, 1991), 11–17; Sam I. Gellens, "Egypt, Islamization of," *CoptEncyc* 3:936–942; Christian Décobert, "Sur l'Arabisation et l'Islamisation de l'Égypte

médiévale," in *Itinéraires d'Égypte Mélanges offerts au père Maurice Martin s.j.*, ed. idem (Cairo, 1992); John Iskander, "Islamization in Medieval Egypt."

42. Frantz-Murphy, "Conversion in Early Islamic Egypt," 11–17; Dennett, *Conversion and Poll Tax*, 82–8.
43. John of Nikiou mentions several early conversion accounts: John, a pro-Chalcedonian monk who converted to Islam (*Chronicle*, §§121.10; 114.1; 121.11); Sergios "the apostate" and Kosmas (*Chronicle*, §109.19–20); and "Theodore the apostate" (§121.3). The biography of Patriarch Alexander II (705–30 CE) provides additional examples of notables who were forced to convert: Peter the magistrate of Upper Egypt, his brother Tawdara (Theodore), and the unnamed son of Theophanes governor of Maryūṭ (HP I.3:306).
44. John of Nikiou, *Chronicle*, §114.1, states that the Arabs were accompanied by "Egyptians who had apostatized from the Christian faith and embraced the faith of the beast."
45. *Apocalypse of Athanasios*, 528.
46. See Chapter Two. There is some ambiguity as to whether the *mawālī* or their *wālī* paid the *jizya*. Ibn ʿAbd al-Ḥakam, *Futūḥ*, 156 (cf. Abū Yūsuf, *Kharāj*, 132), mentions that ʿAbdallah ibn Saʿd had Christian *mawālī* whom he liberated and it was then that they had to pay the *jizya* (*fa-a'taqahum fa kana 'alayhim al-kharaj*—the terms *jizya* and *kharāj* are interchangeable in the context of the seventh and early eighth centuries and it is unlikely that these individuals were landowners). Additionally, conversion assured slaves their emancipation (Abū Yūsuf, *Kharāj*, 144), and prisoners of war (*asīr*) their lives (Abū ʿUbayd, *Amwāl*, §367).
47. Such a working unit is mentioned in al-Kindī, *Wulāt*, 70. It would seem that the ʿAbbāsids killed large numbers of *mawālī* in Palestine because of their association with the Umayyads. Theophanes, *Chronicle*, AM 6243 (750–1 CE): Τούτῳ τῷ ἔτει τοὺς πλείους τῶν Χριστιανῶν ὡς συγγενεῖς τῶν προαρξάντων ἀνεῖλον οἱ προσφάτως κρατήσαντες, δόλῳ τούτους χειρωσάμενοι εἰς Ἀντιπατρίδα τῆς Παλαιστίνης (L.12–4). See also P. Crone, *Slaves on Horses: The Evolution of the Islamic Polity* (Cambridge, 1980), ch. 8. Al-Kindī often references *mawālī*; e.g. 70, 84, 87, 90. As P. Crone noted, for the period at hand, "there was no such thing as an Arab Mawlā" (*Slaves on Horses*, 56).
48. A. Noth, *Arabic Historical Tradition*, 147–67; Ibn ʿAbd al-Ḥakam, *Futūḥ*, 65–6, 83–4, 89; cf. Eutychios, *Naẓm al-jawhar*, II.10, 23, 25. Most early proselytization accounts are likely factious, though a few may have been historical. P. Crone noted evidence from Gaza: *Slaves on Horses*, n. 68, citing H. Delehaye, "Passio sanctorum sexaginta martyrum," *Analecta Bollandiana* 23 (1904), 289–307, at 302.
49. Ibn ʿAbd al-Ḥakam, *Futūḥ*, 46, 65–6, 83–4, 86, 89; cf. John of Nikiou does not mention such invitations, but he documents a few conversions (e.g. *Chronicle*, §121.10–11); cf. Ibn ʿAbd al-Ḥakam, *Futūḥ*, 83, 168—the case of the hesitant convert.

50. See Ibn ʿAbd al-Ḥakam, *Futūḥ*, 152–6. At the time of ʿAbd al-Malik ibn Marwān, the *jizya* was not required of monks (*Futūḥ*, 156); though there is substantial documentary evidence proving that monks paid this tax. Al-Hajjāj ibn Yūsuf (in al-Sawād/Irāq) was purportedly the first official to collect the *jizya* from converts. On the status of land, see Ibn ʿAbd al-Ḥakam, *Futūḥ*, 154. One account maintains that a convert's land should remain with his next of kin in the village. This is likely an early tradition. Until the early eighth century, taxes in Egypt were often levied on the whole village, not individual farmers. Another tradition states that the land of a convert was *fay'* to the Muslims. Often, early converts left their villages, see n. 105 below.
51. There are singular incidents; see HP II.2:215/115r and HCME 51b, 152. At one juncture, two villages threatened to convert if their bishops were not removed (HP I.4:604–5). Theophanes, *Chronicle*, §416 (741/2 CE) remarks: "Kosmas the patriarch of Alexandria and his city became orthodox, emerging from the wicked doctrines of the Monothelites, which had held sway since the time of Cyrus." Kosmas was the first pro-Chalcedonian patriarch to reside in Alexandria under Arab rule (see Eutychios, *Naẓm al-jawhar*, II.45). Eutychios offers conflicting accounts (cf. *Naẓm al-jawhar* II.13 with 28–29), but he seems to favor a tradition that Monothelitism remained for forty six years, which would place its condemnation among the Melkites of Alexandria near the end of the seventh century.
52. An equally discernable shift occurred in Nubia. For the conversion of Nubia to Christianity, see John of Nikiou, *Chronicle*, 142 ch. 90; John of Ephesos, *History*, IV. As for the adoption of an anti-Chalcedonian hierarchy, see Grillmeier, *Christ in Christian Tradition*, II.4:263–78. Eutychios (*Naẓm al-jawhar*, II.46) documents this fact; see Chapter Nine, n. 108, below.
53. HP I.3:259. Patriarch Isaac also appointed a large number of bishops; HP I.3:300.
54. See the discussion of the Aphrodito and Qurra papyri in Chapter Seven.
55. HP I.2:233.
56. Agathon I: HP I.3:258–9. In one incident, Patriarch Agathon indiscriminately ransomed fugitives—Gainites and Barsanuphians—along with the orthodox. This act of philanthropy prompted some to convert. John III: HP I.3:273. Isaac I: *Life of Isaac of Alexandria*, 59, Bell 65. Khaīl I: HP I.3:393, 451. Mark II: HP I.4:543. This ninth-century text demonstrates the overlapping of Institutional Conversion (assuming that the "Roman" refugees were pro-Chalcedonians) and Tradition Transition.
57. *Life of Isaac of Alexandria*, 59, Bell 65, modified. The village of Psanasho, near Samannūd, is singled out as an Akephaloi stronghold; they also had a contingency in Miṣr (HP I.4:529).
58. Conversion due to the influence of a Holy man is documented in John of Nikiou, *Chronicle*, §§89.11; 89.36; cf. Cyril of Scythopolis' *Lives of the Monks of Palestine*.
59. HP I.3:273.

60. HP II.1:24/117v. They were rebaptized and Patriarch Shinūda I (re)consecrated a church and a priest for them. See Chapter Ten, n. 122, below.
61. John of Ṣā is incorrectly identified as a bishop in R. Stewart, "Dumyaṭ," *CoptEncyc* 5:925–6. This tax is identified as a *jizya* by Ibn ʿAbd al-Ḥakam.
62. HP I.3:316–7. Cities named: Ṣā, al-Munā, Wādī Habīb, Banā, Buṣir, Samannūd, Rosetta, and Damietta.
63. HP I.3:382–4. Negotiations with Julianists and Melitians are described in HP I.3:383–84, 452.
64. The ἀκέφαλοι/ⲚⲒⲀⲦⲀⲪⲈ had a bishop in Nioubershenoufi; *Life of Isaac of Alexandria*, 72, Bell 70.
65. *Life of Isaac of Alexandria*, 30, Bell 53.
66. I believe Bell correctly identified Abba John, Isaac's "spiritual brother" ⲠⲈϤⲤⲞⲚ ⲘⲠ̄Ⲛ̄ⲀⲦⲒⲔⲞⲚ, with Iannē. See *Life of Isaac of Alexandria*, 88, Bell 76 and n. 140.
67. HP I.3:383–4.
68. HP I.3:460. Some Melitians were reconciled during this period due to the efforts of Bishop Moses of Wasīm (HP I.3:454). Apparently, the only negotiations that succeeded (even temporarily) were those in which Khaīl I was not involved.
69. See HP I.2:210–11. Centered in the Eastern Delta, the Barsanuphnians separated from the Akephaloi and formed a separate hierarchy in the second half of the sixth century.
70. HP I.4:528–9.
71. It is unclear if George was a widower or if he separated from his wife. In the *Life of Isaac of Alexandria* (52, Bell 62) a candidate for the patriarchate was disqualified because "above all he was a married man and also had some very wicked children." Conversely, Isaac is described as "a pure virgin from his childhood" (55, Bell 63). The biography of Patriarch Demetrios I (189–231 CE), HP I.1:57–61, part of which was compiled under Arab rule, indicates this emphasis on episcopal celibacy; see M.S.A. Mikhail "Demetrios of Alexandria" (*forthcoming*); *Life of John Khame*. In the ninth century CE, though backed by two powerful bishops, the only obstacle to eventually derail Lord Isḥāq ibn Andunā's bid for the patriarchate was the fact that he was married and had children (HP I.4:593); see Chapter Three.
72. HP I.4:528–9.
73. HP I.4:528. Later, Ibrāhīm ibn Bishr was promised a diocese but was not ordained until one became vacant (HP II.2:176–7/147v); the same was true for Isḥāq ibn Andunā (see Chapter Three). This was not completely novel in the early church; a few individuals were ordained bishops without a diocese—though such instances were far from normative, and typically a nominal see was still identified.
74. The reforms of ʿUmar II sparked a number of conversions; Michael the Syrian, *Chronicle*, 11.19.
75. HP I.3:370: *lā tuʾkhaz minhu baʿdan jizyātan*.

76. HP I.3:370–1 notes that 24,000 Christians converted in "Miṣr and its suburbs." Even if the number of converts is likely exaggerated, it must have been significant nonetheless. The HP's biography of Khaīl I was composed by a contemporary of the patriarch.
77. For other examples of this type of conversion, see Eutychios, *Naẓm al-jawhar*, I.203–4; HP II.1:6/113v, 12/115r, 39/120v: HP II.2:184–6/149r-v, 192/150v, 195/151r (the same later returned, HP II.2:204/153r).
78. HP I.3:443. The account continues: "in consequence of the cruel extortions and burdens imposed upon them, many of the rich and poor denied the faith of Christ." Cf. HP II.1:39/120v; II.2:192/150v, 195/151r.
79. Kindī, *Wulāt*, 413–5.
80. HP II.1:9/114r and HCME 39b-40a, 127–8. Sociologists maintain that conversion proceeds along preexisting social networks; see Stark, *Rise of Christianity*, 55–6. In regard to female conversion, Maya Shatzmiller ("Marriage, family, and the faith: women's conversion to Islam,"*Journal of Family History* 21.3 (1996), 235–66) forwarded an opposing viewpoint, maintaining that Christian women were generally more resistant to conversion than men. The Egyptian evidence, while admittedly slim, does not support that conclusion.
81. See Yohanan Friedmann, *Tolerance and Coercion in Islam: Interfaith Relations in the Muslim Tradition* (Cambridge, 2003), ch.5.
82. In addition to the *P.Cair.Arab.* contracts cited below, Walter Till provides translations for the five texts identified as of 1948, and Balogh and Kahle provide two additional Coptic texts (a third is not a marriage contract proper). To these, *P.Ryl.Copt.*139 should be added. Finally, Abbott provides two additional Arabic contracts. See W. Till, "Die Koptischen Eheverträge," in *Die Osterreichische Nationalbibliothek: Festschrift Josef Bick* (Vienna, 1948); 627–38; E. Balogh and P.E. Kahle, "Two Coptic Documents relating to Marriage," *Aegyptus* 33 (1953), 331–40; Nabia Abbott, "Arabic Marriage Contracts among Copts," ZDMG 95 (1941), 59–81. Although concerned with a much later period, also see A.H. Green, "A Late 19th-Century Coptic Marriage Contract and the Coptic Documentary Tradition," *Muséon* 106 (1993), 361–71; and R.Y. Ebied, "Some Observations on 'A Late 19th-Century Coptic Marriage Contract and the Coptic Documentary Tradition,'" *Parole de l'Orient* 25 (2000), 727–32.
83. During Late Antiquity, Pagan converts to Christianity often changed their names (Paphnutios, *Histories of the Monks*, 17b, Vivian 42). Under Umayyad rule (and occasionally later), converts retained their patronymic, which aids in identifying them: e.g. see *P.Cair.Arab.*I.41; Ibn ʿAbd al-Hakam, *Futūḥ*, 135. Converts under ʿAbbāsid rule typically took Arabic names. *P.Giss.Arab.*5, dated 2–3/8–9 c., contains a list of converts with their Christian and new Islamic names.
84. Some narrative accounts may predate the documentary texts. The first is the doubtful account of Mariyya al-Qibṭiyya and her sister Shīrīn, discussed above.

Although not examples of intermarriage per se, both women allegedly converted shortly after traveling to Arabia (Ibn ʿAbd al-Ḥakam, *Futūḥ*, 48–52). ʿAbd al-ʿAzīz ibn Marwān had built a palace (Qaṣr Mariyya) for a Roman concubine, Mariyya, who bore him a son (Ibn ʿAbd al-Ḥakam, *Futūḥ*, 112).

85. This was often the case; Abbott, "Arabic Marriage Contracts," 59.
86. Grohmann's observation that "Christian," as a designation, is rare in Arabic papyri undermines this rationale (see *P.Cair.Arab.*I.54 n. 3).
87. Some Christian contracts do include a divorce clause; e.g. *P.Bal.*152. Christian divorce documents are also extant; e.g. *P.Cair.Masp.*III.67311; cf. *O.Crum.* 72 and Ad. 1.
88. On the history and evolution of the term, see Daniel Pipes, "Mawlas: Freed Slaves and Converts in Early Islam," *Slavery and Abolition* 1 (1980), 132–77; repr. R. Hoyland, ed., *Muslims and Others in Early Islamic Society* (Burlington, 2004), ch. 13.
89. This same couple is in *P.Cair.Arab.*I.56, dated 239/854, discussed below.
90. HP I.3:306. This was during the patriarchate of Alexander II (705–30 CE); Theophanes, *Chronicle*, AM 6232 (739/40 CE), notes other attempts at forced conversion under the Caliph Hishām.
91. HP I.3:305; cf. *Chronicle of Zuqnīn* 236, 254; Theophanes, *Chronicle*, AM 6264 (771/2 CE); HP I.3:322–5, where the governor Usama is accused of perpetrating similar atrocities against monks; cf. C.F. Robinson, "Neck-Sealing in Early Islam," JESHO 48.3 (2005), 401–41.
92. Kindī, *Wulāt*, 51, 54.
93. HP I.4:641–3.
94. For al-Mutawakkil, see HP II.1:6/113v, 8/114r, 9/114r; for al-Ḥākim bi Amr Allāh, see HP II.2:184–6/149r-v, 192/150v. On the reign of al-Ḥākim, see M. Conrad "al-Ḥākim bi-Amr Allāh," EI^2 3:76b-81b; S.A. Assaad, *The Reign of al-Hâkim bi-Amr Allâh. A Political Study* (Beirut, 1974), esp. 93–107; Paul E. Walker, *Caliph of Cairo: Al-Hakim bi-Amr Allah, 996 -1021* (Cairo, 2009).
95. HP I.3:403–4. Upon mocking an icon of the Crucifixion, the man was suspended between heaven and earth and experienced the pains of a crucifixion. He converted and went to a monastery directly after his baptism.
96. HP II.2:152–69/143r-146v.
97. HP II.1:87–8/130r-131r.
98. Abū Yūsuf, *Kharāj*, 179–82; Abū ʿUbayd, *Amwāl*, §§484–85; Yaḥyā ibn Ādam, *Kharāj*, §54 (cf. §56); Mahmoud Ayoub, "Religious Freedom and the Law of Apostasy in Islam," *Islamochristiana* 20 (1994), 75–91; Rudolph Peters and Gert J.J. De Vries, "Apostasy in Islam," *Die Welt des Islams* n.s. 17.1 (1976–1977), 1–25; Antoine Fattal, *Le statut légal des non-musulmans en pays d'Islam*, 2nd ed. (Beirut, 1995; 1958), 163–8; Friedmann, *Tolerance and Coercion*, ch. 4; *Martyrdom of John of Phanijōit*; Febe Armanios and Boğaç Ergene, "A Christian Martyr under Mamlūk Justice: The Trials of Salīb (d. 1512) according to Coptic and Muslim Sources," *Muslim World* 96.1 (2006): 115–44; Frank Griffel, "Toleration and Exclusion."

99. John of Nikiou, *Chronicle*, §121.10; HP II.2:120/137r. Under Ayyubid and Mamluk rule, some Muslims were suspicious of converts, viewing them as nominal Muslims (cf. *Martyrdom of John of Phanijōit*). Such attitudes appear to have been confined to the first generation of converts.
100. *Life of Isaac of Alexandria*, 70, Bell 69–70. The man must have been prominent in his own right. After Patriarch Isaac healed his younger son, who was demon-possessed, "the pious man besought the archbishop to write for him the gospel according to John" as a blessing; a request the patriarch apparently obliged.
101. *Life of Isaac of Alexandria*, 71–2, Bell 70: ⲠⲈⲔⲤⲚⲞϤ ⲈϨⲢⲎⲒ ⲈϪⲰⲔ ⲠⲀϢⲎⲢⲒ. ⲒⲤϪⲈⲚ ϮⲚⲞⲨ ⲔⲞⲒ ̀ⲚϢⲈⲘⲘⲞ ̀ⲈⲢⲞⲒ ϦⲈⲚ ⲠⲀⲒ ̀ⲈⲰⲚ ⲚⲈⲘ ⲪⲎ ⲈⲐⲚⲎⲞⲨ.
102. Cf. Gerrit J. Reinink, "Following the Doctrine of the Demons; Early Christian Fear of Conversion to Islam," in *Cultures of Conversion*, ed. J.N. Bremmer *et al.*, 127–38.
103. *Synaxarion*, Baramhāt 6.
104. HP I.4:493–4, my emphasis.
105. Converts under Umayyad rule gravitated toward urban centers; Abū Yūsuf, *Kharāj*, 181; Abū ʿUbayd, *Amwāl*, §§432–9.
106. This biography was written by John "the Writer" in 865–6 CE.
107. *Apocalypse of Samuel*, 389, my translation.
108. See Chapters Three, Six, Seven, and Eight.
109. Kindī, *Wulāt*, 68. See Chapters Seven and Eight below.
110. Ibn ʿAbd al-Ḥakam, *Futūḥ*, 108, 129, 116, 141–3; al-Maqrīzī, *Bayān*, §59–63; ʿAbd Allah Khurshīd al-Barrī, *al-Qaba'il al-ʿarabiyah fi misr fi al-qurun al-thalathah al-ulā lil-hijrah* (Cairo, 1992). Upon his appointment as governor in 25/646, ʿAbdallāh ibn Saʿd came to Egypt with a sizable contingency of his clansmen and relatives (HP I.2:237; al-Kindī, *Wulāt*, 11–13). Similarly, in 64/684, governor ʿAbd al-Raḥmān ibn ʿUtbā brought a large number of Meccan Khārijītes with him (al-Kindī, *Wulāt*, 41).
111. Kindī, *Wulāt*, 69.
112. Morony, *Iraq after the Muslim Conquest*, 187, 190; Robinson, *Empire and Elites*, ch. 4.
113. Frantz-Murphy, "Conversion in Early Islamic Egypt," 14.
114. See the incident discussed in al-Kindī, *Wulāt*, 70.
115. In general see, CMR and S.H. Griffith's *Church in the Shadow of the Mosque*.
116. Sidney H. Griffith, "The Gospel in Arabic: An Inquiry into its Appearance in the First Abbasid Century," *Oriens Christianus* 69 (1985), 126–67; idem, "The Monks of Palestine and the Growth of Christian Literature in Arabic," *Muslim World* 78 (1988), 1–28; idem, "From Aramaic to Arabic: The Languages of the Monasteries of Palestine in the Byzantine and Early Islamic Periods," DOP 51 (1997), 11–31.
117. See G.J. Reinink, "The Beginnings of Syriac Apologetic Literature in Response to Islam," *Oriens Christianus* 77 (1993), 165–87. Bilingual responses commenced in the middle of the eighth century CE. See Sidney H. Griffith, "Disputes with Muslims in Syriac Christian Texts: from Patriarch John

(d. 648) to Bar Hebraeus (d. 1286)," in *Religionsgespräche im Mittelalter*, ed. B. Lewis and F. Niewöhner (Wiesbaden, 1992). For Greek apologies, see D.J. Sahas, *John of Damascus on Islam* (Leiden, 1972); idem, "Bartholomeus of Edessa on Islam: A Polemicist with Nerve!" *Graeco-Arabica* 7–8 (1999–2000), 467–83. For the first Christian Arabic apology, see Samir Khalil Samir, "The Earliest Arab Apology for Christianity (c. 750)," in *Christian Arabic Apologetics during the Abbasid Period (750–1258)*, ed. S.K. Samir and J.S. Nielsen (Leiden, 1994). For Theodore Abū Qurra's Arabic apologies, see John C. Lamoreaux, trans., *Theodore Abu Qurra* (Provo, 2005).

118. M. Krause, "Koptische Literatur," *Lexikon der Ägyptologie* 3:694–728; T. Orlandi, "Literature, Coptic," *CoptEncyc* 5:1450–60; idem, "Coptic Literature," in *Roots of Egyptian Christianity*, ed. Pearson and Goehring.
119. *Apocalypse of Samuel*, 389; my translation. On the dating of this text, see Chapter Five, ns. 101 and 102.
120. For Sawīrus, *miṣbāḥ al-'aql*, see Sidney H. Griffith, "Kitāb Misbāh al-'Aql of Severus Ibn al-Muqaffa': A Profile of the Christian Creed in Arabic in Tenth Century Egypt," *Medieval Encounters* 2.1 (1996), 15–42. The latter two texts are erronously attributed to Sawīrus ibn al-Muqaffa'. *Kitāb al-īḍāḥ* has been published under the title *Kitāb al-dūrr al-thamīn fī īḍāḥ al-dīn*, ed. M. Jirjis (Cairo 1925; 1971; 1992); the comments on religious confusion are on pages 10–11 and 161. The preface to the *History of the Patriarchs* is likewise erroneously attributed to Sawīrus; see the discussion of the HP in Chapter One.
121. HP II.1:30/118v.
122. HP II.1:31/119r.
123. HP II.1:31–2/119r. The bishops of Samannūd and Minyat Ṭānah were excommunicated and died before returning to their dioceses; this divine punishment—premature death—functions to legitimize their removal.
124. HP II.1:40–1/121r.
125. "A multiplicity of views has spread among the Copts at this time. Each abides by a different belief and makes an infidel out of the other ... None of them know what is read to them in church in Coptic. They hear but do not comprehend; because of this they have lost the knowledge of Christian doctrine." Pseudo-Sawīrus, *K. al-īḍāḥ*, 161, my translation; see the following chapter.
126. On the controversy between Ibn al-Qunbar and Metropolitan Michael of Damietta, see Mark N. Swanson, "*Telling (and Disputing) the Old, Old Story*: A Soteriological Exchange in Late Twelfth-Century Egypt," *Coptica* 6 (2005), 69–82.
127. HCME 9a-17a, 20–43; see also Chapter Five. The depictions of Murqus and Bishop Michael of Dumyāṭ in publications by Coptic authors over the past two centuries are often inaccurate. These works consistently cite Murqus as an advocate for the practice of confessing over a censor, while positioning the bishop as the champion of the orthodox practice of confession before a priest.

Historically, it was the bishop who advocated confession before a censor and called Murqus' beliefs a "heresy."

128. Stark, *Rise of Christianity*, 55; Stark and Finke discuss religious "capital" in *Acts of Faith*, 118–25.
129. M.G. Morony, *Iraq after the Muslim Conquest*, 8–9, 512–4.
130. Cf. David Zeidan, "Typical Elements of Fundamentalist Islamic and Christian Theocentric Worldviews," *Islam and Christian-Muslim Relations* 13.2 (2002), 207–28.
131. Similarities increased after the eleventh century, as Islam developed a mystical, sometimes ascetic *Sufī* tradition and the Fāṭimids focused on the veneration of saints (see Ibn Zulāq, *Faḍā'il miṣr*). At a later period, it is recorded that Christians and Muslims made pilgrimages to the same shrines and invoked the same saints. See Huda Lutfi, "Coptic Festivals of the Nile: Aberrations of the Past?" in *The Mamluks in Egyptian Politics and Society*, ed. T. Philipp and U. Haarmann (New York, 1998) and Boaz Shoshan, *Popular Culture in Medieval Cairo* (New York, 1993); Paula Sanders, *Ritual, Politics, and the City in Fatimid Cairo* (New York, 1994), ch. 5; J.W. McPherson, *The Moulids of Egypt (Egyptian Saints-Days)* (Cairo, 1941; 1995); Febe Armanios, *Beyond Persecution and Tolerance: Coptic Christianity in Ottoman Egypt* (Oxford, 2011); also Chapter Eleven below.
132. The cost/benefit terminology is based on Stark and Finke, *Acts of Faith*, ch. 5; cf. Durk Hak, "Conversion as a Rational Choice: An Evaluation of the Stark-Finke-Model of Conversion and (Re-) affiliation," in *Paradigms, Poetics, and Politics of Conversion*, ed. J.N. Bremmer *et al.*, 13–24; J.J.G. Jansen, "The History of Islam in the Light of the Rational Choice Theory," in *Cultures of Conversion*, ed. J.N. Bremmer *et al.*
133. See Speros Vryonis Jr., *The Decline of Medieval Hellenism in Asia Minor* (Berkeley, 1971), ch. 5; Nehemia Levtzion, "Toward a Comparative Study of Islamization," in *Conversion to Islam*, ed. idem (New York, 1979).
134. There is mention of such an act in al-Ṭabarī, *Ta'rīkh*, I.2583.1–8. In his *Early Arabic Historical Tradition* (pgs. 13–4), A. Noth argues that the account is not authentic, but even if it is accepted as historical, it is doubtful that such marginal proselytizing efforts made much of an impact on the population.
135. Kindī, *Wulāt*, 190, 192; al-Maqrīzī, *Khiṭaṭ*, IV.1002; HP I.4:602, 606–9. Also see Michael C. Dunn, "The Struggle for Abbasid Egypt" (Ph.D. diss., Georgetown University, 1975), 50, 83, 164–8; Friedman, "A note;" also Chapters Six and Nine below.
136. Anti-Chalcedonian political ideology is addressed in Chapters Nine.
137. *Apocalypse of Samuel*, 380.
138. Cf. Pierre Chuvin's discussion in *A Chronicle of the Last Pagans* (Cambridge, 1990), 37, 41 with the frequent reports of abandoned and dilapidated churches in the HCME.
139. Pipes, "Mawlas: Freed Slaves," 147–51.

140. For conversion during later centuries, see Yaacov Lev, "Persecutions and Conversion to Islam in Eleventh-Century Egypt," *Israel Asian and African Studies* 22 (1988), 73–91; Donald P. Little, "Coptic Conversion to Islam under the Baḥrī Mamlūks, 692–755/1293–1354," BSOAS 39 (1976), 552–69; L.S.B. MacCoull, "The Rite of the Jar: Apostasy and Reconciliation in the Medieval Coptic Orthodox Church," in *Peace and Negotiation*, ed. D. Wolfthal (Turnhout, 2000), 145–62; M. Brett, "Population and Conversion to Islam in Egypt in the mediaeval Period," in *Egypt and Syria in the Fatimid, Ayyubid and Mamluk Eras IV*, ed. U. Vermeulen and J. van Steenbergen (Louvain, 2005); Tamer el-Leithy, "Coptic Culture and Conversion in Medieval Cairo, 1293–1524 A.D." (Ph.D. Diss., Princeton University, 2005); Y.N. Youssef, "The Acceptance of the non-Jacobite to the Coptic Denomination," *Collectanea Christiana Orientalia* 3 (2006), 317–34.

Chapter 5 Language, Identity, and Assimilation

1. On the use of Latin in Late Antique Egypt, see J.N. Adams, *Bilingualism and the Latin Language* (Cambridge, 2003), ch. 5. On relevant Pahlavi texts, see E. Venetis, "The Sassanid Occupation of Egypt (7th Cent. A.D.) According to Some Pahlavi Papyri Abstracts," *Greco-Arabica* 9–10 (2004), 403–12.
2. Cf. I.M. Lapidus, "Conversion of Egypt to Islam" with G. Frantz-Murphy, "Conversion in Early Islamic Egypt."
3. This took place some time in 86–7/705–6; Ibn ʿAbd al-Ḥakam, *Futūḥ*, 122; al-Kindī (*Wulāt*, 58–9) maintains that Egypt's records were kept in Coptic, though the surviving papyri leave little doubt that the administration, while relaying in part on that language, was largely Greek.
4. The last bilingual protocol is dated 114/734; the oldest all-Arabic protocol is dated 114/732; *P.World*, pg. 38. The last Greek/Arabic administrative papyrus is dated 385/996; Bénédicte Verbeeck, "Greek Language," *CoptEncyc* 4:1168.
5. Eutychios, *Naẓm al-jawhar*, II.10, 25.
6. See ʿUbayd Allāh, *Amwāl*, §§465, 477; Eutychios, *Naẓm al-jawhar*, II.10.
7. K. Morimoto, "Dīwāns as Registers."
8. Qurra's Arabic correspondences (e.g. *P.Cair.Arab*.III.146–55 and III.160–3) were incomprehensible to the individuals and villages to which they were addressed, but his Greek letters, equally unintelligible to most villagers, could be read by administrators and village elites.
9. See Leslie S.B. MacCoull, "Law, Coptic," *CoptEncyc* 5:1428–32.
10. E.g. *P.CLT*.3; *P.Ryl.Copt*.321, 116; *P.Cair.Arab*.III.164–66; Klass A. Worp, "P.Vindob.G39743: Ein Neuer Rashid-Papyrus," ZPE 58 (1985), 83–5.
11. *P.Lond*.IV contains over seventy correspondences from Qurra ibn Sharīk to Basillios, the magistrate of Aphrodito. Some texts were addressed directly to the villagers of Aphrodito, a few were sent in Coptic, others were sent in Arabic (e.g. *P.Qurra* and in *P.Cair.Arab*).

12. S.H. Skreslet, "Greeks in Medieval Islamic Egypt," 270. For Melkite communities beyond Egypt, see Hugh Kennedy, "The Melkite Church from the Islamic Conquest to the Crusades: Continuity and Adaptation in the Byzantine Legacy," in *The 17th International Byzantine Congress: Major Papers* (New York, 1986), 325–43.
13. This should not be interpreted as indicative of "ethnicity" or creed. Many Egyptian anti-Chalcedonians, individuals and families, used Greek as their primary language.
14. Theodore Abū Qurra (ca. 750–820), the Melkite bishop of Ḥarrān, wrote in Arabic well over a century prior to the appearance of the first Christian-Arabic texts in Egypt. In general, see Sidney H. Griffith's *Arabic Christianity in the Monasteries of Ninth-Century Palestine* (Brookfield, 1992), esp. II, III, VIII, XI; idem, *Church in the Shadow of the Mosque.*
15. Eutychios, *Naẓm al-jawhar*, II.69–70, 87; Aziz S. Atiya, "Ibn Baṭriq, Sa'id," *CoptEncyc* 4:1265–6.
16. The *Apocalypse of Samuel* is certainly the most notable text in this regard, but its pro-Coptic language passages were copied by several later apocalypses.
17. Tito Orlandi, "Literature, Coptic," *CoptEncyc* 5:1450–60, esp. 1453.
18. Orlandi, "Literature, Coptic," *CoptEncyc* 5:1454. Such sentiments are ubiquitous. C. Steed, *History of the Church in Africa* (Cambridge, 2000): "[In Egypt] the Church acquired a national language of its own, Coptic, which became identified with as a symbol of their struggle for autonomy over the language and culture of the Imperialists, the 'Melkite' Greeks in Alexandria" (p. 22).
19. See John of Shmūn, *Encomium on St. Antony*; T. Orlandi, "John of Shmun," *CoptEncyc* 5:1369.
20. On Coptic literature, see Orlandi, "Literature, Coptic;" Fr. Shenouda Maher, *al-Adab al-qibṭī* (Cairo, 1998), 75–6; idem, "The Evolution of the Coptic Language," *Coptologia* 16 (2000), 61–2: "After [the Council of Chalcedon] the Copts lost interest in the translation from Greek." Here, Orlandi traces the existence of Egyptian nationalism to the very beginnings of Coptic literature, presenting it as the impetus for the genre (pg. 1451). On the Melkite community, see Skreslet, "Greeks in Medieval Islamic Egypt," 49, 82, 221, 265. Although a very valuable dissertation, it is fully enveloped by the nationalist paradigm; e.g. the analysis of the Arab conquest (pgs. 53–5, 78–9). Moreover, it frequently draws a direct connection between "ethnicity," language, and creed (also in Martiniano P. Roncaglia, "Melchites and Copts," *CoptEncyc* 5:1583). Nonetheless, not all Greek speakers were pro-Chalcedonian nor were all Egyptians anti-Chalcedonian. On these issues, see Chapters Two, Four, and Five.
21. See D.W. Johnson, "Anti-Chalcedonian Polemics," in *Roots of Egyptian Christianity*, ed. Pearson and Goehring, 216–34.

22. Stephen Emmel, "Nag Hammadi Library," *CoptEncyc* 6:1771–3; James M. Robinson, ed., *The Nag Hammadi Library in English*, 3rd rev. ed. (San Francisco, 1988).
23. Johnson, "Anti-Chalcedonian," 226–8.
24. As with Severos, Theodosios' theological writings are primarily preserved in Syriac: see Albert van Roey and Pauline Allen, eds., *Monophysite Texts of the Sixth Century* (Louvain, 1994). Only his popular sermons survive in Coptic: Theodosios, *Homily on the Virgin* and the *Panegyric on John the Baptist*.
25. There are some exceptions, usually anthologies of patristic excerpts. See Paul de Lagarde, *Catenae in Evangelia Aegyptiacae quae Supersunt* (Göttingen, 1886; Osnabrück, 1971).
26. HP I.2:209–13; E.R. Hardy, "Damian," *CoptEncyc* 3:688–9. For the surviving texts attributed to Patriarch Damian, see *P.Mon.Epiph*, pgs. II.148–52, 331–37.
27. Anastasios (HP I.4: 214–9) had been appointed to the city council, while Andronikos (HP I.4: 220–2) worked as a scribe prior to becoming a deacon in the Angelion Church in Alexandria and, later, patriarch. HP I.2:214–19, 220–2; Aziz S. Atiya, "Anastasius," *CoptEncyc* 1:125–6; idem, "Andronicus," *CoptEncyc* 1:131–2.
28. *Life of Isaac of Alexandria*, 8, 28; Bell 44, 52, my translation.
29. *Life of Isaac of Alexandria*, 36; Bell, 55. As discussed above, paschal letters were composed in Greek through the first quarter of the ninth century and likely long after that. This gloss may indicate that John of Samannūd lacked fluency in Greek, though the description that he was learned in "ecclesiastical and civil" wisdom (HP I.3:260), would necessitate a degree of proficiency in that language.
30. The *Letter of Alexander II* may be dated to 713, 719, or 724 CE.
31. L.S.B. MacCoull, "Redating the Inscription of El-Moallaqa," ZPE 64 (1986), 230–4; Charalambia Coquin, "Church of al-Muʿallaqah," *CoptEncyc* 3:557–60.
32. HP I.4:523.
33. HP I.4:590–665; Subhi Y. Labib, "Yusab I," *CoptEncyc* 7:2362–3.
34. HP I.4:597; Patriarch Mark II (799–819 CE) may have been part of this group (see HP I.4:597). In general, the Greek language had an even more rigorous presence among the Nubians: Stanley M. Burstein, "When Greek was an African Language: The Role of Greek Culture in Ancient and Medieval Nubia," *Journal of World History* 19.1 (2008), 41–61.
35. School exercises and bilingual (Coptic/Greek) wordlists demonstrate that learning Greek remained (at least for some) a priority from the eighth to the eleventh centuries CE: *P.Clackson*.35; *P.Rain.UnterrichtKopt*.119, 124, 132, 133, 228, 229; cf. 232, 236, 237, 238, 247, 262. Text 260, dated 10–11th c. CE, is a long bilingual Greek/Sahidic wordlist; cf. 261, 263, 264; cf. Athanasios of Qūṣ, *Qilādat al-taḥrīr*.
36. HP I.4:639; cf. HP I.3:386, in the biography of Khaīl I (744–68 CE), interpreters facilitated communicate with Arab officials.

37. This may be assumed, but is also observed in HP I.4:639. When angered, the patriarch lashed out at Zacharias bishop of Buḥayra in Coptic.
38. As discussed above, few theological texts were translated into Coptic, and Christian-Arabic writings would not emerge for another century after his death.
39. See Jutta Henner, *Fragmenta Liturgica Coptica*, (Tübingen, 2000); Ugo Zanetti, *Les lectionnaires coptes annuels Basse-Egypte* (Louvain-la-Neuve, 1985); Hans Quecke, *Untersuchungen zur koptischen Stundengebet* (Louvain, 1970); Grillmeier, *Christ in Christian Tradition*, II.4: ch. 3.
40. W.F. Macomber, "The Greek texts of the Coptic Mass of the Anaphoras of Basil and Gregory According to the Kacmarcik Codex," OCP 43 (1977), 308–34; idem, "The Anaphora of Saint Mark According to the Kacmarcik Codex," OCP 45 (1979), 75–98; Cf. Paul J. Fedwick, "The Translations of the Works of Basil Before 1400," in *Basil of Caesarea, Christian Humanist, Ascetic*, ed. idem, 2 vols. (Ontario, 1981) 2:439–512, esp. 485–89; cf. *O.Crum*. 516–22, Ad. 39.
41. One explanation maintains that Greek diaconal responses were added to help Greek-speakers participate in the Coptic liturgy. Others maintain that they simply testify to the antiquity of the Coptic rite, or function as a reminder of the pre-Chalcedonian unity of the past. If anything, however, it was the Greek liturgy that was translated to accommodate Coptic speakers. There is no record of an all-Coptic liturgy prior to the Arab conquest.
42. There are several 9–10th century bilingual (Coptic/Greek) lectionaries and Gospels: *P.MorganLib*.22, 54, 263, 269, 278. Some Coptic and Coptic/Arabic manuscripts contain *kephalaia* numbers in Greek as well as Coptic (Greek in Red/Coptic in Black). The earliest of these (based on the use of the *jenkim*) are: *P.MorganLib*.280, 281, 282–5, 291–2.
43. Mounir Shoucri, "Cyril IV," *CoptEncyc* 3:677–9; Fr. Zakhariyyas al-Anṭunī, *al-Bābā Kyrillus al-rābi abū al-iṣlāḥ* (Cairo, 1994). On these relatively recent hymns, see Oswald H.E. Burmester, "The Greek Kirugmata, Versicles and Responses, and Hymns in the Coptic Liturgy," OCP 2 (1936), 363–94; Ugo Zanetti, "Bohairic Liturgical Manuscripts," OCP 61 (1995), 88; Youhanna Nessim Youssef, "Romanos in the Coptic Church," *Bulletin of Saint Shenouda the Archimandrite Coptic Society* 5 (1998–99), 41–4; idem, "Liturgical Connections between Copts (anti-Chalcedonian) and Greeks (Chalcedonian), After the Council of Chalcedon," *Ephemerides Liturgicae* 114.4 (2000), 394–400; Sherief Sorial, "Coptic Psalmodia: Annual - TCC vol. CR2, Project Update," *Bulletin of Saint Shenouda the Archimandrite Coptic Society* 4 (1997–98), 67–79 and 5 (1998–99), 109–16.
44. N. Gonis ("A Fragment of the "Great Doxology" in the Bodleian Library," ZPE 130 (2000), 172–4) discusses a Greek version of the Great Doxology copied for private use under early Islamic rule by a scribe more fluent in Coptic than Greek. Gonis also references the Greek Easter Hymn in *PKöln*.IV.173.
45. Also see *P.MorganLib*.57, 60, but especially 59 s. III.

46. Henner, *Fragmenta Liturgica Coptica*, *passim*, esp. 141.
47. *P.Ryl.Copt.*34; cf. *P.Lond.Copt.*I.160. There are two *Trisagions* in the liturgical rite. The older hymn, echoing Isaiah 6:3, is chanted in the Liturgy of the Eucharist by both confessions. Soon after the Chalcedonian schism, a second *Trisagion* began to be chanted prior to the reading of the Gospel during the Liturgy of the Word. Two versions of that *Trisagion* exist and is supported by an independent origination narrative. The pro-Chalcedonian version is addressed to God the Trinity, while the anti-Chalcedonian *Trisagion* is addressed to Christ (cf. Rev. 4:8) and, thus, commemorates his birth, death, and resurrection. Assuming that the anti-Chalcedonian version was also addressed to the Trinity, pro-Chalcedonians erroneously accused their opponents of attributing the incarnation, death, and resurrection to God the Father—cf. the Theopascite controversy. The anti-Chalcedonian tradition, which maintains that Joseph of Arimathea and Nicodemius heard the hymn as they were taking the body of Jesus to the tomb (Mk. 15:42–6; Lk. 23:50–3; Jn. 19:38–42), is clear in that the hymn is addressed to God the Son. This is the basis for *Golgotha*, the final hymn chanted in the Coptic rite of Good Friday. See the Syrian writer Mōshē bar Kēphā's (d. 903 CE) *Commentary on the Liturgy*; Ibn Sabbā', *al-Jawhara al-nafīsa*, §68; cf. Robert F. Taft, "Trisagion," *Oxford Dictionary of Byzantium* 3:2121. E.M. Ishaq's "Trisagion" (*CoptEncyc* 7:2278–9) provides an accurate description of the hymn's modern and medieval usage, but is inaccurate in discussing its origins.
48. *P.Ryl.Copt.*39, dated to the 10–11th century. The verso contains an earlier Arabic text.
49. *P.Lond.Copt.*I.154–60; *P.Ryl.Copt.*19, 22, 25, 26–36; also see C.H. Roberts and B. Capelle, *An Early Euchologium: The Dêr-Balizeh Papyrus Enlarged and Reedited* (Louvain, 1949).
50. *P.Lond.Copt.*I.514 is a tenth-century all-Greek liturgical text commemorating Patriarch Khaīl III (881–909 CE). Also see, C. Detlef G. Müller, "La position de l'Égypte chrétienne dans l'orient Ancient," *Muséon* 92 (1979), 121.
51. *P.Ryl.Copt.*28–33, 58. Later, the Gradual Psalm was only chanted in Coptic; cf. Zanetti, "Bohairic Liturgical Manuscripts," 74.
52. See Burmester, "Greek Kirugmata." The orthography of Greek words is more diverse in Bohairic texts.
53. Ibn Sabbā', *al-Jawhara al-Nafīsa*, §80 (pg. 236); CMR 4:918–23. Earlier, at the beginning of the twelfth century CE, the letter of appointment of the patriarch was read to the congregation in Greek, Coptic, and Arabic (HP III.1:7/186v). By the late eleventh century, the fact that Kyrillus II blessed the congregation in Coptic was noteworthy (HP II.3:366/179v).
54. Cf. David J. Wasserstein, "Why did Arabic Succeed where Greek Failed? Language Change in the Near East after Muhammad," *Scripta Classica Israelica* 22 (2003), 257–72.
55. T. Orlandi, "Literature, Coptic" 5:1455–6.

56. This conservatism discouraged the composition of new biblical and theological commentaries, not the language in which these works were composed.
57. Rufus of Shotep, *Homilies*; John of Shmūn, *Encomium on St. Mark* and *Encomium on St. Antony*; T. Orlandi, "John of Shmun," *CoptEncyc* 5:1369.
58. Rufus of Shotep, *Homilies*, Intro. pg. 32–3.
59. I believe that P. Luisier's redating of Rufus' commentaries to the fourth rather than the sixth century (Review of Mark Sheridan, *Rufus of Shotep: Homilies on the Gospel's of Matthew and Luke* (Rome, 1998), OCP 64 (1998), 471–3) has been adequately addressed in M. Sheridan's "Influence of Origen on Coptic Exegesis in the Sixth Century: the Case of Rufus of Shotep," in *Origeniana Octava: Origen and the Alexandrian Tradition*, ed. L. Perrone *et al.* (Louvain, 2003), 1023–33, at 1032–3.
60. This seems to have been initiated by Rufus of Shotep.
61. HCME 14b, 35; Georg Graf, *Ein Reformversuch innerhalb der koptischen Kirche im zwölften Jahrhundert* (Paderborn, 1923); S. Khalil Samir, "Vie et oeuvre de Marc ibn al-Qumbar," in *Christianisme d'Égypte. Hommages à René-George Coquin* (Louvain, 1995), 123–58; Mark N. Swanson, "Ibn al-Qunbar," *Coptica* 5 (2006), 150–72; Vincent Frederick, "Murqus ibn Qanbar," *CoptEncyc* 6:1699–1700; see Chapter Four, ns. 126–7.
62. cf. T. Orlandi, "John of Shmun," *CoptEncyc* 5:1369; and René-Georges Coquin and S. Khalil Samir, "Constantine of Asyuṭ," *CoptEncyc* 2:590–3; S. Khalil Samir, "Arabic Sources for Early Egyptian Christianity," in *Roots of Egyptian Christianity*, ed. Pearson and Goehring.
63. *P.Qurra*.2.18, dated 91/709, is an Arabic text written by Basil the scribe. Another text, dated 91/709–10, was written by Ibn Labnan, a convert to Islam: see *P.Qurra*.3.17–18, n. 18; Yusuf Ragib, "Lettres nouvelles de Qurra b. Šarīk," JNES 40.3 (1981), 173–87 (§3 line 10 and n.14). In general, see A. Papaconstantinou, ed., *The Multilingual Experience in Egypt from the Ptolemies to the Abbasids* (Burlington, 2010), and ns. 80, 81, and 130 below.
64. Wilson Bishai, "The Transition from Coptic to Arabic," *Muslim World* 53.2 (1963), 149; idem, "Notes on the Coptic Substratum in Egyptian Arabic," JAOS 80 (1960), 229; idem, "Coptic Lexical Influence on Egyptian Arabic," JNES 23 (1964), 47, agrees that bilingualism was not widespread in Egypt. He believes that Muslims became numerically dominant due to immigration from abroad and a declining Coptic population, but he is vague as to how the Coptic population decreased, citing only economic hardship as a factor (which would have led to conversion). Samuel Rubenson, "The Transition from Coptic to Arabic," *Égypte/Monde arabe* 27–28 (1996), 79 and n. 8, states that "the simultaneous use of Coptic and Arabic in different areas of a person's life would have been a normal phenomenon." But in the footnote it appears that his analysis is based on a misunderstanding of Bishai's point.
65. Studies of Arabic loanwords in late Coptic are extremely lacking, but see Tonio Sebastian Richter, "*O.Crum AD. 15* and the Emergence of Arabic Words in

Coptic Legal Documents," in *Papyrology and the History of Early Islamic Egypt*, ed. Sijpesteijn and Sundelin; idem, "Arabische Lehnworte und Formeln in Koptischen Rechtsurkunden," JJP 31 (2001), 75–98; idem, "Coptic, Arabic Loan-words in," *Encyclopedia of Arabic Language and Linguistics* (Leiden, 2006), I:495–501; Werner Vycichl, "Vocabulary Copto-Arabic," *CoptEncyc* 8:215; Rodolphe Kasser, "Vocabulary Copto-Greek," *CoptEncyc* 8:215–22.

66. Some estimate the percentage of Greek loanwords in Coptic texts to be as high as 25%.

67. Sofia Torallas Tovar, "Egyptian Lexical Interference in the Greek of Byzantine and Early Islamic Egypt," in *Papyrology and the History*, ed. Sijpesteijn and Sundelin; S.G. Kapsomenos, "Das Griechische in Ägypten," *Museum Helveticum* 10.3–4 (1953), 248–63; Francis Thomas Gignac, "Phonology of the Greek of Egypt, Influence of Coptic on the," *CoptEncyc* 8:186–8.

68. Bishai notes that Turkish had a much greater effect on Egyptian Arabic than Coptic. For the effects of Arabic on Coptic, see Adel Sidrous, "L'influence arabe sur la linguistique copte," in *History of the Language Sciences*, ed. S. Auroux *et al.* (New York, 2000).

69. See Sarah G. Thomason, *Language Contact: An Introduction* (Washington D.C., 2001), chs. 4, 9; Chris Reintges, "Code-Mixing Strategies in Coptic Egyptian," *Lingua Aegyptia* 9 (2001), 193–237.

70. W. Bishai, "Transition," 149, and "Coptic Lexical Influence," states that there are 109 valid Coptic loanwords in Egyptian Arabic. A much higher number is claimed by E.M. Ishaq, "Egyptian Arabic vocabulary, Coptic influence on," *CoptEncyc* 8:112–8. Also see P. Behnstedt, "Weitere koptische Lehnwörter im Ägyptisch-Arabischen," *Die Welt des Orients* 12 (1981), 81–98. More recently, F. Corriente, "Coptic Loanwords of Egyptian Arabic in Comparison with the Parallel Case of Romance Loanwords in Andalusi Arabic, with the True Egyptian Etymon of Al-Andalus," *Collectanea Christiana Orientalia* 5 (2008), 59–123—enumerated 250 words. Whatever the actual number of loanwords may be, they constitute a relatively minute percentage of the Arabic vocabulary in circulation. Moreover, all these lists—as the scholars themselves usually point out—retain many terms that were never popular outside of limited geographic regions, scores relate to agriculture, while others are simply obscure or limited to ecclesiastical usage.

71. As in HP I.3:386; *P.Ryl.Copt*.214; *P.Fay.Monast*.I.19.

72. See *P.Lond.Copt*.I.580, 584, 662, 664, 666, cf. 587, 591, 598, 599, 612, 631, 660, 668. Converts under Umayyad rule typically kept their patronym, while under the ʿAbbasids they took Arabic/Islamic names; see the previous chapter.

73. *CPR*.XVI.4 is an Arabic personal letter from Yazīd ibn Aslam to Buṭsīr (ПЄТОСІРІС) dated 1–2/7–8 c. It reads as a cordial letter between friends. There is no mention of whether or not Buṭsīr was a convert. *CPR*.XVI.9, dated to the same period, was written to a convert.

74. Kindī, *Wulāt*, 54; HP I.3:305: al-Aṣbagh sought out books that they might be read to him: "he read the Paschal Epistles (*al-arṭistīkat* < ἑορταστικαί) in

order to see whether or not the Muslims were insulted in them" (cf. *Chronicle of 1234*/History of Dionysios, 263, Palmer §90). On the *artịstīkat*s of the Coptic church, see Joseph Moris Filtas, "Rasa'l al-arṭistīkat tarīkhiyyan - ʿaqīdiyyan," in *Actes de la 7e rencontre des amis du patrimoine arabe-chrétien*, ed. Wadiʿ Abullīf (Cairo, 1999), 35–52; Alberto Camplani, "Coptic Fragments from a Festal Letter of the Late Sixth Century (John Rylands Library, Coptic Suppl. N. 47–48): Damian or Eulogius?" *Coptic Studies*, ed. Immerzeel *et al.*, I:317–27; several are in Anon., *Iʿtirāf al-abā'* (Cairo, 2002).

75. HP I.3:375, also see Chapter Eleven below.
76. HP I.4:639.
77. "Arabization" and "Islamization" are defined as separate cultural processes in Chapter Six.
78. See *P.Ryl.Copt.*324, 346.
79. A. Mingana, "An ancient Syriac translation of the Ḳur'ān exhibiting new verses and variants," *Bulletin of the John Rylands Library* 9 (1925), 188–235; J.D. Pearson, "Ḳur'ān," EI^2 5:430b-432b.
80. See Y. Raghib, "Quatres papyrus arabes d'Edfou," *Annales Islamologiques* 14 (1978), 1–14. The second text, dated 222/837, is from Edfū and was witnessed in Arabic by the convert Afyaḥ ibn Buṭrus.
81. *P.Qurra*.3.17–18, n.18. Al-Ṣabāḥ was a convert who likely benefited from his language skills. He was appointed over the tax revenue of Fayyūm at the end of the eighth century; see *Chrest.Khoury*.II.26 dated 180/796.
82. Cf. the incident in HP I.4:639, see ns. 36 and 37 above.
83. *Chrest.Khoury*.I.68.
84. For a later period and more generally, see Gary Leiser, "The Madrasa and the Islamizaiton of the Middle East the Case of Egypt," JARCE 22 (1985), 29–47; G. Makdisi, *Rise of Colleges: Institutions of Learning in Islam and the West* (Edinburgh, 1981); idem, *The Rise of Humanism in Classical Islam and the Christian West* (Edinburgh, 1990); Michael Chamberlain, *Knowledge and Social Practice in Medieval Damascus, 1190–1350*, New Edition (Cambridge, 2002).
85. *Apocalypse of Samuel*, 379; translated below.
86. Early (pre-Genizah) documentary papyri from the Delta are extremely scars. Only a few ostraca and texts have survived (e.g. *P.Khalili*.I).
87. Rubenson, "Transition from Coptic to Arabic," 77–91; idem, "Translating the Tradition: Some Remarks on the Arabization of the Patristic Heritage in Egypt," *Medieval Encounters* 2.1 (1996), 4–14; also see Samir, "Arabic Sources"; cf. Tonio Sebastian Richter, "Greek, Coptic, and the 'Language of the Hijra': the Rise and Decline of the Coptic Language in Late Antique and Medieval Egypt," in *From Hellenism to Islam*, ed. H.M. Cotton *et al.* (Cambridge, 2009).
88. Completed prior to 1028 CE, GCAL 2:320–1. Note that Abū Ṣulḥ's father's name, "ʿAbdallāh," is also Arabic. Arabic and Arabized Christian names were commonplace in the Delta by the fourth/tenth century.
89. Christodoulos, *Canons*; those of his successor were likewise in Arabic, see Cyril II, *Canons*.

90. *Itirāf al-abā'* (Cairo, 2002).
91. See Chapter One.
92. R.-G. Coquin and A.S. Atiya, "Synaxarion, Copto-Arabic," *CoptEncyc* 7:2171–90; Vincent Frederick, "Buṭrus Sawirus al-Jamīl," *CoptEncyc* 2:431; Gawdat Gabra, "Untersuchungen Zum Difnar der Koptischen Kirche I: Quellenlage, Forschungsgeschichte und künftige Aufgaben," BSAC 35 (1996), 37–52 and 37 (1998), 49–68.
93. De Lacy O'Leary, ed., *The Difnar (Antiphonarium) of the Coptic Church*, 3 vols. (London, 1926–30); Maria Cramer and Martin Krause, ed./trans., *Das koptische Antiphonar* (Münster, 2008), dated 892 CE, this is the earliest extant manuscript of the work.
94. Monks were no more competent in the Coptic language than the average individual (Lennart Sundelin had elaborated on this at the 2002 annual MESA meeting). Still, monasteries continued to produce all-Coptic liturgical texts (and *Psalmudīs*) long after Coptic ceased functioning as a living language. Today, many monks still view preservation of the language as their duty. One priest informed me that during his customary forty days in the monastery after ordination, the monk assigned to teach him the liturgy instructed him to always pray the Institution Narrative in Coptic or the liturgy would be invalid; this is certainly a marginal perspective, however.
95. Some of the *Synaksār*'s entries provide highly reliable accounts, while others enshrined spurious traditions; e.g. the entry for John the Baptist (Ba'ūna 30), which is based on a historically and biblically confused apocryphal narrative: see *P.Ryl.Copt.*72 and F. Robinson's *Coptic Apocryphal Gospels* (Cambridge, 1896).
96. In the *Canons* of Cyril III, written in 1238, the Seventh Question discusses a priest in a large town who, "does not know Arabic, and makes many mistakes in Coptic." The pressing need for Arabic-literate clergy and declining fluency in Coptic are unmistakable. The use of the Coptic script to write Arabic (cf. *karshuni* in Syria), a phenomenon observed in Egypt over centuries, gained some momentum but the practice never prevailed. On such texts, see Joshua Blau, "Some Observations on a Middle Arabic Egyptian Text in Coptic Characters," in *Studies in Middle Arabic and Its Judaeo-Arabic Variety*, ed. idem (Jerusalem, 1988).
97. Henri Munier, *La Scala copte 44 de la Bibliotheque nationale de Paris* (Cairo, 1930); Arnold van Lantschoot, *Un Précurseur d'Athanase Kircher: Thomas Obicini et la scala Vat. copte 71* (Louvain, 1948); Werner Vycichl, "Sullam," *CoptEncyc* 8:204–7; idem, "Muqaddimah," *CoptEncyc* 8:166–9; Adel Sidarus, "Medieval Coptic Grammars in Arabic: The Coptic Muqaddimāt," *Journal of Coptic Studies* 3 (2001), 63–79; idem, "Coptic Lexicography in the Middle Age: The Coptic Arabic Scalae," in *The Future of Coptic Studies*, ed. R. McL. Wilson (Leiden, 1978).
98. S. Rubenson, "Transition," 85.

99. The later development of *nomocanons* is an altogether different phenomenon; cf. Chapter Seven below; C. de Clercq, "Copte (droit canonique)," *Dictionnaire de Droit canonique* 4 (1944), 594–601; René-Georges Coquin, "Nomocanons, Copto-Arabic," *CoptEncyc* 6:1799; F.J. Cöln, "The Nomocanonical Literature of the Copto-Arabic Church of Alexandria," *The Ecclesiastical Review* 56 (1917), 113–41; Wilhelm Riedel, *Die Kirchenrechtsquellen des Patriarchats Alexandrien* (Leipzig, 1900; 1968).

100. Zanetti, "Bohairic Liturgical Manuscripts," 66 n. 4, 67; idem, "Liturgy at Wadi al-Natrun," in *Christianity and Monasticism*, ed. Mikhail and Moussa, 122; Rubenson, "Transition," 82.

101. HP II.2:204/152v, cf. 192/150v.

102. F. Nau's dated the tract to the first half of the eighth century. Both Christian Décobert and Francisco Javier Martinez have dated it to the ninth century, while John Iskander prefers an early eleventh-century date; Zaborowski favors a later date still. Van Lent and Papaconstantinou favor a late tenth early eleventh century date. Cf. CMR 2:746–7; F. Nau, "Note sur el'Apocalypse de Samuel," ROC 20 (1915–1917), 405–7; C. Décobert, "Sur L'Arabisation et L'Islamisation de l'Egypte mediévale," *Itineraires d'Egypte*, 287; F.J. Martinez's Introduction to *Apocalypse of Athanasios*, pg. 267 n. 53; J. Iskander, "Islamization in Medieval Egypt;" J. van Lent, "Nineteen Muslim Kings;" A. Papaconstantinou, "'They Shall Speak the Arabic Language and Take Pride in it': Reconsidering the Fate of Coptic after the Arab Conquest," *Muséon* 120.3–4 (2007), 273–99; J.R. Zaborowski, "From Coptic to Arabic in Medieval Egypt," *Medieval Encounters* 14.1 (2008), 15–40; cf. J. van Lent's passing comments in Grypeou *et al.* eds., *Encounter of Eastern Christianity with Early Islam*, 310.

103. J. Iskander's argument for an early eleventh-century date, though certainly not without merit, relays on some questionable evidence, such as the numerical value of al-Ḥākim's name (= 666), which is a frequent apocryphal *topoi* (the names "Muhammad" and "Marwan" likewise have the same numerical value).

104. See n. 114 below and Chapter One, above.

105. *Apocalypse of Samuel*, 379, 380, 384. The author was particularly annoyed with the use of Arabic in the sanctuary (*haykal*)—that is, during the liturgy.

106. *Apocalypse of Samuel*, 381, 384, 388.

107. On the Arabization of names, see the last section of this chapter.

108. *Apocalypse of Samuel*, 380. This is said to take place in Upper Egypt.

109. *Apocalypse of Samuel*, 380.

110. *Apocalypse of Samuel*, 379, 380; cf. Ps.-Sawīrus, *K. al-Īḍāḥ*, 10, 161.

111. Edward Pococke completed a Latin translation of *Naẓm al-jawhar* (*Annals*) in 1658 CE (PG 111:889–1232). John Selden had completed an earlier translation in 1642 CE.

112. In Syria, similar texts were translated into Arabic, which speaks against the assumption that genre or audience alone prevented the translation of such texts into Coptic.

113. E.g. the Bohairic *Martyrdom of John of Phanijōit* (d. 1209 CE) and the *Triadon* hymn, which was composed (or translated?) in Sahidic in 722/1322; Peter Nagel, *Das Triadon: ein sahidisches Lehrqedicht des 14. Jahrhundert* (Halle, 1983); Leslie S.B. MacCoull, "The *Triadon*: An English Translation," *Greek Orthodox Theological Review* 42 (1997), 83–148; M. Chaine, "Le Triadon: son auterur, la date de sa composition," BSAC 2 (1936), 9–24.
114. The attribution to Sawīrus and the title under which the text published are both erroneous: *Kitāb al-dūrr al-thamīn fī īḍāḥ al-dīn*, ed. M. Jirjis (Cairo, 1925; 1971; 1992).
115. Pseudo-Sawīrus, *Kitāb al-īḍāḥ*, 10, my translation. The anonymous author of this work may have been familiar with the *Apocalypse of Samuel*, as the language of the two texts, in this passage, is very similar.
116. Pseudo-Sawīrus, *Kitāb al-īḍāḥ*, 161, my translation.
117. HP I.1:17, my translation. The Fourth Preface (HP I.1:22) states that translations were made from Coptic, but there is no mention of Greek.
118. Athanasios of Qūṣ, *Qilādat at-taḥrīr*, pg. 245.
119. *P.Teshlot*; L.S.B. MacCoull, "The Teshlot Papyri and the Survival of Documentary Coptic in the Eleventh Century," OCP 55 (1989), 201–6; Tonio Sebastian Richter, "Spatkoptische Rechtsurkunden neu bearbeitet: BM Or.4917 (15) und P.Med.Copt. inv. 69.69," JJP 29 (1999), 85–95. The corpus has been edited by Green and again by Richter (see bibliography, *P.Teshlot*). Green did not provide any Gregorian dates. The dates glossed by MacCoull are off by fourteen years, as the Hijra is a lunar, not a solar calendar. Richter provides accurate dates.
120. *P.Lond.Copt.*I.xiv, and Chapters Seven and Ten.
121. Green misread the title as "to Agathon from Soucine." See Michael H. Thung, "An Arabic Letter of the Rijksmuseum van Oudheden, Leiden," *Oudheidkundige Mededelingen der Rijksmuseum van Oudheiden* 76 (1996), 63–8. I am thankful to Lennart Sundelin for bringing this article to my attention.
122. Christian Gaubert and Jean-Michael Mouton, "Présentation des archives d'une famille copte du Fayoum à l'époque fatimide," in *Coptic Studies*, ed. Immerzeel *et al.*, I:505–17; also discussed in Chapter Seven.
123. In *P.Fay.Monast.*I.19 (dated 335/946), the Arabic text was translated (*turjam*) to the Christian man. The other two documents included by Abbott do not contain this clause.
124. *P.Cair.Arab.*II.73.
125. Ecclesiastical usage favors "translation," but the term's meaning in legal texts needs further study.
126. *P.Cair.Arab.*I.41.14–15; cf. the same clause in all-Coptic texts, e.g. *P.KRU* 12, 13, 66, 77, 68, 106.
127. E.g. *P.Cair.Arab.*I.54, 58, II.73–5, 86, 119, 122, 138.
128. *P.Cair.Arab.*II.114, dated 241/855–6. He may have been a convert (see also *Chrest.Khoury.*I.47), but by that late date converts tended to adopt new Arabic, if not explicitly Islamic names. See Chapter Four above.

129. *P.Cair.Arab.*II.127, dated 247/861, four Christians witness and sign in Arabic; II.132 dated 330/942, III.198, dated 246/860–1, was written by David the treasurer (*qusṭāl*). *P.Prag.Arab.*10.3–4 date 322/934; 61.3 dated 3/9 century. Also Būlus ibn Isma'īl and Yūsuf ibn Isma'īl may be cited as examples, although they were probably converts to Islam. See *P.Fay.Monast.*3.16–17.
130. *P.Ryl.Copt.*156, 285, 306; Klass A. Worp, "P.Vindob.G39743: Ein Neuer Rashid-Papyrus," ZPE 58 (1985), 83–5.
131. *P.Ryl.Copt.*214 mentions ⲚⲒϬⲈϨ ⲠⲦⲎⲢⲔⲞⲨⲘⲀⲚ (*mutarjim*), "Nicheh the translator."
132. Cf. the slightly later *P.Ryl.Copt.*234 and 243.
133. "'Abd Allāh" is the Arabic equivalent of the Coptic "Shenoute." The popular etymology of the name (Shenoute = "son of God") is inaccurate, it should be, "servant of God."
134. *P.Prag.Arab.*32.21, dated 4–5/9–10, documents Abū al-Khayr the deacon and baker; cf. *P.Cair.Arab.*VI.370 and *P.Ryl.Copt.*309, discussed above.
135. Also see *P.Cair.Arab.*III.199, dated 346/958; and III.202, dated 320/932–3, which is a poll tax list; thus 'Abd al-Khāliq must have been a Christian.

Chapter 6 The Long Eighth Century: A Cultural Bridge

1. Cf. the reaction of Patriarch Sophronios in mid-seventh century Jerusalem, with the schemes in the *Apocalypse of Pseudo-Methodios* and, in Egypt, the *Apocalypse of Athanasios*.
2. E.g. N. Levtzion, "Toward a Comparative Study of Islamization," in *Conversion to Islam*, ed. idem; Georges C. Anawati, "Factors and Effects of Arabization and Islamization in Medieval Egypt and Syria," in *Islam and Cultural Change in the Middle Ages*, ed. Speros Vryonis Jr. (Wiesbaden, 1975); Sam I. Gellens, "Egypt, Islamization of," *CoptEncyc* 3:936–42; G.R. Hawting, *The First Dynasty of Islam: The Umayyad Caliphate AD 661–750*, 2nd ed. (London, 2000), esp. 1–9. Hawting (pg. 1) defines "Islamization" as referring to "both the extension of the area under Muslim rule and to the acceptance of Islam as their religion by peoples of different faiths."
3. Hawting (*First Dynasty*, 9–11) defines "Arabization" as a cultural phenomenon.
4. Defining Arabization as a linguistic rather than a religious process allows for a contextual discussion of the Arabic versions of Jewish and Christian scriptures, and the processes by which the Greek, Coptic, and Syriac patristic traditions were translated into Arabic.
5. See Ulrich Haarmann, "Regional Sentiment in Medieval Islamic Egypt," BSOAS 43.1 (1980), especially pgs. 55–66; idem, "Medieval Muslim Perceptions of Pharaonic Egypt," in *Ancient Egyptian Literature: History and Forms*, ed. A. Loprieno (Leiden, 1996), 605–27; Michael Cook, "Pharaonic History in Medieval Egypt," *Studia Islamica* 57 (1983), 67–103; Joseph

Schacht, *An Introduction to Islamic Law* (Oxford, 1964), e.g. 26–7, 49. Haarmann ("Regional Sentiments," 60) and Schacht employ "Islamization" in a manner consistent with the definition employed here.

6. Oleg Grabar uses the term in this sense in much of his *Formation of Islamic Art*, 2nd rev. ed. (New Haven, 1987), e.g. 54, but he is not always consistent.
7. See Abū ʿUbayd, *Amwāl*, §§47, 49, cf. §§140, 198, 223; and Cl. Cahen, "Djizya," EI^2 2:559a-562a—for the suggestion that the last clause is a later addition: *wa hum ṣaghirūn*, "while they are little/small/humiliated." Under Fāṭimid rule, the *jizya* was paid to an official seated on a high chair (Saleh, "Government Relations," 107), a manifestation of the literal reading.
8. Those forbidding harassment include Abū Yūsuf, *Kharāj*, 123, 125; Abū ʿUbayd, *Amwāl*, §§110–11, 114–20. Traditions that advocate discrimination tend to date to the fifth/eleventh century and beyond: see Arthur S. Tritton, *The Caliphs and their non-Muslim Subjects* (London, 1930; 1970), 227. Still, some forms of discrimination are attested much earlier; see Abū ʿUbayd, *Amwāl*, §§134–40; J. Schacht, *Islamic Law*, 131.
9. Abū Yūsuf, *Kharāj*, 120, 122; Yaḥyā ibn Ādam, *Kharāj*, §§36, 37, 38, 33, 45, 206, 210; Abū ʿUbayd, *Amwāl*, §§62–75, 1695–1721.
10. *P.Strasb.*660; *P.Laur.* III.112; *CPR* XXII.1, cf. A. Papaconstantinou, "Administering the Early Islamic Empire: Insights from the Papyri," in *Money, Power and Politics in Early Islamic Syria: A Review of Current Debates*, ed. J. Haldon (Burlington, 2010); N. Gonis, "Two Poll-Tax Receipts from Early Islamic Egypt," ZPE 131 (2000), 150–4; idem., "Five Tax Receipts from Early Islamic Egypt," ZPE 143 (2003), 149–57; Simonsen, *Caliphal Taxation*, 85–6, 127; Kosei Morimoto, *The Fiscal Administration of Egypt in the Early Islamic Period* (Koyoto, 1981), 64–6.
11. *CPR* IX.52.
12. D.C. Dennett, *Conversion and the Poll Tax*; Simonsen, *Caliphal Taxation*, 85–8, 99; Hossein Modarressi Tabātabā'i, *Kharāj in Islamic Taxation* (London, 1983), 87; cf. *O.Medin.HabuCopt*. pgs. 28–9.
13. See the Qurra papyri and K. Morimoto, *Fiscal Administration*, ch. 2, pgs 41–7, 66–82; C. Wickham, *Framing the Early Middle Ages*, 134–7.
14. N. Gonis, "Reconsidering Some Fiscal Documents from Early Islamic Egypt," ZPE (2001), 225–8; discusses and definitively dates SB XVI 13018—the first tax-note issued to an individual—to 95/714.
15. On *kharāj*, see Qur'ān 23:72, and, according to some readings, 18:94. For the diverse meanings of *kharāj* in documentary sources and among the legal schools, see Tabātabā'i, *Kharāj in Islamic Taxation*, 1–3, 87–96. The term is common in literary sources but rare in papyri. In Umayyad papyri, it is usually referred to as "*jizyat arḍ*" (as opposed to *jizyat ra's*), an expression that may have been unique to Egypt (Morimoto, *Fiscal Administration*, 136–7). *Jizya* is identified in Umayyad papyri as *jizyat ra's*, and later as *jāliya*; see the relatively late examples in P.M. Sijpesteijn, "Shaping a Muslim State," documents 22,

23, 33; Morimoto, *Fiscal Administration*, 136, 176; cf. *Chronicle of Zuqnīn*, Harrak pg. 147 (year 691–2 CE).

16. Cf. Simonsen, *Caliphal Taxation*, 80, 99, 130; Morimoto, *Fiscal Administration*, 61–2; N. Gonis, "Reconsidering Some Fiscal Documents," 226–7. It is doubtful that the average individual viewed the *jizya* as a payment in lieu of military service or for protection, as later jurists claim. Indeed, *sūra* 9:29 does not cite either reason for its collection. By the first quarter of the eighth century, most Arabs did not serve in the army either.
17. See A. Noth, *Early Arabic Historical Tradition*; C.F. Robinson, *Empire and Elites*, esp. ch. 1.
18. F.M. Donner, *Narratives of Islamic Origins*, 174–83.
19. Ibn ʿAbd al-Ḥakam, *Futūḥ*, 79, presents the conquest as the consequence of prayer.
20. John of Nikiou, *Chronicle*, §120.33; §121.2; cf. §121.7–8; HP I.2:228–9; Michael the Syrian, *Chronicle*, 11.3; *Life of Samuel of Qalamun*; A.J. Butler, *Arab Conquest of Egypt*; R.G. Hoyland, *Seeing Islam*; A.M. Guenther, "Christian Experience and Interpretation." Also see J.C. Lamoreaux, "Early Eastern Christian Responses to Islam," in *Medieval Christian Perceptions of Islam*, ed. J.V. Tolan. This is an important survey, but it overemphasizes the differences between pro- and anti-Chalcedonian responses at the expense of diminishing their commonalities, and does not read early Islamic sources critically.
21. This is a later view. Seventh-century Egyptian *pro*-Chalcedonian literature is lacking.
22. See Donner, *Narratives*, 171–3.
23. This opinion eventually prevailed, but various notions were in circulation. Some wanted to define the land based on the water source it relied upon, others sought to base it on the religion of the landowner; hence, the status of the land would change upon the owner's conversion. Eventually the Ḥanafī opinion prevailed. Land was defined as *kharāj* or *ʿushr* irrespective of the religion of the owner or the water source from which it was irrigated. See Tabātabā'i, *Kharāj in Islamic Taxation*, 143–4, 110–11, 122–36.
24. A. Noth, "Some Remarks on the 'Nationalization' of Conquered Lands at the Time of the Umayyads," in *Land Tenure and Social Transformation in the Middle East*, ed. Tarif Khalidi (Beirut, 1984), 224.
25. On *fay'*, see Qur'ān 59:6–8; Tabātabā'i, *Kharāj in Islamic Taxation*, 11–24; F. Løkkegaard, "Fay'," EI^2 2:869a-870a.
26. Ibn ʿAbd al-Ḥakam, *Futūḥ*, 84–90; cf. al-Balādhurī, *Futūḥ*, 213–4, 216; D.R. Hill, *The Termination of Hostilities in the Early Arab Conquests A.D. 634–656* (New York, 1971), 34–53.
27. For *ṣulḥ* traditions, see Ibn ʿAbd al-Ḥakam, *Futūḥ*, 84–5, and Abū ʿUbayd, *Amwāl*, §385 (cf. §387) transmit a *ṣulḥ* tradition complete with witnesses and stipulations. A major transmitter of this *ṣulḥ* tradition is al-Layth ibn Saʿd, see Abū ʿUbayd, *Amwāl*, §392. For *ʿanwa* traditions, see Ibn ʿAbd al-Ḥakam,

Futūḥ, 88–90; Abū ʿUbayd, *Amwāl*, §§127 (cf. 277), 380–7, stipulates that Egypt was conquered without *ʿaqd* or *ʿahd*.

28. Albrecht Noth, "Zum Verhältnis von Kalifaler Zentralgewalt und Provinzen in umayyadischer Zeit: Die 'Ṣulḥ'-'ʿAnwa'-Traditionen für Ägypten und den Iraq," *Die Welt des Islams* 14 (1973), 150–62; ibid, "Some Remarks," in *Land Tenure*, 223–8; idem with L.I. Conrad, *Early Arabic Historical Tradition*, 48–9; Werner Schmucker, *Untersuchungen zu einigen wichtigen bodenrechtlichen Konsequenzen der islamischen Eroberungsbewegung* (Bonn, 1972), 45–7.
29. Ibn ʿAbd al-Ḥakam, *Futūḥ*, 143; al-Kindī, *Wulāt*, 76–7; Morimoto, *Fiscal Administration*, 182–3; 153, 225.
30. Morimoto, *Fiscal Administration*, 183–4.
31. Ibn ʿAbd al-Ḥakam, *Futūḥ*, 88; Abū ʿUbayd, *Amwāl*, §§488–502.
32. Ibn ʿAbd al-Ḥakam, *Futūḥ*, 89, 90; Abū ʿUbayd, *Amwāl*, §380, cf. §§368, 467; al-Kindī, *Wulāt*, 32; al-Ṭabarī, *Ta'rīkh*, I.2584; A. Noth, "Zum Verhältnis," 155 n. 1, 3.
33. On taking a fifth, *khums*, see Qur'ān 8:41 and Tabātabā'i, *Kharāj in Islamic Taxation*, 132–3.
34. Khalīfa ibn Khayyaṭ, *Ta'rīkh*, I.136.11–14. Also al-Balādhurī, *Futūḥ*, 217; cf. al-Kindī, *Wulāt*, 32, though concerned with "Barbarians," this reference may provide the origin for the tradition. One is tempted to name Ṭarābulūs as the nexus of this specific tradition.
35. Pipes, "Mawlas: Fred Slaves," 149.
36. See Abū Yūsuf, *Kharāj*, 127, 138–49; see Chapter Ten below.
37. See Eutychios, *Naẓm al-jawhar*, II.39, 42.
38. Although granted various liberties, non-Muslims were clearly not treated as equals. See Abū Yūsuf, *Kharāj*, 164, 166; Yaḥyā ibn Ādam, *Kharāj*, §224.
39. See Fred M. Donner, "The Formation of the Islamic State," JAOS 106 (1986), 289–93, and C.F. Robinson, *ʿAbd al-Malik* (Oxford, 2005) on the political implications and ideological grounding of some of the evidence discussed below.
40. M.G.S. Hodgson, *Venture of Islam*, I: 247–51, aptly labeled the Umayyad opponents as "piety-minded."
41. H.A.R. Gibb, "ʿAbd al-Malik b. Marwān," EI^2 1:76a-77b; Hawting, *First Dynasty*, ch. 5; C.H. Becker, "ʿAbd Allāh b. ʿAbd al-Malik b. Marwān," EI^2 1:42a; C.F. Robinson, *ʿAbd al-Malik*.
42. See Warren C. Schultz, "The Monetary History of Egypt, 642–1517," in *The Cambridge History of Egypt*, vol. 1, ed. C.F. Petry; O. Grabar, *Formation of Islamic Art*, 89–91. This reform made the weights and measures of al-Ḥijāz standard throughout the caliphate. See G.R. Hawting, "The Umayyads and the Hijaz," *Proceedings of the Seminar for Arabian Studies* 2 (1972), 39–46. For early glass weights, see A.H.Morton, *A Catalogue of Early Islamic Glass Stamps* (London, 1985), and P.Balog, *Umayyad, 'Abbasid, and Tûlûnid Glass Weights and Vessel Stamps* (New York, 1976). On Islamic coins, see the extensive bibliographies

and links at The American Numismatic Society <http://numismatics.org> and the Islamic Coins Group <www.islamiccoinsgroup.50g.com>.

43. Clive Foss, *Arab-Byzantine Coins* (Washington D.C., 2008), ch. 11–12.
44. J.R. Phillips, "The Byzantine Bronze Coins of Alexandria in the Seventh Century," *Numismatic Chronicle*, 7th ser, 2 (1962), 225–41; George C. Miles, "Early Islamic Bronze Coinage of Egypt," in *Centennial Publications of the American Numismatic Society*, ed. H. Inghold (New York, 1958), 471–502; Jere L. Bacharach and H.A. Awad, "The Early Islamic Bronze Coinage of Egypt: Additions," in *Near Eastern Numismatics, Iconography, Epigraphy and History: Studies in Honor of George C. Miles*, ed. D. Kouymjian (Beirut, 1974), 185–92; Lidia Domaszewicz and Michael L. Bates, "Copper Coinage of Egypt in the Seventh Century," in *Fustat Finds*, ed. J.L. Bacharach (Cairo, 2002).
45. John Walker, *A Catalogue of the Arab-Sassanian Coins* [*in the British Museum*] (London, 1941); idem, *A Catalogue of the Arab-Byzantine and Post-Reform Umaiyad Coins* [*in the British Museum*] (London, 1956).
46. An equivalent to the modern, "This note is legal tender."
47. C. Foss, *Arab-Byzantine Coins*, 69–74.
48. *48.* Balādhurī, *Futūḥ*, 466. At least nine Companions were still alive in Medina: see Khalīfa ibn Khayyāṭ *Ta'rīkh*, I:349, 357, 380, 382, 398, 399; II:8.
49. Balādhurī, *Futūḥ*, 467; al-Maqrīzī, *Khiṭaṭ*, I.571; al-Ya'qūbī, *Ta'rīkh*, II.348; *Chronicle of 1234/History of Dionysios*, Palmer §135 and *Chronicle of 819*, AG 1008; P. Grierson, "The Monetary Reforms of 'Abd al-Malik," JESHO 3 (1960), 241–64; G.C. Miles, "Early Islamic Bronze Coinage," 471–502; J.L. Bacharach and H.A. Awad, "Early Islamic Bronze Coinage of Egypt: Additions," 185–92; M.L. Bates. "History, Geography, and Numismatics in the First century of Islamic Coinage," *Revue Suisse de Numismatique* 65 (1986), 231–62; M.L. Bates, *Islamic Coins* (New York, 1982); Michael L. Bates, "The Coinage of Syria under the Umayyads, 692–750 A.D.," in *The History of Bilad al-Sham During the Umayyad Period*, ed. M.A. Bakhit and R. Schick (Amman, 1989), 195–228.
50. Schultz, "Monetary History of Egypt," 325.
51. Cf. Qur'ān 9:33.
52. See G.C. Miles, "Early Islamic Bronze Coinage of Egypt," 473.
53. Balādhurī, *Futūḥ*, 469–70. While amputation of the violator's hands was suggested as an appropriate punishment, this severe punishment was only implemented once.
54. Common in *P.KRU*; also see M.L. Bates, "The 'Arab-Byzantine' Bronze Coinage of Syria: An Innovation by 'Abd al-Malik," in *A Colloquium in Memory of G.C. Miles* (New York, 1976), 16–27.
55. In the *Life of John Khame* (pg. 346) the Virgin Mary miraculously gave three coins with crosses on them to the saint; they were kept as relics at his monastery. John Khame lived in the mid-ninth century, but his *Life* was drafted in the tenth; see. M.S.A. Mikhail, "A Lost Chapter in the History of

Wadi al-Natrun (Scetis): The Coptic *Lives* and Monastery of Abba John Khame," *Muséon (forthcoming)*.

56. Schultz, "Monetary History of Egypt," 326, adds that the first *dīnārs* may have been minted in Egypt as early as 170/786, though the earliest incontestable Egyptian *dīnārs* were struck in 199/814.
57. See the examples gathered by Miles, "Early Islamic Bronze Coinage of Egypt," 480, 481, 479, 499, 484. A mint may have also existed in Ḥulwān, see Miles, n.16.
58. Balādhurī, *Futūḥ*, 468.
59. Maqrīzī, *Khiṭaṭ*, I.571; *Chronicle of 1234/History of Dionysios*, Palmer §135; Theophanes, *Chronicle*, AM 6183 (690/91 CE).
60. O. Grabar, "Ḳubbat al-Ṣakhra," EI[2] 5:298a-299b; idem, *Formation of Islamic Art*, 46–63; idem, "The Umayyad Dome of the Rock in Jerusalem," *Ars Orientalis* 3 (1959), 33–62; idem, "The Meaning of the Dome of the Rock," in *The Medieval Mediterranean*, ed. M.J. Chiat and K.L. Reyerson (Minnesota, 1988); idem, *The Shape of the Holy: Early Islamic Jerusalem* (Princeton, 1996), 52–116; Said Nuseibeh (photography) and O. Grabar (essay), *The Dome of the Rock* (New York, 1996); Richard Ettinghausen and O. Grabar, *The Art and Architecture of Islam: 650–1250* (London, 1987).
61. O. Grabar, "al-Masdjid al-Aḳṣā," EI[2] 6:707a-708a; idem, *Shape of the Holy*, 117–22; R.W. Hamilton, *The Structural History of the Aqṣā Mosque* (London, 1949); K.A.C. Creswell, *Early Islamic Architecture*, 373–80; H. Stern, "Recherches sur la Mosquee al-Aqṣā et ses mosaieques," *Ars Orientalis* 5 (1963), 27–47.
62. An inscription in the Dome of the Rock proclaims the superiority of Islam: "He it is who has sent His messenger with the guidance and the religion of truth, so that he may cause it to prevail over all religion, however much the idolaters may hate it" (Qur'ān 9:33, or possibly 61:9); O. Grabar, *Formation of Islamic Art*, 50–4.
63. Inscriptions are of Qur'ān 112, 4:169–71, 19:34–7, 33:54, 17:3, 64:1, 67:2, 57:2, 3:16–7, 9:33.
64. HP I.3:279, my emphasis.
65. This is the title of the third chapter of O. Grabar's *Formation of Islamic Art*.
66. Kindī, *Wulāt*, 49, 51, 59, 60; HP I.3:296; Eutychios, *Naẓm al-jawhar*, II.40.
67. Kindī, *Wulāt*, 58–59; Ibn ʿAbd al-Ḥakam, *Futūḥ*, 122; cf. *Chronicle of 1234/History of Dionysios*, Palmer §145. See also Chapters Three and Five.
68. See Chapter Three, above.
69. Kindī, *Wulāt*, 59; cf. *Chronicle of 1234/History of Dionysios*, Palmer §134.
70. Kindī, *Wulāt*, 79. Also see Chapter Three, above. SPP X 222, an early eighth-century text, references a certain Sulaymān, identified as the first identifiable Muslim tax collector in Upper Egypt. See N. Gonis, "Reconsidering Some Fiscal Documents," 225–8; text 4.
71. Theophanes, *Chronicle*, §367 (year 693/4); *Chronicle of 1234/History of Dionysios*, Palmer §135; *Chronicle of AD 819*, AG 1015; Michael the Syrian,

Chronicle, 11.16; Abū ʿUbayd, *Amwāl*, §265, cf. §§263–64. On 29 April 2009, the Egyptian government slaughtered over a quarter of a million pigs—kept exclusively by Christian garbage collectors—presumably to hinder the spread of the "Swine Flu" (H1N1 virus). Aside from the unfortunate nomenclature, that strain of the flu cannot be spread by swine. At the time of the slaughter, Egypt did not have a single reported case of the disease.

72. Qur'ān 16:116, 7:146, 5:4, 2:168. On prohibiting pork, see Richard A. Lobban Jr., "Pigs and their Prohibition," IJMES 26.1 (1994), 57–75; Paul Diener and Eugene E. Robkin, "Ecology, Evolution, and the Search for Cultural Origins: The Question of Islamic Pig Prohibition," *Current Anthropology* 19.3 (1978), 493–540.
73. Through Roman rule, pork was the most common "meat" consumed in Egypt; see Maged S.A. Mikhail, "Some Observations Concerning Edibles in Late Antique and Early Islamic Egypt," *Byzantion* 70 (2000), 116–7. It is still eaten by Copts, though its consumption never attained the socio-religious resonance prevalent among the Christians of Spain.
74. HP II.2:188/150r; HCME 96b, 267.
75. See Yaḥyā ibn Ādam, *Kharāj*, §§215, 216, 220–3; Abū ʿUbayd, *Amwāl*, §§263–4, 266–8, 279–93; some of these traditions relate to events that took place during the tenure of ʿUmar b. ʿAbd al-ʿAzīz.
76. HP I.3:326–7, cf. 279—in both cases; al-Kindī, *Wulāt*, 71; Ibn ʿAbd al-Ḥakam, *Futūḥ*, 114; al-Maqrīzī, *Khiṭaṭ*, IV.999–1000.
77. See U. Haarmann, "Regional Sentiments," 62–5, summarizes later iconoclastic incidents. On the possible stimuli for the edict, see A.A. Vasiliev, "The Iconoclastic Edict of the Caliph Yazid II, A.D. 721," DOP 9–10 (1956), 25–47; see also O. Grabar, *Formation of Islamic Art*, 75–103; Sidney H. Griffith, "Images, Islam and Christian Icons: a Moment in the Christian/Muslim Encounter in early Islamic Times," in *La Syrie de Byzance à l'Islam VIIe VIIIe*, ed. Pierre Canivet and Jean-Paul Rey-Coquais (Damascus, 1992), 121–38; P. Crone, "Islam, Judeo-Christianity, and Byzantine Iconoclasm," JSAI 2 (1980), 59–95; G.R.D. King, "Islam, Iconoclasm." Cf. Sidney H. Griffith, "Theodore Abu Qurrah's Arabic Tract on the Christian Practice of Venerating Images," JAOS 105.1 (1985), 53–73; idem, "Eutychius of Alexandria on the Emperor Theophilus and Iconoclasm in Byzantium: A Tenth Century Moment in Christian Apologetics in Arabic," *Byzantion* 52 (1982), 154- 90.
78. Kindī, *Wulāt*, 71–2.
79. A. Vasiliev ("Iconoclastic Edict") questions the date of the edict. Most Arabic authors favor 104/723, though 102/721, noted in the Syrian *Chronicle of 1234*, is likely more accurate. Sidney Griffith ("Theodore Abu Qurrah") discounts any substantive link between this edict and Iconocalism in Byzantium.
80. On women in early Islam, see Nabia Abbott's, "Women and the State on the Eve of Islam," *American Journal of Semitic Languages and Literature* 58 (1941), 259–84; eodem, "Women and the State in Early Islam," JNES 1.1 (1942),

106–126; and JNES 1.3 (1942), 341–68; Leila Ahmed, "Women and the Advent of Islam," *Signs: Journal of Women in Culture and Society* 11 (1986), 665–91. For the Fāṭimid period, see Delia Cortese and Simonetta Calderini, *Women and the Fatimids in the World of Islam* (Edinburgh, 2006); cf. the chapters by G. Nashat and J.K. Choksy in *Women in Iran from the rise of Islam to 1800*, ed. G. Nashat and L. Beck (Urbana, 2003).

81. Kindī, *Wulāt*, 69; Nāṣir-i Khusraw, *Safarnāma*, 59; cf. Ibn Jubayr, *Riḥla*, 57 (Eng. 64); Ibn Ḥawqal, *Ṣūrat al-arḍ*, 147. On later periods and other regions, see Fikret Yegül, *Baths and Bathing in Classical Antiquity* (Cambridge, 1992); Heinz Grotzfeld, *Das Bad im arabische-islamischen Mittelalter* (Wiesbaden, 1970); Edmond Pauty, *Les hammams du Caire* (Cairo, 1933); J. Sourdel-Thomime and A. Louis, "Ḥammām," EI^2 3:139b-144b.
82. At one point, al-Ḥākim bi Amr Allāh forbade women from frequenting public baths (HP II.2:188/149v), and later extended the prohibition to include all non-Muslims (HP II.2:189/150r).
83. See Michael C. Dunn, "Struggle for ʿAbbāsid Egypt;" Morimoto, *Fiscal Administration*, 145–72.
84. E.g. Boulos Ayad Ayad, "The Revolts of the Copts," *Coptic Church Review* 25 (2004), 48–53; Bishop Yu'annis, *Tarīkh al-kannīsa al-qibṭiyya baʿd majma khalqīduniya* (Staten Island, 1989), 44.
85. Cl. Cahen, "Djizya," EI^2 2:559a-562a; Cl. Cahen, "*Kharādj*," EI^2 4:1030b-1033a; Dennett, *Conversion and the Poll Tax*, ch. 5.
86. G. Frantz-Murphy, Introduction, *CPR* XXI.
87. Maged S.A. Mikhail, "Notes on the *Ahl al-Dīwān*: The Arab-Egyptian Army of the Seventh through Ninth Centuries CE," JAOS 128.2 (2008), 273–84.
88. A. Noth, "Zum Verhältnis," 154–6; idem, "Remarks on the 'Nationalization' of Conquered Lands;" idem, *Early Arabic Historical Tradition*, 223–8; *CPR* XXI, 25–30.
89. H.I. Bell, "Two Official Letters of the Arab Period," *Journal of Egyptian Archeology* 12 (1926), 266–75 (SB III.7240); idem, "The Administration of Egypt under the Umayyad Khalifs," *Byzantinisch Zeitschrift* 28 (1928), 285.
90. Kindī, *Wulāt*, 73–74; HP I.3:329–32; al-Maqrīzī, *Khiṭaṭ*, I.212–13; IV.999.10–12.
91. The magnitude of the tax-increase is not clear. The HP states that ʿUbayd Allāh doubled the tax, while al-Kindī states that he increased a carat/*qirāṭ* to each *dinar* (a 4% increase). Land surveys provide the government with a stricter means of assessing taxes as well as an opportunity for avaricious surveyors to extort money from farmers. A land survey also sparked the eleventh revolt.
92. See Chase F. Robinson, "Neck-Sealing in Early Islam," JESHO 48.3 (2005), 409–41.
93. On this population, see M.S.A. Mikhail, "Notes on the *Ahl al-Dīwān*," 273–84; Khalil ʿAthamina, "Some Administrative, Military, and Socio-Political Aspects of Early Muslim Egypt," in *War and Society in the Eastern*

Mediterranean, 7th-15th Centuries, ed. Y. Lev (Leiden, 1997), 101–13. More generally, see Hugh Kennedy, *The Armies of the Caliphs: Military and Society in the Early Islamic State* (London, 2001); Michael Bonner, ed., *Arab-Byzantine Relations in Early Islamic Times* (Burlington, 2004); Patricia Crone, *Slaves on Horses*. Muslim participation was likely due to Yamanī-Qaysī feuding.

94. Cl. Cahen, "'aṭā'," EI[2] 1:729a-730a.
95. This occurred in 109/728. Nine years earlier, in 100/719, 5,000 individuals (possibly families) came to Egypt; see al-Kindī, 68, and Chapters Seven and Eight below.
96. This same policy was followed in the Sawād (in Irāq) when it rebelled.
97. Kindī, *Wulāt*, 81; al-Maqrīzī, *Khiṭaṭ*, I.213.4–5; IV.1000.11–12; Dunn, "Struggle for 'Abbāsid Egypt," 165–6. The HP does not mention this revolt, but it provides ample evidence to place it in context; it documents tax increases during years of successive famine and drought (HP I.3:348–9, 351–2).
98. The 252/866 uprising (see al-Kindī, *Wulāt*, 205–6) was primarily an anti-Turkish campaign. Since the *fitna*, Turkomen soldiers began to dominate the ranks of the army as well as all major posts. Later, in 253/867, an 'Alid sparked a violent revolt in Ahnās. Aḥmad ibn Tūlūn sent an army and killed that rebel: Ibrahīm ibn Muḥammad ibn Yaḥyā ibn 'Abdallāh ibn Muḥammad ibn 'Umar ibn 'Alī ibn Abī Ṭālib (al-Kindī, 219).
99. Kindī, *Wulāt*, 94; al-Maqrīzī, *Khiṭaṭ*, IV.1000.13.
100. Kindī, *Wulāt*, 94.
101. Kindī, *Wulāt*, 95–96; al-Maqrīzī, *Khiṭaṭ*, I.213.8–9; HP I.3:410–11, 414–16, 419.
102. Kindī, *Wulāt*, 102; cf. HP I.3:410–11; Dunn, "Struggle for 'Abbāsid Egypt," 20. Morimoto treats the revolt in the HP and that in the *Wulāt* as two separate events. I read them as referencing the same incident. Both (1) occurred in the same region, Samannūd (2) are within a narrow temporal window (3) were led by men with similar names, Abū Mina and Mina ibn Baqīrā (< Apacyrus: the "apa-" of Apacyrus is often rendered in Arabic as "Abū") (4) with at least three revolts taking place within eighteen months, it would be understandable if two accounts are slightly confused.
103. Kindī, *Wulāt*, 116–7; al-Maqīzī, *Khiṭaṭ*, I.213.10–5, IV.1001.11; Dunn, "Struggle for 'Abbāsid Egypt," 25–26. Not mentioned in the HP.
104. Kindī, *Wulāt*, 101; HP I.3:442.
105. E.g. HP I.3:370–1. 24,000 purportedly converted to Islam and enrolled in the *dīwān* (see Chapter Four above). On the fiscal problems of this period, see Dunn, "Struggle for 'Abbāsid Egypt."
106. P.M. Sijpesteijn, "Shaping a Muslim State," ch. 2; cf. Ibn Jubayr, *Riḥla*, 39 and 62 (Eng. 31, 55) and the Tithe Collectors in *Chronicle of Zuqnīn*, Harrak, pgs. 235, 255, 259–61.
107. HP I.3:442–3.
108. Kindī, *Wulāt*, 117.

109. Kindī, *Wulāt*, 119; al-Ya'qūbī, *Ta'rīkh*, II.483; al-Maqrīzī, *Khiṭaṭ*, I.213.15–16 (cf. IV.1001.2), calls them *'askar*. The *ahl al-dīwān* was not abandoned overnight (al-Kindī, 126), but their deployment, even in this incident, was secondary to that of the soldiers of Fusṭāṭ.
110. Dunn, "Struggle for 'Abbāsid Egypt," 26.
111. Kindī, *Wulāt*, 170. The armies of Jarawī suppressed the ninth revolt; al-Afshīn put down the tenth.
112. Kindī, *Wulāt*, 125–6; Dunn, "Struggle for 'Abbāsid Egypt," 28; *CPR* XXI, pgs. 27–8, this may have been the first *kharāj* levied on Muslims in Egypt.
113. The first attestation of *kharāj* in a documentary text dates to this same year; see *CPR* XXI, 827; Frantz-Murphy, "Land Tenure in Egypt in the First Five Centuries of Islamic Rule (Seventh-Twelfth Centuries AD)," in *Agriculture in Egypt From Pharaonic to Modern Times*, ed. A. Bowman and E. Rogan, (Oxford, 1999), 247.
114. Kindī, *Wulāt*, 125.13 and 126.11–12.
115. Turkish and Persian soldiers had not yet come to dominate the Egyptian army.
116. Kindī, *Wulāt*, 136; al-Ya'qūbī, *Ta'rīkh*, II.496–7; Dunn, "Struggle for 'Abbāsid Egypt," 40.
117. *CPR* XXI, pg. 33. The last text dealing with a tax in kind is dated 182/797.
118. Flax became a major export under Fāṭimid rule; Moshe Gil, "The Flax Trade in the Mediterranean in the Eleventh Century A.D. As seen in Merchants' Letter from the Cairo Geniza," JNES 63.2 (2004), 81–96; P. Mayerson, "The Role of Flax in Roman and Fatimid Egypt," JNES 56.3 (1997), 201–7.
119. *CPR* XXI, pgs. 30–1.
120. *CPR* XXI, pgs. 35–6.
121. Kindī, *Wulāt*, 140–1. Not mentioned in the HP, but al-Layth comes across as an extremely sympathetic governor; see HP I.4:514–5, 518–22.
122. Kindī, *Wulāt*, 140.18.
123. Kindī, *Wulāt*, 143–44.
124. Kindī, *Wulāt*, 146–147.
125. Kindī, *Wulāt*, 147.
126. Kindī, *Wulāt*, 149–50. By that date, taxes were assessed and collected in cash only (*CPR* XXI.34).
127. Kindī, *Wulāt*, 151, 153. There was another rebellion in 202/817 (al-Kindī, 168).
128. Kindī, *Wulāt*, 170. While the number is likely exaggerated, the basic premise remains valid: a significant number of Arab Muslims revolted alongside the Copts.
129. Kindī, *Wulāt*, 185–8.
130. Kindī, *Wulāt*, 189.
131. Kindī, *Wulāt*, 185–92, esp. 190, 192; al-Maqrīzī, *Khiṭaṭ*, I.213.17–9, IV.1002.10–12; HP I.4:601–2, 609; Eutychios, *Naẓm al-jawhar*, II.57; Michael the Syrian, *Chronicle*, 12.17; see Dunn, "Struggle for 'Abbāsid Egypt," 3, 50, 81–5; Ohta Keiko, "The Coptic Church and Coptic Communities in the

Reign of al-Ma'mūn: A Study of the Social Context of the Bashmūric Revolt," *Annals of Japan Association for Middle East Studies* 19.2 (2004), 87–116.

132. Kindī, *Wulāt*, 191, provides the sequence of the various battles.
133. See Chapters Four, Nine, and Eleven.
134. Kindī, *Wulāt*, 192; al-Ya'qūbī, *Ta'rīkh*, II.569.
135. Kindī, *Wulāt*, 193.15–6. Payments were no longer made to *ṭubūl al-muslimūn*, but rather became "the Sulṭān's installments" *nujūm al-sulṭān*; *CPR* XXI, pgs. 36–9.
136. See M.S.A. Mikhail, "Notes on the *Ahl al-Dīwān*," on the problems of defining the *dīwān* payment.
137. Kindī, *Wulāt*, 194.
138. Cf. al-Kindī, *Wulāt*, 125 and 150, with 81 and 116–7.
139. Kindī, *Wulāt*, 158, 162–4, 166, 170, 172, 184. They were a problem for over a decade (199–212/814–827).
140. HP I.4:542.
141. Kindī, *Wulāt*, 170.
142. Kindī, *Wulāt*, 76.
143. Maqrīzī, *Bayān*, §§59–63.
144. Judith Herrin, *The Formation of Christendom* (Princeton, 1987), 4–6, 111–3; Daniel P. McCarthy, "The Emergence of *Anno Domini*," in *Time and Eternity: the Medieval Discourse*, ed. G. Jaritz and G. Moreño-Riano (Turnhout, 2003), 31–53.
145. E.g. *Chronicon Paschale*, 71, 81, 134; Dindorf 581, 591, 685.
146. W. Montgomery Watt, "Hidjra," EI^2 3:366a-367a.
147. J. Schacht *et al.* "Djāhilliya," EI^2 2:383b-384a.
148. See Edward G. Richards, *Mapping Time: the Calendar and its History* (Oxford, 1998); Nachum Dershowitz and Edward M. Reingold, *Calendrical Calculations* (Cambridge, 1997); Arno Borst, *The Ordering of Time*, trans. Andrew Winnard (Chicago, 1993); S.H. Taqizadeh, "Various Eras and Calendars used in the Countries of Islam," BSOS 9.4 (1939), 903–22 and 10.1 (1939), 107–32.
149. On the systems used in late antique Egypt, see Roger S. Bagnall and Klaas A. Worp, *Chronological Systems of Byzantine Egypt*, 2nd ed. (Leiden, 2004), ch. 1; on the indiction system see Chapters Three to Five.
150. *P.Lond.Copt.*I.389 is dated by indiction and "Year of the Saracens," ετου σαρακ/, to 161/777; see also *P.Lond.Copt.*I.398, 405. Text 408 is dated by indiction and the Year of Diocletian to 757 CE. All the texts in *P.Bawit Clackson* (eighth century) are dated by indiction; *O.Medin.HabuCopt.* 61, 81, 82, 83; *O.Crum.* 40, 304, 306, Ad. 17; Tombstones dated by Indiction, *O.Brit. Mus.Copt.*I Plate VI 2 (no. 604); Plate IX 1 (No. 1046); Plate IX 2 (407); Plate XI 5 (no. 823).
151. Klaas A. Worp, "Hegira Years in Greek, Greek-Coptic, and Greek-Arabic Papyri," *Aegyptus* 65 (1985), 107–15; E.B. Allen, "Available Coptic texts involving dates," *Coptic Studies in Honor of W.E. Crum* (Boston, 1950), 3–33.
152. K. Worp, "Hegira years," 114–15; this study covers 641–780 CE.

153. 153.*O.Brit.Mus.Copt.*I Plate VII 1 (No 1208) 457 AD / 741 CE; Plate IX 5 (No 408), Greek, AD 472 / 756 CE; See Bagnall and Worp, *Chronological Systems*, ch 8; L.S.B. MacCoull, and K.A. Worp, "The Era of the Martyrs," *Papyrologica Florentina* 19 (Florence, 1990), II:375–408, at table I; ibid., "The Eras of Diocletian and the Martyrs: Addenda & Corrigenda," *Analecta Papyrologica* 7 (1995), 155–65. Initially, it was primarily used by Pagan priests in casting horoscopes.
154. On occasion, the lunar *hijra* calendar was treated as if it were solar: Worp, "Hegir years," 114.
155. Bagnall and Worp, *Chronological Systems*, 63–82. Attested since 306/7 CE, the earliest document under Islamic rule is dated 657/8 CE. *SB Kopt.* I contains a number of ostraca dated by this system to the first half of the eighth century; *SB Kopt.*I.551, dated 716, is the earliest of them. Also see, N. Gonis and K.A. Worp, "P.Bodl. I 77: The King of Kings in Arsinoe under Arab Rule," ZPE 141 (2002), 173–6, which is dated Year of Diocletian 387 (=670/1 CE).
156. Theophanes' *Chronicle* begins with Diocletian's tenure, and occasionally cites the era; see *Chronicle*, AM 5983 (490/1 CE) and AM 6010 (517/8 CE); as does al-Masʿūdī, *Murūj al-dhahab*, II.376, 377.
157. See Ibn Ḥawqal, *Ṣūrat al-arḍ*, 136–37; Ibn al-Kindī, *Faḍā'il miṣr*, 210; al-Maqrīzī, *Khiṭaṭ*, I.731–9; cf. Ibn Mammātī, *Kitāb qawānīn al-dawāwīn*, esp. ch. 6; Terry G. Wilfong, "Agriculture among the Christian Population of Early Islamic Egypt: Practice and Theory," in *Agriculture in Egypt*, ed. Bowman and Eugene, 217–35.
158. The remaining five (and a quarter) days constituted the Short Month, or *ayam al-nasy*: ЄΠⲀΓΟΜЄΝΗ, ⲀΠⲀΓΟΜЄΝΟΝ (αἱ ἐπαγομέναι); Arabized as *Abū Ghamnā* (al-Maqrīzī, *Khiṭaṭ*, I.711.22). Masʿūdī (*Murūj al-dhahab*, III.399) knew them as the "Blind Days" (العميا). Every four years the Short Month contained six days.
159. Much of al-Maqrīzī's account (*Khiṭaṭ*, I.740–63) is concerned with instances in which the problems of using two calendars—lunar and solar—came to the forefront.
160. *Ashhur al-ʿajam*: *P.Marchands*.I.7.5 dated 258/871; *Chrest.Khoury*.I.24. *Ashhur al-qibṭ*: *P.Cair.Arab*.VI.369 and *Chrest.Khoury*.I.33, cf 34, 45.
161. Most of the documents in *CPR* XXI are dated by the *hijra*.
162. *P.Cair.Arab*.II.101, dated 273/886, is a contract between two Muslims only dated by the Coptic-date clause (also *Chrest.Khoury*.II.7, 9). *P.Cair.Arab*.II.143, dated 298/912, from al-Ashmūnayn concerns a debt of wheat between two Muslims. It is dated by the Muslim calendar (l.4), but the monthly payments are due according to Coptic months (l.3); also see *P.Cair.Arab*.VI.369, 408; see also note 172 below.
163. *P.Prag.Arab*.6, date 288/901; *P.Prag.Arab*.10 dated 322/934; A. Grohmann. "Arabishce Papyri aus den Staatlichen Museen zu Berlin," *Der Islam* 22 (1934), no. 12, dated 461/1078–9 from al-Ashmūnayn; *P.Cair.Arab*.V.345—dated 207/823; V.346, 355; II.89 dated 209/824; *Chrest.Khoury*.II.27.

164. *P.Prag.Arab*.47 and 49, dated 440/1049 and 449/1057. Also see *Chrest.Khoury*. I.27, 37; *P.Cair.Arab*.II.143.

165. Double dates are first attested in the HP's biography of Shinūda I (HP II.1:44/122r, written in 866 CE). The colophon in John of Nikiou's *Chronicle*, is dated 1318 AM, 980 AH (§123.8). But throughout that work, the Era of Diocletian is used (e.g. §116.2). Also see *P.Lond.Copt*.I.489, 490, dated to the early twelfth and eleventh centuries CE respectively. An early-eleventh century tombstone dated by that date of the Martyrs and "Sarasans" is in *O.Brit.Mus. Copt*. I Plate VII 4 (No. 1336). *P.KRU* 106 (dated 734 CE) is dated by year of Diocletian (451) and that of the Saracens. In general, double dating appears to have prevailed from the tenth through the thirteenth centuries; see note 184 below.

166. D. Remondeon, "Cinq documents arabes d'Edfou," *Mélanges Islamologiques* 2 (1954), 103–14 (§§2–4).

167. Use of lashane's name to date texts with the ⲛⲁϩⲣⲉⲛ ⲡⲗⲁϣⲁⲛⲉ formula: *O.Medin.HabuCopt*. (Intro. Pg. 2–3), 50, 51, 52, 60, 70, 71, 73, 75; cf. *P.KRU* 38, 74. The *nahren* can be misleading; but it is clear (especially in papyri where the *lashane* are identified but do not sign) that it should be translated as "under" or "during the tenure of" a certain *lashane* rather than "before" or "in front" of him/them. Tombstone dated just by date and month: *O.Brit.Mus. Copt*. I Plate 6.1 (no. 404); Plate 8.1 (No. 26791); Plate 8.3 (no. 607); Plate 9.3 (no. 1256).

168. Cf. *P.KRU* 106. A major exception is Eutychios' *Naẓm al-jawhar*, which is arranged according to caliphal tenure and the *hijra* calendar. He did not cite the Era of the Martyrs, though he dated his own birth (II.69–70) according to: *hijra* year, a solar equivalent, Era of Diocletian, years since "the time of our Lord Jesus Christ" (beginning with the Resurrection, or possibly the Ascension), Era of Alexander, years since the Babylonian Exile, years since the reign of King David, years since the Exodus, years since Abraham, years since the Great Flood, years since the destruction of Sodom and Gomorrah, years since Adam.

169. Line 12 provides the *hijra* date of the contract; also see *P.Cair.Arab*.II.143, dated 298/912. *Chrest.Khoury*.I.63, 3/9 century, is a rent agreement for a house belonging to a mosque in Ashmūnayn; the rent was due according to Coptic months.

170. See HCME 1b, 1 and 4b, 8; Eutychios, *Naẓm al-jawhar*, II.75; *P.Lond.Copt*. I.487 a Coptic text dated 287 AH (900 CE); the eleventh-century Coptic texts of *P.Teshlot* are all dated according to the *hijra*.

171. Maqrīzī, *Khiṭaṭ*, I.750–63, chronicles several attempts to reconcile the two systems: *al-shamsiyya* / *al-kharājiyya* with *al-'arabiyya/al-hilāliyya*. Agapios notes that he went through great strides to correlate the solar and lunar dates he employs in his chronicle (*Kitāb al-'unwan*, 223).

172. ⲁⲡⲟ ⲙ̅ⲣ̅ (= ⲙⲁⲣⲧⲩⲣⲱⲛ), which parallels ἀπο Διοκλητιανοῦ, was likely the original form of the clause. MacCoull and Worp, "Era of the Martyrs," 401 ns.

2 and 3, arguing that the alleged earlier attestations in *P.KRU*.14, 15, 70, 106, *P.Ryl.Copt*.175, *P.Lond.Copt*.1226, 673, were based on faulty reconstructions of the date clauses; see the following note.

173. The Era of the Martyrs is first attested on Nubian tombstones dated 505 AM/785–6 CE and 513 AM/796–7 CE. Bagnall and Worp, *Chronological Systems*, 67, cf. 82; Adam Łajtar, "Greek Funerary Inscriptions from Old Dongola: General Notes," *Oriens Christianus* 81 (1997), 107–26; Bagnall and Worp (pgs. 86–7) have discounted the earliest references cited in MacCoull and Worp, "Era of the Martyrs."

174. MacCoull and Worp, "Era of the Martyrs," n.3, the "Era of the Martyrs" was not ubiquitous until the eleventh century CE; this is further discussed below. On al-Maqrīzī's general assessment of the Coptic calendar, see *Khiṭaṭ*, I.706–10.

175. Bagnall and Worp, *Chronological Systems*, 67; L.S.B. MacCoull, "Three Cultures under Arab Rule: The Fate of Coptic," BSAC (1985), n.7. For the inscription, see H.G. Evelyn White, *Monasteries*, II.308, III.194. On occasion, the date cited in that publication is erroneously recorded as 869: 575 AM = 859 CE.

176. HP I.3:410, cf. 424, 447, 468. All previous references are to the Era of Diocletian: see HP I.3:304, 315, 321, 359. Often, the reference is to the "year of Diocletian, the slayer of the Martyrs" (HP I.3:300; cf. I.3:219, 229).

177. Era of Diocletian is referenced in HP I.3:359.

178. The first explicit date cited in the biographies written by Deacon John—in 865/6 CE—is found in the biography of Patriarch John IV (775–99 CE); see HP I.4:516.

179. Cf. A. Papaconstantinou, "Historiography," 79, where this designation and its implications are assumed to have prevailed much earlier. Perhaps the designation sparked the use of *al-sana al-hilāliyya* among Muslims, discussed below. The symbolism of the crescent-moon (*al-hilāl*) remains ubiquitous in Islam.

180. Cf. n. 168 above.

181. Maqrīzī, *Khiṭaṭ*, I.710.9–10.

182. *SB Kopt*.I.610 dated 866, 612 dated 872, 613 dated 878, 614 dated 891; cf. *SB Kopt*. I.747. The last documented use of the designation was in 1166/7 CE (MacCoull and Worp, "Era of the Martyrs," 384).

183. Bīrūnī, *al-Āthār al-bāqiya*, 29, 141, 196; Eng. 33, 137, 176.

184. This designation may have been used earlier. Egypt's administrations always relied upon a solar calendar in fiscal matters. Elsewhere, dependence upon the *hijra*/lunar calendar led to great confusion as it was incrementally out of synch with harvest season. Hence, in 281/895 the Caliph al-Muʿtaḍid ordered the use of a solar calendar in all fiscal matters; Tabātabā'i, *Kharāj in Islamic Taxation*, 40; A. Grohmann, *Arabische Chronologie* (Leiden, 1966), 30. The designation is attested in *P.Cair.Arab*.II.85 dated 348/958; *P.Prag.Arab*.47 dated 440/1049 and *P.Prag.Arab*.49 dated 449/1057 are from Ashmūnayn; HP II.3:337/175r, 352/178r, 385/183r, 388/183v, 389/183v, 394/184v;

HP III.1:4/186r, cf. 9/186v. It is frequently attested in HP II.3, where several events are double dated to the Era of the Martyrs and *al-sana al-kharājiyya* (cf. *O.Brit.Mus.Copt.* I Plate VII 4 [No. 1336]).

185. Maqrīzī, *Khiṭaṭ*, I.746; Hassanein Rabie, *The Financial System of Egypt AD 1169–1341* (Oxford, 1972), 133; Taqizadeh, "Various Eras," 905–15.
186. On Diocletian in Coptic literature, see J. Schwartz, "Dioclétien dans la littérature copte," BSAC 15 (1958–60), 151–66; Youhanna Nessim Youssef, "La genèse de la légende sur le roi Dioclétien," BSAC 28 (1986–1989), 107–10; Gonnie van den Gerg-Onstwedder, "Diocletian in the Coptic Tradition," BSAC 29 (1990), 87–122; also al-Maqrīzī, *Khiṭaṭ*, I.710–12.
187. The Melitians identified themselves as "the Church of the Martyrs." See also Theofried Baumeister, *Martyr invictus: der Martyrer als Sinnbild der Erlösung in der Legende und im Kult der frühen koptischen Kirche* (Münster, 1972); A. Camplani, "L'autorappresentazione dell'episcopato di Alessandria tra IV e V secolo: questioni di metodo," *Annali di storia dell'esegesi* 21.1 (2004), 147–85. Willy Clarysse, "The Coptic Martyr Cult," in *Martyrium in Multidisciplinary Perspective*, ed. M. Lamberigts and P. van Deun (Leuven, 1995), notes the apparent increase in the collection and copying of early martyrdom accounts post 700 CE. The Coptic Arabic *synaksār*, and its precursors, commemorate martyrs almost daily.
188. For the caliphate of al-Mutawakkil, see HP II.1 and al-Ṭabarī, *Incipient Decline*, *Ta'rīkh al-rusul wa-al-mulūk*, vol. 34, trans. Joel L. Kraemer (Albany, 1989).
189. Anti-Chalcedonian political ideology is discussed in Chapter Nine.
190. Qur'ān 105; Donner, *Narratives of Islamic Origins*; also see Khalifa ibn Khayyāṭ, *Ta'rīkh*, I.14–15. This pattern persisted even after the *hijra* calendar was in use (*Ta'rīkh*, I.378).
191. Yaʿqubī, *Ta'rīkh*, II.165–6.
192. Grohmann, *Chronologie*, 13–14; cf. Yannis E. Meimaris, "The Arab (Hijra) Era Mentioned in Greek Inscriptions and Papyri from Palestine," *Graeco-Arabica* 3 (1984), 177–89.
193. Most of the Arabic Qurra papyri may be used as an example. Greek documents usually followed the formula, "written in (day) of (Coptic month), indiction X." The eighth-century Coptic legal texts of Jēme (*P.KRU*) are dated in a similar fashion.
194. This expression was also used in Arabic papyri, *P.Cair.Arab.*III.160.10–11.
195. Worp, "Hegira Years," 114; Grohmann, *Chronologie*, 14.
196. *Chrest.Khoury.*I.41, 59, 75. Papyri 45 is dated 389/999, a year in which the two systems—*al-kharājiyya* and the *hilāliyya*—coincided. In passing, al-Maqrīzī (*Khiṭaṭ*, I.746) uses *hilāliyya* as a synonym for *qamariyya*; cf. Taqizadeh, "Various Eras," 908. *Al-hilāliyya* is also attested in Christian narrative sources, e.g. HP II.3:369/180r.

Chapter 7 Muslim Elites, Urban Administration, and Rural Justice

1. On the early bureaucracy, see Hugh Kennedy, "Egypt as a Province in the Islamic Caliphate, 641–868," in *Cambridge History of Egypt*, ed. C.F. Petry; idem, "Central Government and Provincial Elites in the Early ʿAbbāsid Caliphate," BSOAS 44 (1981), esp. 31–8; F. Donner, "Formation of the Islamic State"; P.M. Sijpesteijn, "New Rule over Old Structures."
2. Evident in several of the riots discussed in Chapter Six.
3. As governor Qurra ibn Sharīk put it, "The first duty of the official is the collection of the public taxes" (*P.Lond.*IV.1394). In the riot of 186/801, the governor's failure to collect taxes ultimately led to his dismissal (al-Kindī, *Wulāt*, 140). The above referenced functions of the governor were also shared by *duces* and pagarchs; see *P.Apoll.*, *P.Lond.*IV, and the documents in P.M. Sijpesteijn, "Shaping a Muslim State."
4. Evident in several Qurra texts, e.g. *P.Heid.Arab.*I.10 and *P.Qurra.*3; *P.Apoll.*18, 22–4, 57, 58, 66; *P.KRU* 25, 42, 45, 46, 50; also see Donner, "State Formation," 288.
5. Kindī, *Wulāt*, 11–12.
6. Khalīfa ibn Khayyāṭ, *Ta'rīkh*, I.235.12–4.
7. Khalīfa ibn Khayyāṭ, *Ta'rīkh*, I.247–8, 269.5–7. This was very apparent in 57/677.
8. Kindī, *Wulāt*, 38–9.
9. Kindī, *Wulāt*, 102.
10. In 43/663, ʿUtba ibn Abū Sufyān was the first governor to be appointed solely over the ṣalāt (al-Kindī, *Wulāt*, 35). He was followed by several others: Saʿīd b. Yazīd al-Azdī in 62/682 (*Wulāt*, 40); Ayyūb ibn Shuraḥbīl in 99/718 (*Wulāt*, 68); Muḥammad ibn ʿAbd al-Malik in 105/724 (*Wulāt*, 72); al-Ḥurr ibn Yūsuf, 105/724 (*Wulāt*, 73); Ḥāfiṣ ibn al-Walīd 108/727 (*Wulāt*, 74); ʿAbd al-Malik ibn Rafāʿa, 109/728 (*Wulāt*, 75); al-Walīd ibn Rafāʿa, 109/728 (*Wulāt*, 76); ʿAbd al-Raḥmān ibn Khālid ibn Musafir (al-Fahmī) 118/737 (*Wulāt*, 79).
11. Ibn ʿAbd al-Ḥakam, *Futūḥ*, 178; al-Balādhurī, *Futūḥ*, 223—here instead of "another," it reads "*al-amīr*."
12. On ʿUbayd Allāh, see N. Abbott, "A New Papyrus and a Review of the Administration of ʿUbaid Allah ibn al-Ḥabḥāb," in *Arabic and Islamic Studies in Honor of Hamilton A.R. Gibb*, ed. G. Makdisi (Leiden, 1965), 21–35; R.G. Khoury, "ʿUbayd Allāh b. Ḥabḥāb," EI^2 10:762b.
13. Kindī, *Wulāt*, 74.
14. Kindī, *Wulāt*, 75. This well illustrates the loyalty that at times characterized the relationship between a *wālī* and his appointee, *ṣāḥib al-shurṭa*.
15. There is some discussion as to whether or not ʿUbyad Allāh held the office of governor while in Egypt, as he later did in Ifriqyā in 116/734. Based on a reference to ʿUbyad Allāh as *amīr*, R.G. Khoury (EI^2 10:762b) has maintained

that he was appointed governor of Egypt "at a date not exactly known." Still, while *amīr* frequently denotes the governor, it was not exclusive to that officeholder (e.g., see the usage in *P.KRU* 42; *P.Khalili*.II.42, 44 and pg. 93; also P. Sijpesteijn, "Shaping a Muslim State," 77–8, cf. n.154). In his *Wulāh*, al-Kindī consistently describes ʿUbyad Allāh as *ṣāḥib al-kharāj* (also al-Maqrīzī, *Khiṭaṭ*, I.201, 565; 2.51–2); moreover, he provides a list of ruling governors that spans the entirety of ʿUbyad Allāh's career, which does not leave room for him to have assumed the post. There is one oddity that may have led to confusion though. *Wulāt* 76.10 and *Khiṭaṭ*, 1.214 state that the Caliph Hisham *walla* ʿUbyad Allāh over Miṣr, which could mean an "appointment as governor" or simply an "appointment" (see usage on the same page: *Wulāt* 76.2). Ibn ʿAbd al-Ḥakam, *Futūḥ*, 217, maintains that ʿUbyad Allāh was still *ṣāḥib al-kharāj* up until the point he departed for Ifriqyā.

16. ʿĪsā ibn Abī ʿAṭa' was appointed over the *kharāj* in 125/743 and reappointed until 128/746.
17. Walīd ibn al-Rafiʿ, *ṣāḥib al-kharāj* in 96/715, was apparently also appointed *ṣāḥib al-shurṭa*, though there is no mention of his appointment, only his dismissal from that post (al-Kindī, *Wulāt*, 66). This may have also been the case with ʿUqba ibn ʿAmir (*Wulāt*, 37).
18. Emil Tyan, *Histoire de l'organisation judiciaire en pays d'Islam*, 2nd rev. ed. (Leiden, 1960), 581–5.
19. Tyan, *Histoire de l'organisation*, 573–616; J.S. Nielsen, "*Sh*urṭa" EI^2 9:510b; Donner, "Formation of State," 285–6.
20. ʿAbd al-Malik ibn Rafāʿa al-Fahmī (al-Kindī, *Wulāt*, 64, 66); Ḥanẓala ibn Ṣafwān al-Kalibī (*Wulāt*, 69, 70); Ḥāfiẓ ibn al-Walīd (*Wulāt*, 74); al-Walīd ibn Rifāʿa (al-Kindī, 66, 76); ʿAbd al-Raḥmān ibn Khālid ibn Musafir ibn Khālid ibn Thabit ibn Ẓaʿin al-Fahmī (*Wulāt*, 76, 79); ʿAbdallāh ibn ʿAbd al-Raḥmān ibn Muʿāwiya ibn Ḥudayj (*Wulāt*, 111, 117).
21. Kindī, *Wulāt*, 64, 101.
22. Tyan, *Histoire de l'organisation*, 595–607.
23. *P.Oxy*.XVI.1919 (XVI.2056 is a list of prisoners), XXVII.2478; *CPR* XXII.43; *P.Cair.Arab*.III.150; *P.Prag.Arab*.19, 27, 31, 87; *P.Mon.Apollo*.31; *P.Mon.Epiph*.176 discusses the abuses of prison (cf. 177, 181, 187, 219, 466; 163 and 167); *Chrest.Khoury*.I.68; C. Foss, "Egypt under Muʿāwiya, Part I," 13; idem, "Egypt under Muʿāwiya, Part II," 261; P.M. Sijpesteijn, "Shaping a Muslim State," ch. 1, n.129, and document 7.5 commentary; S. Torallas Tovar, "Las prisones en el Egipto Bizantino según los papiros griegos y coptos," *Erytheia* 19 (1999), 47–55; eodem, "Violence in the Process of Arrest and Imprisonment in Late Antique Egypt," in *Violence in Late Antiquity: Perceptions and Practices*, ed. H.A. Drake (Burlington, 2006), 103–12; idem, "The Police in Byzantine Egypt," in *Current Research in Egyptology 2000*, ed. A. McDonald and C. Riggs (Oxford, 2000), 115–23; Lucian Reinfandt, "Crime and Punishment in Early Islamic Egypt (AD 642–969): The Arabic Papyrological

Evidence," in *Proceedings of the Twenty-Fifth International Congress of Papyrology, Ann Arbor 2007* (Ann Arbor, 2010), 633–40.

24. See al-Kindī, *Wulāt*, 6; Tyan, *Histoire de l'organisation*, 578.
25. Tyan, *Histoire de l'organisation*, 579–81.
26. Kindī, *Wulāt*, 64.
27. It appears that the *ṣāḥib al-shurṭa* had direct control over the stipends of the army.
28. Especially clear during the governorships of ʿAbd al-ʿAzīz ibn Marwān and al-Layth ibn al-Faḍl.
29. See al-Kindī, *Wulāt*, 109, where *ṣāḥib al-shurṭā* took to the *minbar* during the *khuṭba*.
30. Cf. Tyan, *Histoire de l'organisation*, 585–6; though this should not be taken as an absolute, as Tyan himself points out.
31. Kindī, *Wulāt*, 39; *Quḍāt*, 311. This is the first reference to the *quḍāt* in the *Wulāh*; as discussed below, the office underwent several transformations over the first two hundred years; hence, a *qāḍī* in a seventh-century CE social context was a very different official than his successor in the mid-ninth century.
32. ʿAbd al-ʿAzīz ibn Marwān (al-Kindī, *Quḍāt*, 313); Yūnus ibn ʿAṭiyya (*Quḍāt*, 322); ʿAbd al-Raḥmān ibn Muʿawiya ibn Ḥudayj, who was appointed by ʿAbd al-ʿAzīz ibn Marwān over the *quḍāt* and *shurṭa* (*Quḍāt*, 324); and ʿImran ibn ʿAbd al-Raḥmān al-Ḥasanī (*Quḍāt*, 327). Two others worthy of mention are ʿIyaḍ ibn ʿUbayd Allāh al-Azdī, who was appointed over the government and *quḍāt* during his second appointment (*Quḍāt*, 333); and ʿAbdallāh ibn ʿAbd al-Raḥmān ibn Ḥujayra, who was appointed over the *quḍāt* and *bayt al-māl* during his second appointment (*Quḍāt*, 332).
33. The Fāṭimids did draw a distinction.
34. Kindī, *Wulāt*, 74–5, 82–4, 86–7.
35. See Tyan, *Histoire de l'organisation*, chs. 2 and 7; J. Schacht, *An Introduction*, ch. 25; Raif Georges Khoury, *ʿAbd Allāh ibn Lahīʿa (97–174/715–790): juge et grand maître de l'école égyptienne* (Wiesbaden, 1986); on their pay, see W. al-Qāḍī, "Salaries of Judges in Early Islam."
36. Kindī, *Quḍāt*, 305. Another *ḥakam* was al-Aqraʿ ibn Ḥabis, see Tyan, *Histoire de l'organisation*, 51.
37. Ibn ʿAbd al-Ḥakam, *Futūḥ*227; al-Kindī, *Quḍāt*, 300. As H. Kennedy notes, the appointment of judges at such an early time was not universal ("Provincial Elites," 29, n.22). In Mawṣul, the first *qāḍī* was not appointed until 140/757.
38. Tyan, *Histoire de l'organisation*, 119–28, 155; J. Schacht, *Islamic Law*, 24–7, 50–2, 188–90.
39. Tyan, *Histoire de l'organisation*, 41–51.
40. Tyan, *Histoire de l'organisation*, 97–8, 101. This is unmistakable in the career of ʿAbd al-ʿAzīz ibn Marwān, who initially served as the head of the *quḍāt*, and later appointed several individuals to the position (see al-Kindī, *Quḍāt*, 313, 324).

41. The populace objected when this was not the case: see al-Kindī, *Quḍāt*, 369, cf. 428; Tyan, *Histoire de l'organisation*, 112–8.
42. Kindī, *Quḍāt*, 307, 308. Another tradition states that he would read the Qur'ān four times every night, performing the ritual washing every time (*Quḍāt*, 312, 372). Other traditions regarding the frequency of Qur'ānic recitation are summarized in M.G. Morony, *Iraq after the Muslim Conquest*, 448–9.
43. G.H.A. Juynboll, *Muslim Tradition: Studies in Chronology, Provenance, and Authorship of Early Ḥadīth* (Cambridge, 1983), 79–83, estimates that only 30% of Egyptian *quḍāt* specialized in *ḥadīth*.
44. See Michael Cook, *Commanding the Right and Forbidding Wrong in Islamic Thought* (Cambridge, 2000).
45. See Schacht, *Islamic Law*, 19–22, ch. 11.
46. Still, the influence of the Ḥanafī's, who were favored by the ʿAbbāsids, must not be underestimated. In Egypt, Ismāʿīl ibn al-Yasah al-Kindī, appointed in 164/781, was the first *qāḍī* to follow the Ḥanafī school (al-Kindī, *Quḍāt*, 371).
47. Tyan, *Histoire de l'organisation*, 128–9; Schacht, *Islamic Law*, 50–1. The title of *qāḍī al-quḍāt* is first attested under Hārūn al-Rashīd, when it was applied to Abū Yūsuf, the *qāḍī* of Baghdad. The title is appeared in Egypt under the Fāṭimids. Nonetheless, in 177/792 the Egyptian *qāḍī* Muḥammad ibn Masrūq is described as *waliyyan 'alā al-quḍāt*, "in charge of the judges" (al-Kindī, *Quḍāt*, 388).
48. Tyan, *Histoire de l'organisation*, 433–525; J.S. Nielsen. "Maẓālim," EI^2 6: 933b-35a; Schacht, *Islamic Law*, 51. The institution is best attested under the ʿAbbāsids.
49. Kindī, *Wulāt*, 13–4.
50. See Martin Hinds, "The Murder of the Caliph ʿUthman," IJMES 3 (1972), 450–69.
51. Kindī, *Wulāt*, 19; he was later killed by Muʿāwiya.
52. See ʿAbdallāh ibn Qīs ibn al-Ḥarith ibn ʿAyyash ibn Dubīʿ al-Tujībī (al-Kindī, *Wulāt*, 35); ʿAbd al-Raḥmān ibn Ḥassan ibn ʿAtahiya ibn Ḥazn al-Tujībī (*Wulāt*, 51); ʿAbd al-Raḥmān ibn Muʿāwiya al-Tujībī (*Wulāt*, 53); Ziyād ibn Ḥinaṭa ibn Sayf al-Tujībī (*Wulāt*, 49, 51).
53. Kindī, *Wulāt*, 64.
54. In 103/722, ʿUqba ibn Muslim al-Tujībī was appointed over Alexandria (al-Kindī, *Wulāt*, 71), and in 122/741, Qays ibn al-Ashʿath al-Tujībī was appointed over Alexandria (*Wulāt*, 81).
55. Kindī, *Wulāt*, 64.
56. Kindī, *Wulāt*, 66.15–6.
57. Kindī, *Wulāt*, 75–6.
58. ʿAbdallāh ibn Abī Sumīr al-Fahmī was later dismissed and replaced by ʿAbd al-Raḥmān ibn Khālid ibn Musafir ibn Khālid ibn Thabit ibn Ẓaʿin al-Fahmī.

59. Tyan, *Histoire de l'organisation*, 587, interprets the nepotism surrounding this office in a similar light.
60. Even in urban centers, primary contact would have been with the *'arīf*, discussed above, and various members of the *shurṭa*.
61. See Introduction, *P.Lond.*IV.xxvii. There were exceptions, such as al-Mughirā ibn Salīm ἐπικειμένῳ τοῦ Ἀρσινοίτου, Pagarch of Arsinoë/Fayyūm (*P.Lond.* IV.1383), and 'Abd al-Raḥman ibn Ilyas governor of Clysma, see *P.Lond.* IV.1414.57.
62. Simonsen, *Caliphal Taxation*, 117–26; S. Steinwenter, "Lasane-Protokomet-Ape," in *Studien zu den koptischen Rechtsurkunden aus Oberagypten* (Amsterdam, 1967; 1920), 38–51; *O.Crum* 119 and his note 2.
63. E.g. *P.Cair.Arab.*III.181.11; 184.8; 185.6; 189; 190; 192.8; 193.7; 194.7; 195.4; 196.8; 198.1; 199.3–4; also the examples in *O.Medin.HabuCopt.* pgs. 29–30; *O.Crum.* 409, 411, 410, 413, 419. 429; C. Wickham, *Framing the Early Middle Ages*, 422–4.
64. E.g. *P.Cair.Arab.*III.185.6 dated 261/875; III.193.7 dated 313/926; III.194.7 dated 405/1015; also see Simonsen, *Caliphal Taxation*, 117–26.
65. *P.CLT.*5.50–1.
66. *P.CLT.*5.136–9: ⲆⲎⲖⲞⲚ ⲆⲈ ⲞⲦⲒ Ⲧ̅Ⲛ̅ⲞⲨⲰⲚϨ ⲆⲈ ⲈⲂⲞⲖ Ⲙ̅ⲠⲈⲒⲔⲈⲪⲀⲖⲀⲒⲞⲚ ⲦⲚⲦⲀⲢⲔⲞ ⲆⲈ ⲚⲀⲢⲬⲰ ⲚⲒⲘ ϨⲒⲈⲠⲒⲤⲔⲞⲠⲞⲤ ⲈϤⲞⲨⲀⲀⲂ ϨⲒⲆⲀⲔⲀⲤⲦⲎⲤ Ⲛ̅Ⲑ-ⲈⲞⲪⲞⲂⲞⲤ ϨⲒⲖⲀϢⲀⲚⲈ ⲈϤⲚⲀϪⲰⲚ̅Ϥ̅ ⲈⲦϬⲞⲘ ⲠⲈⲒⲈⲄⲄⲢⲀⲪⲞⲚ̅ Ⲛ̅Ϥ̅Ϣ ϢⲚ̅ⲚⲈ-ⲦⲤⲎϨ ⲈⲢⲞϤ. "We now clearly present this declaration. We swear to every magistrate or holy bishop or God-fearing court or *lashane* who shall examine into the validity of this document." Also see *P.Oxy.*VI.893; *P.KRU* 36, 44, 105; *O.Medin.HabuCopt.* 83.
67. *P.Lond.*IV.1339, 1356, 1384, 1400. For ⲀⲠⲈ (pl. ⲀⲠⲎⲨⲈ) see *P.Ryl.Copt.*127, 173, 278, 281, 319; *P.CLT.*3, 5, 6; *P.Heid.Arab.*I. The situation in Iraq was very similar, see Morony, "Religious Communities," 126; repr. Hoyland, ed., *Muslims and Others*.
68. Kindī, *Wulāt*, 69. *Mawārīth* was corrected by C. Becker, "Historische Studien über das Londoner Aphroditowerk," *Der Islam* 2 (1911), 363–4, to read "*mawāzīt*" (μειζότεροι); as in *P.Qurra.*5.21. This term also appears in HP I.3:388, and was translated as "superintendents of inherited property;" again, *mawāzīt* is a better reading.
69. See *P.Lond.*IV, *P.Heid.Arab.*I, *P.Qurra*; idem, "Arabische Papyri des Aphroditofundes," *Zeitschrift für Assyriologie und Verwandte Gebiete* 20 (1907), 68–104; idem, "Neue arabische Papyri des Aphroditofundes," *Der Islam* 2 (1911), 245–68; idem, "Historische Studien über das Londoner Aphroditowerk," *Der Islam* 2 (1911), 359–71; H.I. Bell, "Two Official Letters."
70. Cf. Petra M. Sijpesteijn, "Landholding Patterns in Early Islamic Egypt," *Journal of Agrarian Change* 9.1 (2009), 120–33, at 122–3.
71. For an appraisal of Qurra and his tenure, see Abbott's *P.Qurra*, ch 3.

72. *P.Apoll.*26, 29, 40, 50; *P.Lond.*IV.1338, 1339, 1340, 1346, 1348, 1362, 1364, 1365, 1370, 1380, 1394, 1397, 1398, 1405; *P.Qurra.*4.
73. *P.Lond.*IV.1394, cf. 1356, 1380. Similarly, Qurra believed that "cultivation by the people of the land is their chief duty, after their duty to God" (*P.Qurra.*2.13–5).
74. Cf. *P.Apoll.*9. Like Basilios a generation later, Papas shrugged off the governor's threats and repeated requests to present himself at Fusṭāṭ (*P.Apoll.*6).
75. Kindī, *Wulāt*, 64; here, Qurra put a hundred men to the sword.
76. *P.Apoll.*14, 20; *P.Lond.*IV.1333, 1339, 1343, 1344, 1359, 1361, 1372, 1381, 1383, 1384; *P.Cair.Arab.*151; *O.Medin.HabuCopt.* 136; *O.Crum.* 107, 108, 110, 111, 113, Ad. 43; HP I.3:318; A.A. Schiller, "The Coptic ⲗⲟⲅⲟⲥⲙⲡⲛⲟⲩⲧⲉ Documents," in *Studi in memoria di Aldo Albertoni*, vol. 1 (Padua, 1935), 303–45; W.C. Till, "Koptische Schutzbriefe," *Mitteilungen des Deutschen Archäologischen Instituts für ägyptische Altertumskunde in Kairo* 8 (1938), 71–146; Y. Raghib "Sauf-conduits d'Égypte omeyyade et Abbasside," *Annales Islamologiques* 31 (1997), 143–68; S. Schaten, "Reiseformalitäten im frühislamischen Ägypten," BSAC 37 (1998), 91–100; C. Wickham, *Framing the Early Middle Ages*, 142–43; Alain Delattre, "Les "lettres de protection" coptes," *Akten des 23 Internationalen Papyrologenkongresses*, ed. Bernhard Palme (Vienna, 2007), 173–178.
77. *P.Lond.*IV.1333, 1343, 1344; HP I.3:318, mentions one such bounty hunter, ʿAbd al-ʿAzīz.
78. *P.Lond.*IV.1343, 1384.
79. *P.Lond.*IV.1343, 1384; lit. "count" or "consider the dead happy."
80. *P.Cair.Arab.*I.42 dated 274/888 from Ashmūnayn; I.54 dated 448/1056 from Fayyūm—the same *mu'adhdhin* is attested two years later in I.67.21 dated 450/1058; II.92 dated 3/9 c.; V.320 dated 328/940; II.121 dated 284/897; *P.Prag.Arab.*32.23; *P.Marchands.*I.6.8 and I.5.12; Y. Raghib, "Trois documents dates du Louvre," *Annales Islamologiques* 15 (1979), 1–10 (§1).
81. Clerics were commonly employed and/or functioned as scribes and witnesses in Byzantine and early Islamic Egypt; cf. the authors and witnesses recorded in *P.Teshlot*; *O.Crum.* 62, 70, 163, 175, 304, 429, Ad. 14, cf. 29; *O.Medin. HabuCopt.* 58, 65, 66, 75.
82. A.S. Tritton, *Caliphs and their non-Muslim Subjects*; A. Arthur Schiller, "The Courts are No More," in *Studi in onore di Edoardo Volterra* (Milano, 1971), I.469–502; S.D. Goitein, "Minority Selfrule and Government Control," *Studia Islamica* 31 (1970), 102;, S.D. Goitein, "The Muslim Government as Seen by its Non-Muslim Subjects," *Journal of the Pakistan Historical Society* 12 (1964), 1–13; Gladys Frantz-Murphy, "Settlement of Property Disputes in Provincial Egypt: The Reinstitution of Courts in the Early Islamic Period," *al-Masāq* 6 (1993), 95–105; Daniel Earl Miller, "From Catalogue to Codes to Canon: the Rise of the Petition to ʿUmar Among Legal Traditions Governing Non-

Muslims in Medieval Islamicate Societies" (Ph.D. dissertation, University of Missouri-Kansas City, 2000).

83. Néophyte Edelby, "L'autonomie législative des chrétiens en terre d'islam," *Archives d'histoire du droit oriental* 5 (1950–51), 307–51; trans. in R. Hoyland, ed., *Muslims and Others in Early Islamic Society*; A. Fattal, *Le statut légal des non-musulmans*.
84. On the Syrian tradition, see Uriel I. Simonsohn, *A Common Justice: The Legal Allegiances of Christians and Jews Under Early Islam* (Philadelphia, 2011); Arthur Vööbus, *The Synodicon in the West Syrian Tradition*, 2 vols. (Louvain, 1975–76); J.B. Chabot, *Synodicon Orientale* (Paris, 1902).
85. Edelby, "L'autonomie legislative," e.g. pgs. 317, 319, 320, 323 / Eng. trans. 11, 13, 14, 17.
86. On law in the Byzantine Empire, see Jones, *Later Roman Empire*, ch. 14; J. Beaucamp, "Byzantine Egypt and Imperial Law," in *Byzantine Egypt*, ed. Bagnall; C. Humfress, "Law and Legal Practice in the Age of Justinian," in *Cambridge Companion to the Age of Justinian*; C. Humfress, *Orthodoxy and the Courts in Late Antiquity.*
87. The *Synodicon Orientale* preserves canons issued in 554, 576, 585, 596, 605, 676, 775, 790 CE.
88. See U. Simonsohn, *A Common Justice*; M.G. Morony, *Iraq After the Muslim Conquest*, ch. 12; A.S. Atiya, *A History of Eastern Christianity*; Samuel H. Moffett, *A History of Christianity in Asia: Volume I: Beginnings to 1500* (San Francisco, 1992); Wilhelm Baum and Dietmar W. Winkler, *The Church of the East: A Concise History* (London, 2003); M.-L. Chaumont, *La Christianisation de l'empire Iranien* (Louvain, 1988).
89. Gabriel Ibn Turayk, *Nomocanon*; Ibn al-ʿAssāl, *al-Majmūʿ al-ṣafawī* was translated into Ethiopic as the *Fetha Nagast* and functioned as the official law code of Ethiopia until the adoption of the 1931 constitution: Abba Paulos Tzadua, trans., *Fetha Nagast* (Addis Ababa, 1968). Other important compilations include: Pseudo- Athanasios, *Canons*; Christodoulos, *Canons*; Cyril III, *Canons*; W. Riedel, *Die Kirchenrechtsquellen*. Also see, F.J. Cöln, "The Nomocanonical Literature of the Copto-Arabic Church of Alexandria," *The Ecclesiastical Review* 56 (1917), 113–41; René-Georges Coquin, "Nomocanons, Copto-Arabic," *CoptEncyc* 6:1799; Oswald H.E. Burmester, "The Laws of Inheritance of Gabriel ibn Turaik," OCP 2 (1935), 315–27.
90. Stefan Leder, ed./trans., *Die arabische Ecloga: das vierte Buch der Kanones der Könige aus der Sammlung des Makarios* (Frankfurt, 1985); L. Burgmann, *Ecloga: Das Gesetzbuch Leons III. Und Konstantinos' V* (Frankfurt, 1983); E.H. Freshfield, *A Manual of Roman Law: The Ecloga Published by the Emperors Leo III and Constantine V of Isauria at Constantinople A.D. 726 rendered into English* (Cambridge, 1926).
91. On the absence of this order from Rome and Alexandria, see Jean LaPorte, *The Role of Women in Early Christianity* (New York, 1982), 111; Tadros Y. Malaty, *The School of Alexandria,* vol. 1, *Before Origen* (New Jersey, 1994), 271.

92. HP I.3:258 describes the election of Patriarch Agathon: "the faithful God-fearing people, by the command of the Lord, took that God-fearing priest Agathon, and enthroned him as patriarch." It appears that Agathon personally selected John III as his successor. John III's biography lacks details, but see HP I.3:262–3.
93. HP I.3:278.
94. Kindī, *Wulāt*, 79.
95. Cf. A.A. Schiller's "Courts are No More" with G. Frantz-Murphy's "Settlement of Property Disputes," which argues that Islamic courts began to dominate the public sphere by the early eighth century CE, and that Copts routinely used them at that early date.
96. The term is used to designate legal practice from the 6th to the 9th c. CE: see Leslie S.B. MacCoull, "Law, Coptic," *CoptEncyc* 5:1428–32; A. Arthur Schiller, "Coptic Law," *The Juridical Review* 43 (1931), 211–40.
97. On arbitration and the *episcopalis audientia*, see G. Schmelz, *Kirchliche Amtsträger*, ch. 7; C. Humfress, *Orthodoxy and the Courts in Late Antiquity* (Oxford, 2007); Jill Harries, *Law and Empire in Late Antiquity* (Cambridge, 1999), chs. 5, 9, 10; Traianos Gagos and Peter van Minnen, eds., *Settling a Dispute; Toward a Legal Anthropology of Late Antique Egypt* (Ann Arbor, 1994), 41–42, 45; R.S. Bagnall, *Egypt in Late Antiquity*, 161–172; John C. Lamoreaux, "Episcopal Courts in Late Antiquity," *Journal of Early Christian Studies* 3.2 (1995), 143–67; cf. Tyan, *Histoire de l'organisation*, 84–85, 89–91, 98. For examples of this type of court in Egypt, see Leontios, *Life of John the Almsgiver*, §§5, 18, 24; Paphnutios, *Histories of the Monks*, 19a, Vivian 93; cf. 48a-b, Vivian 128–9.
98. Gagos and van Minnen, *Settling a Dispute*, 44. In Paphnutios' *Histories of the Monks* (48b, Vivian §115), an account of arbitration concludes with: "And in this way *both men profited*, and they left Abba Aaron, glorifying God." My emphasis.
99. Gagos and van Minnen, *Settling a Dispute*, 39–40.
100. Gagos and van Minnen, *Settling a Dispute*, 44; alluding to Matt. 5:25–6, Lk. 12:57–9.
101. Also see *P.Mon.Epiph.*257.
102. Taking grievances to the local governor was a late antique practice that survived into the early Islamic period; see ns. 4 and 85 above.
103. *P.CLT.*1.95–97; see also *P.CLT.*5.136–39.
104. Cf. Alexander Kazhdan, "Court, Law," *Oxford Dictionary of Byzantium* 1:543.
105. In *P.Mon.Epiph.*431, a man asks Apa Psan the anchorite to intercede in his affairs: "for I rely upon God, I rely upon the Great Man, and (upon) your holy fatherhood."
106. This was not an egalitarian utopia, however. The *lashane* were elected from among the more affluent villagers and were rewarded with tax-exemptions: cf. Morimoto, *Fiscal Administration*, 74, 82–3.

107. *P.CLT.*1.82–92. Similar clauses are in *P.CLT.*2.11–15, 18–20, 22–3; *P.CLT.*5.125–32; *Testament of Apa Abraham*, §6; *P.KRU* frequently reiterates these penalty clauses: e.g. *P.KRU* 37, 66, 77, 105, 106.
108. *P.Mon.Epiph.*141, 147, 151, 162, 163, 165, 172, 188, 196, 229, 257, 261, 271, 300, 431, 458, 462; *O.Crum.* 49, 61, 115, 116, Ad. 60; cf. 69, 154, 381; *O.Medin.HabuCopt.* 5, (cf. *P.KRU* 37, 44).
109. E.g. *P.Cair.Arab.*III.167 dated to the second/eighth century; *P.KRU* 3, 5, 66, 77,
110. See *P.Teshlot*; L.S.B. MacCoull, "Teshlot Papyri;" T.S. Richter, "Spätkoptische Rechtsurkunden neu bearbeitet: BM Or.4917 (15);" Michael H. Thung, "An Arabic Letter of the Rijksmuseum van Oudheden, Leiden," *Oudheidkundige Mededelingen der Rijksmuseum van Oudheiden* 76 (1996), 63–8; also see Chapter Five above.
111. Abū Yūsuf, *Kharāj*, 164. G. Frantz-Murphy, "Settlement of Property Disputes," demonstrates that a shift in the witness clauses of Coptic contracts at the early eighth century conformed to Islamic rather than Byzantine norms.
112. Some Christian contracts do retain a divorce clause; see *P.Bal.*152, dated 2nd/3rd c. Divorce agreements are also extant; e.g. *P.Cair.Masp.*III.67311.
113. Although late, see A.H. Green, "A Late 19th-Century Coptic Marriage Contract."
114. Antoine Fattal, "Comment les Dhimmis étaient jugés en terre d'Islam," *Cahiers d'histoire égyptienne* 3 (1951), 321–41; trans. in R. Hoyland, ed., *Muslims and Others*, 83–102.
115. See Cyril III, *Canons*, chapter *On Inheritance*, §§2, 3; O.H.E. Burmester, "Laws of Inheritance." For inheritance laws and the accompanying scholarly debates, see David S. Powers, *Studies in Qur'an and Hadith: the Formation of the Islamic Law of Inheritance* (Berkeley, 1986); J. Schacht, *Islamic Law*, ch. 23. On the use of Islamic courts by the Copts during the Ottoman and modern periods, see Mohamed Afifi, "Reflections on the Personal Law of Egyptian Copts," in *Women, the Family, and Divorce Laws in Islamic Egypt*, ed. Amira El Azhary Sonbol (Syracuse, 1996).
116. The meager regulations pertaining to business law in Coptic Arabic Nomocanons are directly borrowed from Islamic law.
117. Kindī, *Quḍāt*, 351; cf. Nāṣir-i Khusraw, *Safarnāma*, 69.
118. The *qāḍī* Muḥammad ibn Masrūq inaugurated this in 177/792 (al-Kindī, *Quḍāt*, 390, 391); cf. Fattal, *Le statut légale des non-musulmans*, 91–3.
119. The scene of Christians and Jews waiting and being judged by a *qāḍī* at the entrance of a mosque must have been a spectacle to passers-by.
120. T.S. Richter, "Koptische Rechtsurkunden als Quellen der Rechtspraxis im byzantinischen und frühislamischen Ägypten," in *Quellen zur byzantinischen Rechtspraxis*, ed. C. Gastgeber, F. Mitthof and B. Palme (Vienna, 2009), 39–59.
121. *P.Cair.Arab.*I.54, 57, 58; here Christians entering into contracts with each other were sure to draft their contracts "in accordance to Islamic law."
122. Cf. A.H. Green, "A Late 19th-Century Coptic Marriage Contract," 361–71.

Chapter 8 Metamorphosis of the Muslim Community

1. Early Islamic historiography is addressed in Chapters One and Two.
2. Well utilized in K. Morimoto's *Fiscal Administration of Egypt*; G. Frantz-Murphy's *CPR* XXI, J.B. Simonsen's *Studies*; and P.M. Sijpesteijn's "New Rule over Old Structures."
3. See al-Maqrīzī's *Bayān*, Introduction, ch.2. On the history of Arabs prior to Islam, see Irfan Shahid's multi-volume *Byzantium and the Arabs* (Washington D.C., 1984–2010); Jan Retsö, *The Arabs in Antiquity: their History from the Assyrians to the Umayyads* (London, 2003); Robert G. Hoyland, *Arabia and the Arabs: From the Bronze Age to the Coming of Islam* (London, 2001); Timothy Power, *The Red Sea from Byzantium to the Caliphate, AD 500–1000* (Cairo and New York, 2012).
4. Ibn ʿAbd al-Ḥakam, *Futūḥ*, 53–5; Ibn al-Kindī, *Faḍā'il miṣr*, 199; cf. Ibn Zulāq, *Faḍā'il miṣr*, 24–5.
5. Kindī, *Wulāt*, 36; Ibn ʿAbd al-Ḥakam, *Futūḥ*, 130–1.
6. On the Islamic navy, see David Bramoullé, "Recruiting Crews in the Fatimid Navy (909–1171)," *Medieval Encounters* 13.1 (2007), 4–31; Frank Trombley, "Mediterranean Sea Culture between Byzantium and Islam c. 600–850 A.D.)," in *The Dark Ages of Byzantium, 7th - 9th c.*, ed. E. Kountoura-Galake (Athens, 2001), 133–69; W.B. Kubiak, "The Byzantine Attack on Damietta in 853 and the Egyptian Navy in the 9th century," *Byzantion* 40 (1970), 45–66; Adel Allouche, "Umayyad Fleet, Coptic Contribution to," *CoptEncyc* 7:2286; Darwīsh al-Nakhlī, *al-Sufun al-islāmīya 'alā ḥurūf al-mu'jam* (Alexandria, 1974); Aly Mohamed Fahmy, *Muslim Sea-Power in the Eastern Mediterranean: From the Seventh to the Tenth Century AD* (Cairo, 1966).
7. Władysław Kubiak, *Al-Fustat: Its Foundation and Early Urban Development* (Cairo, 1987); George T. Scanlon, *Fustat Expedition Final Report* (Winona Lake, 1986); J. Jomier, "al-Fusṭāṭ," EI^2 2:957b -959a; also see the voluminous publications by Roland-Pierre Gayraud, especially his reports on the excavations of Isṭabl ʿAntar (Fusṭāṭ), which have appeared in *Annales Islamologiques* 22 (1986), 1–26; 23 (1987), 55–71; 25 (1991), 57–87; 27 (1993), 225–32; 28 (1994), 1–27; 29 (1995), 1–24; 42 (2008), 299–312; idem, "Fostat: évolution d'une capitale arabe du VIIe au XIIe siècle d'après les fouilles d'Istabl ʿAntar," *Colloque international d'Archéologie islamique* (Cairo, 1998), 435–60; idem, "La nécropole des Fatimides à Fostat," *Dossiers de l'archéologie* 233 (1998), 34–41; idem, "La transition céramique en Égypte. VIIe-IXe siècle," *VIIe Congrès international sur la Céramique médiévale en Méditerranée* (Athens, 2003), 558–62.
8. See *P.Bal.*174, 187, 240; *P.Lond.Copt.*I .549, 593;*Life of Isaac of Alexandria*, 56, Bell 63.
9. Ibn ʿAbd al-Hakam, *Futūḥ*, 132, cf. 41, 42, 91, 131, 135; Eutychios, *Naẓm al-jawhar*, II.27.
10. H. Kennedy, "From *Polis* to *Madina*," 15–6.

11. Ibn ʿAbd al-Ḥakam, *Futūḥ*, 98, 141–3; a similar pattern may be observed in other *amṣār*. Cf. the Tabernacle, which served as the point of orientation around which the tribes of Israel were encamped.
12. Kindī, *Wulāt*, 49; Eutychios, *Naẓm al-jawhar*, II.40–41; also see HP I.3:278, 291, 296; J.M.B. Jones, "Ḥulwān," EI^2 3:572a; R.-G. Coquin, M. Martin, and P. Grossmann, "Ḥilwan," *CoptEncyc* 4:1232–5.
13. Cf. Muhammad Qasim Zaman, "*Maghāzī* and the *Muḥaddithūn*: Reconsidering the Treatment of "Historical" Materials in Early Collections of Hadith," IJMES 28 (1996), 1–18.
14. Qur'ān 9:90, 97–8, 101, 120; 34:20; 48:11; 49:14; Ibn ʿAbd al-Ḥakam, *Futūḥ*, 162; S. Bashear, *Arabs and Others in Early Islam*, ch. 1; Khalil ʿAthamina, "*Aʿrāb* and *Muhājirūn* in the Environment of *Amṣār*," *Studia Islamica* 66 (1987), 13–5.
15. On the tribes (and clans) that immigrated to Egypt, see ʿAbdallāh Khurshid Barrī, *al-Qaba'il al-ʿarabiya fi miṣr fi al-qurun al-thalatha al-ula lil-hijra* (Cairo, 1967; repr. and enlarged, 1992); and Mamduḥʿ Abd al-Raḥmān ʿAbd al-Raḥīm Riti, *Dawr al-qaba'il al-ʿarabiya fi saʿid miṣr . . .21–358/641–969* (Cairo, 1996).
16. The four editions of the *dīwān* during the first Islamic century were under ʿAmr ibn al-ʿĀṣ, ʿAbd al-ʿAzīz ibn Marwān, Qurra ibn Sharīk, and Bishr ibn Ṣafwān; see al-Kindī, *Wulāt*, 92; al-Maqrīzī, *Khiṭaṭ*, I.252; K. Morimoto, "*Dīwān*s as Registers"; M.S.A. Mikhail "Notes on *Ahl al-Diwān*."
17. For *'aṭā'*, see *P.Oxy.*IV.1349, 1357, 1373; *rizq* is documented in *P.Oxy.*IV.1394, 1404, 1407; P. Mayerson, "POYZIKON and POΓA in the Post-Conquest Papyri," ZPE 100 (1994), 126–8; idem, "An Additional Note on POYZIKON (Ar. *Rizq*)," ZPE 107 (1995), 279–81.
18. *P.Oxy.*IV.1337, 1348, 1353, 1376, 1393.
19. *P.Oxy.*IV.1374; cf. 1337; in *P.CLT* 6, 17 men fulfilling the naval conscription demanded that all should be paid the same rate.
20. HP I.3:324–5.
21. Theophanes, *Chronicle*, §397.6–7; Nikephoros, *Short History*, §54.
22. For the redating of *P.Apoll.* to the 660s, see J. Gascou and K.A. Worp, "Problèmes de documentation apollinopolite," ZPE 49 (1982), 83–95; Clive Foss, "Egypt under Muʿāwiya, Part I: Flavius Papas and Upper Egypt," BSOAS 72.1 (2009), 1–24. More generally on the early Umayyad period: Jeremy Johns, "Archaeology and the History of Early Islam: The First Seventy Years," JESHO 46.4 (2003), 411–36; Robert Hoyland, "New Documentary Texts and the Early Islamic State," BSOAS 69.3 (2006), 395–416. C. Foss, "Egypt under Muʿāwiya, Part II: Middle Egypt, Fusṭāṭ and Alexandria," BSOAS 72.2 (2009), 259–78; idem, "Muʿāwiya State," in *Money, Power and Politics*, ed. J. Haldon.
23. *P.Apoll.*9, 30, 29, 38; *P.Lond.*IV.1336, 1341, 1366, 1391, 1410, 1411.
24. *P.Lond.*IV.1336, 1342, 1353; cf. 1337, 1348.
25. On dock workers, see *P.Lond.*IV.1336, 1410, 1414; cf. 1376. On the port of Clysma, see Philip Mayerson, "The Port of Clysma (Suez) in Transition from Roman to Arab Rule," JNES 55.2 (1996), 119–126; N. Gonis, "P. Vindob. G 14965 (=*CPR* IX 6) + 18880: Requisitioned Workers in Eighth-Century

Egypt," ZPE 145 (2003), 209–11. For those assigned to building projects, see *P.Lond.*IV.1342, 1362, 1378. Carpenters sent to work on the mosque of Damascus are mentioned in *P.Lond.*IV.1341, 1368, 1411. Those sent to work on the mosques of Jerusalem are mentioned in *P.Lond.*IV.1366, 1403, 1414. See also 1334.

26. See *P.Lond.*IV.1368, 1378, 1378.
27. In *P.Apoll.*33, 36, 95 some commodities, such as firewood, had to be sent; also see Y. Ragib, "Lettres nouvelles," §1. For other supplies, cash was preferred (*P.Apoll.*52, 86.88); C. Foss, "Egypt under Mu'āwiya, Part I," 14–5.
28. E.g. *P.Lond.*IV.1375; also in M.S.A. Mikhail, "Notes on the *Ahl al-Dīwān*," 277–8.
29. Ibn 'Abd al-Ḥakam, *Futūḥ*, 143; al-Kindī, *Wulāt*, 76–7; al-Maqrīzī, *Bayān*, §§59–63; Yūsuf Fadl Hasan, *The Arabs and the Sudan: From the Seventh to the Early Sixteenth Century* (Edinburgh, 1967), 33–4.
30. 'Athamina, "*A'rāb* and *Muhājirūn*," 5–25.
31. Ibn 'Abd al-Ḥakam, *Futūḥ*, 116; al-Maqrīzī, *Bayān*, §§18, 22.
32. Ibn 'Abd al-Ḥakam, *Futūḥ*, 128, 118–9.
33. Kindī, *Wulāt*, 76, cf. 68; Ibn 'Abd al-Ḥakam, *Futūḥ*, 143; Khalil 'Athamina, "Arab Settlement during the Umayyad Caliphate," JSAI 8 (1986), esp. 200–4; idem, "Some Administrative, Military and Socio-Political Aspects of Early Muslim Egypt," in *War and Society*, ed. Y. Lev, 107–11.
34. See Patricia Crone, "Were the Qays and Yemen of the Umayyad Period Political Parties?" *Der Islam* 71 (1994), 1–57.
35. See M.C. Dunn, "Struggle for Abbasid Egypt," 165, 182, 191–200.
36. Especially true for the tribe of Mudlij and some of the Ḥimyar; Ibn 'Abd al-Ḥakam, *Futūḥ*, 142, cf. 126; 'Athamina, "Arab Settlement," 202. Some early traditions suggest that farming was an occupation unbefitting an Arab (warrior): Abū 'Ubayd, *Amwāl*, §55; Ibn 'Abd al-Ḥakam, *Futūḥ*, 162; al-Bukhārī, *Ṣaḥīḥ*, bāb *al-muzāra'*a, §2; K. 'Athamina, "*A'rāb* and *Muhājirūn*," 13–15; S. Bashear, *Arabs and Others*, ch. 1. This warrior ethos is also evident in such themes as the popular single combat *topos* along with the *maghāzī* and *akhbār* accounts; see A. Noth, *Early Arabic Historical Tradition*, 129, 145, 168.
37. Yaḥyā ibn Ādam, *Kharāj*, §§156–63, 168–9, 175, 176, 178; Abū 'Ubayd, *Amwāl*, §§433, 434, 437.
38. Abū Yūsuf, *Kharāj*, 61, 65; Yaḥyā ibn Ādam, *Kharāj*, §§26, 197, 198, 199; Norman Calder, *Studies in Early Muslim Jurisprudence* (Oxford, 1993), ch. 6.
39. Abū Yūsuf, *Kharāj*, 65–6; Yaḥyā ibn Ādam, *Kharāj*, §§40, 42, 43, 57.
40. Kindī, *Wulāt*, 74.
41. Kindī, *Wulāt*, 94–5.
42. Kindī, *Wulāt*, 101.
43. The ideological bent is evident in Ibn 'Abd al-Ḥakam, *Futūḥ*, 65–6, 71, 75, 115.

44. On the early *dīwān*, see Gerd-Rüdiger Puin, *Der Dīwān von 'Umar Ibn al-Haṭṭāb* (Bonn, 1970); H. Kennedy, *Armies of the Caliphs*, 60–88; and Morimoto, "*Dīwān*s as Registers."
45. Ibn 'Abd al-Ḥakam, *Futūḥ*, 127.
46. Ibn 'Abd al-Ḥakam, *Futūḥ*, 121.
47. Ibn 'Abd al-Ḥakam, *Futūḥ*, 119, 121, 122, 129.
48. Ibn 'Abd al-Ḥakam, *Futūḥ*, 122, 129 (cf. Ibn Ḥawqal, *Ṣūrat al-arḍ*, 146); here there is mention of *masjid al-zanj* and *masjid al-fārisiyyīn*. The reference to *masjid al-zanj* is especially noteworthy as it challenges another ideologically inspired tradition transmitted by Ibn 'Abd al-Ḥakam (*Futūḥ*, 66), which emphasizes the colorblindness of Islam as opposed to the prejudice of non-Muslims.
49. *Mawlā* was retained throughout the Umayyad period, demarcating non-Arab converts from the privileged Arab Muslims. This aspect of the term was phased out over the first century of 'Abbāsid rule. See Pipes, "Mawlas: Freed Slaves," 152–3; idem, *Slave Soldiers and Islam*, 174–81.
50. On the army, see M.S.A. Mikhail, "Notes on the *Ahl al-Dīwān*;" Y. Lev, ed., *War and Society*; H. Kennedy, *Armies of the Caliphs*; Jere L. Bacharach, "African Military Slaves in the Medieval Middle East: The Cases of Iraq (869–955) and Egypt (868–1171)," IJMES 13 (1981), 471–95.
51. Maqrīzī, *Bayān*, §§3–4, 16, 21, 35.
52. See al-Kindī, *Wulāt*, 325; Ibn 'Abd al-Ḥakam, *Futūḥ*, 102; al-Maqrīzī, *Khiṭaṭ*, I.252.
53. Well discussed by 'Athamina, "*A'rāb* and *Muhājirūn*," 19–23.
54. See Ibn 'Abd al-Ḥakam, *Futūḥ*, 116–7, 127.
55. Allegedly, these were the regulations imposed by 'Umar ibn al-Khaṭṭāb on *ahl al-Shām*. In time, they were interpreted as paradigmatic of the rights and obligations of *ahl al-kitāb* in general. 'Umar II is often identified as the founder of the Covenant. Still, while 'Umar II implemented some of the regulations mentioned in the Covenant, in its full form, the *shūrat* are clearly the product of a much later period.
56. D.E. Miller, "From Catalogue to Codes to Canon"; Fattal, *Le statut légale des non-musulmans*, 97–8.
57. Regulations pertaining to church buildings are discussed in Chapter Ten.
58. Ibn 'Abd al-Ḥakam, *Futūḥ*, 151–2; Abū Yūsuf, *Kharāj*, 127, 144; Abū 'Ubayd, *Amwāl*, §138; Eutychios, *Naẓm al-jawhar*, II: 59, 63; al-Maqrīzī, *Khiṭaṭ*, IV.1017; Ilsa Lichtenstadter, "The Distinctive Dress of Non-Muslims in Islamic Countries," *Historica Judaica* 5 (1943), 35–52; Mark Cohen, "At the Origins of the Distinctive Dress Regulation for Non-Muslims in Islam: the Zunnār, Discrimination or Reinforcement of Community Identity?" in *The Byzantine and Early Islamic Near East* II, ed. L.I. Conrad (Princeton, 1994); M. Kister, "Do Not Assimilate Yourselves...: *lā tashabbahū...*," *Jerusalem Studies in Arabic and Islam* 12 (1989), 321–71; repr. in idem, *Concepts and Ideas at the Dawn of Islam* (Brookfield, 1997), VI; Ḥabīb Zayāt, "Simāt al-naṣārā wa-al-yahūd fī al-islām:

al-ṣalīb, aw al-zunnār, wa al-ʿamāma wa al-ghiyār; shurūt al-ʿumarīya," *al-Machrīq* 43.2 (1949), 161–252; M. J. Saleh, "Government Relations," 98–108.
59. Abū Yūsuf, *Kharāj*, 127; Abū ʿUbayd, *Amwāl*, §137, 139.
60. *Apocalypse of Samuel*, 378–9.
61. Abdel Hamid Saleh, "Les bédouins d'Egpte aux premiers siècles de l'Hégire," *Rivista degli Studi Orientali* 55 (1981), 148–61; trans. "The Bedouins of Egypt during the First Centuries of the Hijra," in *Production and the Exploitation of Resources*, ed. M.G. Morony (Burlington, 2002); also see Barrī, *al-Qaba'il al-ʿarabiya fi miṣr*; Christian Décobert, "Maréotide médiévale. Des Bédouins et des chrétiens," in *Alexandrie médiévale 2*, 127–64.
62. Both retain significant portions of al-Ḥamdānī's (d. 334/945) lost work, *al-Ansāb*, which was dedicated to the topic. See Saleh, "Bedouins of Egypt," 138–40; al-Maqrīzī, *Bayān*.
63. Maqrīzī, *Bayān*, §3 (pg. 3); though al-Balādhurī's *Ansāb al-ashrāf* and Ibn Yūnus' *Tarīkh* are certainly worthy of mention.
64. Of relevance here are, Fred M. Donner, "The Role of Nomads in the Near East in Late Antiquity (400–800 C.E.), in *Tradition and Innovation*, ed. Clover and Humphreys, 73–85; Jibrail S. Jabbur, *The Bedouins and the Desert*, trans. L.I. Conrad (Albany, 1995), ch. 19. For a later period, see Claude Cahen, "Nomades et sedentaires dans le monde musulman du milieu du Moyen-Age," in *Islamic Civilisation 950–1150*, ed. D.S. Richards (Oxford, 1973); Carl F. Petry, "Disruptive 'Others' as Depicted in the Chronicles of the Late Mamluk Period," in *The Historiography of Islamic Egypt (c. 950–1800)*, ed. H. Kennedy (Leiden, 2001), 167–94.
65. Ibn ʿAbd al-Ḥakam, *Futūḥ*, 139–43.
66. Pastoralism had been defamed in the Qur'ān as essentially deceptive and uncultured; see n. 14 above. The pre-Islamic period of tribal blood-feuds and infighting were called *ayyām al-ʿArab*. Later, tales of these feuds were recorded in the ninth-century book by the same name.
67. The HP documents business interactions between Muslim merchants and Coptic monasteries (HP II.1:98/133r); the reference is likely to pastoralists. An indirect reference in HP II.2:210/153v-154r indicates that the Arab pastoralists in the mid-ninth century were somewhat stereotypical; they lived in tents, and needed finished goods, especially weapons and clothing.
68. Scetis (Shihīt / Wādī al-Naṭrūn / Wādī Ḥabīb) was repeatedly attacked throughout the period surveyed: 407, 434, 444, 570, 616, 631, 866, 1069 CE; see Ewa Wipszycka, *Moines et communautés monastiques en Égypte* (Warsaw, 2009), ch 12; William Y. Adams, "Beja Tribes," *CoptEncyc* 2:373–4; Evelyn White, *Monasteries*, II:151–61, 249–51, 297–8, 325–7, 354–6.
69. Alarm spread "for it was the time when they came down from the land of Upper Egypt to the land of Lower Egypt, after putting their beasts out to grass" (HP II.1:52/123v).
70. See HP I.4:552, 565, 582; HP II.1:54/123v. Perhaps the worst period was in the mid-860s, see HP II.1:45–6/122r; 53–6/123v-124r; 57/124r-v,

59–60/125r, 63/125v. Most monasteries in Wādī al-Naṭrūn were abandoned on account of the "Marauding Arabs." Various monasteries and churches, including that associated with St. Menas, were raided and some destroyed (HP II.1:59–60/125r).

71. HP II.2:54–8/124r-v.
72. Maqrīzī, *Bayān*, §33.
73. HCME 82a, 234–5. Marā had paid for the furnishings and icons of the church. Accusations of apostasy led to Marā's arrest by al-Mājīd Fāris. Due to the intervention of Christians and a payment to the *wālī*, however, Marā was released, but he was soon murdered by Bedouins (*'urbān*) in the desert. He was brought to the side of the church he had built and was buried there.
74. HP II.2:168/146r, 182/148v, 193/150v. Khaīl was later restored. In HP II.2:207/153r, he was in the company of the patriarch—his paternal uncle—in the company of other bishops. The whole affair began when John the monk, went to the patriarch and asked to be ordained a bishop without paying any money for the post (simony was quite rampant at that time). Angered by the man's audacity, Bishop Khaīl ordered the man to leave and then handed him over to the *'urbān*. John then went and complained to the Caliph al-Ḥākim bi Amr Allāh, whose persecution was soon to follow. After nine years of persecution, John again asked to be ordained. When Khaīl objected, he was silenced by the other bishops who blamed him for the persecutions of al-Ḥākim. John was ordained a hegumen (HP II.2:207–8/153v). Later, he made an agreement with Shenoute, a patriarchal nominee; John would help him become patriarch, and Shenoute would ordain him a bishop—both kept their ends of the deal (HP II.2:230–31/158r).
75. HP I.4:568.
76. HP II.2:182/148v (Ar. pg. 121). He was handed over to "the Arabs who were the guards of the monasteries (*khufarā al-diyarā*)."
77. It can be argued that the relationship was parasitic or pretorian rather than symbiotic, i.e. the *'urbān* were only protecting the monasteries to exploit them for themselves. Still, the evidence, which is admittedly slim, does point toward a symbiotic relationship, and the positive effect of the protection they afforded Coptic monasteries (for whatever reason) is not in question.
78. HP II.2:200/152r (Ar. pg. 132).
79. HP II.2:201/152r (Ar. pg. 132).
80. G. Zoega, *Catalogus Codicum Copticorum Manuscriptorum qui in Museo Borgiano* (Rome, 1810), 106; A. Hebbelynck and A. van Lantschoot, *Codices Coptici Vaticani Barberiniani Borgiani Rossiani: Tomus I* (Vatican City, 1937), 510; Evelyn White, *Monasteries*, 2:345: "For by the grace of God I came to this holy monastery in great affliction at that time when, he. . .al-Ḥākim (*palhachēm*) destroyed the churches and also the monasteries of the Fayyūm. . .I came to the monastery because of the Body of Christ that I might partake of it. For in no other place do men meet together with confidence before His throne. . .except

[in the Monastery of] our Father Abba Makarios in the Desert." The colophone is dated 730 of Diocletian / 1014 CE.

81. HP II.2:204–5/152v. This prevailed for at least three years during the reign of al-Ḥākim, and for an additional three years Christians had to seek out and receive communion in secret. See the previous note.

Chapter 9 Ideologies and Jurisdictions

1. HP I.4:621, my translation.
2. See Chapter Six. None of the Egyptian uprisings were analogous to the Persian revolts of Bihāfarid (747 CE) or Bābak (816–38 CE), which had overt religious and social aims: see F. Daftary, "Sectarian and National Movements in Iran, Khurasan and Transoxania During Umayyad and Early ʿAbbasid Times," in *History of Civilizations of Central Asia*, vol. 4.1, ed. M.S. Asimov and C.E. Bosworth (Paris, 1998); E. Yarshater, "Mazdakism," in *The Cambridge History of Iran*, vol. 3.2, ed. idem (Cambridge, 1983), 991–1024; cf. J.K. Choksy, *Conflict and Cooperation*, 54–6, 84–6.
3. See Francis Dvornik, *Early Christian and Byzantine Political Philosophy*, 2 vols. (Washington D.C., 1966), esp. vol. 2; Frend, *Monophysite Movement*, ch. 2; F. Kolb, *Herrscherideologie in der Spätantike* (Berlin, 2001), ch. 3. On Syria, see Philip Wood, *"We Have no king but Christ," Christian Political Thought in Greater Syria on the Eve of the Arab Conquest (c. 400–585)* (Oxford, 2011).
4. The Byzantines certainly had alternative (marginal) conceptions for political rule. Faced with three candidates, the soldiers of the Anatolic *thema* declared "We believe in the Trinity. Let us crown all three!" (Theophanes, *Chronicle*, AM 6161 (668/9 CE).
5. See J. Meyendorff, *Imperial Unity*, 29–38; Garth Fowden, *Empire to Commonwealth: Consequences of Monotheism in Late Antiquity* (Princeton, 1993), esp. ch. 4.
6. Persecutions of anti-Chalcedonians are preserved in various hagiographic lives; e.g. the *Panegyric of Makarios of Tikou*, *Life of Daniel of Scetis*, *Life of Samuel of Qalamun*, *Life of Isaac of Alexandria* as well as the *Histories* of pseudo-Zachariah the Rhetor, John of Ephesos, and John of Nikiou. That is in addition to pro-Chalcedonian sources.
7. The population besought God: "Give us a good emperor like Anastasius or else remove the emperor Justin *whom you have given us*" (John of Nikiou, *Chronicle*, §90.20, my emphasis). He continues: "'It is owing to the sins of the city that I have appointed this emperor who is a hater of the virtuous,' thus said the Lord: 'I will give you rulers according to your own hearts'" (cf. Theophanes, *Chronicle* AM 6303 [810/11 CE]). Another passage emphasizes the association between God and emperor: "Let us worship and give praise to Him who gives help and power to kings" (§94.20). Similarly, the HP quotes John, the eleventh-century patriarch of Antioch: "He who resists the king sins; he is like one who resists

the ordinance of God" (HP II.2:216/115r, my translation). The same ideology prevailed among pro-Chalcedonians. Herakleios is reported to have asked: "When a man insults an emperor, whom does he offend?" They answered: "He offends God who has appointed the emperor" Ἡράκλειον... εἰπεῖν λέγεται πρὸς αὐτούς "ὁ βασιλέα ὑβρίζων τίνι προσκρούει;" τοὺς δὲ φάναι "τῷ θεῷ ποιήσαντι αὐτὸν βασιλέα" (Nikephoros, *Short History*, §39).

8. See the Synodal Letter of Patriarch Damian (*P.Mon.Epiph.*II pg. 152; trans. 337), and n. 22 below.
9. *P.KRU* 77, dated 4 December 634 CE.
10. See Chapter One, ns. 6, 7, 46, 47.
11. Such a perspective may be traced back to the beginnings of Second Temple Judaism, where the Persian Cyrus was labeled a Messiah (Is. 45:1); cf. S.D. Goitein, "Minority Selfrule and Government Control," *Studia Islamica* 31 (1970), 102; idem, "The Muslim Government as Seen by its Non-Muslim Subjects," *Journal of the Pakistan Historical Society* 12 (1964), 10.
12. Jan J. van Ginkel, "John of Ephesus on Emperors: The Perception of the Byzantine Empire by a Monophysite," *VI Symposium Syriacum 1992*, ed. René Lavenant, Orientalia Christiana Analecta 247 (1994), 323–33.
13. John bar Penkāyē (684–91 CE): Sebastian P. Brock, "North Mesopotamia in the Late Seventh Century: Book XV of John Bar Penkāyē's Rīš Mellē," JSAI 9 (1987), 51–71; repr. *Studies in Syriac Christianity* (Brookfield, 1992); G.J. Reinink, "East Syrian Historiography in Response to the Rise of Islam: A Case of John Bar Penkaye's Ktābā d-rēš mellē," in *Redefining Christian Identity: Cultural Interaction in the Middle East since the Rise of Islam*, ed. J.J. van Ginkel, H.L. Murre - van den Berg, and T.M. van Lint (Louvain, 2005).
14. Justinian is called "the new Marcian" in the *Chronicle* of John of Nikiou (§92.13). As discussed below, the depictions of Herakleios are mixed. See Gerrit J. Reinink and Bernard H. Stolte, eds., *The Reign of Heraclius (610–641): Crisis and Confrontation* (Louvain, 2002).
15. HP I.2:189, cf. 195. See also, Charles Pazdernik, "'Our Most Pious Consort Given Us by God' Dissident Reactions to the Partnership of Justinian and Theodora, AD 525–548," *Classical Antiquity* 13 (1994), 256–81; Lynda Garland, *Byzantine Empresses: Women and Power in Byzantium, AD 527–1204* (New York, 1998), ch. 1; Susan Ashbrook Harvey, *Asceticism and Society in Crisis: John of Ephesus and The Lives of the Eastern Saints* (Berkeley, 1990), 80–91; eodem, "Theodora the 'Believing Queen': A Study in Syriac Histiographical Tradition," *Hugoye: Journal of Syriac Studies* 4.2 (2001) <http://syrcom.cua.edu/Hugoye>; Volker-Lorenz Menze, *Justinian and the Making of the Syrian Orthodox Church* (Oxford, 2008), ch. 5; G.B. Behnam, *Theodora*, trans. M. Moosa (Piscataway, 2007). Justinian's depiction as the heretical emperor is also found in the *Panegyric on Apollo*, *Life of Daniel of Scetis*, and *Life of Samuel of Qalamun*. His *Monogenēs* hymn is retained by the Copts and is chanted on Good Friday primarily due to an anti-Chalcedonian tradition that attributes it to Severos of Antioch. See Robert F. Taft,

"Monogenes, Ho," *Oxford Dictionary of Byzantium* 2:1397. Severos of Antioch met with Justinian in the hope that "the unbelieving king would be converted from his corrupt doctrine" (HP I.2:188).

16. S.P. Brock, "Christians in the Sasanian Empire: A Case of Divided Loyalties," in *Religion and National Identity*, ed. S. Mews.
17. The depiction in Rev. 17–18 is markedly different. There, the empire is corrupt and the emperor is the beast (the anti-Christ). Nonetheless, this depiction is marginal in historical sources. The *Panegyric on Apollo* (written ca. 600 CE), contains one of the rare attestations. There, the emperor in question is Justinian. In the *Panegyric on Macarius of Tkōw*, II, the indirect references are to the Empress Pulcheria. Būlus al-Būshī's *Commentary on the Apocalypse* does not make any connection to political rule.
18. See J.C. Lamoreaux's "Early Eastern Christian Responses," in *Medieval Christian Perceptions of Islam*, ed. J.V. Tolan, though the analysis is overly polarizing.
19. See L.S.B. MacCoull, "P.Madrid 189 Revisited," ZPE 112 (1996), 285–6, which was used under Islamic rule.
20. This caused a problem for the Syrian patriarch John as he crossed from Arab to Byzantine-controlled territories; see HP II.2:216–21/155r-156r.
21. HP I.2:232–33, though likely a *topos* in this instance; see the discussions in chapters One and Two.
22. HP I.3:438; HP II.2:206/153r; II.3:326/173v; cf. II.1:66/126r-v, 68/126v; Otto F.A. Meinardus, "The Attitudes of the Orthodox Copts towards the Islamic State from the 7th to the 12th century," *Ostkirchliche Studien* 13 (1964), 168–9. Coptic liturgies contain a litany for those in government (*Liturgy of St. Cyril*, the concluding litanies recited in the rite of Pascha, and *P.Lond.Copt.* I.512). The same was true in Jewish communal prayers; see Goitein, "Muslim Government," 11; cf. HP II.2:144/141v. For Syria, see HP II.2:216/155r and 218/155v, which quotes 1 Tim. 2:2.
23. HP II.2:206/153r, cf. II.2:218/155v. In HP II.2:144/141v, Patriarch Afrahām states, "I desire nothing except that God may strengthen your state and give you victory over your enemies." At another juncture, a certain John approached al-Ḥākim stating, "You are the caliph of God on his earth" (HP II.2:193/150v).
24. *P.Oxy.*138, dated 610–11 CE, reads: "To all this I swear by Almighty God and by the supremacy salvation and preservation of our most pious sovereigns, Flavius Heraclius and Aelia flavia" καὶἐπὶ τούτοις πᾶσιν ἐπωμουσάμην πρὸς τοῦ θεοῦ τοῦ παντοκράτορος, καὶ νίκης καὶ σωτηρίας καὶ διαμονῆς τῶν εὐσεβ(εστάτων) ἡμῶν δεσποτῶν Φλαουίου Ἡρακλείου καὶ Αἰλίας Φλαβίας.
25. Another variant, "the health of those who rule over us now and at any time," is also recorded: *P.Bal.*114; cf. 111, 116, 119, 120; see Kahle's Introduction, pgs. 46–47. *P.Bal.*116 reads, "I swear {by} almighty {God} and the health {of our lords} the sovereigns who rule over us {now}." As Kahle notes, Muslim not

Byzantine authorities are intended here. Another version of the formula reads: "our fathers" who rule over us (see Kahle, pg. 47); *P.KRU* 12, 50; cf. *P.Vat.Copti Doresse* 3 in MacCoull, *Coptic Legal Documents*.

26. See *P.Mon.Apollo*.24.9. Clackson noted that the oath is recorded in five mid-ninth century documents from the Hermopolite Monastery of Apa Apollo.
27. This aspect is discussed by A. Papaconstantinou, "'What remains behind': Hellenism and Romanitas in Christian Egypt after the Arab Conquest," in *From Hellenism to Islam*, ed. Cotton *et al.*, esp. 449–54.
28. "Command" *P.KRU* 5, 10, 21, 35, 55, 65, 74; "power" *P.KRU* 21, 36, 38; "by the counsel of God" *P.KRU* 27, 38, 66, 77. My emphases. In general, see Erwin Seidl, *Der Eid im römisch-ägyptischen Provinzialrecht* (Münich, 1935), §10.
29. Meinardus, "Attitudes of the Orthodox Copts," 153–170; cf. Lamoreaux, "Early Eastern Christian Responses;" C.D.G. Müller, "Stellung und Haltung der koptischen Patriarchen des 7. Jahrhunderts gegenüber islamischer Obrigkeit und Islam," in *Acts of the Second International Congress of Coptic Studies*, ed. T. Orlandi and F. Wisse (Rome, 1985), 203–13.
30. M.N. Swanson, *Coptic Papacy*, 4–7, 55–6; M.J. Saleh, "Government Relations," esp. ch. 8; eodem, "Government Intervention in the Coptic Church in Egypt during the Fatimid Period," *Muslim World* 91 (2001), 381–97.
31. The government occasionally used the ecclesiastical infrastructure to disseminate edicts (e.g. *P.Lond*.IV.1343 and 1384; HP I.3:324). In general, clergy were encouraged to resolve disputes whenever possible. Only exceptional cases made their way to Fusṭāṭ. During the patriarchate of Agathon (661–77 CE), the governor commissioned seven bishops to investigate and resolve a problem in Sakhā (HP I.3:263). Cf. Meinardus, "Attitudes of the Orthodox Copts," 167–8.
32. HP I.4:643, my translation.
33. M. Saleh ("Government Relations," 133, 281) cites two passages, one by al-Nuwayrī (d. 732/1332) and another by Ibn al-Naqqāsh (d. 764/1362); cf. Moshe Perlmann, "Notes on Anti-Christian Propaganda in the Mamlūk Empire," BSOAS 10.4 (1942), 843–61. These sentiments are absent from Christian apocryphal literature, which better reflect popular Christian sentiments. A few Copts did voice such sentiments at the dawn of the twentieth century.
34. See Chapter Two above.
35. On Zacharias, See Mark N. Swanson, "Sainthood Achieved: Coptic Patriarch Zacharias according to The History of the Patriarchs," in *Writing 'True Stories': Historians and Hagiographers in the Late Antique and Medieval Near East*, ed. A. Papaconstantinou (Turnhout, 2010).
36. HP II.2:180/148v, my emphasis. This was a pervasive attitude discernible even in documentary texts, e.g. *P.Mon.Epiph*.200 and 216.
37. The biography of Shinūda I (HP II.1) emphatically presents history in a polarizing scheme: Satan vs. church/patriarch.

38. HP II.1:15/115v, citing Ez. 34:27–9. This worldview provides the background for many incidents mentioned in the HP, especially those in which oppressive Muslim rulers are divinely chastised through illness or death.
39. Also see Fattal, *Le statut légale*, 218–31.
40. "The faithful. . .took that God-fearing priest Agathon and enthroned him as patriarch" (HP I.3:258). He appears to have selected John III as his successor. John III's biography is not definitive on that front, but see HP I.3:262–3.
41. HP I.3:278.
42. Cf. *Life of Isaac of Alexandria*, 53, Bell 62; HP I.3:276–7; see the prelude to the election of Zacharias I, HP II.2:176/147v and *Synaxarion*, Hatūr 13. The *Synaxarion*'s entry (Hatūr 9) does not mention the anointing, but states that John III had a vision identifying Isaac as his successor.
43. HP I.3:283–4, my translation. In this context, *malik*, "king" (likely a translation of Coptic *ouro*) does not always designate the caliph (as in the next footnote), but rather the one exercising political authority.
44. HP I.4:640; Arabic reads, "from God and the king."
45. HP I.3:285–6; the author of the famous *Chronicle*.
46. It took three years to attain permission to elect Alexander II in 705 CE (HP I.3:303). In electing Khaīl I (744 CE), the electoral synod first asked permission from the governor (HP I.3:360). Permission was sought before the consecration of Mark II (HP I.4:518). Apparently government permission was also withheld after the death of Patriarch Khaīl II (see HP II.2:114–5/136r). For a later period, see C.E. Bosworth, "Christian and Jewish Religious Dignitaries."
47. E.g. HP II.2:228–9/157v.
48. See HP II.2:174–7/174v; and 228/157v.
49. Hegumen (ἡγούμενος) was originally a title given to the head of a monastery, but here it likely carries the later meaning of an "archpriest:" Ibn Sabbāʿ, *al-Jawhara al-nafīsa*, §50, cf. §78; Pseudo-Sawīrus, *Tartīb al-kahanūt*, ch. 10. The double connotations resonated with the title "Hegumen of Scetis" (Evelyn White, *Monasteries*, 2:178–80).
50. This physical condition may have prevented him from ordination under normal circumstances; cf. Sokrates, *Ecclesiastical History*, 4.23. Ibrāhīm's marital status is unknown; he was certainly a layman not a cleric or monastic.
51. HP I.4:614; also HP I.3:484, citing Rom. 13:2.
52. E.g. HP II.1:15/115v, 77/128v; HP II.2:105, 106/134v.
53. HP I.4:579.
54. HP I.3:406, my translation. Theophanes, *Chronicle*, AM 6240 (747/8 CE), is more precise: Marwān "cut the bridge which was made of boats."
55. HP I.3:407; cf. I Sam. 24:4, 26:8, my translation.
56. HP I.3:407, 440; cf. Eusebios, *Ecclesiastical History*, 9.11; Eusebios, *Life of Constantine*, 1.29–31; Lactantius, *Death of the Persecutors*, 44.
57. HP I.3:430.

58. HP I.3:440, cf. 407, echoing Exodus 12.
59. HP I.3:441.
60. Ibid.
61. HP I.3:443, my translation and emphasis.
62. Eusebios, *Life of Constantine*, 1.28, 31.
63. Eusebios, *Life of Constantine*, 1.30–1, 4.21; Eusebios, *Praise of Constantine*, 6.21 and 9.12 (and H. Drake's Introduction, pgs. 72–3, 43); John Malalas, *Chronicle*, Dindorf 316–7 (13.2).
64. Ibn ʿAbd al-Ḥakam, *Futūḥ*, 176.
65. HP I.4:602–3 and HP II.2:216/155r quote Rom. 13:1–2, 6.
66. Ps. 77:61–2 (LXX); HP I.4:608.
67. Muslim troops needed guides whenever they ventured into that region. In 748–50 CE, the Bashmūrites defeated three separate assaults by government troops (HP I.3:410–11). Similarly, in 830–2 CE, Egyptian troops were repeatedly defeated. Eventually, the Persian general al-Afshīn subdued the rebels with the help of local guides (HP I.4:606–8).
68. HP I.3:393; I.4:609.
69. Eutychios, *Naẓm al-jawhar*, II.57.
70. HP I.3:416. Patriarch Yusāb had written a letter to the rebels (HP I.4:602), but the Bashmūrites assaulted the bishops who delivered it. Later, when al-Ma'mūn arrived in Egypt with the Syrian patriarch Dionysios of Tel-Maḥrē, he sent both patriarchs to negotiate with the Bashmūrites face to face. Again, this was to no avail (HP I.4:607–8). See Chapter Six.
71. HP II.2:131/139r.
72. HP I.4:616.
73. HCME 84a-b, 240; cf. HP I.3:416. The abuses included the imprisonment and torture of Patriarch Khaīl I, destruction of monasteries, murder of monks, and burning Fusṭāṭ. While in his custody, Marwān II forced Patriarch Khaīl to write to the Bashmūrites instructing them to cease their revolt.
74. HP I.3:409, 414–6, 430, 435.
75. The following narrative has had several manifestations; see Georgio Levi Della Vida, "A Christian Legend in Moslem Garb," *Byzantion* 15 (1941), 144–57; Stephen J. Davis, "Variations on an Egyptian Female Martyr Legend: History, Hagiography, and the Gendered Politics of Arab Religious Identity," in *Writing 'True Stories'*, ed. A. Papaconstantinou. The name of the virgin was likely borrowed from St. Febronia of Nisibis, a virgin martyred under Diocletian; cf. Sebastian P. Brock and Susan Ashbrook Harvey, trans., *Holy Women of the Syrian Orient*, rev. ed., (Berkeley, 1987), ch. 7.
76. HCME 84a-86a, 240–242; cf. HP I.3:417–18, 430; al-Maqrīzī, *Khiṭaṭ*, IV.1000–1.
77. There are distinct Byzantine parallels. In his *Chronicle* (AM 6233 [740/1 CE]), Theophanes writes that Constantine V "became emperor by God's judgment on account of the multitude of our sins." Cf. *Chronicle* (AM 6303 [810/11 CE]).

78. The Melkite community was likewise cut off from outside contact. But there were a few exceptions. See Skreslet, "Greeks in Medieval Islamic Egypt," 265, and his discussion of Iconoclasm.
79. Byzantine-Ethiopian relations did have a slight political angel, as when the Ethiopians were recruited to fight against the Persians (Theophanes, *Chronicle*, AM 6064 [571/2 CE]). Still, such marginal political interactions did not directly involve the Alexandrian hierarchy.
80. In addition to bilateral communion, that is, the ability of the members of one jurisdiction to receive the Eucharist in the other, the names of the patriarchs of the sister see were mentioned in liturgical celebrations. See also HP II.3:320/173r, 327/174r.
81. In the Coptic liturgy (Dyptich and Absolution), Patriarch Severos is prominently mentioned ahead of his (older) Alexandrian counterparts: Athanasios, Cyril, and Dioskoros.
82. "Theodosians" and "Jacobites" were the preferred labels well into the Umayyad period (HP I.3:357, 384, 409); the latter continued into the modern period. "Theodosians, meaning 'Copts,'" in the biography of Khaīl I (d. 150/767) is the first reference in the HP to the term "Copt/*qibṭ*" (HP I.3:373); cf. Syriac usage for "Syrians"/Christians and "Arabs"/Muslims (see *Chronicle of Zuqnīn*, Year 724–5 CE, Harrak pg. 155 n.5).
83. E.g. HP II.1:47/122v when the destruction and rebuilding of churches occurred in Syria and Egypt simultaneously; cf. HP I.4:569.
84. By the mid-ninth century, the monastery was reckoned among the major monastic centers of the region (see HP II.1:36/120v); see Evelyn White, *Monasteries*, 2:309–21, 337–8.
85. HP I.3:284, 319, 327; I.4:496, 509, 522, 579–80, 603, 649; HP II.1:5/113v; 25, 23/117v; HP II.2:215/155r, 222/156v; II.3:320/173 r, 327/174r; cf. Kurt J. Werthmuler, *Coptic Identity and Ayyubid Politics in Egypt, 1218–1250* (Cairo, 2010), App. II.A. See the second definition in René Georges Coquin, "Synods, Letters of," *CoptEncyc* 7:2194.
86. The patriarch routinely sent two letters to the kings of Nubia and Ethiopia, but the practice was stopped in the early eleventh century by al-Ḥākim (HCME 106b, 290). It is not clear if a letter was sent to each king separately, or if the letters were biannual; cf. K.J. Werthmuler, *Coptic Identity*, App. II.B.
87. Typically, the delegation brought back a letter from the see it visited. As mentioned in Chapter Five, the letters were exchanged in Greek at least until the mid-ninth century CE(HP I.4:649). Bishop Michael of Tinnīs documented one such trip in which he was a member of the synodal delegation; see HP II.2:211–23/154r-156r. In the mid-eleventh century, during the patriarchate of Khrisṭūdulūs, the synodal letter was written in Syriac by a Syrian monk who was part of the Coptic delegation to Syria (HP II.3:320/173v; cf. 327/174r).
88. HP I.4:606.
89. Fourth century Coptic/Syrian wordlists were discovered in Kellia; see *P.Kell.*II.Syr./Copt.1, 2—the first text is revised in *Addenda and corrigenda* in

*P.Kell.*V (cf. *P.Kell.*II.syr.1, *P.Kell.*II.syr./Gr.1, *P.Kell.*II.Gr.1). See also Karel Innemée and Lucas van Rompay, "La présence des Syriens dans le Wadi al-Natrun (Égypte). À propos des découvertes récentes de peintures et de texts muraux dans l'Église de la Vierge du Couvent des Syriens," *Parole de l'Orient* 23 (1998), 167–202. Trade between Syria and Egypt was constant, not withstanding a few brief junctures; see HP II.1:45/122r; II.2:135/140r. Patriarch Afrahām, the best-known Coptic patriarch of Syrian origins, had been an affluent merchant.

90. Damian, Simon I, Afrahām I, Mark III were all Syrians. Another Syrian, Samuel the Anchorite, was nominated but not elected to the patriarchate in the late eleventh century: J. den Heijer, "Les Patriarches coptes d'origine syrienne," in *Studies on the Christian Arabic Heritage in Honour of Father Prof. Dr. Samir Khalil Samir S.J.*, ed. R. Ebied and H. Teule (Louvain, 2004), 45–63.

91. There was a schism between the Copts and Syrians in the late sixth century; HP I.2: 211–3, 216–7; R.Y. Ebied, "Peter of Antioch and Damian of Alexandria: The End of a Friendship," in *A Tribute to Arthur Vööbus*, ed. R.H. Fischer (Louvain, 1977), 277–82; E.W. Brooks, "The Patriarch Paul of Antioch and the Alexandrian Schism of 575," *Byzantinishe Zeitschrift* 30 (1929–30), 468–76. Another schism commenced in the mid-eighth century over the election of the Bishop of Ḥarrān as Syrian Patriarch. The Coptic patriarch Khaīl I objected to the elevation as contrary to canon law (HP I.3:465–7). Relations were not normalized until both patriarchs passed away.

92. J.M. Fiey, "Coptes et Syriques: Contacts et échanges," *Studia Orientalia Christiana Collectanea* 15 (1972–73), 295–365; J. den Heijer, "Relations between Copts and Syrians in the Light of Recent Discoveries at Dair al-Suryān," in *Coptic Studies*, ed. Immerzeel and Van der Vliet, II.923–38; Lois Farag, "Coptic-Syriac Relations beyond Dogmatic Rhetoric," *Hugoye: Journal of Syriac Studies* http://syrcom.cua.edu/syrcom/Hugoye 11.1 (2008).

93. Most of the examples provided here, and below, are derived from Georg Graf's *Verzeichnis arabischer kirchlicher Termini*, CSCO 147 (Louvain, 1954): hypostasis, أقنوم < ܩܢܘܡܐ; church, بيعة < ܒܝܥܬܐ and كنيسة < ܟܢܘܫܬܐ; abbot, ربيتة = ܪܒܝܬܐ; priest, قسّ < ܩܫܝܫܐ and كاهن = ܟܗܢܐ; homily, ميمر < ܡܐܡܪܐ; semandron (later made out of metal but originally a wooden gong), ناقوس < ܢܩܘܫܐ; sanctuary, هيكال or هيكل < ܗܝܟܠܐ); book (biblical), سفر < ܣܦܪ; apostle, سليح < ܫܠܝܚܐ; psalm, مزمور < ܡܙܡܘܪܐ; "Saint," مار or مارى < ܡܪܝ. The nomenclature so common for Saint Mary in Christian Arabic literature, مرتمريم, is also of Syrian origins < ܡܪܝܡܡܪܬܝ. Perhaps also the use of *āb* (آب) for God the Father, rather the *ab* (اب) is also influenced by Syria (< ܐܒ). Finally, the term for deacon, شماس, may have a Syrian (ܫܡܫ) or a Coptic root (ϢⲘϢⲈ / ϢⲈⲘϢⲒ). Both terms are cognates that have the basic meaning of "to serve" (cf. διακονέω).

94. E.g. metropolitan, مطران < ܡܝܛܪܐܢ < μητροπολίτης; Pascha, فصح < ܦܨܚܐ < πάσχα; monastic schema, إسكيم < ܐܣܟܝܡܐ < σχῆμα.

95. Such as the term *q-r-b*, (قَرب < ܐܬܩܪܒ < ܩܪܒ), "to draw near, approach," which in Syria and Egypt also meant "to receive communion"; to be reposed/dead, نيح < ܢܚ; "to prepare or fill" عمر < ܓܡܪ (especially in preparing the Eucharistic cup); دير < ܕܝܪܐ "monastery." This is in addition to Syriac terms that came into Arabic usage through the Qur'ān, e.g. *kharāj*. See Arthur Jeffery, *The Foreign Vocabulary of the Qur'an* (Baroda, 1938; Lahore, 1977).
96. See Mark Swanson, "'Our Brother, the Monk Eustathius': A Ninth-Century Syrian Orthodox Theologian Known to Medieval Arabophone Copts," *Coptica* 1 (2002), 119–40. Also an anthology translated into Arabic in 1034 CE, *I'tirāf al-abā'* (pg. 392) contains a chapter on the views of the Syrian Orthodox scholar Yaḥyā ibn ʿAdī (893–974 CE).
97. See S. Khalil Samir, "Earliest Arab Apology for Christianity;" Sidney H. Griffith, "Comparative Religion in the Apologetics of the First Christian Arabic Theologians," *Proceedings of the PMR Conference* 4 (1979), 63–87; idem, *Church in the Shadow of the Mosque*.
98. See Chapter Five, n. 47.
99. See Chapter Eleven.
100. Anonymous, *Divine Liturgies of Saints Basil, Gregory, and Cyril*, 2nd ed. (Texas, 2007). "Nature" is understood here as a specific single subject, an individual: see Chapter One.
101. A Nubian king was usually ordained a priest and anointed by the metropolitan at his crowning. The same can be said for the Ethiopian Nagust, who was anointed by the *Abun* (HCME 99a, 272; cf. 105b, 286; Bayru Tafla, "Anointing the Ethiopian Emperor," *CoptEncyc* 1:140–1). There appears to be some confusion in the HCME between the two regions though.
102. Rufinos, *Ecclesiastical History*, 1.9; Bayru Tafla, "Ethiopian Orthodox Church," *CoptEncyc* 3:995–9; Sergew Hable Selassie, *Ancient and Medieval Ethiopian History to 1270* (Addis Ababa, 1971); Otto F.A. Meinardus, "A Brief History of the Abunate of Ethiopia," *Wiener Zeitschrift für die Kunde des Morgenlandes* 58 (1962), 39–65; Grillmeier, *Christ in Christian Tradition*, II.4.4.
103. Ayele' Taklahāymānot, "The Egyptian Metropolitan of the Ethiopian Church," OCP 54 (1988), 175–222.
104. John of Nikiou, *Chronicle*, §90.72, 75–7; al-Maqrīzī, *Khiṭaṭ*, I.517–26; William Y. Adams, *Nubia, Corridor to Africa* (England, 1977), 438–45; idem, "Nubia, Evangelization of," *CoptEncyc* 6:1801–02; Derek A. Welsby, *The Medieval Kingdoms of Nubia: Pagans, Christians and Muslims along the Middle Nile* (London, 2002), 31–8; Grillmeier, *Christ in Christian Tradition*, II.4.3.
105. Other missionaries doubtless preceded Julian, but John of Ephesos' *History*, IV, which provides the most salient information on the topic, contains a long lacuna prior to the reference to Julian. In general see, Salim Faraji, *The Roots of Nubian Christianity Uncovered* (Trenton and London, 2012).
106. Justinian had also commissioned the anti-Chalcedonian Bishop John of Ephesos to evangelize Anatolia.

107. Welsby (*Medieval Kingdoms*, 35–9) discusses the archeological evidence for this phenomenal rate of conversion.
108. In the tenth century, Eutychios (*Naẓm al-jawhar*, II.46) suggested that Nubia became anti-Chalcedonian simply because the Melkites did not have a patriarch in Alexandria during the late seventh century; hence, their conversion was not out of conviction but rather of necessity. He overlooks the fact that anti-Chalcedonians originally evangelized two of the three Nubian kingdoms.
109. Still, HP II.2:218/155v indirectly alludes to the presence of Melkites in the region.
110. Maqrīzī, *Khiṭaṭ*, I.521.13: "Nubia is Maris," *wa hum Maris*. *Bilād al-nūba* and *Bilād al-sūdān* are interchangeable designations in Arabic sources.
111. William Y. Adams, "Nubian Church Organization," *CoptEncyc* 6:1813–4.
112. In the mid-ninth century CE, the oppressive policies of the Caliph al-Mutawakkil forced many to flee. When the policies were halted, many Christians returned to the country (HP II.1:16/116r). Presumably, they had fled to Nubia.
113. See Karel Innemée, *Ecclesiastical Dress in the Medieval Near East* (Leiden, 1992).
114. W.Y. Adams, *Nubia*, 547–91; idem, "Nubia, Islamization of," *CoptEncyc* 6:1802–4.
115. *Scrolls of Bishop Timotheos*.
116. Balādhurī, *Futūḥ*, 237: major battles occurred in 20/641, 27/647, 29/649, 31/652.
117. Ibn ʿAbd al-Ḥakam, *Futūḥ*, 189; al-Balādhurī, *Futūḥ*, 237; al-Maqrīzī, *Khiṭaṭ*, I.542–9; Adams, *Nubia*, 450–3; Welsby, *Medieval Kingdoms*, 68–73; Fattal, *Le statut légale*; Hasan, *Arabs and the Sudan*, ch. 2; Heinz Halm, "Der nubische baqṭ," *Egypt and Syria in the Fatimid, Ayyubid and Mamluk Eras II*, ed. U. Vermeulen and D. de Smet (Louvain, 1998); Jay Spaulding, "Medieval Christian Nubia and the Islamic World: A Reconsideration of the Baqt Treaty," *The International Journal of African Historical Studies* 28.3 (1995), 577–94; Martin Hinds and Hamdi Sakkout, "A Letter from the Governor of Egypt Concerning Egyptian-Nubian Relations in 141/758)," in *Studia Arabica et Islamica: Festschrift fur Iḥsān 'Abbās on His Sixtieth Birthday*, ed. Wadād al-Qāḍī (Beirut, 1981); repr. M. Hinds, *Studies*; F. Løkkegaard, "Baḳṭ," EI^2 1:966a-b; Beshir Ibrahim Beshir, "New light on Nubian-Fāṭimid relations," *Arabica* 22 (1975), 15–24; P. Forand, "Early Muslim Relations with Nubia," *Der Islam* 48 (1972), 111–21; cf. W. al-Qāḍī, "An Umayyad Papyrus," 234–5.
118. Maqrīzī, *Khiṭaṭ*, I.546.1, retains a tradition describing the treaty as a *ṣūlḥ*, which would forbid the enslavement of Nubians; also see Forand, "Early Muslim Relations," 113–4.
119. On the various nuances of *hudnā*, see Gideon Weigert, "A Note on Hudna: Peace Making in Islam," in *War and Society*, ed. Y. Lev.
120. Forand maintains that the treaty was consistently interpreted as a pact among equals, which required reciprocal exchange. The passage he quotes from Bar

Hebraeus is crucial. The shifting perception of the treaty is well documented by al- Maqrīzī, who understands the *baqṭ* as a *ḍarība*: a tax levied on the Nubians (*Khiṭaṭ*, I.542, 547; cf. I.543–4).

121. HP I.3:278. "Maurōtania" (Mauretania), modern day Morocco, is problematic and likely erroneous. It is improbable that two kingdoms that did not share a common border were at war. Further, it is not clear why the Maurōtanians would have traveled all the way to Alexandria with so many other bishoprics much closer. Still, succession within Carthage, which had jurisdiction over Mauretania, is uncertain during this period. A bishop Victor (635 CE) is noted in the seventh century, the next known bishop for the region lived in the eleventh century.
122. This tradition challenges the normative chronology derived from Islamic sources, which dates an incontestable *baqṭ* to the mid-seventh century.
123. *Life of Isaac of Alexandria*, 81, Bell 73.
124. HP I.3:293–94. The government secretaries were presumably Isaac and Athanasios. The *Life of Isaac of Alexandria* (85, Bell 75), maintains that it was Patriarch Isaac himself who explained the situation to the governor. See Chapter Three.
125. Maqrīzī, *Khiṭaṭ*, I.140.10, describes dams that would have theoretically diverted the flow of the Nile. He also recounts a year of a poor inundation in which the Coptic patriarch Khaīl IV traveled to Nubia and caused the Nile to rise, presumably through his influence over the Nubians (*Khiṭaṭ*, IV.1010). In the mid-fifteenth century CE, the *Synaxarion* (Bashans 9) states that the kings of Ethiopia threatened to cut the flow of the Nile on account of the hardships the Christians of Egypt were enduring. The historical and mythical (e.g. Prester John) aspects of this belief are discussed in Richard Pankhurst's "Ethiopia's Alleged Control of the Nile," Benjamin Arbel's "Renaissance Geographical Literature and the Nile," and Emery van Donzel's "The Legend of the Blue Nile in Europe," all are in *The Nile: Histories, Cultures, Myths*, ed. H. Erlich and I. Gershoni (London, 2000). These articles are insightful, but limit themselves to Ethiopian and European sources; Coptic Arabic texts were neglected.
126. HP I.4:657.
127. The "Indian" priest, *min ahl al-hind*, was likely Ethiopian or possibly Nubian. Ancient and medieval sources routinely conflate Ethiopia and India (and even Persia): cf. HCME 108b, 296 and 105a, 285; HP II.2:137–8/137r; *Chronicle of Zuqnīn*, 76; Theophanes, *Chronicle*, AM 6035 (542/3 CE); Phiroze Vasunia, *The Gift of the Nile: Hellenizing Egypt from Aeschylus to Alexander* (Berkeley, 2001), 276–81. The reaction of the caliph, discussed below, would make sense only in the context of Nubia or Ethiopia—not India. A remote possibility is that the Indian priest was from one of the Indian colonies in Iraq; see Morony, *Iraq after the Muslim Conquest*, 271–2, 373. Eusebios (*EH* 5.10) noted that Pantainos the philosopher (ca. 190 CE) traveled on a missionary trip to India. Even if the

account is historical, however, nothing suggests that the trip resulted in any long-term contact between Alexandria and India.

128. HP I.3:290; al-Maqrīzī, *Khiṭaṭ*, IV.999.
129. HP I.3:291.
130. Saleh, "Government Relations," 196–7.
131. HP II.2:115/136r.
132. Theophanes, *Chronicle*, AM 6248 (755/6 CE). Theodore, Patriarch of Antioch, was exiled because he was "accused of frequently communicating Arab affairs by letter to the emperor Constantine."
133. HP I.3:398.
134. HP I.3:398, my translation; cf. HCME 96b-97a.
135. HP I.3:400; cf. HP II.2: 206/153r; HCME 105a, 284; 95b, 264; 99a, 272; *Book of Chrism*, 189; al-Maqrīzī, *Khiṭaṭ*, I.524.15–6. A similar gloss was added to the vulgate recension of Patriarch Demetrios' biography (HP I.1:57) it is lacking in the primitive recension (Seybold 1912).
136. HP II.2:206–7/153r; also HCME 99a, 272; 105a, 285–6.
137. Hasan (*Arabs and the Sudan*, 29) and Adams (*Nubia*, 454) dismiss the account, while Welsby (*Medieval Kingdoms*, 73, 265 n.28) and Saleh ("Government Relations," 191–2) accept its authenticity.
138. Ibn ʿAbd al-Ḥakam, *Futūḥ*, 33, provides a legendary hue by stating that the Nubians invaded in search of hidden treasure—a *topos*: *Futūḥ*, 43; al-Masʿūdī, *Murūj al-dhahab*, II.415–6, 435; HCME 103a, 280; *Apocalypse of Athanasios*, 9.9; al-Maqrīzī, *Khiṭaṭ*, I.49, 199, 201.9; *Chronicle of 1234*, I.224, Palmer §19.
139. Welsby, *Medieval Kingdoms*, 73. A similar incident involving the Ethiopian emperor Sayfa Ar'ad (1342–71) is briefly discussed in R. Pankhurst's "Ethiopia's Alleged Control of the Nile," 29.
140. HP I.3:433.
141. HP I.3:440–1. *Bilād al-sūdān*, literally "land of the Blacks," embraces all of Nubia and Ethiopia.
142. Yaʿqūbī, *Ta'rīkh*, II.415–6; al-Masʿūdī, *Murūj al-dhahab*, VI.163–4.
143. HP I.4:618, my emphasis; cf. HCME 97b, 268–70. Real or imagined, the above-discussed incident involving the Nubian king Kyriakos did have repercussions.
144. HP I.4:618, my translation.
145. George is identified as Jirjā or Qirqī in Arabic sources; HP I.4:619–20; HCME 97b-98a, 268–70; cf. Hasan, *Arabs and the Sudan*, 26.
146. Balādhurī, *Futūḥ*, 238, traces this arrangement back to al-Mahdī, but al-Maqrīzī mentions only al-Muʿtaṣim (*Khiṭaṭ*, I.546–7); cf. Welsby, *Medieval Kingdoms*, 72. Also see M. Brett, "Al-Karāza al-marqusīya: the Coptic Church in the Fatimid Empire," in *Egypt and Syria...IV*, ed. Vermeulen and Steenbergen.
147. Saleh, "Government Relations," 201–2, 211–2.
148. HP II.3:263/163v.; Saleh, "Government Relations," 203.
149. See n. 101 above.

150. See the biography of Patriarch Khrisṭūdulūs: HP II.3:281/166v and HCME 98a, 270; 101a, 276; Hasan, *Arabs and the Sudan*, 92–3. He was accused and later exonerated of prompting the destruction of a mosque in Nubia. Also see ns. 137–9 above.
151. HP I.3:395 (full account on pgs. 394–7). In the mid-ninth century CE, Patriarch Yusāb dealt with similar problems in two bishoprics, Tinnīs and Miṣr, where parishioners threatened to leave the faith if their bishops—Isaac and Theodore—were not removed (HP I.3:604–5).
152. Also see HP II.3:349–50/177v.
153. HP II.2:118/136v, 119–121/137r, and 171–2/147r.

Chapter 10 A Church and Community in Transition

1. On early Egyptian Christianity, see Pearson and Goehring eds., *Roots of Egyptian Christianity*; J.E. Goehring and J.A. Timbie, eds., *The World of Early Egyptian Christianity* (Washington DC, 2007); for Alexandria, see Christopher Haas, *Alexandria in Late Antiquity: Topography and Social Conflict* (Baltimore, 1997); idem, "John Moschus and Late Antique Alexandria," in *Alexandrie médiévale 2*, ed. C. Décobert, 44–59. For some time now, in the average individual's mind the "Pope of Alexandria" is less associated with that city than with Cairo, the location of the Cathedral of St. Mark where all major feasts and ordinations are celebrated.
2. Most of Alexandria's revenue was derived from tariffs on commerce, not land tax (HP II.1:77/128v); see Paula A. Sanders, "The Fāṭimid State, 969–1171," in *Cambridge History of Egypt*, ed. Petry, esp. 161–5.
3. The patriarchate's transfer to Fusṭāṭ-Cairo, discussed below, has been addressed by several scholars, including Cohen (*Jewish Self-Rule*, 67–73, 75) and Saleh ("Government Relations," 273–80). Still, the dominant historiography remains fundamentally incomplete and skewed; see n. 7 below.
4. HP I.3:296.
5. HP III.1:13/187v, cf. 19. Fusṭāṭ had its own bishop at that time.
6. Simon I (d. 701) was identified as, "the patriarch of the Christians who resides in Alexandria" (HP I.3:291).
7. The culminating events took place over nearly forty years. In 1088 CE, Kyrillus II (1078–92) ordained the monk Sanhūt Bishop of Miṣr. Later, Patriarch Khaīl IV (1092–1102) tried to take over the diocese by forcing Sanhūt out of the city, but the population objected: "the patriarch is the Bishop of Alexandria and has precedence over the bishops of the dioceses of Egypt. [However,] *he is not a partner in their sees*, and as it is not permitted for one who has a wife for another to share her [with him], likewise, it is not permitted for a bishop to be a partner with another in his see, which is his bride" (HP II.3:383/183r, my translation and emphasis). Upon Khaīl IV's death, Sanhūt returned to his diocese, where he died in 1111 CE. At that

juncture, Patriarch Makarios II (1102–28) refused to ordain a new bishop for Miṣr-Cairo. Again, notables and clergy, led by Ibn al-Qulzūmī, protested on the same grounds: "We have said that as it is not permitted for a Christian to have two wives, likewise it is not permitted for a bishop to have two dioceses. And this Father, Abba Makarios the Patriarch, he is the Bishop of the City of Alexandria, how is it possible for him to have the Bishopric of Miṣr[-Cairo]?" (HP III.1:24/189r, my translation.) The debate raged for seven years, but Makarios II acquiesced and ordained Yu'annīs ibn Sanhūt bishop of Miṣr in 1118 CE. Yu'annīs died in 1134, early during the patriarchate of Gabriel II ibn Turayk (1131–45), who did not ordain another bishop for the diocese and turned it into a patriarchal seat. There was one later exception. In the mid-thirteenth century, the appalling abuses of Patriarch Kyrillus III, Ibn Laqlaq, led the Coptic synod to place several restrictions on him, effectively forcing him to ordain Būlus al-Būshī bishop of Miṣr (1240 CE). Būlūs was to oversee and sign off on all decisions made by the patriarch (see Cyril III, *Canons*; and HP IV).

8. See HP I.3:267; the *Life of Isaac of Alexandria* is primarily situated in or about Fusṭāṭ and Ḥulwān.
9. HP I.3:463. The biannual synod, which usually convened in Alexandria, convened in Miṣr (HP I.3:448). This was possibly the "Synod of a Hundred." Comprised of all the episcopal sees under Alexandrian jurisdiction, it first convened in the fourth century when Alexander of Alexandria excommunicated Arius (320-21CE). See HP I.3:395; *Life of Isaac of Alexandria*, 65, Bell 67; W.C. Griggs, *Early Egyptian Christianity*, 93.
10. HCME 49a-52a, 145–52. In 1175 CE, the monastery housed five monks "in poor circumstances." It contained eight, possibly ten churches/chapels. Murqus ibn al-Qunbar, the Coptic priest who joined the Melkites in the late twelfth century, resided there for twenty years (HCME 51b, 152). Under the Fāṭimids, the *ra'īs al-yahūd*, the Head of the Jews, also resided in Cairo.
11. The biography of Makarios I (d. 952 CE) states that "none of the patriarchs had sojourned in Alexandria after Abba Khaīl III [d. 907 CE] the patriarch" (HP II.2:121/137v).
12. HP I.4:649.
13. HP I.4:657.
14. Damīrah: HP II.1:4/113r, 16/115v-116r; Mamṭarūn: HP II.1:16/115v; Wādī al-Naṭrūn/Habīb: HP II.2:117/136v, 200/152r; Maḥalāt Danyāl: HP II.2:134/140r; where the *mayrūn* was consecrated (HP II.2:151/143r); Damrū: HP II.2:244/156v, 226/157r, 228/157v.; René-Georges Coquin, "Patriarchal Residences," *CoptEncyc* 6:1912–3; Johannes den Heijer, "Le patriarcat copte d'Alexandrie à l'époque fatimide," in *Alexandrie médiévale 2*, ed. C. Décobert, 84–7, 91–3; Otto F.A. Meinardus. "Patriarchal Cells in the Nile Delta," *Orientalia Suecana* 13 (1964), 51–61; cf. *Book of the Chrism*.
15. HP I.3:277–8 (cf. *Life of Isaac*, 49–53, Bell 61–2), 360–2; HP II.2:115/136r, 136/140r, 150/142v; cf. HP II.1:18–20/116r-v. The committee convened at

several locations for the election of Shinūda II. At times, the candidate was brought in shackles. This would later become a normative aspect, actively integrated into the ordination rite: pseudo-Sawīrus, *Tartīb al-kahanūt*, ch.9, pg. 26.

16. HP II.2:150/142v.
17. HP II.2:115/136r; HP II.3:322/173r. The Monastery of St. Makarios served as the burial place for ten patriarchs, nine of which lived during the centuries under discussion here (e.g. HP II.1:2/113r; HP II.2:118/136v): Khaīl II (849–51); Khaīl III (880–907); Gabriel I (910–20); Quzma III (920–32); Makarios I (932–52); Khrisṭūdulūs (1047–77); Kyrillus II (1078–92); John V (1147–66), Mark III (1166–89); John XV (1619–29). The importance of the Monastery of St. Makarios in the tenth century can be surmised from Eutychios, *Naẓm al-jawhar*, II.201: "[Since] the fifteenth year in the reign of Justinian. . .the Jacobite patriarchate (*kursy*) remained in the Monastery of St. Makarios *until this day*" (also, al-Maqrīzī, *Khiṭaṭ*, IV.997.18–9). While this is a gross oversimplification and is historically inaccurate, it is significant that in the mid-tenth century, the Monastery of St. Makarios—not Alexandria—was viewed as the residence of the Coptic patriarch.
18. For Abū Sarja, see HP II.1:19–20/116v; II.2:136/140r. For al-Muʿallaqa, see HP III.1:40, 193r; cf. Christodoulos, *Canons*, 6–9.
19. Alexandrian clergy claimed the exclusive right to elect patriarchs, see below. The deadlock that occurred in electing a successor to Patriarch Zacharias I (d. 1032 CE) was primarily because "everyone of (the bishops) mentioned one of his relatives or a friend of his with regard to being patriarch" (HP II.2:231/158r). Later, the clergy of Lower Egypt chose Patriarch Kyrillus II (1078 CE) believing that he could be easily manipulated and controlled (HP II.3:332–3/174v).
20. HP II.2:135/140r; *Life of Afrahām*, pgs. 390–1.
21. HP II.2:174–4/147v, my emphasis. The consent/veto authority of the non-electoral party is obvious here. The first Alexandrian nominee, Ibrāhīm ibn Bishr, was not acceptable to the clergy and notables of Miṣr-Cairo, and, hence, another candidate, Zacharias, was chosen.
22. HP II.3:245/160r.
23. HP II.3:321/173r; on the period from Khrisṭūdulūs to Kyrillus II, see J. den Heijer, "Le patriarcat copte d'Alexandrie."
24. HP II.3:371/180v.
25. See J. den Heijer, "Wādī al-Naṭrūn and the *History of the Patriarchs*," in *Christianity and Monasticism*, ed. Mikhail and Moussa, 29.
26. My emphasis. Naming or re-naming candidates (as the case may be) is performed at the heart of the consecration rite, as evidenced by another section in the same biography: "The duration of his patriarchate, from the time of the laying-on of hands upon him *in the Monastery of Abba Makarios*, was fourteen years and three months and a half" (HP II.3:369/180r); cf. J. den Heijer, "Wādī al-Naṭrūn," 33. The same pattern is evident in the biography of Khaīl

IV, where the placement of the episcopal vestments is immediately followed by consecration ("they clothed him in the garment and they consecrated him patriarch") and then the candidate was taken and consecrated again at Alexandria, the Monastery of St. Makarios, and finally at al-Muʿallaqa (HP II.3:385/183r).

27. HP II.3:325/173v.
28. HP II.3:326/174r.
29. Beyond the attestations in the HP, see the odd description of these ordinations in al-Maqrīzī's *Khiṭaṭ*, IV.1010.11–14, 1011.4–6, 1011.7–8, 1011.10, 1011.13, 1012.1–2, 1013.17. In each case, the ordination is to be "completed" at a second location. The same language of "completion" is used in Christian sources.
30. Den Heijer, "Wādī al-Naṭrūn," 28–9; Evelyn White, *Monasteries*, II.347, 349; Meinardus, *Christian Egypt*, 101.
31. HP II.2:121/137v, my emphasis.
32. Theophanios's biography was intentionally abbreviated. Elderly at the time of his ordination, he quickly demonstrated signs of advanced senility (or perhaps mental illness), and became an embarrassment for the church. He was sent to live in a monastery, where he was killed by suffocation. Long after his patriarchate, perfectly qualified candidates were excluded simply on account of their age. The biographies of Mīnā II and Afrahām state that they were taken to Alexandria in fetters for ordination, while those of Philotheos and Zacharias focus on electoral politics rather than the rites of ordination. Of all these biographies, however, their author, Michael of Tinnīs, is best suited to comment on the rituals he personally witnessed, including that of Shinūda II, which clearly documents the practice of multiple ordinations.
33. Under Byzantine rule, a controversy in the ordination of the anti-Chalcedonian Patriarch Dioskoros II led to his re-ordination: "Dioskoros went to St Mark's and the clergy arrived and invested him *a second time and ordained him again*; and so he came to St John's and celebrated the service" (Theophanes, *Chronicle*, AM 6009 (516/7 CE), pg. 247, my emphasis). The evidence for Coptic patriarchs is documented throughout this section. For Egyptian bishops under Islamic rule, bishops Badīr of Asyūṭ (HP II.2:233–4/158v) and Sanhūt of Cairo (HP II.3:346–7/177r) had multiple ordinations, as evidenced by the Arabic accounts written by contemporaries. Among the Melkites of Egypt: "In the nineteenth of Jumadī the Second, Īliyyā ibn Manṣūr became [the Melkite] Patriarch of Jerusalem and was [later] sent to Alexandria. The Alexandrians said, "We do not agree nor [will we] repeat the Prayers of the Patriarchs upon him," but *they did repeat the Prayers* of the Patriarchs in the fourth (day) of Ramadan, year 294 [/907]" (Eutychios, *Naẓm al-jawhar*, II.75, my translation and emphasis). Also see, Michael the Syrian, *Chronicle*, XV.1, Appendix III, pgs. 472–3; HP I.3:461, 466–7.
34. E.g. HP II.3:260/162v.
35. He read, translated, and freely conversed in Coptic (HP II.3:288/167v).

36. Several biographies only date the ordination in Alexandria. Nonetheless, this was not always the case, in the biography of Makarios II *each* consecration is dated; cf. n. 32 above.
37. HP III.1:40, 193r; cf. Christodoulos, *Canons*, 6–9; al-Maqrīzī employed the same language; see n. 29, above.
38. This process is evident in the multi-layered *Book of the Chrism*, the earliest text in which (pg. 190–8) describes that rite as it unfolded in 1257 CE at the Monastery of St. Makarios (cf. the section focused on the preparation in 1178 CE [pg. 197]). Later, the consecration shifted to various churches in Cairo-Miṣr. Intriguingly, the later rites deviated from, and even criticized, the ritual as it unfolded at the monastery.
39. See Khaīl V (HP III.1:62–3/107r); John V (HP III.1:69/198r); Murqus ibn Zar'ah (HP III.2:103/205r); John VI (HP III.2:166/219v).
40. A new bishop's arrival at his diocese was doubtless an occasion for celebration, though documentation for ritualized "enthronements" is scares during this period. Some documentation is early (e.g. Paphnutios, *Histories*, §§72, 82), though the clearest attestations stem from the fourteenth century CE: see U. Zanetti, "Liturgy at Wadi al-Natrun," 136 and Y.N. Youssef, "Consecration of the Myron at Saint Macarius," 114–5, both in *Christianity and Monasticism*, ed. Mikhail and Moussa.
41. In general see, Georg Schmelz, *Kirchliche Amtsträger*, and Ewa Wipszycka, *Études sur le christianisme dans l'Égypte de l'antiquité tardive* (Rome, 1996).
42. HP I.4:597. In the mid-ninth century CE, a Coptic deacon taught the "Children of the [Patriarchal] Cell" to read and write in Greek; see Chapter Five.
43. *P.Oxy*.I.134, VIII.1130, XXXVI.2780, LI.3641, XX.2270—written by a subdeacon; *P.Lond.Copt*.I.449, 450; *P.Bal*.103, 104, 142; *P.KRU* 3, 5; cf. *P.Teshlot*. Deacon Theodore ibn Mīnā served as secretary for the synod (HP II.2:168/146r).
44. In HP I.3:309, Deacon George interceded with the governor and accompanied the patriarch throughout Egypt collecting funds for the imposed fine. HP I.3:415 mentions Valentinos the deacon and secretary of the Patriarchal Cell. Patriarch John III also had a deacon for a secretary (HP PO 5.1: 268). Both of Khaīl I's secretaries were deacons: Theodore (HP I.3:424), and Peter, who attempted to usurp the patriarchate and later converted to Islam (HP I.4:476–94; see Chapter Four). Another erring deacon, described as the disciple of Patriarch Ya'qūb, is mentioned in HP I.4:568. Shinūda I took his deacon/secretary on sensitive missions (HP II.1:35/120r).
45. Such as the biographies of Alexander II (HP I.3:344–5), Simon I (HP I.3:301), Khaīl I (HP I.3:433, I.4:474). Mawhūb authored the biographies of patriarchs Khrisṭūdulūs and Kyrillus II.
46. Deacons who became patriarchs: Peter III, "Peter Mongos" (John of Nikiou, *Chronicle*, §88.58), Theodosios (John of Nikiou, *Chronicle*, §92.1), Damian I (HP I.2:209), Andronikos (HP I.2:220), Simon II (HP I.4:590), Kosmas II (HP II.1:3/113r). Among the pro-Chalcedonians: Apollinaris (John of Nikou,

Chronicle, §92.9) and Kosmas (HP I.3:372). Deacons who became bishops: Simon, (HPI.3:348), Theodore bishop of Miṣr (HP I.3:374), John bishop of Sakhā (HP I.4:504, cf. 587), and Isḥāq ibn Andunā (HP I.4:611, 616). In the sixth century, Julian of Halekarnassios ordained Gaianos, the archdeacon of Alexandria and founder of the Gainite sect. He contended with Theodosios for the patriarchate, but Gaianos eventually relinquished his claim.

47. Deacon George, Patriarch Isaac's rival for the patriarchate, was ordained a priest and clothed with the monastic habit on the day before he was to be ordained patriarch (cf. HP I.3:276–7 and *Life of Isaac*, 50–1, Bell 61). Patriarch Yusāb was ordained a deacon and later a priest before his elevation to the patriarchate (HP I.4:598). Another candidate, Deacon Mark, was bound with chains and ordained a priest, but he managed to escape before his ordination as bishop (HP I.4:510, 598). Khaīl II was ordained a priest; later (possibly much later), he was ordained patriarch (HP II.1:1/112v). In the first two cases, ordination to the priesthood was in preparation for the episcopacy—the men did not serve as priests. Later, as is the case today, the rank of deacon was seen as an ordination en route to the priesthood; candidates are typically ordained deacons on, or a few days prior, to ordination to the priesthood. This does not appear to have been the norm during the period at hand. The modern Coptic Orthodox Church has very few deacons, the title being usurped by subdeacons, readers, and chanters who do not properly hold the rank. The few Coptic deacons that do exist are usually referred to as "archdeacon," "full deacon," or *diyākun*.
48. *O.Crum* 29, 106, 139; HP I.4:630; G. Schmelz, *Kirchliche Amtsträger*, ch. 6.
49. HP I.4:617; HCME 38b, 125; and 45b, 139.
50. HP I.4:496 calls a deacon "*al-shaykh al-kāhin*;" also see pseudo-Athanasios, *Canons*, §70; cf. *P.Mon.Epiph*.192.
51. *P.Oxy*.LI.3640, dated 533 CE, mentions "John, deacon and archimandrite of the Monastery of Apa Hierax."
52. HP I.4:499, 565.
53. For Archdeacon Simon, see HP I.3:348; I.4:610–11. The anonymous deacon is discussed in HP I.4:580, 582. Also see HP I.3:313. Priests likewise served in this capacity (HP I.3:297).
54. HP I.3:276, my translation.
55. HP I.3:277, cf. 363–4, in which the archdeacon of the Church of St. Sergios was part of the nominating committee. Also see *Life of Isaac of Alexandria*, 51–2, Bell 61–2; HP I.4:517.
56. Cf. HP III.1:64/197r. A section of the rite for the ordination of priests should be prayed by a deacon. In the earliest surviving Coptic Arabic manual for ordination (dated 1364 CE), the archdeacon still retains an important function; see *Ordination Rite*. Ibn Sabbāʿ states that the archdeacon is to be seated to the left of the patriarch and that the patriarch should consult him in ordinations. In addition, "No one should have a staff in the church except the patriarch and the archdeacon—the shepherd of the rites (*ṭuqūs*). It is proper

that he should have a staff in his hand, [as he is] the keeper of the flock (*qaḍīb al-ra'īya*) and the patriarch has the staff as he is the shepherd of shepherds" (*al-Jawhara al-nafīsa*, §48; cf. pseudo-Sawīrus, *Tartīb al-kahanūt*, ch.10, pg. 29 and ch. 12, pgs. 34–5).

57. HP I.4:499; Benjamin, *On Cana of Galilee*, 19r. Later, priests gained the option to read the Gospel, or to delegate it to a deacon who could read and interpret the text; cf. Ibn Sabbā', *al-Jawhara al-nafīsa*, §§47, 68; pseudo-Sawīrus, *Tartīb al-kahanūt*, ch.13, pg. 35.
58. E.g. HP II.2:166/146r; Ibn Sabbā', *al-Jawhara al-nafīsa*, §47, also §§64, 76.
59. Gabriel II, *Canons*, §2. Here *Isbādīqun* < ⲤⲠⲞⲨⲆⲒⲔⲞⲚ < δεσποτικόν is the middle portion of the eucharistic oblation that is placed into the chalice and (now) consumed by the celebrating priest or bishop.
60. HCME 61b, 182; *Chronicle of 1234/History* of *Dionysios*, Palmer §§70 and 159; Ibn Sabbā', *al-Jawhara al-nafīsa*, §65; pseudo-Sawīrus, *Tartīb al-kahanūt*, ch. 13, pg. 36.
61. Pseudo-Athanasios, *Canons*, §106; Ibn Sabbā', *al-Jawhara al-nafīsa*, §83 (pg. 258–60); Thomas Halton, "The Kairos of the Mass and the Deacon in John Chrysostom," in *Diakonia: Studies in Honor of Robert T. Meyer*, ed. T. Halton and J.P. Williman (Washington D.C., 1986), 57–8.
62. *Apocalypse of Athanasios*, 59; Pisentios' *Discourse on Saint Onnophrios* repeatedly asserts that it was the deacon who issued the command (pg. 183), while in the HP (II.2:223/156r) an eleventh-century bishop, demonstrating the liturgical shift, is the speaker. In Ibn Sabbā', *al-Jawhara al-nafīsa*, §84 (pg. 281), both the priest and the deacon are involved: "Then the deacon says, 'Go in peace, and again, Go in Peace,' and the priest will permit the congregation and read the blessing over them."
63. Makīn, *Mukhtaṣar al-bayān*, IV.156, 316.
64. Cf. Ibn Sabbā', *al-Jawhara al-nafīsa*, §§44, 47 and pseudo-Sawīrus, *Tartīb al-kahanūt*, ch. 13, pg. 35.
65. E.g. Abba Jacob the priest (HP I.3:356) and John the Hegumen of the Enaton (HP I.3:281, 336).
66. Patriarch Agathon was a priest (HP I.2:238). Three patriarchs served as priests in the Monastery of St. Makarios prior to their elevation: Khaīl I (HP I.3:365), Ya'qūb I (HP I.4:555), and Yusāb I (HP I.4:572, 593). Epimachos, hegumen of the Monastery of St. Makarios, later became a bishop (HP I.3:356, cf. 336). Theodore bishop of Miṣr in the mid-eighth century CE was hegumen of Fusṭāṭ and priest in the Church of St. Sergios (HP I.3:464). Also see HP I.3:433–4, 456.
67. Griggs, *Early Egyptian Christianity*, 92–3; Davis, *Early Coptic Papacy*, 135–6.
68. HP I.3:279, cf. 274: John III was headquartered at Alexandria. HP I.3:267 notes that it was customary for the patriarch to meet the governor upon his arrival in the city.
69. HP I.3:360.
70. HP I.3:362; cf. Ibn Sabbā', *al-Jawhara al-nafīsa*, §80 (pg. 235).

71. HP I.3:362.
72. The HP identifies five constituencies: the clergy of Alexandria, bishops of northern Egypt, bishops of southern Egypt, the archdeacon of the Church of St. Sergios, and the notables *(arakhinā)* Menas and Paul.
73. The clergy of Miṣr also gained prestige, and are often positively depicted, e.g. HP I.3:367; HCME 43b, 135.
74. For the rise and function of bishops in Late Antiquity see: Peter Brown, *Power and Persuasion in Late Antiquity: Towards a Christian Empire* (Madison, 1992); Wolfgang Liebeschuetz, "The Rise of the Bishop in the Christian Roman Empire and the Successor Kingdoms," *Electrum* 1 (1997), 113–25; Claudia Rapp, *Holy Bishops in Late Antiquity* (Berkeley, 2005).
75. K. A. Worp, "A Checklist of Bishops in Byzantine Egypt (A.D. 325 - c.750)," ZPE *100* (1994), pp. 283–318. E.g. *P.Mon.Epiph.*254, 469; *P.Oxy.*XVI.1900. The titles used are often indicative of rank: θεοφόρος was employed for bishops, archimandrites, and monastic leaders, while ὁσιώτατος was usually reserved for bishops alone. *P.Oxy.*XVI.1871: θεοσεβεστάτου ἐπισκόπου, "most pious bishop." Χριστοφόρος / ⲉⲧⲫⲟⲣⲉⲓ ⲙⲡⲉⲭ̅ⲥ̅, "Christ bearer," was usually reserved for bishops: *O.Brit.Mus.Copt.*I Plate 41.5 (No. 21245), Plate 52.6 (No. 21200).
76. E.g. the above-mentioned Ibrāhīm ibn Bishr who became the Bishop of Minūf al-ʿUlyā (HP II.2:174–7/147v-48r).
77. See Anbā Kyros (HP I.3:460); Isḥāq ibn Andūna (HP I.4:591–2, 610–11); cf. HP I.4:525; HCME 30b, 105; 37b, 122; also 61b, 182; cf. HP III.1:64/197r.
78. Most prominent were patriarchs Afrahām ibn Zarʿah and his relative Murqus ibn Zarʿah (Mark III). Isḥāq ibn Andūna was a layman, married with children, prior to his ordinations (HP I.3:591). Deacon Gregory was likewise married with children (HP I.3:276; *Life of Isaac of Alexandria*, 50–1, Bell 61); cf. ns. 46 and 47 above.
79. HP I.3:465–7. The Syrian patriarch Isaac was succeeded by another bishop as patriarch in 758 CE, Athanasios IV Sandēlāiā (Sandalia is a town in N. Syria: *Chronicle of Zuqnīn*, Harrak pgs. 192 n.4, 176, n.2). Thus, the schism between the two sees continued until the tenure of the Coptic patriarch John IV and his Antiochene counterpart, George.
80. Paphnutios, *Histories of the Monks*, fol. 33b, Vivian §76.
81. Both elements, nomination by a predecessor and popular election, may be observed in the account of Bishop Isaiah in Upper Egypt: Paphnutios, *Histories*, fol. 32b, Vivian §74.
82. Many patriarchs, including Shinūda I (HP II.1:23/117r) and Afrahām (HP II.2:136/140r) attacked the practice of Simony, but clearly failed to root it out. Instances of abuse are noted in HP II.2:108/135r (involving ten bishoprics); HP II.2:117/136v, 150–1/143r, 169–70/146v. Bishop Michael of Tinnīs roundly condemned the practice, singling it out as the cause for God's wrath that allowed for al-Ḥākim's persecution (HP II.2:177/147v-148r and 180/148v). But he also forwarded a rationale for the practice: "The patriarchs

of the Copts and their fathers did not cease from acting according to this commandment up to the time of the oppression by the authorities of the Muslims from Aḥmad ibn Ṭūlūn up to the days of al-Ḥākim. . .Necessity caused them to do what they did in this (matter) on account of what was demanded of them in the way of money and of what they undertook in the way of burdens" (HP II.2:233/158v). Also see Ewa Wipszycka, "Fonctionnement de l'Église égyptienne aux IVe-VIIIe siècles (Sur quelques aspects)," in *Mélanges offerts au Père Maurice Martin* (Cairo, 1992), 115–45; repr. in eodem, *Études sur le christianisme*; Otto F.A. Meinardus, "The Χειροτονία among the Copts: A Necessary Evil?" *Ekklesiastikos Pharos* 59 (1977), 437–49.

83. See the account of Bishop Isaiah, n. 81 above. In HP II.2:233–4/158v the diocese of Asyūṭ refused to accept a bishop who bought the office.
84. T.A. Kane, *Jurisdiction*; Nicea, Canon 6; there were a few exception to this general pattern.
85. In HP II.2:103/133v-134r, the Bishop of Sakhā rebuked the patriarch for praying in his diocese without his "command or presence."
86. HP I.3:358 (cf. 464): Theodore bishop of Miṣr was the first of three bishops with that name who consecutively occupied that diocese, and as many as five bishops of Nikiou were named "John" in the seventh century. There were at least three bishops named "Abraham" that successively served in Fayyūm during the late seventh and early eighth centuries CE. The modern St. Abra'am bishop of Fayyūm (d. 1914 CE) follows in that tradition as is the current bishop of Fayyūm, who is likewise named Abra'am.
87. At the end of the seventh century, the Copts had sixty-four (HP I.3:288) and were later reduced to sixty (HCME 12b, 30). At the end of the seventh century, the Melkites had one bishop, but by the second half of the ninth century they had six (HP II.2:115/136r.).
88. HP II.2:133/139v; cf. 179/148r and 181/148v.
89. HP I.3:348.
90. HP I.3:332. Bishop Shamūl was arrested and publicly tortured by ʿUbayd Allāh ibn al-Ḥabḥāb.
91. *Life of Isaac of Alexandria*, 56, Bell 64, n.97; *Life of Samuel*, Cop. 25, Eng. 101–2.
92. HP I.4:517–8.
93. HP I.4:519.
94. On the title, see Chapter Three, n. 22.
95. T. Derda and E. Wipszychka, "L'emploi des titres *Abba*, *Apa* et *Papas* dans l'Egypte byzantine," JJP 24 (1994), 23–56.
96. HP I.3:358–9.
97. Deacon Peter's bribe to the governor secured his ordination (HP I.4:633–4). Likewise, Theodore bishop of Wasīm gained his office due to government pressure on the patriarch (HP I.4:633–5). On the tenure of Kyrillus III, see HP IV; M.N. Swanson, *Coptic Papacy*; K.J. Werthmuler, *Coptic Identity*.
98. These assistants often functioned as advisors; e.g. Mark, the advisor to John IV (HP I.4:500).

99. HP I.2:226; I.3:292, 381; II.1:92/132r; Benjamin, *On Cana of Galilee*, fol. 20r. In some instances, the relationship was biological rather than simply spiritual—as stated above, the elevation of widowers was not uncommon: e.g. the sons of bishops Isḥāq ibn Andūna and Sanhūt of Misr.
100. Isaac I, the spiritual son of Bishop Zacharias, became a monk at Zacharias' hands before the latter became Bishop of Saïs: HP I.3:273; *Life of Isaac of Alexandria*, 19–20, Bell 48–9.
101. Mark III spent Lent at the Enaton (HP I.4:519–20). Most likely, Simon I also spent Lent there since that monastery became his primary residence (HP I.4:556). Ya'qūb I (819–30 CE) spent the Forty Days at the Monastery of St. Makarios "as the custom of the patriarchs." The same was true of Isaac I (686–9 CE) (*Life of Isaac of Alexandria*, 39, 41, Bell 57, which has two references), and Yusāb I (HP I.4:630). Also see HP II.1:2/113r; 52/123v; II.3:326/174r; Evelyn White, *Monasteries*, II.350.
102. HP I.4:621; Ibn Sabbā', *al-Jawhara al-Nafīsa*, §51: "None of the bishops or metropolitans has authority to approach the ruler (*al-sulṭān*) except with the permission and advice [of the patriarch]."
103. Patriarch Khaīl I was blamed for the Bashmūric revolt of 748–50 CE; Yusāb I was accused of sparking the 216/831 revolt; Khrisṭūdulūs was arrested because of the destruction of a mosque in Nubia.
104. HP I.4:640; "caliph," lit. "king." After Patriarch Yusāb's exoneration from the charge that he incited the Bashmūric revolt 216/831, the Caliph al-Ma'mūn "commanded that a decree should be written, directing that the patriarch should be honored and respected, and that none should oppose him in his judgments or with regard to those whom he should appoint or depose" (HP I.4:615). Caliph Hārūn al-Wāthik reissued the decree (HP I.4:640–1).
105. HP I.3: 367, 389.
106. Nonetheless, several biographies portray patriarchs who were very human and a number who were clearly an embarrassment to the faithful, such as the avaricious Philotheos and the mentally decaying Theophanios (HP II.2). These frank portrayals go a long way in establishing the historical credibility of the biographies written by Bishop Michael of Tinnīs.
107. HP I.4:637–41; see Chapter Three, n. 72.
108. Bannā bishop of Miṣr, supported by Pachomius of Busta, George of Ṭaḥa, George of Ahnās, Zacharias of al-Buḥayrah, Menas of al-Bahnasā, and presumably Theodore (ibn Isḥāq ibn Andūna) of Wasīm. Patriarch Yusāb was supported by Menas of Tana, Shenoute of Ṣā, and "the rest."
109. See Chapter Three. While Patriarch Yusāb prevailed, the followers of Banā caused tremendous difficulties for him (see HP I.4:649–51, 656–7).
110. HP II.2:231/158r; III.1:6/186r.
111. Taken for granted today, the patriarchate's relocation to Cairo was a prolonged and extremely controversial process, see n. 7 above.
112. See Jacques Jarry, "Inscriptions commémoratives de destruction d'idoles à Akoris," BSAC 34 (1995), 29–31; Zbigniew Borkowski, "Local Cults and

Resistance to Christianity," JJP 20 (1990), 29–30; Elisabeth R. O'Connell, "Transforming Monumental Landscapes in Late Antique Egypt: Monastic Dwellings in Legal Documents from Western Thebes," JECS 15.2 (2007), 239–73; J. Hahn, S. Emmel and U. Gotter, eds., *From Temple to Church: Destruction and Renewal of Local Cultic Topography in Late Antiquity* (Leiden, 2008). Further up the Nile, the Temple of Isis was converted into a church; Welsby, *Medieval Kingdoms*, 35.

113. Dwight W. Young, "A Monastic Invective against Egyptian Hieroglyphs," in *Studies Presented to Hans Jakob Polotsky*, ed. idem (East Gloucester, 1981), 353. Jacob of Serug makes similar comments in his *Discourse on the Fall of Idols*.
114. E.g. see Jean Gascou, "Metanoia, Monastery of the," *CoptEncyc* 5:1608–11; cf. events in Syria see *Chronicle of 1234/History of Dionysios*, I.236–7; Palmer, §§40, 42; J.J. van Ginkel, "Persuasion and Persecution: Establishing Church Unity in the Sixth Century," in *All those Nations: Cultural Encounters within and with the Near East*, ed. H.L.J. Vanstiphout *et al.*, pgs. 60–9 (Leiden, 1999).
115. Eutychios, *Naẓm al-jawhar*, I.201; al-Maqrīzī, *Khiṭaṭ*, IV.992.
116. See Chapters Two and Three, above.
117. Eutychios, *Naẓm al-jawhar*, II.45–6, 52; HP I.3:373, 377; al-Maqrīzī, *Khiṭaṭ*, IV.997; *Chronicle of 1234/History of Dionysios*, Palmer, §70, pg. 159; Fattal, *Le statut légale*, 181.
118. Melkites are undocumented beyond the Delta under Islamic rule, and the HCME repeatedly refers to the diminutive size of that community (28a, 97; 40b, 129). Skreslet states that the Melkites had fifteen churches and several monasteries ("Greeks in Medieval Islamic Egypt," 270). The HCME notes eleven churches, many of which were later destroyed or converted into mosques, and two monasteries: 2b, 5; 28a, 97; 50a, 147; 53a, 157 (Eutychios, *Naẓm al-jawhar*, II.41); 56a-b, 165–66; 71a, 205; 64b, 188. The two monasteries are the Monastery of al-Quṣayr near al-Muqaṭṭam (49a-52a, 145–152), and that of John the Baptist, which was likely acquired by the Melkites in the tenth century CE. It housed Melkite nuns until al-Ḥākim bi Amr Allāh turned it into a mosque (40a-41a, 128–30). Additionally, the Monastery of St. Catherine in Sinai also attracted Egyptian Melkites, such as the tenth century Yuḥannis ibn Buqtur (S. Khalil Samir, "Yuḥannis ibn Buqtur al-Dimyatī," *CoptEncyc* 7:2358).
119. HP I.2:214; Evagrios, *Ecclesiastical History*, 4.11 (and Whitby n. 31–2).
120. HP I.2:238.
121. See Chapter Four, ns. 19–22.
122. See Y.N. Youssef, "Les rituels de la reconsécration," in *Ägypten und Nubien in spätantiker und christlicher Zeit*, ed. S. Emmel *et al.*, 2 vols. (Wiesbaden, 1999), 1:511–515; L.S.B. MacCoull, "'A dwelling place of Christ, a healing place of knowledge': the Non-Chalcedonian Eucharist in Late Antique Egypt and its setting," in *Varieties of Devotion in the Middle Ages and Renaissance*, ed. S.C. Karant-Nunn (Turnhout, 2003).
123. HP I.4:529.

124. See HP I.3:267–72, chapters Three and Four above, and the discussion of ecclesiastical properties below.
125. *Chronicle of 1234/History of Dionysios*, I.237; Palmer, §42. The account continues, "In this way the Orthodox were robbed of the great Church of Edessa and that of Ḥarrān; and this process continued throughout the west, as far as Jerusalem." The Church of Edessa had come under Melkite control shortly before the Arab conquest.
126. HP I.3:266.
127. See the examples in the *Life of Isaac of Alexandria*, 49, 65, 70, 85–6, Bell 61, 67, 69, 75.
128. Eutychios, *Naẓm al-jawhar*, II.41; also HP I.3:278, 296. Most sources focus on the construction of churches in Lower Egypt; projects in Upper Egypt were largely undocumented in narrative sources.
129. Eutychios, *Naẓm al-jawhar*, II.45, my emphasis; also al-Maqrīzī, *Khiṭaṭ*, IV.1001. Later, Hārūn al-Rashīd granted possession of several churches to another Melkite patriarch, Politianus (Biltiyan): Eutychios, *Naẓm al-jawhar*, II.51–52; al-Maqrīzī, *Khiṭaṭ*, IV.1002. A similar dynamic is attested under the Fāṭimids (HP II.2:171/146v; al-Maqrīzī, *Khiṭaṭ*, IV.1006). In large measure, ecclesiastical properties allocated by the government to one faction or another hardly need discussion; influence with (or bribes to) governing authorities dictated the outcome of events. Of greater interest are disputed properties; see Chapter Eleven.
130. See Abū Yūsuf, *Kharāj*, 139–49; Abū ʿUbayd, *Amwāl*, §259, 269; Fattal, *Le statut légale*, 174; Tritton, *Non-Muslim Subjects*, 37–8. Several legal opinions maintain that the restoration of churches and synagogues depended on whether the land was conquered by *sulḥ* or *ʿanwa*, see Chapter Six.
131. John of Nikiou preserves eight stipulations (*Chronicle*, §120.18–21): 1) A fixed tribute. 2) Muslims are not to intervene in any matter for eleven months. 3) Byzantine (lit. "Roman") troops in Alexandria were to keep their possessions and wealth, and leave Egypt by sea, and no other Byzantine army was to return. Those who journeyed by land had to pay a monthly tribute. 4) Muslims were to take 150 soldiers and 50 civilians as hostages and make peace. 5) Byzantines were to cease warring against the Muslims. 6) Muslims were to desist from seizing Christian churches. 7) and not meddle in any the Christian affairs 8) Jews were allowed to stay in Alexandria. Ibn ʿAbd al-Ḥakam (*Futūḥ*, 85–86, cf. 151–2) retains two versions of the agreement, neither of which addressed the building or repair of ecclesiastical properties. See also Trittion, *Non-Muslim Subjects*, 38–42.
132. *Nuqūs* (Gr. *simandron*; Cop. *shenthōouti*) were wooden gongs used to call the faithful to prayer. Later, the word came to designate the metal cymbals used in chanting certain liturgical hymns.
133. Construction or restoration projects are attested in practically every patriarchal biography. The present discussion focuses on the first two centuries under Islam, but the pattern is clear until the fifth/eleventh c.: HP II.1:17/116r,

27/118r; 47/122v, 68/126v; II.2:144–45/141v; 163/145v; 179/148r; 205/153r; 208–9/153v.

134. On the destruction of churches, see Fattal, *Le statut légale*, 191–92. Al-Ḥākim abruptly reversed his discriminatory policies in 411/1020. There is also the case of the wazīr Yazūrī, who closed all churches for eight years (442–50/1050–58); Fattal, *Le statut légale*, 198–99.

135. In his *Mas'ala fī al-kana'is*, Ibn Taymiyya states, "[Muslim religious scholars] are in agreement that if the *imām* would destroy every church in lands conquered without treaty (*bi arḍ al-ʿanwa*), such as in Egypt, Nubia (*al-sūwad*), and ʿIraq, the coast of Syria. . .that would not be unrighteous (*ẓulman*) of him, but he should be obeyed. And if they refrain from the rule of Muslims over them, they would be breaking the agreement (*ʿahd*) and their blood and goods would be permissible" (102); see Seth Ward, "Ibn al-Rifʿa on the Churches and Synagogues of Cairo," *Medieval Encounters* 5 (1999), 70–84; idem, "Construction and Repair of Churches and Synagogues under Islam: A Treatise by Tāqī al-Dīn ʿAlī b. ʿAbd al-Kāfī al-Subkī" (Ph.D. diss., Yale University, 1984).

136. This may simply be the bias of the sources. For much of the period at hand, the Coptic church had tremendous financial resources that produced income independent of the donations and gifts of the faithful. See Ewa Wipszycka, *Les Ressources et les activités économiques des églises en Egypt du IVe au VIIe siècle* (Brussels, 1972). For monasteries in particular, see Jean Gascou, "Monasteries, Economic Activities of," *CoptEncyc* 5:1639–45. Also see *P.Mon.Apollo*, which includes a number of papyri that document tithing to the Monastery of St. Apollo. The term *pakton*, frequently employed in these documents, is understood and translated as "tithing." In at least some instances, however, it may be better understood as the fulfillment of a religious vow, which often included the remittance of an annual amount of wheat or money to the monastery.

137. HP I.3:236, 246. *Synaxarion*, Tubah 8; (pseudo-)Agathon, *Book of Consecration*.

138. Agathon (HP I.3:262), John III (I.3:272), Isaac I (I.3:278), Simon I (I.3:287).

139. Ibn ʿAbd al-Ḥakam, *Futūḥ*, 132; HCME 23b, 86. Maslamā's tenure is treated in al-Kindī, *Wulāt*, 38–40. This contradicts Abū ʿUbayd (*Amwāl*, §263, cf. 264, 268) who (later) maintains that no churches should be built in the *amṣār* of Muslims.

140. *Life of Isaac of Alexandria*, 70, 87; Bell 69, 75. The request was repeated to Simon I in HP I.3:296. The Christian funded these projects.

141. Trittion, *Non-Muslim Subjects*, 42–3. He permitted the building of the church of mār Jirjis—*kanīsat al-farrāshīn* (cf. HCME, 53a, 157)—for the Melkites and the Church of Abū Qīr for the Copts (Eutychios, *Naẓm al-jawhar*, II.41). On Isaac and Athanasios, see Chapter Three.

142. HP I.3:316, 403. Clergy were forced to use wooden and glass vessels. Marble was a Byzantine export lacking in Islamic lands; hence, it was often confiscated from churches and reused in mosques and palaces. The confiscation of marble

is documented in HP I.3:321; and again under Yusāb I (HP I.4:627–29). Over a two year span, 92–94/711–3, Qurra demolished and enlarged a portion of *al-masjīd al-jami'* (al-Kindī, *Wulāt*, 65). It may be assumed that the confiscated marble and pillars were used to complete that project; both materials were commonly used in the adornment of mosques and government palaces; see Ibn 'Abd al-Ḥakam, *Futūḥ*, 132, 135; Theophanes, *Chronicle*, AM 6183 (690/1 CE).

143. Kindī, *Wulāt*, 77.
144. Eventually, al-Walīd and Wuhayb were killed (al-Kindī, *Wulāt*, 77–78). This took place five years after 'Ubayd Allāh ibn Ḥabḥāb settled Qaysīs in Egypt, and may have been the first violent Yamanīs-Qaysī clashe in Egypt.
145. HP I.3: 373, 403. Here, what was damaged during the reign of Qurra ibn Sharīk was repaired and new churches constructed.
146. HP I.3:436, 438.
147. HP I.4:497–9, 502, 504, 508.
148. E.g. *Synaxarion*, Misra 19 and 29; *Life of John the Little*, Mikhail and Vivian, Appendix 5; Evelyn White, *Monasteries*, II.292–96.
149. HP I.4:499, 502.
150. HP I.4:503.
151. HP I.4:512. It is unclear whether the policy shift was due to the new governor, or if Hārūn al-Rashīd had let up on his edict.
152. HP I.4:522, 529, 532–3, 545–6, 548.
153. HP I.4:533.
154. HP I.4:574–5, discussed in Chapter Three.
155. HP I.4:574.
156. HP I.4:627–9; cf. I.3:321. See n. 142 above.
157. HP I.4:633–5. See Chapter Three.
158. Kindī, *Wulāt*, 131.
159. HP II.2:193/150v; 194–95/151r; 208/153v. Many churches and synagogues were closed, and were later destroyed.
160. Kindī, *Wulāt*, 131–2. The account mentions the Church of Mary and the churches in Maḥras Qustantīn, which were rebuilt with the *mashurā* of al-Layth ibn Sa'd and 'Abdallāh ibn Lahi'ā.
161. HP II.1:6/113v; 36/120r; 45–47/122r-v; 52–58/123v-124v. The destruction reached the churches of Upper Egypt (HP II.1:60/125r); it had economic repercussions, particularly for merchants (HP II.1:45/122r; cf. 77/128v).
162. HP II.2:193–95/150v-151r. Saleh ("Government Relations," 81–86, 96) and Fattal (*Le statut légale*, 103–4) discuss al-Ḥākim's destruction of churches and the conversion of some into mosques.
163. Saleh, "Government Relations," 79.
164. Due to the Miracle at al-Muqaṭṭam; see Chapter Eleven.
165. HP II.2:145/142r.
166. Al-Mu'allaqa was also restored, but apparently without much commotion.
167. HP II.2:145/142r, my translation; *Life of Afrahām*, pgs. 39–40.

168. Ibn Taymiyya, *Mas'ala fī al-kana'is* (see n. 135 above); cf. Richard J.H. Gottheil, "Dhimmis and Moslems in Egypt," in *Old Testament and Semitic Studies in Memory of William Rainey Harper*, ed. R.F. Harper, F. Brown, and G.F. Moore (Chicago, 1908), II:353–414; idem, "An Answer to the Dhimmis," JAOS 41 (1921), 383–457.

Chapter 11 Polemics and the Construction of Communal Identities

1. See R. Lane Fox, *Pagans and Christians* (New York, 1987); Pierre Chuvin, *A Chronicle of the Last Pagans*, trans. B.A. Archer (Cambridge, 1990); David Rokeah, *Jews, Pagans, and Christians in Conflict* (Leiden, 1982); J. Lieu, J. North, and T. Rajak, eds., *The Jews Among Pagans and Christians in the Roman World* (London, 1992); S.H. Griffith, *Church in the Shadow of the Mosque*. On polemical texts among the three traditions, see the volumes in CMR; Heinz Schreckenberg, *Die christlichen Adversus-Judaeos Texte und ihr literarisches und historisches Umfeld*, 2 vols. (Frankfurt am Main, 1982–88); Moritz Steinschneider, *Polemische und apologetische Literatur in arabischer Sprache* (Leipzig, 1877; Liechtenstein, 1966).
2. F.E. Peters, *The Children of Abraham: Judaism, Christianity, Islam*, New Ed. (Princeton, 2004), chs. 1–2.
3. See F.E. Peters, *Judaism, Christianity and Islam*, 3 vols. (Princeton, 1990); idem, *The Monotheists: Jews, Christians, and Muslims in Conflict and Competition*, 2 vols. (Princeton, 2003); Jacques Waardenburg, *Muslims and Others: Relations in Context* (Berlin, 2003), ch. 1–2; idem, "Christians, Muslims, Jews, and their Religions," *Islam and Christian-Muslim Relations* 15 (2004), 13–33.
4. Cf. Ex. 20:3, Jn. 14:6, Qur'ān 1:5–7.
5. See al-Mas'ūdī, *Murūj al-dhahab*, II.386–91; Mark R. Cohen and Sasson Somekh, "Interreligous Majālis in Early Fatimid Egypt," in *Majlis*, eds. H. Lazarus-Yafeh *et al.*
6. Gabriel Said Reynolds, *A Muslim Theologian in a Sectarian Milieu: 'Abd al-Jabbār and the Critique of Christian Origins* (Leiden, 2004); David Thomas, *Early Muslim Polemic against Christianity: Abū 'Īsá al-Warrāq's "Against the Incarnation"* (Cambridge, 2002); idem, *Anti-Christian Polemic in Early Islam: Abū 'Īsá al-Warrāq's "Against the Trinity"* (Cambridge, 1992); Rifaat Ebied and David Thomas, eds., *Muslim-Christian Polemic during the Crusades The Letter from the People of Cyprus and Ibn Abi Talib al-Dimashqui's Response* (Leiden, 2005).
7. Pseudo-Sawīrus, *Kitāb al-īḍāḥ*; Mark Swanson, "A Copto-Arabic Catechism of the Later Fatimid Period: 'Ten Questions which One of the Disciples Asked of His Master,'" *Parole de l'Orient* 22 (1997), 473–501; idem, "Three Sinai

Manuscripts of Books 'of the Master and the Disciple' and their *membra disiecta* in Birmingham," OCP 65 (1999), 347–61.

8. There is now a sizable bibliography on the various nuances of "identity:" e.g. see James D. Fearon, "What is Identity (As We Now Use the Word)?" unpublished paper, 1999; Frank Welz, "Rethinking Identity: Concepts of Identity and "the Other" in Sociological Perspective," *The Society: An International Journal of Social Sciences* 1 (2005), 1–25; A.M.Y. Lin, ed., *Problematizing identity: Everyday struggles in language, culture, and education* (New York, 2008); Gladys Frantz-Murphy, "Identity and Security in the Mediterranean World ca. AD 640 - ca. 1517," in *Proceedings of the Twenty-Fifth International Congress of Papyrology*, ed. T. Gagos and A.Hyatt (Ann Arbor, 2010), 253–64.
9. E.g. *P.Lond.Copt*.I.250; Pseudo-John III, *Questions of Theodore* and *Disputation of Patriarch John*; cf. Theophanes, *Chronicle*, AM 6248 (755/6 CE); S.H. Griffith, "Disputing with Islam in Syriac: The Case of the Monk of Bêt Ḥālê and a Muslim Emir," *Hugoye: Journal of Syriac Studies* 3.1 (2000) <http://syrcom.cua.edu/Hugoye/>; idem, "Disputes with Muslims in Syriac Christian Texts: from Patriarch John (d. 648) to Bar Hebraeus (d. 1286)," in *Religionsgespräche im Mittelalter*, ed. F. Niewohner, 251–73; Wafik Nasry, *The Caliph and the Bishop. A 9th Century Muslim-Christian Debate: Al-Ma'mūn and Abū Qurrah* (Lebanon, 2008).
10. E.g. J. den Heijer noted that this type of literature is "hardly as edifying as 'real' apologetic literature" ("Apologetic Elements in Copto-Arabic Historiography: the Life of Afrahām ibn Zurʿah, 62nd Patriarch of Alexandria," in *Christian Arabic Apologetics*, ed. Samir and Nielsen, 202).
11. J.C. Lamoreaux, *Theodore Abu Qurrah*; HP II.2:164/145v.; several works are attributed to Sawīrus, including the *Book on the Differences of the Sects*, *Refutation of the Nestorians*, *Refutation of the Jews*, *Refutation of Saʿīd ibn Baṭrīq* (P. Chébli, ed./trans.); cf. GCAL 99.2 and 100; CMR 2: 496–8.
12. S.H. Leeder, *Modern sons of the Pharaohs* (London, 1918; 1973), 68–70.
13. Also, *lex orandi legem credendi constituit*, "the rule of prayer is the rule of faith." While this formulation is credited to St. Prosper of Aquitaine (d. 465 CE), its underlying assertion was universal to the early church; see Jaroslav Pelikan, *Credo: Historical and Theological Guide to Creeds and Confessions of Faith in the Christian Tradition* (New Haven, 2003), ch. 6.2; Rebecca Lyman, "*Lex orandi*: Heresy, Orthodoxy, and Popular Religion," in *The Making and Remaking of Christian Doctrine*, ed. S. Coakley and D.A. Pailin (Oxford, 1993), 131–42; Alister E. McGrath, *The Genesis of Doctrine: A Study in the foundation of Doctrinal Criticism* (Oxford, 1990; Grand Rapids, 1997); Baby Varghese, *West Syrian Liturgical Theology* (Burlington, 2004), ch. 4–5.
14. Melkite churches and monasteries were usually named after saints held in common with the Copts, e.g. the Monastery of St. John the Baptist (HCME 40a-b, 129) or the Church of St. Menas (HCME 56a-b, 165–6). A possible exception was a church named after St. Sabas (HCME 50b, 150)—though the

designation of "the Alexandrian" likely eliminates its identification with the pro-Chalcedonian Saint Sabas (439–532 CE) who was of Cappadocian origins and led a monastic community in Palestine. The names of Melkite bishops and patriarchs followed the same pattern: e.g. Joseph, Eustathios, Eutychios, Kosmas, Theodore, Arsenios.

15. See Chapter Five. Aside from the names in the Dyptichs, the two versions of the *Trisagion* provided the earliest tangible liturgical difference between the two groups.
16. Makīn (the Younger), *Mukhtaṣar al-bayān*, IV.242–4; Subhi Y. Labib, "Abraham, Saint," *CoptEncyc* 1:10–11; J. den Heijer, "Apologetic Elements."
17. S.P. Brock, "The 'Nestorian Church,'" 23–35; also Chapter One above.
18. *Chronicle of Sīrt*, II.313; S.P. Brock, "Christians in the Sasanian Empire," 17; Michael G. Morony, "History and Identity in the Syrian Churches," in *Redefining Christian Identity*, ed. J.J. van Ginkel *et al.*, 10 n.67. Morony notes that Sabhrīshōʿ may have been following a precedent set by another East Syrian catholicos, Ezekiel (570–81 CE). Another, mid-seventh century reference is found in the Armenian *History* of Sebios, ch. 50 (pg. 145).
19. Makīn (the Younger), *Mukhtaṣar al-bayān*, IV.64.
20. Bishop Basilios' "Fastings" (*CoptEncyc* 4:1093–7), is informed by medieval Coptic authors and current practice, but it does not reflect the historical origins or development of the fasts it discusses.
21. Maged S.A. Mikhail, "A New Historiography of Lent in Alexandria and the Alleged Reforms of Patriarch Demetrius." In *The Future of Coptic Studies: Theories, Methods, Topics*, ed. Nelly van Doorn-Harder (*forthcoming*). The study challenges the thesis of a post-Epiphany Lent in Alexandria.
22. Cf. Sokrates, *Ecclesiastical History*, 5.22; Sozomen, *Ecclesiastical History*, 1.7; *Chronicle of 640*, 15; cf. John Malalas, *Chronicle*, Dindorf 482–83 (18.96); Theophanes, *Chronicle*, AM 6038 (545/6 CE), AM 6156 (663/4 CE), AM 6252 (759/60 CE), AM 6259 (766/7 CE); *Chronicle of Zuqnīn*, Harrak, (545–6 CE), pg. 235; (772–3 CE), pgs. 255, 259–60; Egeria, *Diary*, ch. 27. Gingras (n. 321) convincingly argues that Egeria described but one of several contemporary observations in fourth century Jerusalem (382–383 CE); M.G. Morony, *Iraq after the Muslim Conquest*, 374; Paul F. Bradshaw and Maxwell E. Johnson, *The Origins of Feasts, Fasts and Seasons in Early Christianity* (Collegeville: Liturgical Press, 2011), chs. 10–12; Thomas J. Talley, *The Origins of the Liturgical Year*, 2nd ed. (Collegeville, 1991), part 3.
23. Patriarch Athanasios introduced the forty-day Lent into Egypt: Athanasios, *Festal Letters*, 2.8 (dated 330 CE); 3.6 (331 CE); 6.13 (334 CE); cf. with his *Letter to Serapion* and Sokrates, *Ecclesiastical History*, 5.22. David Brakke, "Jewish Flesh and Christian Spirit in Athanasius of Alexandria," *Journal of Early Christian Studies* 9.4 (2001), 453–81; esp. 457–64; Alberto Camplani, "Sull' origine della Quaresima in Egitto," in *Acts of the Fifth International Congress of Coptic Studies*, ed. David W. Johnson, 2 vols. (Rome, 1993), 2.105–

21. The designation of Lent as the "Forty Days," or "the Holy Forty," prevails in Greek, Coptic, and Arabic sources.

24. Alberto Camplani, "Coptic Fragments from a Festal Letter of the Late Sixth Century (John Rylands Library, Coptic Suppl. N. 47–48): Damian or Eulogius?" *Coptic Studies*, ed. Mat Immerzeel *et al.*, I: 317–27.

25. A. Camplani, "La Qaresima egiziana nel VII secolo: note di cronologia su Mon.Epiph. 77, Manchester Ryland Suppl. 47–48, P.Grenf. II 112, P.Berol.10677, P.Köln 215 e un'omelia copta," *Augustinianum* 32 (1992): 423–32; favoring the tenure of Benjamin or Agathon. Camplani favors a mid-seventh century date. Still, P.Mon.Epiph 77 may be dated later. The remains of Patriarch Benjamin's *Sixteenth Festal Letter* lack any reference to Lent. A key reference in his lost *Thirty Fifth Festal Letter* depends on two date-clauses cited in *De sacris ieiuniis* (PG 95:63–78, §505), attributed to John of Damascus (d. 749 CE). Noting a discrepancy in the date clause, but confident in its attribution to Benjamin, scholars have followed A. Rahlfs lead in correcting the date clause so that it would fall within Benjamin's tenure (A. Rahlfs, "Die alttestamentlichen Lektionen der griechischen Kirche," *Nachrichten von der Königlichen Gesellschaft der Wissenschaften zu Göttingen. Philologisch-historische Klasse aus dem Jahre* (1915), 28–136; here pg. 86 n.3). Still, it is equally likely that the date clauses are accurate, but that the attribution to Benjamin is erroneous. That would date the letter cited in *De sacris ieiuniis* to the first quarter of the eighth century, coinciding with the earliest unambiguous evidence for an Egyptian eight-week observance, the *Letter of Alexander II* (dated to 713, 719, or 724 CE).

26. Ibn al-ʿAssāl, *al-Majmūʿ al-ṣafawī*, I.171.

27. Makīn, *Mukhtaṣar al-bayān*, IV.238–9, 241; Ibn Kabar, *Muṣbāḥ al-ẓulmā*, II.141; "for it seems that the Copts fasted (that week) before Herakleios." Nicea sought to establish a common date for the Easter celebration, not the length of Lent, though its Fifth Canon provides the first attestation for the "Forty Days" (*Decrees*, I.8). Still, considerable differences in the length of Lent and the means by which it was observed persisted for well over a century after Nicea (Sokrates, *Ecclesiastical History*, 5.22).

28. Gabriel Ibn Turayk, *Nomocanon*, ch. 19 cf. 30; Ibn al-ʿAssāl, *al-Majmūʿ al-ṣafawī*, ch. 15. Lent is referenced in Coptic Arabic literature by both designations ("Forty" and "Fifty Days"): Christodoulos, *Canons*, §§6, 10; HCME 5b, 11, and 66a, 194; al-Makīn (the Younger), *Mukhtaṣar al-bayān*, IV.231, 238.

29. HCME 15b, 38–39, my emphasis; cf. 40b-41a, 129 and the account of Abū Yāsir in 46a, 140. On Ibn al-Qunbar, see Chapter Four, ns. 126–7, and Chapter Five, n. 61.

30. Makīn (the Younger), *Mukhtaṣar al-bayān*, IV.38–68, cf. 316–8; cf. Pseudo-Sawīrus, *Tartīb al-kahanūt*, ch. 21.

31. The current Coptic Lectionary for Lent contains readings for Sunday evening (before sunset).

32. Christodoulos, *Canons*, §1 (cf. Ex. 3:5). In current Coptic practice, shoes are not worn in the sanctuary, but are regularly worn in parish churches, though the older practice still dominates in monastic churches. Melkite practice also persisted; they continue to wear shoes in church and sanctuary.
33. Perhaps a symbolic reenactment inspired by Jn. 18:22–4.
34. The Copts recognized a reserved sacrament until the eleventh century when it was forbidden by Patriarch Khrisṭūdulūs, possibly on account of various abuses that crept in; e.g. Sokrates, *Ecclesiastical History*, 5.22; Benjamin, *On Cana of Galilee*; Pseudo-Sawīrus, *Tartīb al-kahanūt*, ch. 21, pg. 57.
35. Irregularities crept in even among the Copts of Upper Egypt and their coreligionists in the Delta: Makīn (the Younger), *Mukhtaṣar al-bayān*, IV. 223–24; *Chronicle of 1234/History of Dionysios*; Palmer, §188 (664 CE); cf. Michael the Syrian, *Chronicle*, 11.12b: E.g. Otto Neugebauer, *Abu Shaker's "Chronography;"*. . .(Vienna, 1988), 77–86, 90–95, 97, 100, 151–52, 160—this volume is a summary of the work, not a translation; also see n. 22 above.
36. Neugebauer notes that the parameters for Abū Shākir's calculations were often random.
37. Jewish factions were embroiled in their own calendrical disputes; see Marina Rustow, *Heresy and the Politics of Community: the Jews of the Fatimid Caliphate* (Ithaca, 2008), 15–20, 57–65.
38. This is clear from Neugenbauer's summary. Unfortunately, the relevant sections of Abū Shakir's *Chronography*, which survives in Ethiopic, have not been translated as of yet.
39. This issue is discussed from another vantage point in A. Papaconstantinou "Historiography," esp. 80–1, where Coptic claims are described as "legendary" and posed as if they were novel, first emerging under Islamic rule. Here it is taken for granted that Copts and Melkites were participating in the same debate since Byzantine rule, each positioning itself as the sole legitimate successor to the pre-Chalcedonian fathers.
40. HP I.3:373 states that he was also known as Theophylact.
41. Eutychios, *Naẓm al-jawhar*, II.45, my emphasis; cf. al-Maqrīzī, *Khiṭaṭ*, IV.1001; see Chapters Three and Ten above.
42. HP I.3:373–86; Skreslet, "Greeks in Medieval Islamic Egypt," 111–20.
43. The saint is often referenced among the Copts as *mārī Mīnā al-ʿagaybī*, "St. Mina the miraculous/wonderworker." As the HP records, "that church had great fame, (was famous for) many miracles, and was endowed with property (*awqāf*) everywhere." HP I.3:373, my translation. Also see HP I.4:549, 565, 582–3, 627; HP II.1:3/113r. Interruption of pilgrimage to St. Menas caused financial difficulty for the whole church (HP I.4:582–83). The fulfillment of religious vows must have also brought a sizeable income. During the caliphate of al-Ḥāfiẓ, a well at the complex of St. Menas was dug at the expense of Shaykh Abū al-Ṣayrafī (HCME 30b, 105) in fulfillment of such a vow. The church was likewise restored when al-Walīd ibn Rufāʿa was *wālī* in 106/725 (HCME 29b, 103). In 559/1164, the whole complex burned down under

Ṣalāḥ al-Dīn Yūsuf ibn Ayyūb (Saladin) and was restored by Shaykh Ṣalīb, Karīm al-Dawla ibn 'Ubayd ibn Qurrūṣ al-Jullāl, Manṣūr ibn Salīm al-Jullāl and the patriarch, who contributed to the effort from proceeds gained from Simony (HCME 31a, 106–7). See also, Peter Grossmann, "The Pilgrimage Center of Abū Mīnā," in *Pilgrimage and Holy Space*, ed. D. Frankfurter (Leiden, 1998), 281–302; idem, *Abu Mina*, 2 vols. Archäologische Veröffentlichungen 44, 54 (Mainz, 1989–2004); Arietta Papaconstantinou, *Le culte des saints en Égypte: des Byzantines aux Abbassides* (Paris, 2001), 146–54.

44. A portion of Patriarch Michael's letter is preserved in HP I.3:376–7.
45. HP I.3:378. He is identified as a *qāḍī* (pg. 385), and praised for his impartiality.
46. HP I.3:386, my emphasis; *Synaxarion*, Ba'unā 15.
47. HP I.3:378.
48. HP I.3:344.
49. Heirship is also an issue in the *Life of Isaac of Alexandria*: "His understanding was illumined with regard to the holy teachings, just like the great Athanasios and the wise Cyril, *whose successor he was*" (59, Bell 65, my emphasis); "I will believe in him as in *Athanasios, Cyril, Ignatios, and Severos*" (63, Bell 66). The authorities cited in Benjamin's *Sixteenth Festal Letter* (Müller, 322) and the *Letter of Alexander II* also prove as much.
50. Also see, HP I.3:375. The HP depicts the proceedings as a theological debate in which "The orthodox with their arguments from the Holy Scriptures prevailed over the [pro-]Chalcedonians."
51. See CMR; Abdelmajid Charfi, "La fonction historique de la polémique islamochrétienne à l'époque abbasside," in *Christian Arabic Apologetics*, ed. Samir and Nielsen; Lasker, "Jewish Critique of Christianity under Islam"; Mark R. Cohen, *Under Crescent and Cross: the Jews in the Middle Ages* (Princeton, 1994).
52. There exists a tremendous volume of historical literature on the Nile: Ibn al-Kindī, *Faḍā'il miṣr*, 203–6; Ibn Zulāq, *Faḍā'il miṣr*, 74–6; al-Mas'ūdī, *Murūj al-dhahab*, cf. II.358–62 with VI.272–4; Ibn Ḥawqal, *Ṣūrat al-arḍ*, 147–8; Danielle Bonneau, *La crue du Nil*; eodem, *Le fisc et le Nil: incidences des irrégularités de la crue du Nil sur la fiscalité foncière* (Paris, 1971); eodem, *Le régime administratif de l'eau du Nil dans l'Egypte grecque, romaine et byzantine* (Leiden, 1993); H. Erlich and I. Gershoni, eds., *The Nile*; Haggai Erlich, *The Cross and the River: Ethiopia, Egypt, and the Nile* (London, 2002); also see the references in ns. 65, 68, and 71 below.
53. The ancient Egyptians personified the inundation in the god Hapy; see John L. Foster, *Hymns, Prayers, and Songs: An Anthology of Ancient Egyptian Lyric Poetry* (Atlanta, 1995), hymns 51, 52. Herodotus, (*Histories*, 2.90.1) mentions the "Priests of the Nile" who were alone responsible to bury anyone killed by a crocodile. The Copts and Melkites had analogous rituals to bless the Nile: for the Coptic rite, see W.B. Roshdi Dous, "The Nile Service: Ἀκολουθία τοῦ Νείλου," in *Actes du huitième congrès international d'études coptes*, ed. N. Bosson

and A. Boud'hors (Louvain, 2007), 2:425–38; a Melkite counterpart is in G. Margoliouth, "The Liturgy of the Nile," *Journal of the Royal Asiatic Society* (1896), 677–731.

54. Throughout the HCME, the Nile is qualified as "blessed," 46b, 140; 163, 55b; 69a, 201; 95b, 265; 100a, 273; 275, 100b; 102a, 277. The HCME (20a-b, 67–68; 26b-27a, 93–94), Ibn Zulāq (*Faḍā'il miṣr*, 74–6), Ibn al-Kindī (*Faḍā'il miṣr*, 203, 205–6), and al-Maqrīzī's (*Khiṭaṭ*, I.130–159) comment at length on the Nile's "virtues." Also see, Leslie S.B. MacCoull, "*Stud. Pal.* XV 250ab: A Monophysite Trishagion for the Nile Flood," *Journal of Theological Studies* 40 (1989), 129–35.
55. The traditional measure is "Sixteen cubits" (1 Egyptian *dhirā'* = .54 m): Herodotus, *Histories*, 2.13.1; Pliny, *Natural History*, 36.11; HP I.3:448; al-Masʿūdī, *Murūj al-dhahab*, II.362, 367; al-Maqrīzī, *Khiṭaṭ*, I.159.2–3, 161.13–5, 186.17. For the documentary evidence, see Orsamus M. Pearl, "The Inundation of the Nile in the Second Century AD," *Transactions and Proceedings of the American Philological Association* 87 (1956), 51–9; Étienne Bernand, *Inscriptions grecques et latines d'Akôris* (Cairo, 1988), no. 29–41. Still, there are some minor discrepancies; Nāṣir-i Khusraw, *Safarnāma*, 52, 53; Ibn Jubayr, *Riḥla*, 47 (Eng. 55); cf. Ibn Ḥawqal, *Ṣūrat al-arḍ*, 136.
56. Henry Maguire, "The Nile and the Rivers of Paradise," in *The Madaba Map Centenary, 1897–1997: Traveling Through the Byzantine Umayyad Period*, ed. M. Piccirillo and E. Alliata (Jerusalem, 1999), 179–84. The "Litany of Water" is annually prayed in the Coptic liturgy from the 12th of Ba'ūna through the 9th of Bābah; it reads, "Graciously, Lord, bless the waters of the river this year."
57. Ibn ʿAbd al-Ḥakam, *Futūḥ*, 150.
58. Paphnutios, *Histories of the Monks*, fol. 53b-54a, 54a-55b, Vivian §§131, 132–5.
59. *Synaxarion*, Amshīr 2.
60. *Apocalypse of Athanasios*, 12.5—only in the Coptic version. Cf. *Synaxarion*, Misra 12; al-Maqrīzī, *Khiṭaṭ*, I.182.6–9; Leeder, *Modern Sons*, 70. Archangel Michael is often commemorated on the twelfth of Coptic months, but this is the only explicit reference to his intercession for the Nile.
61. Eutychios, *Naẓm al-jawhar*, II.74.17–19. For "prayed for water" (استسقوا). *Ṣalāt al-istisqā'* was a prayer for rain; cf. al-Masʿūdī, *Murūj al-dhahab*, II.363.
62. Offering ecumenical prayers at times of hardship was noted by Leeder at beginning of the twentieth century (*Modern Sons of the Pharaohs*, 69–70).
63. Eusebios, *Life of Constantine*, 4.25.2–3. The *Historia Monachorum* 8.25, Russell, 74 (cf. Paphnutios, *Histories of the Monks*, Vivian, Introduction, 31) describes Pagan priests as they carried an idol in a state of ecstasy through various villages "no doubt performing the ceremony to ensure the flooding of the Nile." Abba Apollo is said to have miraculously brought an end to the rite, and was able to convert the Pagans to Christianity. Cf. Athanasios, *Life of Antony*, §39; S. Emmel, "Shenoute of Atripe and the Christian Destruction of

Temples in Egypt: Rhetoric and Reality," in *From Temple to Church*, ed. J. Hahn *et al.*, 161–201 (esp. Frag. 2.5).

64. HP I.3:448–51.
65. The HP depicts Abū al-ʿAwn favorably, but his secretaries are said to have negatively influenced him; cf. HP I.3:442–4 and I.4:482, 490. At several junctures, the level of the Nile was interpreted as an omen indicating God's favor or displeasure. Here, a low Nile betrayed God's anger with the two secretaries. Its miraculous increase is attested at a number of events: e.g. the arrival of the Khurāsāniyya, the arrival of Badr al-Jamālī in Egypt, and the elevation of Patriarch Peter VI (HP III.3:286/261r).
66. HP I.3:448; HCME 59b-60a, 175–6.
67. HP I.3:449, my emphasis; the true agenda of these narratives is just beneath the surface.
68. HP I.3:449–50: "O God, the only One, who hast no companion, creator of heaven and earth, you know that we associate no other with you, and worship none besides you, and that we do not say, as the Christians do, that you have a son, or that you were born, but we confess you to be one, and worship your unity. We desire this day to see your wonders, which you work, that we may know and prove that there is no religion like ours, which we inherit from our fathers; and we pray you to work a miracle for us, as you did yesterday for the Christians, who are our enemies and the enemies of our creed, for they set beside you another God, begotten by you from the beginning, whom they call Christ born of Mary, saying that he is your son, with the Holy Spirit and that you are the third of them, with many such doctrines. We pray you to give us a sign and miracle in this water."
69. Bishop Moses of Wasīm is very prominent in the biography of Patriarch Khaīl I. He is commemorated in the *Synaxarion*, Misra 11. That entry does not reference this event, however. See also Gawdat Gabra, "Bemerkungen zum Text des Difnars über Moses, Bischof von Awisim—ca. 740–770," BSAC 32 (1993), 63–71. Eutychios presents an interesting parallel situated within the context of the second century CE. He states that during a prolonged period of plague and drought Roman authorities asked the Christians to intercede with God. Subsequently, rain fell and the plague ceased (*Naẓm al-jawhar*, I.104.3–6).
70. HP I.3:448.
71. Ibn ʿAbd al-Ḥakam, *Futūḥ*, 150–1; cf. Ibn Zulāq, *Faḍāʾil miṣr*, 74–5; al-Maqrīzī's *Khiṭaṭ*, I.152.11–154.18. This is a *topos*. The outline of the narrative—throwing a virgin into the river or to a dragon—is found in diverse legends, including some associated with Ss. George and Theodore of Shoteb (*Synaxarion*, Abīb 20); cf. the mythology surrounding the festival for *Wafaʾ al-nīl*.
72. Ibn ʿAbd al-Ḥakam, *Futūḥ*, 150.14.
73. Ibn ʿAbd al-Ḥakam, *Futūḥ*, 150.18–20.
74. Ibn ʿAbd al-Ḥakam, *Futūḥ*, 151.6–7.

75. The association with the Feast of the Cross is implicit.
76. Cf. S.H. Griffith, *Church in the Shadow of the Mosque*, 162–6.
77. Maqrīzī, *Khiṭaṭ*, I.183–5; Aziz S. Atiya, "Martyr, Feast of the," *CoptEncyc* 5:1547–8; H. Lutfi, "Festivals of the Nile," in *Mamluks in Egyptian Politics and Society*, ed. Philipp and Haarmann, esp. 263–268; the assertion that John was a martyr under Islam is not attested in Coptic sources or the *Synaxarion*, the context of which suggests that he was martyred during the Diocletian persecutions; cf. ns. 81 and 85 below.
78. Maqrīzī, *Khiṭaṭ*, I.183.2–4. The first attestation is in the biography of Michael V (1145–6 CE), though it references a reform introduced by his predecessor, Gabriel II (1131–45 CE): HP III.1:64–65/196v.
79. Cf. the celebrations of *'Id al-Ghitas* (al-Masʿūdī, *Murūj al-dhahab*, II.364–5) and the Nayrūz (Shoshan, *Popular Culture*, ch. 3).
80. *Synaxarion*, Bashans 8, mentions only the saint's martyrdom and that his body is "now in Shurbā al-Khaymā," but there is no reference to the river or the festival.
81. *Martyrdom of John of Phanijōit*; L.S.B. MacCoull, "Rite of the Jar," in *Peace and Negotiation*, ed. D. Wolfthal, 154–5; Hany N. Takla, "The Thirteenth-Century Coptic (?) Martyrdom of John of Phanidjoit, Reconsidered," in *Ägypten und Nubien in spätantiker und christlicher Zeit*, ed. S. Emmel *et al.* (Wiesbaden, 1999). Both are named "John" and are commemorated a day apart. Furthermore, John of Sanhūt is mentioned in the *Martyrdom of John*, §128. At one point in the *Martyrdom*, John of Phanijōit's body was thrown in the river, but there is no mention of the Nile rising.
82. Maqrīzī, *Khiṭaṭ*, I.184.6–7.
83. Maqrīzī, *Khiṭaṭ*, I.184.9–10; "relic" is literally "finger."
84. Maqrīzī, *Khiṭaṭ*, I.185.9; the confiscated ecclesiastical *awqāf* amounted to 25,000 *faddans*.
85. P. Sanders, *Ritual, Politics, and the City in Fatimid Cairo*, 100–5; Michael Winter, *Egyptian Society Under Ottoman Rule, 1517–1798* (London, 1992), 242–3; H. Lutfi, "Festivals of the Nile," 269–73; E.W. Lane, *Manners and Customs of the Modern Egyptians* (London, 1908), 495–6; J.W. McPherson, *The Moulids of Egypt (Egyptian Saints-Days)* (Cairo, 1941; 1995), esp. 228; McPherson surveys well over a hundred Christian and Muslim *mawlids*.
86. Atiya, "Martyr, Feast of the," 48; Lutfi, "Festivals of the Nile."
87. In the mid-eleventh century, Nāṣir-i Khusraw (*Safarnāma*, 61–62, 64–65) knew it as a civil celebration devoid of religious connotations; cf. P. Sanders, *Ritual, Politics, and the City*, ch. 5.
88. *Synaxarion*, Baramhāt 28; HP III.3:305–6/267r.
89. In Arabic, *ifranj*, "Franks," may also denote "westerners" or "foreigners" in general.
90. Peter Brown "The Rise and Function of the Holy Man in Late Antiquity," *Journal of Roman Studies* 61 (1971), 80–101; repr. idem, *Society and the Holy in Late Antiquity* (London, 1982); idem, "The Saint as Exemplar in Late

Antiquity," *Representations* 1 (1983), 1–25; idem, "The Rise and Function of the Holy Man in Late Antiquity, 1971–1997," *Journal of Early Christian Studies* 6.3 (1998), 353–76.

91. See *Life of Afrahām*; Maryann M. Shenoda, "Displacing Dhimmī, Maintaining Hope: Unthinkable Coptic Representations of Fatimid Egypt," IJMES 39.4 (2007), 587–606. J. den Heijer's "Apologetic Elements," discusses the Garshūnī version of this story.
92. Copts celebrate the Fast of the Nativity (Christmas) on Kyahk 29 (January 7). Cf. Averil Cameron, *Christianity and the Rhetoric of Empire* (Berkeley, 1991), ch. 3.
93. He had entered Cairo in 972 CE: HP II.2:138–45/140v-142r; HCME, 34b-35a, 116–7; *Synaxarion*, Kyahk 6. On these *majālis* see, H. Lazarus-Yafeh *et al.*, eds., *Majlis: Interreligious Encounters*.
94. Mu'izz insisted upon the civility of the proceedings, HP II.2:139/140v.
95. Even in the presence of the patriarch (HP II.2:139/140v-141r), Sawīrus took the lead in such proceedings. HP II.2:138/140v.
96. Absent in the *Life of Afrahām*. *Qāḍī al-quḍāt* is first attested in Egypt under the Fāṭimids.
97. HP II.2:138/140v; "efficacy" is lit. "strength."
98. On Ibn Killis (d. 380/991), see Mark R. Cohen and Sasson Somekh, "In the Court of Ya'qūb Ibn Killis: A Fragment from the Cairo Genizah," *Jewish Quarterly Review*, n.s. 80 (1990), 283–314; Yaacov Lev, "The Fatimid vizier Ya'qub b. Killis and the Beginning of the Fatimid Administration in Egypt," *Islam* 153 (1981), 237–49; M. Canrad, "Ibn Killis, Abū 'l-Faradj Ya'ḳūb b. Yūsuf," EI^2 3:840b-841b.
99. HP II.2:139/141r.
100. On scriptural polemics, see Cohen, *Under Crescent and Cross*, ch. 9; Griffith, *Church in the Shadow of the Mosque*. The bishop's words echo the scriptural polemics exchanged between Christians and Jews—but ever so slightly.
101. HP II.2:142/141v; Y.N. Youssef, "The Miracle of Ibn Zar'ah in Coptic Tradition: Texts and Icons," *Coptica* 8 (2009), 81–96. The tanner had plucked out his eye when he lusted after a woman; a literal enactment of Matt. 5:29 and parallels. Each morning, he would deliver water to the poor and shut-ins, and every evening he would keep only enough money to buy bread and give the rest in alms.
102. Ibn 'Abd al-Ḥakam, *Futūḥ miṣr*, 182; Eutychios, *Naẓm al-jawhar*, II.70; Ibn al-Kindī, *Faḍā'il miṣr*, 206–7; HCME 145, 48b; Ibn Yūnus, *Tarīkh*, I. §1026; Ibn Mammātī, *Kitāb qawānīn al-dawāwīn*, ch. 2 (pg. 82–3).
103. HP II.2:144/141v, my emphasis; cf. *Life of Afrahām*, pg. 400.
104. HCME 34b-35a, 116–17; cf. *Life of Afrahām*, pg. 398–9.
105. Cf. *Life of Afrahām*, pg. 40; Evelyn White, *Monasteries*, 2:346. A tradition maintains that after hearing a recitation of the Gospels and the Qur'ān, al-Mu'izz converted to Christianity and was baptized in the baptistery next to the Church of St. John (Butler, *Ancient Coptic Churches*, 1:126); cf. André Binggeli,

"Converting the Caliph: A Legendary Motif in Christian Hagiography and Historiography of the Early Islamic Period," in *Writing 'True Stories'*, ed. A. Papaconstantinou.

106. Clearly identified in the HCME: "the mountain moved: namely, that part of the Muqaṭṭam hills which is near the hill of al-Kabsh, between Cairo and Miṣr."
107. Also in the *Life of Afrahām*, pg. 397.
108. An oral tradition claims that the tanner, fearing being tempted by vainglory, was instructed by an angel to walk under the elevated mountain before it came down for a last time. The hem of his garment is said to protrude at the base of the mountain even today.

Chapter 12 Webs of Significance

1. Clifford Geertz, *The Interpretation of Cultures* (New York, 1973), 5: "Man is an animal suspended in webs of significance he himself has spun."
2. HCME 102a-b, 278–9. It adds: "on the night of the Feast of the Holy Nativity, every year, the Muslims, as well as the Christians, burn candles, and lamps, and logs of wood in great numbers."
3. This was normative among the Shafiʿī and Malikī schools, which dominated in Egypt. The Ḥanifī's demanded the same *diyya* regardless of the victim's religious affiliation, while the Ḥanbalī's only required a fourth.
4. Discussed in M. Cohen's *Crescent and Cross*.
5. I agree with A. Papaconstantinou ("Historiography") in that the adoption of the era documents a significant shift, though we date the prevalence of that designation in society and interpret the contours of that shift in very different ways.
6. Ibn Yūnus, *Tarīkh*, I. §949.
7. G.E. von Grunebaum, *Medieval Islam: A Study in Cultural Orientation*, 2nd ed. (Chicago, 1969), 184.

SELECT BIBLIOGRAPHY

Primary Sources

Papyri and Ostraca

Papyrological Checklists and Standard Abbreviations

Greek and Coptic: http://scriptorium.lib.duke.edu/papyrus/texts/clist.html
Arabic Ostraca and Papyri: www.ori.uzh.ch/isap/isapchecklist.html
Arabic Documentary Database: http://orientw.uzh.ch/apd/project.jsp

Chrest.Khoury.I: *Chrestomathie de papyrologie arabe*, R.G. Khoury. Leiden, 1993.

Chrest.Khoury.II: *Papyrologische Studien. Zum privaten und gesellschaftlichen Leben in den ersten islamischen Jahrhunderten*, R.G. Khoury. Wiesbaden, 1995.

CPR VIII: *Koptische Texte*, vol. 1; *Rechtsurkunden*, vol 2, W. Krall. Vienna, 1895.

CPR.XVI: *Arabische Briefe aus dem 7.—10. Jahrhundert*, ed. W. Diem. Vienna, 1993.

CPR.XXI: *Arabic Agricultural Leases and Tax Receipts from Egypt, 148–427 A.H./ 765–1035 A.D.*, ed. G. Frantz-Murphy. Vienna, 2001.

CPR.XXII: F. Morelli, ed./trans. *Documenti greci per la fiscalità e la amministrazione dell'Egitto arabo*, F. Morelli. Vienna, 2001.

CPR XXX: *L'Archivio di Senouthios* Anystes *e Testi Connessi*, ed. F. Morelli. Berlin, 2010.

O.Brit.Mus.Copt.I= *Coptic and Greek Texts of the Christian Period from Ostraka, Stelae, etc. in the British Museum*, ed. H.R. Hall. London 1905.

O.Crum.: *Coptic Ostraca from the Collections of the Egypt Exploration Fund, the Cairo Museum and Others*, ed. W.E. Crum (London, 1902).

O.Medin.HabuCopt.: *Coptic Ostraca from Medinet Habu*, ed. E. Stefanski and M. Lichtheim (Chicago, 1952).

P.Apoll.: *Papyrus grecs d'Apollônos Anô*, ed. R. Rémondon. Cairo, 1953.

P.Bal.: *Bala'izah: Coptic Texts from Deir el-Bala'izah in Upper Egypt*. 2 vols., P.E. Kahle. London, 1954.

P.Bawit Clackson: S.J. Clackson, *It is our Father who Writes: Orders from the Monastery of Apollo at Bawit*. Cincinnati, 2008.

P.Cair.Arab.: *Arabic Papyri in the Egyptian Library*, A. Grohmann. 6 vols. Cairo, 1934–1961.

P.Cair.Masp.: *Papyrus grecs d'époque byzantine, Catalogue général des antiquités égyptiennes du Musée du Caire*, ed. Jean Maspero. 3 vols. Cairo, 1911–1916.

P.Clackson.: *Monastic Estates in Late Antique and Early Islamic Egypt: Ostraca, Papyri, and and Essays in Memory of Sarah Clackson (P.Clackson)*, eds. A. Boud'hors, J. Clackson, C. Louis, P. Sijpesteijn. Cincinnati, 2009.

P.CLT.: *Ten Coptic Legal Texts*, ed. A. Arthur Schiller. New York, 1932; 1973.

P.Fay.Monast.: *The Monasteries of the Fayyum*, ed. N. Abbott. Chicago 1937.

P.Giss.Arab.: *Die arabischen Papyri aus der Giessener Universitätsbibliothek,* ed. A. Grohmann. Giessen, 1960.

P.Heid.Arab.I: *Papyri Schott–Reinhardt I*, ed. C.H. Becker, Heidelberg, 1906.

P.Kell.: *Papyri from Kellis*, eds. I. Gardner *et al.,* Oxford.
 II. *Kellis Literary Texts*, 1996.
 V. *Coptic Documentary Texts from Kellis* I, 1999.

P.Khalili.I.: *Selected Arabic Papyri*, ed. Geoffrey Khan. Oxford, 1992.

P.Khalili.II.: *Bills, Letters, and Deeds: Arabic Papyri of the 7th to 11th Centuries*, ed. Geoffrey Khan. New York, 1993.

P.KRU.: *Koptische Rechtsurkunden des achten Jahrhunderts aus Djême (Theben)*, ed. W.E. Crum and George Steindorff. Leipzigs, 1912; 1973; W.C. Till, *Die koptischen Rechtsurkunden aus Theben*. Vienna, 1964.

P.Lond.Copt.I.: *Catalogue of the Coptic Manuscripts in the British Museum*, ed. W.E. Crum. London, 1905.

P.Lond.Copt.II.: *Catalogue of Coptic literary manuscripts in the British Library acquired since 1906*, ed. B. Layton. London, 1987.

P.Lond.IV.: *Greek Papyri in the British Museum*, vol. IV, *The Aphrodito Papyri*, ed. H.I. Bell. With an Appendix of Coptic Papyri edited by W.E. Crum. London 1910; Milan 1973. Partial English trans. H.I. Bell. "Translations of the Greek Aphordito Papyri in the British Museum." *Der Islam* 2 (1911), 269–83, 372–84; 3 (1912), 132–40, 369–73; 4 (1913), 87–96; 17 (1928), 4–8.

P.Marchands.I – V.: *Marchands d'étoffes du Fayyoum au IIIe/IXe siècle d'après leurs archives (actes et lettres)*, ed. Yusuf Raghib. Cairo, 1982–1996.

P.Mon.Apollo.: *Coptic and Greek texts relating to the Hermopolite Monastery of Apa Apollo*, ed. S.J. Clackson. Oxford, 2000.

P.Mon.Epiph.: *The Monastery of Epiphanius at Thebes,* Part II, eds. W.E. Crum and H.G. Evelyn White. New York, 1926.

P.MorganLib.: *Catalogue of Coptic Manuscripts in the Pierpont Morgan Library*, ed L. Depuydt. Louvain, 1993.

P.Oxy.: *The Oxyrhynchus Papyri*.

P.Prag.Arab.: A. Grohmann. "Arabische Papyri aus der Sammlung Carl Wessely im Orientalishcen Institute zu Prag." *Archiv Orientální* 10 (1938), 149–62; 11 (1940), 242–89; 12 (1941), 1–112; 14 (1043), 161–260.

P.Rain.UnterrichtKopt.: *Neue Texte und Dokumentation zum Koptisch-Unterricht*, ed. Monika R.M. Hasitzka. Vienna, 1990.

P.Qurra.: *Ḳurrah Papyri from Aphrodito in the Oriental Institute*, ed. Nabia Abbott. Chicago, 1938.

P.Ryl.Copt.: *Catalogue of the Coptic Manuscripts in the Collection of the John Rylands Library*, ed. W.E. Crum. Manchester, 1909.

P.Sarga.: *Wadi Sarga, Coptic and Greek Texts*. Eds./trans. W.E. Crum and H.I. Bell. Copenhagen, 1922. (*Coptica* III).

P.Teshlot.: Tonio Sebastian Richter, "Spätkoptische Rechtsurkunden neu bearbeitet (II): Die Rechtsurkunden des Teschlot-Archive," JJP 30 (2000), 95–148; Michael Green, "A Private Archive of Coptic Letters and Documents from Teshlot," *Oudheidkundige Mededelingen der Rijksmuseum van Oudheiden* 64 (1983), 61–122.

P.World.: A. Grohmann, *From the World of Arabic Papyri*. Cairo, 1952.

SB Kopt.I.: *Koptisches Sammelbuch* I, ed. Monika R.M. Hasitzka. Vienna, 1993.

Literary Sources

Abū ʿUbayd al-Qāsim ibn Sallām. *Kitāb al-amwāl*. Beirut, 1981.

Abū Yūsuf, *Kitāb al-kharāj*. Beirut, 1979; cf. A. Ben Shemesh, trans. *Abū Yūsuf's Kitāb al-kharāj*. Leiden, 1969. Shemesh rearranged the text.

(Pseudo-) Agathon. *Book of Consecration*: René-Georges Coquin, ed. *Livre de la Consécration du Sanctuaire de Benjamin*. Cairo, 1975.

Agapios [Maḥbūb ibn Qusṭanṭīn], *Kitāb al-ʿunwān* [Part 2], ed./trans. Alexander Vasiliev, PO 7.4. Paris, 1911.

Anonymous, *Life of John the Almsgiver*: H. Delehaye ed. "une vie inédite de Saint Jean l'Aumonier." *Analecta Bollandiana* 45 (1927), 5–74; E. Dawes and N.H. Baynes. *Three Byzantine Saints*. Oxford, 1949; Crestwood, 1996. [Also see Leontios]

[Third] *Apocalypse of Athanasios*: Bernd Witte, *Die Sünden der Priester und Mönche: Koptische Eschatologie des 8. Jahrhunderts nach Kodex M 602 pp. 104–154 (ps. Athanasius) der Pierpont Morgan Library*. Altenberge, 2002; F.J. Martinez ed./ trans. "Eastern Christian Apocalyptic in the Early Muslim Period: Pseudo-Methodius and Pseudo-Athanasius." Ph.D. diss., Catholic University of America, 1985.

Apocalpyse of Samule (of Qalamūn): J. Ziadeh, "L'Apocalypse de Samuel, Supérieur de Deir-el-Qalamoun." ROC 20 (1915–17), 374–403.

Athanasios, *Life of Antony*: *Vie d'Antoine*, ed./trans. G.J.M. Bartelink. SC 400. Paris, 1994; Tim Vivian and Apostolos N. Athanassakis, *The Life of Antony: The Coptic Life and the Greek Life*. Kalamazoo, 2003.

(Pseudo-) Athanasios, *The Canons of Athanasius of Alexandria*, trans. Wilhelm Riedel and W.E. Crum. Oxford, 1904.

Athanasios of Qūṣ, *Qilādat at-taḥrīr fī ʿilm at-tafsīr: eine koptische Grammatik in arabischer Sprache aus dem 13./14. Jh.*, ed./trans. Gertrud Bauer. Tübingen, 1972.

Balādhurī. *Futūḥ al-buldān*, ed. M.J. de Goeje. Leiden, 1866; P.K. Hitti and F.C. Murgotten, *The Origins of the Islamic State*. New York, 1916–1924; 1969.

Benjamin (Patriarch), *On Cana of Galilee*: C. Detlef G. Müller, ed./trans. *Die Homilie über die Hochzeit zu Kana und weitere Schriften des Patriarchen Benjamin I von Alexandrien*. Heidelberg, 1968; Maged S.A. Mikhail, "*On Cana of Galilee*: A Sermon by Patriarch Benjamin I." *Coptic Church Review* 23.3 (2002), 66–93.

Benjamin (Patriarch), *Sixteenth Festal Letter*: C. Detlef G. Müller, ed./trans., *Die Homilie über die Hochzeit zu Kana*, pgs. 302–350. Heidelberg, 1968.

Bīrūnī, *al-Āthār al-bāqiya ('an al-qurūn al-khāliya), Chronologie orientalischer Völker von Albērūnī*, ed. C. Edward Sachau. Leipzig, 1878; 1923; Baghdad; 1963; idem, trans. *The Chronology of Ancient Nations*. London, 1879; Frankfurt, 1969.

Book of the Chrism: A. van Lantschoot. "Le ms. Vatican copte 44 et le Livre du Chrême (ms. Paris arabe 100)." *Muséon* 45 (1932), 181–234.

Būlus al-Būshī, *Commentary on the Apocalypse*: Shawqi Najib Talia. "Būlus al-Būšī's Arabic Commentary on the Apocalypse of St. John: An English Translation and Commentary." Ph.D. diss., Catholic University of America, 1987.

Bukhārī. *Ṣaḥīḥ*, ed. Muhammad Muhsin Khan. 9 vols. Lahore, 1979.

Christodoulos [Khrisṭūdulūs], *Canons*: O.H.E. Burmester, "The Canons of Christodulos, Patriarch of Alexandria (AD. 1047–1077)." *Muséon* 45 (1932), 1–14.

Chronicle of 640: "A Chronicle Composed AD 640." In *The Seventh Century in West-Syrian Chronicles*, ed./trans. A. Palmer, 13–23. Liverpool, 1993.

Chronicle of 819: J.B. Chabot, ed. *Anonymi auctoris chronicon ad annum Christi 1234 pertinens*, 1 (CSCO 81). Paris, 1920; 3–22; In *The Seventh Century in West-Syrian Chronicles*, ed./trans. A. Palmer, 13–23. Liverpool, 1993.

Chronicle of 1234: J.B. Chabot, ed. *Chronicon ad annum Christi 1234 pertinens*, 2 vols, CSCO 81–82, *scr. syri* 36–37. Paris, 1916–20; Latin translation of the first volume by Chabot, CSCO 109, *scr. syri* 56, (Paris, 1937); French translation of the second volume by A. Abouna, CSCO 354. Louvain, 1974; English translation of a reconstructed *Secular History* based on the text of the *Chronicle of 1234* in *The Seventh Century in West-Syrian Chronicles*, ed. Andrew Palmer. Liverpool, 1993.

Chronicle of Sīrt: Addaï Scher, *Histoire Nestorienne (Chronique de Séert) Seconde Parte I*, PO 7.2. Paris, 1950; *Parte II*, PO 13.4. Paris, 1950.

Chronicon Paschale, ed. L. Dindorf, 2 vols. Bonn, 1832; Michael and Mary Whitby, trans. Liverpool, 1989.

Chronicle of Zuqnīn (Parts III and IV), trans. A. Harrak. Toronto, 1999; J.-B. Chabot, *Incerti auctoris chronicon anonymum pseudo-Dionysianum vulgo dictum* II. CSCO 104. Paris 1933.

Cyril of Scythopolis, *Lives of the Monks of Palestine*: E. Schwartz ed., *Kyrillos von Skythopolis*. Leipzig, 1939; R.M. Price. *Cyril of Scythopolis: Lives of the Monks of Palestine*. Intro. and notes by J. Binns. Kalamazoo, 1991.

Cyril II [Kyrillus], *Canons*: O.H.E. Burmester. "The Canons of Cyril II, LXVII Patriarch of Alexandria," *Muséon* 49 (1936), 245–88,

Cyril III [Kyrillus], *Canons*: O.H.E. KHS-Burmester. "The Canons of Cyril III Ibn Laklak, 75th Patriarch of Alexandria A.D. 1235–1250." BSAC 12 (1946–47), 31–136; 14 (1958), 113–50.

Decrees of the Ecumenical Councils, ed. N.P. Tanner. 2 vols. Washington D.C., 1990.

Eusebios, *Ecclesiastical History*: Gustave Brady ed./trans. *Historia Ecclesiastica*. SC 31, 41, 55, 73. Paris, 1952–60; Roy J. Deferrari, trans. *Eusebius Pamphili: Ecclesiastical History*. 2 vols. New York, 1953–55.

Eusebios, *Praise of Constantine*: Ivar A. Heikel, ed. *Oratio de laudibus Constantini*, in *Eusebius' Werke I*, pgs. 195–223. GCS 7. Leipzig, 1902; H.A. Drake, trans. *In Praise of Constantine: A Historical Study and New Translation of Eusebius's Tricennial Orations*. Berkeley, 1979.

Eusebios, *Life of Constantine*: F. Winkelmann, ed. *Über das Leben des Kaisers Konstantins*. GCS Eusebius 1/1. Berlin, 1975: rev. 1992; Averil Cameron and Stuart G. Hall, trans. *Eusebius: Live of Constantine*. Oxford, 1999.

Eutychios, *Naẓm al-jawhar* [*Annals* or *Ta'rīkh*] (Antiochene recension): Eutychius/ Sa'īd ibn Baṭrīq, *Eutychii Patriarchae Alexandrini annales (Tārīkh)*, ed. L. Cheikho, B.C. de Vaux, and H. Zayat. CSCO 50 [=I], 51 [= II]. Beirut, 1906, 1909.

Eutychios, *Naẓm al-jawhar* (Alexandrian recension): *Das Annalenwerk des Eutychios von Alexandrien*, ed./trans. M. Breydy, CSCO 471, 472. Louvain, 1985.

Egeria, *Diary*: Egérie, *Journal de voyage*, ed./trans. Pierre Maraval. SC 296. Paris, 1997; George E. Gingras, trans. *Egeria: Diary of a Pilgrimage*. New York, 1970.

Futūḥ al-Bahnasā: (Pseudo-) al-Wāqidī, *Futūh al-sham wa miṣr wa al-bahnasa*, 3rd ed. Cairo, 1925; E. Galtier, trans. *Foutouh al-Bahnasa*. Cairo, 1909.

Gabriel Ibn Turayk, *Nomocanon*; Patriarch Gabriel II Ibn Turayk. *Le Nomocanon du patriarche copte Gabriel II Ibn Turayk (1131–1145)*, ed. Antonios Aziz Mina. 2 vols. Beirute, 1993.

Historia Monachorum in Aegypto, ed. A.J. Festugière. Brussels, 1961; Norman Russell, trans. *The Lives of the Desert Fathers*. Kalamazoo, 1981.

History of Dionysios (of Tel-Maḥrē) see *Chronicle of 1234*.

History of the Patriarchs [HP]

I.1–4 = *History of the Patriarchs of the Coptic Church of Alexandria*, ed./trans. B. Evetts in PO I.2 [=1], I.4 [=2], V.1 [=3], X.5 [=4]. Paris, 1947–1959.

II.1–3 = *History of the Patriarchs of the Egyptian Church*, ed./trans. O.H.E. KHS-Burmester and Yassā 'Abd al-Masīḥ (A.S. Atiya participated in the third volume). Cairo, 1948–59.

III.1–3 = *History of the Patriarchs of the Egyptian Church*, ed./trans. O.H.E. KHS-Burmester and Antoine Khater. Cairo, 1968–1970.

IV.1–2 = *History of the Patriarchs of the Egyptian Church*, ed./trans. O.H.E. KHS-Burmester and Antoine Khater. Cairo, 1974.

Hisory of the Patriarchs (Primitive Recension): C.F. Seybold, ed. *Severus ibn al-Muqaffa': Alexandrinische Patriarchengeschichte von S. Marcus bis Michael I (61–767), nach der altesten 1266 geschriebenen Hamburger Hanschrift im arabischen Urtextherausgegeben*. Hamburg, 1912.

History of the Churchs and Monasteries of Egypt [HCME]: B.T.A. Evetts (and A.J. Butler). *Abū Sālih: The Churches and Monasteries of Egypt*. Oxford, 1895; 1969; New Jersey, 2002; Abū Sāliḥ/Abū al-Makārim. *Tārīkh al-kanā'is wa al-adyurah*, ed. Samu'īl al-Suryānī. Egypt 1984.

Ibn 'Abd al-Ḥakam, *Kitāb futūḥ miṣr wa akhbāruhā* [*The History of the Conquest of Egypt, North Africa and Spain*], ed. Charles C. Torry. New Haven, 1922; New Jersey, 2002.

Ibn al-'Assāl, *al-Majmū' al-ṣafawī*, ed. Jirjis Filūthā'ūs 'Awaḍ. 2 vols. Cairo, n.d.; cf. Abba Paulos Tzadua, trans., P.L. Strauss, ed. *Fetha Nagast: The Law of the Kings*. Addis Ababa, 1968.

Ibn Ḥawqal, *(Kitāb) Ṣūrat al-arḍ*: *Opus georgaphicum auctore Ibn Ḥauḳal...Liber imaginis terrae*, ed. J.H. Kramers. 3rd ed. BGA II. Leiden, 1967; J.H. Kramers and G. Wiet, trans. *Configuration de la terre*. 2 vols. Beirut and Paris, 1964.

Ibn Jubayr, *Riḥla*: William Wright, ed., M.J. de Goeje, rev. *The Travels of ibn Jubayr*. Leiden, 1907; R.J.C. Broadhurst, trans. *The Travels of Ibn Jubayr*. London 1952.

Ibn Kabar (Abū al-Barakāt), *Muṣbāḥ al-ẓulmā fī īḍāḥ al-khidmā*, ed. Samu'īl al-Suryanī. 2 vols. Cairo, 1998.

Ibn al-Kindī, *Faḍā'il miṣr (al-maḥrūsa)*: J. Østrup. "Umar ibn Muhammed al-Kindis Beskrivelse af Ægypten." *Oversigt over det Kongelige Danske Videnskabernes Selskab Forhandlinger* 4 (1896), 173–245.

Makīn [the Younger]: Jirjis ibn al-ʿAmīd al-Makīn, *al-Mawsuʿā al-lahutiyyā al-shahīra bī al-ḥāwī,* ed. A Monk from the Monastery of al-Muḥarraq, 4 vols. Egypt, 1999–2001. Printed text is erroneously attributed to Ibn al-Makīn "the Elder" (d. 1273: GCAL II § 113). It is also known as, *Mukhtaṣar al-bayān fī taḥqīq al-īmān* (late 14th c.: GCAL II § 139.3)

Ibn Mammātī, *Kitāb qawānīn al-dawāwīn*, ed, A.S. Atiya. Cairo, 1943; R.S. Cooper, "Ibn Mammātī's Rules for the Ministries: Translation with Commentary of the Qawānīn al-dawāwīn." Ph.D. diss., University of California, Berkeley, 1973.

(Pseudo-) Ibn al-Rahib, *Chronicon Orientale*: L. Cheikho ed. *Petrus Ibn Rahib: Chronicon Orientale.* CSCO 45, 46. Beirut, 1903; Louvain, 1955.

Ibn Sabbāʿ, *al-Jawharah al-nafīsah*: Yuḥannā ibn Abī Zakariyya ibn Sabbāʿ. *al-Jawharah al-nafīsah fī 'ulūm al-kanīsah/Pretiosa Margarita de scientiis ecclesiasticis*, ed. Vincentio P. Mistriḥ. Cairo, 1966.

Ibn Taymiyya, *Mas'alat al-kanā'is*: In *Majmūʿat fatāwā shaykh al-Islam Aḥmad ibn Taymiyya*, vol. 28:632–46. Riyāḍ, 1966; Benjamin O'Keeffe trans. "Aḥmad ibn Taymiyya, Mas'alat al-kanā'is (the Question of the Churches)." *Islamochristiana* 22 (1996), 53–78.

Ibn Yūnus al-Miṣrī, *Tarīkh*, 2 vols. Beirut, 2000.

Ibn Zulāq, *Faḍā'il miṣr (wa akhbāruhā wa khawaṣuhā)*, ed. Ali M. Umar. Cairo, 1999.

Iʿtirāf al-abā': A monk from Dayr al-Muḥarraq, ed. *I'tirāfāt* [sic] *al-abā'*. Cairo, 2002.

Jacob of Serug, *Discourse on the Fall of Idols*: P. Martin. "Discourse de Jacques de Saroug sur la chute des idoles." ZDMG 29 (1876), 107–147.

(Pseudo-) John III, *Questions of Theodore*: A. van Lantschoot, ed./trans. *Les Questions de Théodore*. Vatican, 1957.

(Pseudo-) John III, *Disputation of Patriarch John*: Evelyn White, *Monasteries of the Wadi 'n Natrun*, I:171–75; MS Paris Ar.250 (on microfiche).

John of Ephesus, *Ecclesiastical History*: *Iohannis ephiesini historiae ecclesiasticae pars tertia*, ed. E.W. Brooks, CSCO 105. Paris, 1935; R. Payne Smith, trans. *The Third Part of the Ecclesiastical History of John Bishop of Ephesus*. Oxford, 1860.

John Malalas, *Chronicle*: L.A. Dindorf, ed. *Ioannis Malalae Chronographia*. Bonn, 1831 [=PG 97:9–718]; Elizabeth Jeffreys, Michael Jeffreys and Roger Scott, trans. *The Chronicle of John Malalas*. Melbourne, 1986.

John of Nikiou, *Chronicle*: Ethiopic with Fr. trans. in *Chronique de Jean évêque de Nikiou*, ed./trans. H. Zotenberg. Paris, 1883; Eng. trans. *The Chronicle of John (c. 690 AD) Coptic Bishop of Nikiu*. R.H. Charles trans. London, 1916; Amsterdam, 1981.

John of Shmūn, *Encomium on St. Antony*: G. Garitte, "Panégyrique de saint Antoine par Jean, évêque d'Hermopolis." OCP 9.3 (1943), 100–134, 330–65; Tim Vivian. "An Encomium on Saint Antony." in *The Life of Antony: The Coptic Life and the Greek Life*, trans. T. Vivian and Apostolos N. Athanassakis. Kalamazoo, 2003.

John of Shmūn, *Encomium on St. Mark*: Tito Orladi. *Studi Copti. 1. Un encomio de Marco Evangelista. 2. Le fonti copte della Storia dei Patriarchi de Alessandria. 3. La leggenda di S. Mercurio.* Milan, 1968.

Khalīfa ibn Khayyāṭ, *Ta'rīkh*: Suhayl Zakkār ed. *Ta'rikh Khalīfa ibn Khayyāṭ*. 2 vols. Damascus, 1967.

Kindī, Muḥammad ibn Yūsuf, al-. *Kitāb al-wulāt wa kitāb al-quḍat* [*The Governors and Judges of Egypt*], ed. Rhuvon Guest. Leiden, 1912.

Leontios, *Life of John the Almsgiver*: A.J. Festugière, ed. *Vie de Jean de Chypre, dit L'Aumonier*. Paris, 1974; E. Dawes and N.H. Baynes. *Three Byzantine Saints*. Oxford, 1949; Crestwood, 1996.

Letter of Alexander II: C. Schmidt and W. Schubart. *Altchristliche Texte*, ch. 5. Berlin, 1910; L.S.B. MacCoull. "The Paschal Letter of Alexander II, Patriarch of Alexandria; a Greek Defense of Coptic Theology under Arab Rule." DOP 44 (1990), 27–40; eodem. *Coptic Perspectives on Late Antiquity*. Brookfield, 1993.

Letter of Pisentios: Augustin Périer, ed./tr., "Lettre de Pisuntios, eveque de Qeft, a ses fideles." ROC 19 (1914), 80–87, 88–92, 302–16, 316–36, 445–46

Life of Afraham the Syrian (62 Patriarch of Alexandria): L. Leroy, ed. "Histoire d'Abraham le Syrien, patriarche copte d'Alexandrie." ROC 14 (1909), 380–400; 15 (1910), 26–41, 218–20.

Life of Daniel of Scetis: M. Ignazio Guidi. "Vie et récits de l'Abbé Daniel, de Scété (vi siècle)." ROC 5 (1900), 535–64; Tim Vivian, *Witness to Holiness: Abba Daniel of Scetis*. Kalamazoo, 2008.

Life of Isaac of Alexandria (by Mina of Nikiou): E. Porcher ed./trans. *Vie d'Isaac, Patriarche d'Alexandrie de 686 à 689*. PO 9.3. Paris 1914; 1974; David N. Bell. *The Life of Isaac of Alexnadria and The Martyrdom of Saint Macrobius*. Kalamazoo, 1988.

Life of John Khame, ed./trans. M.H. Davis. PO 14.2. Paris, 1920.

Life of John the Little: Maged S.A. Mikhail and Tim Vivian, *The Holy Workshop of Virtue: The Life of John the Little by Zacharias of Sakhā*. Collegeville, 2010.

Life of Samuel of Qalamun (by Isaac the presbyter): A. Alcock, *Life of Samuel of Kalamun*. England, 1983.

Life of Shenoute: J. Leipoldt and W.E. Crum. *Sinuthii Archimandritae Vita et Opera Omnia*. CSCO 41. Louvain, 1951; David N. Bell. *The Life of Shenoute by Besa*. Kalamazoo, 1983.

Lactantius, *Death of the Persecutors*: Lactantius. *On the Death of the Persecutors*. ed. and trans. J.L. Creed. Oxford, 1984.

Mas'ūdī, *Murūj al-dhahab* (*wa ma'ādin al-jawhar*): C. Barbier de Meynard and Pavet de Courteille, ed./trans. *Les prairies d'or*, 9 vols. Paris, 1861-77; A. Sprenger, trans. *El-Mas'udi's Historical Encyclopaedia Entitled: Meadows of Gold and Mines of Gems*. London, 1841 [books 1–17]; P. Lunde and C. Stone, trans. *The Meadows of Gold: The Abbasids*. London, 1989. [Books 108–132].

Martyrdom of John of Phanijōit: Jason R. Zaborowski, ed./trans. *The Coptic Martyrdom of John of Phanijōit: Assimilation and Conversion to Islam in Thirteenth-Century Egypt*. Leiden, 2005.

Maqrīzī, *al-Bayān wa-l-i'rāb 'ammā bi arḍ misṛ min al-a'rāb*, ed. 'Abd al-Majīd 'Ābdīn. Cairo, 1961.

Maqrīzī, *Dhikr qibṭ miṣr*: See last volume of al-Maqrīzī's *Khiṭaṭ*; partial English translation in S.C. Malan. *A Short History of the Copts and their Church*. London, 1873.

Maqrīzī, *Khiṭaṭ*: al-Maqrīzī. *Al-Mawā'iẓ wal-I'tibār fī Ḏikr al-Ḫiṭaṭ wal-Aṯār*. 4 vols., ed. Ayman Fu'ād Sayyid. London, 2002–04.

Michael the Syrian, *Chronicle*: Jean-Baptiste Chabot ed./trans. *Chronique de Michel le Syrien*. 4 vols. Paris, 1899–1924.

Moses of Abydos, *Dossier*: Mark Moussa. "Abba Moses of Abydos." M.A. thesis, Catholic University of America, 1998; idem. "The Coptic Literary Dossier of Abba Moses of Abydos." *Coptic Church Review* 24.3 (2003), 66–90.

Mōshē bar Kēphā, *Commentary on the Liturgy*: Richard H. Connolly, ed./trans. *Two Commentaries on the Jacobite Liturgy*. Oxford, 1913; New Jersey, 2002.

Nāṣir-i Khusraw, *Safarnāma: Book of Travels*, ed./trans. W.M. Thackston. Costa Mesa, 2001.

Nikephoros, *Short History*: Cyril Mango, ed./trans. *Nikephoros Patriarch of Constantinople Short History*. Washington D.C., 1990.

Ordination Rites of the Coptic Church: Coptic Text, Translation and Annotation, ed. O.H.E. Burmester. Cairo, 1985.

Panegyric on Apollo: K.H. Kuhn ed./trans. *A Panegyric on Apollo Archimandrite of the Monastery of Isaac by Stephen Bishop of Heracleopolis Magna*. CSCO 394, 395. Louvain, 1978.

Panegyric on St. John the Baptist: K.H. Kuhn, ed./trans. *A Panegyric on John the Baptist Attributed to Theodosius Archbishop of Alexandria*. CSCO 268, 269. Louvain, 1966.

Panegyric on Macarius of Tkōw: David W. Johnson. *A Panegyric on Macarius Bishop of Tkōw Attributed to Dioscorus of Alexandria*. CSCO 415/416. Louvain, 1980.

Paphnutios, *Histories of the Monks* (of Upper Egypt): E.A. Wallis Budge. *Miscellaneous Coptic Texts*. Vol. 5.1, pg. 432–495. London, 1915; New York, 1977; Tim Vivian, trans. *Paphnutius: Histories of the Monks of Upper Egypt and the Life of Onnophrius*. 2nd ed. Kalamazoo, 2000.

Pisentios, *Discourse on Saint Onnophrios*: W.E. Crum. "Discours de Pisentius sur Saint Onnophrius'." ROC ser. 2, 10.2 (1915–17), 38–67; Tim Vivian trans. *Paphnutius: Histories of the Monks of Upper Egypt and the Life of Onnophrius*. 2nd ed. Kalamazoo, 2000.

Rufus of Shotep. *Homilies on the Gospels of Matthew and Luke*, ed. Sheridan, J. Mark. Rome, 1998.

Sawīrus ibn al-Muqaffa', *(Kitāb) miṣbāḥ al-'aql* [*The Lamp of Understanding*], ed. Samir Khalil Samir. Cairo 1978; R.Y. Ebied and M.J.L. Young, eds. and trans. *The Lamp of the Intellect of Severus ibn al-Muqaffa', Bishop of al-Ashmūnain*. CSCO 356/357. Louvain, 1975.

Sawīrus ibn al-Muqaffa', *Refutation*: P. Chébli, ed. *Réfutation de Sa'îd ibn-Batriq (Eutychius): (Le Livre des conciles)*. PO 3.2. Paris, 1909.

(Pseudo-) Sawīrus ibn al-Muqaffa', *Kitāb al-Īḍāḥ*= Ps.-Sawīrus, *Kitāb al-dūrr al-thamīn.*

(Pseudo-) Sawīrus ibn al-Muqaffa', *Kitāb al-dūrr al-thamīn fī īḍāḥ al-dīn*, ed. M. Jirjis. Cairo 1925; 1971; 1992.

(Pseudo-) Sawīrus ibn al-Muqaffa', *Tartīb al-kahanūt*: *Ein altes liturgisches Handbuch der koptischen Kirche*, ed. Julius Assfalg. Cairo, 1955.

Scrolls of Bishop Timotheos, ed. J. Martin Plumley. London, 1975.

Sebeos, *History*: *Patmut'iwn Sebēosi*, ed. G.V. Abgaryan. Erevan, 1979; *The Armenian History Attributed to Sebeos*, 2 vols. trans. R.W. Thomson, commentary by J. Howard-Johnston. Liverpool, 1999.

Sokrates, *Ecclessiastical History:* Sokrates, *Kirchengeschichte*, ed. Günther Christian Hansen with contributions by Manja Širinjan. GCS vol. 1. Berlin, 1995; A.C. Zenos in *Nicen and Post-Nicen Christian Fathers*, ed. P. Schaff and H. Wace, ser. 2 vol.2. New York, 1890.

Sozomen, *Ecclesiastical History*: Sozomène. *Histoire ecclésiastique*, trans. André-Jean Festugière, annotation by Guy Sabbah. SC 306, 418. Paris, 1983; 1996; Chester D. Hartranft in *Nicene and Post-Nicene Christian Fathers*, ed. P. Schaff and H. Wace, ser. 2 vol.2. New York, 1890.

Synaxarion: Iacobus Forget, ed./trans., *Synaxarium*. CSCO vols. 47–48, 67, 78, 90. Louvain, 1905–1926.

Ṭabarī, *Ta'rīkh al-rusul wa al-mulūk*. 15 vols., ed. M.J. de Goeje. Leiden, 1879–1901.

Theophanes, *Chronicle*: *Theophanis Chronographia*, ed/trans. C. de Boor, 2 vols. Leipzig, 1883; C. Mango and R. Scott trans. *The Chronicle of Theophanes Confessor*. Oxford, 1999.

Timothy Ailuros, *Letters*: R.Y. Ebied and L.R. Wichham, "A Collection of Unpublished Syriac Letters of Timothy Aelurus." *Journal of Theological Studies* n.s. 21 (1970), 321–369; idem. "Timothy Aelurus: Against the Definition of the Council of Chalcedon." In *After Chalcedon: Studies in Theology and Church History offered to Professor Albert van Roey for his Seventieth Birthday*, ed. G. Laga, J.A. Munitiz and L. van Rompay, 115–166. Louvain, 1985.

Theodosios, *Homily on the Virgin*: W.H. Worrell. "A Homily on the Virgin by Theodosius Archbishop of Alexandria." In *The Coptic Manuscripts in the Freer Collection*, ed. idem. London, 1923; New York, 1972.

Theodosios, *A Panegyric on John the Baptist Attributed to Theodosius Archbishop of Alexandria*, ed./trans. K.H. Kuhn. CSCO 268, 269. Louvain, 1966.

(Pseudo-) Theophilos, *Sermon on the Three Youth*: H. de Vis, ed./trans. "Thèophile, archevêque d'Alexandrie: Sermon sur les Trois Enfants de Babylone." In *Homélies coptes de la Vaticane*, 2 vols. Louvain, 1990.

"*Testament of Apa Abraham*, Bishop of Hermonthis, for the Monastery of St. Phoibammon near Thebes, Egypt," trans. L.S.B. MacCoull. In *Byzantine Monastiac Foundation Documents*, eds. J.P. Thomas, A. Constantinides Hero, G. Constable. Washington DC, 2000.

Triadon: Oscar von Lemm, *Das Triadon*. St. Petersburg, 1903; Peter Nagel. *Das Triadon*. Halle, 1983; Leslie S.B. MacCoull. "The *Triadon*: An English Translation." *Greek Orthodox Theological Review* 42 (1997), 83–148.

Ya'qūbī, *Ta'rīkh Aḥmad ibn Abī Ya'qūb* [*Ibn Wadhih qui dicitur al-Ja'qubi Historiae*], ed. M.Th. Houtsma. 2 vols. Leiden, 1883; 1969.

Yaḥyā ibn Ādam. *Kitāb al-kharāj*, ed. Aḥmad Muḥammad Shākir. Beirut, 1979.

(Pseudo-) Yusāb of Fuwwā, *Tarīkh al-abā' al-batārikā li al-anbā Yusāb usquf Fuwwā*, eds. Ṣamū'īl al-Suryānī and Nabih Kamil. Cairo, 1987.

(Pseudo-) Zachariah Rhetor. *Chronicle*: *Historia ecclesiastica Zachariae rhetoric vulgo adscripta*, ed. E.W. Brooks, CSCO 83, 84. Paris 1919–21; *The Syriac Chronicle Known as that of Zachariah of Mitylene*, trans. F.J. Hamilton and E.W. Brooks. London, 1899; New York, 1979.

Secondary Sources

Abbott, Nabia. "A New Papyrus and a Review of the Administration of ʿUbaid Allah ibn al-Ḥabḥāb." In *Arabic and Islamic Studies in Honor of Hamilton A.R. Gibb*, ed. G. Makdisi, 21–35. Leiden, 1965.

——— "Arabic Marriage Contracts among Copts." ZDMG 95 (1941), 59–81.

Adams, William Y. *Nubia, Corridor to Africa*. Great Britain, 1977.

Alexander, Paul J. *Religious and Political History and Thought in the Byzantine Empire*. Brookfield, 1978.

Anawati, Georges C. "Factors and Effects of Arabization and Islamization in Medieval Egypt and Syria." In *Islam and Cultural Change in the Middle Ages*, ed. Speros Vryonis Jr. Wiesbaden, 1975.

Assaad, Sadik A. *The Reign of al-Hākim bi-Amr Allāh. A Political Study*. Beirut, 1974.

Atiya, Aziz S. *A History of Eastern Christianity*. London, 1968; 1980.

———, ed. *The Coptic Encyclopedia*. 8 vols. New York, 1991.

ʿAthamina, Khalil. "Arab Settlement during the Umayyad Caliphate." JSAI 8 (1986), 185–207.

———. "*Aʿrāb* and *Muhājirūn* in the Environment of *Amṣār*." *Studia Islamica* 66 (1987), 5–25.

———. "Some Administrative, Military and Socio-Political Aspects of Early Muslim Egypt." In *War and Society in the Eastern Mediterranean, 7th Centuries*, ed. Yaacov Lev, 101–113. Leiden, 1997.

Ayoub, Mahmoud. "Religious freedom and the Law of Apostasy in Islam." *Islamochristiana* 20 (1994), 75–91.

Bacharach, Jere L. "African Military Slaves in the Medieval Middle East: The Cases of Iraq (869–955) and Egypt (868–1171)." IJMES 13 (1981), 471–495.

———, ed. *Fustat Finds: Beads, Coins, Medical Instruments, Textiles, and Other Artifacts from the Awad Collection*. Cairo, 2001.

Bagnall, Roger S. "Religious Conversion and Onomastic Change in Early Byzantine Egypt." *Bulletin of the American Society of Papyrologists* 19 (1982), 105–124.

———. *Egypt in Late Antiquity*. Princeton, 1993.

———, ed. *Egypt in the Byzantine World, 300–700*. Cambridge, 2007.

———, ed. *The Oxford Handbook of Papyrology*. Oxford, 2009.

———. and Klaas A. Worp. *Chronological Systems of Byzantine Egypt*. 2nd ed. Leiden, 2004.

Balog, P. *Umayyad, ʿAbbasid, and Tûlûnid Glass Weights and Vessel Stamps*. New York, 1976.

Banaji, Jairus. *Agrarian Change in Late Antiquity: Gold, Labour, and Aristocratic Dominance*. Oxford, 2001.

Barnes, Timothy D. "Late Antiquity and Early Islam: A Review Essay." *al-Masāq* 9 (1996–97), 191–99.

Barrī, ʿAbdallāh Khurshid. *al-Qabāʾil al-ʿarabiyyā fi miṣr fi al-qurūn al-thalathā al-ulā lil-hijrā*. Cairo, 1967; repr. and enlarged, 1992.

Bashear, Suliman. *Arabs and Others in Early Islam*, SLAEI 8. Princeton, 1997.

Bates, Michael L. "History, Geography, and Numismatics in the First century of Islamic Coinage." *Revue Suisse de Numismatique* 65 (1986), 231–62.

———. "The 'Arab-Byzantine' Bronze Coinage of Syria: An Innovation by ʿAbd al-Malik." In *A Colloquium in Memory of G.C. Miles*. New York, 1976.

———. *Islamic Coins*. New York, 1982.
Becker, Carl H. "Arabische Papyri des Aphroditofundes." *Zeitschrift für Assyriologie und Verwandte Gebiete* 20 (1907), 68–104.
———. "Historische Studien über das Londoner Aphroditowerk." *Der Islam* 2 (1911), 359–71.
———. "Neue arabische Papyri des Aphroditofundes." *Der Islam* 2 (1911), 245–68.
Behnstedt, Peter. "Weitere koptische Lehnwörter I Ägyptisch-Arabischen." *Die Welt des Orients* 12 (1981), 81–98.
Beihammer, Alexander D. *Quellenkritische Untersuchungen zu den ägyptischen Kapitulationsverträgen der Jahre 640–646*. Vienna, 2000.
Bell, H.I. "Two official Letters of the Arab Period." *Journal of Egyptian Archaeology* 12 (1926), 265–81.
———. "The Administration of Egypt under the Umayyad Khalifs." *Byzantinisch Zeitschrift* 28 (1928), 278–86.
Berg, Herbert. *Method and Theory in the Study of Islamic Origins*. Leiden, 2003.
Beshir, Beshir Ibrahim. "New light on Nubian-Fāṭimid relations." *Arabica* 22 (1975), 15–24.
Bishai, Wilson. "Coptic Lexical Influence on Egyptian Arabic." JNES 23 (1964), 39–47.
Blau, Joshua. "Some Observations on a Middle Arabic Egyptian Text in Coptic Characters." In *Studies in Middle Arabic and Its Judaeo-Arabic Variety*. Jerusalem, 1988.
Breydy, Michel. *Études sur Saʿīd ibn Baṭrīq et ses sources*. CSCO 450. Louvain, 1983.
Brock, Sebastian P. "Christians in the Sasanian Empire: A Case of Divided Loyalties." In *Religion and National Identity*, ed. Stuart Mews. Oxford, 1982.
———. "The 'Nestorian Church: A Lamentable Misnomer." *The Bulletin of the John Rylands Library Manchester* 78.3 (1996), 23–35.
Brooks, E.W. "The Patriarch Paul of Antioch and the Alexandrian Schism of 575." *Byzantinishe Zeitschrift* 30 (1929–30), 468–76.
Brown, Peter. *The World of Late Antiquity, AD 150–750*. New York, 1971; 1989.
Bulliet, Richard W. *Conversion to Islam in the Medieval Period*. Cambridge, 1979.
Burmester, Oswald H.E. "The Greek Kirugmata, Versicles and Responses, and Hymns in the Coptic Liturgy." OCP 2 (1936), 363–94.
Butler, Afred J. *The Arab Conquest of Egypt and the Last Thirty Years of the Roman Dominion*. 2nd ed. P.M. Fraser. Oxford, 1978; 1998.
———. *The Ancient Coptic Churches of Egypt*. 2 vols. Oxford, 1884; 1970.
Calder, Norman. *Studies in Early Muslim Jurisprudence*. Oxford, 1993.
Choksy, Jamsheed K. *Conflict and Cooperation: Zoroastrian Subalterns and Muslim Elites in Medieval Iranian Society*. Columbia, 1997.
Clover, Frank and R. Stephen Humphreys. "Toward a Definition of Late Antiquity." In *Tradition and Innovation in Late Antiquity*, ed. F.M. Clover and R.S. Humphreys, 3–19. Madison, 1989.
Cohen, Mark R. *Jewish Self-Government in Medieval Egypt*. Princeton, 1980.
———. "At the Origins of the Distinctive Dress Regulation for Non-Muslims in Islam: the Zunnār, Discrimination or reinforcement of Community Identity?" In *The Byzantine and Early Islamic Near East II*, ed. L.I. Conrad. Princeton, 1994.
———. *Under Crescent and Cross: The Jews in the Middle Ages*. Princeton, 1994.

Cöln, F.J. "The Nomocanonical Literature of the Copto-Arabic Church of Alexandria." *The Ecclesiastical Review* 56 (1917), 113–41.

Connerton, Paul. *How Societies Remember.* Cambridge, 1989.

Conrad, L.I. "The Conquest of Arwād: A Source-Critical Study in the Historiography of the Early Medieval Near East." In *The Byzantine and early Islamic Near East I: Problems in the Literary Source Material*, eds. A. Cameron and L.I. Conrad, 317–401. Princeton, 1992.

Cook, Michael. *Commanding the Right and Forbidding Wrong in Islamic Thought.* Cambridge, 2000.

———. "Pharaonic History in Medieval Egypt." *Studia Islamica* 57 (1983), 67–103.

Creswell, K.A.C. *Early Muslim Architecture.* 2 vols., 2nd ed. with a contribution by Marguerite Gautier-van Berchem. Oxford, 1969.

Crone, Patricia. *Slaves on Horses. The Evolution of the Islamic Polity.* Cambridge, 1980.

———. "Were the Qays and Yemen of the Umayyad Period Political Parties?" *Der Islam* 71 (1994), 1–57.

Crone, Patricia and Michael Cook. *Hagarism: the Making of the Islamic World.* Cambridge, 1977.

Décobert, Christian. "Sur l'Arabisation et l'Islamisation de l'Égypte médiévale." In *Itinéraires d'Égypte Mélanges offerts au père Maurice Martin s.j.*, ed. idem. Cairo, 1992.

———. ed. *Alexandrie médiévale 2*. Cairo, 2002.

Den Heijer, Johannes. *Mawhub ibn Mansur ibn Mufarriğ et l'historiographie Copto-Arabe: Étude sur la composition de l'Histoire des Patriarches d'Alexandrie.* Louvain, 1989.

———. "The Influence of the *History of the Patriarchs of Alexandria* on the *History of the Churches and Monasteries of Egypt* by Abū l-Makārim (and Abū Ṣāliḥ?)." *Parole de l'Orient* 19 (1994), 415–439.

———. "Coptic Historiography in the Fātimid, Ayyūbid, and Early Mamlūk Periods." *Medieval Encounters* 2 (1996), 67–98.

———. "Apologetic Elements in Copto-Arabic Historiography: the Life of Afrahām ibn Zurʿah, 62nd Patriarch of Alexandria." In *Christian Arabic Apologetics during the Abbasid Period*, eds. Samir and Nielsen.

Dennett, Daniel C. *Conversion and the Poll Tax in Early Islam.* Cambridge, 1950.

Donner, Fred M. "The Formation of the Islamic State." JAOS 106 (1986), 283–96.

———. *Narratives of Islamic Origins: the Beginnings of Islamic Historical Writing.* Princeton, 1998.

———. "From Believers to Muslims: Confessional Self-Identity in the Early Islamic Community." *al-Abhath* 50–51 (2002–03), 9–53.

Dunn, Michael C. "The Struggle for ʿAbbāsid Egypt." Ph.D. diss., Georgetown University, 1975.

Duri, ʿAbd al-ʿAziz. *The Rise of Historical Writing among the Arabs*, trans. by Lawrence I. Conrad. Princeton, 1983.

Ebied, R.Y. "Peter of Antioch and Damian of Alexandria: The End of a Friendship." In *A Tribute to Arthur Vööbus*, ed. Robert H. Fischer, 277–282. Louvain, 1977.

Ebied, R.Y. and H. Teule, eds. *Studies on the Christian Arabic Heritage in Honour of Father Prof. Dr. Samir Khalil Samir S.J.* Louvain, 2004.

Erlich, Haggai and Israel Gershoni, eds. *The Nile: Histories, Cultures, Myths.* London, 2000.

Evelyn White, Hugh G. *The Monasteries of the Wâdi 'n Natrûn*, 3 vols., ed. by Walter Hauser. New York, 1926–1933; 1973.

Fahmy, Aly Mohamed. *Muslim Sea-Power in the Eastern Mediterranean: From the Seventh to the Tenth Century AD*. Cairo, 1966.

Fattal, Antoine. *Le statut légal des non-musulmans en pays d'Islam*, 2nd ed. Beirut, 1995; 1958.

Forand, P. "Early Muslim Relations with Nubia." *Der Islam* 48 (1972), 111–21.

Clive Foss, *Arab-Byzantine Coins: An Introduciton with A Catalogue of the Dumbarton Oaks Collection*. Washington D.C., 2008.

———. "Egypt under Muʿāwiya, Part I: Flavius Papas and Upper Egypt." BSOAS 72.1 (2009), 1–24; "Egypt under Muʿāwiya, Part II: Middle Egypt, Fusṭāṭ and Alexandria." BSOAS 72.2 (2009), 259–78.

Fowden, Garth. *Empire to Commonwealth: Consequences of Monotheism in Late Antiquity*. Princeton, 1993.

Frantz-Murphy, Gladys. "Settlement of Property Disputes in Provincial Egypt: The Reinstitution of Courts in the Early Islamic Period." *al-Masāq* 6 (1993), 95–105.

———. "Land Tenure in Egypt in the First Five Centuries of Islamic Rule (Seventh-Twelfth Centuries AD)." In *Agriculture in Egypt From Pharaonic to Modern Times*, eds. A. Bowman and E. Rogan. Oxford, 1999.

———. "The Economics of State Formation in Early Islamic Egypt." In *From al-Andalus to Khurasan: Documents from the Medieval Muslim World*, eds. P.M. Sijpesteijn, L. Sundelin, S.T. Tovar, A. Zomeño. Leiden, 2007.

———. "Nationalism as a Factor in Anti-Chalcedonian Feeling in Egypt." In *Religion and National Identity*, ed. S. Mews. Oxford, 1982.

Frend, W.H.C. *The Rise of the Monophysite Movement*. 2nd rev. ed. Cambridge, 1979.

Friedmann, Yohanan. *Tolerance and Coercion in Islam: Interfaith Relations in the Muslim Tradition*. Cambridge, 2003.

Gabra, Gawdat. "Untersuchungen Zum Difnar der Koptischen Kirche I: Quellenlage, Forschungsgeschichte und künftige Aufgaben." BSAC 35 (1996), 37–52; "Untersuchungen Zum Difnar der Koptischen Kirche II: zur Kompilation." BSAC 37 (1998), 49–68.

Gagos, Traianos and Peter van Minnen, eds., *Settling a Dispute; Toward a Legal Anthropology of Late Antique Egypt*. Ann Arbor, 1994.

Gascou, Jean. "Les Grands Domaines, la Cité et l'État en Égypte Byzantine." *Travaux et Mémoires* 9 (1985), 1–89.

Gascou, Jean and K.A. Worp. "Problèmes de documentation apollinopolite." ZPE 49 (1982), 83–95.

Gaubert, Christian and Jean-Michael Mouton. "Présentation des archives d'une famille copte du Fayoum à l'époque fatimide." In *Coptic Studies on the Threshold of a New Millennium*, eds. M. Immerzeel and J. van der Vliet, I:505–517. Louvain, 2004.

Gayraud, Roland-Pierre. Excavation Reports for Isṭabl ʿAntar (Fusṭāṭ) have appeared in Annales Islamologiques 22 (1986), 1–26; 23 (1987), 55–71; 25 (1991), 57–87; 27 (1993), 225–232; 28 (1994), 1–27; 29 (1995), 1–24; 42 (2008), 299–312.

———. "Fostat: évolution d'une capitale arabe du VIIe au XIIe siècle d'après les fouilles d'Istabl ʿAntar." *Colloque international d'Archéologie islamique* (Cairo, 1998), 435–460.

———. "La nécropole des Fatimides à Fostat." Dossiers de l'archéologie 233 (1998), 34–41.

Geary, Patrick J. *Phantoms of Remembrance: Memory and Oblivion at the End of the First Millennium*. Princeton, 1996.

Geertz, Clifford. *The Interpretation of Cultures*. New York, 1973.

Gervers, M. and R.J. Bikhazi, eds. *Conversion and continuity: indigenous Christian communities in Islamic lands, eighth to eighteenth centuries*. Toronto, 1990.

Goitein, S.D. *A Mediterranean Society: The Jewish Communities of the Arab World as Portrayed in the Documents of the Cairo Geniza*. 6 vols. Berkeley, 1967–1993.

Gonis, N. "Reconsidering Some Fiscal Documents from Early Islamic Egypt." ZPE 137 (2001), 225–28.

———. "Five Tax Receipts from Early Islamic Egypt." ZPE 143 (2003), 149–57.

Gonis, N. and K.A. Worp. "P.Bodl. I 77: The King of Kings in Arsinoe under Arab Rule." ZPE 141 (2002), 173–76.

Gottheil, Richard J.H. "Dhimmis and Moslems in Egypt." In *Old Testament and Semitic Studies in Memory of William Rainey Harper*, eds. R.F. Harper, F. Brown, and G.F. Moore, II: 353–414. Chicago, 1908.

———. "An Answer to the Dhimmis." JAOS 41 (1921), 383–457.

Grabar, Oleg. *The Formation of Islamic Art*. 2nd rev. ed. New Haven, 1987.

Graf, Georg. *Geschichte der christlichen arabischen Literature*. 5 vols. Vatican, 1944–1953.

Gray, Patrick T.R. *The Defense of Chalcedon in the East (451–553)*. Leiden, 1979.

———. "Neo-Chalcedonianism and the Tradition: From Patristic to Byzantine Theology." *Byzantinische Forschungen* 8 (1982), 61–70.

Green, A.H. "A Late 19th-Century Coptic Marriage Contract and the Coptic Documentary Tradition." *Muséon* 106 (1993), 361–71.

Grierson, P. "The Monetary Reforms of ʿAbd al-Malik." JESHO 3 (1960), 241–64.

Griffel, Frank. "Toleration and Exclusion: al-Shāfiʿī and al-Ghazālī on the Treatment of Apostates." BSOAS 64 (2001), 339-54.

Griffith, Sidney H. "Kitāb Misbāh al-ʿAql of Severus Ibn al-Muqaffaʿ: A Profile of the Christian Creed in Arabic in Tenth Century Egypt." *Medieval Encounters* 2.1 (1996), 15–42.

———. "Apologetics and Historiography in the Annals of Eutychius of Alexandria: Christian Self-Definition in the World of Islam." In *Studies on the Christian Arabic Heritage*, eds. R. Ebied and H. Teule.

———. *Church in the Shadow of the Mosque: Christians and Muslims in the World of Islam*. Princeton, 2008.

Griggs, W.C. *Early Egyptian Christianity*. Leiden, 1990.

Grillmeier, Aloys with Theresia Hainthaler. *Christ in Christian Tradition*. Vol. II.2, *The Church of Constantinople in the Sixth Century*, trans. P. Allen and J. Cawte. Louisville, 1995.

Grillmeier, Aloys with Theresia Hainthaler. *Christ in Christian Tradition*. Vol. II.4, *The Church of Alexandria with Nubia and Ethiopia after 451*. Trans. O.C. Dean. Louisville, 1996.

Grillmeier, Aloys and H. Bacht, eds. *Das Konzil von Chalkedon: Geschichte und Gegenwart*. 3 vols. Würzburg, 1951–54; 1979.

Grohmann, Adolf. *Handbuch der Orientalistik* 1:1–2 (I. *Arabische Chronologie*, II. *Arabische papyruskunde*). Leiden, 1966.

Grossmann, Peter. "The Pilgrimage Center of Abū Mīnā." In *Pilgrimage and Holy Space*, ed. D. Frankfurter, 281–302. Leiden, 1998.

———. *Abu Mina*, 2 vols. Mainz, 1989–2004.

Grypeou, Emmanouela, Mark Swanson and David Thomas, eds. *The Encounter of Eastern Christianity with Early Islam, 600 – 900*. Leiden, 2006.

Guenther, Alan M. "The Christian Experience and Interpretation of the Early Muslim Conquest and Rule." *Islam and Christian-Muslim Relations* 10.3 (1999), 363–378.

Haarmann, Ulrich. "Regional Sentiments in Medieval Islamic Egypt." BSOAS 43.1 (1980), 62–65.

Haas, Christopher. *Alexandria in Late Antiquity: Topography and Social Conflict*. Baltimore, 1997.

Halbwachs, Maurice. *On Collective Memory*. Chicago, 1992.

Haldon, J. ed., *Money, Power and Politics in Early Islamic Syria: A Review of Current Debates*. Burlington, 2010.

Hardy, E.R. *The Large Estates of Byzantine Egypt*. New York, 1931; 1968.

Harries, Jill. *Law and Empire in Late Antiquity*. Cambridge, 1999.

Hasan, Yūsuf Fadl. *The Arabs and the Sudan: from the Seventh to the Early Sixteenth century*. Edinburgh, 1967.

Hawting, G.R. *The First Dynasty of Islam: The Umayyad Caliphate AD 661–750*. 2nd ed. London, 2000.

Henner, Jutta. *Fragmenta Liturgica Coptica: Editionen und Kommentar liturgischer Texte der Koptischen Kirche des ersten Jahrtausends*. Tübingen, 2000.

Hill, D.R. *The Termination of Hostilities in the Early Arab Conquests A.D. 634–656*. New York, 1971.

Hinds, Martin. *Studies in Early Islamic History*, eds. J. Bacharach, L.I. Conrad, P. Crone. SLAEI 4. Princeton, 1996.

Hodgson, Marshall G.S. *The Venture of Islam*. 3 vols. Chicago, 1974.

Howard-Johnston, James. *Witnesses to a World Crisis: Historians and Histories of the Middle East in the Seventh Century*. Oxford, 2010.

Hoyland, Robert G. *Seeing Islam as Others Saw It: A Survey and Evaluation of Christian, Jewish and Zoroastrian Writings on Early Islam*. SLAEI 13. Princeton, 1997.

———. ed. *Muslims and Others in Early Islamic Society*. Burlington, 2004.

Innemée, Karel and Lucas van Rompay. "La présence des Syriens dans le Wadi al-Natrun (Égypte). À propos des découvertes récentes de peintures et de texts muraux dans l'Église de la Vierge du Couvent des Syriens." *Parole de l'Orient* 23 (1998), 167–202.

Isidhūrus, (Bishop). *al-Kharrīdah al-nafīsah fī tarīkh al-kanīsah* [*Precious Pearls in the History of the Church*]. Cairo, 1883; 1964; 1991.

Iskander, John. "Islamization in Medieval Egypt: the Copto-Arabic 'Apocalypse of Samuel' as a Source for the Social and Religious History of Medieval Copts." *Medieval Encounters* 4.3 (1998), 219–227.

Johnson, David W. "Anti-Chalcedonian Polemics in Coptic Texts 451–641." In *The Roots of Egyptian Christianity*, eds. Pearson and Goehring, 216–234. Philadelphia, 1986.

———. "Further Fragments of a Coptic History of the Church: Cambridge OR. 1699 R." *Enchoria* 6 (1976), 7–17.

Jones, A.H.M. "Were Ancient Heresies National or Social Movements in Disguise?" *Journal of Theological Studies* n.s. 11 (1959), 280–98.

———. *The Later Roman Empire*. 2 vols. Baltimore, 1986.

Juynboll, G.H.A. *Muslim Tradition: Studies in Chronology, Provenance, and Authorship of Early Ḥadīth*. Cambridge, 1983.

Kennedy, Hugh. "Central Government and Provincial Elites in the Early ʿAbbāsid Caliphate." BSOAS 44 (1981), 26–38.

———. "Egypt as a province in the Islamic Caliphate, 641–868." In *The Cambridge History of Egypt*, ed. C.F. Petry.

———. "From *Polis* to *Madina*: Urban change in late Antique and Early Islamic Syria." *Past and Present* 106 (1985), 3–27.

———. "The Melkite Church from the Islamic Conquest to the Crusades: Continuity and Adaptation in the Byzantine Legacy." In *The 17th International Byzantine Congress: Major Papers*, 325–343. New York, 1986.

———. *The Armies of the Caliphs: Military and Society in the Early Islamic State*. New York, 2001.

———. *The Prophet and the Age of the Caliphates*. 2nd. London, 2004.

Khalidi, Tarif. *Arabic Historical Thought in the Classical Period*. New York, 1994.

Khoury, Raif Georges. *ʿAbd Allāh ibn Lahīʿa (97–174/715–790): juge et grand maître de l'école égyptienne*. Wiesbaden, 1986.

King, G.R.D. "Islam, Iconoclasm and the Declaration of Doctrine." BSOAS 48.2 (1985), 267–277.

Kister, Menahem. "Do Not Assimilate Yourselves...: *lā tashabbahū*...." JSAI 12 (1989), 321–71; idem. *Concepts and Ideas at the Dawn of Islam*. Brookfield, 1997.

Krause, Martin. "Koptische Literatur." *Lexikon der Ägyptologie* 3:694–728.

Kubiak, Wladyslaw. *Al-Fustat: Its Foundation and Early Urban Development*. Cairo, 1987.

Łajtar, Adam. "Greek Funerary Inscriptions fro Old Dongola: General Notes." *Oriens Christianus* 81 (1997), 107–126.

Lamoreaux, John C. "Early Eastern Christian Responses to Islam." In *Medieval Christian Perceptions of Islam*, ed. John Victor Tolan. New York, 1996; 2000.

Lane-Poole, Stanly. *A History of Egypt in the Middle Ages*. London, 1901; 5th ed. 1936.

Lapidus, I.M. "The Arab Conquests and the Formation of Islamic Society." In *Studies on the First Century of Islamic Society*, ed. G.H.A. Juynboll. Illinois, 1982.

———. "The Conversion of Egypt to Islam." *Israel Oriental Studies* 2 (1972), 248–62.

Lasker, Daniel J. "The Jewish Critique of Christianity under Islam in the Middle Ages." *Proceedings of the American Academy for Jewish Research* 57 (1990–91), 121–153.

Lazarus-Yafeh, H., M.R. Cohen, S. Somekh, and S.H. Griffith, eds. *The Majlis: Interreligious Encounters in Medieval Islam*. Wiesbaden, 1999.

Leiser, Gary. "The Madrasa and the Islamization of the Middle East: The Case of Egypt." *Journal of the American Research Center in Egypt* 22 (1985), 29–47.

Lev, Yaacov. "Persecutions and Conversion to Islam in Eleventh-Century Egypt." *Israel Asian and African Studies* 22 (1988), 73–91.

———. "The Fatimid vizier Ya'qub b. Killis and the Beginning of the Fatimid Administration in Egypt." *Der Islam* 153 (1981), 237–49.

Lichtenstadter, Ilsa. "The Distinctive Dress of Non-Muslims in Islamic Countries." *Historica Judaica* 5 (1943), 35–52.

Little, Donald P. "Coptic Conversion to Islam under the Bahrī Malūks, 692–755/1293–1354." BSOAS 39 (1976), 552-69.

Løkkegaard, Frede. *Islamic Taxation in the Classic Period, with Special Reference to Circumstances in Iraq*. Copenhagen, 1950.

Lutfi, Huda. "Coptic festivals of the Nile: Aberrations of the Past?" In *The Mamluks in Egyptian Politics and Society*, eds. T. Philipp and U. Haarmann. Cambridge, 1998.

MacCoull, Leslie S.B. *Coptic Perspectives on Late Antiquity*. Brookfield, 1993.

———. "The Rite of the Jar: Apostasy and Reconciliation in the Medieval Coptic Orthodox Church," in *Peace and Negotiation: Strategies for Coexistence in the Middle Ages and the Renaissance*, ed. Diane Wolfthal, 145–62. Turnhout, 2000.

———. "'A dwelling place of Christ, a healing place of knowledge': the Non-Chalcedonian Eucharist in Late Antique Egypt and its setting." In *Varieties of Devotion in the Middle Ages and Renaissance*, ed. S.C. Karant-Nunn. Turnhout, 2003.

———. *Coptic Legal Documents: Law as Vernacular Text and Experience in Late Antique Egypt*. Turnhout, 2009.

Macomber, W.F. "The Anaphora of Saint Mark According to the Kacmarcik Codex." OCP 45 (1979), 75–98.

———. "The Greek texts of the Coptic Mass of the Anaphoras of Basil and Gregory According to the Kacmarcik Codex." OCP 43 (1977), 308–34.

Mayerson, Philip. "The Port of Clysma (Suez) in Transition from Roman to Arab Rule." JNES 55.2 (1996), 119–126.

Meinardus, Otto F.A. "A Brief History of the Abunate of Ethiopia." *Wiener Zeitschrift für die Kunde des Morgenlandes* 58 (1962), 39–65.

———. "The Attitudes of the Orthodox Copts towards the Islamic State from the 7th to the 12th century." *Ostkirchliche Studien* 13 (1964), 153–170.

———. *Christian Egypt Ancient and Modern*. 2nd rev. ed. Cairo, 1977.

———. *Christian Egypt: Faith and Life*. Cairo, 1970.

Meyendorff, John. *Imperial Unity and Christian Divisions*. Crestwood, 1989.

Mikhail, Maged S.A. "A Historical Definition for the 'Coptic Period'." *Orientalia Lovaniensia Analecta* 133 (2004), 971–981.

———. "A Reappraisal of the Current Position of St. Peter the Apostle in the Coptic Orthodox Church." *Bulletin of the St. Shenouda the Archimandrite Coptic Society* 5 (1999), 53–72.

———. "Some Observations Concerning Edibles in Late Antique and Early Islamic Egypt." *Byzantion* 70 (2000), 105–121.

———. "Notes on the *Ahl al-Dīwān*: The Arab-Egyptian Army of the Seventh through Ninth Centuries CE." JAOS 128.2 (2008), 277–78.

———. "An Orientation to the Sources and Study of Early Islamic Egypt (641–868)." *History Compass* 8.8 (2010), 929–50.

———. "A Lost Chapter in the History of Wadi al-Natrun (Scetis): The Coptic *Lives* and Monastery of Abba John Khame." *Muséon* (*forthcoming*).

———. "A New Historiography of Lent in Alexandria and the Alleged Reforms of Patriarch Demetrius." In *The Future of Coptic Studies: Theories, Methods, Topics*, ed. Nelly van Doorn-Harder (*forthcoming*).

———. and Mark Moussa, eds. *Christianity and Monasticism in Wadi al-Natrun*. Cairo, 2009.

Miles, George C. "The Early Islamic Bronze Coinage of Egypt." In *Centennial Publication of the American Numismatic Society*, ed. Harald Ingholt, 471–502. New York, 1958.

Miller, Daniel Earl. "From Catalogue to Codes to Canon: the Rise of the Petition to ʿUmar Among Legal Traditions Governing Non-Muslims in Medieval Islamicate Societies." Ph.D. diss., University of Missouri-Kansas City, 2000.

Morimoto, Kosei. "The *Diwān*s as Registers of the Arab Stipendiaries in Early Islamic Egypt." *Itinéraires d'Orient. Hommages à Claude Cahen*. Res Orientales 6 (1994), 353–365.

———. *The Fiscal Administration of Egypt in the Early Islamic Period*. Kyoto, 1981.

Morony, Michael G. *Iraq after the Muslim Conquest*. Princeton, 1984.

———. "History and Identity in the Syrian Churches." In *Redefining Christian Identity: Cultural Interaction in the Middle East since the Rise of Islam*, eds. J.J. van Ginkel, H.L. Murre – van den Berg, T.M. van Lint. Louvain, 2005.

Morton, A.H. *A Catalogue of Early Islamic Glass Stamps*. London, 1985.

Müller, C. Detlef G. "La position de l'Égypte chrétienne dans l'orient Ancient." *Muséon* 92 (1979), 105–25.

Naguib, Saphinaz-Amal. "The Martyr as Witness: Coptic and Copto-Arabic Hagiographies as Mediators of Religious Memory." *Numen* 41 (1994), 225–254.

Nau, F. "Dans quelle mesure les Jacobites sont-ils Monophysites?" ROC 10 (1905), 113–134.

Neugebauer, Otto. *Abu Shaker's "Chronography;" A Treatise of the 13th Century on Chronological, Calendrical, and Astronomical Matters, written by a Christian Arab, preserved in Ethiopic*. Österreichische Akademie der Wissenschaften, Philosophische-Historische Klasse Sitzungsberichte 498. Vienna, 1988.

Noth, Albrecht. "Zum Verhältnis von Kalifaler Zentralgewalt und Provinzen in umayyadischer Zeit: Die 'Ṣulḥ'-'ʿAnwa'–Traditionen für Ägypten und den Iraq." *Die Welt des Islams* 14 (1973), 150–62.

———. "Some Remarks on the 'Nationalization' of Conquered Lands at the Time of the Umayyads." In *Land Tenure and Social Transformation in the Middle East*, ed. Tarif Khalidi. Beirut, 1984.

———. *The Early Arabic Historical Tradition: A Source-Critical Study*. 2nd rev. ed. with L.I. Conrad. Princeton, 1994.

Nuseibeh, Said and O. Grabar. *The Dome of the Rock*. New York, 1996.

Olick, Jeffrey and Joyce Robbins. "Social Memory Studies: from 'Collective Memory' to the Historical Sociology of Mnemonic Practices." *Annual Review of Sociology* 24 (1998), 105–140.

Orlandi, Tito. "Coptic Literature." In *The Roots of Egyptian Christianity*, ed. B. Pearson and J.E. Goehring. Philadelphia, 1986.

———. *Storia della Chiesa di Alessandria*. Testo copto, traduzione e commento, I. *Da Pietro ad Atanasio*, II. *Da Teofilo a Timoteo II*. Milan, 1968–1970.

———. *Studi Copti. 1. Un encomio di Marco Evangelista. 2. Le fonti copte della Storia dei Patriarchi di Alessandria. 3. La leggenda di S. Mercurio.* Milan, 1968.

Palmer, Andrew, ed./trans. *The Seventh Century in West-Syrian Chronicles.* Liverpool, 1993.

Papaconstantinou, Arietta. *Le culte des saints en Égypte: des Byzantines aux Abbassides.* Paris, 2001.

———. "'What remains behind': Hellenism and Romanitas in Christian Egypt After the Arab conquest," in *From Hellenism to Islam: Cultural and Linguistic Change in the Roman Near East*, ed. H.M. Cotton *et al.*, Cambridge, 2009.

———, ed. *The Multilingual Experience in Egypt from the Ptolemies to the Abbasids.* Burlington, 2010.

———, ed. *Writing 'True Stories': Historians and Hagiographers in the Late Antique and Medieval Near East.* Turnhout, 2010.

Pearson, B.A. and J.E. Goehring, eds. *The Roots of Egyptian Christianity.* Philadelphia, 1986.

Perlmann, Moshe. "The Medieval Polemics between Islam and Judaism." In *Religion in a Religious Age*, ed. S.D. Goitein. Cambridge, 1974.

Petry, Carl F., ed. *The Cambridge History of Egypt*, vol. 1, *Islamic Egypt 641–1517.* Cambridge, 1998.

Phillips, J.R. "The Byzantine Bronze Coins of Alexandria in the Seventh Century." *Numismatic Chronicle*, 7th ser, 2 (1962), 225–41.

Powers, David S. *Studies in Qur'an and Ḥadith: the Formation of the Islamic Law of Inheritance.* Los Angeles, 1986.

Puin, Gerd-Rüdiger. *Der Dīwān von 'Umar Ibn al-Haṭṭāb: ein Beitrag zur frühislamischen Verwaltungsgeschichte.* Bonn, 1970.

Qāḍī, Wadād, al-. "Population Census and Land Surveys under the Umayyads (41–132/661–75)." *Der Islam* 83 (2006), 341–416.

———. "An Umayyad Papyrus in al-Kindī's *Kitāb al-Quḍāt.*" *Der Islam* 84.2 (2007), 200–45.

———. "The Salaries of Judges in Early Islam: The Evidence of the Documentary and Literary Sources." JNES 68 (2009), 9–30.

Quecke, Hans. *Untersuchungen zur koptischen Stundengebet.* Louvain, 1970.

Raghib, Yusuf. "Trois documents dates du Louvre." *Annales Islamologiques* 15 (1979), 1–10.

———. "Quatres papyrus arabes d'Edfou." *Annales Islamologiques* 14 (1978), 1–14.

Rambo, Lewis R. "Conversion." In *The Encyclopedia of Religion*, ed. Mircea Eliade. 4:73–79. New York, 1987.

———. *Understanding Religious Conversion.* New Haven, 1993.

Rapp, Claudia. *Holy Bishops in Late Antiquity: the Nature of Christian Leadership in an Age of Transition.* Berkeley, 2005.

Reinink, G.J. "The Beginnings of Syriac Apologetic Literature in Response to Islam." *Oriens Christianus* 77 (1993), 165–87.

Reinfandt, Lucian. "Crime and Punishment in Early Islamic Egypt (AD 642–969): The Arabic Papyrological Evidence." In *Proceedings of the Twenty-Fifth International Congress of Papyrology, Ann Arbor 2007*, pg. 633–40. Ann Arbor, 2010.

Richards, D.S. "The Coptic Bureaucracy under the Mamlūks." In *Colloque International sur l'Histoire du Caire*, ed. André Raymond *et al.*, 373–81. Cairo, 1972.

Richter, Tonio Sebastian. "Spatkoptische Rechtsurkunden neu bearbeitet: BM Or.4917 (15) und P.Med.Copt. inv. 69.69." JJP 29 (1999), 85–95.

———. *Rechtssemantik und forensische Rhetorik: Untersuchungen zu Wortschatz, Stil und Grammatik der Sprache koptischer Rechtsurkunden*. Wiesbaden, 2008.

———. "Koptische Rechtsurkunden als Quellen der Rechtspraxis im byzantinischen und frühislamischen Ägypten." In *Quellen zur byzantinischen Rechtspraxis*, eds. C. Gastgeber, F. Mitthof and B. Palme. Vienna, 2009.

———. "Greek, Coptic, and the 'Language of the Hijra': the Rise and Decline of the Coptic Language in Late Antique and Medieval Egypt." In *From Hellenism to Islam: Cultural and Linguistic Change in the Roman Near East*, eds. H.M. Cotton *et al.*, Cambridge, 2009.

Riedel, Wilhelm. *Die Kirchenrechtsquellen des Patriarchats Alexandrien*. Leipzig, 1900; 1968.

Riti, Mamduḥ ʿAbd al-Raḥmān ʿAbd al-Raḥīm. *Dawr al-qaba'il al-'arabiyah fi sa'id misr mundhu al-fath al-islami … 21–358/641–969*. Cairo, 1996.

Roberts, Colin H. and Bernard Capelle. *An Early Euchologium: The Der-Balizeh Papyrus Enlarged and Reedited*. Louvain, 1949.

Robinson, Chase F. *Empire and Elites after the Muslim Conquest*. Cambridge, 2000.

———. *Islamic Historiography*. Cambridge, 2003.

Rokeah, David. *Jews, Pagans, and Christians in Conflict*. Leiden, 1982.

Rubenson, Samuel. "The Transition from Coptic to Arabic." *Égypte/Monde arabe* 27–28 (1996), 77–91.

Rustow, Marina. *Heresy and the Politics of Community: the Jews of the Fatimid Caliphate*. Ithaca, 2008.

Saleh, Abdel Hamid. "Les bédouins d'Egpte aux premiers siècles de l'Hégire." *Rivista degli Studi Orientali* 55 (1981), 148–61; "The Bedouins of Egypt during the First Centuries of the Hijra." In *Production and the Exploitation of Resources*, ed. Michael G. Morony. Burlington, 2002.

Saleh, Marlis J. "Government Relations with the Coptic Community in Egypt during the Fātimid Period (358–567/969–1171)." Ph.D. diss., University of Chicago, 1995.

Samir, S. Khalil. "The Role of Christians in the Fātimid Government Services of Egypt to the Reign of al-Hāfiz." *Medieval Encounters* 2.3 (1996), 177–192.

———. "Vie et oeuvre de Marc ibn al-Qumbar." In *Christianisme d'Égypte. Hommages à René-George Coquin*, 123–158. Louvain, 1995.

Samir, S. Khalil and Jørgen S. Nielsen, eds. *Christian Arabic Apologetics during the Abbasid Period (750–1258)*. Leiden, 1994.

Samuel, V.C. *The Council of Chalcedon Re-Examined*. Madras, 1977; 2001.

Sarris, Peter. *Economy and Society in the Age of Justinian*. Cambridge, 2006.

Scanlon, George T. *Fustat Expedition Final Report*. Winona Lake, 1986.

Schacht, Joseph. *An Introduction to Islamic Law*. Oxford, 1964.

Schacht, Joseph. *The Origins of Muhammadan Jurisprudence*. Oxford, 1953.

Schiller, A. Arthur. "Coptic Law." *The Juridical Review* 43 (1931), 211–240.

———. "The Courts are No More." *Studi in onore di Edoardo Volterra* I, 469–502. Milano, 1971.

Schmelz, Georg. *Kirchliche Amtsträger im spätantiken Ägypten nach den Aussagen der griechischen und koptischen Papyri und Ostraka*. Münich, 2002.

Schmucker, Werner. *Untersuchungen zu einigen wichtigen bodenrechtlichen Konsequenzen der islamischen Eroberungsbewegung*. Bonn, 1972.

Schoeler, Gregor. *The Oral and the Written in Early Islam*, trans. Uwe Vagelpohl, ed. J.E. Montgomery. London, 2006.

Schultz, Warren C. "The Monetary History of Egypt, 642–1517." In *The Cambridge History of Egypt*, vol. 1, ed. C.F. Petry.

Schwartz, J. "Dioclétien dans la litérature copte." BSAC 15 (1958–60), 151–66.

Shoshan, Boaz. *Popular Culture in Medieval Cairo*. New York, 1993.

———. "The 'Politics of Notables' in Medieval Islam." *Asian and African Studies* 20 (1986), 179–215.

Sidarus, Adel. "Coptic Lexicography in the Middle Age: The Coptic Arabic Scalae." In *The Future of Coptic Studies*, ed. R. McL. Wilson. Leiden, 1978.

———. "Medieval Coptic Grammars in Arabic: The Coptic Muqaddimāt." *Journal of Coptic Studies* 3 (2001), 63–79.

———. "L'influence arabe sur la linguistique copte." In *History of the Language Sciences*, ed. Sylvain Auroux *et al.,* Berlin, 2000.

Sijpesteijn, Petra M., "Shaping a Muslim State: Papyri Related to an Eighth-Century Egyptian Official." Ph.D. diss., Princeton University, 2004.

———. "Landholding Patterns in Early Islamic Egypt." *Journal of Agrarian Change* 9.1 (2009), 120–33.

———. "New Rule over Old Structures: Egypt after the Muslim Conquest." In *Regime Change in the Ancient Near East and Egypt*, ed. H. Crawford. Oxford, 2007.

———. "The Arab Conquest of Egypt and the Beginning of Muslim Rule." In *Egypt in the Byzantine world*, ed. R.S. Bagnall.

Simonsen, Jørgen Bæk. *Studies in the Genesis and Early Development of the Caliphal Taxation System*. Copenhagen, 1988.

Skreslet II, Stanley H. "The Greeks in Medieval Islamic Egypt: A Melkite Dhimmi Community under the patriarch of Alexandria (640–1095)." Ph.D. diss., Yale University, 1987.

Spaulding, Jay. "Medieval Christian Nubia and the Islamic World: A Reconsideration of the Baqt Treaty." *The International Journal of African Historical Studies* 28.3 (1995), 577–594.

Stark, Rodney and Roger Finke. *Acts of Faith: Explaining the Human Side of Religion*. Berkeley, 2000.

Suermann, Harald. "Copts and the Islam of the Seventh Century." In *The Encounter of Eastern Christianity with Early Islam*, eds. Emmanouela Grypeou *et al.*

Swanson, Mark N. "'Our Brother, the Monk Eustathius': A Ninth-Century Syrian Orthodox Theologian Known to Medieval Arabophone Copts." *Coptica* 1 (2002), 119–40.

———. "A Copto-Arabic Catechism of the Later Fatimid Period: 'Ten Questions which One of the Disciples Asked of His Master'." *Parole de l'Orient* 22 (1997), 473–501.

———. "Three Sinai Manuscripts of Books 'of the Master and the Disciple' and their *membra disiecta* in Birmingham." OCP 65 (1999), 347–61.

———. *The Coptic Papacy in Islamic Egypt 641–1517*. Cairo, 2010.

Tabātabā'i, Hossein Modarressi. *Kharāj in Islamic Taxation*. London, 1983.

Taklahāymānot, Ayele'. "The Egyptian Metropolitan of the Ethiopian Church." OCP 54 (1988), 175–222.

Thomas, David, *et al.*, ed. *Christian-Muslim Relations: A Bibliographical History*, 4 vols. Leiden, 2009–2012.

Till, W.C. "Die Koptischen Eheverträge." In *Die Osterreichische Nationalbibliothek Festschrift Josef Bick*. Vienna, 1948.

———. "Erbrechtliche Untersuchungen auf Grund der koptischen Urkunden." *Österreichische Akademie der Wissenschaften, Philosophisch-historische Klasse, Sitzungsberichte* 229.2. Vienna, 1954.

Timm, Stefan. *Das Christlich-Koptische Ägypten in Arabischer Zeit*. Wiesbaden, 1984–1992.

Tritton, Arthur S. *The Caliphs and their non-Muslim Subjects*. London, 1930; 1970.

Trombley, Frank. "Mediterranean Sea Culture between Byzantium and Islam c. 600–850 A.D.)." In *The Dark Ages of Byzantium, 7th–9th c.*, ed. E. Kountoura-Galake, 133–169. Athens, 2001.

Tyan, Emil. *Histoire de l'organisation judiciaire en pays d'Islam*. 2nd rev. ed. Leiden, 1960.

Udovitch, A.L., ed. *The Islamic Middle East, 700–1900: Studies in Economic and Social History*. Princeton, 1981.

Van den Gerg-Onstwedder, Gonnie. "Diocletian in the Coptic Tradition." BSAC 29 (1990), 87–122.

Van Ginkel, Jan J. "John of Ephesus on Emperors: The Perception of the Byzantine Empire by a Monophysite." [*VI Symposium Syriacum 1992*, ed. René Lavenant] *Orientalia Christiana Analecta* 247 (1994), 323–33.

Vasiliev, A.A. "The Iconoclastic Edict of the Caliph Yazid II, A.D. 721." DOP 9–10 (1956), 25–47.

Vila, David H. "Christian Martyrs in the First Abbasid Century and the Development of an Apologetic against Islam." Ph.D. diss., Saint Louis University, 1999.

———. "The Struggle over Arabisation in Medieval Arabic Christian Hagiography." *al-Masāq* 15 (2003), 35–46.

Von Lemm, Oscar. *Koptische Fragmente zur Patriarchengeschichte Alexandriens.* Mémoires de l'Académie impériale des sciences de St. Pétersbourg ser. 7, 36.11. St. Petersburg, 1888.

Vryonis, Speros Jr. *The Decline of Medieval Hellenism in Asia Minor and the Process of Islamization from the Eleventh through the Fifteenth Century*. Berkley, 1971.

Walker, Joel. "The Limits of Late Antiquity: Philosophy between Rome and Iran." *Ancient World* 33 (2002), 45–69.

Walker, John. *A Catalogue of the Arab-Byzantine and Post-Reform Umaiyad Coins*. London, 1956.

Wansbrough, John. *The Sectarian Milieu: Content and Composition of Islamic Salvation History*. Oxford, 1978.

Ward, Seth. "Construction and Repair of Churches and Synagogues under Islam: A Treatise by Tāqī al-Dīn 'Alī b. 'Abd al-Kāfī al-Subkī." Ph.D. diss., Yale University, 1984.

———. "Ibn al-Rif'a on the Churches and Synagogues of Cairo." *Medieval Encounters* 5 (1999), 70–84.

Watson, Andrew. *Agricultural Innovation in the Early Islamic World*. Cambridge, 1983.

Werthmuler, Kurt J. *Coptic Identity and Ayyubid Politics in Egypt, 1218–1250*. Cairo, 2010.

Weigert, Gideon. "A Note on Hudna: Peace Making in Islam." In *War and Society in the Eastern Mediterranean, 7th–15th Centuries*, ed. Y. Lev. Leiden, 1997.

Weitzmann, K. ed., *Age of Spirituality: A Symposium*. New York, 1979; Princeton, 1980.

Welsby, Derek A. *The Medieval Kingdoms of Nubia: Pagans, Christians and Muslims along the Middle Nile*. London, 2002.

Wickham, Chris. *Framing the Early Middle Ages: Europe and the Mediterranean, 400–800*. New Edition. Oxford, 2007.

Wiet, Gaston. *L'Égypte arabe de la conquête arabe a la conquête ottomane 642–1517 de l'ère chrétienne*. Paris, 1937.

Wilfong, Terry G. *Women of Jeme: Lives in a Coptic Town in Late Antique Egypt*. Ann Arbor, 2002.

———. "The non-Muslim Communities: Christian communities." In *The Cambridge History of Egypt*, vol. 1, ed. Carl F. Petry.

Wipszycha, Ewa. "Le Nationalisme A-t-Il Existe Dans L'Egypte Byzantine?" JJP 22 (1992), 83–128.

———. "La christianisation de l'Égypte aux IV–VI siècles: Aspects sociaux et ethniques." *Aegyptus* 68 (1988), 117–165.

———. *Les Ressources et les activités économiques des églises en Egypt du IVe au VIIe siècle*. Brussels, 1972.

———. *Études sur le christianisme dans l'Égypte de l'antiquité tardive*. Rome, 1996.

———. *Moines et communautés monastiques en Égypte*. Warsaw, 2009.

Worp, Klaas A. "Hegira Years in Greek, Greek-Coptic, and Greek-Arabic Papyri." *Aegyptus* 65 (1985), 107–115.

Youssef, Youhanna Nessim. "Liturgical Connections between Copts (anti-Chalcedonian) and Greeks (Chalcedonian), After the Council of Chalcedon." *Ephemerides Liturgicae* 114.4 (2000), 394–400.

———. "Romanos in the Coptic Church." *Bulletin of Saint Shenouda the Archimandrite Coptic Society* 5 (1998–99), 41–44.

———. "Consecration of the Myron at Saint Macarius." *Coptica* 2 (2003), 106–121.

Yu'annis, (Bishop). *Tarīkh al-kannīsā al-qibṭiyyā ba'd majma' khalqīdunyā*. Staten Island, 1989.

Zanetti, Ugo. "Abū l-Makārim et Abū Sālih." BSAC 34 (1995), 85–138.

———. "Bohairic Liturgical Manuscripts." OCP 61 (1995), 65–94.

Zayāt, Ḥabīb. "Simāt al-naṣārā wa-al-yahūd fī al-islām: al-ṣalīb, aw al-zunnār, wa al-'amāma wa al-ghiyār; shurūt al-'umarīya." *al-Machrīq* 43.2 (1949), 161–252.

PAPYROLOGICAL INDEX

Page numbers are in italics.

Chrest.Khoury. (*276*) **I**.24 (*327*), 27 (*328*), 33 (*327*), 34 (*327*), 37 (*328*), 41 (*330*), 45 (*330*, *327*), 47 (*315*), 59 (*330*), 63 (*328*), 68 (*312*, *332*), 75 (*330*); **II**. 7 (*327*), 9 (*327*), 26 (*312*), 27 (*327*)

CPR **IX**.52 (*317*); **XVI**: 4 (*311*), 9 (*311*); **XXI**: (*288*, *323*, *325-27*, *340*), 34 (*325*); **XXII**: 1 (*317*), 43 (*332*); **XXX** (*288*)

O.Brit.Mus.Copt. I. Plate VI 1, no. 404 (*328*); VI 2, no. 604 (*326*); VII 1, no. 1208 (*327*); VII 4, no. 1336 (*330*, *328*); VIII 1, no. 26791 (*328*); VIII 3, no. 607 (*328*); IX 1, no. 1046 (*326*); IX 2, no. 407 (*326*); IX 3, no. 1256 (*328*); IX 5, no. 408 (*327*); XI 5, no. 823 (*326*); XLI.5, no. 21245 (*365*); LII 6, no. 21200 (*365*)

O.Crum. 29 (*363*), 40 (*326*), 43 (*156*), 49 (*339*), 61 (*339*), 62 (*336*), 69 (*339*), 70 (*336*), 72 (*301*), 86 (*156*), 106 (*363*), 107 (*336*), 108 (*336*), 110 (*336*), 111 (*336*), 113 (*336*), 115 (*339*), 116 (*339*), 119 (*335*), 139 (*363*), 154 (*339*), 163 (*336*), 175 (*336*), 295 (*156*), 304 (*326*, *336*), 306 (*326*), 381 (*339*), 409-11 (*335*), 413 (*335*), 419 (*335*), 429 (*335*, *336*), 516-22 (*308*), Ad. 1 (*301*), Ad.14 (*336*), Ad.15 (*310*), Ad.17 (*326*), Ad.29 (*336*), Ad.39 (*308*), Ad. 43 (*336*)

O.Medin.HabuCopt. (*317*, *335*), 5 (*339*), 50 (*328*), 51 (*328*), 52 (*328*), 58 (*336*), 60 (*328*), 61 (*326*), 65 (*336*), 66 (*336*), 70 (*328*), 71 (*328*), 73 (*328*), 75 (*328*, *336*), 81 (*326*), 82 (*326*), 83 (*326*, *335*), 136 (*336*)

P.Apoll. (*147*, *164*, *331*, *341*), 6 (*336*), 9 (*336*, *341*), 14 (*336*), 18 (*331*), 20 (*336*), 22-4 (*331*), 26 (*336*), 29 (*336*, *341*), 30 (*341*), 33 (*342*), 36 (*342*), 38 (*341*), 40 (*336*), 50 (*336*), 52 (*342*), 57 (*331*), 58 (*331*), 66 (*331*), 86 (*342*), 95 (*342*)

P.Bal. 103 (*181*, *362*), 104 (*362*), 111 (*348*), 114 (*348*), 116 (*348*), 119 (*348*), 120 (*348*), 142 (*362*), 152 (*301*, *339*), 174 (*340*), 187 (*340*), 240 (*340*)

P.Bawit Clackson. (*326*)

P.Cair.Arab. (305), **I**.38 (66), 40 (65), 41 (66, *300*, *315*), 42 (66, *157*,

336), 43 (*65*), 48 (*66*, *70*), 54 (*66*, *157*, *301*, *315*, *336*, *339*), 56 (*70*, *301*), 57 (*157*, *339*), 58 (*157*, *315*, *339*), 67 (*336*); **II**.73 (*315*), 74-75 (*315*), 85 (*329*), 86 (*315*), 89 (*327*), 97 (*130*), 101 (*327*), 114 (*315*), 119 (*315*), 121 (*336*), 122 (*315*), 127 (*316*), 132 (*316*), 138 (*315*), 143 (*327*, *328*); **III**.146-55 (*305*), 150 (*332*), 151 (*336*), 160 (*305*, *330*), 161 (*305*), 162 (*305*), 164-66 (*305*), 167 (*104*, *339*), 181 (*335*), 184 (*335*), 185 (*335*), 189 (*335*), 190 (*335*), 192 (*335*), 193 (*335*), 194 (*335*), 195 (*335*), 196 (*335*), 198 (*316*, *335*), 199 (*316*, *335*), 202 (*316*); **V**.320 (*336*), 345 (*327*), 346 (*327*), 355 (*327*); **VI**. 369 (*327*), 370 (*316*), 408 (*327*)

P.Cair.Masp. III.67311 (*301*, *339*)

P.Clackson. 35 (*307*), 45 (*145*)

P.CLT. 1 (*155*, *162*, *338*, *339*), 2 (*339*), 3 (*182*, *305*, *335*), 5 (*335*, *338*, *339*), 6 (*335*, *341*)

P.Fay.Monast. I.19 (*311*, *315*), 3 (*316*)

P.Giss.Arab. 5 (*300*)

P.Heid.Arab. I: (*335*), 10 (*331*)

P.Kell. II.Syr./Copt.1, 2 (*352*); II Syr.1 (*353*); II Syr./Gr. 1 (*353*); II Gr.1 (*353*)

P.Khalili. (*312*), **I**.21 (*266*); **II**.38 (*266*), 42 (*332*), 44 (*332*)

P.Köln.IV.173(*308*)

P.KRU. (*181*, *182*, *320*, *330*), 3 (*339*, *362*), 5 (*339*, *349*, *362*), 10 (*349*), 12 (*315*, *349*), 13 (*315*), 14 (*329*), 15 (*329*), 21 (*349*), 25 (*331*), 27 (*349*), 35 (*349*), 36 (*335*, *349*), 37 (*339*), 38 (*328*, *349*), 42 (*146*, *331*, *332*), 44 (*335*, *339*), 45 (*331*), 46 (*331*), 50 (*331*, *349*), 66 (*315*, *339*), 55 (*349*), 65 (*349*), 66 (*349*), 68 (*315*), 70 (*329*), 74 (*328*, *349*), 77 (*315*, *339*, *347*, *349*), 105 (*335*, *339*), 106 (*315*, *328*, *329*, *339*)

P.Laur. III.112 (*317*)

*P.Lond.Copt.*I. (*147*, *315*), 154-160 (*309*), 160 (*309*), 389 (*326*), 398 (*326*), 405 (*326*), 408 (*326*), 449 (*362*), 450 (*362*), 487 (*328*), 489 (*328*), 490 (*328*), 512 (*348*), 514 (*309*), 549 (*340*), 250 (*373*), 580 (*311*), 584 (*311*), 587 (*311*), 591 (*311*), 593 (*340*), 598 (*311*), 599 (*311*), 612 (*311*), 631 (*311*), 660 (*311*), 662 (*311*), 664 (*311*), 666 (*311*), 668 (*311*), 673 (*329*), 1226 (*329*), 1339 (*335*), 1356 (*335*), 1384 (*335*), 1394 (*331*), 1400 (*335*)

P.Lond. IV.: (*164*), 1333 (*336*), 1335 (*165*), 1336 (*341*), 1336 (*341*), 1337 (*341*), 1338 (*336*), 1339 (*336*), 1340 (*336*), 1341 (*341*, *342*), 1342 (*341*, *342*), 1343 (*336*, *349*), 1344 (*336*), 1346 (*336*), 1348 (*336*, *341*), 1353 (*341*), 1356 (*336*), 1359 (*336*), 1361 (*336*), 1362 (*336*), 1364 (*336*), 1365 (*336*), 1366 (*341*, *342*), 1368 (*342*), 1370 (*165*, *336*), 1372 (*336*), 1375 (*342*), 1376 (*341*), 1378 (*342*), 1380 (*336*), 1381 (*336*), 1383 (*335*, *336*), 1384 (*336*), 1386 (*165*), 1391 (*341*), 1392 (*164*, *165*, *288*), 1394 (*336*), 1397 (*164*, *165*, *336*), 1398 (*336*), 1403 (*342*), 1404 (*165*), 1405 (*336*), 1410 (*341*), 1411 (*341*), 1412 (*289*), 1413 (*289*), 1414 (*335*, *341*), 1447 (*289*, *290*), 1448 (*284*), 1592 (*290*)

P.Marchands. **I**.5 (*336*), 6 (*336*), 7 (*327*)

P.Mon.Apollo. (*182*, *218*, *370*), 31 (*332*), 24 (*349*)

*P.Mon.Epiph.*I. 77 (*375*), 88 (*155*, *156*), 131 (*289*), 133 (*289*), 141 (*339*),

143 (*289*), 147 (*339*), 151 (*156*, *339*), 162 (*339*), 163 (*156*, *332*, *339*), 165 (*339*), 167 (*332*), 172 (*339*), 176 (*332*), 177 (*332*), 181 (*332*), 187 (*332*), 188 (*339*), 192 (*363*), 196 (*339*), 200 (*349*), 216 (*349*), 219 (*332*), 229 (*339*), 254 (*365*), 257 (*338*, *339*), 261 (*339*), 264 (*155*), 271 (*339*), 300 (*339*), 431 (*338*, *339*), 458 (*339*), 462 (*339*), 466 (*332*), 469 (*365*); **II**.148-52, 331-37 (*307*); 152, 337 (*347*)

P.MorganLib. 22, 57, 59, 60, 280, 281, 282-5, 291-2 (*308*)

P.Oxy. **I**.130 (*287*), 133-9 (*287*), 134 (*362*), 138 (*348*); **IV**. 1337 (*341*), 1348 (*341*), 1349 (*341*), 1353 (*341*), 1357 (*341*), 1373 (*341*), 1374 (*341*), 1376 (*341*), 1393 (*341*), 1394 (*341*), 1404 (*341*), 1407 (*341*); **VI**.893 (*335*); **VIII** 1130 (*362*); **XVI** (*287*), 1871 (*365*), 1900 (*365*), 1919 (*332*), 2056 (*332*); **XX** 2270 (*362*); **XXVII**. 2478 (*332*); **XXXVI** 2780 (*362*); **LI** 3640 (*363*), 3641 (*362*)

P.Prag.Arab. 6 (*327*), 10 (*316*, *327*), 19 (*332*), 27 (*332*), 31 (*332*), 32 (*316*, *336*), 47 (*328*, *329*), 49 (*328*, *329*), 87 (*332*)

P.Rain.UnterrichtKopt. 119, 124, 132, 133, 228, 229, 232, 236, 237, 238, 247, 260-64 (*307*)

P.Qurra. (*305*), 2 (*310*, *336*), 3 (*310*, *312*, *331*), 4 (*336*), 5 (*335*)

P.Ryl.Copt. 19 (*309*), 22 (*309*), 25 (*309*), 26-36 (*309*), 39 (*309*), 58 (*309*), 72 (*313*), 116 (*305*), 127 (*335*), 139 (*300*), 156 (*316*), 173 (*335*), 175 (*329*), 214 (*311*, *316*), 221 (*104*), 234 (*316*), 236 (*104*), 243 (*316*), 267 (*156*), 278 (*335*), 281 (*335*), 285 (*316*), 306 (*316*), 309 (*104*, *316*), 319 (*335*), 321 (*305*), 324 (*104*, *312*), 346 (*104*, *312*), 401 (*104*)

*P.Strasb.*660 (*317*)

P.Teshlot. (*315*, *328*, *336*, *339*, *362*), 6 (*102*)

P.Vat.CoptiDoresse. 3 (*349*)

P.World. (*305*)

*SB Kopt.*I. 551 (*327*), 610 (*329*), 612-14 (*329*), 747 (*329*)

SPP X 222 (*321*)

INDEX

Abbreviations: *Archd.* = Archdeacon, *bp* = bishop, *C* = Coptic, *dcn* = deacon, *Emp.* = Emperor, *gov.* = governor, *M* = Melkite, *Pat* = patriarch

ʿAbbāsids, 5, 25, 30, 41, 58, 62–65, 69–73, 76–78, 86, 106, 111, 120, 121, 126, 128, 137, 138, 142, 143, 152, 157, 162, 167, 170, 187, 188, 193, 206, 225, 227, 230, 244, 259, 263, 265, 285, 297, 300, 302, 312, 334

Abbott, N., 6, 66, 300, 301, 315, 322, 331, 336, 384.

ʿAbd al-Aʿalī ibn Khālid ibn Thābit ibn Ẓaʿīn al-Fahmī, 145

ʿAbd al-ʿAzīz, bounty hunter, 336

ʿAbd al-ʿAzīz al-Jarawī, 45, 291, 325

ʿAbd al-ʿAzīz ibn Marwān, gov., 7, 29, 39–44, 50, 68, 113, 116, 120, 141, 153, 162, 184–6, 197–99, 205, 206, 224–6, 274, 282–4, 286, 287, 289, 333, 341

ʿAbd al-Khāliq, 316

ʿAbd al-Malik ibn Marwān, caliph, 68, 113–7, 148, 153, 166, 199, 266

ʿAbd al-Malik ibn Marwān ibn Mūsā, gov., 199

ʿAbd al-Malik ibn Mūsā ibn Naṣīr, gov., 240

ʿAbd al-Malik ibn Rifāʿa ibn Khālid ibn Thābit ibn Ẓaʿīn al-Fahmī, gov., 145, 331, 332

ʿAbd al-Raḥmān ibn Ḥassan ibn ʿAtahiya ibn Ḥazn al-Tujībī, 334

ʿAbd al-Raḥman ibn Ilyas, 335

ʿAbd al-Raḥmān ibn Khālid ibn Musāfir ibn Khālid ibn Thabit ibn Ẓaʿin al-Fahmī, 145, 331, 332, 334

ʿAbd al-Raḥmān ibn Muʿawiya ibn Ḥudayjal-Tujībī, 332, 333, 334

ʿAbd al-Raḥmān ibn ʿUtba ibn Jaḥdam, 140, 302

ʿAbdallāh ibn ʿAbd al-Malik, 43, 113, 116, 144, 145

ʿAbdallāh ibn ʿAbd al-Raḥmān ibn Muʿāwiya ibn Ḥudayj, 332, 333

ʿAbdallāh ibn Abī Sumīr al-Fahmī, 334

ʿAbdallāh ibn Lahiʿā, 371

ʿAbdallāh ibn Marawān, 200–1

ʿAbdallāh ibn Qīs ibn al-Ḥarith ibn ʿAyyash ibn Dubīʿ al-Tujībī, 334

ʿAbdallāh ibn Saʿd ibn Abī Sarḥ, 138, 196, 302

ʿAbdallāh ibn Ṭāhir, 187, 291

'Abdallāh ibn Yasar al-Fahmī, 145
'Ābis ibn Sa'īd al-Murādī, 140, 141
Abra'ām, secretary, 9th c., 49
Abraham, OT Patriarch, 232, 258, 329
Abraham bp (Barsanuphian then Coptic), 63–64
Abraham bp of Fayyūm, 8th c., 216, 217, 366
Abraham bp of Hermonthis (Armant), 217
Abū al-'Awn 'Abd al-Malik ibn Yazīd, gov., 138, 244, 379
Abū al-Barakāt ibn Kabar, 237, 275, 375
Abū al-Bishr, 99; *see* Sawīrus ibn al-Muqaffa'
Abū Ḥusayn, 240
Abū al-Khayr, dcn/baker, 316
Abū al-Khayr, dcn/convert, 69–70, 366
Abū Mīnā, rebel leader, 121, 324; cf. Mīnā ibn Baqīrā
Abū Muslim, 187–8, 259
Abū al-Nady *mawlā* Balī, 123
Abū al-Ṣayrafī, notable, 376
Abū Shākir Buṭrusibn al-Rāhib, 239, 376
Abū Ṣulḥ Yūnus ibn 'Abdallāh, 96, 312
Abū 'Ubayd al-Qāsim ibn Sallām, 117, 284, 297, 301, 302, 305, 317, 318, 319, 322, 323, 331, 342, 343, 344, 366, 369, 370
Abū Yāsir, priest, 375
Abū Yumīn, 104
Abū Yūsuf, *qāḍī al-quḍāt*, 112, 284, 297, 298, 301, 302, 317, 319, 334, 339, 342–4, 369
Abullīf, W., 312
Adams, J.N., 305
Adams, W.Y, 344, 354, 355, 357
Administration, ch. 7*passim*, 116, 145–7
Afifi, M., 339
Afrahām ibn Za'rah, CPat, 208, 218, 230, 236, 249, 251, 252, 253, 348, 353, 360, 361, 365, 371, 373, 381, 382
al-Afshīn, general, 125, 325, 351
Afyaḥ ibn Buṭrus, convert, 312
Agapios, 21, 282, 283, 328
Agathon I, (Pseudo-), *Book of Consecration*, 282, 283, 294, 295, 370
Agathon I, CPat, 40, 60, 61, 153, 184, 223, 226, 288, 298, 338, 349, 350, 364, 370, 375
Agrarian Revolts *see* Revolts
Ahl al-dhimmā, see *Dhimmā*
Ahl al-dīwān, 120–2, 323, 325, 341
Ahl al-Ḥarās, 65, 269
Ahl al-kitāb, 112, 171, 343
Aḥmad ibn 'Alī al-Mardānī, notable, 49, 292
Aḥmad ibn Marwān al-Qurayshī, 66
Aḥmad ibn Ṭūlūn, 48, 49, 324, 366
Ahmad, L., 323
'Ajam (pl. *a'ājim*), 112, 115, 129, 241, 327
Akephaloi, 14, 54, 62, 63, 277, 293, 298, 299
Alexander I, Pat, 359
Alexander II, CPat, 6, 14, 41, 86, 92, 276, 278, 290, 297, 301, 307, 350, 362, 375, 377
Alexander, P.J., 276, 286
Alexandria, xii, 14, 19, 27, 23, 24, 27, 38, 40, 47, 53, 54, 56, 76, 82, 89, 91, 92, 115, 124, 126, 140, 143, 144, 151, 161, 163, 164, 168, 174, 189, 194, 199, 204–18, 220, 221, 223–25, 227, 229, 236, 243, 283, 285, 290, 295, 334, 337, 355–65, 369
Alexandrian Clergy, 89, 215–7, 221, 360
'Alī ibn Abū Ṭālib, caliph, 134
'Alī ibn Sulaymān, gov., 229
'Alī ibn Yaḥyā al-Armannī, 48
Allen, E.B., 326
Allen, P., 280, 294, 295, 307

al-Amīn, caliph, 124
ʿAmr ibn al-ʿĀṣ, 19, 21, 23, 24, 25, 26, 27, 81, 111, 138, 143, 144, 161, 162, 181, 245, 247, 341
ʿAmr ibn Suḥayl ibn ʿAbd al-ʿAzīz ibn Marwān, 120
Anastasios, CPat, 85, 307
Anastasios, Emp, 287, 346
Anawati, G.C., 316
Anderson, B., 273, 282
Andronikos, CPat, 85, 307, 362
Annals see *Eutychios*
ʿAnwa see *Ṣulḥ*
Apacyrus, pagarch, 25, 283
Apacyrus ibn Isḥāq ibn Andunā, 48
Apion family, 55, 287, 294
Apocalypse of Athanasios, 8, 59, 72, 76, 215, 297, 314, 316, 357, 364, 378
Apocalypse of Samuel, 8, 70, 72, 73, 76, 91, 93, 95, 98, 99, 100, 101, 172, 267, 268, 286, 302, 303, 304, 306, 312, 314, 315, 318, 344, 347
Apollinaris, MPat, 362
al-Aqraʿ ibn Ḥabis, 333
Arab Conquest, ch.2*passim*, 109–10, 259–62; *early post-conquest interactions*, 7, 24–25, 28, 39–44, 60, 147–9, 167–9, 184, 223, 222–5; *depictions of*, 109–12, 167–8
Arabization, 3, 14, 52, 71, 80, 82, 90, 92, 93–105, 107, 116, 133, 170, 193, 263, 290, 312, 314, 316, 327
Arbitration *see* Litigation
Arians, 54, 293
Armanios, F., 301, 304
Armenians, 11, 54, 56, 174, 270, 278, 294, 296, 374
al-Aṣbagh ibn ʿAbd al-ʿAzīz, gov., 66, 92, 311
Assaad, S.A., 301
ʿaṭāʾ, 65, 111, 126, 163, 324
ʿAṭā, secretary of gov. Ṣāliḥ ibn ʿAlī, 188
ʿAṭā ibn Shurāḥbīl, secretary of Abū al-ʿAwn, 244
ʿAthamina, K., 323, 341, 342, 343
Athanasios (pseudo-), *Canons*, 337, 363, 364
Athanasios I, Pat, 53, 85, 194, 237, 240, 352, 374, 377, 378
Athanasios IV "Sandēlāiā," Syr Pat, 353, 365
Athanasios Bar Gūmōyē, secretary, 39–44, 50, 116, 198, 225, 287–90, 356, 370
Athanasios bp of Qūṣ, 101, 307, 315
Atiya, A.S., 273, 306, 307, 313, 337, 380
Awad, H.A., 320
Awqāf (sg. *waqf*), 141, 239, 247, 376, 380
Ayad, B.A., 323
Ayoub, M. 301
ʿĀʾyshā bint Yūsuf, 66
Ayyūb ibn Shuraḥbīl, gov., 331
Ayyūbids, 49, 132, 226, 275, 295, 302
al-ʿAzīz, Fāṭimid caliph, 252

Babylon (Miṣr), 14, 18, 26, 161, 162, 284, 291
Bacharach, J.L., 320, 343
Badīr bp of Asyūṭ, 361
Badr al-Jamālī, general, 174, 379
Bagnall, R.S., 272, 273, 274, 276, 281, 289, 293, 326, 327, 329, 337, 338
al-Balādhurī, Aḥmad ibn Yaḥyā, 21, 31, 58, 111, 114, 115, 283, 284, 319, 320, 321, 331, 344, 355, 357
Balog, P., 319
Banaji, J., 272, 284, 294
Bannā *see* Wannā
Banū Taghlib, 108
Baptism/rebaptism, 44, 59, 61, 62, 301
Baptistery, 238, 381
Baqṭ (*pakton*), 196, 197, 201, 202, 355, 356
Bar Hebraeus, 303, 355–6, 373
Barnes, T.D., 273
Barrī, ʿA.K., 302, 341, 344

Barsanuphians, 14, 54, 63, 224, 298, 299
Bashear, S., 58, 274, 296, 341, 342
Bashmūr Revolts *see* Revolts
Basil, scribe, 310
Basilios bp of Nikiou, 294, 295
Basilios magistrate of Aphrodito, 81, 82, 147, 148, 305, 336
Bates, M.L., 320
Baths, 117–18
Battle at the Zab River, 187
Battle of Tours, 198
Bauer, W., 280
Baum, W., 296, 337
Baumeister, T., 330
Beaucamp, J., 337
Becker, C.H., 319, 335
Behnstedt, P., 311
Beihammer, A.D., 281
Bell, D.N., 281, 288–90, 295, 298, 299, 302, 307, 340, 350, 356, 359, 363, 365–7, 369, 370, 377
Bell, H.I., 284, 323, 335
Benjamin I, CPat, 7, 13, 17, 18–26, 40, 53, 56, 61, 92, 181, 226, 260–1, 276, 281, 282, 283, 285, 288, 293, 294, 364, 367, 375, 376, 377; *On Cana of Galilee*, 19, 23, 38, 276, 281, 282, 288, 293, 294, 364, 376; *Festal Letter*, 281, 375, 377
Benjamin, dcn, early 8th c., 92
Bernand, É., 378
Beshir, B.I., 355
Betz, H.D., 276
Bilingual(ism), 72, 82, 85, 91–2, 96, 102, 211, 302, 305, 307, 308, 310
Binggeli, A., 381
al-Bīrūnī, Abū Rayḥān, 132, 329
Bishai, W., 310, 311
Bishay ibn Shinūda, scribe, 104
Bishop(ric) of Miṣr, 47, 48, 63, 211, 218, 220, 358, 359, 363, 364, 366, 367
Bishops, 215–8; *not considered for patriarch*, 217; *jurisdiction* 217, 358–9, 366
Bishr ibn Ṣafwān, 341
Biyamā, 189–91
Blau, J., 313
Bolman, E.S., 277
Bonneau, D., 283, 377
Bonner, M., 274, 324
Bonosos, general, 25
Book of Chrism, 359, 362
Book of Daniel, 106
Bosworth, C.E., 274, 287, 346, 350
Bradshaw, P., 374
Brakke, D., 374
Brakmann, H., 275
Bramoullé, D., 340
Bremmer, J.N., 292, 302, 304
Brett, M., 305, 357
Brock, S.P., 279, 347, 348, 351, 374
Brooks, E.W., 353
Brown, P., 272, 365, 380, 381
Brunschvig, R., 281
Bukām of Būrah, 45–46, 50, 228
al-Bukhārī, Abū ʿAbdallāh, 342
Bulliet, R.W., 295, 296
Būlus al-Būshī bp of Miṣr, 348, 359
Burmester, O.H.E., 308, 309, 337, 339
Burstein, S.M., 307
Butler, A.J., 16, 18, 20, 24, 281–4, 318, 381
Byzantine Egypt/Period/Rule: 1, 2, 17, 21–6, 31–6, 39, 41, 54, 55–6, 58, 90–1, 106, 115, 129, 133–4, 159, 161, 163, 179, 190–1, 198–9, 210, 223, 226, 235, 255, 262, 265, 268, 270; *historiography*, 17, 21, 22, 31–2, 91, 106, 133–4, 178–9, 188, 191, 255, 262; *also see* Nationalism

Cahen, C., 289, 317, 323, 324, 344
Cairo, 162, 205–9, 212, 221, 246, 277, 358–62, 367, 381, 382

Calder, N., 342
Calendars/Chronology, 127–35, 238–9
Callahan, A.D., 275
Cameron, A., 272, 274, 277, 381
Camplani, A., 312, 330, 374, 375
Canrad, M., 381
Chabot, J.-B., 337
Chagnon, L., 16, 281
Chaine, M., 315
Chalcedon, Council/Schism of, xii, 12, 13, 17, 22, 34, 51–5, 76, 80, 83, 84, 87, 89, 109, 150, 178, 191, 195, 204, 206, 221, 222, 232, 235, 256, 258, 278, 280, 306, 309: *Neo-Chalcedonianism*, 279
Charfi, A., 377
Charles Martel, 198
Cheïkho, L., 288–91
Children, 47, 48, 65, 94, 95, 99, 100, 125, 155, 183, 190, 215, 217, 249, 287, 299, 365
"Children of the [Patriarchal] Cell," 86, 362
Choksy, J.K., 281, 323, 346
Christianization, 53–4, 154, 221
Christodoulos *see* Khrisṭūdulūs
Chronicle of 1234, 19, 20, 22, 224, 282, 283, 289, 290, 312, 320, 321, 322, 357, 364, 368, 369, 376
Chronicle of 640, 374
Chronicle of 819, 295, 320
Chronicle of John of Nikiou, 19, 23, 25, 26, 27, 30, 31, 32, 36, 59, 185, 214, 279, 282–9, 291, 293, 294, 297, 298, 302, 318, 328, 346, 347, 350, 354, 362, 363, 366, 369
Chronicle of Sīrt, 374
Chronicle of Zuqnīn, 293, 294, 301, 318, 324, 352, 356, 365, 374
Chronicon Paschale, 294, 326
Church of the East, "Nestorians," East Syrians, 11, 56, 150, 151, 236, 279, 337, 373, 374
Churches; 40–1, 55–56, 112, 115–16, 221–31, 239–41, 289, 294, 369–71, 376; *building and restoration*, 225–31; (*Coptic*): Angelion (Evangelion) in Alex., 42, 215, 307; St. John in Damascus, 112; St. Johnin Cairo, 381; John the Baptist, 381; Mary Magdalene in Jerusalem, 45; St. Mark in Alex., 38, 215, 226, 285; St. Mary, 371; St. Michael in Alex., 186, 228; St. Menas, 214; St. Mina at Maryūṭ, 239–240, 376; Abū Mīnā's in Ḥamrā', 227; Church at Maḥras Qustantīn, 371; Mu'allaqa (The Suspended Church), 86, 205, 207, 208, 209, 212, 228, 251, 252, 307, 360, 361, 371; Abū Sarja (Sergios), 205, 207, 209, 360, 363–5; Church at Shubra Khayma, 247; St. Shinūda at Miṣr, 216; St. Merkurios at Miṣr, 229–30, 252; Abū Qīr, 370; Peter in Fusṭāṭ, 244; Virgin at Ḥārat al-Rūm, 205, 209, 291; (*Melkite*): 224, 294–5, 368, 369, 373–4; Mār Jirjis/*Kanīsat al-farrāshīn*, 370; St. Menas, 373; St. Sabas, 373
Chuvin, P., 304, 372
Clover, F., 272, 344
Cohen, M.R., 277, 343, 358, 372,377, 381, 382
Coinage, 113–15
Cöln, F.J., 314, 337
Communal Autonomy, 149–54
Connerton, P., 285
Conrad, L.I., 274, 282, 319, 343, 344
Conrad, M., 301
Constantine, Emp, 16, 178, 180, 187, 188, 243, 247, 259, 350, 351, 357, 378
Constantine V, Emp, 351
Constantine bp of Asyūṭ, 90, 310

Constantine bp of Miṣr (Melkite then Coptic), 63, 280
Constantinople, 46, 56
Conversion, ch. 4, 42, 94–5, 170, 175, 217, 223–4, 263; *converting clergy*, 62–64; *women*, 65; *intermarriage*, 65; *coercion*, 66–67; *converts to Christianity*, 67, 174–5, 345; *incentives*, 44, 62, 65, 74–5, 77
Cook, M., 274, 316, 334
Coptic – Melkite relations, 55–56, 228, 235–41, 294
Coptic – Syrian relations, 191–4, 207, 352
Coptic communication beyond Egypt, 184, 197–9, 201
"Coptic" Revolts *see* Revolts
Copts/Coptic, 21, 26, 112, 118, 125, 129, 245, 258, 274, 284, 327; *earliest use*, 352
Coquin, R.-G., 310, 313, 314, 337, 341, 352, 359
Corriente, F., 311
Cortese, D., 323
"Council of a Hundred [Bishops]," 14, 359
Courbage, Y., 295
Covenant of ʿUmar, 171, 225, 230, 343
Creswell, K.A.C., 321
Crone, P., 274, 297, 322, 324, 342
Crum, W.E., 273, 290
Crusades, 161, 183, 226, 306
Cursus, 161–4
Cyril *see also* Kyrillus
Cyril I, Pat., 6, 11, 13, 14, 85, 53, 240, 280, 352, 377
Cyril of Scythopolis, 54, 299

Daftary, F., 346
Damian I, CPat.,13, 85, 281, 307, 312, 347, 353, 362, 375
Daniel of Scetis, st, 346, 348
David (Dawūd) the treasurer (*qusṭāl*), 316
Davis, D., 296
Davis, S.J., 278, 292, 351, 365
De Ste. Croix, G., 278
De Clercq, C., 314
Deacons and Archdeacons, 6, 47, 48, 69, 73, 86, 92, 102, 149, 156, 175, 213–5, 217, 220, 238, 290, 307, 316, 329, 354, 362–6; *secular roles*, 102, 156
Décobert, Christian, 276, 296, 314, 344, 358, 359
Delattre, A., 336
Della Vida, G.L., 351
Demetrios I, Pat, xiii, 53, 237, 259, 293, 299, 357
Demographics, 2, 4, 12–15, 51, 54, 58, 76, 120, 127, 133–4, 144, 156, 172, 197, 223, 263–5, 270, 296, 366
Den Heijer, J., 6, 275, 276, 282, 283, 353, 359, 360, 361, 373, 374, 381
Dennett, D., 59, 292, 296, 297, 317, 323
Dhimmā, (*dhimmī, dhimmī*s), 27, 71, 108, 112, 123, 133, 150, 151, 152, 171, 222, 230, 231, 234, 241, 267, 269, 274, 339, 372, 381; *Ahl al-dhimmā*, 78, 112
Dhull Regulations, 171, 343
Diaconal hymns and responses, 87, 214–5, 308
Didaskalia, 96
Difnār, 96, 270, 313, 379
Dihqāns, 71
Dīnah of Maḥallat Danyāl, notable, 49
Dionysios of Tel-Maḥrē, Pat of Antioch, 125, 193, 282, 351; *see also History of Dionysios/Chronicle of 1234*
Dioskoros I, CPat, xii, 6, 13, 85, 88, 293, 352
Dioskoros II, CPat, 361.
Dioskoros of Aphrodito, 55, 276, 294
Dioskoros, neo-martyr, 69
Dīwān, 39, 43, 44, 111, 116, 126, 146, 163, 168, 169, 289, 290, 305, 341

Doctrine/dogma/theology, 10–13, 22, 33, 55, 56–7, 72, 73–4, 75, 84, 85, 87, 89, 91, 96, 101, 179, 191–4, 204, 209–12, 232, 234, 235, 238, 241, 243, 245, 253, 256, 258, 261, 264, 265, 277, 278, 279, 280, 286, 293, 298, 303, 307, 308, 310, 354, 377, 348, 373, 379
Donner, F.M., 109, 274, 281, 283, 318, 319, 330, 331, 332, 344
Dous, W.B.R., 377
al-Dumaḥis ibn al-ʿAzīz al-Kinānī, 120
Dunn, M.C., 304, 323, 324, 325, 342
Duri, ʿA.ʿA., 274
Dvornik, F., 346

East Syrians *see* Church of the East
Ebied, R.Y., 300, 353, 372
Edelby, N., 149–52, 337
Egeria, 4th c. pilgrim, 375
Ekloga, 151
Ekthesis, 57
Elias, gov. of Alex., 46
Elites, chs. 3 and 7 *passim*, 59, 71; *rural* 146–9; *female*, 49
Embolē, 163, 165
Emmel, S., 307, 368, 378, 380
Era of Diocletian, 129–133, 194, 328, 329
Era of the Martyrs, 131–4, 269–70, 327, 328, 329, 330
Ergene, B., 301
Erlich, H., 356, 377
Ethiopia(n), 15, 34, 53, 58, 67, 177, 179, 191, 192, 194–203, 236, 287, 352, 356, 337, 354, 357, 377
Eucharist(ic), 87, 96, 192, 215, 248, 295, 309, 352, 354, 364, 368
Eusebios of Caesarea, xiii, 178–9, 180, 188, 243, 244, 350, 351, 356, 378
Eutychian(s), xii, 54, 279
Eutychios, MPat, xii, 5, 27, 32, 45, 46, 83, 99, 132, 190, 222, 225, 242, 284, 298, 328, 379; *Naẓm al-jawhar*, xiii, 27, 32, 45, 83, 132, 225, 242, 284, 289, 291, 292, 297, 298, 300, 305, 306, 314, 319, 321, 325, 328, 340, 341, 343, 351, 355, 360, 361, 368, 369, 370, 376, 378, 379, 381
Evagrios, 54, 368
Evelyn White, H.G., 281, 329, 344, 345, 350, 352, 361, 367, 371, 381
Ezekiel, East Syr. Catholicos, 374

Fahm Tribe, 140, 145, 331, 332, 334
Fahmy, A.M., 340
Farag, L., 353
Faraji, S., 354
Faramā (Pelusium), 23, 24, 86, 115
Fargues, P., 295
Farhadian, C.E., 292
Fasting/feasting, 74, 187, 193, 232, 235–8, 249–51, 253, 374, 375, 381; *Lent*, 219, 235–8, 367, 374, 375; *Fast of Nineveh*, 193, 235–38; *Fast of Herakleios*, 193, 236–8, 259; *anti-fasts*, 236–8
Fāṭimids, 3, 49, 67, 91, 131, 132, 137, 142, 162, 174, 182, 190, 201, 206, 212, 213, 225, 229, 230, 268, 275, 277, 287, 295, 304, 305, 315, 317, 323, 325, 333, 334, 340, 349, 355, 357–9, 369, 372, 376, 380, 381
Fattal, A., 149, 152, 301, 337, 339, 343, 350, 355, 368–71
fay', 110, 126, 298, 318
Fearon, J.D., 373
Feast (*ʿĪd*): 238, 358, 374, 380, 382; *of the Cross*, 244–5, 380; *of the Martyr*, 246–7, 265; *Ghitās* (Epiphany), 265
Febroniaof Nisibis, st, 351
Fedwick, P.J., 308
Fibrūniyā, st., 190–1, cf. Febronia
Filtas, J.M., 312
Firdawsī, Ḥakīm Abū al-Qāsim, 296

Forand, P., 355
Foss, C., 320, 332, 341, 342
Fowden, G., 346
Frantz-Murphy, G., 119, 123, 276, 288, 296, 297, 302, 305, 323, 325, 336, 338–40, 373
Fraser, P.M., 17, 23, 281–3
Frend, W.H.C., 10, 273, 278, 279, 283, 346
Friedmann, Y., 295, 300, 301, 304
Frumentios (Salama I), bp/missionary Ethiopia,194
Fusṭāṭ, 82, 115, 121, 122, 124, 125, 137, 140, 147, 148, 155, 162–4, 168, 185, 205–9, 212, 218, 220, 223, 226, 228, 229, 244, 320, 325, 336, 340, 341, 349, 351, 358, 359, 364
Futūḥ miṣr see Ibn ʿAbd al-Ḥakam

Gabra, G., 313, 379
Gabriel I, CPat, 360
Gabriel II Ibn Turayk, CPat, 96, 151, 201, 209–12, 337, 359, 364, 375, 380
Gagos, T., 154, 338, 373
Gainites, 45, 199, 298, 299, 363
Garland, L., 347
Gascou, J., 294, 341, 368, 370
Gaubert, C., 315
Gayraud, R.-P., 340
Geary, P., 29, 285
Geertz, C., 255, 382
Gellens, S.I., 296, 316
George, st, 175, 379
George bp of Ahnās, 367
George bp of Ṭaḥa, 367
George bp (Barsanuphian then Coptic), 63, 64
George, 7th c. patr.nominee, 42, 184, 214, 289, 299, 363
George, Archd., *see* Jirja
George, dcn of Sakhā, 214
George, dcn, 9th c., 86
George, Nubian prince, 201, 357
George, Patr. of Antioch, 365
George, prefect (*eparchos*), 43, 284
Gershoni, I., 356, 377
Gervers, M., 295, 296
Ghiyār, 171, 267–8, 344
Gibb, H.A.R., 319, 331
Gil, M., 277, 325
Goehring, J.E., 272, 275, 303, 306, 310, 358, 381
Goitein, S.D., 152, 277, 336, 347, 348
Gonis, N., 308, 317, 318, 321, 327, 341
Gottheil, R.J.H., 372
Grabar, O., 317, 319, 321, 322
Gray, P.T.R., 278, 279
Graf, G., 310, 353
Green, A.H., 300, 315, 339
Gregory bp of Kaïs, 214, 218, 290, 292
Grierson, P., 320
Griffel, F., 293, 301
Griffith, S.H., 269, 280, 291, 302, 303, 306, 322, 354, 372, 373, 380, 381
Griggs, W.C., 292, 359, 364
Grillmeier, A., 278, 279, 280, 293, 298, 308, 354
Grohmann, A., 65, 70, 276, 301, 327, 329, 330
Grossmann, P., 341, 377
Grypeou, E., 274, 282, 287, 314
Guenther, A.M., 286, 318

Haarmann, U., 304, 316, 317, 322, 380
Haas, C., 358
Ḥabīb Mikhāʾīl ibn Budayr al-Damanhūrī, 96
al-Ḥāfiẓ, Fāṭimid claiph, 201, 376
Ḥāfṣ ibn al-Walīd ibn Yūsuf al-Hadramī, gov., 64, 139, 141, 331, 332
Hainthaler, T., 293
al-Hajjāj ibn Yūsuf, 298
Hak, D., 304

al-Ḥākim bi Amr Allāh, 46, 67, 99, 117, 133, 134, 171, 175, 183, 200, 226, 229, 269, 301, 314, 323, 345, 346, 348, 352, 365, 366, 368, 370, 371
Halbwachs, M., 285
Haldon, J., 317, 341
Halm, H., 355
al-Ḥamdānī, Abū Muḥammad al-Ḥasan ibn Aḥmad ibn Ya'qūb, 173, 344
Hamilton, R.W., 321
Hanīdā bint Sarī, 66
Ḥanẓala ibn Ṣafwān al-Kalibī, 332
Hardy, E.R., 273, 294, 307
Harries, J., 338
Harthama ibn al-A'yan, general, 122
Hārūn al-Rashīd, caliph, 45, 123, 124, 227–29, 231, 334, 369, 371
Harvey, S.A., 347, 351
Hasan, Y.F., 342, 355, 357, 358
Ḥātim ibn Ḥarthama, gov., 124
Hawting, G.R., 316, 319
Henner, J., 308, 309
Henotikon, 57
Heraklas, Pat, 218
Herakleios, Emp., 22, 25, 56, 61, 114, 179, 180, 193, 235–38, 259, 283, 347, 375
Heresy, Upper Egypt/Medieval, 73
Herrin, J., 326
Hierarchies, 12–15, 239–41, 366
Hill, D.R., 318
Hinds, M., 334, 355
Hishām, caliph, 144, 145, 165, 225, 239, 301, 332
Hishām (*Iszem*) ibn Bīlal, 104
Histories of the Holy Church, 6, 13
Historiography: 2–3, 5, 8–9, 31–32, 91, 109–112, 268–71; *anti-Chalcedonian*, 21, 24–26, 28–30, 33–36; *of Byzantine rule*, 17, 21, 22, 31–2, 36, 91, 106, 133–4, 178–9, 188, 191, 255, 262
History of Dionysios [of Tel-Maḥrē] see *Chronicle of 1234*
History of the Churches and Monasteries of Egypt, 49, 190–1, 226, 252, 266, 284, 287, 292, 296, 298, 300, 303, 304, 310, 322, 328, 345, 351, 352, 354, 356–9, 363–6, 368, 370, 373, 375–9, 381, 382
History of the Patriarchs [HP], xii, xiii, 4, 5, 7, 19, 21–3, 36, 38, 39, 42, 45, 57, 61–3, 69, 73, 92, 96, 101, 115, 119–20, 125–6, 131, 174, 175, 177, 183, 187, 187–91, 197, 200, 202, 203, 206, 210, 211, 213, 215, 216, 220, 227–9, 236, 240, 244, 245, 248, 249, 252, 259, 275–381 *passim*; *Composition and recensions*, 5–7
Hodgson, M.G.S., 273, 319
"Holy Man," 157, 249, 253, 298, 380
Howard-Johnston, J., 274, 296
Hoyland, R., 19, 23–24, 274, 281, 282, 283, 286, 288, 301, 318, 335, 337, 339, 340, 341
Ḥulwān, 162, 185, 205, 206, 207, 223, 226, 321, 341, 359
Humfress, C., 337, 338
Humphreys, R.S., 272, 344
al-Ḥurr ibn Yūsuf, gov., 139, 331
al-Ḥusayn ibn Jamīl, gov., 123
Hymns, 13, 88–89, 222, 309, 309, 315, 369, 377; *E Agape*, 87; *Christos Anesti*, 88; Gradual Psalm, 89, 309; *Monogenēs*, 347–8; *E Parthenos*, 88; *Tenēn*, 88; *Trisagion*, 88, 235, 278, 309, 374; *Triadon*, 315; also *see* Diaconal hymns *and* responses

Iannē, 62–63, 299
Ibn 'Abd al-Ḥakam, 4, 19–21, 23, 24, 26, 27, 30, 31, 35, 58, 59, 110, 141, 162, 171, 189, 200, 226, 245, 295–9, 301, 302, 305, 318, 319,

321, 322, 332, 333, 340–4, 351, 355, 357, 369, 370, 371, 378, 379, 381; *historiography/themes*, 21, 24, 26–8, 31, 35, 59, 342
Ibn al-ʿAssāl, al-Asʿad, 96
Ibn al-ʿAssāl, al-Ṣafī, 151, 237, 337, 375
Ibn al-Kindī, ʿUmar ibn Muḥammad, 282, 296, 327, 340, 377, 378, 381
Ibn Ḥawqal, Muḥammad Abū al-Qāsim, 323, 327, 343, 377, 378
Ibn Jubayr, Abū al-Ḥusayn Muḥammad, 323, 324, 378
Ibn Kabar *see* Abū al-Barakāt ibn Kabar
Ibn Labnan, convert, 310
Ibn Mammātī, 327, 381
Ibn al-Qulzūmī *see* Yūḥannā ibn Ṣāʿīd al-Qulzūmī
Ibn al-Rāhib *see* Abū Shākir
Ibn Sabbāʿ, Yūḥannā ibn Abī Zakariyyā, 96, 248, 252, 270, 289, 290, 302, 313, 350, 356, 370, 371, 377, 378, 379, 380, 381
Ibn Sallām *see* Abū ʿUbayd al-Qāsim ibn Sallām
Ibn Taymiyya, Taqī al-Dīn Aḥmad, 231, 370, 372
Ibn Yarbuʿ al-Fazarī, 43, 116
Ibn Yūnus al-Miṣrī, 271, 344, 381, 382
Ibn Zūlāq, 1, 304, 340, 377–9
Ibrahīm king of Nubia, 202
Ibrāhīm ibn Bishr, notable/bp of Minūf al-ʿUlyā, 186, 299, 360, 365
Ibrahīm ibn Muḥammad ... ibn Abī Ṭālib, 324
Ibrahīm ibn Sawīrus, 44
Iconoclasm, 46, 117, 278, 322, 352
Īliyyā ibn Manṣūr, MPat of Jerusalem, 361
Ilyās ibn Yazīd, gov., 291
Immerzeel, M., 277, 312, 315, 353, 375
Immigration/settlement (Arab), 52 58, 71, 93, 120, 127, 143–5, 157, 163, 165, 166, 169, 170, 192, 266, 296, 310, 341
ʿImran ibn ʿAbd al-Raḥmān al-Ḥasanī, 333
Innemée, K., 353, 355
Intermarriage, 65–66, 94, 301
ʿĪsā ibn Abī ʿAṭa', 332
ʿĪsā ibn ʿĀmir, 240
ʿĪsā ibn Manṣūr, 125
ʿĪsā ibn Yazīd al-Julūdī, gov., 125
Isaac I, CPat, (and *Life of Isaac*), 40–43, 61, 62, 68, 69, 85, 153, 184, 185, 186, 197, 198, 205, 214, 215, 218, 226, 281, 288, 289, 290, 295, 298, 299, 302, 307, 340, 346, 350, 356, 359, 363, 365, 366, 367, 369, 370, 377
Isaac, secretary, 41–4, 198, 225, 289, 290, 370
Isaac bp of Ḥarrān, 217
Isaac bp of Tinnīs, 358
Isaiah bp, 365, 366
Isbādīqun, 214, 215, 364
Isḥāq ibn Andunā, notable/ bp of Wasīm, 45–48, 220, 292, 299, 363, 367
Isḥāq ibn Damāna, 94
Isḥāq ibn Sulaymān, gov., 122
Ishmaelites, 283
Iskander, J., 295, 297, 314
Islamization, 103, 107–18, 170, 245–7, 295, 296, 297, 304, 312, 314, 316, 317, 355
Ismāʿīl ibn al-Yasah al-Kindī, 334
Ismaʿīl *mawlā* Aḥmad ibn Marwān al-Qurayshī, 66
Iʿtirāf al-abā', 96, 312, 313, 354
ʿIyaḍ ibn ʿUbayd Allāh al-Azdī, gov./ *qāḍī*, 333

Jabbur, J.S., 344
Jacob Baradaeos, 13, 192
Jacob of Serug, 368
Jacobites, xii, 10, 192, 200, 225, 239, 352, 360
Jansen, J.J.G., 304

Jarry, J., 367
Jawhar, general, 137, 213
Jerome, st, 215
Jirja, Archd., 6, 213, 362
Jizya, 44, 59, 64, 74, 77, 104, 107–9, 112, 113, 119, 258, 267, 297–9, 317, 318, 323
"John" *see also* "Yu'annīs" *and* "Yūḥannā"
John "the Writer," monk, 6, 131–2, 302, 329, 345
John bar Penkāyē, 347
John bp of Nikiou, see *Chronicle of John of Nikiou*
John bp of Old Dongola, 202
John bp of Pshati, 218
John bp of Sakhā, 363
John bp of Samannūd, 8th c., 63, 307
John bp of Terenouti *see* Iannē
John III (pseudo-), *Questions of Theodore*, and the *Disputation*, 233, 373
John III, CPatr, 6, 40–42, 61, 62, 85, 153, 184, 185, 214, 225, 226, 275, 298, 307, 338, 350, 362, 364, 370
John IV, CPatr, 218, 226, 227, 228, 269, 329, 365, 366
John Khame, st, 299, 320–1
John Malalas, 32, 54, 280, 294, 351, 374
John Moschos, 55
John of Ephesos, 179, 298, 346, 354
John of Phanijōit, neo-martyr, 246, 301, 302, 315, 380
John of Ṣā, notable, 44, 62, 65, 77, 299
John of Samannūd *see* John III
John of Sanhūt, martyr, 246, 380
John of Shmūn, 84, 89, 90, 306, 310
John the Almsgiver, MPat, 55, 58, 61, 224, 294, 295, 338
John the Baptist, 313, 307, 368, 373
John the Deacon, 8th c., 6
John the Little, st, 371
John V, CPatr, 360, 362
John VI, CPatr, 362
John XV, CPatr, 360
John, dcn/Archimandrite, 363
John, Hegumen of the Enaton, 185, 364
John, monk/convert mid-7th c., 297
John, Pat of Antioch, 346, 348
Johnson, D.W., 272, 275, 306, 307
Johnson, M.E., 374
Jones, A.H.M., 273, 274, 292, 337
Jones, J.M.B., 341
Judaism/Jewish, 9–10, 53, 72, 79, 82, 99, 105, 112, 113, 115–8, 149, 151, 157–8, 178–9, 181, 183, 232, 234, 241–5, 248, 250–3, 262, 267, 271, 277, 316, 339, 347, 348, 359, 369, 376, 381
Julian of Halikarnassos, 277, 279, 293, 363
Julian, priest/missionary, 195, 354
Julianists *see* Gainites
Jumlat al-qawānīn, 96
Jurisprudence: Ḥanafī, 318, 334, 382; Ḥanbalī, 382; Malikī, 264, 382; Shafī'ī, 264, 382
Justin I, Emp., 55, 287, 346
Justin II, Emp., 47
Justinian, Emp., 13, 35, 133, 180, 195, 204, 222, 347, 348, 354, 360
Juynboll, G.H.A., 334

Ka'b ibn Ḍinnā, 141
Kaegi, W.E., 281, 283, 284
Kahle, P.E., 300, 348–9
Kane, T.A., 293, 366
Karīm al-Dawla ibn 'Ubayd ibn Qurrūṣ al-Jullāl, notable, 377
Kasser, R., 311
Kaydur Naṣr ibn 'Abd Allāh, gov., 126
Kazhdan, A., 338
Keiko, O., 325
Kennedy, H., 273, 281, 286, 306, 324, 331, 333, 340, 343, 344
Khaīl bp. of Sakhā, 175, 345

Khaīl I, CPat, 6, 62, 63, 131, 181, 188, 190, 199, 200, 202, 206, 207, 216, 217, 220, 240, 244, 276, 298, 299, 300, 307, 350–3, 362, 364, 367, 377, 379
Khaīl II, CPat, 6, 350, 360, 363
Khaīl III, CPat, 48–49, 275, 309, 359, 360
Khaīl IV, CPat, 6, 209, 210, 356, 358, 361
Khaīl V, CPat, 362, 380
Khālid ibn al-Walīd, 112
Khalidi, T., 274, 318
Khalīfa ibn Khayyāṭ, 111, 319, 320, 330, 331
Kharāj, 39, 107–13, 119, 121–4, 132, 137, 138, 139, 144, 145, 166, 167, 291, 297, 317, 318, 325, 329, 330, 354; *ṣāḥib al-kharāj*, 119, 137–9, 145, 291, 332; *dīwān al-kharāj*, 39; also see Abū Yūsuf, Abū ʿUbayd, and Yaḥyā ibn Ādam
Khayr ibn Nuʿaym, *qāḍī*, 158
Khoury, R.G., 331, 333
Khrisṭūdulūs (Christodoulos), CPat., 6, 96, 97, 202, 208–10, 312, 338, 352, 358, 360, 362, 367, 375, 376
Khurāsāniyya, 121, 122, 188, 190, 200, 259, 379
Khusraw II Parvez, 58
Kinanā ibn Bishr ibn Salāman, 144
al-Kindī, Abū ʿUmar Muḥammad ibn Yūsuf, 4, 117, 118, 141, 124, 125, 141, 157, 158, 284, 289, 297, 300, 301, 302, 304, 305, 311, 319, 321–6, 331, 336, 338–43, 370, 371
King, G.R.D., 277, 322
Kister, M., 344
Kitāb al-dūrr al-thamīn see *K.al-īḍāḥ*
Kitāb al-īḍāḥ (Pseudo-Sawīrus), 73, 99, 101, 233, 303, 314, 315, 372
Kitāb misbāḥ al-ʿaql see Sawīrus ibn al-Muqaffaʿ
Klein, K.L., 285
Kosmas *see* Quzmā(n)
Krause, M., 273, 303, 313
Kubiak, W.B., 340
Kyriakos bp of Nubia, 202
Kyriakos king of Nubia, 199, 200, 357
Kyrillus II, CPat, 6, 7, 93, 96, 181, 206, 209, 210, 309, 312, 358, 360, 362
Kyrillus III, Ibn Laqlaq, CPat, 219, 220, 313, 337–339, 359, 366
Kyrillus IV, CPat, 88, 308
Kyrillus VI, 258
Kyros, MPat-prefect, 19–22, 24, 27, 56, 57, 133, 222, 223, 283, 284, 286, 294, 295
Kyros bp of Jawjar, 365
Kyros bp of Nikiou, 56

Labib, S.Y., 307, 374
Labor and Pay, 163–5
Lactantius, 350
Łajtar, A., 329
Lamoreaux, J.C., 286, 287, 303, 318, 338, 348, 349, 373
Lane-Poole, S., 282
Language: ch. 5*passim*, 133, 90–91, 255–8
Lapidus, I.M., 297, 305
Lashane, 37, 130, 142, 147, 149, 153, 155–7, 328, 335, 338
Lasker, D.J., 377
Late Antiquity, 2, 9, 32, 34, 50, 54, 76, 114, 115, 117, 118, 129, 149, 151, 154, 162, 174, 184, 189, 191, 204, 212, 214, 222, 232, 242, 258–9, 269, 272, 277, 300, 305, 326, 338, 365
al-Layth ibn Faḍl, gov., 123, 325, 333
al-Layth ibn Saʿd, 318, 371
Leder, S., 337
Leeder, S.H., 234, 373, 378
Leiser, G., 312
Leithy, T., el-, 305

Lent *see* Fasting
Leontios of Neapolis, 294, 295, 338
Letter of Pisentios, 33–34, 287
Lev, Y., 305, 324, 342, 343, 356, 381
Levtzion, N., 304, 316
Lichtenstadter, I., 343
Liebeschuetz, W., 365
Life of Isaac of Alexandria see Isaac I
Litigation, 87, 154–7
Little, D.P., 305
Liturgical language(s), 88–91, 257–8
Liturgical manuscripts, 87–88, 98–9
Løkkegaard, F., 318, 355
Longinos, priest/missionary, 195
Loprieno, A., 316
Lowenthal, D., 285
Luisier, P., 310
Lutfi, H., 304, 380

MacCoull, L.S.B., 276, 287, 294, 305, 307, 315, 327, 329, 338, 339, 348, 349, 368, 378, 380
Macomber, W.F., 308
Madlajā/Madlij Arabs, 124, 127, 174, 175
Maher, S., 306
Maḥfūẓ ibn Sulaymān, 123
al-Mājīd Fāris, 345
Makarios the Great, 45
Makarios I, CPat, 209, 210, 359, 360
Makarios II, CPat, 209, 359, 362
Makdisi, G., 312, 331
al-Makīn Jīrjis "the Younger," 14th c., 215, 237, 238, 364, 374, 375, 376
Malaty, T.Y., 337
al-Malik al-Nāṣir Yūsuf ibn al-ʻAzīz, 174
Mamlūks, 71, 132, 173, 174, 182, 226, 247, 274, 275, 287, 301, 302, 305, 344, 349
al-Ma'mūn, caliph, 45, 124, 125, 193, 326, 351, 367, 369
Manicheans, 54, 84, 257, 293
al-Manṣūr, caliph, 69
Manṣūr ibn Salīm al-Jullāl, notable, 377
Manuel the Eunuch, general, 19
Maqāra ibn Sāth of Nabarūh, notable, 45, 228
Maqāra ibn Yu'annīs, secretary, 9th c., 49
Maqāra ibn Yūsuf, notable, 44–6, 50
al-Maqrīzī, Taqī al-Dīn Aḥmad, 115, 120, 125, 131, 132, 169, 173, 246, 247, 274, 283, 291, 296, 302, 304, 320–30, 332, 340–5, 351, 354, 360, 361, 362, 368, 369, 376, 378, 379, 380
Marā, convert(?) to Christianity, 174, 345
Marawān II, caliph, 133, 187, 188, 190, 191, 200, 201, 240, 350, 351
Marcian, Emp., 133, 180, 240, 347
Mariyya al-Qibṭiyya, 58, 59, 296, 300
Mariyya, Roman concubine, 301
Mark (Murqus) II, CPat, 48, 61, 63, 181, 228, 298, 350
Mark (Murqus) III ibn Zaʻrah, CPat, 218, 353, 360, 362, 365
Mark bp of Faramā, 86
Mark bp of Tinnīs, 86
Mark, Archd., 214
Mark, dcn, 214
Martinez, F.J., 287, 314
al-Masʻūdī, ʻAlī ibn al-Ḥusayn, 274, 282, 327, 357, 372, 377, 378, 380
Maslama ibn Mukhallad al-Anṣārī, gov., 138, 140, 370
Maurice, Emp., 296
Mawhūb ibn Manṣūr, 6, 7, 96, 210, 211, 213, 275, 362
Mawlā (*mawālī*), 59, 66, 72, 81, 93, 121, 124, 148, 168, 169, 297, 301, 304, 343
Mayerson, P., 325, 341
McCarthy, D., 326
McPherson, J.W., 304, 380
Meimaris, Y.E., 330

Meinardus, O.F.A., 182, 273, 279, 348, 349, 354, 359, 361, 366
Meletians, 53, 54, 62, 78, 257, 293, 330
Melkites: xii, xiii, 3, 5, 12–15, 17, 19, 20, 27, 28, 35, 38–41, 44–6, 49, 50, 52, 55, 58, 60, 64, 82–4, 87, 88, 90, 98, 100, 133, 190, 195, 199, 206, 210, 215, 222–5, 228, 232, 234–41, 246, 256, 258, 260, 264, 265, 280, 286, 298, 306, 352, 355, 359, 361, 366, 368, 369, 370, 373–4, 376, 377; *see also* Monasteries, Churches, *and* Coptic-Melkite Relations
Memory Studies, 17, 29–30, 34–6, 285
Menas, monk, 6
Menas, gov. Lower Egypt, 288
Menas, notable, 365
Menas bp of Bahnasā, 367
Menas bp of Memphis, 244
Menas bp of Tana, 367
Menesōn, *chartularius*, 43
Meyendorff, J., 56, 273, 279, 294, 346
Michael bp of Damietta, 303
Michael bp of Miṣr, 218
Michael bp of Tinnīs, 5, 6, 7, 73, 183, 210, 220, 275, 352, 361, 365, 367
Michael ibn Bukām, 45
Michael the Syrian, Syr Pat, 279, 281, 282, 300, 318, 321, 325, 361, 376
Michael, Archangel, 228, 242, 245, 378
Miles, G.C., 320, 321
Miller, D.E., 336, 343
Mīnā I, CPat, 6
Mīnā II, CPat, 49, 218, 361
Mīnā ibn Baqīrā, rebel leader, 324; cf. Abū Mīnā
Moeller, C., 279
Monasteries, 22, 44, 48, 53, 55, 57, 67, 112, 147, 174–6, 202, 208, 217, 218, 221, 222, 226, 227, 229, 231, 268, 270, 291, 301, 313, 344, 345, 350, 351, 359, 361, 362, 367, 368, 370, 374; (*Coptic*): Apa Apollo, 349, 370; Enaton (*dayr al-zujāj*), 185, 219, 364, 367; Epiphanios, 156; Apa Hierax, 363; John Khame, 320; Makarios, 175, 207–10, 112, 219, 226, 346, 360–2, 364, 367; Menas church/complex, 239–41, 345; Metras, 22, 57; Samuel at Qalamūn, 57, 295; (*Syrian*), 192, 352; (*Melkite*), 368, 373–4: St. Catherin's, 368; John the Baptist, 368, 373; Quṣayr, 207, 359, 368
Monenergism, 28, 56, 61, 110
"Monophysite," erroneous application to the Copts, 10–12, 277–80
Monothelitism, 28, 56, 61, 110
Morelli, F., 383
Morimoto, K., 81, 289, 290, 305, 317, 318, 319, 323, 324, 338, 340, 341, 343
Morony, M., 74, 281, 288, 296, 302, 304, 334, 335, 337, 344, 356, 374
Morton, A.H., 319
Moses bp of Awsīm (or Wasīm), 6, 216, 244, 299, 379
Moses of Abydos, 293
Moses of Nisibis, 192
Moses, OT Prophet, 232, 245, 295
Mōshē bar Kēphā, 309
Mosque (*masjid*), 116, 130, 149, 158, 162, 164, 222, 225, 295, 296, 321, 328, 339, 342, 343, 359, 367, 368, 370, 371
Moussa, M., 273, 314, 360, 362
Mouton, J.-M., 295, 315
Mu'adhdhin, 149, 230, 336
Muʿawiya ibn Abī Sufyān, caliph, 296
Muʿāwiya ibn Mālik ibn Ḍamḍam al-Judhāmī, gov., 122
al-Muʿizz, Fāṭimid caliph, 137, 229, 249, 251, 381

al-Mughirā ibn Salīm, 335
al-Muhajir ibn Abī al-Muthannī al-Tujībī, 144
Muhājirūn, 163, 165, 341–3
Muḥammad, Prophet, 21, 58, 67, 108, 114, 116, 144, 134, 163, 261, 284
Muḥammad ibn ʿAbd al-Malik, gov., 331
Muḥammad ibn ʿAbdallāh, *qāḍī*, 219, 220
Muḥammad ibn Masrūq, *qāḍī*, 334, 339
al-Muktafī, caliph, 242
Munier, H., 313
Müller, C.D.G., 273, 309, 349, 377
Muqaddima, 96, 313
Muqaṭṭam, 207, 241, 244, 249–53, 368, 371, 382
al-Muqawqas, 20, 58
Murqus ibn al-Qunbar, 90, 238, 303–4, 310, 359, 375
Mūsā, secretary, 9th c., 49
Mūsā ibn ʿĪsā ibn Mūsā, gov., 229
Mūsā ibn Muṣʿab al-Khathʿamī, gov., 122
Mūsā al-Yahūdī, 250, 252
al-Muʿtaḍid, caliph, 329
al-Muʿtaṣim, caliph, 48, 201, 357
al-Mutawakkil, Caliph, 44, 67, 132, 133, 134, 171, 229, 269, 290, 301, 330, 355
al-Muṭīʿ, caliph, 137
Muẓaffar ibn Kaydur, 126

Nāṣir Muḥammad ibn Qalāwūn, 246
Nāṣir-i Khusraw, 323, 339, 378, 380
Nasry, W., 373
Nationalism/Nationalist; pgs. 3, 9, 10, 17–18, 22, 24, 83, 84, 90, 179, 191, 224, 273, 279, 283, 306, 348; see chs. 1, 2, 3, 5
Nau, F., 278, 314
Naẓm al-jawhar see Eutychios
Nersēs, Armenian Catholicos, 294
"Nestorians" see Church of the East
Neugebauer, O., 376
Nicheh, 8th c. translator, 316
Nikephoros, Pat of Constantinople, 294, 341, 347
Niketas, general, 25
Nile, 25, 125, 161, 167, 188, 198, 253, 356, 359, 368, 377–80; *blessing the N.*, 377–9; *Ethiopian threat*, 198, 356, 357; *festivals*, 247, 304, 379–80; *increase as omen*, 188, 244, 379, 380; *sixteen cubits*, 242, 244, 245, 378; *N. topos*, 241–9, 259, 271
Nomocanon, 151, 158, 159, 237, 314, 337, 339, 375; *see also* Synodicon
Noth, A., 20, 110, 274, 282, 285, 296, 297, 304, 318, 319, 323, 342
Nubia, 15, 53, 54, 67, 117, 131, 138, 177, 184, 191, 192, 194–203, 298, 307, 329, 352, 354, 355, 356–8, 367, 370

O'Connell, E.R., 368
O'Leary, De L., 313
O'Sullivan, S., 295
Old Dongola, 195, 199, 202, 329
Olick, J., 285
Ordination, 54; *multiple ordinations*, 209–12
Orlandi, T., 275, 281, 303, 306, 309, 310, 349

Pachomius, C bp, 199
Pact of Union, 56, 57
Palmer, A., 282, 283, 289, 290, 312, 320, 321, 357, 364, 368, 369, 376
Panegyric on Apollo, 280, 347, 348
Panegyric on John the Baptist, 307
Panegyric on Makarios of Tikou, 346, 348
Panegyric on the Three Holy Youth, 36
Pankhurst, R., 356–7
Papaconstantinou, A., 273, 280, 281, 310, 314, 317, 329, 349, 351, 376, 377, 382

Papas, magistrate, 336
Paphnutios (*Histories*), 277, 293, 300, 338, 362, 365, 378
"Patriarch," 42, 289
Patriarchal elections, 205, 208–9, 215–16; *interference in*, 153, 184–6, 205, 219
Patriarchal residences, 206–7, 358–9
Paul of Samannūd, 25
Paul, notable, 365
Pazdernik, C., 347
Pearson, B.A., 272, 303, 306, 310, 358
Pearson, J.D., 312
Pelikan, J., 279, 373
Perlmann, M., 349
Persian, 1, 60, 79, 93, 125, 126, 128, 169, 270, 296, 325, 346, 347, 351, 352; *Occupation*, 60–1, 226 *also see* Sasanian
Peter III "Mongos", CPat, 362
Peter (Buṭrus) VI, CPat, 379
Peter (Buṭrus) VII, CPat, 248
Peter son of Athanasios Bar Gūmōyē, 290
Peter the Iberian, 13
Peter, dcn/convert, see Abū al-Khayr
Peter, gov. Upper Egypt, 66, 297
Peters, F.E., 296, 372
Petry, C.F., 273, 277, 287, 319, 331, 344, 358
Phantasiasts *see* Eutychians
Phillips, J.R., 320
Philotheos (Fīlūtā'us), CPat, 186, 203, 361, 367
Philoxenos, Prefect of Arcadia, 288
Phokas, 25
Pigs, 117
Pipes, D., 301, 304, 319, 343
Pisentios bp of Koptos (Qifṭ), 216, 287, 364
Politianos (Biltiyān), MPat, 369
Political ideology, 32–5, 178–84
"Pope," title and use, 54, 218, 289, 358
Post-Conquest relations (early) *see* Arab Conquest
Powers, D.S., 339
Price, R., 280
Pseudo-Samuel see *Apocalypse of Samuel*
Puin, G.-R., 343

Qāḍī, 67, 87, 92, 137, 140–3, 156–9, 185, 219, 220, 231, 250, 292, 333, 334, 339, 377; *qāḍī al-quḍāt*, 65, 142, 250, 334, 381
al-Qāḍī, Wadād, 276, 277, 296, 333, 355
al-Qalqashandī, Aḥmad ibn ʿAbdallāh, 173, 274
Qays ibn al-Ashʿath al-Tujībī, 334
Qays(ī)s, 116, 122, 124, 167, 169, 227, 263, 266, 324, 334, 342, 371; *migration/settlement*, 71, 120, 166, 371; *political ascent*, 116, 143–45
qibṭ see Copts
Qishlām, notable of Tinnīs, 49
Quecke, H., 308
Qur'ān(ic): 1, 5, 66, 93, 108, 109, 113, 115, 142, 149, 152, 153, 157, 159, 271, 317–22, 330, 334, 341, 344, 354, 372, 381
Qurra ibn Sharīk, gov., 44, 50, 62, 81, 133, 144, 145, 147, 148, 226, 305, 310, 312, 317, 330, 331, 335, 336, 341, 371
Quzmā I, CPat, 44
Quzmā II, CPat, 362
Quzmā III, CPat, 203
Quzmān, MPat, 14, 62, 225, 239–40, 363

Raghib, Y., 312, 336
Rambo, L.R., 292
Rapp, C., 365
Rashīd, *pagarch/amīr*, 104
Rebaptism *see* Baptism
Reinink, G.J., 302, 347
Reinfandt, L., 332

Relics, 227, 246–7, 269, 320, 380
Revolts, 19, 75–76, 144, 165, 166, 167, 169, 170, 174, 178, 179, 186, 189–90, 227, 229, 268, 323–6, 346, 351, 367; *Agrarian Revolts*, 118–27, 169, 263, 266, 268, 270; *Bashmūr Revolts*, 75–76, 121, 125, 189–191, 326, 351, 367
Reynolds, G.S., 372
Richards, D.S., 287, 344
Richards, E.G., 326
Richter, T.S., 310, 312, 315, 339
Riedel, W., 314, 337
Riti, M.ʿA., 341
Roberts, C.H., 309
Robbins, J., 285
Robinson, C., 247, 281, 283, 285, 301, 302, 318, 319, 323
Robinson, F., 313
Robinson, J.M., 307
Rokeah, D., 372
Rubenson, S., 95, 97, 310, 312, 313, 314
Ruffini, G.R., 294
Rufus of Shotep, 89–90, 310
Rukn al-Dawla Baybars al-Jāshankīr, 246–7
Rustow, M., 376

al-Ṣabāḥ, convert, 312
Sabas, st, 373–4
Sabhrīshōʿ metropolitan of Bēth Garmē, 236, 374
Ṣadaqa, 108, 109, 121
Ṣadqan, 194
al-Ṣāfī, secretary of Abū al-ʿAwn, 244
Ṣafī, secretary of Ṣāliḥ ibn ʿAlī, 188
Sahas, D.J., 282, 303
Ṣāḥib al-kharāj, 119, 137–9, 144–5, 332
Ṣāḥib al-ṣalāt, (al-wālī), 137–8, 145
Ṣāḥib al-shurṭa, 139–41, 145, 332–3
Saʿīd ibn Baṭrīq *see* Eutychios
Saʿīd ibn Yazīd al-Azdī, gov., 140, 331
Ṣalāḥ al-Dīn Yūsuf ibn Ayyub (Saladin), 377
Saleh, A.H., 172, 173, 344
Saleh, M.J., 182, 287, 288, 291, 317, 344, 349, 357, 358, 371
Ṣalīb, notable, 377
Ṣāliḥ ibn ʿAlī, gov., 167
Ṣāliḥ ibn Shīrzad, 124
Samir, K.S., 287, 292, 303, 310, 312, 354, 368, 373, 377
Samuel of Qalamūn (pseudo-) see *Apocalypse of Samuel*
Samuel of Qalamūn, st, (*Life*) 57, 294, 295, 346, 366
Samuel the Anchorite, 353
Samuel, V.C., 278, 280
Sanders, P.A., 304, 358, 380
Sanhūt bp of Miṣr, 358, 367
Saracens, 68, 326, 328
Sarkissian, K., 278
Sarris, P., 294
Sasanian, 26, 58, 113–5, 150, 151, 153, 180, 296; *Occupation*, 60–1, 226
Sawīrus ibn al-Muqaffaʿ bp of al-Ashmūnayn, 5, 72, 73, 99, 100, 101, 233, 249, 250, 251, 275, 303, 373, 381
Sayfa Ar'ad, Emp. of Ethiopia, 357
Scanlon,G.T., 276, 340
Scetis *see* Wādī al-Naṭrūn
Schacht, J., 317, 326, 333, 334, 339
Schick, R., 281, 320
Schiller, A.A., 336, 338
Schmelz, G., 338, 362, 363
Schmucker, W. 110, 319
Schoeler, G., 274
Schultz, W.C., 319–21
Schwartz, J., 330
Sebeos, 286, 296
Selassie, S.H., 354
Sellers, R.V., 278
Sergios, convert, 297

Sergios, Pat of Constantinople, 56
Severos of Antioch, Syr. Pat., xii, 34, 85, 192, 277, 279, 307, 347, 348, 352, 377
Severos son of Bane, 104
Seybold, C.F., 283, 357
Shahārija, 71
Shamūl bp of Wasīm, 217, 366
Shenoda, M.M., 381
Shenoute bp of Ṣā, 367
Shenoute *dux* of Antinöe, 23, 27, 38–39, 226, 285, 288
Shenoute, Prefect of al-Rīf, 288 (Perhaps same as the *dux*, above)
Shenoute of Atripe, 90, 221, 378
Shenoute, entomology of the name, 316
Sheridan, M., 310
Shinūda I, CPat, 6, 275, 345
Shinūda II, CPat, 6, 209, 275
Shīrīn, concubine, 58, 59, 296, 300
Shoshan, B., 287, 304, 380
Shoucri, M., 308
Shūrat al-'Umariyya see *Covenant of 'Umar*
Sidarus, A., 311, 313
Sijpesteijn, P.M., 276, 277, 281, 284, 288, 295, 311, 318, 324, 331, 332, 335, 340
Simon "the Tanner," st, 252, 358, 362, 382
Simon I, CPat, 6, 41, 42, 153, 185, 186, 198, 205, 226, 290, 353, 363, 367, 370
Simon II, CPat, 362
Simon, Archd., 214, 363
Simonetta, C., 323
Simonsen, J.B., 276, 284, 317, 318, 335, 340
Simonsohn, U.I., 337
Simony, 217, 221, 269, 345, 365, 377
Skreslet II, S.H., 274, 291, 306, 352, 368, 376
Smith, A.D., 273
Sokrates, 179, 350, 374–6
Somekh, S., 372, 381
Sophronios, Pat. of Jerusalem, 20, 24, 55, 56, 282, 288, 316
Spaulding, J., 355
Stark, R., 292, 300, 304
Stephanos son of Athanasios Bar Gūmōyē, 290
Stern, H., 321
Stewart, R., 290, 291, 299
Suermann, H., 274, 287
Suḥayl ibn 'Abd al-'Azīz ibn Marwān, 120
Sulaym ibn 'Iṭr, *qāḍī*, 142
Sulaymān ibn 'Amr al-Tujībī, 144
Sulaymān, tax collector, 321
Ṣulḥ / *'anwa* traditions, 107, 109–13, 119, 225, 230, 231, 318, 319, 369, 370
Sullam, 96, 313
Sundelin, L., 276, 277, 311, 313, 315
Swanson, M.N., 7, 182, 274, 275, 276, 283, 303, 310, 349, 354, 366, 372
Synaxarion (*sinaksār*), 96, 248, 252, 270, 289, 290, 302, 313, 330, 350, 356, 370, 371, 477, 378–81
Synodicon, 151, 294, 337
Syriac Common Source, 19, 21
Syrians, East, *see* Church of the East
Syrians, West, 56, 150, 151, 179–80, 236, 237, 337, 373

al-Ṭabarī, Abū Ja'far Muḥammad ibn Jarīr, 31, 126, 282, 304, 319, 330
Tabātabā'i, H.M., 317, 318, 319, 329
Tafla, B., 354
al-Tāj ibn Sa'īd al-Dawla, 246
Takla, H.N., 380
Taklahāymānot, A., 354
Ṭanūs ibn Yuḥannis, 103
Taqizadeh, S.H., 326, 330
Ṭarābulūs, 112, 319
Tartīb al-kahanūt, (pseudo-Sawīrus), 12, 280, 350, 360, 364, 375, 376
Tattoos, 267

Tax fugitives, 148
Teshlot, 102–3, 156, 315, 328, 336, 339, 362
Theodore, convert, 297
Theodore, gov. of Alex., 40, 41
Theodore Abū Qurra bp of Ḥarran, 233, 291, 303, 306, 322, 373
Theodore bp of Miṣr, 47, 358, 363, 364, 366
Theodore bp of Philae, 195
Theodore [ibn Isḥāq ibn Andūna] bp of Wasīm, 48, 228, 365, 366, 368
Theodore ibn Mūsā, dcn, 362
Theodore of Shoteb, st, 379
Theodosios, CPat, xii, 56, 85, 192, 279, 293, 307, 352, 362, 363
Theology *see* Doctrine
Theophanios, CPat, 361, 367
Theophanes Confessor, 1, 21, 279, 280, 282, 284, 294, 297, 298, 301, 321, 327, 341, 346, 350, 351, 352, 356, 357, 361, 371, 373, 374
Theophanes, gov. of Maryūṭ, 40, 50, 66, 297
Thomas, D., 274, 372
Thung, M.H., 315, 339
Till, W.C., 300, 336
Timbie, J.A., 275, 381, 358
Timm, S., 290, 291
Timothy I, Pat, 240
Timothy II, "Ailuros," CPat, 6, 13, 240, 279, 280, 293, 294
Timothy bp of Qasr Ibrīm (Phrim), 196, 355
Torrance, I., 278
Tovar, S.T., 277, 311, 332
Tritton, A.S., 317, 336, 369
Trombley, F., 277, 340
Ṭūlūnids, 48
Tyan, E., 139, 332–5, 338
Typos, 57

ʿUbayd Allāh al-Azdī, 333
ʿUbayd Allāh ibn al-Ḥabḥāb, 119, 139, 145, 160, 165, 263, 323, 331–2, 366, 371; question of his appointment as governor, 331–32
ʿUbayd Allāh ibn Marawān, 201
Udovitch, A.L., 296
ʿUmar I, Ibn al-Khaṭṭāb, caliph, 108, 117, 134, 161, 171, 245, 282, 284, 296, 343
ʿUmar II, caliph, 44, 299, 343
ʿUqba ibn ʿAmir, 332
ʿUqba ibn Muslim al-Tujībī, 334
ʿUqba ibn Nafīʿ, 138
ʿUrbān, 163, 167, 172–6, 229, 271, 345
Usāma ibn Zayd, 164, 301
ʿUshr, 110, 111, 119, 166, 318
ʿUtba ibn Abū Sufyān, gov., 331
Uthemann, K.-H., 279
ʿUthmān ibn ʿAffān, caliph, 138, 144, 334
ʿUthmān ibn al-Mustanīr al-Judhamī, rebel leader, 124

Valentinos, dcn of Pat. Cell, 362
Van den Gerg-Onstwedder, G., 330
Van der Vliet, J., 277, 353
Van Ginkel, J.J., 179, 180, 281, 347, 368, 374
Van Lent, J., 276, 287, 314
Van Minnen, P., 154, 338
Van Rompay, L., 280, 353
Varghese, B., 373
Vasiliev, A.A., 322
Vasunia, P., 356
Victor bp of Carthage, 356
Victor bp of Fayyūm, 56, 356
Victor bp of Nikiou, 295
Vincent, F., 310, 313
Vivian, T., 300, 338, 365, 371, 378
Von Grunebaum, G.E., 382
Vööbus, A., 337, 353
Vryonis, S., Jr., 304, 316
Vycichl, W., 311, 313

Wādī al-Naṭrūn (Scetis), 40, 67, 175, 192, 273, 281, 314, 321, 344, 345, 350, 353, 359–62
Wāḍiḥ ibn Rajā, 67
al-Walīd I, caliph, 116
Walīd ibn al-Rafi', 332
al-Walīd ibn Rifā'a ibn Khālid ibn Thābit ibn Ẓa'īn al-Fahmī, gov., 145, 227, 331, 332, 371, 376
Walker, Joel, 272, 301
Walker, John, 320
Walker, P.E., 301
Wannā (Bannā), dcn/bp of Miṣr, 48, 220, 292, 367
Wansbrough, J., 275
Ward, S., 370
Ware, K., 279
Wardān *mawlā* 'Amr ibn al-'Āṣ, 81
Wasserstein, D.J., 309
al-Wāthik, caliph, 367
Watson, A., 296
Weigert, G., 356
Weitzmann, K., 278
Welsby, D.A., 354, 355, 357, 368
Werthmuler, K.J., 352, 366
Wertsch, J.V., 285
Wesche, K.P., 279
Whitby, M., 272, 278, 368
Wickham, C., 273, 285, 294, 317, 335, 336
Wilfong, T.G., 276, 278, 327
Winkelmann, F., 273
Winter, M., 380
Wipszycha, E., 273, 293, 344, 362, 366, 370
Women, 49, 58, 65, 118, 125, 190, 287, 300, 301, 322, 323, 337, 339, 351
Worp, K.A., 305, 316, 326–30, 341, 365
Wuhayb al-Yaḥṣubī, rebel leader, 227, 371

Yaḥyā ibn Adām, 301, 317, 319, 322, 342
Yaḥyā ibn 'Adī, 354
Yaḥyā ibn al-Wazīr al-Jarawī, 126, 325
Yaman(ī), 122, 124, 143, 166, 167, 169, 227, 263, 266, 324, 342, 371
Ya'qūb I, CPat, 45, 46, 175, 214, 228, 362, 364
Ya'qūb ibn Isḥāq, 66
Ya'qūb bp of Arwāṭ, 214
Ya'qūb ibn Isḥāq ibn Yaḥyā, 66
al-Ya'qūbī, Aḥmad ibn Abī Ya'qūb ibn Wāḍiḥ, 320, 325, 326, 330, 357
Ya'qūb ibn Killis, 250, 252, 381
Yazīd ibn 'Abdallāh, pagarch of Akhmīn, 104
Yazīd (II) ibn 'Abd al-Malik, caliph, 117, 322
Yazīd ibn Ḥātim, gov., 121
Yazīd ibn Qāsim, 66, 70
Yazūrī, *wazīr*, 370
Young, D.W., 368
Youssef, Y.N., 305, 308, 330, 362, 368, 381
Yu'annīs, secretary, 9th c., 49
Yūḥannā ibn Buqtūr, 368
Yūḥannā al-Dimyāṭī, gov. Lower Egypt, 288
Yūḥannā ibn Ṣā'īd al-Qulzūmī, 6, 210, 359
Yūḥannā bp of Samannūd, 13th c., 96
Yūḥannā al-Samannūdī, rebel leader, 8th c., 120
Yu'annīs ibn Sanhūt bp of Miṣr, 359
Yunā bint Ḥalyṣ, 66, 70
Yūnus ibn 'Aṭiyya, 333
Yusāb I, CPat, 6, 47, 48, 67, 86, 87, 92, 125, 182, 185, 187, 198, 201, 207, 219, 220, 228, 291, 292, 307, 351, 358, 363, 364, 367, 371
Yusāb bp of Fuwwā (Pseudo-), 275

Zabban ibn 'Abd al-'Azīz, 117
Zaborowski, J.R., 280, 295, 314
Zacharias bp of Buḥayra, 92, 308, 367

Zacharias bpof Sakhā, 43
Zacharias bp of Saïs, 367
Zacharias bpof Wasīm, 47
Zacharias (Rhetor) bp of Mitylene, (pseudo-), 279, 346
Zacharias I, CPat, 181, 183, 186, 208, 349, 350, 360, 361
al-Ẓāhir Baybars, 174
Zakariyya ibn Yaḥnnis king of Nubia, 201
Zanetti, U., 308, 309, 314, 362
Zayāt, Ḥ., 343
Zeno, Emp, 57
Ziyād ibn Ḥinaṭa ibn Sayf ibn Halawa al-Tujībī, 334
Zoega, G., 345

www.ingramcontent.com/pod-product-compliance
Lightning Source LLC
Chambersburg PA
CBHW050133240426
43673CB00043B/1653